THE TIBETAN ASSIMILATION OF BUDDHISM

The Tibetan Assimilation of Buddhism

Conversion, Contestation, and Memory

MATTHEW T. KAPSTEIN

OXFORD
UNIVERSITY PRESS
2000

OXFORD
UNIVERSITY PRESS

Oxford New York
Athens Auckland Bangkok Bogotá Buenos Aires Cape Town
Chennai Dar es Salaam Delhi Florence Hong Kong Istanbul Karachi
Kolkata Kuala Lumpur Madrid Melbourne Mexico City Mumbai Nairobi
Paris São Paulo Shanghai Singapore Taipei Tokyo Toronto Warsaw

and associated companies in
Berlin Ibadan

First published in 2000 by Oxford University Press, Inc.
198 Madison Avenue, New York, New York 10016

First issued as an Oxford University Press paperback, 2002

Library of Congress Cataloging-in-Publication Data
Kapstein, Matthew.
The Tibetan assimilation of buddhism : conversion, contestation, and memory / Matthew T. Kapstein.
p. cm.
Includes bibliographical references and index.
ISBN 0-19-513122-3; 0-19-515227-1 (pbk.)
1. Buddhism—China—Tibet—History. I. Title.
BQ7576.K37 2000
294.3'923'09—dc21 99-33551

1 3 5 7 9 8 6 4 2

Printed in the United States of America
on acid-free paper

To the memory of Michael Aris
March 27, 1946–March 27, 1999
beloved friend to all friends of Tibet

༄༅། ། ཀྱེ་ཧུད་ཡིད་བཞིན་ནོར་བུ་མཆོག །གློ་བུར་ཆུ་ལ་ཤོར་བ་ལས། །
ལྷག་པའི་འགྱོད་པ་གཏིང་ནས་སྐྱེས། །མིག་ནས་མཆི་མ་ཆར་བཞིན་བབས། །
དེ་ལྟར་ཐམས་ཅད་མི་རྟག་པའི། །ཚུལ་ལ་བསམས་ནས་ལྷ་ཆོས་བྱེད། །
ལྷ་ཆོས་བྱས་པའི་བསོད་ནམས་ཀུན། །སྐལ་ལྡན་ཁྱེད་ལ་ཕན་ཕྱིར་བསྔོ། །
ཞབས་དཀར་བས་སོ། ། དགེའོ། །

Preface

By what pathways and processes does a society appropriate unto itself what is alien, transforming the other even as it is transformed by it? The Tibetan assimilation of Buddhism offers compelling subject matter for reflection about this question, a question that is now especially pertinent to the study of society and culture. At a time when public discourse, in many domains, including popular interest in Tibet, seems to fix upon notions of hard and fast cultural or ethnic identities, it is well to remind ourselves that our identities have always been fluid constructions, whose vitality and ongoing creation demand internal change and responsiveness to external forces.

Much excellent work in the contemporary human sciences, throughout a broad spectrum of research, has been consecrated to explorations of cultural transmission and adaptation. It would be difficult to mention all that has in one way or another influenced my thinking in this area, not to speak of all that I probably should have read but still have not. To clarify the concerns informing the present book to some extent, however, two works come to mind that, though treating different historical problems from quite different perspectives, equally contribute to our thinking on the general question I have posed. I refer to Erik Zürcher's *The Buddhist Conquest of China* and Serge Gruzinski's recent *The Conquest of Mexico* (originally *La colonisation de l'imaginaire*). With the former, I share here an interest in the spread of Buddhism in early medieval Asia, and the crucial role played, not so much by foreign Buddhist missionaries, but by the formation of an indigenous Buddhist cultural elite who came to articulate their originally foreign faith in their own terms. And whereas Gruzinski examines the response of a colonized people to the culture of the colonizers, an issue that must be wholly distinguished from our present subject matter, the transformations of indigenous Mexican memory and imagination that were entailed by the processes he describes present a striking analogy to the transformation of the Tibetan *imaginaire* that was catalyzed by the promulgation of Buddhism.

Literary production in the thirteen centuries during which Tibetan has been written has been vast. At the present time, we have access to many thousands of printed volumes and manuscripts, containing many tens of thousands of individual works of different types: biographies and histories, medical treatises, books on astrology and divination, poems and works on poetics, grammars and dictionaries, ritual handbooks, and writings on all aspects of Tibetan religious life and thought are extensively represented, including those writings devoted strictly to Buddhist doctrine and scholastic philosophy. The study of this great legacy is only now emerging from its infancy, and though many particular problems remain unresolved, the general contours of

Tibetan literary and cultural history are in important respects becoming clear to those familiar at least in a general manner with the range of works now available in the Tibetan language. One of my aims in the present work is to convey to readers who are not Tibetanists some impression of the broad domain of Tibetan religious thought that has now begun to come into view.

Throughout this book, I therefore discuss aspects of the historical development of Buddhism in Tibet, but, unlike the two books I have mentioned, I do not propose to present here an historical account of my topic overall. My interest lies first in the varied textures of Tibetan Buddhist thought, and only secondarily in history per se. For this reason I have proceeded by way of a series of case studies, for the most part originally conceived as independent essays, that nevertheless reflect one another in their concerns. In a separate publication I shall explore in some detail the history of Tibetan Buddhist doctrinal thought in a more restricted sense. Here, however, in the first chapter I seek to introduce the history of Buddhist thought in Tibet as a question for critical reflection, and I suggest some of the ways in which historical change in the field of Tibetan thought may itself be conceived. In part 1, "Conversion and Narrative," I consider traditions concerning the eighth-century Tibetan adoption of Buddhism in relation to the late, legendary accounts of the conversion, as well as aspects of the earliest evidence that contributes to our understanding of eighth-century events. Part 2, "Sources of Contestation," offers studies of topics relating to doctrinal transmission, interpretation, and dispute, in order to illustrate aspects of Buddhist thought in Tibet as defining, not a body of static dogmatics, but a much contested field. In part 3, "Myth, Memory, Revelation," our concern will be with mythic and philosophical aspects of the Nyingmapa, or Ancient, school of Tibetan Buddhism, in whose revealed scriptures the formerly alien Indian religion is decisively transfigured to become a matter of Tibetan cultural, and even personal, memory.

The photograph that appears on the cover of this book provides a view of the great monastic complex of Samye. As Tibet's first Buddhist monastery, founded during the late eighth century, it is a unique symbol of Tibet's adoption of Buddhism. Not long after its foundation, it became the site of Tibet's first great doctrinal dispute, in which the Chan tradition of China confronted Indian Buddhist scholasticism. Finally, as a center of pilgrimage, even today it remains a focal point of Tibetan historical memory. In its three-storeyed structure, then, Samye embodies our key themes of conversion, contestation, and memory.

The chapters of this book draw on materials gathered throughout the entire course of my involvement in the study of Tibet, beginning almost three decades ago. To recall all that has been generously given to me that should be acknowledged here would require a thorough reconstruction of the magical net (*māyājāla*) of intellectual encounters woven throughout this time. In several chapters, for instance, I refer to an old chronicle called the *Testament of Ba* (*Sba-bzhed*). Though I only began to consider this important early text in depth five or six years ago, I was first introduced to it in 1972, when, as an undergraduate college student, I had the good fortune to attend James Bosson's courses on classical Tibetan at the University of California, Berkeley. While at Berkeley, too, I was able to study Buddhist texts with Lewis Lancaster, who also encouraged my studies in Nepal. I shall refrain, however, from lengthy autobiographical reflection just now, and, with apologies to teachers and friends who remain unnamed herein, mention those whose counsel and encouragement most directly contributed to these pages.

Over the years I have been privileged to study and discuss Tibetan Buddhist history and thought with some of the leading representatives of traditional Tibetan learning. Though I write within the tradition of European scholarship, my reading of all things Tibetan is indelibly marked by the abundant instructions and comments of H. H. Dudjom Rinpoche Jikdrel Yeshe Dorje (1904–1987), H. H. Karmapa XVI Rangjung Rikpei Dorje (1927–1981), H. H. Dilgo Khyentse Rinpoche Tashi Peljor (1910–1992), Ven. Kalu Rinpoche Rangjung Künkhyap (1905–1989), Ven. Dezhung Rinpoche Kunga Tenpei Nyima (1906–1987), Ven. Tulku Urgyen Rinpoche (1920–1996), and Rev. Serlo Lama Sangye Tenzin (1924–1990). I often imagine, when I become immersed in the works of the figures discussed in these pages—past masters like Sakya Paṇḍita, Karma Pakshi, Dölpopa, or Longchenpa—that one or more of these men is reading over my shoulder, challenging me to "turn not to the words, but to meaning." I cannot pretend to comprehend the meaning of their tradition as they would, much less to communicate that understanding here, but at the least I hope to convey that Tibetan Buddhist writings do mean to challenge us in ways that require our contemporary reflections to unfold in sustained dialogue with tradition.

Ongoing conversations over many years with fellow Tibetanists have crucially influenced the reflections gathered in this book. I am particularly grateful in this regard for the friendship of Anne-Marie Blondeau, Ronald Davidson, Gyurme Dorje, David Germano, Steven Goodman, Janet Gyatso, Yoshiro Imaeda, David Jackson, Samten Karmay, Per Kværne, Alexander Macdonald, Fernand Meyer, Katsumi Mimaki, David Seyfort Ruegg, E. Gene Smith, Heather Stoddard, and Tashi Tsering. I similarly wish to mention colleagues whose insights into Buddhism in East Asia have often caused me to rethink perspectives on the history of Buddhism in Tibet, especially Ryuichi Abe, Carl Bielefeldt, Raoul Birnbaum, Robert Buswell, Bernard Faure, John McRae, and Stephen Teiser.

My mother, Dorothy Hammer, has always reminded me of the virtues of fine craftsmanship in the English language. If I nevertheless fall into the tar pit of academic prose, I have only myself to blame. Christine Mollier has graciously given me references to pertinent Chinese materials, suggestions regarding the book's title, and inspiration to think things anew.

The three chapters of part 1, "Conversion and Narrative," were first presented as the Numata Lectures at the Divinity School of the University of Chicago in January 1997. Gratitude is due to the Numata Foundation, to Clark Gilpin, Dean of the Divinity School, and to the Divinity School's Numata Committee: Steven Collins, Paul Griffiths, and Frank Reynolds. These scholars, together with Philip Gossett, Dean of the Division of the Humanities, and Sheldon Pollock, Chair of the Department of South Asian Languages and Civilizations when I returned to the University of Chicago in 1996, have made this a particularly propitious setting in which to complete this book. The presence in Chicago and the friendship of Margot Pritzker and Thomas J. Pritzker, whose deep connections with Tibet and neighboring lands are well known among those involved in Tibetan Studies, have further contributed to these fortunate circumstances.

Generous awards from a number of bodies have directly supported the research upon which this book is based. I acknowledge, in particular, the Committee for Scholarly Communication with China for its support of my research in Tibetan regions of

China in 1990 and 1992. In 1994–1995 I had the good fortune to be a member of the Institute for Advanced Study in Princeton, and I am especially grateful to Peter Schäfer, who invited me to join his seminar there, and to the physicist Piet Hut for freewheeling conversations throughout that year. A major grant from the National Endowment for the Humanities, supporting my translation work in 1994–1997, enabled me to complete a substantial volume of translation, from which many of the text selections included in the present book are drawn. All translations given here, unless otherwise noted, are my own.

Several chapters or chapter sections of this book were previously published as separate articles. I thank the editors and publishers of the journals and books in which they first appeared for permission to reproduce them here:

"Religious Syncretism in 13th Century Tibet: *The Limitless Ocean Cycle*," in B. N. Aziz and M. Kapstein, eds., *Soundings in Tibetan Civilization*, pp. 358–371. New Delhi: Manohar, 1985.
"Remarks on the *Maṇi-bka'-'bum* and the Cult of Avalokiteśvara in Tibet," in S. Goodman and R. Davidson, eds., *Tibetan Buddhism: Reason and Revelation*, pp. 79–93, 163–169. Albany: SUNY Press, 1992.
"The Purificatory Gem and Its Cleansing: A Late Tibetan Polemical Discussion of Apocryphal Texts," *History of Religions* 28/3 (February 1989): 217–244.
"Samantabhadra and Rudra: Innate Enlightenment and Radical Evil in Tibetan Rnying-ma-pa Buddhism," in Frank E. Reynolds and David Tracy, eds., *Discourse and Practice*, pp. 51–82. Albany: SUNY Press, 1992.
"The Amnesic Monarch and the Five Mnemic Men," in Janet Gyatso, ed., *In the Mirror of Memory*, pp. 239–269. Albany: SUNY Press, 1992.
"From Dol-po-pa to 'Ba'-mda' Dge-legs: Three Jo-nang-pa Masters on the Interpretation of *Prajñāpāramitā*," in Helmut Krasser, Michael Torsten Much, Ernst Steinkellner, and Helmut Tauscher, eds., *Tibetan Studies: Proceedings of the Seventh Seminar of the International Association for Tibetan Studies*, vol. 1, pp. 457–475. Vienna: Austrian Academy of Science, 1997.

The first two have been incorporated into chapters 6 and 8, respectively. The next three appear here, with revisions, as chapters 7, 9, and 10. Some passages in chapter 6 are derived from the last mentioned.

To Cynthia Read, editor for philosophy and religion at the Oxford University Press, and to her associates at the Press, I am indebted for their care in bringing about the fruition of this work.

One of many fortunate encounters during the early 1970s, not long after I had embarked on the path of Tibetan Studies, was with Michael Aris, later of St. Anthony's College, Oxford, to whom this book is dedicated, and whose tragic passing occurred while it was being prepared for the press. During my last conversation with Dr. Aris, in July 1998 at the meeting of the International Association for Tibetan Studies, an organization that he had founded, we discussed this book in manuscript, which, with characteristic generosity, he had recently read. He offered me both kind encouragement and thoughtful advice for its final revision. I have attempted as best I know how to achieve a standard that in some small measure reflects the excellence he exemplified for all those who knew him.

Chicago, Illinois M. T. K.
April 1999

Contents

9 Samantabhadra and Rudra: Myths of Innate Enlightenment and Radical Evil 163
Fragments from a Myth of Tibet 163
The Myth of Samantabhadra 167
The Matricide Rudra 170
Must the Message Be Mythic? 176

10 The Amnesic Monarch and the Five Mnemic Men: "Memory" in the Great Perfection Tradition 178
Preliminary Orientations 178
Mnemic Engagement in the *Wide-Open Tantra of Universal Liberation* 180
An Allegorical Re-presentation 187
Mnemic Engagement in the Practice of Prayer 193
By Way of Conclusion 194

Appendix: *The Prayer of Great Power* 197

Notes 203

Chinese Glossary 273

Bibliography 275
Tibetan References 275
Sanskrit References 283
Chinese References 283
Western Language References 284

Index 305

A Note on Pronunciation

One of the greatest challenges for the non-Tibetanist who wishes to read scholarship on Tibet is to wrestle with names and terms that often seem to have been generated by the random sorting of the roman alphabet. Correspondingly, one of the greatest challenges for the Tibetanist is to find a way in which to represent words and names of the Tibetan language that can be read by nonspecialists without at the same time earning the scorn of peers, who prefer exact transcriptions. If the present book offers only the latest example of failed compromise, I may console myself nevertheless that failure along these lines enjoys some very good company indeed.

Tibetan, like English and French, is written with a roughly phonetic script that is not employed phonetically. Just as we write *thought* where *thawt* should suffice, so the Lhasan writes *thugs-bsam*, but pronounces, very roughly, *thusam*. This in itself would present not much difficulty, if there were a consensus among scholars as to a system of simplified Tibetan phonetic romanization, but regrettably this is not the case. On the one hand, Tibetan pronunciation varies considerably from one region to another, so that a phonetic script must be limited with respect to dialect. On the other, because the actual sounds of Tibetan do not correspond too closely with the sounds normally represented by the roman script as used for English, special conventions of usage must be stipulated, and Tibetanists have not so far agreed about these.

For the purposes of this book, I have based my transcription on an approximation of modern Central Tibetan pronunciation, retaining the exact transcription of the root-consonant (*ming-gzhi*) wherever this seems feasible. The following conventions should be noted:

The vowels *a*, *i*, *e*, *o*, *u* are pure vowels, never diphthongs, and their pronunciation is similar to that in Italian. The final *e* must always be pronounced, never silent. Thus *dorje* should be pronounced *dorjé*, never *dorj*. The vowels *ö* and *ü* are pronounced as in German.

The consonants *kh* and *ph* are similar to English *k* and *p*. The *h* in each case merely represents aspiration, and *kh* should never be pronounced like the guttural *ch* in

German *Nachlaß*, nor *ph* like the English *ph* in *phlox*. *Th* is used as it is in the English name *Thomas*, but never as in *thralldom* or *blather*. *Ts* and *dz* both resemble the sound in English *adze*, while *tsh* resembles that in *bets*. In the same way, *tr* and *dr* resemble the sound in *drill*, while *trh* is more like that in *trill*. *Ng* is as in English *sing*, though English speakers often find it difficult to pronounce in initial position, as in the common Tibetan name *Ngawang*.

K and *g* are closely similar to the English hard *g* in *gulf*, and those not actually seeking to master the Tibetan language may pronounce these two letters in just the same manner. (In Lhasa dialect they differ as to the tone of the syllable they begin, a distinction not made in English.) Similarly: *c* and *j* resemble English *j*, *p* and *b* resemble English *b*, *s* and *z* resemble English *s*, and *sh* and *zh* resemble English *sh*. *T* and *d* are closer to the French or Italian *d* than to the English.

Ch, *h*, *m*, *n*, *ny*, and *w* have approximately the same values they have in English.

The use of these conventions is limited to Tibetan proper nouns occuring in the main body of the text. Their precise Tibetan orthography is given in the general index. Book titles and terms used only parenthetically, and all Tibetan words used in the notes, are given in exact transcription following the system described in Wylie 1959.

Sanskrit words are transcribed here according to the standard system favored in scholarship concerning India. For those wishing to become familiar with the essentials of Sanskrit pronunciation, a convenient guide may be found in Olivelle 1996, pp. xiv–xv.

Chinese is given in the official Pinyin romanization, using tone accents only when citing words and phrases not used as titles or proper nouns. A Chinese glossary will be found at the end of the book.

A Brief Chronology of Tibetan Buddhism

The topics considered in this book for the most part belong to the history of Tibetan Buddhism prior to 1400. The timeline from 650 to 1400 provides a sketch of Tibetan Buddhist history during this period, and the closing paragraphs summarize developments after 1400 to which I also refer herein. Familiarity with this chronology will enable the reader to situate the particular topics discussed in the main body of the book within the Tibetan historical framework overall.

Tibetan traditions and legends trace, for more than thirty generations, the
ancient origins of the dynasty that succeeded in unifying Tibet as an im-
650 perial power during the reign of Songtsen Gampo (c. 617–649/650). The
Tibetan writing system is invented at this time, and, according to later legendary tradition, Buddhism is first introduced by the emperor's Chinese
bride, the princess of Wencheng (d. 684).

700 During the time of the emperor Düsong (d. 704), some temples are probably established. Under his son Trhi Detsuktsen (reigned 705–755/756) the princess of Jincheng (d. 739) promotes both Chinese culture and Buddhism.

750 The emperor Trhi Songdetsen (reigned 755/756–797) adopts Buddhism, probably in 762. In 763 his armies overrun the Chinese capital, Chang'an. He establishes Tibet's first Buddhist monastery, Samye (c. 779), and during the 780s conquers Dunhuang, a major center of Chinese Buddhism. The Chinese Chan master Moheyan is invited to central Tibet and becomes involved in a debate or discussion at Samye with the Indian Buddhist philosopher Kamalaśīla. The Tibetan occupation of Dunhuang leads to the preservation there of numerous Tibetan manuscripts, whose discovery in 1907 provides our richest source of Tibetan documentation for this period.

800 Under Trhi Songdetsen's greatest successors, Trhi Desongtsen (reigned 804–815) and Relpacen (reigned 815–838), Buddhism continues to flour-

ish with royal patronage. In the reign of Lang Darma (838–842), patronage of the monasteries is reduced or withdrawn, and later tradition recounts that there was a persecution of Buddhism culminating in Lang Darma's assassination in 842 by a Buddhist monk.

850 The collapse of the Central Tibetan royal dynasty follows, with the ensuing
900 power vacuum persisting for a full four hundred years, until the Sakyapas, backed by China's Mongol rulers, emerge as Tibet's supreme rulers during the late thirteenth century.

950 The revival of monastic Buddhism in Central Tibet begins towards the middle of the tenth century. During the late tenth and early eleventh centuries, Tibetan Buddhism enters a new period of rapid development and change. Local lords vie for ascendency, and religious authority is no less contested than temporal power. From the late tenth century onwards we find Tibetan translators and pilgrims journeying to India and Nepal in search of gurus, scriptures, and esoteric lore.

1000 These developments are particularly prominent in Western Tibet, where the great translator Rinchen Zangpo (958–1055) is patronized by the monarchs of the Guge kingdom. The Indian scholar and adept Atiśa (982–1054) is invited to teach there beginning in 1042. The careers of these two notable Buddhist monks mark the beginning of what Tibetan historians call the "later spread of the teaching," or the age of the "new translations." In reaction to these new developments the older Tibetan religious traditions—the Bön religion and the Nyingmapa, or "ancient," school of Buddhism—reassert themselves.

1050 The new infusion of Indian Buddhist teaching gives rise to a number of new Tibetan Buddhist sects and schools. Among the most prominent are the Kadampa, stemming from Atiśa's successors, the Sakyapa, representing the tradition of the Khön family's monastery at Sakya (founded in 1073), and the Kagyüpa, maintaining the tantric teachings of the translator Marpa (1012–1097).

1100 The Kadampa monastery at Sangphu is founded in 1071 or 1073 and swiftly emerges as the leading center for the study of logic and other philosophical topics. Marpa's successors proliferate into a large number of Kagyüpa sublineages following Gampopa (1079–1153), the foremost disciple of the poet Milarepa (1040–1123). During the same period Khyungpo Neljor (d. c. 1135) independently establishes the Shangpa Kagyüpa tantric tradition.

1150 The reassertion of the Bön and Nyingmapa traditions is advanced by means of rediscovered "treasures" (*gter-ma*), texts and religious objects said to have been cached in earlier times and now recovered. Nyangrel Nyima Özer (1124–1196) in this way produces a tremendous body of historical and legendary literature that exerts a very considerable influence on the later development of both historiography and religious thought.

1200 In 1204, the Kashmiri scholar Śākyaśrī arrives in Tibet with a retinue of learned Indian followers, and their visit helps to catalyze a new enthusiasm for Indian scholarship. An heir to the Khön family of Sakya, who becomes famed as Sakya Paṇḍita (1182–1251), devotes himself to the advancement in Tibet of Indian intellectual traditions.

1250 In 1246, Sakya Paṇḍita is invited to visit the Mongol ruler, thus initiating the relationship between Sakya and Mongol power that dominates Tibetan politics for the next century. His nephew, Chögyel Phakpa (1235–1280), becomes state preceptor under Khubilai Khan. Members of non-Sakyapa sects also maintain relations with the Mongol lords; examples are the second Karmapa hierarch, Karma Pakshi (1204–1283), and his successor, Karmapa III Rangjung Dorje (1284–1339).

1300 During the period of the Mongol-Sakyapa hegemony, Tibetan Buddhist scholastic philosophy comes into flower. The many famous figures active during this period include the Kadampa scholiast Rikpe Reldri (early fourteenth century), the redactor of the Tibetan Buddhist canon, Butön (1290–1364), the founder of the controversial "extrinsic emptiness" teaching, Dölpopa (1292–1361), and the master of the Great Perfection system, Longchenpa (1308–1363).

1350 Under the leadership of Tai Situ Changchub Gyeltshen of the Phakmodrupa order, Tibet is freed from the Sakyapa-Mongol regime. The historical writings "rediscovered" by Orgyen Lingpa (b. 1323) contribute to the mythologizing of the 8th-century Tibetan empire. Scholastic philosophy continues to thrive, particularly in the monastic centers allied with the scholarly traditions of Sakya.

1400 Je Tsongkhapa (1357–1419) founds the Ganden monastery to the east of Lhasa (1409), which soon gives rise to a new Buddhist order, the Gelukpa, and emphasizes its continuities with the older Kadampa school. Though greatly revered for his vast learning and rigorous standard of practice, relations between his disciples and some representatives of the other orders grow increasingly contentious. The fifteenth and sixteenth centuries witness intensive doctrinal debate between the Gelukpas and their Sakyapa and Kagyüpa rivals.

The rise of the Gelukpa order coincides with a period of sustained civil war in Tibet. By the sixteenth century, important powers in the central Tibetan province of Ü are allied with the Gelukpas, while the kings of Tsang in the west support hierarchs of the Kagyüpa and other schools. One of the leading Gelukpa hierarchs, Sonam Gyamtsho, becomes a missionary to the Mongols and, on winning the allegiance of the chieftain Altan Khan (1578), receives the Mongolian title Dalai Lama ("oceanic guru"). Because the title is bestowed posthumously on his predecessors, he becomes the third in the line. The connection forged with the Mongols encourages the renewed interest of the Mongolian leadership in Tibetan affairs, and in 1642 Gushri Khan of the Khoshot tribe conquers all of Tibet, establishing the Fifth Dalai Lama (1617–1682) as ruler of the reunified realm.

In 1717, the Mongolian Dzungar tribe invades Tibet, bringing renewed civil war and intersectarian violence. The Manchu rulers of China's Qing dynasty (1644–1911) become directly involved in the events in Tibet and during the 1720s consolidate direct rule over large parts of the eastern Tibetan provinces of Amdo and Kham. Throughout the eighteenth and nineteenth centuries, however, these regions emerge as new centers of creative energy in the development of Tibetan Buddhist thought.

The Tibetan Assimilation of Buddhism

1

Introduction

Death, Literacy, and Tibet's Buddhist Elite

Before Buddhism made its presence felt in Tibet, as it did during the eighth and ninth centuries C.E., and even as the Buddha's teaching began to establish itself there, it was but one of several foreign ways of culture with which the Tibetans were becoming familiar. Besides Tibet's ancient indigenous traditions, that are still perceptible both in their persistent survivals and in elements of the earliest written records,[1] early medieval Tibet knew of Chinese historiography and Greek medicine, Nepalese sculpture and Sogdian textiles, Nestorian Christianity and Manichaeism.[2] The penetration by Buddhism of Tibetan culture, so that the two would become to all intents and purposes indivisibly associated, was not yet previsioned, and to explain the success and thoroughness of Buddhism's Tibetan conquest remains a central problem for the historical study and interpretation of Tibetan civilization. The sketches of three key issues given here may serve as an introduction, delineating some important aspects of the rise of Buddhism in Tibet, and providing a point of departure for the studies that follow in later chapters.

Like some who have in recent years considered the relations among systematic and narrative modes of discourse,[3] I am concerned throughout this book with the study of a particular cultural sphere that is not our own, in this instance the realm of Tibetan Buddhism. Investigations such as these tend to underscore the apparent gulf separating descriptive and documentary scholarship from the domain of theory and interpretation, while at the same time they call into question any such deep divide. In the study of cultural history, this emerges wherever the question of contextualization imposes itself upon us, as it does whenever complex domains of discourse—worlds of thought in which myth and science, history and metaphysics, logic and poetry intersect, blend, and rebound—become subject matter for our reflections. We know that contextual background plays a crucial role in understanding, so we can't eliminate it. But we can't seem to come up with a decisive formulation of what that role is to be, so often we'd like to. I very much doubt that we shall ever be able to provide a purely methodological account of contextualization that would also serve as an acceptable guide to practice.[4] The scholar as contextualizer must in the end be a myth maker, spinning tales of reason, truth, and history, in virtue of which the actions, arts, sciences, and, myths of persons elsewhere and elsewhen may become somehow more intelligible for us than they would have been otherwise. In this regard, not all myths are equal: some succeed relatively better than others in the task of making the foreign intelligible to us, and thereby opening our own world of discourse to voices previously unheard.

Before turning to some of my own myths, I must briefly mention certain widespread conceptions of the history of Buddhism in Tibet that in our present context can be misleading, obscuring for us the real complexities of historical processes and cultural patterns.[5] On the one hand, Tibetan Buddhism is often presented as an arch-conservative tradition, preserving unchanged for a full millenium the religious culture of northeastern India's great Buddhist monasteries. It is urged that only the Buddhism of Tibet, at least in its orthodox forms, authentically embodies the totality of the Indian Buddhist heritage, faithfully maintained throughout the centuries with little appreciable innovation or deformation.[6] This viewpoint is certainly fostered by the genuine conservatism of many aspects of ritual and practice, but also by the ideology of monastic Buddhism in Tibet, in this respect an ideology that often appears to systematically devalue innovation and personal inventiveness, considering them sources of deviation and of the transgression of the genius of the past.[7] From this perspective, the brilliance of Tibetan Buddhism has been precisely its unalterable adherence to the form and content of Indian Buddhism, as sanctioned by the Buddha himself. It is a viewpoint that is radically ahistorical. It is, in short, a form of religious perennialism.

Opposed to this, it has also often been held that Buddhism in Tibet was the result of radical transformations in which the character of the Indian Buddhist tradition was all but lost. Tibetan Buddhism, it is said, was indeed the product of Indian Buddhism, but liberally mixed with large doses of Hindu tantrism and indigenous Tibetan demonology and superstition.[8] By contrast, contemporary popular Buddhism in the West has in recent years begun to elaborate a more generous interpretation of change within Buddhist traditions, maintaining that the various Buddhisms of the Asian past, of which Tibetan Buddhism is offered as a paradigmatic example, must be seen as creative traditions that for good reason did not merely replicate their Indian sources but ingeniously adapted them to local conditions. This, it is sometimes argued, provides an historical warrant for the current fabrication of a distinctively Western Buddhism.

What I wish to emphasize here is that the Tibetan Buddhist tradition was not, for all its conservatism, a static replication of Indian antiquity, nor, in its dynamic aspects, was it the product of deliberate contrivance on the part of Tibetans motivated to construct a uniquely Tibetan form of Buddhism.[9] Buddhism in Tibet developed through a sustained and subtle process, whereby the foreign religion achieved a decisive cultural hegemony but was at the same time, as conquerors almost always are, transformed by its own success. Aspects of that process, as evidenced within the sphere of Tibetan Buddhist thought, will be our chief concern in these pages.

We may begin, however, by reflecting upon a single general problem: what sorts of evidence do we find of historical change in Tibetan thought as a result of the advent of Buddhism? Some may argue, of course, that the initial presence of Buddhism in Tibet did not really change much of anything at all.[10] My own view is that it did, and that it did so profoundly. To illustrate this, let us consider briefly three topics that may stand as examples: death, literacy, and aspects of the formation of the Tibetan cultural elite.

The Uncertain Fate of the Dead

Both the archaeological record and the earliest written documents demonstrate the importance to pre-Buddhist Tibet of mortuary rites.[11] The *Old Tibetan Chronicle*, found at Dunhuang and dating perhaps to the late eighth or early ninth century, opens with an account of the death of the first mortal king, whose forebears had passed directly to the heavens leaving no earthly remains, and it recounts the origins of royal burial practice: the monarch's hair was to be braided and his face painted with vermilion; his body was preserved in a mausoleum, with offerings of food and drink.[12] The documents from Dunhuang also include a description of the program to be followed at royal funerals, which required the services of an elaborate and specialized priesthood.[13] The royal funerals, as we know from other sources, often followed death by several years, and the two events, death and the culminating performance of the last rites, were scrupulously recorded in the imperial annals, reinforcing our impression that these were especially solemn moments for the old Tibetan monarchy.[14] Later Tibetan historiography clearly reflects this, for one of the details mentioned in connection with most of the early monarchs is the construction and placement of their mausoleums.[15] These ancient tombs, in fact, have remained hallowed places of pilgrimage down to our own times.[16]

The careful attendance of the dead, their provision with adequate nutrition, and also the traditions concerning the direct bodily ascent of the most ancient kings to the heavens—these convince us that early on there must have been well-formed Tibetan beliefs concerning the fate of the dead. Just what those beliefs were, however, remains unclear.[17] As will be seen in chapter 3, there is some reason to hold that the possibility of reincarnation, at least in the event of neonatal death, was maintained, further supporting the impression that there was indeed a conception of the persistence of some type of soul. Even in this case, however, it is clear that the stable continuity of the family, and not speculation about the afterlife, was the central concern.[18] Indeed, as the later Tibetan institution of an incarnate religious hierarchy demonstrates, the Buddhist teaching of transmigration would itself eventually be made to serve an ancient and autochthonous Tibetan interest in stable succession.[19] Whatever the uncertainties of these matters when seen from our present perspective, however, several of the earliest Tibetan Buddhist documents clearly treat the Buddhist conception of a repeating cycle of birth, death, and rebirth as alien to earlier Tibetan belief. A particularly striking example, now well known to Tibetanists through the work of Yoshiro Imaeda, is *The Cycle of Birth and Death,* whose opening canto recounts this tale:

> Throughout numberless aeons in the past,
> All corporeal beings and all of the gods,
> Because they live for many years,
> Have not beheld the phenomena of birth and death.

Thus they hope to remain alive forever.
The lord of their realm, Light Blazing King,[20]
Dwelt in the heavenly mansion of Exalted Light,
Radiating with fine light, unbearable to behold.
All those dwelling, above and below,
Appeared there as if in a mirror.
The windows are adorned with sun and moon;
It is a fine place, a happy dwelling—no end to what can be said!
All wealth appears just as you think it—
All of it is magical stuff!
His body is as if blazing with golden light,
And his thousand sons and retinue of ten thousand relations,
Thus appearing with magical power,
All hope to remain this way forever!
At some time the Light Blazing King of that realm
Fell upon the time when his life had run out:
Unable to demonstrate his qualities of magical power,
The excellent bodily light that had blazed now dimmed.
Forgetting to speak and even the movement of breath,
He thought all of this was startling.
Though he asked each and every one,
"What was my fault? How to fix it?"
No one knew how this was to be fixed.
The whole retinue of his thousand sons and ten thousand relations
Fell into an ocean of woe;
Beating their breasts and beating their arms, they lamented,
And hoped that what had been would come again.
Among the gods was one of long life,
Called Dutara the Great Wizard.
He came to Light Blazing's dwelling
And explained to them their error and bewilderment.
"All of you are sullied with ignorance!
Everyone in this realm
After seventy thousand aeons have passed
Comes to be just like this!
This is called the principle of birth and death.
I know not what benefits it."
When he'd explained this many times,
The best son of Light Blazing King,
Whose name was Precious Jewel,[21]
Having listened thoughtfully with respect
Knew that it was really true.
"When the time of birth and death thus befalls us,
What's there to do? What's fit?
By doing what will we be happy?"
So he asked the Great Wizard with respect.
Dutara answered back,

"Having discovered the existence of birth and of death,
I've not found what's of use.
If you wish to inquire about the principle of birth and death,
Then [depart] from here, by goodness.
There is the Lord of the Gods, Wizard of the Three Realms,
Who is a very great and venerable wizard;
It would be best to ask and inquire of him."
This was explained most perspicaciously,
And then the son of the gods, Precious Jewel,
Moved with respect by his father's woe
Thought not at all of happy realms.
Striving to examine the principle of birth and death,
With a retinue of many skilled in wizardry,
He went off to [to seek out that] wizard,
Not recalling at all the way home.[22]

Whatever earlier Tibetan beliefs may have been, the Buddhist conception of re-death,[23] of death after death striking even the gods, must have been a terrifying discovery. Precious Jewel ultimately finds the goal of his quest in India, meeting there with the Buddha of the present age, Śākyamuni. The Buddha, in conclusion, assuages the fears of the Tibetan gods by teaching to them a tantric funeral ritual that will insure the future well-being of the deceased.[24]

Another Dunhuang manuscript contains a short collection of Buddhist texts connected with funerary rituals.[25] It is of considerable interest, for while presaging in some respects the developed Tibetan literature on the *bar-do*, the "intermediary state" intervening between death and rebirth, it also contains, in its later passages not quoted here, a critique of more ancient Tibetan beliefs.[26] At the same time, however, as Imaeda once more has pointed out, it seems to incorporate elements that cannot be traced in properly Buddhist mortuary rituals but that may be of archaic Tibetan origin, namely, its direct calls addressed to the deceased.[27] This would later emerge as a hallmark of the rites of the *bar-do:*

Now listen, you who are deceased! Fickle impermanence, the real nature of the whole world, has at this time befallen you, the deceased. The illusion of the five conditioned bundles has been undone. It's time to provide you with the great refuge for one who journeys from this world to the next. Your lords and refuges, in journeying as one without a second to uncertain domains, are the Buddhas, who are transcendent lords, the bodhisattvas, who are great heroes, and the exalted arhats. None are greater than these. Therefore, you who are deceased, do not let your mind stray, do not allow your thoughts to rebel, but at all times think on the Three Precious Jewels, and, turning to those Precious Jewels, let the mind's path tend to nothing else whatsoever! Do not unbalance the scales of thought!

Hear more, you who are deceased! Obtaining illusory bodies in this prison of the three realms, all who are born die in the end. No one is free from that! Journeying thus from one birth to the next, the path of birth and death is oppressive. Remember that that's how it is!

Eighty-thousand *yojana* beneath this Rose-Apple Continent is the place of great hell, where the ground is blazing iron. There, in a blazing iron house, numberless hundreds of thousands are cooked, burned, and tormented by many most powerful demons. In unbearable suffering they utter loud cries and moan in lamentation. Because there exists such a hellish place, O you who are deceased, take care not to miss your path and to stumble!

But if, perchance, you fear you might fall, there is a bodhisattva called the exalted Avalokiteśvara, who will protect you straight away from that great hell. Remember his name, pray to him . . . , recite his mantra, beseech him for refuge, and you will be freed from that awful place.[28]

Following this, the soul is guided to avoid falling into birth among the tormented spirits (*yi-dwags*, Skt. *preta*) and animals. Escaping thus the infernal realms, the final goal to which the deceased is now conducted is indeed the goal of the Buddhist path, nirvāṇa, but interestingly it is very closely associated in this case with paradise,[29] as is reflected in one of the titles by which this rite is designated, the "teaching of the path to the gods' realm" (*lha-yul-du lam bstan-pa*). The text here continues:

From this Rose-Apple Continent, there is in the north Mount Meru. It is the king of mountains, made of four sorts of precious gems. On its summit is the gathering place of the gods of the excellent religion, where the lord of the gods, Indra, and his thirty-two ministers open the way and show the paths of gods and men and of the world. There that king of the gods will teach the instructions of the doctrine to you, O worthy son, and the power of [your] merits will be emptied. O worthy son! then on the northern summit of Mount Meru, there is the palace called Alakāvatī, where the transcendent lord, glorious Vajrapāṇi, dwells with a retinue of many wrathful ones.[30] Worthy son, he will confer empowerment upon you, granting all desires to your heart's content. Then, worthy son, owing to the blessing of Vajrapāṇi, continue your journey, and in the divine abode of Tuṣita there is the religious regent of Buddha Śākyamuni, who is called sublime Maitreya. His retinue includes the bodhisattvas Vasumitra and Siṃhāntara, the 996 bodhisattvas of the Auspicious Aeon, and others, as well as numberless godlings. In a jeweled palace, with flowing godly robes, the enjoyment of varied musical instruments, and other such things unimaginable, the perfect provisions of happiness, in that holy, divine land may you be cautious about those many joys!

Worthy son, do not be complacent with divine enjoyment and its delights alone, but convey yourself and all sentient beings to perfect nirvāṇa! Establish an attitude that never tires of seeking the accumulations of merit and gnosis! May you obtain, too, freedom from the passions.[31]

Unlike the later Tibet traditions of the *bar-do*, which direct the deceased to avoid all realms of rebirth, and to attain the highest enlightenment without falling into either infernal or divine abodes, the "teaching of the path to the gods' realm" regards divine rebirth as a passage through which one must journey in order to arrive at Buddhism's supreme end.

From the late tenth century onwards, Tibet became the stage for the renewed transmission of Buddhist teachings and esoteric lore from India. Rituals, meditations, and yogic practices, including many that were intended to forestall death or to ensure that the deceased would realize an auspicious path, were now introduced in great numbers, and accordingly the funerary rites of Tibetan authorship respond to or absorb these new sources. The so-called *Tibetan Book of the Dead*, redacted during the fourteenth century, is only the most famous product of this process.[32]

One of the many colorful figures involved in the revived transmission of tantric esotericism during this period was Khyungpo Neljor, "the yogin of the Eagle clan."[33] Though there is considerable uncertainty about his precise dates, the main period of his activity seems to have been the late eleventh through early twelfth centuries. Originally an adherent of the Bön religion, he converted to Buddhism and became at first a follower of the ancient Nyingmapa school. Like many others of his generation, however, he regarded India as the source of uniquely authoritative Buddhist teachings, and so he left Tibet to pursue his path in the Kathmandu Valley of Nepal, and in India proper.

Among Khyungpo Neljor's surviving writings is a brief collection of instructions concerning the *bar-do* teachings as derived from the systems of tantric yoga he had studied.[34] Though he does clearly refer there to Indian works that had been introduced to Tibet before the end of the eleventh century, the text is striking for its continued development of the apparently indigenous Tibetan tradition of calling the dead. It incorporates, too, the Chinese Buddhist custom of practicing the death rites for seven weeks, by mentioning the possibility that the *bar-do* will itself last for seven weeks, a temporal specification that is well known in connection with the later *Book of the Dead.*[35] It further presages the *Book of the Dead* by its constant reference to the sophisticated metaphysical doctrines of Mahāyāna Buddhism, inasmuch as these had been incorporated into later Indian Buddhist tantrism.[36] For instance, in one passage Khyungpo Neljor writes:

> Now, if the intermediate state is brief it lasts one week, and if long, then after experiencing the varied pains and manifestations of the intermediate state for seven weeks you will take birth again. What's more, if at that time you should think "I'm dead!" then those of you who possess the instructions will be reached at that time by the voice of the guru, saying, "Know the intermediate state to be the intermediate state! Meditatively cultivate the conqueror's body of rapture!" and so you will know not to be frightened, because here is a time for awakening as a buddha. Hence, you will petition the guru and cultivate the contemplation that all the appearances of the intermediate state are your own projections, and that all your own projections are nonveridical apparition and dream. You will place your devotion in the emanations and transformations of the meditational deity, and especially think to meditate upon the outer environment as the celestial palace, the inner inhabitants as gods and goddesses, and your own body as the threefold deity. Just then, owing to the powers realized in the cultivation of [the yoga of] the dream during your previous life, you may naturally arise in the conqueror's body of perfect rapture, adorned with major and minor marks, apparent but insubstantial, without hankering for veridical existence—this is a divine body, the great seal (*mahāmudrā*), whose essence is the body of reality (*dharmakāya*), whose phenomenal features are the body of rapture (*sambhogakāya*), whose activities are the emanational body (*nirmāṇakāya*), and which, in their indivisibility, is the body of great bliss (*mahāsukhakāya*). Thereby, until the sea of saṃsāra is emptied, training each in accord with his or her needs, you will bring sentient beings to maturation and liberation.[37]

With the wide distribution of the *Book of the Dead* and similar works, such conceptions came to pervade both Tibetan beliefs regarding the possible fate of the dead, and the formulation of ritual means whereby the lasting peace of the dead might best be secured.[38] But the changes we have surveyed here were not the result of the importation of Buddhist beliefs and practices plain and simple; they were the product, rather, of an ongoing process of accommodation, in which the alien and the indigenous came by stages to suffuse one another.

Literacy and Learning in a Dark Age

As the foregoing sketch of the history of death in Tibet makes clear, there were two periods of great and profound historical change that formed the background for the particular transformations we have examined. The first of these occurred with the rise and expansion of the old Tibetan empire in the seventh to ninth centuries and the second a century or so after its fall, with the revival of the transmission of Indian Buddhism to Tibet towards the end of the tenth century. The remaining chapters of this book take up various aspects of Buddhism under the empire and during the period of post–tenth-century revival. One of the great puzzles in the study of Tibetan history, however, remains the "dark age" of a century or so intervening between the two. Because only a small number of documents can be assigned with reasonable certainty to this period, for the most part our conclusions about it must of necessity be derived indirectly. Reflection on the maintenance of literacy, and on the uses of literacy for the representation and organization of knowledge, are particularly suggestive in this regard.

According to tradition, the Tibetan language was first written during the early seventh century, when the monarch Songtsen Gampo (c. 617–649/650) commanded that a standard script be devised. His minister Thönmi Saṃbhoṭa is said to have been dispatched to Kashmir, where he studied Indian systems of writing and the Sanskrit language. On the basis of his studies under brahman masters, he invented a Tibetan alphabet and also composed a series of grammars for the new literary language. Though the veracity of this account has been regarded with skepticism in recent scholarship, there can be no doubt that the seventh and eighth centuries saw the development of written Tibetan as a vehicle for both administration and the transmission of culture, and that the growth of Tibetan literacy contributed to great and enduring changes in the Tibetan world. Literacy facilitated the redaction and regularization of indigenous Tibetan laws and traditions; the governance of the tremendous territory ruled by the old Tibetan empire, with its diverse peoples and customs, until its collapse in the ninth century; and, crucially, the absorption by the Tibetans of vast quantities of alien learning. We shall return to these and other questions posed by the development of Tibetan literacy during this period in chapter 4.

Traditional accounts of early postimperial Tibetan history, repeated throughout later Tibetan historical writing, maintain that, following a persecution of Buddhism that was supposed to have occurred at the order of the emperor Lang Darma, and in the wake of his assassination, probably in 842, Buddhist activity in Tibet virtually ground to a halt, not to be revived for perhaps a hundred years.[39] The few monks who both survived and continued to uphold their vows are said to have fled Central Tibet to find refuge in the far northeast, in what is today Qinghai. Their presence there formed the seed for a Tibetan monastic revival, which brought about a reestablishment of Buddhism in Central Tibet during the mid–tenth century.[40] Besides the transmission of the monastic vows, traditional sources concur that some Tibetan Buddhist educational activity also continued throughout the "dark age" in far eastern Tibet, though there is disagreement about the extent and precise nature of such activity. In particular, there is reason to hold that some elements of Buddhist scholastic learning—for instance, the formal study of the regulations of the Vinaya and of the "meta-doctrine," or Abhidharma, as well as of the important Perfection of Wisdom treatise, the *Abhisamayālaṃkāra* (The Ornament of Emergent Realization)—did indeed remain alive in the east.[41]

It is clear, though, that matters must have been far more complex than this account alone suggests: how, for example, was the knowledge of the imposing Buddhist translation literature that had been created under the empire preserved over a span of three or four generations in the absence of all but a smattering of ongoing Buddhist education in the Tibetan far east? Though some religious communities in the east no doubt preserved important traditions of Tibetan Buddhist learning established earlier while the empire still held sway, it seems unlikely that book learning was exclusively sustained in this way. Deeper reflection on the available evidence suggests that Tibetan Buddhism, once established under the empire, never really vanished. Though the period in question was a sort of Tibetan "dark age," it is clear that, as was the case for its counterpart in Europe, even in the darkness the light was never entirely extinguished.

One sign that Tibetan remained alive as a literary language during this time, primarily in surviving (and perhaps even growing) Buddhist circles, is that the literary Tibetan that develops after the tenth century is to a great degree derived from what had earlier been a language of scriptural translation. At the same time, the archaic literary Tibetan known from Dunhuang, the old royal inscriptions, and other early sources, gradually falls out of use, becoming increasingly obscure to later generations of Tibetans. Thus, it seems plausible that following the collapse of the dynasty, as the archaic language used by the civil and military adminstration became obsolete and a literate culture was preserved largely among Tibet's Buddhists, Buddhist usage gradually emerged as the standard, even in writing about subjects such as history that had previously been written in the language employed by the state bureaucracy.[42] Some such development would have contributed to the iconizing of Buddhism and its originally Indian context as the paradigms of learned (that is, literate) and prestigious culture. The persistence of Tibetan literacy to a degree that permitted knowledge of sophisticated Buddhist texts to be preserved, including some knowledge of Tibetan-Sanskrit lexicography,[43] must certainly count as prima facie evidence that Tibet's dark age was not nearly so bleak as the traditional historiography would have us suppose. Several other considerations support this same conclusion.

To begin, the earliest available sources by no means establish the persecution of Buddhism by Lang Darma, a crucial event for later Tibetan historical consciousness, to have in fact occurred. Several scholars have now argued that little more than a reduction of patronage may have been at stake, and that there is good evidence showing Lang Darma himself to have been initially a Buddhist king who enjoyed the good wishes of the clergy.[44] This, however, may go too far in the way of rehabilitating the apostate king: we must note that there is one manuscript from Dunhuang, dating probably to the end of the tenth century, that strikingly does *not* mention Lang Darma in an enumeration of Tibet's royal patrons of Buddhism, though at the same time it contains no suggestion of a persecution.[45] It seems possible that the persecution, despite its great importance in later thought, was in essence a withdrawal of patronage, no doubt due to a poor current accounts balance rather than to anti-Buddhist sentiment,[46] which came to be very much exaggerated in its retellings.

In addition, as the historiography of the Nyingmapa tradition underscores, the persecution is not supposed to have much affected lay adherents of tantric Buddhism, and other sources, too, emphasize familial lineages of tantric practioners active during this time.[47] Many of the Dunhuang Tibetan tantric manuscripts probably are also to be attributed to the period between the fall of the dynasty and the cultural renaissance in western Tibet towards the end of the first millenium.[48] However we interpret reports, beginning as early as the late tenth century, that the Tibetan tantrism of this period had grown degenerate,[49] we may nevertheless attribute to tantric circles some role in maintaining basic skills of alphabetization. Just as the Japanese *kana* syllabary is supposed to have been derived from principles used in the phonetic representation of Buddhist mantras, so in the Tibetan case the ritual requirements of esoteric Buddhism, though not involved in the initial formation of the script, may well have contributed to its maintenance and promotion.[50]

Further, let us note that Lang Darma's successors, who ruled variously truncated portions of the old empire, mostly seem to have maintained clearly Buddhist identities, and to have sponsored projects including temple building and calendrical rectification that surely would have required the services of persons with some formal learning. Though later historical traditions tended to forget or to ignore the evidence in this area, the earliest available records provide indications of such activities continuing even in the midst of the dark age in Central Tibet.[51]

Finally, we must add that there are indications, derived from Chinese sources reporting on Tibetan populations in far northeastern Tibet during the tenth century, that Buddhist activity in those parts was in fact far more extensive than the later Tibetan histories would have us believe.[52] In short, there were likely several different cultural formations in early postimperial Tibet that were able to maintain to varying degrees basic skills in the use of the written language, and these were mostly, so far as we can now determine, tied to Buddhism in one way or another.

I have already suggested that the written language itself was transformed as a result of the dominance of what had at first been an artificial language of translation. Are there other important changes that seem due to the tie now forged between Buddhism and Tibetan literacy? There are, certainly, many examples that may be adduced in response to this question, and the later chapters of this book show some of the extent to which narratives and ideas derived from Buddhist writings became the naturalized media for Tibetan self-expression. Suffice it to add in brief here one illustration that indicates something of the depth of the impact made by the Buddhist domination of literacy upon the formation of Tibetan thought.

As is well known, there is in Tibet an organized religion besides Buddhism that is regarded by Tibetans as the religion of pre-Buddhist Tibet, namely, Bön. In contemporary scholarship, doubts have been expressed about whether there was in fact an *organized* Tibetan religion prior to the introduction of Buddhism, and whether the term *bon*, as used in archaic documents, names such a religion.[53] These questions need not detain us here, for it seems relatively clear that, once Buddhism had established itself in Tibet, the indigenous religious traditions, whether organized or not, underwent enormous transformations that were in large measure catalyzed by Buddhism's presence. The Bön religion as we now know it, with its monastic institutions, tantric rituals, and scriptural canons, is surely the most remarkable outcome of such transformations. At the same time, this must not be taken to suggest that the Bön religion came into existence merely as a nativist reaction to Buddhism. The formation of Bön involved an intricate synthesis of archaic Tibetan tradition not only with Buddhism, but with other cultural influences flowing into Tibet as well.[54]

The massive collections of Bönpo scriptures that have become recently available have not yet been adequately studied.[55] General remarks about them are of necessity unsure, and the investigation of the Bönpo textual traditions promises to provide fertile subject matter for Tibetan Studies for many years to come. Nevertheless, on the basis of what is already known, it is evident that the formation of the Bönpo corpus, while preserving and recording vast quantities of indigenous Tibetan tradition, among many other matters, was also responsive to Buddhist textual models throughout. This becomes especially clear with the revelation, from the late tenth century onwards of the Bönpo versions of the *Prajñāpāramitā* and other important canonical sūtras.[56] Though there are indications that there was indeed a literate Bön (or "proto-Bön") priesthood active during the early postimperial period, and perhaps even before,[57] it seems sure that their literary production came increasingly to fall under a Buddhist star. This may be seen, for instance, in examining the analysis in early Bön and Buddhist sources of approaches to spiritual practice in terms of various schemes involving nine sequential "vehicles" (*theg-pa rim-pa dgu*).[58] Though the metaphor of the vehicle as a spiritual path is certainly derived from Indian Buddhism,[59] it is likely that the ninefold enumeration was a Tibetan innovation. In sources plausibly composed in the tenth century, or soon thereafter, there is considerable disagreement about how the nine are to be enumerated, though the various systems overlap considerably. An early Buddhist version from Dunhuang, for instance, declares:

> One might ask, to what does "nine sequential vehicles" refer? The nine vehicles are the vehicle of men, the vehicle of gods, the vehicle of pious attendants (*śrāvaka*), the vehicle of the self-realized ones (*pratyekabuddha*), the vehicle of the sūtras, the vehicle of the bodhisattvas, and then the Yoga, Kriyā and Upaya.[60]

Another Buddhist text, the *Man-ngag lta-ba'i phreng-ba* (The Garland of Views: An Esoteric Precept), attributed to Padmasambhava and certainly in circulation prior to the eleventh century,[61] adopts a different scheme of enumeration:

> The numberless erroneous views of sentient beings in the realms of the world may be gathered into four categories: indifferent, materialistic, nihilistic, and extremist. . . . [But] in the path transcending the world, there are two: the dialectical vehicle and the vehicle of indestructible reality (*vajrayāna*). And in the dialectical vehicle there are three: (1) the vehicle of the pious attendants, (2) the vehicle of the self-realized ones, and (3) the vehicle of the bodhisattvas. . . . In the vehicle of indestructible reality there are also three aspects: (4) the vehicle of the Kriyātantra, (5) the vehicle of Ubhayatantra, and (6) the vehicle of Yoga. . . . The view of those who have entered into the vehicle of the Yogatantra is twofold: outer yoga, which is the

> vehicle of the tantra of austerity; and inner yoga, which is the vehicle of the tantra of means. . . . The view of those who have entered the vehicle of the inner yoga, the tantra of means, is threefold: (7) the way of creation, (8) the way of perfection, and (9) the way of great perfection.[62]

These may be compared now with the account given in the *Theg-pa'i rim-pa mngon-du bshad-pa'i mdo-rgyud* (The Canon Expounding the Sequence of Vehicles), a Bönpo treatise of the "Central Treasure" (*dbus-gter*), whose Tibetan rendition is attributed to the eighth-century translator Vairocana, and which was perhaps redacted sometime after the late tenth century:[63]

> In the great abode, the unsurpassed expanse of essential Bön,
> Dwelt the supreme teacher, Shenlha Ökar.
> To his circle of emanational embodiments, [who are] entirely [of his] gnosis,
> He proclaimed this teaching, a sūtra expounding fully the sequence of vehicles . . . .
> "All the sequences of the vehicles,
> If explained in sum, are gathered in two:
> The outer extremists and the inner adherents of Shenrap. . . .[64]
> Concerning the perverse view [of the outer extremists]:
> Formerly, there was a son of the gods, the sage Shega Rapden,
> Who clairvoyantly saw destruction
> When a being, transmigrating, came to be disembodied.
> Then, to the circle of ladies who always befriended him, Shega said:
> 'Oh! lasting friends, my fair princess, and you ladies attendant,
> Until death let us rejoice and make love!
> For after death there is no scope for action;
> When the body, destroyed, passes away like dust,
> What revitalization will there be?
> The mind will not endure when bodily continuity halts.'
> So saying they seized upon this perversely. . . .
>
> "If the inner vehicle of Shenrap be summarized, there are two,
> For it is explained that there are both cause and fruition.
> The causal vehicle also includes two:
> The greater vehicle and lesser vehicle.
> The fruitional vehicle includes two as well,
> For it is explained that there are both outer and inner.
> Therefore, one speaks of the trio of outer, inner, and secret vehicles.
> The lesser vehicle comprises two:
> (1) the vehicle relying on other gods and men,
> And (2) the vehicle of the self-realized Shenrap.
> The greater vehicle also has two:
> (3) The greater vehicle of compassionate spiritual warriors,
> And (4) the unelaborate vehicle of auspicious spiritual warriors.
> There are two vehicles of the outer fruitional mantra:
> (5) The vehicle of original Bön, involving rituals and purifications,
> And (6) the vehicle of supernormal cognition, complete in all aspects.
> The inner vehicle of secret mantra has three:

(7) The vehicle of compassionate play, involving actual creation,
(8) The vehicle of complete perfection, which is exceedingly profitable,
And (9) the original great perfection, the unsurpassed, highest pinnacle."[65]

There are many intriguing features of this text that illustrate both the manner in which Bönpo doctrinal authors during the period with which we are concerned sought to achieve a distinctive synthesis and the degree to which the field of textual interraction among differing traditions was now largely defined by the modalities of Buddhist knowledge.[66] The opening passage, for instance, with its account of the divine sage Shega Rapden, appears to accord well with developing conventions of Tibetan narrative and reminds us to some extent of the Buddhist tale of the god Precious Jewel, which we have examined earlier. The reader may not notice, however, that Shega's expression of hedonism is borrowed almost verbatim from Sanskrit sources, and that this sage among Bönpo divinities is in fact a redescription of the *ṛṣi* Bṛhaspati, legendary founder of India's materialist philosophies.[67]

A comparison of these three schemes of nine vehicles, which originate during roughly the same age, but in different traditions, demonstrates at once their affinities (tab. 1).

What, in our present context, is the significance of the similarities and differences we find here? I have argued that, during the period following the collapse of the empire, there was, contrary to impressions derived from the later historiography, an ongoing maintenance of elements of literacy and formal learning, primarily in Buddhist circles. In the formation of the various nine-vehicle schemes, it is evident that such communities were not, however, simply repeating what was to be derived from earlier Buddhist sources, but also were engaged in actively exploring, to varying degrees on the basis of those sources, ways of reformulating and expressing religious traditions that were felt to be congenial to Tibetan ways of thinking. This process rendered it possible for the evolving field of literate agency increasingly to involve the participation of some who asserted the supremacy of the non-Buddhist traditions with which they were identified and which were the established basis for their status and authority, over and against the alien presence of Buddhism. Of course, what was important was not the fact of the foreign or native origin of religious ideas and practices—here, as in so much of our experience, it was the feel of the thing that mattered, and not the historical actualities.

This is not to say, of course, that the emerging Bönpo corpus was mere imitation or that the Bönpo authors lacked originality: recent investigations of relatively early Bönpo dialectical texts, for instance, have demonstrated some excellent examples of genuinely novel developments, even if these were inspired ultimately by still earlier Buddhist sources.[68] In some cases, too, we know that Tibetan Buddhist literature liberally borrowed from Bönpo texts.[69] What seems most impressive, given our emerging knowledge of the formation of the Bönpo tradition, is the range of topics about which Bönpo thinkers ventured to formulate original statements, even if these formulations, consisted, as certainly they sometimes did, in giving literary expression to Buddhist conceptions in distinctively Tibetan terms. In this passage, for instance, we have a delightful summary of exegetical methods applied to the teaching of the spiritual paths and meditational practices of the Great Perfection (*rdzogs-chen*) traditions of Bön, for which the intuitive realization of the "mind of enlightenment" is the focal concern of both study and contemplative practice:

Table 1. Comparison of Three Enumerations of the Nine Vehicles

Dunhuang	*Padmasambhava*	*Bönpo Central Treasure*
	I. WORLDLY VEHICLES "numberless erroneous views of sentient beings"	I. WORLDLY VEHICLES "outer extremists"
	II. DIALECTICAL VEHICLES	II. CAUSAL BÖN
		II.a. *The lesser vehicle*
1. vehicle of men		1. vehicle relying on other gods and men
2. vehicle of gods		
3. vehicle of pious attendants	1. vehicle of pious attendants	
4. vehicle of self-realized ones	2. vehicle of self-realized ones	2. vehicle of the self-realized Shenrap
5. vehicle of sūtras		II.b. *The greater vehicle*
6. vehicle of bodhisattvas	3. vehicle of bodhisattvas	3. greater vehicle of compassionate spiritual warriors
		4. unelaborate vehicle of auspicious spiritual warriors
	III. VAJRAYĀNA	III. FRUITIONAL BON
7. Yoga	4. vehicle of Kriyātantra	III.a. *Outer fruitional mantra*
8. Kriyā	5. vehicle of Ubhayatantra	5. vehicle of original Bon
9. Upaya	6. vehicle of Yoga:	6. vehicle of supernormal cognition
	6.a. Outer Yoga	
	6.b. Inner Yoga	III.b. *Inner vehicle of secret mantra*
	7. way of creation	7. vehicle of compassionate play, involving actual creation
	8. way of perfection	8. vehicle of complete perfection
	9. way of great perfection	9. the original great perfection, the unsurpassed, highest pinnacle

This "mind of enlightenment" (*byang-chub-kyi sems, bodhicitta*) is said to be explained in five ways. First is the explanation that resembles garuḍa's flight: the explanation is offered by traversing in a bound the general extent of the ground [and realizing] the abiding nature of the view [which comprehends that ground]. In the explanation that follows the lion's leap, you collect together the examples and topics that are scattered out of order, and explain the text, restoring order to it. Explanations that proceed with the duck's waddle delimit the topics, lead straight down the path, remove sources of error with scriptural citations, provide a guideline of personal instruction, and so explain the text in full detail. Explanations according to the cuckoo's warble disclose truth with respect to the unerring significance of the mind of enlightenment,[70] so that these explanations excel beyond [those of] the eight [lower] vehicles. Finally, explanations in the manner of the turtle's withdrawal [into its shell] provide the fortunate individual with just the abbreviated pith of the text.[71]

Indian works on Buddhist scriptural exegesis had first been translated into Tibetan during the late eighth and early ninth centuries and clearly provided the initial impetus for Tibetan reflection on such matters.[72] Nevertheless, what we see here is evidence of a process of creative appropriation. However the precise debts of one tradition to the other be apportioned, this should not obscure for us the fact that Buddhist written representations of religious ideas decisively established the framework for later literary developments, but within that framework had also to make room for competing voices.

Elite Buddhism and the Expression of Authority

We know from the old Tibetan documents found at Dunhuang, and from later epic traditions as well, that Tibet had early on elaborated a conception of sacral kingship, profoundly tied to the ideals of an heroic and aristocratic society. The earliest known version of the myth of the first Tibetan king shows not only men, but the entire natural world, leaning in homage towards the king, in honor of his inherent charisma.[73] In both the *Old Tibetan Chronicle* from Dunhuang and the later *Epic of Gesar*, the values of cunning, magical effulgence, and power, and the dangers of the hubris that arises from these, are frequently encountered themes.[74] And once we move from legendary to historical time in the seventh to the ninth centuries, we find that the emperors styled themselves "divine rulers of magical sagacity."[75]

Following the breakup of the old Tibetan empire, those vying for authority sought to recapture elements of this confluence of divinity, wisdom, and power, and connections with Buddhist learning and with those who had reputations for spiritual attainment emerged as important signifiers of merit. This had indeed been presaged in the later empire's adoption of the Buddhist religion. The association of Buddhism with the old monarchy and its successors, its mastery of literacy and learning in this world and of one's destiny hereafter—these are among the factors that help to explain the cultural ascendancy that Buddhism had achieved in Tibet by the eleventh century, when the historical record returns to the light. Personal mastery of Buddhist learning and ritual, above all in forms that were believed to represent authoritative Indian Buddhist sources, now became the preeminent marker of personal excellence, and hence the defining feature of an emerging cultural elite. This is reflected in a passage from the life of Khyungpo Neljor, whose work on the intermediate state following death we have referred to above:

> From the start, since my paternal ancestors were all Bönpo masters, I had a hankering or disposition [for Bönpo teachings]. At age thirteen I studied all the outer and inner Bön teachings with the master Yungdrung-gyel and became learned in them. An assembly of about seven hundred who possessed ritual skull-cups gathered around me, and I composed many rites, treatises, and commentaries, and so caused the Bön teachings to be spread throughout the three provinces of Tibet. I became a Bön scholar and adept, and produced many learned pupils. . . .
>
> Though I actually saw many assemblies of deities and my occult powers became unlimited, so that I became an indisputable [master of Bön], nevertheless some doubts arose in my own mind. I thought, "Bön has not been translated by the paṇḍitas [of India] or by the undisputed translators [of Tibet.] People say that I am not a man of the Dharma, but that I am a Bönpo. So now, as prophesied by the adept Amogha, I must go to India."[76]

Ritual mastery and learning by themselves, it appears, are now insufficient. It is the undisputed possession of Buddhist teachings stemming directly from India that verifies one's worth.

The dichotomy between autochthony and Indian origin, however, was neither equivalent to nor effaced the tension between magical or ritual sources of authority and clerical prestige. That this was a source of continuing rivalry is clearly indicated by the biographies of the eleventh-century masters of the Zur lineage of the Nyingmapa, where we find opposing factions formed even among the disciples of a single master:

> At first, the teacher and his students . . . mainly devoted themselves to study; so there were few who were adept at the rites of enlightened activity. When discussions were held in the teaching court, those who did know the rites were seated among the ignorant, who did not participate in the discussions. [In retaliation] the ritualists would not allow the others to chant when they assembled for the daily *torma* offerings. At this Lama Zurpoche said, "One may be liberated by arriving at the culmination of any subject. It is not right to scorn one another. . . ."[77]

But scorn one another they certainly did. The opposition that we encounter here runs throughout the later history of Tibetan Buddhism and has been interpreted variously by students of Tibetan religion.

Geoffrey Samuel, in his wide-ranging book *Civilized Shamans*, has emphasized the distinction between what he characterizes as "shamanic" and "clerical" Buddhism.[78] Though I now think the former is an unfortunately confusing term that perhaps should be abandoned in this context,[79] I believe that Samuel nevertheless rightly describes an important dichotomy within Tibetan Buddhism, as suggested by the anecdotes just given and also by our earlier examinations of death and of literacy. We may say that, on the one hand, Tibetan Buddhism came to define itself soteriologically, as concerned with the practical attainment of freedom, whether from the ills of this life, or from evil rebirth, or from saṃsāra altogether, and that this was for the most part expressed in terms of ritual mastery. On the other hand, it defined itself in terms of the control of knowledge. In Tibetan terms, this distinction accords broadly with that between the accomplished adept's attainment (*grub-pa*) and skillful mastery of the branches of learning (*mkhas-pa*): both are terms Khyungpo Neljor uses in the passage quoted above. To the extent that these may be represented as two disparate ideals that demand different types of virtuosity, we do find much evidence of competition between adepts and clerics. Nevertheless, Tibetan Buddhism came in time to promote a synthesis; the greatest masters were to be "gurus endowed with both learning and attainment" (*mkhas-grub gnyis-ldan-gyi bla-ma*). It was this synthesis that eventually came to define Tibet's Buddhist elite.

The study of Tibetan Buddhism in the United States has often emphasized the forms of knowledge and the practices sanctioned and promoted by the clerical, scholastic wing of the tradition.[80] To the extent that this book is based upon texts that were produced by and consumed within such circles, it cooperates with such a perspective; nevertheless, I am particularly concerned not to lend support to the widespread belief that the sophisticated Buddhist philosophical culture of highly trained monk-scholars was, to all intents and purposes, identical to Tibetan religious culture overall. This would be misleading, for the culture of Tibet was always considerably more diversified, in both its religious and popular manifestations, than the study of its rich Buddhist intellectual history alone would suggest.

Historians and anthropologists, of course, have been very much aware that it has been to the detriment of the study of Tibetan civilization to identify that civilization one-sidedly with the learned dimensions of its religion: phenomena of historical and social importance, including often popular religious phenomena, in many cases seem to be at best only tangentially connected with materials derived from specialized doctrinal writings, and the monastic educational traditions that favored such writings.[81] Nevertheless, because the learned elite was invested with great prestige and often also with great power, symbolic or real, within the Tibetan world, it is not more inappropriate that its manifestations should receive special emphasis in the history of Tibetan civilization in general, than it is for us to emphasize in other settings the contributions of rather small intellectual and religious communities.

At all events, it would be an error to insist upon driving too deep a wedge here between adepts and scholars, or between elite and nonelite cultural formations. Tibetan religious culture, as we have seen, sought to affirm an ideal that mended the former divide, so that although there was real and sustained opposition, it was an opposition that in principle and in practice was regularly dissolved. The latter gulf, too, was bridged in several ways, and many of the topics discussed in this book belong in fact to the common ground shared throughout much of the Tibetan cultural sphere. This was true, for instance, of the great legendary narratives of Tibet's imperial past; although only relatively small numbers of persons were familiar with the historical accounts of the royal dynasty, as given in the precise texts I often cite, there were nevertheless innumerable retellings, in both popular religious literature and oral tradition, that were known by Tibetans of varied educational background and social status.[82]

Besides this, there were many channels whereby elite and nonelite segments of Tibetan religious society flowed into and interacted with one another. The monastic colleges, for instance, whatever their rapport with incarnate hierarchy or noble clans, always also had powerfully meritocratic tendencies, so that in every generation we find monks of humble background taking their place among the most highly revered teachers.[83] At the same time, we find many instances of famed Buddhist masters taking special interest in instructing persons of varied social backgrounds.[84] It is important that we recall, too, in this context, the important function of fame: the epistemological writings of a celebrated master like Sakya Paṇḍita (chapter 6), for instance, were perhaps well known only in the monastic philosophical colleges, but Sakya Paṇḍita himself was universally renowned, and his fame in turn encouraged some to study his works and to emulate him.

The formation of the Tibetan Buddhist elite, therefore, should not be seen as strictly opposed to popular, or nonelite, Buddhism. The prestige, and in some cases the actual power, derived from religious mastery—scholastic or ritual as the case may be, and preferably both at once—by the eleventh and twelfth centuries had become a fundamental source of authority within the Tibetan world, with important ramifications for all segments of Tibetan society, and so it continues to be.

The Tibetan assimilation of Buddhism is in evidence throughout the entire range of Tibetan writing during the past millenium. Whether we turn to medical treatises, manuals of divination, law codes, or poetry, not to speak of properly religious works, we are likely to encounter at least some token of Buddhism's presence. The three topics just surveyed briefly suggest some of the ways and means of its great diffusion. In the chapters that follow, I do not propose to trace that diffusion in detail—to do so would be to write an encyclopedia of Tibetan Buddhism—but I do offer some further sketches that will help to characterize the landscape of Buddhist thought in Tibet overall.

PART I

CONVERSION AND NARRATIVE

2

The Chinese Mother of Tibet's Dharma-King

The Testament of Ba *and the Beginnings of Tibetan Buddhist Historiography*

When scholars of religion speak of conversion, we most often have an individual's conversion in mind, and this in turn is almost always thought to involve profound and frequently dramatic changes of personal feeling and thought. Students of late antiquity and early medieval religions, however, must frequently attempt to understand reports of not only individual conversion, but also the conversions of peoples, whether due to popular movements, royal fiat, or elements of both. Changes of individual feeling and thought certainly play an important role here, as will be underscored in chapter 3, but so too do social, economic, and political phenomena that have perhaps only indirect relationships with individual religious experience. Thus, instead of personal conversion accounts, the transformations of national narratives must sometimes serve as the primary records of conversion to be interpreted.[1]

In this and the chapter that follows, it is the transformation of narratives in the wake of the adoption of Buddhism by the Tibetan court during the late eighth century that concerns us.[2] After considering two episodes that reflect the manner in which some Tibetan Buddhists understood the conversion of the court within a century or two thereafter, and that inform the creation of a distinctive Buddhist historiography in Tibet, we shall turn, in the fourth chapter, to address aspects of the conversion itself, attempting so far as is possible to penetrate the veil of later legend.

History's Mirrorwork

In the study of early medieval Tibet, that is, Tibet during the age of the so-called Yarlung dynasty that ruled through the mid-ninth century and its immediate aftermath,[3] and in many instances even when we turn to a later age, history often cannot be clearly distinguished from legend.[4] Not only are we far removed—in time, place, and the entire complex of conditions contributing to the possibilities of our understanding—from the authors of the documents upon which our investigations rely, but, in most cases, those authors were themselves far removed from the creation of the documents and oral traditions upon which they in turn depended.[5] Indeed, not infrequently we can be sure that there must have been many authorial acts intervening between the ancient events described in our sources and those sources themselves. Thus the study of early medieval Tibet may be compared without much exaggeration to the view from one end of a great hall of mirrors: there is little basis initially for determining which of the many reflections one perceives actually originate from the opposite end of the hall, which only reveal persons and objects situated in the intervening corridor, which are just optical illusions, and, finally, which are in fact the observer's own reflection coming back upon himself. Some such state of affairs, of course, characterizes historical research in general, so that there is nothing very remarkable in this regard about the study of Tibet,[6] save, perhaps, for the still relatively slight degree to which Tibetanists have so far reflected upon it.

The Tibetan hall of mirrors, however, does have some special features that capture our attention at the outset. The far end appears to be closed off by a curtain, which, so far as we can tell from our vantage point, is translucent and at the same time reflective, with several small gaps through which some parts of the enclosed hallway may be seen. Among other things, we can discern that, in the area immediately behind the curtain, all the mirrors are shattered. The curtain, perhaps, was set in place by an architectural restoration firm that was never able to complete its work.

Tibetanists will perhaps understand this extended metaphor without requiring further interpretation, but for others, following the conventions of the allegorist, I provide here a key: the far end of the corridor is the history of the early medieval Tibetan empire; the rubble partially visible behind the curtain is the original documentation that survives—above all, the Dunhuang Tibetan manuscripts and the Central Tibetan pillar inscriptions;[7] the curtain is woven of the great historical myths of the early empire that were elaborated in the centuries following its collapse, and that established the patterns that would dominate all later Tibetan historiography;[8] its translucency represents the incorporation within these myths of authentically ancient traditions; while its reflectivity represents the distinctive perspective of the postimperial period during which they were redacted.

Despite the elements of concealment involved here, our position now seems comparable to that of an observer who possesses a reasonably reliable plan of large parts of the hall, and who is thus at a great advantage over one whose perspective precludes even the determination of the position of the mirrors; for the Tibetanist, in most cases, may console himself with the thought that his knowledge of the authorship of post-eleventh-century historical works, and of the time and place of their composition, is in most cases sound.[9] And even in the case of the anonymous historical writings from the early medieval period recovered at Dunhuang, we know generally when they were written and, as Géza Uray has well argued, we can be reasonably certain in some instances that we are dealing with official records of the Tibetan imperial administration.[10]

There are, however, also cases in which the position of an entire panel within the hall gives rise to considerable uncertainty. A notable example of this is the *Sba bzhed* (The Testament of Ba), a famous and exceedingly influential account of the establishment of Buddhism as the Tibetan state religion during the reign of Trhi Songdetsen

(742–c. 797), in the second half of the eighth century. Named for one or another of the two major actors in the story whose clan names were Ba—Ba Selnang and Ba Sangshi—to either of whose authorship traditional Tibetan scholars have frequently attributed it, the *Testament of Ba* is often thought to be the earliest developed historical record of the period it describes that has come down to us.[11] In its essence, the *Testament of Ba* is a narrative account of the long reign of Trhi Songdetsen, during which time, we know through the two versions of the *Tang Dynasty Annals* (*Tangshu*) and the Dunhuang Tibetan documents, Tibet not only challenged Chinese power in Inner Asia, but in 763 also succeeded briefly in occupying the Tang capital of Chang'an, and setting an emperor of Tibetan choosing upon the throne.[12] From a later Tibetan perspective, however, Trhi Songdetsen is primarily famed as the monarch who definitively established Buddhism as the Tibetan national religion, and who to achieve this brought the monk Śāntarakṣita and the tantric master Padmasambhava to Tibet; founded the first Tibetan Buddhist monastery, Samye (c. 779); sponsored copious translations of Buddhist scriptures and commentaries; and adjudicated the debate between the Indian philosopher Kamalaśīla, who was Śāntarakṣita's leading disciple, and the Chinese Chan master Moheyan. It is this tale, the primary elements of which are certainly based upon actual events, that is the central concern of the *Testament of Ba*.

The study of the *Testament of Ba* and its place in Tibetan historiography thus points at once in two directions, according to whether we consider it in its relationship to the beginnings of Tibetan historiography during the early medieval period so far as we know them, or turn instead to its impact upon the works of later historians, for whom it does often seem a virtual beginning. Seen from this dual perspective, it has been clear since its first publication that the later Tibetan Buddhist historiographical tradition, at whose inception the *Testament of Ba* must be situated, is in crucial respects discontinuous with the older traditions of Tibetan historical writing known from Dunhuang.[13] While much that it reports is certainly fiction, its fictions are often old ones, and so of considerable interest in themselves. We must, I think, accept the general assessment of Stein, who has summarized his conclusions regarding the *Testament of Ba* in these words:

> It is a relatively ancient, novelized narrative of the events of the 8th century. It has been obviously manipulated, but contains historical elements verified by independent and ancient sources.[14]

In short, the *Testament of Ba* may be read as a work of historical fiction, which must be used very cautiously whenever it is precise factual information that is at issue, though it was certainly written on the basis of earlier documents that were much closer to the history it narrates.[15]

In this and the chapter that follows, then, I shall seek to characterize more fully the double relationship of the *Testament of Ba* to the period whose history it narrates, on the one hand, and to the later Tibetan construction of the history of the Buddhist conquest of the empire, on the other. While a thorough discussion of the questions that are raised here would require a relatively complete analysis of the *Testament of Ba,* and much else besides, in the present instance our reflections will be, for the most part, limited to the consideration of just a few paradigmatic themes and episodes.

China's Nephew

The *Testament of Ba* opens with prophecy: in the treasury of Chimphu (the valley in which Samye would be situated), King Trhi Detsuktsen (705–755, a.k.a. Me Aktshom, the "Bearded Ancestor"), discovers a hidden testament of his ancestor, King Songtsen Gampo (c. 617–649/650), engraved on a copper tablet:

> In the time of my descendants, in the time of a king named "De" (*Lde*), the authentic, divine doctrine will emerge, and many renunciates following the Tathāgata, shaven headed and barefoot, wearing the royal banner of ochre on their bodies, will come forth as the objects of worship of gods and men. . . .[16]

The king reflects that he must be the very "De" mentioned in the prophecy and dispatches Trenka Muleko and Nyak Jñānakumāra to India to receive the Dharma.[17] They go only as far as Mount Kailash, to the west of Tibet, where they meet Buddhagupta and Buddhaśānti, two hermits, who refuse to accompany the envoys back to Central Tibet.[18] They do, however, bestow on them some teachings that form the basis for the foundation of five temples in Lhasa, Chimphu, and so on.[19] The king is criticized for this by a prominent noble, who jests that the king, given his religiosity and ugliness, really must be a brahman. Trhi Detsuktsen, annoyed by the imputation, swears that, if he in fact deserves to be called a brahman, he should produce an even uglier son with greater faith, but that if he has been an upstanding king, his son should be beyond ministerial reproach. His oath results in the birth to Queen Trhitsün of Jang of an exceedingly handsome prince, whose name, Jangtsha Lhawön, highlights his superhuman good looks, "the nephew of Jang, the heir to the gods."[20]

Because the Tibetan people are said to be descended from the union of a monkey and an ogress of the rocks,[21] the king decides that no Tibetan bride can be worthy of the prince, and that only a Chinese princess will do, especially because the best of his ancestors, King Songtsen Gampo, who was Ārya Avalokiteśvara's emanation,[22] had also taken a Chinese princess (*gōngzhǔ*) as his wife. Accordingly, envoys are dispatched and return sometime later with the princess of Jincheng,[23] the bride chosen for their prince. By the time they return, however, the prince has been slain by a magical missile launched by an adept of mantras,[24] and the princess is greeted not by her betrothed, but by an old graybeard (*mes ag-tshom-can*), the king. She consoles herself with song and, pondering the distance both to India, where there is the Dharma, and to her homeland, sings of the sinfulness of the Tibetan ministers. The king, learning of this, offers to send her back to China with lavish gifts, but the Jincheng princess has now made up her own mind: one's karma cannot be overturned; she marries the old king. Sometime later, she rediscovers the Jowo Śākyamuni statue that her own ancestral aunt, the princess of Wencheng,[25] had brought to Tibet and, moved by compassion, institutes before it funerary rites called *tshe* for the Tibetan nobility.[26]

Still later, the princess gives birth to a son in Yarlung, whereupon a clairvoyant Chinese Buddhist monk declares to the king, who is dwelling in Drakmar at the time,[27] that this is certainly a bodhisattva. But by the time the king arrives to see his new son, the baby has been stolen by one of the co-wives, Zhiteng of the powerful Nanam clan, who declares the boy to be her own. The ministers, to resolve the dispute, place the infant in a hollow and have the two women race to see who will take possession of him first. The Jincheng Gongzhu succeeds, but Zhiteng tries to pull the child from

Figure 2.1 *Above*: The Jowo Śākyamuni statue in the central shrine of the Lhasa Jokhang Temple. *Below*: The Chinese princess of Wencheng as enshrined in the Jokhang.

her, whereupon the Chinese princess, fearing that he might be injured, immediately relaxes her grasp; it is this that, in Solomonic fashion, establishes the Jincheng Gongzhu's genuine maternity. After a year, the celebration of the baby's first steps is held, whereupon relations of the Nanam clan (who apparently have not yet ceded their claim) arrive with a child's robes as gifts and call to him, saying, "Come sit on uncle's lap!" The little prince responds with a well-known couplet:

> Trhi Songdetsen is China's nephew.
> Pray what's for the Nanam uncles to do?[28]

Whereupon he goes to sit in his Chinese mother's lap, having just conferred upon himself the regnal name by which he would later be known.

I have paraphrased these first pages at length in order to convey something of the narrative richness of the *Testament of Ba*. In my estimation, perhaps owing to the work's archaicism, and also to the prejudgement involved in the classification of it as a book of "history," its extraordinary achievement as a relatively early work of Tibetan literature has not been sufficiently appreciated. It will emerge, in fact, that this is an essential key to advancing our understanding of it.

First, however, let us return to the episode just related, and see what other sources have to tell us about these events.

Tibet's Son

According to the account found in many of the well-known Tibetan histories produced from the twelfth century onward,[29] Trhi Songdetsen was the son of Trhi Detsuktsen and his Chinese bride, the Jincheng Gongzhu. She was, according to the same traditions, in fact brought to Tibet to marry the crown prince, Jangtsha Lhawön, whose untimely death required that she marry his father instead. Her child is said to have been stolen from her by her co-wife of the Tibetan Nanam clan and to have become known as Trhi Songdetsen. Some versions of the tale add that the princess's discovery that she was to marry not a handsome, young prince, but instead an old graybeard explains Trhi Detsuktsen's epithet, Me Aktshom, "Bearded Ancestor," and that the princess recovered her son after his abduction by the Nanam queen following a Solomonic judgement of her rightful claim of maternity.[30] Of course, if this all now seems familiar, it is because the entire later Tibetan historical tradition resorts to the authority of the *Testament of Ba* regarding these matters. A brief version of the story first became well known to Western scholars through Obermiller's 1932 translation of the history of the famous fourteenth-century polymath, Butön Rinchendrup (1290–1364).[31]

Twenty years after Obermiller's publication of Butön's account, the incomparable Paul Demiéville, in an article-length footnote, demonstrated that the tale found there was most unlikely to be at all true.[32] We shall consider the entire matter in more detail as we proceed, but suffice it here to mention just these points noted by Demiéville: that the *Old Tibetan Annals* from Dunhuang, which had become known through the pioneering 1940 edition and translation of Bacot, Thomas, and Toussaint, give the year of the Chinese princess's death as 739, her funeral as 741, and the birth of Trhi Songdetsen as 742,[33] and that the general correlations between the dates found in this document and those given in the two versions of the *Tang Dynasty Annals* tended to support its veracity.[34] Moreover, the Dunhuang geneological table, also first studied in the publication just mentioned, states flatly that Trhi Songdetsen was the son of the Nanam queen.[35] Finally, Demiéville takes stock of the pronouncedly anti-Chinese standpoint attributed by later Tibetan historians to Trhi Songdetsen and suggests that this circumstantially calls into question the traditions regarding his Chinese matriliny.[36] But here we must remark that if Demiéville is correct about this last point, we also have good grounds for doubting that the very Tibetan historians who attributed this sinophobia to one of the great Tibetan culture heroes would have so cheerfully countenanced a Chinese maternal line for him, so long as a Tibetan aristocratic line, that of the Nanam clan, was also available to them.[37] The account is thus an inherently conflicted one, and it is this that calls for our deeper consideration.

The relationship between the Chinese princess and Trhi Songdetsen is only one of many difficulties one encounters in the study of the early sources: careful comparison of the Dunhuang Tibetan documents, the two versions of the *Tang Dynasty Annals*, and the later Tibetan histories reveals numerous inconsistencies in the accounts of the reign of Trhi Detsuktsen and the succession of his son Trhi Songdetsen. For present purposes, however, we may forego the detailed study of the eighth-century Tibetan monarchy that examination of this material would require and instead briefly summarize some relevant conclusions of earlier scholarship.

With regard to the basic tale of the princess's arrival in Tibet, the premature death of her betrothed, and her marriage instead to his father, the old king, the Japanese Tibetanist Yamaguchi Zuihō has fairly demonstrated that something like this did in fact occur, but to a different princess, during the reign of another king, some six decades before:[38] the Tang princess of Wencheng was recorded in the annals from Dunhuang to have arrived in Tibet to marry, not the great emperor Songtsen Gampo, but his son, in whose favor the monarch abdicated. Upon the son's death soon after ascending the throne, however, Songtsen returned to rule and married his daughter-in-law, too. Yamaguchi argues that the author of our tale was simply in error in transferring the episode to the princess of Jincheng. In this, he is no doubt correct, but one wonders why such an error became the authoritative tale that it did, embellished with a Tibetan version of the judgement of Solomon. Something more than a mere mix-up is surely at stake here.

Christopher Beckwith, a scholar of early Tibetan history, has advanced a complicated and intriguing argument that addresses this issue. He believes that the several incidents of crisis in the succession of the monarchy during the early eighth century suggest that it faced grave obstacles to maintaining its claims of legitimacy. Trhi Songdetsen's adoption of a universal religion, Buddhism, his construction of the Samye monastery, with what Beckwith rightly terms its "kosmokrator symbolism," and the later attribution to him of maternal descent from the Chinese imperial line may all be seen as part of an effort to restore the dynasty's shaken credibility.[39] There are two important points, I think, that should be stressed here: first, despite the several documented crises of the early eighth century, it is by no means clear that the monarchy was in fact challenged by the accusation of illegitimacy. Second, there is no evidence whatever suggesting that the tale of the emperor's birth to a Chinese princess came into circulation while the empire still held sway.[40] On the contrary, the imperial record is quite clear in maintaining that Trhi Songdetsen was the son of the Tibetan Nanam queen, and almost contemporary Chinese records are equally clear about this.[41]

To understand, therefore, why later Tibetan historians chose in this case to publish not the truth but a legend, we must turn to consider the episode from another perspective.

Solomon on the Silk Road

Begging the indulgence of my readers, I propose that we embark at this point on a detour into the no-man's land between historical scholarship and historical fiction, a terrain that we've been skirting all along in any case.

The *Testament of Ba* opens with a Solomonic judgement regarding disputed maternity; it culminates in a blow-by-blow description of the construction of the Samye temple, lovingly describing the preparation of building materials and the temple's intricate iconography; and it reaches its denouement in the schism between Chinese and Indian Buddhism in Tibet.[42] Now, described in this way, the *Testament of Ba* at once appears to bear an uncanny resemblance to the First Book of Kings, which opens with Solomon's judgment, culminates in the construction of the first temple, and reaches its denouement in the division of the kingdom. This raises a fascinating, if seemingly loony, question: is there even a shadow of a possibility that 1 Kings might have indirectly inspired the *Testament of Ba*? Of course, the indisputable facts—that the monastery of Samye was founded during Trhi Songdetsen's reign, and that there was some sort of dispute between Chinese and Indian Buddhist factions, as well as many telltale points of detail, such as the *Testament of Ba*'s account of a meeting with the Korean Chan master Kim in Chengdu[43]—rule out the possibility of speculating that the *Testament of Ba* might be a wholesale confabulation based upon a foreign model; but this does not preclude the possibility that the author used a foreign model to help structure and embellish a tale, some of which was indeed factually accurate. Other examples of this are not unknown: for instance, Tsuguhito Takeuchi has established beyond reasonable doubt that something of this sort was precisely what took place in the composition of the *Old Tibetan Chronicle* from Dunhuang, where the author reworked for his own purposes a passage from the *Shiji* of the great Chinese historian Sima Qian.[44] Thus there is no question but that the arsenal of early Tibetan literary technique included the appropriation of foreign narrative frames for the elaboration of Tibetan stories. The question therefore inevitably arises: what may the Tibetans of the early medieval period have known of the Bible?

In fact, Tibetan literature does include any number of what at first glance appear possibly to be Bible stories: Per Kværne has remarked on the resemblance between the tale of the translator Vairocana's unfortunate encounter with the queen Tshepongza and the episode of Joseph and Potiphar's wife;[45] in an episode in the *Yarlung Jo-bo'i Chos-'byung* (The Yarlung Lord's History of the Doctrine), a new star appearing at the birth of the boy who would later become the first king of the Western Xia dynasty is taken as an evil omen by the astrologers of the Chinese court, whereupon the emperor commands a slaughter of male infants;[46] and, in the historical and legendary traditions of the Nyingmapa school, Garap Dorje, who is virtually a savior figure, is born to a virgin, deposited at birth in a pit where he is protected and worshipped by deities, and, while still a child, goes to the temple to debate with the wise.[47] But, as Kværne has convincingly demonstrated, it is almost certainly an Indian tale that figures in the background of the story of Vairocana. And none of the other examples seem so compelling as to eliminate the possibility that there were alternative, even if not yet identified, sources of inspiration, or independent origins of some of these motifs among the Tibetans themselves.

Nevertheless, we should note too that the transmission of biblical lore to Tibet during the age in question cannot quite be ruled out: assuming that the military confrontation between Arabs and Tibetans during the eighth century did not result in Islam's becoming a source of Tibetan knowledge of Western religious tradition,[48] there were still three other possible sources of such knowledge available to the Tibetans during the period concerned, namely, Nestorian Christians, Manichaeans, and Jewish merchants operating along the Silk Road.

Nestorianism and Manichaeism had become major religious movements in Inner Asia during the Tang period and were to remain important there until the Chinggis Khanite invasions of the early thirteenth century.[49] What's more, the researches of Tucci, Stein, and Uray have established that there were both Nestorian and Manichaean contacts with Tibet, that adherents of these religions may have even made a bid to convert the Tibetans, and that the Tibetans were to some extent at least familiar with them.[50] Significantly, in the case of Manichaeism, we even have good reason to believe that King Trhi Songdetsen himself knew of its denunciation in China.[51] The possibility that Nestorian or Manichaean motifs might turn up in ancient Tibetan sources is thus one that no student of early Tibetan cultural history will dismiss out of hand.

Nevertheless, it seems unlikely that the events narrated in Kings or Chronicles would have been among biblical traditions widely transmitted by either Nestorians or Manichaeans. Though Inner Asian and Chinese Nestorians did sometimes use Hebrew personal names—there was even a Chinese priest named Solomon[52]—the extent of their knowledge of the history of Israel remains unclear. Catholic visitors to the court of the Khans during the thirteenth century reported that, while the Nestorians possessed the entire biblical text in Syriac, they understood little of its contents.[53] This may well have been a sectarian calumny, but even if true during the thirteenth century we have little idea whether or to what extent it can be read back into the eighth. Boris Marshak has shown that the scene of Joshua at the gates of Jericho was a royal emblem of the Nestorian Karluks, who depicted it on exquisite silver medallions,[54] and much evidence shows that the Karluks had extensive, though often antagonistic, relations with the Tibetans.[55] Beyond such slender markers, however, the trail apparently grows cold.

The Manichaeans for their part, though certainly familiar with elements of New Testament lore, seem not to have known much of the traditions of Israel, excepting the tale of the creation, and perhaps some apocrypha such as the *Book of Enoch*.[56] The evidence as we know it offers nothing to support the supposition that any significant Manichaean transmission of Hebrew lore occurred in Inner Asia generally, much less in Tibet in particular.

Aurel Stein's discovery at the Dandān-Oïlik site in Khotan of an eighth-century Judeo-Persian merchantile document provided the first proof positive of a Jewish presence in an area that was intermittently under Tibetan sway during the age with which we are concerned.[57] It remains a mystery just how extensive that presence was, or what the nature of these Central Asian Jewish merchants' contact, if any, may have been with the Tibetans who sometimes ruled the territories which they traversed. But Pelliot's discovery at Dunhuang of a Hebrew penitential prayer, with references to Psalms and to the Prophets, and now attributed to the ninth or perhaps the tenth century, leads us to posit sustained, even if low-level, Jewish Silk Road activity.[58] It seems not unreasonable to assume that Jewish merchants plying the Silk Road would have been, like Jewish merchants in other parts of the medieval world, generally knowledgeable about the history of Israel;[59] and the traditions of Solomon and the first temple were, of course, prominent features of that history. Whether that knowledge would have been communicated to non-Jews, however, is an altogether different matter. I should note, too, that in the records of medieval Jewish travelers with which I have become acquainted so far, Tibet is not mentioned prior to the twelfth century, and that in a reference not suggesting direct contact,[60] though an early ninth-century Arabic writer does explicitly associate Jewish mercantile activity in the farther east with the musk trade, and musk was a peculiarly Tibetan commodity.[61] At the same time, we have no evidence that the Tibetans knew anything of Judaism, or of the Jews as a distinct people, before our own age, unless we were to admit in this context, as certainly we should not, the disguised occurence of the names Adam and Moses in the *Kālacakratantra* (and even this would be too late for the purposes of the present discussion).[62] From all this we may conclude that, though there well could have been some knowledge of Hebrew historical tradition among the Jews who journeyed along the fringes of the late first-millenium Tibetan world, and perhaps among their Nestorian contemporaries as well, we are not entitled to posit any more than that bare possibility, and even so there is no suggestion that such knowledge was ever transmitted to Tibet.

If this brief inquiry into the prospects for locating a biblical model for the *Testament of Ba* has drawn a blank, however, let us not conclude that the detour was fruitless. For, though there was probably no historical connection that would account for the superficial similarities between 1 Kings and the *Testament of Ba*, even if, in the case of the maternity dispute, there is one very striking resemblance, reflection about this still discloses an historiographical analogy between them. It is this, I believe, that will help us to make sense of our earliest elaborate history of Buddhism in Tibet.

The Religious Transformation of History

In his Sather Lectures, Arnaldo Momigliano, certainly the most incisive recent interpreter of ancient historiography, wrote:

> In pre-exilic times the Jews had had chronicles of their kings. The author or authors of the present Books of Kings used them. But the Books of Kings we read now are not comparable with the ordinary Royal Chronicles we know from Assyria and must assume to have existed in Persia. The Books of Kings are a record of events connected with the relationship between Jehovah and the Hebrew nation as a whole. This of course

> applies even more to the definite postexilic products which we call the Books of Ezra and Nehemiah and Chronicles. These are histories of a religious society. Two or three centuries later the author of the First Book of Maccabees showed that this tradition of the political and religious historian was still alive among the Jews.[63]

This is perhaps not a good example of the great distinctiveness of scholarly vision that characterizes much of Momigliano's work; his description here of Deuteronomistic historiography conforms well with prevailing views. Herbert Butterfield, for instance, expresses a similar orientation in slightly different terms when he writes:

> To a considerable extent [Judges and Kings] represent what is really a commentary, or something like a sermon, on the history of the monarchy. . . . [I]n fact, the straight narrative history—of which there must have existed a great amount—has largely disappeared. What survives is a specialised kind of religious meditation on parts of the story.[64]

Keeping these thoughts before us, and recalling, too, what was said earlier of the insufficient attention that has been paid to the *Testament of Ba* as a literary text, it becomes clear, I think, that the halting progress Tibetanists have made towards achieving an adequate assessment of the *Testament of Ba* so far has been due in part to an exaggerated emphasis upon its place as a book of history, despite the reservations of R. A. Stein and others about this. It is, however, no doubt best regarded as, in Butterfield's phrase, "a specialised kind of religious meditation on parts of the story" of Trhi Songdetsen's career, one that indeed seeks to advance the rudiments of a distinctively Buddhist interpretation of Tibetan history in general. Seen from this perspective, it appears that the *Testament of Ba* is among the first of a line of Tibetan writings, culminating in the great legendary accounts of imperial Tibet, the production of which reached its apogee during the twelfth through the fourteenth centuries, with such apocryphal works as the *Maṇi Bka'-'bum* (The Maṇi Kambum) and the several versions of the *Padma bka'-thang* (The Testimonial Record of Padmasambhava), but including also some works often thought of simply as "histories," like the *Rgyal-rabs gsal-ba'i me-long* (The Mirror Clarifying Royal Geneology). In connection with the *Maṇi Kambum* (twelfth–thirteenth centuries), for instance, a compilation focusing upon King Songtsen Gampo as the embodiment of the bodhisattva Avalokiteśvara, we find the elaboration, in the absence of the order provided by an actual monarchy, of a vision of a world ordered by the agency of the buddhas and bodhisattvas, a vision that was projected back upon the earlier monarchy itself. What these books achieve is to engender an understanding of Tibet and its place in the world, according to which the destiny of the Buddha's teaching and that of the Tibetan people themselves are realized to be inextricably interlinked. (This is a topic to which we shall return in chapter 8.) It is by placing the *Testament of Ba* within the context of the religio-historical polemic that was elaborated by Tibetan Buddhists in the early postimperial period, and not by reference to supposed problems of legitimation while the empire still held sway, or to simple confusion about the historical record, that we can begin to formulate an adequate interpretation of the Tibetan monarch's contested maternity.

The *Testament of Ba* offers us a number of themes that merit consideration in this connection: three that are closely interrelated, and that may help to shed some light on its tale of the emperor's maternity, are its treatment of the question of karma and rebirth, its view of Tibet as a stage for the dramatic activity of bodhisattvas, and its remarkable emphasis on the Chinese role in the buddhicization of Tibet.

(1) The first of these will be a central theme in the following chapter, and so I will say only a few words about it here: the Dunhuang Tibetan documents provide striking evidence of the active promotion of the Buddhist teachings of karma and saṃsāra among the Tibetans during the last centuries of the first millenium. The implication of the texts concerned seems to be that these doctrines were to some extent still contested or were at least felt in some ways to be problematic. Though emphatic propagation of the karma-saṃsāra cosmology would always remain a prominent dimension of Tibetan Buddhist doctrinal instruction, in both its popular and scholastic facets, later Tibetan historians mostly seem to have forgotten that the conceptions of karma and saṃsāra were once controversial.[65]

Not so in the case of the *Testament of Ba*. It is noteworthy that this work, almost uniquely among the narratives of Tibet's conversion, stresses precisely the centrality of karma and saṃsāra as contested categories.[66] Indeed, this is one of the features of the *Testament of Ba* that convinces me that, even if the author did not witness the events related therein, the book must nevertheless be relatively ancient.[67]

(2) A corollary to the *Testament of Ba*'s promotion of the karma-saṃsāra framework is its insistence upon the dynamic role of the bodhisattvas as agents of salvation within that framework, and, what is more, upon Tibet itself as a field for the activity of such agents. The *Testament of Ba* is among the relatively early works that clearly formulate King Songtsen Gampo's bodhisattvahood,[68] and, as we have seen, a Chinese monk announces Trhi Songdetsen's similar status at the time of his birth.[69] Later in the book, Śāntarakṣita, at his first meeting with the Tibetan minister Ba Selnang, states that he, Selnang, and the king form what amounts to a bodhisattvic triumvirate whose task is to guarantee the establishment of Buddhism in Tibet through the foundation of the Samye monastery, a theme that would come to be greatly elaborated in later literature.[70] Again, the examples can be multiplied, and, as before, it seems plausible to read the *Testament of Ba* not as a naive historical romance carelessly repeating established tradition, but as a work that seeks to create a well-formed historical vision, according to which the historical destiny of Tibet is bound to the salvific activity of bodhisattvas. If the *Maṇi Kambum* represents a relatively advanced vision of the constitution of Tibet as a fundamentally spiritual polity, the *Testament of Ba* may be regarded as a surviving rough draft on the way to that policy statement.

(3) As Demiéville remarked, later Tibetan sources sometimes impute a pronouncedly anti-Chinese stance to the reign of Trhi Songdetsen. The main reason for this impression, which indeed has its apparent origin in the *Testament of Ba,* is the traditional tale of the confrontation between Heshang Moheyan and Śāntarakṣita's leading Indian disciple, Kamalaśīla.[71] Their debate culminates in a royal decision authorizing Tibetans to adhere to the Indian tradition, while commanding the suppression of Chinese Buddhism. In fact, the *Testament of Ba* is not so clear on this point as it might at first seem, for it is altogether ambiguous about whether it is Chinese Buddhism in general that was condemned, or only the particular tradition propounded by Moheyan. Though it does seem strongly to suggest that the condemnation entailed a general recall of Chinese Buddhist books throughout the country, it

specifies that those books were then concealed in the treasury of Samye, emphatically not destroyed.[72]

But, with the sole exception of the Samye debate, the *Testament of Ba* takes what appears to be an entirely favorable position with respect to the influence of Chinese Buddhism in Tibet: the princess of Jincheng and the Heshang who declares Trhi Songdetsen to be a bodhisattva are only two among the half dozen or so Chinese Buddhist protagonists who play noteworthy roles,[73] and, with the exception of Moheyan and his cohorts, these figures are positively valued by the author of the *Testament of Ba*. Indeed, the *Testament of Ba*'s emphasis on these persons and their fine contributions to the Dharma in Tibet apparently puts the lie to any stereotyping of early Tibetan Buddhist historiography as one-sidedly anti-Chinese.[74]

The author of the *Testament of Ba* was perhaps also aware of materials such as the so-called *Dbon-zhang-rdo-ring* (The Nephew-Uncle Pillar Inscription), which preserves the Sino-Tibetan treaty of 821/822 in both Tibetan and Chinese and emphasizes the quasi-familial relationship that had been established between the Chinese emperor and the Tibetan monarch.[75] The author of the inscription, Trhi Songdetsen's grandson Trhi Tsukdetsen (Relpacen, d. 838), records there that their relationship of uncle and nephew had been established by his ancestor Songtsen Gampo's marriage to the Wencheng Gongzhu and his great-grandfather Trhi Detsuktsen's to the Jincheng Gongzhu, and that this relationship, despite the unfortunate fact that "now and then the frontier ministers on both sides caused some mischief,"[76] had been maintained by the successive Tibetan monarchs down to and including himself. The convention that the rulers of China and Tibet were thus related as uncle and nephew may have provided one additional and, given the other materials we have considered, possibly compelling reason for the author of the *Testament of Ba* to think of the king as having been, quite literally, the "nephew of China."[77] Indeed, it is not unimaginable that the entire story originated with someone's reading a double entendre into lines 33–34 of the East Inscription, which begin,

> And since they [the Chinese and Tibetan emperors] were thus connected as kinsmen, the Tsenpo my father, the miraculously wise divinity Trhi Songdetsen himself, formed his firm resolution in strict accord with that relationship of Nephew and Uncle. . . .[78]

To restate these points in precise relation to the question of Trhi Songdetsen's maternity, it appears likely that the princess of Jincheng had become a heroine for Tibetan Buddhists during the later imperial period and immediately thereafter: she was remembered for having promoted Buddhist funerary rites among the nobility even before the conversion of the Tibetan court, and thus to have adopted a definite stance in the internal Tibetan debate on the contested issues surrounding mortuary ritual and the Buddhist cosmology of karma and saṃsāra. Though not explicitly referred to as a bodhisattva, at least in the *Testament of Ba*, she was therefore nonetheless viewed as an agent of the Buddha's teaching, and indeed as one of a number of Chinese missionaries and masters who had helped to secure the ascendancy of the Dharma in Tibet. Given the established euphemism that the Chinese emperor and the Tibetan Tsenpo were related as uncle and nephew, it now involved but a small step to think of her as the true mother of Tibet's Dharma-king.

And to all this we must add that there was indeed a *Buddhist*, and not a biblical tale, available to be employed in the elaboration of the *Testament of Ba*'s account, for the story of the contested maternity and its Solomonic resolution is known in the Pali tradition from the commentary on the *Mahommaggajātaka* and is familiar to many students of the Pali language from Andersen's *Pali Reader*, where it bears the title "Mahosadha's Judgement."[79] That a variant of the same story was also found in a Tibetan canonical version was first reported to Western folklorists in an almost forgotten St. Petersburg publication of the 1880s, a collection of tales from the Tibetan Vinaya translated into German by Anton Schiefner, that also appeared some years later in an English translation.[80] The text in question had been translated from Sanskrit into Tibetan during the reign of Trhi Songdetsen.[81]

In sum, the author of the *Testament of Ba* (or his source) had appropriated a canonical Buddhist tale to justify a claimed Buddhist geneology for a Buddhist king.

History and Identity

In his intricate and intriguing study of the formation of our modern identity, *Sources of the Self*, Charles Taylor briefly criticizes the arguments of Derek Parfit and other contemporary heirs to the empiricist tradition who hold, in a manner suggestive of Buddhist Ābhidharmika philosophy, that "personal identity" is a metaphysical illusion, that there is no necessary and sufficient condition of our ongoing identity through time. He maintains that "[i]t seems clear . . . that there is something like an a priori unity of a human life through its whole extent" and insists that

> as a being who grows and becomes I can only know myself through the history of my maturations and regressions, overcomings and defeats. My self-understanding necessarily has temporal depth and incorporates narrative.[82]

This is not the occasion for detailed examination of the philosophical puzzles of identity; my point in introducing Taylor's remarks in this context is to note that whatever it is that "is something like an a priori unity of a human life through its whole extent" is something we seek in, or project upon, not only our own lives, but also the stories of our clans, tribes, and nations. That is to say, through our narratives we do not just orient ourselves to the world, but in large measure we create the very world to which we orient ourselves. It has been the task of every author of national history to do much more than describe the facts;[83] for national history underwrites, at least among those who belong to or feel strong affinity with the nation in question, the sense that one participates in a community in which certain desirable values may be actualized. The values and ends that seem possible objects of individual striving are precisely those engendered by the world in which the individual lives and acts, and that world is in turn engendered by its past, present, and possible actors.

Géza Uray has argued that the old Tibetan royal annals, represented in fragmentary form by the *Old Tibetan Annals* and *Chronicle* from Dunhuang, served as instruments of bureaucratic practice and of the art of government.[84] Their development coincided with and reflected the organization of the empire during the period of expansion beginning in the mid-seventh century. We may add that, with the fall of the empire during the ninth century, Tibetans were faced not only with a practical political and economic crisis, but, as are all those whose communities experience great and traumatic change, with a crisis of understanding as well. The sophisticated cosmology and soteriology of Buddhism provided one possible way of making sense of the Tibetan world as a domain of meaningful agency and possible excellence, which began during and continued even after its tryst with imperial greatness. The stunning achievement of Tibetan Buddhist historians was to create a compelling and enduring articulation of this vision, and it is to the author of the *Testament of Ba* that we owe what was perhaps its first full, and for Tibetans still vital, formulation.

3

The Mark of Vermilion

Rebirth and Resurrection in an Early Medieval Tale

As we have seen in the previous chapter, it has long been evident that Tibetan historical traditions concerning the first millennium of the common era contain much in the way of self-contradiction, factual inaccuracy, legend, and sheer fancy. While contemporary academic historians of Tibet have generally felt it their charge to get at the facts of the matter to the extent possible, it has sometimes not been sufficiently considered that the apparent inaccuracies, legends, and fancies *are* among the facts of the matter. Tibetan historians without doubt often published legends, where we would prefer to find truth according to our own lights; but our task is not solely to pick away at what they wrote, for the legends themselves, above and beyond the questions that may be raised concerning the literal veracity of their affirmations and denials, were proposed and became authoritative in response to genuinely obtaining states of affairs in the communities in which they were elaborated. In short, the Tibetanist must strive to illuminate not only Tibetan history, but Tibetan historiography as well.

The Mark of Vermilion

Early on in the *Sba-bzhed* (The Testament of Ba), the same work we have described earlier, while recounting the events leading up to Trhi Songdetsen's adoption of Buddhism, there is a lovely tale concerning a great tragedy in the household of the minister Ba Selnang, and its ultimately happy outcome.[1] The text recalls that during the repression of Buddhism that followed the death of Emperor Trhi Detsuktsen, when his successor, Trhi Songdetsen, was still in his minority, the performance of Buddhist funerary rites was suppressed. These rites, as we have seen, had been instituted by the late emperor's Chinese bride, the princess of Jincheng. After her arrival in Tibet, during a visit to the image of Śākyamuni that had been installed in Lhasa by her distant ancestral relation, the princess of Wencheng, she had been moved by compassion for the fate of the deceased Tibetan nobility, who died without benefit of the Buddha's teaching. The rites she instituted, to be performed on a weekly basis for seven weeks following a death, were known as *tshe*. As Stein has argued, this is certainly not the familiar Tibetan term for "lifespan" that occurs in the names of rituals of longevity (*tshe-sgrub, tshe-dbang*) and in a common generic term for funerary rituals, literally, "rites for those whose lifespan has passed" (*tshe-'das-kyi cho-ga*). Rather, it is most likely a transcription of the Chinese *zhāi*, defined in the dictionaries as "a fast of abstinence," as in the idiom *dǎzhāi,* "to perform rituals to deliver souls in purgatory," and in other Chinese Buddhist expressions.[2] The *Testament of Ba* holds that these rites were specifically banned by ministerial decree.

Now, it is at this time, just following the proclamation of the ban, that both of Ba Selnang's children, a boy and girl, suddenly die. Ba becomes very much preoccupied with the truth or falsehood of Buddhist notions of rebirth and seeks the counsel of an elderly Chinese monk, who assures him that the Buddhist teachings about these matters are true.[3] He arranges for the monk to perform the last rites in the family's private quarters in secret, while a Bön funeral—that is to say, a funeral according to the pre-Buddhist rites of Tibet[4]—is staged at the entrance to the household as a ruse. When the monk asks whether the minister wishes his children to return as gods or as human beings, Ba chooses divine rebirths for them, but his wife wishes them to return as her own children once more. To console both, the monk suggests that he lead the son to a godly realm, but that the daughter take birth in the family again. As he performs the ceremony, there is a miraculous transformation of the son's remains into *śariram*, relics,[5] indicating his rebirth as a god. The monk then takes a pearl, smears it with a solution of vermilion, and places it in the left cheek of the mouth of the daughter's corpse. After the monk performs a ritual "as a mark of faith," the infant is placed in an urn and buried beneath her mother's bed. Months later, a child is born into the family with a pearl in its mouth spotted red; the urn is disinterred and found to be empty. When the child completes her first year,[6] she recognizes places and persons she has seen before, without having been instructed about them. In this way, Ba Selnang comes to see for himself the truth of the doctrine of rebirth, and he secretly requests instruction in meditation from the Chinese monk.

In the light of what we already know of the *Testament of Ba*, we would be warranted to regard this tale of the vermilion-marked pearl simply as one of its several fictions, possibly a quaint bit of folklore, but certainly not *history* in anything but a euphemistic sense. Very well, but we may still ask whether it is a fiction that in some fashion reflects or responds to circumstances that actually obtained in eighth-century Tibet, or whether it is perhaps a tale borrowed from some other source or one composed at some other time, and thus possibly alien even to the period it purports to describe.

Recently, in an exceptional article, A.-M. Blondeau has described a group of rituals specially practiced in connection with the death of neonates and has shown that such rituals certainly form the background for the tale of Ba's daughter.[7] In brief, the deceased child is either regarded as a bearer of the family's wealth and good fortune, so that its corpse is mummified and kept, sometimes in the wall of the house, so as to preserve those blessings despite the infant's untimely passing, or else it is a question of securing the child's rebirth in the same family, in which case the corpse is preserved only temporarily, and it is marked with various substances and designs—in one version a vermilion solution is used to paint its palms.[8] The reborn child will have birthmarks resembling the markings applied to its past embodiment's corpse, a phenomenon attested in an event recounted by no less than the present Dalai Lama.[9] We may note, however, that the motif of the vermilion-marked pearl in the mouth, a striking image in the *Testament of Ba*'s account, is nowhere to be found in the fascinating documentation assembled by Blondeau.

While I have not located a sure model for the tale of the vermilion-marked pearl that would support the suggestion that it might have been more or less directly borrowed from either a specific ritual practice or an earlier literary account, I suspect that the symbolism of the pearl, as it is used here, is of non-Tibetan inspiration. The foreignness of the pearl is underscored by the word for "pearl" in Tibetan, *mu-tig*, from Sanskrit *muktā,* though this is no doubt an old loan that may well have been naturalized in Tibetan long before the eighth century. Hans Jonas, in his study of the "Hymn of the Pearl" found in the Acts of the Apostle Thomas, shows that in Gnostic lore the pearl had come to symbolize the soul, pure in its essential nature, that was nevertheless now mired in the darkness of the world.[10] As such, it is an image also known from Manichaean documents, including the hymn cycle *Angad Rôšnân*, in which the doctrine of rebirth is explicitly discussed.[11] The manuscript of this work was found at Turfan, in contemporary Xinjiang, and so was transmitted in regions that fell close to the sphere of imperial Tibet, where, as Stein and Uray have demonstrated, Manichaeism was certainly to some extent known (see ch. 2, n. 50). Moreover, as will be seen below (p. 192), there are striking parallels between the "Hymn of the Pearl" itself and certain allegories of the Tibetan Great Perfection tradition, and, as will become clear later in this chapter, this association with the Great Perfection is itself highly suggestive in this instance. Nevertheless, despite the obvious similarity of symbolism, taken very generally, there is no compelling resemblance between the specific imagery of the pearl in the Gnostic and Manichaean hymns and that of the tale we are now considering. Those conversant with Indian ayurvedic and tantric lore may also find the vermilion-marked pearl reminiscent of the descriptions in Indian embryology of the intermingling of blood and semen at the moment of conception, though I am not aware of actual reference in India to the pearl as a symbol in this context.[12]

Still, though I have not yet encountered a Chinese version of our story, my supposition is that, if there indeed is a foreign model for the motif of the pearl placed in the mouth, it is most likely Chinese. Those familiar with the sculpted lions and dragons that adorn traditional Chinese temples and palaces will recognize that the image of the gem in the mouth is an important symbol of wealth, good fortune, and power.[13] In a Chinese folktale that I know only through a recent source, a primer of literary Chinese published early in this century, there is a discussion of a wondrous pearl brought from the West, about which it is said that, "By keeping it in the mouth one can have no thirst" (*hán zhī kě bù kě*).[14] The character that means "to hold in the mouth" (*hán*) in this phrase is also employed in the composition of a homonym (*hán*) that refers specifically to the insertion of gems into the mouths of corpses.[15] As the evidence derived from the former Han dynasty tombs makes clear, this was a well-established custom in ancient times, though the gem in question was generally a jade tablet, not a pearl.[16]

There is an additional reason, indeed a puzzling one, for suspecting some element of Chinese inspiration to be at work here; for the Chinese pearl really appears to include a mark of vermilion, that is, the character for "pearl," *zhū,* combines the jade-radical (*yù*), its semantic component, with the character for vermilion, *zhū*, as its phonetic. Though we must entertain the possibility that this is merely coincidental, still, given the *Testament of Ba*'s many incorporations elsewhere of materials that in one way or another point back to China, even though it is clear that the *Testament of Ba*'s author often either misunderstands or deliberately misconstrues these materials,[17] we cannot rule out the possibility that the odd convergence of the structure of a symbolic motif with that of a Chinese graph may be something more than chance. Suggestive, too, in this context, is the notion of the cinnibar elixir pearl (*dān-zhū*), related to alchemical means to achieve bodily immortality and found in early Taoist sources as the proper name for a divinity residing in the mouth.[18]

Clearly, then, the motif of the gem placed in the mouth of the dead points to Chinese inspiration, especially given the officiating role of the Chinese monk and the performance of the Chinese Buddhist memorial fast. Nevertheless, the smear of vermilion equally echoes more ancient Tibetan practices, which remain current, as we have seen, in the rituals discussed by Blondeau. We may add that it is well known that the Tibetans once painted their faces with vermilion; the Khotanese in fact called them "red-faces,"[19] and the practice was also described by the Chinese.[20] The custom is said to have been proscribed by the kings at the urgings of the Tang princesses brought to Tibet, who detested it.[21] Also significant for us here is the testimony of the *Old Tibetan Chronicle* from Dunhuang, which records that the face of the king's corpse was to be painted with vermilion in preparation for its entombment.[22]

Whatever the exact origins of the several motifs it employs, it seems plausible that the story of Ba Selnang's conversion does include some elements indicating that a recollection of actual circumstances in Tibet's early history is invoked here, however indistinctly. In sum, there can be no doubt that Ba Selnang was an historical figure and that he was to play a great role in the eighth-century establishment of Buddhism as the state religion of Tibet. A manuscript from Dunhuang (*IO* 689/2), which has been relatively well studied,[23] lists him according to his religious name of Yeshewangpo as the first in an enumeration of Tibetans in the lineage of Śāntarakṣita, and according to the *Testament of Ba*'s account, it was Ba Selnang who first met that master in Nepal, and who later was among the first Tibetans to receive monastic ordination from him.[24] Moreover, much of the available documentation affirms that Trhi Songdetsen came to the throne (in 755/756) during a phase of anti-Buddhist reaction.[25] That phase, however, appears to have been entered more than a decade before, even prior to his birth, at the time of the death, significantly, of the princess of Jincheng in 739. Invaluable evidence about the decease of the princess and the persecution that followed comes from the histories and prophecies of Buddhism in Khotan found in several Tibetan versions at Dunhuang and in the later Tibetan canons, which have had a long history of study in the West.[26] A manuscript found by Pelliot tells us:

> At about that time [during the events in Khotan described earlier in the text] the divine Tsenpo of Tibet and the lord of China formed [the relationship of] nephew and uncle, at which the Chinese princess, too, became the divine Tsenpo's bride. The Chinese princess built one great temple in Tibet and established its provisions. The whole saṃgha went there, whereupon the princess also provided rations. The doctrine of the Mahāyāna having thus blossomed in Tibet, for a period of twelve years

> both the saṃgha and ordinary layfolk practiced the doctrine and so were exceedingly happy. But even there Māra's host became agitated, and Māra sent forth the black pox and many other sorts of disease. As for the princess, she died after the black pox appeared at her heart. After that, the laity lost faith and said that the occurrence of the black pox and many sorts of disease was an evil due to the arrival in Tibet of the host of the saṃgha. It was ordained that not even one member of the saṃgha be permitted to remain in Tibet. After they were banished, one and all, the entire saṃgha traveled to Gandhāra in India.[27]

Other versions specify that the plague, which was almost certainly an Inner Asian outbreak of what European medievalists now term the Justinian Plague, afflicted the children of the nobility in particular, and that the expulsion of the saṃgha was at the urging of the ministers close to the royal family.[28]

It seems possible, then, that the *Testament of Ba* reflects a distant memory of the plague that occurred in Tibet in 739 and that claimed the life of the Jincheng Gongzhu, or of a subsequent outbreak during the years immediately following. Assuming this to have been the case, then the sudden loss of the children of the family, even if not representing literally a particular tragedy in the history of the Ba clan, nevertheless may well reflect a disaster that afflicted many Tibetans of high standing at that time. Indeed, the *Old Tibetan Annals* from Dunhuang records the death of a royal prince, perhaps the crown prince, whom the *Testament of Ba* considers to have been slain by sorcery, together with the decease of the princess of Jincheng.[29] What seems most certain is that, beginning no later than 739 and continuing no doubt for some years thereafter, some of the leading Tibetan clans were stricken with an epidemiological catastrophe that defied their comprehension, and, like Ba Selnang according to the account of the *Testament of Ba*, under such circumstances, some would have no doubt experienced a crisis of faith, given especially an environment in which alternative religious systems were already competing with one another. As the European experience of the Black Death during the fourteenth century teaches us, plague can act as a powerful catalyst for spiritual ferment.[30]

Cosmology, Karma, and Conversion

That there was considerable spiritual ferment in Tibet during the eighth century is something about which we can be certain: the evidence of this is abundant. Interpreting that evidence, however, is another matter altogether. As was suggested earlier, one of the main difficulties we confront here is the authority of later Tibetan historiography, which offers us a much mythologized construction of eighth-century events. In attempting to discern what relationship the tale of the vermilion-marked pearl might have to what we can plausibly argue to have been the case during the period it describes, above and beyond its probable reference to the Justinian Plague, let us survey in brief the thematic role of the episode under consideration in the narrative of the *Testament of Ba* itself, and the nature of the relationship between the themes in question and what may be gleaned from authentic late eighth- and early ninth-century sources.

(1) The narrative of the *Testament of Ba* is developed episodically without any division of the work into chapters or marked sections, but we may nevertheless speak of it as a composition in three movements. The first, to which the tale of the vermilion-marked pearl belongs, concerns the events surrounding the birth and childhood of Trhi Songdetsen, culminating in his personal adoption of Buddhism.[31] Here the *Testament of Ba* places great emphasis, as we have seen in chapter 2, on funerary rites and the truth of the Buddhist teaching regarding the round of rebirth, saṃsāra. Not surprisingly, it also has much to say about the propagation of the teaching of karma, the principle that fitting results ultimately issue from the moral quality of willful action. According to the narrative of the *Testament of Ba*, it is in fact Trhi Songdetsen's early childhood interest in and later adult acceptance of this teaching that signal a religious orientation culminating in the monarch's conversion.[32] The second broad division of the *Testament of Ba* recounts the invitations extended to the Indian masters Śāntarakṣita and Padmasambhava, their activities in Tibet, and the foundation of the Samye monastery, including the inception of the Tibetan Buddhist saṃgha.[33] The final movement relates the great schism between adherents of the Chan propounded by the Heshang Moheyan and the followers of the gradual path of Indian Mahāyāna, and the royal resolution of the conflict in favor of the Indian faction.[34] The unifying warp that runs through this narrative fabric emphasizes, I believe, the contested appropriation by the Tibetan court of the Indian cosmological framework that Buddhism required as its proper context, that is to say, the conception of the world as a well-ordered domain of rebirth governed by the lawlike operation of karma. This is clear and explicit in the first movement of the *Testament of Ba*, to which our tale belongs, but note, too, as the *Testament of Ba* itself underscores, that the Samye monastery is in its design a cosmogram, a three-dimensional model of the Mount Meru world system through which beings revolve, and of the compresent maṇḍala of the buddha Vairocana, which is the same world in its "pure" or awakened aspect.[35] Finally, in the doctrinal battle between the Heshang Moheyan and Kamalaśīla, it is the apparently antinomian character of the former's teaching that stands condemned; that is to say, the radical Chan of the Heshang is presented as undermining precisely the order of things that had been constructed in the preceding movements.[36]

We may remark, too, that the structure of the *Testament of Ba* seems to recapitulate—whether intentionally or not is uncertain—the pattern of traditional Tibetan monastic debate, according to which one first refutes (*dgag*) the incorrect position of one's opponent, which in this case is that of the Tibetan ministers who opposed the Buddhist teaching of karma and rebirth; then establishes (*gzhag*) the correct view held by one's own party, here represented by the cosmogram of Samye; and finally refutes (*spang*) objections to and misapprehensions of one's position, as Kamalaśīla does in rebuking the Heshang.[37] The tale of the vermilion-marked pearl, whatever its original inspiration, thus must be read as integral to the *Testament of Ba*'s central argument.

While this much seems generally correct, there is a very important objection to this interpretation of the text that must be addressed. As Blondeau has rightly argued, neither the tale that we find in the *Testament of Ba*, nor the rituals that Tibetans actually practice in connection with neonatal deaths, really has anything to do with karma. Rather, it seems to be the case that preexisting Tibetan religious beliefs had already assumed that persons may be reborn, at least under some conditions, and that this, even prior to Buddhist doctrinal influences, explains in part the great importance that notions of rebirth and reincarnation would later assume in Tibetan society.[38] The Buddhist polemic, therefore, was concerned to demonstrate less the mere fact that rebirth occurs, than that rebirth is a *universal* phenomenon that itself demonstrates the truth of the entire karma-saṃsāra cosmology, and hence the superiority of Buddhism as a soteriological system.[39] The *Testament of Ba* simply seems to ignore the inconvenient fact that the episode under discussion by itself really does not contribute to the case it is advanced to support. We shall return to this problem, for it will emerge that later writers would indeed seek to modify the episode accordingly. For the moment, however, let us continue to examine the background for what I have termed the *Testament of Ba*'s central argument.

(2) From the perspective of normative Buddhist doctrine, cosmology is thought of above all in terms of moral causation, involving, in traditional terms, the crucial teaching of rebirth. It is of some importance, then, that, beginning perhaps in the last half of the eighth century—that is, still during the reign of Trhi Songdetsen—we start to find evidence of the production of an indigenous Tibetan didactic literature whose primary aim is the propagation of the doctrines of rebirth and moral causation. As examples, we may mention once more *The History of the Cycle of Birth and Death* and add the *'Phrul-gyi byig-shu mi phyi-ma-la bstan-pa'i mdo* (The Sūtra Taught by the Monk of Magical Sagacity for Future Persons), a work of which there are also multiple copies or fragments in the Dunhuang collections.[40] This short text in verse, treating the essential Buddhist themes of impermanence, rebirth, and karma, presages in some respects the popular post-eleventh-century sermonizing concerning what came to be known in short as "the four reversals of attitude" (*blo-ldog rnam-bzhi*).[41] Noteworthy, too, is the Dunhuang collection of brief Buddhist funerary texts that we have examined in chapter 1 (pp. 7–8), which anticipates the later literature on the intermediate state (*bar-do*) and includes a remarkable polemical passage pointedly criticizing the pre-Buddhist funeral rites of Tibet as sacrifices incapable of securing the ends for which they were intended.[42] Steinkellner has edited, from among the manuscripts collected by Aurel Stein, the highly interesting *'Jig-rten pha-rol sgrub-pa* (The Proof of a World Beyond) by one Prajñāsena, a work that, though clearly inspired by Indian philosophical models, was no doubt intended, in the form in which it was preserved, for Tibetan consumption.[43] The late eighth- and early ninth-century ascent of the cosmology of karma and rebirth seems also evident in the numerous liturgical texts discovered at Dunhuang, which make it clear that one of the key roles for which the monks received official patronage was to perform confessional services for whatever evils were committed by the Tsenpo and his ministers, and to magnify their merits, for, assuredly, in the business of running the empire, sin and merit were to be gathered aplenty.[44]

The *Old Tibetan Chronicle* from Dunhuang states that Trhi Songdetsen sought "to propagate the dharma by constructing temples throughout the center and the frontiers, having made it accepted that the Buddha's dharma is unsurpassed. Guiding all through compassion, he freed them from birth-and-death, and secured them in perpetual deliverance."[45] That the emperor was much impressed with Buddhism for the manner in which it described the world as a well-ordered and intelligible system of moral causation and rebirth finds confirmation in the small number of available documents that may be attributed with relative security to the monarch's command, and perhaps to his pen. Foremost are the edicts concerning the royal conversion to Buddhism, which, in the form in which they are preserved by Pawo Tsuklaktrhenga (1504–1566), have been generally thought to be authentic.[46] It seems probable, too, that the author of the *Testament of Ba* was familiar with the text of these same edicts.[47] Though some details of their interpretation are open to question, the main points are clear: following the death of Trhi Detsuktsen in 755/756, Buddhism was suppressed by a ministerial conspiracy. When his son, Trhi Songdetsen, reached his twentieth year, that is, in 761/762, various evil omens arose that could not be controlled by the established rituals, whereupon the ban on Buddhist worship was lifted and things changed for the good. The emperor then took up the study of the doctrine and came to conclude that it did not accord with the old religion of Tibet in its cults and ritual (*sku lha gsol ba dang cho ga myi mthun pas*), and so it was suspected (*dogs*) of leading the Tibetans to an evil fate, bringing epidemic and famine upon them (p. 53). By contrast, the Tsenpo continues, the Buddha has taught:

> Investigating the reality of the doctrine—for what is known from the doctrine is not found in the realms of the worldly—the states of sentient beings are beyond number. All those born in the four ways and subject to rebirth are as they are, beginninglessly and endlessly, owing to their own deeds (*las, karman*).[48]

Following this is a brief disquisition on the three types of deeds, the six realms of rebirth, and the merit and wisdom accumulated by the Buddhas, bodhisattvas, and arhats who transcend the world.[49]

Trhi Songdetsen's favorable inclination to essentially scholastic Buddhism is further in evidence in the most extensive written work plausibly attributed to him, the *Bka' yang-dag-pa'i tshad-ma* (The Authentic Proof of the Scriptures).[50] Because this difficult treatise, which has been little studied as yet, is listed as his composition in a catalogue of Buddhist texts that was compiled at the order of his second son and grand-successor within two decades of his passing,[51] we must, I think, accept that, if not composed literally by the emperor, it was at least ghostwritten for him with his knowledge and approval. What is most remarkable about it in connection with our present subject matter is its sustained concern with Buddhist discussions of reasoning and of causation. Like a convert to the Galilean system eagerly embracing the newly propounded intelligibility of the heavens, the author of the *Authentic Proof of the Scriptures* delights in the very idea of reason (here: Tib. *rigs-pa* = Skt. *yukti*) that he finds articulated in Buddhist scriptures:

> To express particular reasons is to exercise power with respect to all phenomena; for just as in the world whatever it is that kings uphold according to their own reason is then implemented by the force of command, so, in the same way, adherence to one's own party, with respect to any principle, is established by the authority of the reasons to which one holds.[52]

It seems entirely consistent with what we otherwise know that a Buddhist missionary of the philosophical stature of Śāntarakṣita would have appealed to his royal patron by accentuating the analogy of the legislative role of reason, as understood in Indian Buddhist scholastic circles, with that of the monarch himself.[53] Prominent among the determinations of that reason is the reasonableness of the karma-saṃsāra cosmology:

> To determine, he writes, that ordinary beings, proceed to another world when their lifeforce is exhausted . . . [you must know that] it is the formless component, consciousness, that so proceeds. For instance, the wind, though lacking ostensible form, moves about, carrying with it whatever odor it chances to meet, be it the fragrance of flowers or the stench of corruption, which one comes to smell without perceiving any form of wind or of scent. Nevertheless, so long as the continuum of the wind is uninterrupted, one smells the sweet or foul odors respectively, each without change. Similarly, though neither consciousness nor karma possesses form, it is apparent that ripening must accord with [that cause which is subject to] maturation. Moreover, owing to whatever karma was committed, which is the cause, one is born in the life beyond in a certain form, just as there is correspondence between the form that appears in a mirror and the form the mirror faces, or between a seal and the impression it makes in clay.[54]

Of course, compared with later Tibetan scholasticism, this is perhaps not very elegant. What is of interest to us is not so much the degree of the monarch's philosophical perspicacity as the great fascination evidenced here with an apparently newfound ability to describe the world, however imperfectly, as an ordered process whose complexity is nevertheless intelligible. And, unless we find some basis for doubting the attribution of the *Authentic Proof of the Scriptures* at least to the court of Trhi Songdetsen, we must accept its testimony, particularly given what we otherwise know of the symbolism of Samye, that Buddhist conceptions of cosmological and causal order indeed did play a significant role in the Tsenpo's decision to adopt the foreign religion.

In sum, then, there is a compelling body of evidence dating to the period under discussion that supports the conclusion that conceptions of rebirth and retribution, that is to say, the saṃsāra-karma cosmological scheme and all that it entailed in reference to notions of natural causation and human conduct, were both contested among eighth-century Tibetans and aggresively propagated by the proponents of Buddhism, with the Tsenpo first and foremost among them. The *Testament of Ba*, though much fictionalized, on this account may well preserve a genuine reflection of the climate of Tibetan thought during the age of the royal conversion to Buddhism.

From Rebirth to Resurrection

The later Tibetan historical tradition was produced almost entirely by authors for whom the saṃsāra-karma cosmology was beyond any possibility of serious contestation, so it is not surprising that they did not find a satisfying leitmotif in the *Testament of Ba*'s emphasis upon its verification in the face of denial.[55] With their re-visioning of the history of the Buddhist conquest of Tibet, the tale of the vermilion-marked pearl is for the most part forgotten. Putön alludes to it briefly, but without recounting it in full.[56] Pawo Tsuklaktrhenga, writing in the mid-sixteenth century, repeats it at length, but that is only because he reproduces whole sections of the *Testament of Ba* verbatim in his work.[57] A century later, the Fifth Dalai Lama, critical of Pawo's use of the *Testament of Ba*, a work that he finds at once fascinating and suspect, mentions our tale, but because he regards it as indicative of the *Testament of Ba*'s inconsistencies: if the Buddhist clergy had been expelled from Tibet following a ban on their religion, he asks, what was the old Chinese monk still doing in Lhasa? For this and other reasons, he concludes that, though the *Testament of Ba* may well be genuinely ancient in its origins, it has been much contaminated in the course of its transmission by its later editors.[58]

The vermilion-marked pearl, though buried once more, was by no means entirely lost, however, even disregarding the brief disinternments just mentioned. Its peculiar recovery, to which we now turn, clearly indicates a stunning transformation in the Tibetan conception of Tibet's imperial past. We may even say that, like Ba Selnang's poor daughter, her story was itself marvelously reborn.

I have argued that, during the period in which Buddhism was adopted as the dominant religion of the old Tibetan state, it was the world-ordering dimension of Buddhist teaching that was of greatest interest to the emperors and that defined the pattern of their adherence to and patronage of their new religion. Soteriological Buddhism was, officially at least, primarily a matter for the monks, whose pursuit of perfect enlightenment helped to ensure that the saṃgha was a worthy object for the generosity of noble patrons anxious to earn merit and repent of misdeeds. This is not to say that there were no soteriological orientations in evidence outside of officially sponsored monastic institutions: the fashion of Chan in the late-eighth-century court certainly involved nonmonastic practitioners from the royal family and nobility,[59] and many of the Dunhuang fragments of Tibetan esoteric texts seem likely to have emanated from outside of the state-sanctioned monastic mainstream.[60] Nevertheless, it is clear that, adopting Spiro's categories, "kammatic" and not "nibbanic" Buddhism was in the forefront of official Tibetan religious interest during the eighth and ninth centuries.[61] By the eleventh century, however, much had changed. The old empire had long since collapsed and there simply was no central source of political authority in the Tibetan world.[62] The Buddhist karma-saṃsāra cosmology had increasingly become normative for Tibetans, so that, while it was still actively propagated, as it would be down to the present day, its propagation was no longer a matter of active contestation, as the author of the *Testament of Ba* considers it to have been, and as several of the Dunhuang manuscripts mentioned here confirm that indeed it was. At the same time, the broadening dissemination of esoteric doctrine and practice effected a reorientation in which soteriological Buddhism became a matter of immediate concern for Tibetan Buddhists more generally, while at the same time those who were thought to be guardians of esoteric salvific teaching became esteemed in both temporal and religious spheres, so that the lama (*bla-ma*) now increasingly emerged as the common locus of actual power, worldly and spiritual.[63]

With this in mind, then, we turn to a story that comes into wide circulation in the early fourteenth century. This is the account of the origins of an esoteric teaching of the Nyingmapa school of Tibetan Buddhism, a teaching of the Great Perfection (*rdzogs-chen*) system of meditation, called the *Mkha'-'gro snying-thig* (The Innermost Spirituality of the Ḍākinī).[64] The textual sources of this teaching are prominent among the "treasures," or revealed doctrines, that began to proliferate from about the twelfth century on,[65] these in particular having been revealed by the enigmatic Pema Lendreltsel, who flourished in Central Tibet towards the turn of the thirteenth to the fourteenth century. The corpus he "discovered" was given its definitive redaction and then widely popularized in the mid-fourteenth century by Longchen Rabjampa (1308–1363), the greatest scholastic master of the Nyingmapa school.

According to the tale that is narrated there, the monarch Trhi Songdetsen had a daughter, called Princess Pemasel, who died when she was just eight. The ruler, becoming utterly distraught, at once sends for his guru, the Indian tantric master Padmasambhava, who explains at length the nature of the king's karmic connection with the daughter who is at once so well loved, and through her death has caused the monarch so much grief. The master then inscribes the mantra syllable NṚ in vermilion at the little girl's heart-center. Recalling her consciousness from the intermediate state by means of his Gnostic abilities, he coerces her to reanimate her corpse. After she reawakens, he transmits the liberating teaching of the *Innermost Spirituality of the Ḍākinī* to her, and it is through her later rebirths as Pema Lendreltsel and as Longchen Rabjampa himself that this teaching is made available for the general edification of the faithful.[66]

Now, I think it is clear that we are in essence dealing with one and the same story here and in the *Testament of Ba*'s tale of the vermilion-marked pearl. The structural connections between the two are unmistakeable, and the transformations of the tale both intriguing and illuminating. Consider:

(1) Ba Selnang	→	Trhi Songdetsen
(2) Ba's daughter	→	Princess Pemasel
(3) Chinese Heshang	→	Padmasambhava
(4) vermilion-marked pearl	→	vermilion mantra-syllable
(5) rebirth	→	resurrection
(6) vindication of rebirth (a cosmological doctrine)	→	vindication of Great Perfection (a soteriological doctrine)

Moreover, the story of Princess Pemasel, by making fully explicit the karmic background of the episode, responds precisely to the objection that, as we have seen, may be raised against the Buddhist credentials of the account given in the *Testament of Ba*.

Of course, it is possible that the author of the *Innermost Spirituality of the Ḍākinī* did not in fact know the *Testament of Ba*'s account, and that his version of the story was independently composed on the basis of the same ritual to which that account refers. This, however, in no way alters my basic thesis: in either case, we are dealing with essentially similar material, reflecting in its origins indigenous Tibetan beliefs and practices, as appropriated by self-consciously Buddhist authors writing of them in different periods in markedly differing ways. The variations of this simple tale, therefore, aptly illustrate the manner in which the royal conversion to Buddhism as the imperial religion during the eighth and ninth centuries became thoroughly reformulated by later Tibetan chroniclers so as to accord, in significant respects anachronistically, with the needs and interests of their own day.

From the eleventh century onward, the Tibetan vision of the old order became increasingly defined by the ongoing elaboration of two great cycles of myths of imperial Tibet: an Avalokiteśvara cycle, focusing primarily on the reign of Songtsen Gampo, and a Padmasambhava cycle, concerning the reign of Trhi Songdetsen. (These will be examined in chapter 8.) Throughout the latter, it is the apotheosis of Padmasambhava, now the "precious guru" of the Tibetan people as a whole, who dominates even the figure of the Tsenpo.[67] It is his teaching of esoteric means to achieve swift liberation that becomes doctrinally preeminent. The role of the Chi-

Figure 3.1 The trinity of the Tibetan conversion: Padmasambhava (*center*), Śāntarakṣita (*lower left*), and Trhi Songdetsen (*lower right*). Nineteenth century (after *Bod-kyi thang-ga*).

nese in the conversion of Tibet, accentuated by the *Testament of Ba*, is now mostly effaced, and it is no accident that this occurs while China's Mongol emperors of the thirteenth and fourteenth centuries hold at least nominal sway over Tibet.[68] Indeed, in later times the Chinese monks who had come to Tibet would be caricatured as buffoons. In the narratives of the foundation of Samye, too, the old ministerial clans are either forgotten altogether or receive a poor second billing after the legendary adepts of Padmasambhava's immediate circle.[69] Thus even the *Testament of Ba*, a work that seems to have nothing but praise for the great master, ultimately comes to be disparaged by later adherents of his cult, not for its inconsistencies, but because it is thought to represent the "sullied perspective" of the ministers.[70] The transformations noted here in the tale of the mark of vermilion thus may serve to delineate a general and thoroughgoing transformation of Tibetan historical consciousness.

Our tale, however, was still subject to one more rebirth. In the most famous of the accounts of Padmasambhava, the epic *Padma bka'-thang* (The Testimonial Record of Padmasambhava) revealed by Orgyen Lingpa (fl. mid-fourteenth cent.), the story of Princess Pemasel is told once more, mostly following the version we have just summarized, but in the *Testimonial Record of Padmasambhava* there is no mark of vermilion, no resurrection, no transmission to her of the liberating teaching of the Great Perfection.[71] Rather, in what remains of the *Innermost Spirituality*'s lengthy narrative, Padmasambhava, the omniscient master who knows past, present, and

Figure 3.2 Mi-tshe-ring, the "long-life man," derived from the Chinese god of longevity Shouxing, is a buffoon figure in monastic dance-dramas. He is popularly (though incorrectly) identified with the eighth-century Chan master Moheyan, and so has come to represent the Chinese false teacher.

future, consoles the distraught monarch by revealing his daughter's miserable condition in past lives, and her good fortune to enjoy a birth in the royal family, if only for a short time, owing to a karmic debt (*lan-chags*) that the monarch has now unwittingly repaid. The princess, having formed a connection with Padmasambhava, will henceforth continue to improve her condition in subsequent lives, to take birth eventually, as the earlier version had affirmed, as Longchen Rabjampa, referred to here by his proper name, Drime Özer. Though the tale seems to emphasize rebirth and karma once again, it is with a view no longer to vindicate those doctrines, so much as to accentuate the magnificence of Padmasambhava, knower of the three times, ultimate agent of the salvation of the Tibetan people. The archaic ritual dimension of the early version, concerned to secure the rebirth of a deceased infant in the same family into which she had been already born, is now mostly lost to history. It survived, however, as Blondeau has shown, where it first arose, in the continuing practices of Tibetan funerary ritual.

4

Plague, Power, and Reason

The Royal Conversion to Buddhism Reconsidered

The Puzzle of the Tibetan Conversion

In the preceding chapters I have emphasized primarily the representation in later Tibetan writings of themes connected with the Tibetan imperial conversion, though by focusing upon the *Sba-bzhed* (The Testament of Ba), I have also sought to suggest something of the manner in which in its early phases the growing myth of the conversion indeed referred back to aspects of the religious situation under the old Tibetan empire. In concluding part 1, let us turn now to the conversion itself, adhering so far as is possible to evidence derived from texts and artifacts that, for the most part, assuredly do stem from the period concerned.[1] On the basis of this material, I shall attempt to sketch out here, not so much a history of events, but rather a speculative reconstruction of the intentions that the early Tibetan adoption of Buddhism involved.

The conversion of Trhi Songdetsen and its ramifications for the Tibetan empire have been much discussed by contemporary Tibetanists. Those investigating the earliest available sources have succeeded in recent decades in bringing a substantial body of relevant material to light that not so long ago had either seemed altogether incapable of adequate decipherment or was otherwise buried in obscurity.[2] Nevertheless, despite the materials that are now at our disposal, prejudgements about Tibetan history, whether stemming from an earlier phase in our knowledge of Tibet or from popular misrepresentations, remain in wide circulation.

A prominent aspect of the Western myth of Tibet is that the Tibetans were a nation of semibarbarous warriors who were civilized and thus tamed by the gentle teachings of Buddhism.[3] Whatever partial truths may have contributed to this myth, the actual historical record makes perfectly clear that it would be an absurdity to describe the conversion of the empire in any such terms: after all, Trhi Songdetsen's armies sacked the Chinese capital in 763, that is, within two years of his adoption of the religion of peace. And his son, Trhi Desongtsen, whom we know to have been raised as a child under the tutelage of Buddhist monks,[4] was not in the least hesitant to continue to assert Tibetan military power in Inner Asia. That he at least saw no contradiction here is clearly indicated by the introduction to his commission of a lexical guide to Buddhist scriptural translations, which tells us:

> In the horse year the Emperor Trhi Desongtsen dwelt in the Öncangdo palace in Kyi. The old armies of east and west had been rotated and the brigands quelled. The messenger(s) of the Karluk offered homage. The Great Ministers . . . and others brought much tribute from the territories, and offered camels, horses and cattle to His Majesty. As a follow-up to the awards that he granted to each according to rank from Zhanglön on down, he gave his command that . . . those who had become master translators . . . should write a catalogue of the Tibetan translations and coinages deriving from the Sanskrit of the Greater and Lesser Vehicles.[5]

The assumption that Buddhism and imperium might be incompatible is one that would not have occurred to these Buddhists, and, indeed, it is one that few serious students of Buddhist history would countenance today.[6]

Nevertheless, there is a more subtle version of this view that does, I think, continue to lurk in the background of the study of early Tibet. The argument runs something like this: Tibet rose to imperial greatness, ruling much of Inner Asia and successfully challenging even such potent adversaries as the Arabs and the Chinese, largely on the strength of its indigenous resources and traditions. (This premise seems in essence true.) Within a few generations of the conversion to Buddhism, however, the empire grew weak, and, riven by factional feuds among the nobles, it collapsed. (True as well.) Evidently, the later monarchs' religious concerns led them to divert too much in the way of resources to the monks and monasteries, and to devote too little to the maintenance of Tibet's earlier strengths.[7] This conclusion, however, is a non sequitur.

Available evidence does not permit a neat and clear clarification of all the issues raised here, but certainly several elements of the argument are suspect. Factional feuding of the nobility, for instance, is known to have preceded and accompanied the rise of the empire, and so it was by no means uniquely tied to the presence of Buddhism.[8] It is more likely the case that religious faction was above all the result, and not the cause, of deeper divisions among Tibet's lords. That is to say, religion became a means for the representation of political difference. We do not yet have sufficient knowledge of the imperial economy to determine to what extent patronage of Buddhism may have drained the exchequer. But at the same time, it is clear that the Tibetan armies at the frontiers were massively dependent upon corvée labor, the forced impression of conquered peoples into military service, and the expropriation of animals, goods, and commodities in the conquered territories, arrangements that were no doubt well suited to an empire still expanding into new territory, but probably destabilizing once the pace of imperial expansion slowed.[9] The primary reason, in fact, to single out Buddhism as having had a special causal relation with the decline of the empire is that the predominant Tibetan historical myth, in *both* its Buddhist and Bönpo versions, does just that;[10] but the myth accentuates the supposed role of religious dispute precisely because it was composed by religious partisans, for whom religion was a uniquely compelling concern.[11] In Tibet, as in religious societies elsewhere, such concern fundamentally shaped the manner in which history came to be written, but it is less clear that the history we are now examining was itself so shaped.

It seems, then, preferable to leave the question of the relationship between Buddhism and the empire's decline to one side, until at least there is more advance in the study of some issues of certain relevance to this, such as the imperial economy, old Tibetan civil and military institutions, and the formation of the early aristocracy.[12] But by our raising these questions, the role of Buddhism under the Tibetan empire is itself problematized, and it is this that introduces the matter to be considered here: if the old traditions of Tibet were, as seems the case, entirely adequate to support the early growth of the empire, and if the Buddhism adopted under the empire was, as I have suggested, in any case compatible with Tibet's martial culture,[13] why did the emperors judge it to be desirable to adopt the foreign religion at all? What was Buddhism's special appeal to them?

The Power of Plague

We have seen earlier that occurrences of plague and epidemics were among the circumstances that the *Testament of Ba* recalled in connection with events leading up to the emperor's conversion, and that the earliest sources offer some confirmation in this regard. The emperor himself, in his later edict discussing the conversion, had said:

> That [Buddhism] was not the old religion. Because it did not accord with the propitiations and rites of the tutelary deities, all suspected it to be no good. They suspected it would harm [me, His Majesty]. They suspected it would threaten governance. They suspected [that it brought about] epidemics and cattle plagues. They suspected it, when famine suddenly fell upon them.[14]

It is characteristic of our modern sensibility to think that, for the most part, epidemics and the like were outside the domain of human rational control until very recently. Many of us tend to harbor a perspective according to which—from the standpoint of public health policy and similar matters—shamanic healing, Buddhist merit making, and contact with the relics of long deceased Catholic saints represent essentially similar, quasi-magical efforts to manipulate one's environment in the absence of sound scientific knowledge. It is important for us to recall, therefore, that medieval peoples certainly did not see things in this way. They, like ourselves, held that some beliefs and practices were sensible and others foolish. Destructive diseases were, as they indeed still are, particularly terrifying deformations of human existence, and the belief, true or false, that we have won or are in the process of winning some degree of apparently rational mastery over them counts for a great deal among us. And, generally speaking, this was true, too, of medieval peoples.

I emphasize these simple points because we too often tacitly accept the modern religionists' dichotomy of sacred and profane spheres and read it back into the worlds of our forebears. If we wish to make sense of the preferability of Buddhism to some in medieval Tibet, we need to understand how they thought it rationalized, more adequately than its competitors, the frailties of our concrete existence in the world. The adoption of the cosmology of karma and saṃsāra, as we have seen in the preceding chapter, did not preclude, and in some respects no doubt encouraged, the performance of what *we* might hold to be magical ritual;[15] but also it did appear to make intelligible why it was that among such rituals there were sometimes those that worked and other times those that failed; and did so in a lawlike manner. Furthermore—and this should be borne in mind in connection with all that will follow—the cosmology of karma and saṃsāra comported well with an imperial interest in legislation; that is to say, law and order may be reinforced by assenting to cosmic justice and order.[16]

We may note parenthetically that, despite the emperor's concern to allay fears regarding the cults of the Tibetan protective divinities and his insistence on the explanatory soundness of karma, this conflict is one that in fact has never been fully resolved for the Tibetans, even in our own times. In an address to the Tibetan community as recently as 1996, the present Dalai Lama criticized those who, he said, place too much faith in the supposed agency of divine protectors and attend too little to the management of their own karma.[17] I do not think that he had Trhi Songdetsen's edict in mind; the resemblance of the arguments is coincidental, and for that reason all the more striking.[18]

The Charisma of Reason

Weberian reflections on religion sometimes underscore a broad distinction between spontaneous, charismatic sources of authority, and rational, institutional ones, and in this connection emphasize the conception of a routinization of charisma.[19] With the establishment, for instance, of a trained priesthood or church, the uncanniness of charisma becomes contained and controlled. But this is not to say that it is lost. It is important that we consider in this regard the possibilities afforded for a charismaticization of reason. Imperial Buddhism in medieval Tibet may be taken, I think, as a case in point.

The early Tibetan kings were certainly regarded as divine in their origin, and, as we have seen in chapter 1, much of what we know of pre-Buddhist Tibetan cult relates to the cult of the kings.[20] Tsenpo (*btsan-po*), the proper designation by which the Tibetan monarch was known, a term relating to secure power and strength,[21] may also relate the ruler to the *tsen* (*btsan*), a class of divinities often associated with mountains, high ground, and cliffs, who in contemporary Tibetan religion are commonly regarded as demonic temple protectors.[22] The title was first adopted, it seems, by the rulers of Yarlung and came to refer uniquely to the Tibetan emperor, rather in the manner that "tsar" did to the ruler of the Russian empire.[23] Chinese chroniclers were content to write the phonetic approximation, *zànpŭ*, in Chinese characters, and not to attempt a translation.[24] We must bear in mind, then, that the Tibetan emperor thus enjoyed a unique sacral-political status.[25]

Later Tibetan historiography attributes three great civilizing innovations to the seventh-century ruler Songtsen Gampo (c. 617–649), whose conquests are usually seen as defining the beginnings of the Tibetan empire: the introduction of a system of writing, the codification of the laws, and the inception of Tibetan Buddhism.[26] These themes have been much mythologized in the writings of post-eleventh-century historians, and their accounts can be used only with great caution. Nevertheless, their association of literacy, legislation, and religious change probably does represent a genuine insight into the structural relationships among these three undeniably crucial turns in the cultural history of early medieval Tibet. The burgeoning dimensions of the Tsenpo's realm, and the attendant increase in the complexity of its civil and military administration, and of its relations with its neighbors, most certainly required close attention to the regularization of the practices and policies of the state at many levels. Under such circumstances, writing and recordkeeping became indispensable technologies. The earliest statement of what took place when the empire was born during the early seventh century, as recorded some two centuries later in the *Old Tibetan Chronicle* from Dunhuang, reflects such concerns:

> Formerly, Tibet had no writing, but during the lifetime of this emperor the Great Legislation that was the Sacred Authority of Tibet (*bod-kyi gtsug-lag bka'-grims chad-mo*),[27] as well as the rank-order of ministers, the powers of both great and small, the awards in recognition of excellence, the punishments for misdeeds, the regularization, among farmers and herdsmen, of pelts, acreage and roadways, the measures of volume and weight, etc.—all of the righteous governance of Tibet emerged during the time of the emperor Trhi Songtsen. Because everyone recalled and experienced his beneficence, they called him by the name of "Songtsen the Wise" [Songtsen Gampo].[28]

We may be inclined to assume that the ancient institutions of Tibetan sacral kingship provided a fully adequate ideological basis for the Tibetan empire. An early and important passage such as this one indeed supports that view, as it contains no suggestion that the royal innovations were founded upon anything besides more ancient Tibetan customs and institutions. This reading, however, may be in certain respects naive. For the process whereby the principality of Yarlung grew to become the kingdom of Tibet, continued to expand to include territories and peoples beyond the confines of the Tibetan world, and in so doing required and created a literate imperial administration is scarcely conceivable without being accompanied by significant ideological transformations. The advent of literacy and literate practices were thus consequences of and conditions for great changes in many aspects of the culture of Tibet. Our problem is to understand the nature of such changes in relation to the continuities with the past that seem also to be emphasized in our sources.

Literacy contributed to the emergence of and empowerment of new classes whose makeup is not yet well understood.[29] Certainly, those members of the older dominant classes who became literate—or at least came to depend upon the services of literate persons they employed—were included among them, and we must also suppose there to have been scribes, clerks, supply and taxation officers, et cetera, whose corporate identity was newly engendered above all by their employment in the creation and maintenance of written records. Even assuming, as likely was the case, that many such persons would have been of menial status, their literate labor became a condition for the power of those whom they served.[30] The written word, in short, was a new and powerful technology in the Tibetan world that could not readily be reduced to or subsumed within the sacral, economic, or martial powers that alone had dominated Tibet until the time of Songtsen Gampo.

The archaic, preliterate ideology of Tibetan sacral kingship, centered upon the local cults of the Yarlung valley and its environs, could not have remained perfectly stable for long. The internal constitution and foreign relations of the newly literate empire both increasingly favored writing as a vehicle for the organization not only of established knowledge but also of diplomacy, intelligence, and the assimilation and diffusion of new knowledge within a heterogeneously composed, literate community. Great skill in the techniques of the written word came to be imbued with a peculiar charisma of its own, and it would have been natural to attribute this power to neighboring civilizations whose longer histories of literacy gave them relatively greater advancement here, and who thus offered models for Tibetan emulation.[31] The Chinese chancellery and the Buddhist monastery were certainly not the sole exemplars of mastery over the arts of writing available to Tibetans of the seventh and eighth centuries, but they would have been among the most impressive. That foreign cultural influences, and Buddhist and Chinese influences above all, should have become important forces in Tibet in the wake of the creation of the Tibetan script was thus entailed in some measure by the circumstances attending the growth of the empire itself.[32] Tibet could have maintained its archaic traditions wholly unchanged only by retreating into itself, foregoing the path of imperial expansion.

It is in part owing to the vagaries of later history that in one area alone the evidence bearing on the organization of knowledge in early medieval Tibet is far better preserved than in any other and is extremely impressive. I refer, of course, to the transmission and codification of Buddhist learning during the late eighth and early ninth centuries. For it was here, given the position of Buddhism as the dominant ideology throughout postimperial Tibetan history and the aura of sacrality that came to surround the Buddhism of the imperial period in particular, that the later tradition preserved in relative abundance documents of fundamental importance.[33]

From our own distant vantage point, the reason that the achievement of the empire's Buddhists in the redaction of scriptural learning appears to overwhelm other accomplishments of Tibetan learning thus may be the result of the fortuitous conjunction of superior preservation during a later period with religious charisma acquired after the fact. Despite this, there can be little doubt that the very great efforts made to establish Buddhism and Buddhist learning in the Tibetan empire do reflect in part the value attributed to them by Tibet's rulers during the eighth and ninth centuries: monastic, clerical Buddhism, with its trained scholars and scribes, its language sciences and methods of translation, its libraries and catalogues, its sytematicization of reasoning and debate, provided medieval Tibet with an ideal model of organized knowledge.[34] In a sprawling empire in which the management of knowledge must have been felt as an ever more urgent concern, part of the charisma attributed to Buddhism stemmed from its particular mastery over the arts of the written word, its mastery of reason.[35]

Stephen Teiser has argued recently that the Chinese emperors who sponsored the production of Chinese Buddhist canonical collections did so because it was possible to regard the canon, the Buddhist Scriptural Treasury, precisely as an imperial treasure. The royal possession of the Dharmakāya—the corpus of the Buddha's doctrine—became in effect a new source of royal charisma.[36] Something similar seems to have taken place in Tibet, but we may further specify that possession of the canon signified the incorporation into the monarch's domain of the well-ordered empire of enlightened reason.

Buddhism and Legislation

The themes we are considering are clearly in evidence in connection with the development of the traditions and legends of Tibetan imperial legislation. We have seen earlier that the *Old Tibetan Chronicle*, which attributes the redaction of the laws to

Songtsen Gampo, says nothing at all that would lead us to see the influence of Buddhist ethics at work here. This impression is borne out by surviving fragments of the old laws, which are similarly devoid of references to Buddhism.[37] Later Tibetan tradition, however, while retaining some records of the old laws, asserts them to have been built upon foundations derived from basic Buddhist morality and the traditions of Indian Dharmaśāstra. This transformation is particularly intriguing, however, for as Stein has clearly shown, the incremental evolution of the traditions concerning the imperial legislation can be traced in a number of early documents.[38]

Crucial evidence of this process may be found in a manuscript in the India Office Library collection (*IO* 370), first studied by Richardson.[39] This incomplete work found at Dunhuang has the appearance of a school exercise; I have come to think of it as a poem on the rise of Buddhism in Tibet that was to be copied and memorized by young students, perhaps in the early ninth century, though, I must emphasize, we cannot know with any certainty that it was so intended or used. It shows that besides the association of Trhi Songdetsen with the promulgation of Buddhism in Tibet, which we would expect in any case, Songtsen Gampo was already in some circles being thought of as a Buddhist monarch: the seeds of the later legend were no doubt already planted. Of special interest here is the depiction of Tibetan law as harmonized with Buddhist moral principles, also anticipating the later traditions, which seek to find the basis for Songtsen Gampo's legislation in Indian and Buddhist law and morality (though in our present text, the reference to the pillar inscriptions makes it likely that Trhi Songdetsen in fact is the legislator here referred to). The text reads in part:

> The lords of men, sons of the gods and supreme kings,
> The Magically Sagacious King Songtsen
> And the Monarch Trhi Songdetsen,
> In the realm of Tibet, a human land in Jambudvīpa,
> Well proclaimed the supreme greater vehicle,
> The doctrine of the transcendent perfection of discernment,
> The Mother of the Sugatas of the [three] times,
> That, like the Udumbara flower,
> Is an extremely fine and rare panacea,
> Benefiting all beings,
> And that, equipoised regarding suchness,
> Deconstructs the extremes of being and nonbeing;
> Thus they taught the teaching of Gautama, the Śākya.
> Accepting [that teaching], they made it their spiritual commitment,
> And greatly increased it among all beings.
> For there to be firm retention of it,
> It was written on a stone pillar as a compact between the lord and his subjects.
> In the ocean of such sacred scripture,
> The conduct of the lord and his subjects became the world-mountain.
> So doing, an enduring scriptural foundation was established:
> Those born within the realm, Tibet and Kham, were happy,
> Harvests were good, diseases of men and cattle rare,
> The authority and customs of the subjects, too, were great.
> Because divine doctrine and human custom were feared,

They were honored and closely adhered to, so that
Teachers, parents, relations, and friends,
The elderly, and those of higher station
Were gently and respectfully honored in an unerring manner.
Because they had a kindly attitude towards all,
They neither stole from nor plundered one other.
They avoided lying, sexual license, and shamefulness,
And were straightforward, reliable, heroic, and greatly disciplined.
Though human in body, their customs were divine.
In other kingdoms, and among other men,
This was unprecedented, and will not be again;
Even among the gods this is rare.
Because, when his father, the king, died, the son was young,
The fine doctrine and old scriptures declined.
But the supreme path of truth, the virtuous doctrine,
The ten virtues of the discipline, were preserved,
And the royal laws of the king, lord of men,
Oral traditions taught by wise ancestors—
Where else were these performed as in the customs of Tibet?[40]

What we may clearly discern here is an effort on the part of Tibet's Buddhists to demonstrate the harmony that was supposed to have obtained between Buddhism and the laws and customs enacted by the Tibetan court. The demonstration of such an affinity would no doubt have contributed to the rationalization of Buddhism's position within Tibet, that is, it could be seen as not an entirely alien tradition. This in turn paved the way for the development of the mythic readings of Tibetan imperial history we shall examine in chapter 8, in which the innate affinity between the Buddha's teaching and Tibet is given cosmological grounding even prior to the introduction of Buddhism.[41] But in the present context, we must ask, how may Buddhism, in its aspects that emphasized the convergence of law and morality, have served the interests of the Tibetan empire?

In essence, the answer is, I think, a simple one: a requirement of the state is a state of sin. The moral teachings of Buddhism, as those of the other "universal religions," serve as a source of legal and political coercion.[42] So long as Tibet remained a relatively restricted domain whose subjects held a common family of sacred powers in reverence and were subservient to the direct power of their chieftain, there was no need to seek a source of authority beyond what Tibetan tradition itself had to offer. The foundation of a universal state, however, ruling many diverse peoples and in active contact with many more, necessitated a framework of universal law, which Buddhism was able to supply. The legislative value of Buddhism was, in a sense, made evident by Tibet's expansion into the world.

Imperial Cosmopolitanism

The tremendous influence of Buddhism upon the later formation of Tibetan culture tends to obscure for us the role of many other cultural influences that also became available to Tibetans as a result of Tibet's geographical expansion. The evidence suggests that Nestorian Christianity, Manichaeism, Chinese historiography and divination, and Greek medicine were to be counted among numerous foreign ways of knowledge to which the Tibetans were exposed at this time. The establishment and dissemination of a more-or-less standard writing system, of course, greatly facilitated the spread of such "exotic" learning within the Tibetan empire. It is of particular interest, therefore, that among the texts preserved at Dunhuang we find translations and summaries of literary works, histories, and other genres of writing concerned in one way or another with the foreign peoples with whom the Tibetans were now in contact.

The Tibetan empire in Central Asia at various times included the regions of Khotan, the Tarim basin, Lop Nor, and other places with Iranian and Turkic populations.[43] The contribution of these peoples to the formation of the culture of the empire is less clear than the contribution of China or India, though we can be sure that much of the Indian culture known to the Tibetans was in fact transmitted via Central Asia and Khotan.[44] Khotanese artistic influence was sufficient so that, in addition to Chinese and Indian styles, Tibetan sources would speak of a distinctively Khotanese style, as well.[45] Sogdian textiles, renowned for their sophisticated manufacture and design, also made their way to Tibet.[46] There is some evidence that Galenic medicine reached Tibet through Central Asian sources during this period, and this also points to the Iranian world, perhaps through Sogdiana or Khotan.[47] Khotanese literature in Tibetan translation is represented in several works dealing with the history of Buddhism in Khotan.[48] Tibetan interest in the neighboring peoples of Central Asia is further exemplified by a fascinating document in the Pelliot collection in Paris (*PT* 1283), a sort of intelligence report summarizing knowledge of the Turkish population around Beshbaliq, among other sources of evidence.[49] The old Tibetan versions of the Rāmāyaṇa, too, demonstrate Tibet's participation in wider spheres of Asian culture.[50]

I review these facts here because they point to an additional element of importance in interpreting the Tibetan adoption of Buddhism. I have suggested earlier that Buddhism interested the Tibetans in no small measure through its successful promotion of a particular, well-ordered, cosmological framework, which implied the ethical and ritual mastery of the cosmos it promoted, and through its institutional mastery of techniques, which conformed with the bureaucratic requirements of empire. But Buddhism had another feature favoring it that the indigenous Tibetan royal cult did not; Buddhists, so to say, spoke an international language. In fact, given the peculiar position of Tibet, Buddhism in the eighth century would have been the most prominent cultural system known in almost all the surrounding nations; its presence in India and Nepal, China, and Central Asia may well have contributed to an aura of universality.[51] The Chinese princess of Jincheng, as we have seen in chapter 3, brought to Tibet Khotanese Buddhist monks, who departed for Gandhāra in what is today northern Pakistan after their royal patron's demise. And in chapter 5, we shall turn to the tenuous, but nevertheless real, transmission of Korean Buddhist materials to Tibet at this time.

The tale of the Jincheng Gongzhu, however, also made clear that the international spread of Buddhism was not at once appreciated in Tibet. Its significance in this respect could only be disclosed when the Tibetan monarchs began to adopt Buddhist symbols and conventions for the exercise of royal authority, in other words, when it began to emerge that Buddhism facilitated the symbolic expression of imperial power

Figure 4.1 Dunhuang cave 159. A Tibetan Tsenpo in the lower register of a mural depicting the bodhisattva Vimalakīrti as its main theme. Late eighth–early ninth century (after *Dunhuang Mogaoku*).

in a manner that could be understood not only within Central Tibet, but among subject populations and in neighboring realms.[52] That something along these lines occurred is most clearly in evidence in connection with the esoteric cult of the Buddha Vairocana, to which we now turn.

Under the Tibetan empire of the late eighth and early ninth centuries, Mahāvairocana, the Dainichi-nyorai of Japanese Shingon Buddhism, appears to have become the central figure in a new state cult. Textual, archeological, and art historical evidence all tend to support the conclusion that the emperor himself was in some sense homologous with the cosmic Buddha, and that the ordering of the empire was therefore effectively equivalent to the generation of the maṇḍala. This conclusion is indirectly reinforced by the evidence of Indian-influenced imperial cults in other parts of Asia during roughly the same period.[53] I wish to suggest that the Tibetan imperial state itself came to be constituted, through a principle of homology, as the body and maṇḍala of the Buddha Vairocana.

We have seen that Buddhism, during its first century or so in Tibet, was subject to an oscillating fate, sometimes tolerated, occasionally banned, but not permitted to supplant established Tibetan beliefs and practices. The sea change began in 761/762, when the young emperor Trhi Songdetsen adopted Buddhism as the religion of his court. Following this, in the 770s he constructed the first full-fledged monastery in Tibet in which Tibetan monks could receive ordination and extended state patronage to support massive translation projects.[54] The foundation, circa 779, of the Samye monastic complex, with its great three-storey central temple, is remembered by Tibetans as the central event in the conversion of their nation to the foreign religion. Unfortunately, we do not have precise contemporaneous evidence regarding the founding of Samye and its plan, but the *Testament of Ba*'s account of its architecture and design is remarkably detailed and probably in large part authentic.[55] According to this account—and here the later Tibetan histories and the plan of the later restorations of Samye all concur—Samye was designed in a manner that gave special prominence to Vairocana. It was Vairocana who was installed as the central divinity in the second storey, while the four-faced Sarvavid-Vairocana, surrounded by the eight foremost bodhisattvas and other deities, making up a maṇḍala of forty-two, occupied the uppermost shrine. The central divinity on the lowest storey was Śākyamuni, who is in this context also the Nirmāṇakāya, the emanational embodiment, of Vairocana.[56] Of course, the plan of Samye included many other deities who do not seem to have been so closely related to the Vairocana traditions,[57] but it is difficult to resist the impression that esoteric Buddhism was represented at Samye first and foremost by Vairocana. As Richardson has shown, this orientation was recapitulated in several other Central Tibetan temples of the late imperial and early postimperial period,[58] and, indeed, the association of Vairocana with royal cult appears to have endured in West Tibet well into the second millenium.[59]

It is furthermore important to recall in this connection that the Tibetan court appears to have been very restrained in its commitment to the esoteric traditions of tantric Buddhism. The circulation of the tantras was restricted by order of the court, and permission to translate and to transmit them strictly controlled.[60] It is against this background that the apparent prominence of Vairocana becomes particularly significant. In eighth- and ninth-century Tibet, the tantric free-for-all that comes to characterize aspects of Tibetan Buddhism during the eleventh century had not yet occurred,[61] so that the accentuation of particular esoteric traditions in the otherwise intentionally limited field of imperial-period Buddhism gains considerable gravity.

The likelihood that Trhi Songdetsen greatly favored the Vairocana traditions is underscored by more than just the reports of Samye's design. There is, as we have seen (p. 45), one important doctrinal text attributed to the monarch himself, and, although it may certainly have been written by others on his behalf, it is doubtlessly a product of his court and was published under royal authority. Its opening verses of invocation, in the present context, are especially suggestive, given the tradition that the upper storeys of Samye housed the maṇḍala of Vairocana with the eight foremost bodhisattvas and other deities, while the ground floor emphasized Śākyamuni, possibly as the emanational embodiment (*nirmāṇakāya*) of Vairocana. In the invocations at the beginning of the *Authentic Proof of the Scriptures*, we find Śākyamuni once more, accompanied by the eight bodhisattvas and by the wrathful deities Trailokyavijaya and Acala. Both of these last-mentioned deities are exclusively associated with Buddhist tantric materials, and, what is more, they appear elsewhere in strong connection with the Vairocana cult, notably in the Japanese Shingon tradition, where as Gōsanze-myōō and Fudō-myōō they are foremost among the fierce Knowledge-Kings (*vidyārāja*) protecting the maṇḍala.[62] The basis for this association is possibly the *Mahāvairocanābhisambodhi* (The Awakening of the Great Vairocana), where they (and the eight bodhisattvas) are among the deities emphasized.[63] And it will be seen as we proceed that this tantra was central to the officially sanctioned esoteric Buddhism of the Tibetan empire.

The importance of the invocation verses, therefore, is found in the reinforcement that it offers to the thesis that, despite his great caution regarding the way of mantra,

Trhi Songdetsen did sanction some tantric traditions that were well established in a monastic context, and that had become widely associated with royal cult.[64] The tantrism sanctioned by the Tibetan emperor may have to some extent resembled that of the roughly contemporaneous Heian court in Japan—if our dates are accurate, Kūkai (774–835) in fact was a toddler when Samye was built in 779[65]—and may have had some Southeast Asian parallels as well (though the history of Javanese and of Khmer tantrism during this period remains, unfortunately, extremely obscure).

Consider now the two verses of invocation Trhi Songdetsen offers to the wrathful deities Trailokyavijaya and Acala:

> Conqueror of the three realms [= Trailokyavijaya], heroic lord,
> To you, who tames by your splendor, respectfully I bow.
> May we definitely vanquish
> The wrong views of the three worlds.
>
> Sublime Acala, who never trembles at all,
> To you, firmer than the power of Mount Meru, I bow.
> By all means, may we also not tremble
> When confronted by worlds of demons and enemies.[66]

One hesitates to read too much into these and the other short verses opening the *Authentic Proof of the Scriptures*, but it is probably significant that the martial imagery associated with these two divinities is emphasized here (as often it is in Japan as well).[67] The creation of the maṇḍala overcomes adversity and tames the realm, eliminating opposition to a universal, benevolent order. It may well be that ideologically the esoteric Buddhism favored by the court was so favored precisely because it flattered the imperial self-image.

The *Testament of Ba*, we have seen, reports that during the reign of Trhi Songdetsen's father, Trhi Detsuktsen (704–755/756), who assumed the throne as an infant in 705, emissaries were sent to the region of Mount Kailash to invite two Buddhist teachers who dwelt in retreat there to visit Central Tibet. They declined the royal summons but sent books instead, and instructions for founding a number of temples. One of the hermits was named Buddhaguhya, or Buddhagupta, and it is a matter of speculation whether he is to be identified with a teacher of the same name who made great contributions to eighth-century tantric Buddhism in Tibet.[68] Writings attributed to the latter have been found at Dunhuang, and others are preserved in the Tibetan Buddhist canons and in the traditions of the ancient Nyingmapa sect, which traces its roots to this period. The fundamental authenticity of these latter materials in this case finds support at Dunhuang, for some of the documents discovered there and attributed to our author do concern a particular version of the Great Perfection (*rdzogs-chen*) system of meditation that resembles at least some of the material preserved by the later Nyingmapa tradition. This aspect of what we may call the Buddhagupta corpus has begun to be studied in recent years by Samten Karmay and Namkhai Norbu.[69]

More to the point of the present discussion, however, is a considerable body of texts also attributed to this figure and found in the canons. Much of this material is attested in the earliest extant catalogue of scriptures translated into Tibetan, the *Dkar-chag ldan-kar-ma* (The Denkar Palace Catalogue), which was compiled early in the ninth century and reflects primarily the achievement of the translation committees working during the reign of Trhi Songdetsen.[70] Significantly, all of the four tantric commentaries recorded there are works of Buddhagupta, and two of these concern the *Awakening of the Great Vairocana* and the *Sarvadurgatipariśodhanatantra* (The Tantra Purifying All Evil Destinies).[71] The latter tantra, also known from fragments at Dunhuang, has also been one of the primary texts relating to Vairocana in Tibet.[72]

The thorough investigation of the tantric commentaries attributed to Buddhagupta remains an important desideratum and promises to shed much light on Buddhist tantrism during the eighth century.[73] In our present context, however, they are of significance just because their presence in a palace catalogue suggests that the Tibetan court, though in general not very enthusiastic to support the translation of tantric literature, made a great exception on behalf of the commentarial traditions promulgated by Buddhagupta and associated with Vairocana.

The last group of materials I wish to survey in this connection has begun to receive some attention among art historians and archeologists in recent years. The objects in question are a number of reliefs in stone, as well as several important cave murals, all depicting a similar crowned and meditating Buddha, sometimes accompanied by the eight major bodhisattvas. The Buddha is adorned with the ornaments of the Body of Rapture (*sambhogakāya*); his two hands rest in his lap, and his legs are folded in the vajra posture. Iconographically, this figure closely resembles the Buddha who occupies the center of what in the Shingon school is termed the Mahākaruṇa-garbha-maṇḍala (The Womb Maṇḍala of Great Compassion), namely, Mahāvairocana.[74]

The icon in question has been found in at least three locations in far eastern Tibet recently studied by Amy Heller, where it is depicted in relief and accompanied by inscriptions dating to the early ninth century, to the reign of Trhi Songdetsen's son Trhi Desongtsen.[75] In one case, the inscription at Denmatrak, a lineage of masters is mentioned who are otherwise known from a Dunhuang Tibetan Chan text, a work that was first studied and translated by Marcelle Lalou nearly a half century ago.[76] It is possible that the inscription is a slightly later addition, in which case the image of Mahāvairocana at Denmatrak may in fact date to the reign of Trhi Songdetsen. Local folklore attributes it to a much earlier period, to the princess of Wencheng's arrival in Tibet in the early seventh century, but no evidence that has so far come to light makes this very plausible.[77]

Besides these sculpted reliefs, a mural depicting a precisely similar form of Mahāvairocana, again surrounded by the eight bodhisattvas, is also known from Anxi Yulin cave 25 in Gansu Province. This mural dates to the period of Tibetan occupation at the end of the eighth century or the beginning of the ninth.[78] That is, it may also be attributed to the reign of Trhi Songdetsen or that of his son Trhi Desongtsen. Moreover, cave 14 at Dunhuang, although most of its murals date to just after the period of Tibetan occupation, contains a portrait of Vairocana (in this case sometimes identified as Avalokiteśvara in meditation) that appears to resemble so closely the images of Vairocana just mentioned that either it must predate the remainder of the cave, and so be identified among the images under discussion, or else it was executed with deliberate reference to them.[79]

These facts point convincingly, I think, to the conclusion that the cult of Vairocana was widely promulgated with imperial support, and that it expressed a significant homology obtaining between, on the one hand, emperor and empire, and on the other,

Figure 4.2 *Left*: Vairocana, Anxi Yulin cave 25 (after *Anxi Yulinku*). *Right*: Vairocana, Dunhuang cave 14 (after *Dunhuang Mogaoku*).

Vairocana and his maṇḍala or realm. The reliefs at Denmatrak or the murals at Anxi Yulin, were, from this perspective, emblems of the Tibetan emperor's pervasive presence and stern but benevolent authority throughout his domains. It is in this respect that Christopher Beckwith has rightly referred to what he calls the "kosmokrator symbolism" of Samye, that is, its demonstration of the imperial agency of a universal legislator; and he further argues that in this respect Samye was of a piece with religious symbols of imperial power throughout the early medieval world, be it specifically the world of Carolingian Catholicism, Abbassid Islam, or Tibetan Buddhism.[80] We may go further than this, I think, to find evidence here not only of the symbolization of a particular world order, but of the active construction of that order through the imperial promotion of religious monuments and icons. John Strong writes of the legend of Aśoka's stūpa building that,

> in building eighty-four thousand stupas over eighty-four thousand minute relics, Aśoka was trying to reconstruct the Buddha's physical body on the face of his own realm, Jambudvīpa.[81]

And Strong concludes his analysis of the Indian emperor's project in these words:

> No longer are the Buddha's physical remains randomly dispersed here and there; they are now cosmologically organized and spread throughout the kingdom. And no longer does the dharmakāya represent quite so naively just the corpus of the Buddha's Teachings; it is now more cosmological and has been systematically implanted in and identified with the kingdom.[82]

Similarly, but now drawing on the ritual and symbolic resources of the tantras, Trhi Songdetsen and his successors sought not merely to present to their dominions conceptual analogies and symbols, but rather to make use of these in a thoroughgoing "maṇḍalification" of the kingdom that surely also involved the promotion throughout Tibet of temples, teachers, book copying, ritual practices, and much else besides.[83] The conversion of Tibet, therefore, was from this perspective much more than the adoption of an alien religion, as if it were a question of the application of a mere patina or veneer; it was to be the wholesale conversion, the fundamental transformation, of a human domain into a Buddha-realm, an empire governed by superhuman insight, power, and law. For this indeed was the imperial ideal, already latent in indigenous Tibetan conceptions of the Tsenpo's divinity, and Buddhism provided an exceptional vehicle for the expression of it.[84] Though the collapse of the Tibetan empire, and the reaction against Buddhism that it may have to some extent entailed, would in some respects undo this achievement, the fact that later Tibetan Buddhists, in their historical legends, came to see their land in just such terms points to more enduring success.

Converting the Conversion

Earlier, I remarked that customarily, when we think of conversion, it is individual conversion that we have in mind. Following James, we sometimes think of this as a sudden and dramatic reorientation of consciousness, marked by profound changes of sentiment and of faith.[85] By contrast, what I have attempted to illustrate here is that when it is conversion of a nation that is at issue, the gradual transformation of cosmological frameworks, of ritual, intellectual, and bureaucratic practices, and of the historical and mythic narratives through which the national identity is constituted are among the key themes to which we must attend.[86] Moreover, in the case of Tibet, it is now clear that there were in fact two conversions that can perhaps be roughly correlated, but by no means identified, with the so-called earlier and later propagations of the Buddha's teaching in that land.[87] In the first instance, there was the imperial adoption of Buddhism, which corresponded with the expansion of the old Tibetan empire, the formation within it of a literate administration, and the need to represent Tibetan imperial power both within and beyond the frontiers of Tibet. In the second, there was a conversion of the conversion narrative itself, ensuring that the Buddhist conquest of Tibet would endure long after the conquered empire had vanished. It is tempting to speculate that it was the empire's adoption of the rituals and symbols of esoteric Buddhism that in large measure forged the passage between these two movements. That is to say, one of the chief means whereby the old empire represented itself as the realm of the Buddha's knowledge and power helps to explain the myths that were later woven about it.

PART II

SOURCES OF CONTESTATION

5

From Korea to Tibet

Action at a Distance in the Early Medieval World System

Tibetan Buddhism has often been represented, by both Tibetans and non-Tibetan students of Tibetan culture, as the product of a strict and literal transmission of Indian Buddhism, an almost invariant preservation of a perennial tradition, and it is indeed true that leading Tibetan Buddhist teachers have been careful students of Indian Buddhism. Despite the powerful and enduring role of Indian Buddhist sources and precedents, however, it is clear that this view alone is far too simple. "Indian Buddhism" itself was not at all monolithic, and India imparted many and varied influences to Tibet, which the Tibetans themselves received and transformed in many and varied ways. Moreover, as is underscored in this chapter, not all of the Buddhism the Tibetans transmitted came from India.

The transmission of Buddhism in Tibet was always a dynamic process that involved the ongoing selection, in different places and times, of texts, doctrines, and practices to be emphasized or marginalized, buried or retrieved. Even where the question is one of the transmission of a single element of the tradition, it may nevertheless be subject to changing valuations and interpretations. According to the histories of the various lineages, the interpretations of different masters, the changes of opinion catalyzed by discussion and debate, the institutional culture of particular monasteries and monastic colleges, as well as the interests of patrons, what was transmitted could also be transformed. Evidently, it makes little sense to think of transmission as a process whereby identical learning was reproduced invariantly in each generation, like a series of objects stamped out on a factory conveyor.

Understanding transmission then to be not rigid replication, but a dynamic process in which preservation also involved change, a continuous re-creation of tradition through both selective reappropriation of the past and innovation, all of this book may be said to deal with one or another aspect of this process. In this chapter, I introduce some aspects of it by focusing on materials that were indeed subject to various, and sometimes odd, erasures and recoveries. This chapter also reflects, owing to its concern with East Asian Buddhism in Tibet, certain of the themes touched upon in part 1. It serves as an illustration of Tibet's participation in the international culture of Buddhism, and, at the same time, of the assimilation and transmission in Tibet of materials made available through such participation.

An Island in the Eastern Sea

Recent research has demonstrated that aspects of Korean Buddhism contributed to the formation of Tibetan Buddhism in some instances. The contributions in question all occurred during the Tang period (618–907), were largely forgotten, but exerted discernible influence on Tibetan thought long afterwards nevertheless. Thus, despite their relative obscurity, or perhaps by virtue of it, they exemplify aspects of the general problem of the transmission of religious learning within the Tibetan world. The investigation of the transmission of Buddhist teachings from Korean sources to Tibet during the Tang period and their later legacy there presents us, too, with an interesting case study in cultural influence from the perspective of world-systems theory and so in this respect may offer something more than the footnote to the history of East Asian and Tibetan Buddhism that otherwise is all, I am afraid, one may reasonably hope to find here.

It is appropriate to begin by asking what the Tibetans in fact may have known of Korea. The short answer, of course, is virtually nothing, and, as will become clear, whatever was received from Korea was presumed to be Chinese (or, in the case of the *Vajrasamādhisūtra,* originally Indian). Indeed, this was the case with traditional Tibetan conceptions of most of what we would term "East Asia"; more nuanced descriptions were in general only employed when referring to peoples, like the Mongols or Uighurs, with whom the Tibetans were also directly familiar in non-Chinese contexts and so continued to distinguish carefully even when the general framework for the relationship was a sinitic one. Owing to their station, China's foreign rulers—Mongols during the Yuan Dynasty and Manchus during the Qing—were perhaps treated ambiguously in some contexts: a common expression such as *gyanak gongma* (*rgya-nag gong-ma*), for instance, may be read as either "emperor of China" or "Chinese emperor" and so is altogether indifferent with respect to the rulers' ethnicity.[1]

Nevertheless, it is certain that some of the Tibetans who traveled to the Chinese court during the Tang, Yuan and Ming dynasties would have at least heard of the kingdoms of Korea. To the extent that they left written records of this, however, they are limited to the mere occurrence of the place-name.[2] The explicit descriptions of Korea in traditional Tibetan sources of which I am aware are very late, dating to the mid-Qing dynasty. Sumpa Khenpo Yeshe Peljor (1704–1787), writing a general account of world geography in 1777, refers in a terse phrase to lands lying in and about the eastern ocean, including Manchuria (*man ju'i sa*) and the "little island of Korea" (*gling chung ku'u li*).[3] The work in question is by no means so uninformative about all that it mentions; its discussion of Siberia, for instance, includes what I take to be the first Tibetan reference to polar bears.[4] Sumpa Khenpo, moreover, did succeed in arousing some interest in the study of geography among the Tibetan literati of his time. In the most famous treatise that he inspired, the *'Dzam-gling rgyas-bshad* (A Full Exposition of Jambudvīpa), written in 1830 by the fourth Tsenpo, Tendzin Trhinle (1789–1838), we find discussions of the departments of France, and even a mention of Louisiana.[5] Korea is briefly described in the following entry:

> Proceeding from China to traverse Manchuria, when one travels east, there is *Khro-zhang* (< Ch. *Chaoxian*), the land of those called *Kwo-le* (< Ch. *Gaoli*), or, by the

Indians, Russians, and others, *Ko-ri-ya*. The people of that land are well-proportioned and handsome. Their customs are deep, and their way of dress, script, and so forth, resemble those of China in former times, though the language is of a different type. The women of that land are said never to be seen on any occasion, except by their own parents, husbands, sons, et cetera.[6]

It is clear, then, that Tibetans in China did sometimes hear of Korea and perhaps could gain some slight impression of that land and its people. But it seems equally clear that they never associated these reports with the Buddhist materials we shall consider here. With the understanding, then, that Tibetans would always understand the instances of Korean influence on Tibetan Buddhism to have been Chinese influences, let us turn directly to the cases that have so far come to light.

The Tamer of Tigers

One of the great fascinations of modern scholarship concerning the early history of Tibetan Buddhism has been the often perplexing evidence of the transmission and legacy of Chinese Chan Buddhism in Tibet. During the 1970s, in particular, Japanese researchers devoted considerable energy to this area.[7]

It was Hironobu Obata who first pointed out the importance of a passage in the version of the *Sba-bzhed* (The Testament of Ba) that had been published by Stein.[8] I offer here a translation of the passage in question, following not Stein's text, but the apparently earlier recension that appeared in Beijing in 1980.[9] The episode occurs when, towards the end of the reign of Trhi Detsuktsen, the father of the great Buddhist monarch Trhi Songdetsen, five emissaries headed by Ba Sangshi are sent to China to receive Chinese "wisdom" (*gtsug-lag*).[10] Ba Sangshi is himself a puzzling figure, whom the *Testament of Ba* presents as a Tibetanized Chinese, though some passages seem ambiguous about his origins.[11] Having succeeded in their mission at the court, he and his companions are now en route back to Tibet:

> On the road along which the five emissaries were traveling to Tibet was a rock outcropping around which no one could move.[12] Whoever saw it died in landslides.[13] The powerful Kim Hwa-shang[14] of the city of Eg-chu, who was able to harness a tiger, and who was clairvoyant, entered into meditation for three days at the order of his preceptor.[15] In this way he shattered the rock and then built a temple in the tamed space that was left. He also then had that region put under plough. Separating [some of the fields] as temple-lands, he came back to Eg-chu, whereupon the Tibetan emissaries received a meditation transmission [from him]. When they asked for prognostications about what would then happen, asking whether the Buddha's doctrine would be established in Tibet, or if the life-threatening demons of Tibet might not act up if the Buddha's scriptures were proclaimed, and whether or not the Tsenpo and his son were at ease, the Hwa-shang investigated [these matters] clairvoyantly. Then he responded, "The Tsenpo has passed away. Because the prince has not attained his majority, the ministers who delight in evil have enacted laws whereby they have destroyed the doctrine, tearing down to the foundations a spiritual center called Drakmar Drinzang.[16] If you are to spread the doctrine, take care that the Tsenpo reaches adulthood. Later on, when as king he attains his majority, he will order discussions concerning a doc-

> trine of the non-Buddhist sophists.[17] When that occurs, ask that he hear this, and then faith will be born in the prince. Afterward, request that he listen to this, and the prince will then practice the doctrine." Saying this, he granted them three volumes as prophesied.[18]

After this, following a final prophecy concerning the future arrival in Tibet of Śāntarakṣita, he sends the envoys on their way with adequate provisions. Brokenhearted at the news concerning the destruction of Drakmar Drinzang, they return to Tibet via Wutaishan, a very great detour.[19]

Several of the elements in this account in fact are sufficiently circumstantial so that we may suspect that some knowledge of true events lies in the background. Obata noticed, among other matters, that the place name "Eg-chu" in our text is in fact a fairly good representation of the Tang period pronunciation of Yizhou, **Iäk-tśiau* in Kalgren's reconstruction,[20] that is to say, modern Chengdu, where the Silla master of the northern Chan school, Kim Hwasang (Ch. Jin Heshang), was active during the period of the An Lushan rebellion.[21] The death of the Tibetan emperor Trhi Detsuktsen indeed occurred during just this time, in 755/756,[22] so that it seems certain that our text preserves here an authentic recollection, even if not fully accurate, of actual affairs.

Before taking this any further, however, we should once more recall that the origins and dating of the *Testament of Ba* have remained vexing problems for students of Tibetan historiography. In the episode we are considering here the two available texts are closely similar, and it is difficult to imagine that any late author could have made up the details of the account out of whole cloth, even if the *Testament of Ba* is, as seems likely, a relatively late composition (post–tenth century) in the versions that have become available so far. At the very least, the account must be based on original documents going back to the eighth or ninth century.[23]

That some Tibetans during this period knew of master Kim by reputation, although, as Obata surmised, he probably had no direct Tibetan disciples,[24] is further suggested by some of the Tibetan Chan documents discovered at Dunhuang, as well as by certain later sources. In the most famous of the Tibetan Chan collections from Dunhuang, *PT* 116,[25] we find two quotations attributed to the *Chánlùn* (Chan Discourse)[26] of one Kim-hu(n)-shen-shi. J. Broughton has already proposed that this might refer to master Kim.[27] Their content is consistent with many of the Chan maxims of the period, but in itself this neither supports nor damages the case for attributing them to Kim. I offer translations of them here for the convenience of readers:

I. *From the Chan Discourse of the preceptor Kim-hun-shen-shi:*
If mind is in equilibrium, all principles are in equilibrium.
If there is awareness of the genuine, there is nothing that is not a principle of the buddha.
When the objective is understood, the mind that thirsts and desires does not arise.
Even when you are not immediately involved in the sphere of the genuine, you will not seek it.[28]
If you ask, why is that?
It is because the essential nature of the transcendental perfection of discernment,
Being primordially in equilibrium, is never objectified.[29]

II. *From the Chan Discourse of the preceptor Kim-hu:*
For the man who meditatively cultivates the path,
To be free from all conception of views,
Is called the "sole intuition."[30]
When [you are] thus endowed with that intuition,
None of the afflictions of latent dispositions arise.
That is the path of liberation.[31]

As is characteristic of the Chan teaching elsewhere attributed to master Kim, the emphasis in these passages is on an intuitive realization that is entirely independent of works.[32] Indeed, there is a sense in which some of the Chan teachings of this period resemble in part those of Luther in their insistence upon a radical internal transformation that is neither the product of nor reducible to one's virtuous deeds. And like some of the strains of early Protestantism that were condemned as antinomian,[33] the charge of antinomianism would become central to the condemnation in Tibet of the Chan teaching, above all as it was represented by the Heshang Moheyan.[34]

Only the vaguest memory of master Kim's teaching was preserved among later Tibetans. Both of the passages just cited—assuming that they are indeed Kim's—found their way, with some variations, into the chapter on sudden enlightenment in a famous early manual of the Great Perfection (*Rdzogs-chen*) system, the *Bsam-gtan mig-sgron* (The Lamp for the Eye of Dhyāna), by Nupchen Sang'gye Yeshe (c. tenth century),[35] a work that was very widely transmitted through roughly the thirteenth century, after which time it virtually disappeared. This text, however, was almost certainly the source employed by Orgyen Lingpa (b. 1323; see chapter 9) in the composition of the analogous chapter of his work, the *Blon-po bka'i thang-yig* (The Testimonial Record of the Ministers), which is presented as a rediscovered treasure (*gter-ma*) originally set down in the eighth century. It reproduces the first of our passages with some further deformations.[36] The apocryphal histories of Orgyen Lingpa, however, have remained popular works of literature down to the present day, and so, however obscured and attenuated, some recollection of master Kim's words has possibly been preserved through this source.

It is important, now, that I say something of the general neglect of master Kim in the later Tibetan Buddhist historical literature, for we learn much about the transmission of Buddhism in Tibet by seeking to understand why many things that had been introduced were not transmitted, indeed even erased from the record, later on. Only one of the later histories repeats in any detail the *Testament of Ba*'s account of the meeting with Kim in Chengdu, and this is Pawo Tsuklaktrhenga's *Mkhas-pa'i dga'-ston* (The Scholars' Banquet), a work into which, as we have seen (p. 46), much of the text of the *Testament of Ba* was to all intents and purposes downloaded.[37] The neglect of the episode on the part of other Tibetan historians, particularly Butön, is sometimes taken to be a sign of the purportedly anti-Chinese perspective of these authors. Though such assumptions were certainly tenable not long ago, in the light of our present knowledge of the development of Tibetan historiography they appear to be less sure: as we have seen, late Tibetan views of relatively early Tibetan history, and of Tibet's relations with China, themselves have had a long and complicated history. This is not to say that there were no anti-Chinese sentiments present among Tibetan historical writers; in Butön's day, reaction to the Yuan dynasty's presumptions in Tibet had certainly been given literary expression.[38] We are not justified, however, in seeking to find such sentiments underlying every narrative decision. Why poor master Kim should have borne the brunt of Tibetan antipathy to China's Mongol overlords would need to be better clarified before we can accept this to have motivated his excision from the record.[39]

Beyond the vagaries of human memory, there are several factors that may explain why Tibetan historians generally neglected the tale of the meeting of the envoys with master Kim. To begin, Tibetan religious historiography focused primarily upon lineage history, and there was no enduring Tibetan Chan lineage stemming from Kim's teaching. Though, as we shall soon see, elements of Chan teaching did indeed survive in some Tibetan Buddhist circles, the Chan tradition generally was subject to the criticism of those who favored bona fide Indian teachings. The attenuated survivals of Chan were therefore for the most part disguised. To all intents and purposes, therefore, master Kim had no place in any existing Tibetan lineage and hence no place in any narration of lineage history. The importance of this principle for the reconstruction of the history of the conversion narrative is crucial, for it is clear that the roles played by such figures as Padmasambhava and Vimalamitra, shadowy at best in the earlier versions, expand as they themselves assume greater importance for later Tibetan esoteric traditions.[40]

It is likely, too, that the *Testament of Ba*, in which the meeting with master Kim is found, was composed as a vindication and eulogy of the members of the Ba clan who are often regarded its authors. While it was universally acknowledged that these figures did play a crucial role in the conversion of Tibet, still, as L. Petech has more recently argued, the early second millenium saw the gradual eclipsing of the old ministerial clans of Central Tibet, including the Ba, and the attendant rise of powerful households that were opposed to them.[41] The tale of master Kim probably had few compelling resonances for those who were heirs to families that identified themselves in no way with traditions stemming from eighth-century China, but instead with the circle of Padmasambhava and his disciples, or with the new transmissions of the eleventh century. Under such circumstances, our tale held only antiquarian interest, which accounts for its revival in the work of an antiquarian author like Pawo Tsuklaktrhenga, while it continued to be neglected by historians who were more concerned to retell the history of the old Tibetan dynasty as a myth that reflected their own interests and those of their contemporaries.

Ambitious eleventh-century Tibetan Buddhists were not so much actively opposed to China as they were drawn to India, and this attraction had much to do during the period in question with issues of legitimation and power in Tibet,[42] but such factors as the relative proximity of India and Nepal to West and Central Tibet also must not be neglected; these regions of Tibet during the eleventh century enjoyed a rich cultural and material trade with both Kashmir and the Kathmandu Valley, and thence to other parts of India, that had no parallel in Tibetan relations with the Chinese Song dynasty, which were in any case largely mediated by the Western Xia kingdom.[43] In such times as these, an old story in difficult and perhaps already archaic language about the master of an unknown meditation lineage from China would have been, if nothing else, simply out of fashion.

For all of this, however, master Kim possibly did leave some enduring traces in later popular Tibetan traditions. We have seen already that at least one quotation that is perhaps to be attributed to him remained in circulation. One final item piques our curiosity before we move on: in one of his most well known manifestations, Padmasambhava is depicted as a wrathful suppressor of demons, riding a tiger. Though the evidence is too slender to permit an answer, this raises a question nevertheless: may we discern here a last faint reflection of the ancient tale of a Korean Chan master in Sichuan?[44]

Chan Traces in Later Traditions

Though Tibetan Chan certainly faded away, it would not be quite accurate to say that it ever actually died. Again, recent research makes it clear that the entire story is far more complicated than we had previously imagined it to be, and our sources, though often tantalizing, are seldom so illuminating as we would like.[45] I mention here just a few conclusions that will be required as background, but I will refrain from elaborating the full basis for these conclusions here.

Whether or not the last decades of the eighth century really saw the expulsion of the Heshang Moheyan from Central Tibet and the banning of certain Chan writings there, as the *Testament of Ba* and other sources maintain, it is now clear that the early ninth century witnessed the rise of a syncretic Tibetan Chan lineage based in northeastern Tibet (Amdo) and also active in and around Dunhuang. This lineage seems to have operated very widely in the eastern portions of the Tibetan empire, almost certainly under the patronage of Trhi Songdetsen's son and grand-successor, Trhi Desongtsen, or his representatives.[46] While this line of Chan teaching appears to have preserved a radical teaching of sudden enlightenment, it also seems to have contextualized it within a framework of normative Buddhist cosmology, emphasizing the doctrine of karma, and probably also to have transmitted it in association with some tantric ritual and contemplative disciplines.[47] Assuming this to have been the case, the masters of this tradition may have successfully distanced themselves from some of the tendencies the monarchy is said to have found objectionable in the teaching of Moheyan, specifically, its radically antinomian character.[48] Furthermore, there is some reason to believe that elements of the Chan teaching, perhaps stemming from this very lineage (though positive evidence for this is lacking), remained current in far eastern Tibet at least through the beginning of the eleventh century.[49]

The precise fate of this and other remnants of early Tibetan Chan remains very much a mystery. Not long ago it was widely assumed that it was primarily within the Great Perfection (*rdzogs-chen*) systems of the Nyingmapa and Bön traditions that clear evidence of the continuity of Chan in Tibet was to be found, but it now appears that this is an oversimplification. On the one hand, the Great Perfection is known to involve much more than whatever of its aspects can plausibly be traced back to Chan influence: "Great Perfection" refers to a highly ramified family of systems that are, doctrinally and historically, far too complicated to reduce to a single source or impetus.[50] And on the other hand, it is now clear that the Great Perfection was not alone among the Tibetan meditational traditions in absorbing surviving elements of the Chan teaching; from an early date the Kagyüpa proponents of the Mahāmudrā and, as I shall indicate later, others as well, adopted certain materials from Chan sources.[51] Tracing out the precise legacy of Chan in Tibet is thus an intricate and difficult matter. One of the tracking devices that can be usefully employed here, rather like fluorescent dust on banknotes, interestingly turns out to be the *Vajrasamādhisūtra* (The Sūtra of Adamantine Concentration).[52]

The Korean composition of the *Vajrasamādhisūtra* has been reasonably established by Robert Buswell in his fine book devoted to that scripture.[53] Of course, in the circles in which it was transmitted and enjoyed much popularity during the Tang period, it was not at all thought to be of Korean authorship and was accepted as an authentic Indian sūtra.[54] No doubt its translation from Chinese into Tibetan reflected both its general popularity and, perhaps, too, its importance to some of the Chan lineages that had become influential among at least some Tibetan Buddhists.[55] Its apocryphal character no less than its content may have facilitated its early translation into Tibetan, for there is evidence to suggest that popular, apocryphal sūtras translated from the Chinese were among the first Buddhist texts to become available in Tibet.[56]

Though the version of the *Vajrasamādhi* preserved in the Tibetan canons is without the customary translator's colophon, its inclusion in the early-ninth-century Denkar palace catalogue of Buddhist scriptures confirms that it had been translated from the Chinese sometime earlier.[57] Its citation in Dunhuang Tibetan Chan collections suggests that it was in circulation there during the early ninth century at the latest.[58] Thus, it comes as no surprise to see the *Vajrasamādhi* cropping up in a catechistic section of *PT* 116, the same manuscript that preserves citations from the Chan Discourses we have already examined, for example:

> How is it evident that the Mahāyāna is subsumed in nonconceptualization?
> The *Vajrasamādhisūtra* says:
> Without thought or reflection, arising and sinking will not come about, and one becomes unwavering in just what genuinely is. That is the sūtra of the Mahāyāna.[59]

Despite the preservation of the *Vajrasamādhisūtra* in the later Kanjur collections, there is no evidence that there was ever any tradition of study associated with it in Tibet, most certainly not after the disappearance of the Tibetan Chan lineages towards the end of the first millenium. Nevertheless, because passages from the *Vajrasamādhi,* like some of the sayings of master Kim and other Chan teachers, had been incorporated in the Tibetan Chan anthologies, they later came to be incorporated in the handbooks of certain Tibetan traditions of meditation. In this context, the *Vajrasamādhisūtra* had one very useful feature that the sayings of Kim and the Chinese Chan masters did not: it was believed to be an authentic sūtra spoken by the Buddha himself. For this reason, citations from it could continue to be employed long after Chan itself came to be considered anathematic, even where political correctness or an instinct for self-preservation demanded that many of the other quotations from the old Chan manuals be dropped.

The *Lamp for the Eye of Dhyāna*, as we have seen, clearly employed Chan collections like *PT* 116, and so it comes as little surprise that we find some citations from the sūtra there as well. For instance, we read: "It says in the *Vajrasamādhisūtra:* 'If mind is unwavering in emptiness, then the six transcending perfections are subsumed therein.'"[60]

As D. Jackson has recently observed, moreover, such passages begin turning up in the writings of Milarepa's noted disciple Gampopa (1079–1153) and the latter's Kagyüpa followers as well, often in connection with a much contested doctrine sometimes called the "mahāmudrā of the sūtra tradition" (*mdo-lugs phyag-chen*).[61] This teaching was said to bring about direct insight into the ultimate nature of mind, owing to the impact of an "introduction" (*ngo-sprod;* see chapter 10) conferred by one's teacher, without the disciple's having first traversed the entire sequence of tantric initiation and yogic practice. Thus, in the most widely studied of Gampopa's writings, the *Thar-pa rin-po-che'i rgyan* (The Jewel Ornament of Liberation), the chapter concerning contemplative insight, or discernment (*prajñā, shes-rab*), argues for the identity of the culminating teachings of the sūtras and tantras on this point. It is there that we find just the same passage from the *Vajrasamādhisūtra* once more.[62]

Jackson's argument, with which I generally concur, is that it is very unlikely that Gampopa and his cohorts were deriving such quotations directly from the sūtras cited; rather, they probably were culling them from preexisting meditation manuals, texts like *PT* 116 or the *Lamp for the Eye of Dhyāna*. They were careful only to employ passages attributed to sūtras in this manner, however, for they certainly wished to avoid suggesting that what they were teaching was a rehashing of the Chinese Chan doctrine, which after all had been condemned in the Kadampa tradition of the eleventh-century teacher Potowa (1027 or 1031–1105), a tradition with which Gampopa was himself closely affiliated.[63] This ploy, however, was not fully successful. Sakya Paṇḍita (1182–1251), for one, recognized very clearly that the Kagyüpa teaching drew some of its inspiration from such sources, and so he castigated its "sūtra tradition of the mahāmudrā" as what he termed, with apparent derision, "Chinese Great Perfection" (*Rgya-nag rdzogs-chen*).[64]

The spread of passages from the *Vajrasamādhisūtra,* however, demonstrates that even this is too simple. In a Kadampa meditation manual of the twelfth century, the *Man-ngag rin-chen spungs-pa* (The Jewel Heap of Esoteric Instruction), we have a chapter on sudden enlightenment that includes citations from many sūtras, among which one reads:

> In the *Vajrasamādhisūtra* it says:
>
> If there be no ignorance in the original matrix of mind, then what might one say of the conditioning factors emerging from ignorance, and so on down to birth and death?[65]

There is good reason to believe that the author, one Cegomdzongpa Sherap Dorje, despite his affiliation with the Kadampa line of Potowa, nevertheless was sympathetic to the meditational traditions of the Nyingmapa and Kagyüpa schools.[66] Thus he may have been moved to incorporate the teaching of the nontantric approach to sudden enlightenment, insofar as he could derive it from these traditions, within the otherwise normative Kadampa framework of the gradual path. In this, he was perhaps following Gampopa's lead.[67] Having succeeded in wedging the swift foot of immediacy into the slow-swinging gate of Kadampa gradualism, however, he insured that some element of the Chan teaching would be preserved for posterity by some of its most determined opponents. For in later times the successors to the Kadampa were, above all, the Gelukpa followers of Tsongkhapa (1357–1419), and it is in their tradition alone that Cegomdzongpa's work has continued to be transmitted, even down to the present day.[68] The learned geshe (*dge-bshes*, a Gelukpa scholar who has completed his examinations in doctrine and philosophy) with whom I discussed it admitted that he found the sudden-enlightenment chapter to be in some respects a puzzling inclusion, but he maintained that the Gelukpa treasure the book as a whole for its particularly eloquent synthesis of the Mahāyāna path nonetheless.[69]

The legacy of Chan in Tibet, then, can by no means be regarded, as sometimes it has been, as a matter of a single impetus uniquely imparted to one well-defined tradition. The *Vajrasamādhi* is in no way our only guide to its broad but subtle diffusion. Nevertheless, it is often the case that citations such as those we have just been considering provide a valuable clue—perhaps not quite a smoking pistol—allowing us to trace at least some of its furtive movements.[70]

The Vicissitudes of the Great Chinese Commentary

One final example of Korean sources in the background of the development of Tibetan Buddhism leads us at last away from the Chan traditions but will keep us close to the Gelukpas in Tibet. Wŏnchŭk's (613–696) great commentary on the *Saṃdhinirmocanasūtra* (The Sūtra Which Sets Free the [Buddha's] Intention) is now well known among scholars of East Asian Buddhism to have been rendered in Tibetan by Gö Chödrup, or, as he was known in Chinese, Facheng, a renowned translator based in Dunhuang and active there during the early ninth century.[71] It has been preserved in this translation, no doubt with some changes due to editorial practice, in the printed Tanjur editions of recent times,[72] though the integral text in Chinese was lost long ago.[73] The role that it has played in Tibetan thought is intriguing and merits consideration in relation to the dynamics of Tibetan doctrinal history. In this respect, its position has also been to some degree misunderstood.

The Tibetan canons, to begin, are massive collections that include vast quantities of material that, excepting for the occasional interventions of editors, printers, and copyists, few ever look at, much less read.[74] Indeed, reading the canon—understanding this phrase by analogy to contemporary anglophone conceptions of "reading Scripture"[75]—was generally not a very important cultural practice in Tibet; most literate people read primarily the texts that they had been personally taught to read, including manuals and liturgies for the rituals they performed and meditations they practiced, as well as letters, horoscopes, and sometimes, too, histories, biographies, and storybooks that were thought to be diverting or edifying. Even the minority of monks who pursued programs of doctrinal and philosophical study focused for the most part on a very small number of fundamental texts and the commentaries upon them considered authoritative in the particular colleges in which they were enrolled.[76] Accomplished scholars certainly cultivated greater breadth and often sought to familiarize themselves with the textbooks and commentaries current in various centers of learning, but they seldom devoted much thought to works that were not in vogue in any of the contemporary schools—only the rarest of masters deliberately cultivated the study of rarely studied books. The idea of combing the Tanjur for a big commentary that had no active tradition of transmission might occur to one of our Ph.D. students, swayed by professorial encouragement while shopping for a dissertation topic, but in general it would have seemed a pretty odd thing to do in Tibet.[77]

It is with this in mind that the history in Tibet of Wŏnch'ŭk's great commentary becomes something of a mystery, for, though it was not actually transmitted in any living line of teaching that is known to us, there was a flurry of interest in it during the fourteenth and early fifteenth centuries that has had some legacy in the later scholasticism of the Gelukpa school, in recent centuries the dominant Tibetan Buddhist tradition. The reasons for the occasional references to it found within Gelukpa scholastic textbooks are entirely clear and very well known: Tsongkhapa (1357–1419) cites it in two of his most widely studied treatises, the *Drang-nges legs-bshad snying-po* (The Provisional and the Definitive: The Essence of Eloquence)[78] and the *Yid dang kun-gzhi'i dka'-'grel* (The Commentary on Difficulties in Relation to the Intellect and the Ground-of-All).[79] Later Gelukpa citations of Wŏnch'ŭk, so far as I have been able to ascertain, can all be traced back to the inspiration of these works.[80] The puzzle that must be addressed, therefore, is what was the basis for Tsongkhapa's interest?

This question has been raised previously. R. A. F. Thurman, in his masterful translation of the *Essence of Eloquence*, speculated that Tsongkhapa cited Wŏnch'ŭk in an effort to deliver Chinese Buddhism from the "stigma" of association with the condemned teaching of Heshang Moheyan. But as J. Powers rightly argues in an article devoted to the Great Commentary in Tibet, this was not at all probable.[81] In fact, Powers never clearly states why not, but, as we have seen, the "stigma" was by no means so complete or so uniform as has sometimes been supposed, and so it is not really plausible that Tsongkhapa would have considered this a problem he needed especially to address. Certainly he and his contemporary scholiasts knew well that Chinese Buddhism was not monolithic, and only philosophical simpletons would have identified all of Chinese Buddhism with the teaching of Moheyan.[82] In the two works we are considering, Tsongkhapa was by no means writing for simpletons.

The alternative explanation offered by Powers, however, is also unconvincing. Tsongkhapa was aware, he reasons, that the "Great Chinese Commentary" was the largest commentary on the *Saṃdhinirmocana* preserved in Tibetan, and because he was interested in this sūtra in connection with his study of various problems of doctrinal interpretation, being a "meticulous scholar" he read Wŏnch'ŭk and reported upon his researches in his writings.[83] Now, there can be no doubt that Tsongkhapa was indeed a most meticulous scholar and merits all praise in this regard. Nevertheless, we must take care not to project back upon him a conception of the traditional Tibetan scholar that closely mirrors his contemporary Western counterpart; we must endeavor to avoid, that is, seeing in our Tibetan forebears merely projections of ourselves. Though it is indeed the case that Tibetan scholars did sometimes read books that others neglected, so that we do sometimes find citations that cannot be otherwise explained, the student of Tibetan intellectual history must always start with the assumption that even the greatest of Tibetan monastic scholars were interested above all in the interpretation of received tradition. Before leaping to other conclusions in order to explain the apparently odd fact of Tsongkhapa's recourse to Wŏnch'ŭk, it is therefore first necessary to consider whether it may have played a role in the background of Tsongkhapa's own formation. The question that we must pose about Tsongkhapa in this instance is this: had Wŏnch'ŭk's work come to be actively studied in fourteenth-century Tibet, and, if so, how did this occur?

With this question in mind, when we turn to investigate some of the traditions of fourteenth-century Sakyapa and Kadampa scholasticism with which we know Tsongkhapa to have been familiar, we soon discover that several of the same passages from Wŏnch'ŭk cited by Tsongkhapa had already been placed in circulation by his teachers and predecessors. Tsongkhapa was neither seeking to redeem wrongly disparaged traditions of Chinese Buddhism, nor was he a research scholar engaging in entirely new philological investigations. He was, rather, a Tibetan scholastic interpreter doing what Tibetan scholastic interpreters do best, that is, enlarging and elaborating the commentarial traditions in which he himself had been trained.[84] It is the basis for his predecessors' interest in Wŏnch'ŭk, then, that we must seek to establish.

In the *Essence of Eloquence*, Tsongkhapa was concerned in part with the problem of determining which among the "three turns of the wheel"—the three great phases in the Buddha's disclosure of his teaching—were to be assessed as, respectively, of provisional or definitive meaning.[85] As will be seen in the following chapter (in the section concerning Dölpopa), this had emerged as a focal point of debate during the preceding century owing to sustained disagreements between those who regarded the culminating philosophical teaching of Buddhism to be found in Candrakīrti's interpretations of the Madhyamaka philosophy of Nāgārjuna, and those who, by contrast, sought to discover the highest teaching of the Buddha in the doctrine of Buddha-nature, whose philosophical elaboration was to be found above all in aspects of the tradition stemming from the divine bodhisattva Maitreya and his human disciple Asaṅga.[86] Tibetan proponents of the latter tradition had often turned to a famous passage in the *Saṃdhinirmocana* (given below, p. 113) concerning the three turns in support of their approach to interpretation. An important question this raised, of course, was just how the *Saṃdhinirmocana* itself was to be understood, and so this was one of the areas in which Tsongkhapa turned to the authority of Wŏnch'ŭk. It was not, however, an original move on his part: Tsongkhapa's mentor in the Candrakīrti tradition, the noted Sakyapa master, Remdawa Zhönu Lodrö (1349–1412), had referred similarly to the Korean master in just the same context. In fact at the very beginning of his introduction to his excellent and influential commentary on Candrakīrti's *Madhymakāvatāra* (The Introduction to the Madhyamaka), after briefly introducing the three turns, he remarks:

> The Chinese preceptor [Wŏnch'ŭk] has said that this is explained in the commentary by sublime Nāgārjuna on the skill-in-means chapter of the Transcendent Perfection of Discernment.[87]

And he goes on to cite here Paramārtha (Ch. Zhendi, Tib. Yang-dag-bden)—the Indian master of Yogācāra Buddhism who taught in Canton in the sixth century—reference to whom was also no doubt derived from Wŏnch'ŭk's work.[88] Later he quotes Wŏnch'ŭk once again at length:

> Again, in the commentary on the *Saṃdhinirmocana*, the Chinese preceptor says: "It emerges from the expositions of the Tripiṭaka, concerning those three wheels of doctrine, that about one hundred years after the Buddha's nirvāṇa, the masters of the twenty orders composed the commentaries on the first wheel of doctrine, each according to his own knowledge. Then, when two hundred years had passed after the Buddha's nirvāṇa, the bodhisattva Nāgārjuna composed treatises based on the sūtras of the Prajñāpāramitā, to whit, the commentary on the Prajñāpāramitā, the Madhyamaka, etc. There, the way of the absence of characteristics is well taught, having rejected imputed essences. Then, Āryadeva and others rightly accepted that textual tradition, so that it was transmitted and promulgated from one to the next. When nine hundred years had passed after the Buddha's nirvāṇa, the bodhisattva Maitreya composed

treatises, such as the *Yogācārabhūmi* (The Levels of the Practice of Yoga), the *Madhyāntavibhāga* (The Discrimination of the Middle and Extremes), etc., based upon the *Saṃdhinirmocanasūtra* and others. Master Asaṅga and Vasubandhu rightly accepted that textual tradition and promulgated it. At that time, because the doctrine of the Buddha is of a single savor, there were no conflicts between those proponents of emptiness and of existence."[89]

Clearly, then, Remdawa was very much interested in Wŏnch'ŭk's work. It remains obscure, though, how he came to be so interested. On considering another of the main references to Wŏnch'ŭk in Tsongkhapa's writings, we come across an additional clue, for in the *Commentary on Difficulties* Tsongkhapa relates a minor disagreement between himself and an earlier Kadampa scholar named Comden Rikpei Reldri (active during the late thirteenth and early fourteenth centuries).[90] This occurs in connection with some technical problems in the Yogācāra philosophy of mind, namely, the question of whether, in addition to the eight types of consciousness discussed in the major Indian Yogācāra writings, one had also to assume, as Paramārtha had done, a ninth consciousness, a "taintless consciousness" (Skt. *amala(vi)jñāna*) conceived as a purified correlate of the consciousness of the ground-of-all (Skt. *ālayavijñāna*, Tib. *kun-gzhi'i rnam-par-shes-pa*).[91] The topics at issue are, as before, strongly connected to important points of dispute in Tibet throughout the fourteenth century.[92] Rikpei Reldri had been, in fact, one of the most influential Kadampa scholiasts of the period, and, despite the later neglect of his works, in Tsongkhapa's day they appear to have been still widely studied.

Unfortunately, the writings of Rikpei Reldri that have been published so far do not include his reflections on the ground-of-all consciousness and associated subject matter, so that we do not yet have access to whatever illumination his works provide regarding the particular issues at stake here.[93] The remainder of the argument in this section, therefore, is to some extent speculative and may be confirmed or refuted only by the appearance of new sources.

Among the important disciples and associates of Rikpei Reldri was a scholar named Chim Jamyang, who became the court chaplain of the Yuan emperor Buyantu (reigned 1311–1320).[94] The major work of Chim Jamyang that is now available is his large commentary on the *Abhidharmakośa* (The Treasury of the Meta-Doctrine), the writing of which he began in Sakya but completed during his sojourn in China.[95] He refers clearly here to Paramārtha's nine-consciousness theory,[96] which, as we have seen, Tsongkhapa knew through Wŏnch'ŭk. It is plausible that Chim Jamyang, like many other Tibetan prelates who spent long periods in the Chinese capital during the Yuan dynasty, and again like those who dwelt in Beijing four centuries later under the Qing, had occasion to take more than a casual interest in Chinese Buddhist traditions and so may have read with some care relevant texts preserved in Tibetan.[97] The systematic comparison of the Chinese and Tibetan Buddhist canons had indeed been sponsored by the Yuan court,[98] so that in this setting it would have made good sense to delve into the Great Commentary.[99] Assuming something like this to have been the case, Chim Jamyang may well have been the source of his master Rikpei Reldri's knowledge of Wŏnch'ŭk, and thence of Remdawa's. That these scholars drew upon Wŏnch'ŭk in connection with the theories of the triple turn of the wheel, the nine consciousnesses, and the taintless consciousness, reflects the fact that his work proved to be of interest in the first instance when it addressed topics that were already intensively contested in Tibet in any case. Tsongkhapa's interest in the Korean commentator, therefore, far from being a novelty, reflects his intense participation in the dominant scholastic discourse of his time.[100]

Korea, Tibet, and the Early Medieval World System

What conclusions are to be drawn from these and other, similar cases? In terms of their particulars, nothing I have discussed here is of convincingly deep importance for Korean or Tibetan history as such. Korean Buddhism did make some impact in far-off Tibet, perhaps not a very great impact, but a discernible one nevertheless. And something has been revealed to us of the dynamics of doctrinal transmission in Tibet, of the pattern of selective forgettings, reappropriations, and revaluations of the past that this involved, and of the manner in which these reflect and contribute to larger contests. Besides these discoveries, however, I am inclined to find some further interest here, not so much in virtue of what is revealed about Korea or Tibet in particular, but rather because I believe that these data present us with some excellent examples to ponder in relation to the dynamics of cultural transmission in early medieval Eurasia.

It has by now been much argued that the emphasis in recent times on the writing of national history has obscured the study of international history and has rendered difficult our prospects for understanding the world, in any particular period, as constituting a total system.[101] So-called area studies—though not so constrained as national history—by dividing the world into more or less autonomously conceived blocks nevertheless represent in some respects a still narrow perspective. After all, there have been all sorts of exchanges among different areas throughout human history. An obvious objection to any proposed study of the "world system" as a corrective, however, is just that the system, so understood, is vastly too complex to permit precise and careful investigation, except by dissecting it into smaller morsels, chiefly regions and states. "World-systems theory," it is urged, may be laudable in its intent, but in practice it may too easily degenerate into platitudes and overgeneralizations. In just a few special areas—the study of the Mongol empire in the thirteenth century or the development of the great maritime empires after the fifteenth century might be among the better examples—something like a world-systems perspective is indeed thrust upon us; but the very peculiarity of these cases precludes their invocation as general models for historical study.

It seems to me that there are good intuitions on both sides of the fence here. There can be no denying the necessity of special studies, focusing on precise and well-defined questions, that promise to clarify through their very particularity the larger problems that the investigation of world systems seeks to illuminate. The careful study of cultural transmission in early medieval Eurasia is a fertile ground for such investigations, and relatively simple instances, such as those we have been considering here, offer not a bad point of departure for them. From a certain perspective at least, the mere fact that any relatively sophisticated learning whatsoever could have been transmitted from Korea to Tibet during the eighth century is pretty remarkable.[102] What were some of the relevant, enabling conditions?

Five factors appear at once to merit special consideration: the complex of what we would now think of in terms of ethnicity and nationality; language; religion; polity; and the system of trade and technology. The first I mention primarily to underscore its relative unimportance in the period we are considering. No doubt the presence in a given, continuous geographical area, of people speaking a common tongue, sharing bonds of real or mythical ancestry, and with many common beliefs, would have facilitated the rapid diffusion of new knowledge among the population concerned. Protonationalist sentiment must not be discounted as a possible element in medieval cultural transmission, but, unless we have good reason to posit this as an especially important factor in some particular case, we must take care not to project modern nationalistic conceptions too readily onto the past.[103] In the third of our present examples, for instance, we do not image that the Wŏnch'ŭk thought of his work as particularly "Korean"; certainly his Tibetan readers did not, and by the same token, they did not regard its identification as "Chinese" as precluding its potential relevance to things "Tibetan." Nevertheless, as R. Buswell has argued, the reception of Wŏnch'ŭk's work in China was perhaps impeded by the fact that he was an outsider in Chinese eyes.[104] It seems plausible to hold that medieval protonationalisms served more decisively as principles of exclusion than of inclusion and so were disclosed primarily where boundaries and prerogatives were threatened.[105]

Language was surely a more significant factor in promoting cultural exchange throughout the early medieval period than was nationality. And what was most important for the transmission of knowledge, of course, was not national language, but transnational language. Sanskrit and literary Chinese are perhaps the two most impressive, and the best known, of the transnational languages of Asia during the age in question,[106] but we must recall here that Tibetan had by the late eighth century carved out a very wide niche for itself in Inner Asia. In Dunhuang, for instance, we find that the local Chinese either were regularly employing Tibetan, or in some cases were using the Tibetan script to write Chinese.[107] The domains embraced by such transnational languages were, of course, realms in which the potential for cultural transmission was very great, and this was heightened to a marked degree by the creation of translation "filters," rendering possible transmission between differing linguistic domains. The Tibetans and the Koreans did not generally employ the same transnational language, but the center for the translation of Buddhist Chinese managed by Gö Chödrup and his collaborators at Dunhuang, to mention the concrete instance we know best,[108] gave the Tibetans a receptor for signals emanating from the entire sinitic field, including Korean Buddhist circles.

The possibility of communication, however, does not by itself motivate communication. The three additional factors I have mentioned—religion, polity, and commerce—may serve both to facilitate and to motivate the transmission and spread of cultural knowledge. This much is, I think, clear, and in the present context I may be spared, I trust, the obligation to discuss these at length. The relationships between the Tibetan and Tang states, and between the latter and the Korean kingdoms, the traffic along the northern and southern Silk Roads, the pervasive spread of Buddhism—relatively nuanced accounts of these and much more would be required to fill out our tale. Let us just note, then, that religion, polity, and trade may often be thought to represent virtually autonomous systems themselves, which correspond at best imperfectly and perhaps not at all to national and linguistic bounds. Our conception, therefore, is one of five overlapping subsystems that may be dynamically interactive, and that together form a dense medium through which goods, techniques, and symbols can be transmitted over very great spaces throughout equally great periods of time, despite whatever technological limitations may be thought to have hampered the flow of knowledge during the period concerned.

Seen from such a perspective, the cases considered here stand as tokens—markers of the specific patterns and processes informing an overarching system next to which they in themselves appear trifling. It would be incorrect to allow this perspective to undermine the value of investigating such matters, however. If we think of our subject now as a science of cultural ecosystems, it should be at once clear that these cannot be studied at all, apart from the particular species that both constitute and thrive within a given system taken as a whole.

Turning now to the history of Tibetan Buddhism in particular, we must understand that the three examples taken up in this chapter would have to be multiplied a thousandfold to do justice to the full range of texts and teaching traditions that variously became interwoven or opposed to one another in the fabric of Tibetan thought, from about the eighth through the thirteenth centuries. The few connections between Tibet and Korea are good to think, so to speak, just because they are so much simpler than those between, say, Bengal, Nepal, Kashmir, or China, and Tibet overall. The full complexity of such connections, moreover, must be considered in relation to the full panoply of Tibetan individuals, lineages, and institutions that identified themselves with, rejected, or ignored specific materials that became available through the varied processes of cultural transmission. Once more, our examples from Korea illustrate this in a usefully austere manner. In the chapter that follows, however, it will soon be apparent that in examining just a few aspects of Tibetan Buddhist thought, austerity must soon give way to reflection upon the intricate textures and the numberless tensions that characterize the field overall.

6

What Is "Tibetan Scholasticism"?

Three Ways of Thought

During the eleventh century, Tibetan Buddhism entered a period of renewed development and change. The collapse of the old Tibetan royal dynasty had taken place, according to traditional accounts, following the assassination of the anti-Buddhist monarch Lang Darma, probably in 842,[1] and the ensuing power vacuum persisted for a full four hundred years. Local lords vied for ascendency, and religious authority was no less contested than temporal power. As cultural life was gradually restored, Tibetan seekers and adventurers began to look outside Tibet for authoritative sources of Buddhist teaching, with the result that throughout the eleventh century we find Tibetan translators and pilgrims journeying to India and Nepal in search of gurus, Scriptures, and esoteric lore. These developments were particularly prominent in Western Tibet, where the great translator Rinchen Zangpo (958–1055) was patronized by the monarchs of the Guge kingdom. There, too, the saintly Indian scholar and adept Atiśa (982–1054) was invited to teach, beginning in 1042. The careers of these two notable Buddhist monks mark the start of what Tibetan historians call the "later spread of the teaching" (*bstan-pa phyi-dar*), or the age of the "new translations" (*gsar-'gyur*).

The renewed Buddhist activity of the period, however, was not without its tensions. We have already suggested that competing lines of transmission accounted for this in part. Yet there were many factors operating besides mere difference of religious lineage: regional and clan affiliations, relations with preexisting Tibetan Buddhist traditions versus involvement in the new infusion of Indian teaching, orientations favoring monastic scholarship versus those emphasizing tantric yoga, competition for patronage—these were among the elements informing the developing scene. Indeed, difference of religious lineage can often be interpreted in terms of other, more fundamental oppositions.[2]

The areas of contention in eleventh- and twelfth-century Tibetan Buddhism, however, also fueled a creative dialogue that was characterized in some instances by imaginative and visionary syntheses and restatements of Buddhist teaching, and in others by the effort to clarify that teaching through reasoned analysis, interpretation, and debate. Though these tendencies may be associated in many instances with the divisions between contemplative and scholarly orientations, or between tantric and nontantric traditions, it is important to recognize that neither of these oppositions was absolute, and that in the lives and careers of individual masters differing facets are frequently intermingled. By the thirteenth century, the intellectual and spiritual ferment of the age had issued in a period of unusual creativity whose varied explorations of Buddhist thought will be illustrated through the three sketches presented in this chapter.

It has become customary to characterize the intellectual life of the Tibetan monastic colleges as a type of scholasticism. Though I regard this convention to be generally an appropriate one, I think that our notion of just what counts as Tibetan scholasticism needs to be in some respects problematized, and to do this will be one of my concerns here. We should begin, however, by first clarifying the application of the Western notion of scholasticism to things Tibetan.[3]

Scholasticism, of course, primarily characterizes a dominant form of intellectual practice in the Latin Catholic universities of the thirteenth through sixteenth centuries. Among the features that have been regarded as defining scholasticism, those frequently emphasized have included the effort to elaborate Catholic theology according to purely rational principles, the harmonization of theology with Aristotelian philosophy that this effort involved, the emphasis in this context upon Aristotle's logical writings, or *Organon*, and the primacy of scholia, commentarial glosses on texts, as the written medium for the elaboration and expression of ideas. The word "scholasticism," in fact, derives from "scholium."

It is not difficult to find here strong analogies with important aspects of intellectual practice in the Tibetan monastic colleges that developed from the late eleventh century onwards, where there was a marked concern to emphasize a highly rational approach to Buddhist doctrine, over and against one dominated exclusively by faith.[4] This required the careful study of Indian Buddhist philosophical writings, with the epistemological and logical works of Dharmakīrti (c. 600) supplying the major methodological organ.[5] Finally, as in the Latin West, it was the commentary, in several specific forms, that emerged as the preeminent literary form of philosophical and doctrinal writing. All of this, it seems, makes it entirely reasonable to extend the use of the word "scholasticism" to the non-Christian, non-Aristotelian context of Buddhist Tibet.

Beyond these generalities, when we focus our attention upon some characteristically Aristotelian assumptions, it often appears that they have marked parallels in the thought of Dharmakīrti and his Tibetan successors. Aristotle, for instance, tells us that "[t]he first class of simple propositions is the simple affirmation, the next, the simple denial . . ." and that "it is plain that every affirmation has an opposite denial, and similarly every denial an opposite affirmation."[6] The essential role of the binary opposition of affirmation and negation in the formation of human thought and language has been almost universally presupposed in Western philosophical traditions, from those of the Lyceum down to the logical positivist and structuralist movements of recent times. In the schools of Indian and Tibetan Buddhist thought, too, a similar opposition is often regarded as fundamental, as is suggested in a somewhat whimsical manner in this episode reported in the biography of the famed nineteenth-century Tibetan Nyingmapa thinker, Mipham Gyamtsho (1846–1912):

> When Mipham Rinpoche was looking over the *Exposition of Valid Cognition* [the *Pramāṇavārttika* of Dharmakīrti] he had a dream in which one who was Sakya Paṇḍita in essence appeared to him in the guise of a learned and accomplished master from India, the tip of his nose slightly crooked, and said, "What is there that you do not understand in the *Exposition of Valid Cognition*? It has two parts, refutation and proof." Then, he divided a volume of the *Exposition of Valid Cognition* into two parts and handed it to Mipham, saying, "Combine these two together!" No sooner had he combined them than they turned into a sword, and all things that may be known appeared before him. Swinging that sword once, it appeared to Mipham that he cut through them all in an instant, without impediment. Consequently, he said, there was not a single word in the *Exposition of Valid Cognition* which he did not understand.[7]

The opposition of proof and refutation at the level of demonstrative reasoning structurally parallels that of affirmation and denial at the level of the proposition. Aristotle, who regards affirmation to have priority over negation similarly accords primacy to affirmative demonstration,[8] and in this respect his view differs somewhat from that represented in Mipham's dream, where the two-edged sword is perfectly balanced. Whether this balance was maintained in practice, however, is perhaps another question.

It is significant, too, that it was Sakya Paṇḍita who appeared in Mipham's dream. In the development of the Tibetan scholastic traditions, the contributions of Sakya Paṇḍita Künga Gyeltshen (1182–1251) to the formation of ideals of scholarship and intellectual refinement were enormous, and his writings ranged over rhetoric and the linguistic sciences, music and pedagogy, logic and Buddhist philosophy.[9] In this chapter, we shall follow Mipham's lead and concern ourselves with aspects of Sakya Paṇḍita's contributions to Buddhist logic and epistemology, examining in particular his arguments in connection with the theory of objects, including, in principle at least, books that turn into swords and other objects appearing in dreams.

The remaining two figures to be considered here, Karma Pakshi (1204–1283) and Dölpopa Sherap Gyeltshen (1292–1361), are both renowned as great exponents of yoga and tantric esotericism, in which the cultivation of imagination and vision is most valued. Of course, it has sometimes followed that this emphasis on the visionary, on exploring what the great interpreter of Islamic mysticism, Henry Corbin, has aptly termed the *mundus imaginalis*,[10] has given rise to novelty that resists ready harmonization with more conservative traditions of scriptural exegesis. For this reason, one of the challenges for Tibet's religious visionaries was to elaborate doctrinal apologetics, indeed sometimes polemics, through which to express and to justify their perspectives. It will become apparent here that the distinction between visionary and scholastic approaches to the interpretation of Buddhist teaching was therefore by no means an impermeable one, and to recognize this is one of the ways in which our conception of Tibetan scholasticism needs to become more nuanced.

In these examples it will be found too that each author's style of reflection corresponds in certain respects with his substantive concerns regarding the nature of Buddhist insight. Briefly, we may say that while Sakya Paṇḍita regards a precise mastery of Indian Sanskrit learning to be the bedrock for the formation of the refined Buddhist layman or monk, Karma Pakshi embraces an intuitive, but at the same time skeptical, vision that countenances the possibility that direct insight may be catalyzed by any of a rich plurality of sources. This well comports with the tolerant and plural-

Figure 6.1 Sakya Paṇḍita. Sixteenth century. Now preserved at the Nyingmapa monastery of Mindröling.

istic outlook that he encouraged in his religious dealings with the Mongol empire. Dölpopa, in contrast to both, emphatically privileges particular texts and doctrines within the great corpus of Indian Buddhist scriptures and finds in the contemplation of their inner meaning the key to the understanding of the Buddha's teaching overall.[11]

In describing some of the issues we encounter here, I shall often adopt a comparative approach, suggesting ways in which these three thinkers sometimes touch upon concerns shared by Western philosophers, and reconstructing aspects of their arguments from a contemporary philosophical perspective. This is both a matter of exegetical convenience, referring to things near at hand to explain those farther afield, and a reflection of aspects of my own outlook: relativism and antirelativism, I think, each at best embody partial truths that in the real world require one another. Human culture and thought spin out their magical net in the interweaving of difference and identity. In the three studies that follow, the territory we must traverse will be found, I think, to be at once both familiar and foreign.

Sakya Paṇḍita's Reasons

Objects and Entities in Buddhist Philosophical Logic: Some Problems

Though the Indian logical and epistemological tradition had been introduced to Tibet as early as the eighth century—we have already seen evidence of royal interest in this area (p. 45)—this appears to have been one of the branches of Buddhist learning in which Tibetan activity came to a halt with the fall of the old dynasty. It was during the eleventh century that there was a renewal of interest here, and Tibetans began to study and to translate Indian logical treatises once again. An indigenous Tibetan tradition of philosophical study and debate took root at Sangphu monastery (founded 1071 or 1073) in Central Tibet, which was to remain a singularly influential scholastic center for the next three centuries and more.[12] Sakya Paṇḍita, as a scholar of Sanskrit who revised the Tibetan translation of one of the major treatises of the Indian philosopher Dharmakīrti,[13] while no doubt indebted to the tradition of Sangphu in some respects, became sharply critical of it in others. His *Treasury of Epistemological Reason* (*Tshad-ma-rigs-gter*), which was to be one of the most widely studied philosophical works ever composed by a Tibetan author, delineates and defends the distinctive elements of his own reading of the Indian Buddhist epistemological tradition, frequently opposing the school of Sangphu.[14] In the eleven chapters of his treatise, he surveys a variety of questions pertaining to three central categories: the epistemological object (*shes-bya'i yul*), the subject that knows the object—that is, the mind (*shes-byed-kyi blo*)—and the act of knowledge through which the two are related (*blo des yul rtogs-pa'i tshul*).[15] As it is my primary purpose here to indicate something of the style of argumentation Sakya Paṇḍita employs in this context, my remarks will be limited to a survey of his treatment of the first of these topics, the object.

For philosophers concerned with the fundamental problems of ontology, the problems surrounding the inquiry into just what is, a special set of difficulties arises when our intentional attitudes are considered. The objects of belief, thought, love, and hate need not be concrete physical objects such as this chair, this desk, or this writing tablet. Neither must they be mental events per se, that is, the objects of thought need not be themselves thoughts. Our minds seem to have access to a whole range of objects that, if they exist at all, exist in no ordinary sense. Unhappy with the prospect of ontic superfecundity, the ontologist may wish to deny the existence of such objects altogether. The theory of objects and ontology, it would seem, part company here. Alexius Meinong has put the point succinctly: "[T]he totality of what exists, including what has existed and will exist, is infinitely small in comparison with the totality of the objects of knowledge."[16]

Philosophical concepts related to questions of intentionality had begun to develop in India at an early date, and, no later than the first centuries C.E., Buddhist thinkers had already argued that having an intentional object (*sālambanatvam*) is the mark of the mental.[17] Moreover, intentional objects *as* intentional objects were systematically distinguished from the external objects of the senses by means of the adoption of an appropriate technical terminology whose definitions were rigorously formulated. Sakya Paṇḍita was thus the heir to an already ancient tradition of reflection on the nature and significance of intentional phenomena.

In both India and Tibet, certain of the philosophical schools of Buddhism sought to maintain that some of the more anomalous objects among our ideas, as well as such things as hallucinated objects, really do exist. Sakya Paṇḍita summarizes their views as follows:

> The Tibetans say: "If there do not exist both objective generalities (*don-spyi*), which are the objects of conceptual error, and unreal appearances (*med-pa gsal-snang*), which are the objects of nonconceptual [i.e., perceptual] error, then error becomes groundless. Hence, there exist both [those two types of] apparent object. This is proven perforce of the self-presentations (*rang-rig*) in which both [those types of] erroneous cognition are apprehended."
>
> Moreover, the Saṃmitīya sect among the pious attendants (*nyan-thos, śrāvaka*) and others hold that both general terms (*ming-spyi*) and objective generalities, whose forms are [respectively] words and marks, are concreta [to be classed among] those factors of being which are set apart; for they are set apart from [the classes of] physical forms, minds, and mental events. Moreover, they hold that unreal appearances—even the objects of dreams—are so-called "factors of being which are without the marks of sensible objects," and that these are concreta; and that dream-cognitions are born from these.[18]

It will be useful to consider in this context some of the definitions that have been put forward by Tibetan Buddhist logicians in connection with the theory of objects:

(D1) Object (*yul*) = Def. That of which a mind can be aware.
(D2) Knowable (*shes-bya*) = Def. Possibly an object.
(D3) Intelligible (*rig-bya*) = Def. Possibly comprehended by an epistemic operation.
(D4) Established ground (*gzhi-grub*) = Def. That upon which an epistemic operation is directed.
(D5) Certainly existent (*yod-nges*) = Def. Possibly within the purview of an epistemic operation.[19]

These five terms (D1–D5) are sometimes said to have the same reference. Our next group of definitions distinguishes various types of object:

(D6) Apparent object (*snang-yul*) = Def. That object which appears either as a representation, or directly without representation. (Note: The disjunctive form of this definition insures that it will be applicable in the contexts of both direct realism and representationalism.)
(D7) Apprehended object (*gzung-yul*) = Def. The external object whose representation is directly perceived by the apprehending subject.
(D8) Object of intellection (*zhen-yul*) = Def. That of which a mind can be aware through an intellectual operation which in apprehending it renders it predominant. (This may seem somewhat obscure. The object of intellection is usually said to be an object indirectly referred to through a mediating concept, e.g., the fire referred to when, having seen smoke, one thinks, "There's been a fire.")
(D9) Operational object (*'jug-yul*) = Def. That object which is the predominant [established] ground for an [epistemic] operation directed upon it by a corresponding subject.

It will not be necessary here to examine these definitions in detail. What is of interest in the present context is a problem that flows from the assumption that (D1)–(D5) have the same reference. For then, by simple substitution, we can derive from (D1) and (D5) the equation:

Certainly existent = that of which a mind can be aware.

Buddhist idealists were, of course, not in the least troubled by this: some of them would have surely affirmed Berkeley's formula, *esse est percipi*. The idealists, in other words, would argue that the equivalency derived from (D1) and (D5) follows from the fact that all that certainly exists and all of which a mind can be aware are mental acts. We should note, however, that (D7) may be taken to insist on there being external objects—it is a definition advanced in connection with a realist ontology. To abandon (D7) might open the way for the proposed idealistic recasting of the remaining definitions; but to preserve (D7) while admitting, too, an apparent equation of existence and object, we might be led to assert that there are actual existents corresponding to all cognitive objects.

Some such considerations as these must have motivated the various theories of objects advanced by Buddhist logicians. One approach to the resolution of the ontological problems encountered here was suggested by the eighth-century Indian Buddhist philosopher Dharmottara and was elaborated by Tibetan thinkers of the Sangphu school in the eleventh and twelfth centuries.[20] Their strategy was to elaborate a theory of objects sufficiently rich to accommodate such things as objective generalities and apparitions as real, but peculiar, "objects of apprehension," which they determined to be of three kinds altogether: (1) the concrete particular object of apprehension (*gzung-yul rang-mtshan*), for instance, "the object of apprehension of that sensory direct perception that grasps a vase when a mind immediately perceives a vase"; (2) the general characteristic as an object of apprehension (*gzung-yul spyi-mtshan*), for instance, "the object of apprehension of that thought that grasps the vase as a vase, that is, as an objective generality"; and (3) the nonexistent, apparitional object of apprehension (*med-pa gsal-snang*), for instance, "the object of apprehension of that sensory consciousness to which there appear hairlike lines, when hairlike lines are apparent to the erring sensory consciousness [as in the case of one with cataract]." The use of the term "object of apprehension" in these contexts may suggest that these thinkers were not originally concerned to elaborate an ontological theory, but rather sought merely to create a typology of epistemic objects. Nonetheless, even if that was the case, speaking in terms of there being such objects led to a certain hypostasis, the objects of types (2) and (3) coming to be regarded as real in just the same sense as those of type (1).

Objective Generalities and Illusory Objects

How are we to understand all of this? The term "objective generality" (*don-spyi*) is defined in a great many ways by later Tibetan thinkers. Recent interpreters of Tibetan scholastic documents have sometimes used here the term "generic image," but I think we should be on our guard lest we assimilate the concept to one of mental imagery.[21] Indeed, while some Tibetan writers do single out mental images as paradigm cases of what I here call "objective generalities," others emphasize nonimagistic, discursive paradigms. For the purposes of the present discussion, the various scholastic definitions do not have to be considered in detail. To indicate the sense of "objective generality" and the manner in which the objective generality provides a source of conceptual error, a useful analogy may be found in the empiricist notion of an idea. Consider David Hume's famous example of the golden mountain.

The golden mountain, of course, does not actually exist, but nonetheless I can think of such a thing. How can this be? According to Hume, I combine my idea of gold with that of mountain. Such ideas are of course not identical to the actual things out there in the world, but neither does it make good sense to think of them as self-existent universals. Rather, they are somehow derived from my impressions of the things to which they correspond. Similarly, the Buddhist logician's objective generalities are neither concrete particulars nor Platonic ideas (the existence of which Buddhist philosophers would in any case deny).[22] And, in the present example, these queer objects do not correspond to what is, but rather to what is not. Thus, they are a source of conceptual error. The question that Sakya Paṇḍita will seek to answer, then, is this: is there nevertheless some sense in which these peculiar objects themselves exist?

To clarify further what is meant by "objective generality," as well as the motive for positing that there are such objects, let us consider a commonplace example. Suppose you enter a room and, your feet being tired, you want a chair. Then what is the object of your desire? It is a chair to be sure, but can we say that it is this chair or that chair? The curious thing is that whatever conclusions we might come to with regard to "a chair," the thing that eventually satisfies your desire is *this* chair, even if you didn't have *this* chair in mind when at first you wanted *a* chair. To see just what is at stake here, let us look more closely at some typical sentences:

(**1**) Dechen wants a chair.
(**2**) There is some particular chair that Dechen wants.[23]
(**3**) There is chair number one, and chair number two, et cetera, and Dechen wants chair number one, or chair number two, et cetera.[24]

Sentence 1 is illustrative of the kind of case with which we are here concerned, and sentences 2 and 3 represent attempts to express the sense of sentence 1 using the logical device of existential quantification, without the entire sentence being governed by a verb of intention. (That is, the statement of the chair's existence stands outside of the statement of Dechen's want, and so only the chair, not its existence, is what is wanted.) Sentence 2 exemplifies what has become known as a failure of existential generalization. It says: there *is* something such that Dechen wants *it*. This suggests that Dechen had one particular chair in mind all along, which renders mysterious the fact that her desire may be satisfied by a chair of which she had no previous knowledge, or that she may desire something that does not exist at all. Sentence 3, on the other hand, suggests that when Dechen wants a chair, she wants it-doesn't-matter-which-one of a very large number of things. And there is, of course, a sense in which this is true, although it seems unlikely that sentence 3 has succeeded in capturing just that sense. For supposing that the object of Dechen's want is, as is here proposed, a disjunction, then is it merely a very long disjunction, or is it one that includes (in this case) all chairs? If it does include all chairs, how is it that Dechen knew to do this? But if it does not include all chairs, then why should we suppose that it includes that chair which eventually satisfies Dechen's desire? The failure of sentences 2 and 3 to represent sentence 1 adequately is symptomatic of the unusual ontological status of "a chair."

Do we wish, then, to say that "a chair" really represents some sort of ideal object? This cannot be answered without further determining just what kind of ideal object it might be. Certainly it is not a universal, that is, the property of being a chair. Even if we assume here an extreme Platonist account of universals, we do not say that one's desire for a chair has for its object the ideal form, the universal Chair. Similarly, we may speak of senses, or meanings, or immanent objects, but all alike leave paradoxical the satisfaction of the desire by a concrete particular chair.

The second type of intentional object with which Sakya Paṇḍita will be concerned is the perceptual object that seems to exist but does not exist actually. The apparitional city seen in the midst of a desert, Rāma's vision of an illusory deer, images seen in dreams, various hallucinated sensations—these are just a few of the stock examples. The ontological problems arising in connection with such objects present certain formal analogies to those that arise in connection with the indefinite descriptions just discussed. For example,

(**4**) Rāma sees the illusory deer.

does not seem to say the same thing as

(**5**) There exists something such that Rāma sees it.[25]

In this instance, however, a disjunctive translation along the lines of sentence 3 would be too absurd even to consider, and we will ignore here the suggestion that really it is an abstract object that is seen, perhaps the disembodied principle of deerhood.

Sakya Paṇḍita's Approach to the Problem

Before examining his arguments with respect to objects of these types, it will be useful to consider some essential features of Sakya Paṇḍita's ontology overall. It is clear that he sought to subsume all things that are in the two great classes of mental and physical substances. The former are discrete self-presentations, and the latter are concrete particulars.[26] All abstract objects are to be reduced to one or another of these classes or are held to be in some sense ontologically parasitic. Thus, Sakya Paṇḍita was a sort of reist, though certainly not a pansomatist: that is to say, he believed that only real things exist, but that these need not only be bodies. On the contrary, he believed that a further reduction of the two great classes would result in the elimination of the physical in favor of the mental, the world thus being ultimately constituted only of self-presenting states.[27] This idealist turn, however, need not concern us here; only his dualist ontology is relevant in the present context.

Sakya Paṇḍita advances two main arguments against the thesis that objective generalities and apparitions actually exist. The first depends on the premise that where a real object corresponds to a mental state representing that object, the cognition is veridical,[28] as when one sees a pot under normal conditions. Assuming then, that objective generalities and apparitions are real, the mental states representing them are veridical. This conclusion, however, is counterexemplified by instances of cognitive error. Unless we wish to jettison the correspondence theory, our sole option is to reject the reality of objective generalities and apparitions.

I think that with regard to apparitions the point being made here is clear enough. The assumption that the deer seen by Rāma is a real deer is not consistent with the assumption that Rāma is deluded in his perception of it. This is clearly part of what we mean when we speak of hallucinations. The force of the argument with respect to objective generalities, however, is not quite so straightforward. Sakya Paṇḍita himself saw this and proceeded to elaborate a further line of argument in order to make his case here.

Let us consider someone who, entering a poorly lit chamber, takes a rope in the corner to be a snake. The objective generality that he believes corresponds to his perception is in this case "a snake." And, certainly, his taking the rope to be a snake is an example of an errant cognition. Consider:

(6) Sonam takes the rope to be a snake.

We will generally concur in rendering this as:

(7) There is something that Sonam takes to be a snake.[29]

But

(8) There is something that Sonam takes the rope to be[30]

seems at best ambiguous, and certainly false if "there is something" is taken to mean "there really is a snake here."

In his assumption that objective generalities have some role in cognitive error, then, Sakya Paṇḍita was also pointing to a basic peculiarity of the objects of such intentional states as "taking," "believing," "appearing to," and so forth.

Returning, for the moment, to the initial premise, which concerned the correspondence between veridical states and real objects, Sakya Paṇḍita has a supposed objector draw attention to the peculiar features of the situation exemplified by statement 7: there is a real object of this state of taking to be. Hence, it is not erroneous.[31] He responds that the objection proceeds from a false analysis of the situation. The visual perception of a variegated ropelike (or snakelike) object has been here confounded with the taking of that object to be a snake. True enough, the visual perception of a certain shape and arrangement of color is by no means erroneous, but that is not what is here at issue. The error is Sonam's *taking* the real object to be a snake, when there is no such snake. Hence, the objective generality "a snake" is no real object at all.

Sakya Paṇḍita's second argument is more difficult and involved than the first, and I am not entirely certain about the manner in which it is to be understood. Its fundamental assumption seems to be that real objects belong to the domain of intersubjectivity, in other words, there are no real private objects. If the apparition or objective generality apprehended by Sonam were a real object, then others who are appropriately situated might apprehend that very same object.[32] But there is no reason to suppose that they do. Hence, these are not real objects. In other words, Rāma's deer should be intersubjectively accessible in just the same sense as is any ordinary deer. And so, too, a snake, when Sonam is deluded with respect to the rope.

An objection that is raised here states in effect that although objective generalities and apparitions are real objects, they are not intersubjectively accessible just because they are private (lit., "bound to one's own mind," *bdag-gi blo dang 'brel*), like the insides of our bodies. The response given to this is that first of all the example is a bad one—our internal organs are possibly such that they are perceived by others, for instance, if one is gravely wounded; and in any case we don't even perceive them ourselves under normal circumstances; hence, our innards are not similar to supposed "private objects." And, more importantly, there are simply no such private objects. How is this to be established?

Let us suppose that Dechen takes the rope in the corner to be a snake and that Sonam takes the very same rope to be a snake. Is there any sense to the notion that they are, or are not, referring to the same snake? On the assumption that they are referring to real private objects, it would seem that they are taking one and the same rope to be utterly different things, for each is referring to a discrete private object. Thus, should they attempt to converse with one another, there will be no possibility of understanding, for ex hypothesi they are speaking of utterly disparate things about which they have no common knowledge.[33] Then is communication between them to be explained by supposing there to be a resemblance (*rnam-pa 'dra-ba*) between their nevertheless discrete objects? Sakya Paṇḍita's response to this suggestion is that there can be no possibility whatsoever of establishing any such posited resemblance: I know only the object before my own mind and have no means by which I might compare it to the mysterious private object of which you speak, except by reference to what you say about it. But now we have begun to turn in circles. Only Dechen can in fact ever know what she takes the rope to be, and analogously for Sonam. One wonders: did Meinong and Russell ever puzzle about the same unicorn?

One question that it may be well to pose at this juncture is: how is it established that Sonam and Dechen both refer to the same thing when in fact they do refer to "the very same rope"? The answer that I think Sakya Paṇḍita wants to give here involves a rather strong principle of verification. That they are referring to the same thing is established only when they pick out the same actual being in the world. But in that case the referent is a concrete particular, not an objective generality. The conclusion we must draw is that there is no way to verify the identity of objective generalities; the rules of our common discourse simply demand that we play it as if such an identity obtained. Thus, all reference to such things is wrapped up in error.[34]

Sakya Paṇḍita concludes from this that we must abandon altogether the attempt to conceive of objective generalities and apparitions as real objects. They are to be reduced, he maintains, to the self-presenting (*rang-rig*) states of the subject.[35] Thus if Dechen takes something to be a snake, what we mean to say is that the taking of such-and-such a phenomenon (for instance, a patch of color) to be a snake is self-presenting for Dechen. And analogously in the case of apparitions.

Our consideration of Sakya Paṇḍita's theory of objects points to a number of analogous developments in recent Western philosophy. The problem of objective generalities seems to be rather closely related to that which arises in connection with what Russell calls "indefinite descriptions" or "ambiguous objects." Some of his observations on this subject would be appropriate here:

> [M]any logicians have been driven to the conclusion that there are unreal objects. . . . In such theories, it seems to me, there is a failure of that feeling for reality which ought

> to be preserved even in the most abstract studies. . . . In obedience to the feeling of reality, we shall insist that, in the analysis of propositions, nothing "unreal" is to be admitted. . . . "A unicorn" is an indefinite description which describes nothing. It is not an indefinite description which describes something unreal.[36]

Russell's argument is thus similar to Sakya Paṇḍita's in its negative purpose, that is, to banish unreal objects from our ontology. But the positive aspect of Russell's theory of descriptions is certainly without clear precedent in the material under consideration.

The concept of the objective generality may also have some affinities to that of the common name—perhaps this is what is involved in Sakya Paṇḍita's reference to the doctrine of general terms. If so, I suspect that he would concur here with Reinhardt Grossmann:

> What does it mean to name something commonly? . . . there is no sensible answer to this question. The notion of a common name is inherently confused. I, for one, cannot make sense of the assertion that, say, 'fish' names every single fish, but does not name either this or that particular fish, or the property of being a fish, or the class of all fish.[37]

Sakya Paṇḍita's suspicions with respect to supposed private objects are perhaps in some respects also reminiscent of views advanced by Wittgenstein and his disciples. On what grounds do we say that two people have the same idea, when that idea refers to nothing real? Some philosophers, concurring with Meinong, would insist that this puzzle forces us to acknowledge that there must be some types of nonreal object. According to Meinong:

> [I]n this case there exist two different ideas since there occur two mental acts of presentation. But these two ideas are equal . . . when we say that two persons have the same idea, we can only mean that there occur two ideas of the same entity.[38]

Sakya Paṇḍita would, of course, dissent. He affirms, I believe, something very much like Quine's maxim: "No entity without identity." In the absence of specifiable identity conditions for the entities conceived of by two persons who ponder the golden mountain, we cannot affirm that they conceive of the same thing at all.

Sakya Pandita's theory of objects was not, however, purely negative. He asserted positively that nonreal objects are ontologically dependent upon the self-presenting states of the subject. It seems to me that here his theory has some similarities with the early phenomenology of Edmund Husserl, that of the *Logical Investigations*:

> [T]he object is aimed at, which signifies that the act of aiming at it is an experience; but the object is still only presumed and, in truth, is nothing. . . . I represent the god Jupiter, which is to say that I have a certain experience of representation, which in my consciousness is realized as the representation-of-the-god-Jupiter. . . . But if, in addition, the object aimed at exists, the situation has not necessarily changed from the phenomenological point of view. For consciousness of what is given is essentially the same thing, whether the object represented exists, or if it is imagined and even perhaps absurd.[39]

Before leaving this topic, it may be well to close by asking what all of this has to do with Buddhism. Some Tibetan authorities perhaps believed that mastery of the Dignāga-Dharmakīrti system of logic and epistemology was to be counted among the necessary conditions for progress towards the Buddhist enlightenment, for enlightenment, being perfect knowledge, was to be engendered by flawless reason that frees itself from all error. Sakya Paṇḍita's views about this have been disputed and are less than entirely clear-cut. Though he may have regarded logic and epistemology, like the other "outer" sciences,[40] to have no direct relationship with the final ends of the Buddhist path, he did insist that the ability to reason and to refute what was unreasonable should contribute to one's ability to understand and to interpret rightly the Buddha's teaching.[41] And this conceptual clarity, of course, may well conduce to spiritual advancement, if what is rightly understood is practically applied. It will be seen in what follows, however, that the relationship between natural reason and the teaching's highest insights poses a problem that runs deep within the Tibetan tradition.

Karma Pakshi's Doubts

The Magus Karmapa

In 1978, two rare volumes attributed to the third Karmapa hierarch, Rangjung Dorje (1284–1339), and entitled *Rgya-mtsho mtha'-yas-kyi skor* (The Limitless Ocean Cycle) were published in India. The title, it seemed to me at the time, was suggestive of two famous verses from the *Bhadracaripraṇidhānarāja* (The Regal Aspiration of Fine Conduct), perhaps the most widely known prayer in Tibet:

> Purifying the ocean of fields,
> Liberating the ocean of beings,
> Beholding the ocean of dharmas,
> Immersed in the ocean of gnosis,
> Refining the ocean of conduct,
> Perfecting the ocean of prayer,
> Worshiping the ocean of Buddhas,
> May I practice for an ocean of aeons, never fatigued.[42]

Through the biographical accounts of the third Karmapa, it was known that he had composed a treatise concerning the cosmology of the *Avataṃsakasūtra*,[43] the collection of sūtras from which the *Regal Aspiration* is drawn. Could this *Limitless Ocean Cycle* be Rangjung Dorje's work on the *Avataṃsaka*? Obtaining a copy, I plunged into the text and, as I soon discovered, into an ocean of philological difficulty.

The *Limitless Ocean Cycle* is a collection of treatises that taken together present an exceedingly thorough survey of the nine vehicles (*theg-pa*, Skt. *yāna*) of the Nyingmapa school (see p. 16, table 1). The author's perspective, though, is that of one who has very close ties to the new translation schools that arose after the tenth century, the Kagyüpa in particular. The published manuscript is incomplete—my guess is that it contains about half of the original content—but this much is sufficient to provide us with some understanding of the author's general scheme.[44] As that author, according to the colophons of individual texts making up the cycle, styles himself Karmapa Rangjung Dorje, both the publisher and the U.S. Library of Congress naturally identified him with the third Karmapa hierarch.[45]

Here, however, as I read through the *Limitless Ocean Cycle*, something struck me as being amiss: my previous reading of Rangjung Dorje's work had revealed an exacting thinker and precise stylist, one who was fascinated with the minutiae of astronomical calculations and yogic physiology, and who sought to express these in the clearest manner possible. His concern for exactitude was to be found also in his contemplative works.[46] The author of the *Limitless Ocean Cycle*, however, was clearly a visionary who liked to work in great, broad strokes, who adhered to a well-defined architechtonic, to be sure, but still ventured to make rambling digressions or to conjure up strange associations of ideas in the course of advancing an arcane, yet luminous, doctrine. That doctrine itself is one in which the teachings of all the nine vehicles, of the tantras old and new, and of even the non-Buddhist "extremists" (Skt. *tīrthika*, Tib. *mu-stegs-pa*), come crashing together in the realization of the Great Perfection (*Rdzogs-pa-chen-po*). In short, my initial impression of the author of the *Limitless Ocean Cycle* was that he differed greatly in intellectual temperament from Rangjung Dorje, hardly less than did, say, Eckhart from Aquinas. Nonetheless, in the face of the colophonic data and uncertain of the value of my general impressions, I hesitated to conclude that the *Limitless Ocean Cycle* was not the work of the third Karmapa.

It was quite by accident that several months after beginning to study the *Limitless Ocean Cycle* I came across the following passage, which laid bare the solution to the entire problem. It comes from the *Ri-chos mtshams-kyi zhal-gdams* (Precepts on Solitary Retreat) by the seventeenth-century yogin Karma Chakme. Significantly, as we shall see, it is found in the chapter of that work that treats the teaching of the tantras of the anuyoga-class:

> [What I have set forth here] is merely the kernel, based on my own experience and easily understood. It may be elucidated at length by regarding both the great text of the *Gdams-ngag rgya-mtsho mtha'-yas* (Limitless Ocean of Instructions)[47] and the *Zab-chos rgya-mtsho mtha'-yas* (Limitless Ocean of Profound Doctrines),[48] which include numberless texts, fundamental and ancillary, these being found in the *Collected Works* (*Bka'-'bum*) of the great siddha Karma Pakshi (1204–1283).[49]

Accepting Karma Chakme's attribution as a working hypothesis, it seemed essential to discover why it was that the colophons of the *Limitless Ocean Cycle* were signed "Rangjung Dorje." *The Autobiographical Writings of the Second Karma-pa Karma Pakshi*, published in India at the same time as the *Limitless Ocean Cycle* (and by the same publisher!), provided an answer on the first folio:

> This is the unborn, primordially pure Lion's roar proclaimed by one who is
> In the future to be emanated by Siṃhanāda,
> In the past Düsum Khyenpa [the first Karmapa hierarch] himself,
> At present Rangjung Dorje. . . .[50]

And again, some verses further on:

> I am Rangjung Dorje,
> The vajra-king, one of great might. . . .

"Rangjung Dorje" occurs frequently throughout the *Autobiographical Writings* as the name whereby the author refers to himself,[51] though he also uses "Dharmasiddhi" on occasion,[52] and, in some of the episodes connected with the Mongol court, the famous title "Karma Pakshi."[53] In tales of past lives, "Sempa Rangjung Dorje" is met with frequently, which may lead us to conclude that this is understood to be the proper name of the bodhisattva who in Tibet is manifest as the Karmapa.[54] It is in the light of all this that an episode in the life of the third Karmapa, which is reported by Pawo Tsuklaktrhenga, may be comprehended: the master Orgyenpa (1230–1309), having just identified the youth who would be the third Karmapa as Karma Pakshi's reincarnation declares, "As my guru's esoteric name (*gsang-mtshan*) was Rangjung Dorje, I will name you just that." And so he names him.[55]

Karma Pakshi, known as the rebirth of Karmapa Düsum Khyenpa (1110–1193), one of the four preeminent disciples of Gampopa (1079–1153), is sometimes regarded as the first representative of the most distinctive of Tibetan hierarchical institutions, the identification of a future hierarch as the rebirth, or "emanational embodiment" (*sprul-sku*), of his deceased predecessor. Certainly, with Orgyenpa's recognition of his successor, this began to emerge as a primary means of succession within Tibetan religious institutions.[56] The successive Karmapas, who, like the later Dalai Lamas, are thought to be emanations of Tibet's patron bodhisattva, Avalokiteśvara, played a major role in Tibetan religious, and sometimes also political, life down to the time of the line's recent representative, Karmapa XVI Rangjung Rikpei Dorje (1927–1981). Indeed, the latter's disputed succession demonstrates just how important this office continues to be for Tibetan Buddhists.[57]

Karma Pakshi hailed from far eastern Tibet and during his youth became the pupil of Düsum Khyenpa's illustrious grand-disciple, Pomdrakpa (1170–1249), who initiated him into the Kagyüpa system of yoga and meditation. He later was ordained and continued his studies under one of the leading masters of the Nyingmapa school, Jampabum (1179–1252), the third abbot of Kathok monastery in what is today western Sichuan.[58] Kathok had its own distinctive tradition of doctrinal learning, reaching back to the Nyingmapa lineages that had been active during the period between the fall of the old dynasty and the eleventh-century revival.[59] The hallmarks of the system were the analysis of the entire range of Buddhist teaching in terms of nine progressive approaches to the highest enlightenment called vehicles (*theg-pa*, *yāna*),[60] and a special emphasis on the three highest vehicles, those of esoteric tantras, particularly as these were embodied in the teachings of the *Guhyagarbhatantra* (The Tantra of the Secret Nucleus), the *Mdo dgongs-pa 'dus-pa* (The Sūtra Gathering All Intentions), and the highest contemplative teachings of the Nyingmapa, those of the Great Perfection (*Rdzogs-pa-chen-po*).[61] Karma Pakshi's *Limitless Ocean Cycle* is in most respects, in fact, an elaborate systematization of the Kathok tradition of teaching.

In 1255/56, responding to the invitation of the Mongol ruler Möngke Khan, Karma Pakshi traveled to Sira-ordos (the Mongol imperial camp) to participate in a religious conclave sponsored by the Khan. Though he participated in debates with the adherents of other religions, primarily Taoists but probably also Confucianists and Nestorian Christians, he came to be a strong proponent of the Mongol imperial policy of religious tolerance and praised the Khans for this at several points in his autobiography.[62] With the definitive ascension of the leaders of the Sakyapa school to the predominant position in Mongol-Tibetan affairs, Karma Pakshi was for awhile out of favor, and his relations with Khubilai Khan (1215–1294), the Mongol founder of the

Yuan dynasty in China, seem to have undergone considerable fluctuation. Nonetheless, he adopted and is primarily remembered by the epithet bestowed on him at the Mongol court: Karma Pakshi, "the magus Karmapa."[63]

Karma Pakshi's autobiography reveals that, like many leading Tibetan Buddhist masters, he was prone throughout much of his life to intense visionary experiences, and these formed a major part of his inspiration as a doctrinal author. His writings, no complete set of which is known to be available at the present time, were primarily devoted to esotericism but included at least one treatise on Buddhist logic and epistemology, now lost, and several other opuscules of philosophical interest.[64] He regarded all of his writings as disclosing a unified, comprehensive vision of Buddhist teaching and practice, which is embodied in the *Limitless Ocean Cycle*. According to his own testimony, the text to be discussed in the following section was central to his thought, and this reveals a distinctively skeptical frame of mind.

That the Rangjung Dorje of the *Autobiographical Writings* is definitely none other than the Rangjung Dorje of the *Limitless Ocean Cycle* is confirmed both by direct references to the *Limitless Ocean Cycle* within the *Autobiographical Writings* and by the stylistic and doctrinal similarities between the two. Among the direct references to the *Limitless Ocean Cycle*, we find:

> Having journeyed to the land called "Ke-cu" in China, I remained there for eight months. At that time all of China arose shimmeringly, appearing as the maṇḍalas of Mañjuvajra and Cakrasaṃvara and their assembled deities. I then heard all sounds and voices as the doctrinal wheels of the various vehicles, and of the outer and inner philosophical systems, and I realized them. Thereupon, most of the *Limitless Ocean of the Teaching* (*Bstan-pa rgya-mtsho mtha'- yas*), the doctrinal wheel of the nine vehicles, became clear, and I composed it at length.[65]

Again, he tells us:

> I, the renowned Karmapa, realizing, obtaining the great transmission of myriad transmitted doctrines and so having perfected and analyzed, without adulteration and in particular, the words and the meanings of the trio of nonrealization, mistaken realization, and partial realization, have discussed the *Limitless Ocean of the Teaching*, which accords with the intention of the Buddhas, with the host of ḍākas, ḍākinīs, bodhisattvas, śrāvakas, and pratyekabuddhas, and, in accord with all the philosophical systems, have discovered and realized within myself the Buddha, [who is endowed with] fivefold embodiment.[66]

Finally, we may remark that in one passage he refers to his *Autobiographical Writings* as the background histories (*gleng-gzhi*) for the *Bstan-pa rgya-mtsho mtha'-yas* (The Limitless Ocean of the Teaching) and the *Ye-shes rgya-mtsho mtha'- yas* (The Limitless Ocean of Gnosis).[67]

Let us note, too, that neither Pawo Tsuklaktrhenga, nor even the recent Mendong Tshampa Rinpoche (writing in 1897), was in the least uncertain as to the use of the name Rangjung Dorje, or as to the provenance of the *Limitless Ocean Cycle*. I have uncovered, in fact, no evidence whatever for there having been any confusion about these matters within the tradition itself prior to our own generation. Thus the mistaken identification of the author of the *Limitless Ocean Cycle* must be regarded as a contemporary, and not as a traditional, misattribution.[68]

Skepticism and Breakthrough

What of the actual teaching of the *Limitless Ocean Cycle*? It may be best to begin by making a somewhat rough and subjective observation: the *Limitless Ocean Cycle* is unusual among the Tibetan encyclopedic works that have become available in that it aims not to delimit and then to dissect the knowable, but rather to challenge us throughout with its irreducible, infinite grandeur. This is not to say that the notion that knowledge is without limits is a particularly novel one for Tibetan Buddhist scholasticism; the point here is that while the scholastic pedagogy prefers to treat carefully circumscribed bodies of learning, this is not entirely true of Karma Pakshi. He wishes, instead, to confront us at every turn with what he terms "the trio of nonrealization, mistaken realization, and partial realization" (*ma-rtogs log-rtogs phyogs-rtogs gsum*) and thereby to make of ignorance and doubt catalysts for the emergence of an enlightened awareness.

Let us attempt to see just how this is evidenced within the text itself. One of the opuscules making up the *Limitless Ocean Cycle* is a peculiar work called the *'Dod-pa rgya-mtsho mtha'-yas* (The Limitless Ocean of Tenets).[69] Its relation to the entire cycle is known to us in very general terms through references to it found in other sections of the *Limitless Ocean Cycle* itself, for instance:

> The *Gdams-ngag rgya-mtsho mtha'-yas* (The Limitless Ocean of Instructions), the *Zhus-lan rgya-mtsho mtha'-yas* (The Limitless Ocean of Dialogue),[70] and the *'Dod-pa rgya-mtsho mtha'-yas* (The Limitless Ocean of Tenets) are all-embracing: the exposition of these does not belong to any sequence [that is to say, they do not have set positions within the sequence of the nine yānas]. . . . They are the general framework for the whole. . . .[71]

In what way does the *Limitless Ocean of Tenets* "embrace everything"? What kind of "general framework" does it provide? Turning to the text, we find a strange list of conflicting doctrines, dozens of them, with a minimum of explanation and analysis, for instance:

> It is held that saṃsāra has a beginning and end, and it is held that saṃsāra is without beginning or end. It is held that minds are of identical nature throughout all saṃsāra and nirvāṇa, and it is held that all minds are of differing natures. It is held that sentient beings are newly produced, and it is held that sentient beings are not newly produced.[72] It is held that in understanding and practicing by means of various reasonings, one definitively establishes [the doctrine] by reasoning, and it is held that one definitively establishes it [without relying on natural reason] through the transmitted precepts spoken by all the buddhas, and it is held that the trio of Buddha, doctrine, and teaching has not been experienced as emerging and thus is not. It is held that there is no karma, and it is held that there is karma and the ripening of karma. It is held that when offspring are born to the males and females of all creatures, they are generated by body [alone], and [it is held] that they are generated by both body and mind. It is held that there is a connection between the illusion and the illusionist, and it is held that there is no connection between the illusion and the illusionist.[73] It is held that there is a connection between the echo and the place where the echo occurs, and it is held that there is no connection between the echo and the place where the echo occurs. It is held that there is a connection between the cause and the result, but if there were a connection between the cause and the result, then there would be the fault of

the Buddha reverting into sentient being, just as the result reverts to the cause; and if there were no connection between the cause and the result, there would be the fault of meaninglessness [with respect to the proposition that] all phenomena subsumed in saṃsāra and the path to nirvāṇa are formed [as the results of causes]. It is held that there is a connection between both body and mind, and it is held that there is no connection between body and mind. It is held that there is ultimate truth, and it is held that there is the truth of superficial appearance. It is held that the eight aggregates of consciousness have objects, it is held that they are subjects, and it is held that they have neither object, nor causal conditions. It is held that scriptural authority is true and that reason is untrue, and it is held that reason is true and scriptural authority untrue. It is held that there is a connection between all material substances and their shadows, and it is held that they have no connection with their shadows. It is held that there is a connection between all the particulars of saṃsāra and nirvāṇa and the names by which they are designated, and it is held that there is no connection between all the particulars of saṃsāra and nirvāṇa and the names by which they are designated. It is held that [for some types of sentient creatures] fire relieves the affliction of thirst, and it is held that water makes [those creatures] warm and thirsty. It is held that the phenomena of saṃsāra and nirvāṇa have a beginning and an end; and it is held that if [they] were incessant, then [everything] would have to come to be everywhere; and it is held that, abiding without going and coming [in a state of equipoise], they have come to be all-pervarding. It is held that there is a connection between cloud and sky, and it is held that there is no connection between cloud and sky. It is held that there is no connection between day and night, and it is held that there is a connection between day and night. It is held that there is a connection between this birth and the next, and it is held that there is no connection between this birth and the next, and it is held that there is no birth at all after this one. It is held that there is a connection between fire and smoke, and it is held that there is no connection between fire and smoke. It is held that there are connections among the three poisons [stupidity, hatred, passion], and it is held that there is no connection among the three poisons. It is held that there is a connection between both happiness and suffering, and it is held that there is no connection between both happiness and suffering. It is held that there is a connection between both the locus of a real property and reality per se, and it is held that there is no connection between the locus of a real property and reality per se. Please know, by means of the two types of epistemic authority [perception and inference], the inconceivable extent to which appearances of there being connections are imputed where there are no connections. One who comprehends everything [in this way] is the king of all-knowers and omniscient ones![74]

Occasionally, however, the purpose of this catalogue is made explicit and clear:

It says in the transmission of the *Prajñāpāramitā* (The Perfection of Discernment):

> Tenets are like the edge of a sword. Tenets are like a poisonous plant. Tenets are like a flaming pit. Tenets are like the [poisonous] *kimpaka* fruit. Tenets are like spittle. Tenets are like an impure container. Tenets are reviled by all.[75]

Therefore, whatever tenets—whether good, bad, or mediocre—you might harbor are the causes of good, bad, or mediocre [conditions of] saṃsāra. They are devoid of the life-force of nirvāṇa. Therefore, whatever tenets, hankerings, or particular philosophical positions you hold, they cause you to be buddhaless and make you meet with saṃsāra. You should know the masses of tenets, [each one] in particular.

In all the outer and inner philosophical systems there are various tenets. They appear all mixed together. The wise appear to have tenets; the ignorant appear to have tenets, too. Because tenets are all-pervading, I pray that the wise analyze them. It is held that Buddhahood is attained from having tenets; it is maintained that Buddhahood is attained from not having tenets; and it is maintained that Buddhahood is attained from removing both extremes. I pray that you direct your attention to each and every such tenet in turn. . . . It is held that Buddhahood is attained from gradually traversing the stages and paths; and it is held that Buddhahood is attained naturally, not performing the slightest virtue, not repenting of the slightest sin. The number of tenets is vast; because thought cannot embrace [all] tenets, do you not harbor doubts as to what is genuine?[76]

If you do not doubt, Karma Pakshi seems now to be telling us, you very well ought to do so. Why so?

The genuinely skeptical portion of the argument resembles the tenth mode of classical skepticism in the West, according to which the conflict of views on a particular topic leads us to withhold judgement when we find that there is no uncontested criterion that will resolve the conflict in question.[77] Thus, Karma Pakshi's procedure consists of juxtaposing opinions on diverse topics, such as the limits of the round of rebirth (saṃsāra), the nature of karma, the creation of sentient beings, the relationship between reason and faith, and so on. The insights of the great meditative traditions are to be realized in a breakthrough rendered possible, in part, by this ground-clearing operation, but their achievement is not, in any straightforward sense, the result of the dialectical procedure alone. Thus he continues:

You must realize the perseity of the Buddha. You must realize the perseity of the Dharma and Saṃgha. You must realize the perseity of the deity and of the mantra. . . . There is a limitless ocean of tenets pertaining to the dharmas of saṃsāra and nirvāṇa and to the particular philosophical systems. You must realize it to be neither conjoined with, nor separate from, the limitless ocean of realization, which is free from all acceptance and rejection, and which is spontaneously present gnosis.[78]

Moreover:

Though there appear all the dharmas of saṃsāra and nirvāṇa, various philosophical systems, and the inconceivably many adherences, the root of all of them is the essential abiding nature of actual entities (*dngos-po gshis-kyi gnas-lugs*), naturally and spontaneously present, the expanse of reality (*chos-kyi dbyings*) that is limitlessly extensive and without measure. Without limit and center it can be labeled neither "Buddha" nor "sentient being." All that appear, the dharmas of saṃsāra and nirvāṇa, abiding naturally and essentially, cannot by any means be abandoned or acquired through effort and practice. Such is the essential abiding nature of the actuality of mind. . . .[79]

Thus the truly significant foundation we seek, which can only be known intuitively, is the enlightenment of the Great Seal (Mahāmudrā) and Great Perfection traditions and all that this entails. The *Limitless Ocean of Tenets* embraces the entire content of the *Limitless Ocean Cycle* by calling upon us to question any and all doctrines to which we might adhere before we have gained that realization. Like some of the skeptical fideist philosophers and theologians of seventeenth-century Europe,[80] Karma Pakshi maintains that conflict among differing philosophical and religious doctrines must lead us to doubt and a suspension of judgment. In this case, however, that suspension provides an opening not for Christian faith, but precisely for a letting go of the limiting views and opinions that obstruct our realization of the liberating vision of the Buddhist enlightenment, as taught in the Great Seal and Great Perfection meditational precepts of the Kagyüpa and Nyingmapa traditions. If, then, I am reading Karma Pakshi correctly, doubt provides us with a pathway leading to realization, so that any tenet belonging to the trio of nonrealization, mistaken realization, or partial realization may legitimately become a point of departure for the pursuit of awakening. This approach to doctrine may be exemplified by Karma Pakshi's distinctive attitude towards other religions. While his views here are difficult to interpret precisely, they do appear to confirm my basic thesis. To see this we may turn to the *Bstan-pa rgya-mtsho mtha'-yas* (The Limitless Ocean of the Teaching), where, after making some standard assaults on the non-Buddhist *mu-tek-pa* (*mu-stegs-pa, tīrthika,* "extremist") positions, he continues:

> Birth in the *mu-tek-pa* family has not arisen without cause. Because the causes [for achieving circumstances favorable to enlightenment] are amassed, the *mu-tek-pa* paths tend towards the path, and their philosophical systems bring about a change of mind. One must not, then, disparage the *mu-tek-pas*. Again, they magnify the teaching, for the philosophical systems of *mu-tek-pa* teachers are said to be miraculous displays of the Conqueror. . . . *Mu* is the expanse itself, and *tek* is gnosis.[81]

It will be worthwhile now to inquire briefly into the sources of Karma Pakshi's inspiration. In the foregoing discussion we have several times met with a phrase that occurs often in the *Autobiographical Writings*, that is, the "trio of nonrealization, mistaken realization, and partial realization." It seems in fact to be drawn from a verse that we find repeated on numerous occasions throughout the *Limitless Ocean Cycle*, and that paraphrases a verse from the thirteenth chapter of the *Guhyagarbhatantra* (The Tantra of the Secret Nucleus), the foremost of the Nyingmapa tantras of the mahāyoga class.[82] The cryptic verse in question reads:

> Intention, discipline, and esotericism,
> Nonrealization and mistaken realization,
> Partial realization and not realizing what is genuine
> Give rise to doubts about this absolute![83]

According to the traditional exegesis of the *Secret Nucleus*, each of the terms in the first three lines refers specifically to one or another of the philosophical systems, or vehicles, that is ranked below the mahāyoga.[84] Before Karma Pakshi's age, the paṇḍita Rongzom Chöki Zangpo (eleventh century), in commenting upon Padmasambhava's *Man-ngag lta-ba'i phreng-ba* (The Garland of Views: An Esoteric Precept), had already utilized this passage as the framework for his analysis of the master's presentation of the various philosophical and spiritual systems.[85] Now, Karma Pakshi tells us:

> The words and meanings [of the verse just cited] have been amply set forth in verse in the *Limitless Ocean of the Teaching*. . . .[86]

As that work never attempts, in the available texts, a word-by-word exposition of the key verse, it is plausible to conclude that Karma Pakshi means here that the *Limitless Ocean of the Teaching* is in its *entirety* a revelation of the full implications of the one four-line mnemonic. But if this mnemonic provides some insight into Karma Pakshi's general approach as illustrated earlier with reference to the "extremist" *mu-tek-pa*, that is, his tendency to move from exposition through doubt to the triumphant assertion of the Great Perfection, still it does not reveal the source of his overall architechtonic. This, however, may be reasonably identified with the nine-yāna system of the Nyingmapa, above all as it is elaborated in connection with the exegesis of the anuyoga-tantras.[87] Karma Pakshi's extensive treatment of the anuyoga would in fact be noted by the Nyingmapa polemicist Sokdokpa Lodrö Gyeltshen (b. 1552),[88] and Karma Pakshi himself unequivocally states his opinion concerning the crucial role of the anuyoga as follows:

> Because the anuyoga is the general transmission of all the vehicles, all vehicles and philosophical systems are distinguished and established within the anuyoga. . . . Know that the anuyoga is like a vast ocean, in comparison with which all the other vehicles and philosophical systems are like rivers and streams. All vehicles are subsumed in the anuyoga. The utterly perfect fruit of anuyoga is the Great Perfection. . . .[89]

We may say summarily that Karma Pakshi's view of the general architecture of the path is derived from the *Mdo dgongs-pa 'dus-pa* (The Sūtra Gathering All Intentions) and other fundamental works of the anuyoga, that his treatment of specific systems seems to be grounded in the teachings of the *Secret Nucleus* and its exegetical tradition, belonging to the mahāyoga, and that the goal to which he seeks to guide us is that of the Great Perfection (*Rdzogs-pa-chen-po*, or *atiyoga*). In the *Limitless Ocean Cycle*, then, we have perhaps the grandest attempt, prior to the age of that crown jewel of Tibetan visionaries, Longchen Ramjampa (1308–1363; see chapter 9), to elaborate a syncretic approach to the Buddhist traditions of Tibet, one based upon the peculiar traditions of the Nyingmapa school.[90]

What of Karma Pakshi's Kagyüpa affiliations? Often he refers to himself as one who is blessed by the lineage of Nāropā,[91] Marpa's Indian teacher and the fountainhead of the Kagyüpa tradition; and the tantric transmissions of the new translation schools are considered at length in connection with the mahāyoga sections of the *Limitless Ocean Cycle*.[92] In the *Autobiographical Writings*, he insists, at one point, that the Great Perfection and the Great Seal differ only in name,[93] which no doubt accounts for Karma Chakme's references to Karma Pakshi as a precursor of Chakme's own synthetic teaching of the "coalescence of Great Seal and Great Perfection" (*phyag-rdzogs zung-'jug*).[94] Still, the thrust of the *Limitless Ocean Cycle* is without doubt Nyingmapa, a fact which may explain its extreme rarity even in Karma Kagyüpa circles. While Karma Pakshi certainly anticipates much of the later Kagyüpa/Nyingmapa eclecticism that in time came to pervade the various Kagyüpa lineages,[95] his actual impact on the later masters of these schools remains unclear.[96]

How are we to assess Karma Pakshi's contributions? What is certainly most distinctive about his thought is the robust skepticism we have seen presented in the *Limit-*

less Ocean of Tenets. Though skeptical arguments of many kinds were well known to Tibetan scholars, Karma Pakshi appears to have given much freer rein to this tendency than we find elsewhere, except perhaps in some of the tantras of the Great Perfection teaching, which must be counted among his major sources of inspiration. In his exceptional deployment of skeptical argument, he may perhaps be described in certain respects as an antischolastic. Nevertheless, I am inclined to hold that his doubts were less unusual than his manner of expressing them; for, though the contemplative traditions frequently employed informal skeptical arguments in connection with meditational training, their philosophical articulation tended to be cautiously restrained.[97] One result was that, although the tension between positive reason and skeptical doubt did impart a measure of impetus to the development of Tibetan Buddhist intellectual traditions, this tension seldom emerged so forcefully as it did in the writings of the second Karmapa. The dilemmas posed by the presence of strong skeptical undercurrents within the tradition were resolved in part, as we shall see emphasized in turning now to Dölpopa, by ensuring that one's reflections were securely anchored in the interpretation of scripture.

Dölpopa on the Age of Perfection

Reason and skepticism, which turns reason back against itself, though perhaps sometimes regarded as describing a binary opposition in the field of thought, by no means demarcate the full range of thought's varied ways. In Tibetan Buddhist writing, poetic and hermeneutical modes of reflection are also very well represented. The historical theories of Dölpopa offer a particularly remarkable example of hermeneutical reflection.[98]

To begin to place Dölpopa in the Tibetan world of the fourteenth century, and to understand his own world-making activity, which is reflected in his view of Buddhist history, we need to examine briefly some aspects of his life.[99] The biography included in the first volume of Dölpopa's collected works begins, indeed, with a series of accounts of his past lives, making it one of the documents of special interest for the study of the emergence of the characteristically Tibetan institution of emanational hierarchy (*sprul-sku*).[100] Like Karma Pakshi, Dölpopa regarded himself as the present instantiation of a being whose personal history spanned aeons. And again like the Karmapa, and several other major emanational lines in Tibet, including the Dalai Lamas, Dölpopa identified himself with Tibet's patron bodhisattva, Avalokiteśvara, and his Tibetan emanation in the form of King Songtsen Gampo. He thus was aligned with a cult that had already given cosmological meaning to Tibet in its relation with the Buddhist universe (see chapter 8). Dölpopa was further considered to have been the great Kagyüpa master Drigung Kyopa Jiktensumgön (1143–1217) in his preceding lifetime,[101] and like that master he was also identified with the Indian philosopher Nāgārjuna. Moreover, in the twenty-seventh of the rebirths listed, he had been Kalkī Puṇḍarīka, the "king of the clans" (*rigs-ldan*) of the kingdom of Shambhala, the guardian realm of Kālacakra, the Wheel of Time.[102] This will be seen below to be a detail of special significance. The biography of Dölpopa includes tales of thirty-two lifetimes in all, matching the number of the Buddha's major marks, and so representing the culmination of Dölpopa's course in the attainment of perfect buddhahood.

In its general features, Dölpopa's life story is not at all atypical; its pattern is entirely of a piece with the biographies of other leading lamas, in particular those of the fourteenth century. Born in the region of Dölpo, in what is today far northwestern Nepal,[103] he traveled as a young man to Central Tibet, where for a number of years he studied with one leading teacher after another in succession. His pursuit of Buddhist learning was wide-ranging and open: monastic discipline and the ethical path of the bodhisattva, epistemology and Madhyamaka philosophy, tantric and yogic instruction in a variety of lineages—all figure prominently among his studies. In his thirties, he arrived at the hermitage of Jonang to learn the esoteric teachings of the *Kālacakratantra* (The Tantra of the Wheel of Time) from the adept Yönten Gyamtsho (1260–1327),[104] and it was here that his quest found its end. He became the master's foremost disciple and lineage heir, and it was under Dölpopa's leadership that Jonang began to emerge as the center of a distinct sect and philosophical tradition. The memorial *caitya* that he constructed to honor his teacher became one of Tibet's celebrated religious monuments, graphically representing his vision of the Buddhist cosmos as a whole.[105] During his last thirty years, he taught widely throughout Central Tibet and Tsang, attracting a large following and leaving an enduring impression on Tibetan Buddhist practice and thought.

In some respects, this is the quintessential Tibetan "local boy makes good" story: a youth of humble origins, belonging to a religious family, goes forth to study widely and eventually becomes the disciple of some of the leading masters of his time.[106] Attaching himself to one lineage in particular, he becomes established as a prominent teacher in his own right, and his career begins to unfold as the actualization of the tradition to which he is heir, a cosmic event understood in its relation to a history spanning many lives, and embodying an entire cosmology. Where Dölpopa is perhaps a distinctive figure, if not an entirely unique one, is in the self-conscious determination with which he elaborated this enterprise, so as to generate an altogether distinctive material and doctrinal expression of it.[107] This is above all in evidence in the case of his foundation of the great memorial *caitya* for his teacher, a *caitya* designed as a grand embodiment of the universe with its myriad Buddhas, bodhisattvas, and tantric divinities. Dölpopa's own abundant writings about *caityas* make it entirely clear that he saw its construction as an event of transcending importance,[108] and it is of crucial significance that his distinctive teaching of "extrinsic emptiness" is said to have been proclaimed at this time.[109] Here, however, our chief concern will be the vision of historical time that his cosmic vision entailed.

Doxography and History

In the Indian and Tibetan traditions of Buddhist scholasticism, the study of the several doctrinal and philosophical approaches to the interpretation of the teaching was in large measure a matter of doxography.[110] The perspectives of texts and authors were allocated to distinctive "schools," whereupon the primary task for the doxographer became the characterization of the doctrines of the schools in question. Unremarkably, the doxographic approach tended to flatten out distinctions among authors allocated to a particular school and works attributed to a single author. It tended, too, to ignore history almost entirely. Without much exaggeration, we may say that, though Buddhist philosophy indeed had a history in India and Tibet, there was nevertheless no history of philosophy.

Figure 6.2 Dölpopa. A modern image at Se Monastery in Sichuan.

Or almost none. It is clear, for instance, that the authors of philosophical commentaries in Sanskrit often had knowledge of the earlier commentarial history of the texts with which they were concerned. That is to say, they knew, more or less, the chronological sequence in which the earlier commentaries were composed, and who it was that was refuting or defending whom. So, for instance, Candrakīrti on Buddhapālita and Bhāvaviveka.[111] But we may point, too, to other examples: Haribhadra's references to the earlier commentarial tradition of the *Abhisamayālaṃkāra* (The Ornament of Emergent Realization),[112] for example, or Yasomitra's to that of the *Abhidharmakośa* (The Treasury of the Meta-Doctrine).[113]

One of the contributions the Tibetans certainly made to the Indian traditions they inherited was to accentuate and elaborate the apparently thin historical elements found in Indian commentaries and doxographical writings. Despite the tendency within the monastic colleges to deprecate history as a frivolous distraction,[114] historical and legendary narratives were much loved by Tibetan authors, so that the frequent incorporations of hagiographical and historical elements within Tibetan exegetical writings is not at all surprising. For the most part, in Tibet as elsewhere in the Buddhist world, doctrinal history emphasized the succession of lineages, and here innovation and change were frequently effaced in an effort to establish authority by demonstrating the invariability of what had come down from the past.[115] No doubt, too, the great emphasis on lineage histories as sources of religious legitimation within the esoteric traditions of Tibet did much to encourage this tendency.[116] In some cases, particular currents in Buddhist philosophical thought became the subject matter for lineage history as well, and this perhaps influenced the doxographical literature: we may point to the fourteenth-century *Grub-mtha'* (Philosophical Systems) of Üpa Losel. Here, the first folios provide short accounts of the lives of the great Indian Buddhist philosophers—Nāgārjuna, Āryadeva, and others—drawing upon, for instance, the relevant prophetic verses of the *Mañjuśrīmūlatantra* (The Root Tantra of Mañjuśrī).[117]

Still, the incorporation in doxography of short hagiographical digressions is not what we generally mean when we speak of the history of philosophy. That we do not use this phrase univocally in our own intellectual community, and that history of philosophy in the West is indeed a contested category, has been well and concisely argued by Richard Rorty in an exceptional article entitled "The Historiography of Philosophy: Four Genres."[118] But in the present context, we may be excused if our usage remains a bit rougher than Rorty would countenance there: the history of philosophy may be understood generally as involving the conception that historical change and intellectual change are rather deeply interconnected, that historical time is not just a container in which ideas indifferently occur, like furnishings that may be rearranged anywhere in a room. There is a temporal order to the world, and the historical articulation of ideas reflects it.

Buddhist doctrine, in certain of its aspects, is certainly capable of harmonization with such a perspective.[119] The notion of the decline of the doctrine, for instance, correlated the degeneration of human life in several spheres with the corruption of views. The ramifications of this and allied conceptions were influential far beyond India, where they originated, and shaped East Asian Buddhism in important respects.[120] The belief that a particular scripture or doctrine was especially suited to a particular age was among its important entailments.[121] But this is not quite the same as the effort to read the earlier history of philosophy as a disclosure of the changing shape of lived time.

Now, there are a number of occasions where we do find Tibetan authors going beyond the mere superaddition of hagiography to doxography to suggest, at least, a more genuinely *historical* approach to Buddhist thought: notable in this regard is the work of Serdok Paṇchen Śākya Chokden (1428–1507), who authored important histories of both epistemology and Madhyamaka thought.[122] Gelukpa schoolmen, moreover, though coming from a tradition that generally discouraged the study of history, nevertheless did have opinions about the historical unfolding of the doctrine, which we find very well articulated in such writings as the introduction to the great *Grub-mtha' lhun-po mdzes-rgyan* (Philosophical Systems: The Ornament Beautifying the World Mountain) of Cangkya Rölpe Dorje (1717–1786).[123] Here, the doctrinal history of the teaching is depicted as a series of oscillations between brilliant articulations of the Buddha's intention, and the degeneration of understanding in the generations that followed each such disclosure, this cyclical process reaching its culmination, for the Tibetans at least, with the appearance of Je Rinpoche Tsongkhapa Lozang Trakpa (1357–1419). The repeated movement towards refinement of the doctrine, however, occurs in a contrapuntal relationship with a pattern of general decline, so that we arrive at the only apparently paradoxical conclusion that, as Cangkya writes:

Even as behavior has visibly spread
To new depths of degeneration,
Even now through [Je Rinpoche's] grace,
The secret of the Sage's words has not vanished.[124]

Dölpopa's Teaching and the Four Ages of the Doctrine

The Tibetan Buddhist school generally represented as standing in the most extreme opposition to the Gelukpa in matters of doctrinal interpretation, namely the Jonangpa, was also among those that elaborated a distinctive view of the history of the doctrine.[125] The controversial philosophical teachings of Dölpopa, the first great exponent of a distinctively Jonangpa viewpoint, have aroused growing interest among specialists in Tibetan and Buddhist Studies since Ruegg first described the doctrines of the Jonangpa school as they are reported in the *Grub-mtha' shel-gyi me-long* (The Crystal Mirror of Philosophical Systems) of Tuken Lozang Chöki Nyima (1737–1802) and so established the unique position of the Jonangpa tradition in Tibetan Buddhist thought.[126] The key doctrine of the absolute's "extrinsic emptiness" (*gzhan-stong*) with respect to superficial phenomena was there presented in some detail to contemporary students of Buddhist thought for the first time, though the perspective represented by Tuken was that of a determined opponent of the Jonangpa "heresy." More recent contributions have made it clear that the intellectual and spiritual legacy of Dölpopa has remained influential among the traditions of Tibetan Buddhism down to the present time, whether this be through the extreme antipathy to his views evinced by his philosophical opponents, or through the ongoing attempt to retrieve and reformulate what seem to be his most enduring insights.[127] An entry into his way of thought may be found in his interpretations of the Prajñāpāramitā, the perfection of wisdom, or discernment.

As we have seen in chapter 5 (p. 80), the *Sandhinirmocanasūtra* (The Sūtra Which Sets Free the [Buddha's] Intention) was invoked by scholars who held that the second of the Buddha's three "turns of the wheel of the doctrine" was a provisional teaching surpassed by the third and final turn, which alone was definitive and unsurpassed.[128] The paradigms of the second turn, however, are generally thought to be the Prajñāpāramitā Sūtras, and the most authoritative commentaries on their intention to be the Madhyamaka writings of Nāgārjuna. Like those who opposed his teaching, Dölpopa clearly regarded these to be in some sense definitive too. We may ask then how Dölpopa sought to resolve the apparent conflicts to which his position gave rise. This question, certainly, is of some importance: Tsongkhapa's decisive rejection of Dölpopa's approach to interpretation, and the formation of the Gelukpa commentarial tradition as one in many respects opposed to the Jonangpa, are among the issues that must be related directly to it.[129]

Dölpopa, though perhaps in some respects an eccentric interpreter, was not so overwhelmed by his own vision that he lost sight of the foremost objections that might be raised to it. Scattered throughout his writings are hints about how he thought these were to be met; on the question of the interpretation of the second turn of the wheel, a comment responding precisely to the line of criticism that Tsongkhapa would later refine and defend is found in his most famous work, the *Ri-chos nges-don rgya-mtsho* (Teachings for Mountain Retreat: The Ocean of Certainty):

> Some hold the [*Sandhinirmocana*]*sūtra* to be of provisional meaning, but this is unreasonable, for such has been neither declared [in scripture], nor is it established by reason, and therefore [the sūtra in question] is of definitive meaning and unobjectionable.
>
> It is objected, however, that, because the middle turn is Madhyamaka, and the last Mind Only, then it is the middle that remains of definitive meaning, while the last remains provisional.
>
> But this is most exceedingly unreasonable, because there is neither scriptural authority nor reason [establishing] the final turn to be the proper canon (*rang-gzhung*) of Mind Only, for its teaching surpasses Mind Only, and it teaches the culminating significance of the Great Madhyamaka, and teaches [this] in accord with the culminating significance of the Vajrayāna.[130]

It is clear why some such maneuver appealed to Dölpopa and other Tibetan proponents of similar positions; for sūtras typically considered paradigmatic of the third turn of the wheel, such as the *Laṅkāvatāra* and the *Gaṇḍavyūha*, do indeed teach much that surpasses Mind Only, at least given the relatively restricted perspective on that philosophical school that had come to dominate the doxographical literature. Indeed, these sūtras are not infrequently cited as authorities by major teachers of the Madhyamaka, like Candrakīrti and Śāntideva, and this was taken by Dölpopa and his adherents as providing some support for the conception of a "Great Madhyamaka" tradition surpassing the more widely known Madhyamaka philosophical schools, as understood, once again, according to the doxographical stereotypes.[131] Finally, but certainly not least, there were many in Tibet who held that the Vajrayāna, the way of mantra, was in crucial respects a "higher" teaching than that of the sūtras, and that the apparent affinities of the tantras with at least some of the sūtras of the third turn are more pronounced than with the sūtras of the middle turn.[132] But where does this leave the Prajñāpāramitā itself? Dölpopa's discussion continues:

> The second turn . . . is not taught to be of provisional meaning and surpassed, etc., for the reason that it teaches Prajñāpāramitā, but rather because it teaches that which is not intrinsically empty to be intrinsically empty, and for other such reasons. The Prajñāpāramitā that is unborn, unceasing, primordially pacific, etc., is taught in the third turn and in the Vajrayāna. But it is taught [in these three respective divisions of the teaching] unclearly, clearly, and exceedingly clearly. . . .

In short, Dölpopa suggests that the Prajñāpāramitā Sūtras, in their verbal form, do not always clearly articulate the teaching that is in fact their intention, namely, the teaching of the nucleus or inherent potential for buddhahood shared by all living beings, which is also known as nondual gnosis, the Great Seal, the enlightened mind in its absolute aspect, et cetera.[133] And this he identifies as well with emptiness, reality, Perfection of Discernment, and so on.[134] Dölpopa in this way combines the formulation of a qualitative gradation of the teaching with a type of esotericism:[135] the *Kālacakra Tantra*, for instance, is in many respects held to be superior to the *Aṣṭasāhasrikā Prajñāpāramitā* (The Eight Thousand–Line Perfection of Wisdom), but their essence is suffused with the same radiant light, which just shines more brightly in the former. And this, he goes on to say, is the culminating emptiness-cum-compassion, means-cum-wisdom, that is the coalescent union of bliss and emptiness, the sole savor; and this is also the sole savor of the union of the expanse (*dbyings, dhātu*) and awareness, in which the culminating abiding nature of reality, as noesis and noetic object, is one. Such is the real (*mtshan-nyid-pa*) Prajñāpāramitā, the culmination of the Prajñāpāramitā of the ground and the Prajñāpāramitā of the result, the quiddity of [their] indivisible essence. The path whereby it is disclosed and the canon which teaches these [topics under discussion] are only conventionally designated (*btags-pa-tsam*).

Dölpopa, however, does not provide us merely with such general and idealized accounts of the Prajñāpāramitā teaching; his view of Prajñāpāramitā is developed in impressive detail in four major commentaries and several short commentarial notes devoted to the Prajñāpāramitā literature. The most important of these works are a detailed commentary on the *Abhisamayālaṃkāra*, and separate commentaries on the *Aṣṭadaśasāhasrikā* (The Eighteen Thousand–Line Perfection of Wisdom), the *Pañcaviṃśatisāhasrikā* (The Twenty-five Thousand–Line Perfection of Wisdom), and the *Śatasāhasrikā* (The Hundred Thousand–Line Perfection of Wisdom).[136] While a preliminary survey of this material suggests that Dölpopa generally restrained his inclination to read his philosophy of extrinsic emptiness into these texts, nevertheless he does not hesitate to articulate it when remarking on those passages in which the relative "unclarity" of the Prajñāpāramitā sūtras seems to intimate the "clarity" of the sūtras of the third turn, or the "exceeding clarity" of the tantras. Thus, in a note on the sixth fascicule of the *Śatasāhasrikā* he writes that

> the absolute ground of emptiness is extrinsic emptiness, self-emergent gnosis, the changeless absolute, the nucleus of the [Buddha] who has fared well (*sugatagarbha, bde-bar gshegs-pa'i snying-po*), the Great Madhyamaka, the real Prajñāpāramitā and the culminating Secret Mantra. . . .[137]

And elsewhere, where it is a question of the innate virtue of all dharmas, "which being insubstantial are empty, naturally luminous (*rang-bzhin-gyis 'od-gsal-ba, prakṛtiprakāśa*), and therefore good (*dge-ba, kuśala*)," Dölpopa briefly enumerates the deities of the Kālacakra, Hevajra, and other maṇḍalas, who, like Rūpavajrā ("she who embodies the adamantine essence of form"), are taken to be apotheosized dharmas; for it is precisely the goodness of those dharmas, as disclosed in the Prajñāpāramitā, that is deified in the tantras.[138]

But how do Dölpopa's views about this relate to his peculiar views about Buddhist history? He offers some elements of his response to this question in a letter addressed to his disciples, in which he summarizes his views regarding a wide variety of particular topics:

> Relying upon the determination of the many exalted sources in which the Buddha, the Transcendent Lord, has definitively spoken, and on the autocommentaries that he has clearly spoken, I have had much to teach you that is profound and especially exalted, and generally causes the increase of discriminative intelligence. Concerning that, following the flawless doctrines and persons of the Kṛtayuga [the Perfect Age] endowed as they were with measureless qualities, there emerged, among the famous doctrines and persons of the Tretāyuga [the Third Age] and later ages, those that have had repute while being in fact untrue. So it is inappropriate to have confidence in them.

Now, then, it is well ascertained by pure scriptural authority and reason that the widespread assertion that the third wheel of the transmitted precepts is Mind Only is untrue. The *Mahāyānasūtrālaṃkāra* (The Ornament of Mahāyāna Sūtras) and all the other doctrines of Maitreya are ascertained to be texts of the Great Madhyamaka; the *Buddhāvataṃsaka* (The Bounteousness of the Buddha), the *Mahānirvāṇa* (The Great Decease), etc., that are renowned as the sūtras of Mind Only, are ascertained to be the sūtras of the Great Madhyamaka; and Ārya Asaṅga and his brother [Vasubandhu], and ācārya Dignāga, and others, many of whom are renowned as scholars of Mind Only, are also ascertained to be Mādhyamikas. This widespread assertion that they have commented on Madhyamaka in the manner of Mind Only is also ascertained to be untrue. . . .

It says in the *Sandhinirmocanasūtra*, among pronouncements of the Buddha, the Transcendent Lord: "Then the bodhisattva Paramārthasamudgata said to the Transcendent Lord, 'The Transcendent Lord has at first, in the land of Vārāṇasī in the Mṛgadrava at Ṛṣipatana, on behalf of those who had truly entered the vehicle of the pious attendants, turned the amazing and wonderful wheel of the doctrine teaching the four sublime truths, which had not been turned previously in accord with the doctrine by either any god or any man in the world. That turning of the wheel of doctrine by the Transcendent Lord is surpassed, contextually relative, of provisional meaning, and verbally debatable. Then, beginning with the phenomenal absence of essence, the Transcendent Lord has turned the second most amazing and wonderful wheel of the doctrine, speaking of emptiness on behalf of those who have truly entered the greater vehicle, taking as the point of departure the absence of production, the absence of cessation, primordial quiescence, and the natural, complete attainment of nirvāṇa. That turning of the wheel of doctrine by the Transcendent Lord is surpassed, contextually relative, of provisional meaning, and verbally debatable. Then, the Transcendent Lord, beginning with the phenomenal absence of essence, on behalf of those who have truly entered all vehicles, turned the exceedingly amazing and wonderful third wheel of the doctrine, which is endowed with excellent analysis. This turning of the wheel of doctrine by the Transcendent Lord is unsurpassed, not contextually relative, and of definitive meaning. It is not subject to verbal debate."[139] In these and other ways he has said that [the third turning of the wheel] is endowed with profound distinctions.

Ācārya Dharmamitra and others say that in this passage the middle transmission [referred to] is the Madhyamaka and is of provisional meaning, while the final transmission [referred to] is Mind Only and is of definitive meaning; and they call it a confusion to make [Madhyamaka,] which is not refuted by reason, into provisional meaning, and [Mind Only,] which is refuted, into definitive meaning. But in this case, their rebuttal is directed against the Buddha, the Transcendent Lord, and so will be regarded by believable witnesses as confusion compounded by confusion! For there can be none greater than the Buddha; and he has not taught the final [turning of] the wheel to be Mind Only; and both the middle and the final [transmissions] equally teach absence of essence, nonproduction, noncessation, original quiescence, and the complete nirvāṇa that is naturally attained; and it is a grotesque perversion to hold that he has said what he has not said, namely, that Madhyamaka is of provisional meaning while Mind Only is of definitive meaning. . . .

The intention is to distinguish intrinsic emptiness and extrinsic emptiness. Those who do not do so and say that it is all only intrinsic emptiness, and that emptiness is not determined in terms of extrinsic emptiness, but that only intrinsic emptiness determines emptiness, and maintain that all the [scriptural] statements that ultimately there is existence, permanence, self, purity, and truth are of provisional meaning, while all the statements of nonexistence, impermanence, nonself, impurity, and rottenness are of definitive meaning, and that the nine or twelve absolutes, the ultimate body of reality, the essential body, natural luminosity, natural coemergence, natural great bliss, the naturally innate, natural nirvāṇa, the natural and spontaneously achieved maṇḍala, and so on, as well as the natural abiding buddha-family (*gotra*) with its many classifications, the ultimate nucleus of the Tathāgata (*tathāgatagarbha*) endowed with many attributes, and so forth, are to be held with respect to reality but that reality itself is to be held as intrinsically empty—these and more are so many perverse views, coarse and bad views, without number. *All are to be dispelled by making a genuine witness of the scriptural authority and reason of the Kṛtayuga tradition.* Though there are many who adhere to the evidence of the Tretāyuga and later polluted and flawed scriptural authorities and reasons, these are in fact inappropriate as genuine witnesses. Therefore, do not follow in their path of error![140]

In these concluding sentences, Dölpopa invokes concisely his view of Buddhist history and its implications for Buddhist hermeneutics: he appears to have combined widespread beliefs regarding the decline of the doctrine with the notion of cosmic time, common to several Indian traditions, embodied in the scheme of four yuga, or world ages.[141] The task for the would-be interpreter of the Buddha's teaching, accordingly, is to recover the teaching of the Perfect Age, or Kṛtayuga (*Rdzogs-ldan*), and to shun the misunderstandings foisted upon the teaching by the mundane scholars of the Third Age, or Tretāyuga (*Gsum-ldan*), and later periods.[142] The principles according to which Dölpopa distinguishes among the ages of the doctrine have yet to be adequately determined on the basis of his writings, though my general impression is that in this regard he is primarily concerned with doxographical classification, allocating philosophical doctrines to "aeons" according to purely dogmatic, and not temporal, criteria. The closest Dölpopa ever seems to come to a clear articulation of his conception's general architecture is in his *Bka'-bsdus bzhi-pa'i don bstan-rtsis chen-po* (The Great Calculation of the Teaching, Whose Significance Is the Fourth Gathering of the Transmitted Doctrine).[143] In introducing this work, he writes:

The great four aeons concern the quality of the temporal kalpa,
And the lesser four aeons the quality of the teaching.
The first is in years four million,
Three hundred and forty thousand; its fourth part
Is called a "foot," and one, two,
Three, and four feet are, respectively, called
Kali, Dvāpara, Tretā and Kṛt.
As for the lesser four aeons, concerning the quality of the teaching,
Their duration is of 21,600 human years,
One-fourth of which provides the measure of each of the four aeons.

Faultless, endowed with all virtues, is the doctrine of the Kṛtayuga.
Then, when that fourth has passed, there is the "former" Tretā.
When half has passed, it becomes the "latter" Tretā.
The remainder when three-fourths has passed is Dvāpara,
And when not even one-fourth remains there is the Kaliyuga,
Said to be the evil doctrine of demons and of barbarians.

Having become well aware of these distinctions,
Desiring to purify and to cleanse the teaching,
To establish self and others on the excellent path,
The excellent doctrine of the Kṛtayuga should be accepted as one's sole witness.
The Tretā and what follows are flawed,
Their texts corrupted like milk in the market.
In no case should they be accepted as witnesses.
The superior refutes the inferior,
As superior philosophical systems refute their inferiors.[144]
The Kṛtayuga doctrine is the taintless transmission of the Conqueror,
That has been definitively spoken by the lords of the tenth bhūmi
And by the great, systematic path-breakers.[145]

It is not at all clear how Dölpopa wished to apply the four-aeon scheme to the actual historical interpretation of Buddhism, except through an aprioristic allocation of texts and commentators to aeons on the basis of the doctrines they upheld. Based on what we have seen already, what can be offered in the way of a preliminary statement of the theory's application is a brief list of some of the characteristic writings belonging to the Kṛtayuga doctrine, namely: the teachings transmitted by Śākyamuni himself and their "autocommentaries" (*rang-'grel*, by which Dölpopa seems to refer to those passages in the sūtras offering guides to interpretation); the doctrines of Maitreya; the writings of Nāgārjuna, Asaṅga, Vasubandhu, Dignāga, and perhaps several of the other great paṇḍitas of India. Ārya Vimuktisena, Haribhadra, and some of the other late scholastic masters are named as representing the teachings of the Tretāyuga.[146] Note, however, that they are not so classified owing to the late period in which they lived and worked; one of the last great paṇḍitas of Buddhism in India, Abhayākaragupta, seems certainly to have been considered by Dölpopa to have been a sage of the Kṛtayuga.[147] Significantly, too, Dölpopa persistently labels his own commentarial tradition the Kṛtayuga Tradition (*Rdzogs-ldan-lugs*).[148]

Sources of Inspiration

Where did Dölpopa get his ideas about the history of the doctrine, or were they, rather, the product of wholly unprecedented innovation? He himself answers this question for us:

> What I have said upon careful analysis, that "The greater and lesser four aeons," et cetera, may be found in the great commentary upon the Glorious Kālacakra.[149]

And this is just where one familiar with his work would have thought to look, even if Dölpopa had not mentioned it explicitly. But, we must ask, what does the "great commentary upon the Glorious Kālacakra," that is, the *Vimalaprabhā* (Taintless Light) commentary, in fact say that would support Dölpopa's viewpoint? The relevant passage, found in comments on verses 22–23 of the *Lokadhātupaṭala* (The Chapter on World Systems), proves to be highly suggestive but exceedingly thin:

> On the farther sides of Meru, the one who cannot be conquered by the demons or barbarians roams the earth where the religion of the Tathāgata has been destroyed and their perverse religion is current. In that terrain, the Cakrin roams, his practice during

> the Kaliyuga being irreligion. This is the significance of his "carrying the Kaliyuga." That, indeed, is the Kaliyuga whose nature is irreligion. In whatever region the religion of the barbarians is carried, in that region, especially, he travels. Having slaughtered in battle the barbarians and others, including the demons, he wanders, converting those before him to his own religion. Thus the "other" Kṛt, Tretā, and Dvāpara, and the ["other"] Kaliyuga proceed by connection with time. Here "other yuga," the Kṛt, etc., means that this is not the great Kṛtayuga, etc. This yuga proceeds by connection with time. Time is the circle of the zodiac. . . .
>
> In whichever part [of the earth] the Cakrin dwells in power, there proceeds the Kṛtayuga. The meaning here is that the doctrine of authentic and perfect Buddha (*Samyaksambuddhadharma*), which is called "Kṛtayuga," proceeds. . . .[150]

The essential framework, then, is indeed to be found just where Dölpopa has told us to look. In order to develop a view significantly similar to Dölpopa's on this basis, however, we would need to know just what the *Vimalaprabhā* regards the content of the "doctrine of authentic and perfect Buddha, which is called 'Kṛtayuga,'" to be, and about this that commentary is by no means clear, save to say that the doctrine of the Kālacakra Tantra itself must be at least part of what is intended. One further passage that may have inspired Dölpopa in this connection is the commentary on *Adhyātmapaṭala* (The Chapter of Inner Meaning), verses 161–179, in which a brief doxographical survey of Buddhism and some rival doctrines (including Islam) is to be found.[151] Significantly, verse 161 and its commentary describe emptiness (*śūnyatā*) as "not insentient" (*ajaḍa*, *bem-min*), a locution that would figure prominently in the arguments of the partisans of extrinsic emptiness (*gzhan-stong*), and of their occasional allies, the Kagyüpa Great Seal and Nyingmapa Great Perfection proponents. If it is correct to suppose that Dölpopa took what is in fact by and large a very general account of esoteric Mahāyāna philosophical doctrine, as is that offered in the *Adhyātmapaṭala*, to be a normative dogmatic tract supporting his identification of the philosophical quintessence of the Kṛtayuga doctrine with his own teaching of extrinsic emptiness, then the inspiration for his theory may in fact have been the *Vimalaprabhā* alone. And to this we must add that because in a past life he himself had been the noble king of Shambhala, Kalkī Puṇḍarīka, to whom the authorship of the *Vimalaprabhā* is attributed,[152] he could indeed claim that his teaching was that of the Perfect Aeon, according to the principle that "in whichever part [of the earth] the Cakrin dwells in power, there proceeds the Kṛtayuga."

The Problem of "Mind Only" and the Legacy of the Theory

Dölpopa's original contribution to the development of Buddhist thought in Tibet may be seen as an effort to elaborate an account of the actual content of the *Kālacakratantra's* "teaching of the golden age," philosophically, in terms of extrinsic emptiness and the doctrines allied to it, and hermeneutically, as we have seen, in terms of his classification of Indian Buddhist writings taken to represent that teaching. The picture of the historical degeneration of the doctrine that this involved suggested to Dölpopa, among other things, that the interpretation of the teachings of Maitreya, Asaṅga, and Vasubandhu as representing a Mind Only (*Sems-tsam*, *Cittamātra*) school was itself the product of that degeneration, and that, in conjunction with Nāgārjuna, the works of these thinkers should be interpreted as representative of the Great Madhyamaka teaching (*Dbu-ma-chen-po*).[153] It is this teaching, of course, that Dölpopa proposes to retrieve through the extrinsic emptiness doctrine. Dölpopa's suggestion raises, however, an unavoidable problem in doctrinal history, for just how are we to understand the position of what is called the Mind Only school in the light of the proposed redescription? I emphasize this problem not so much because it is significantly more prominent than others that Dölpopa entertained, but because it presents us with a particularly clear example of the ramifications of Dölpopa's theory for the writing of Buddhist history in Tibet.

In the letter to his disciples, parts of which we have examined here, Dölpopa has much to say about the relationship between the so-called Mind Only school and his theory of the four aeons of doctrine. There we have seen that he writes:

> Ārya Asaṅga and his brother [Vasubandhu], ācārya Dignāga, and others, [who] are renowned as scholars of Mind Only, are also ascertained to be Mādhyamikas. This widespread assertion that they have commented on Madhyamaka in the manner of Mind Only is also ascertained to be untrue. . . .

Later he develops his position as follows:

> Ācārya Haribhadra stated that,
>
> "Vasubandhu, the kinsman benefiting beings,
> Making his own inclination foremost,
> Explicated [the text], having rightly relied
> On the inwardness of the knowable."[154]
>
> As for the assertion, based upon this, that ācārya Vasubandhu is therefore [a proponent of] Mind Only and his textual commentaries are the texts of Mind Only—this is in fact completely untrue. If one thinks it to be true, then have him investigate carefully whether or not the most supreme commentary, the *Gnod-'joms* (The Defeater of Objections) and the autocommentaries that the Buddha, Transcendent Lord, has himself definitively spoken are in accord.[155]

Similar arguments are offered concerning Asaṅga and Dignāga. Dölpopa in effect reasoned that, because we know that Mind Only is manifestly not a correct view, and that Asaṅga, Vasubandhu, and Dignāga were teachers who held correct views, they could not have been proponents of the obviously false teaching of Mind Only. But Haribhadra, for instance, has attributed just that doctrine to Vasubandhu, which shows us that he did not clearly comprehend the teaching of the Kṛtayuga and therefore must be assigned to the belief system of a later, degenerate age. The so-called Mind Only school turns out on this account to be an interpretive mistake, the invention, not of Asaṅga and Vasubandhu, but of those who misread them.

Dölpopa's picture of Buddhist history was to have its own important legacy in Tibet and was to resurface, albeit in modified form, in later authors such as Tāranātha (1575–1634), Jamyang Khyentse Wangpo (1820–1892), and Jamgön Kongtrül Lodrö Thaye (1813–1899).[156] Perhaps most striking among the modifications we find in their works is an alteration in the story that is told to explain the philosophical embarrassment of Mind Only. A recent retelling may be found in the *Jo-nang chos-'byung* (The History of the Jonangpa Tradition), by Khenpo Lodrö Drakpa (1920–1975), who writes:

> Sometime after the three gatherings of the Hīnayāna transmissions were done, there came, moreover, about five hundred teachers of the doctrine, including the great and venerable Avitarka, who propounded the Mahāyāna doctrine. From various places they brought forth and then propogated many sūtras of the Mahāyāna [belonging to] the Mahāyāna Piṭaka, including the *Laṅkāvatāra*, the *Ghanavyūhasūtra*, and so on. From this arose the substantialist idealist tradition (*dngos smra-ba'i sems-tsam-lugs*) of the Mahāyāna school.[157]

The "great Madhyamaka" tradition only arises afterwards, thanks to the continuing disclosures of the definitive significance of the Mahāyāna by Saraha, Nāgārjuna, and Asaṅga. And Khenpo Lodrö Drakpa elsewhere specifies that, though the "substantialist idealist tradition" is known from later commentarial writings, the original treatises of Avitarka and his colleagues were never translated into Tibetan and so are no longer available.[158]

What are we to make of this tale? I am not certain where it in fact originates, or whether it was in circulation prior to the age of Tāranātha (1575–1634).[159] Apparently, Dölpopa knew nothing of it. To understand what may have motivated its acceptance, however, it must be noted that Dölpopa's assault on Haribhadra probably could not be sustained. Indeed, until Dölpopa's own extensive commentaries on the *Abhisamayālaṃkāra* have been thoroughly examined, we cannot even be certain that Dölpopa was entirely consistent on this score. However that may be, there can be no doubt that, given Haribhadra's great prestige for Tibetan commentators on the *Abhisamayālaṃkāra*,[160] and the widespread Indian doxographical evidence for a Mind Only tradition,[161] something better than Dölpopa's story about the supposed late commentarial misreading of Asaṅga and Vasubandhu was required if the historical vision of the Kṛtayuga tradition was to be maintained. Avitarka and the five hundred teachers were, I suspect, literally "made to order."

It was Gilbert Ryle who said of the history of philosophy in the West that "our standard histories of philosophy" were "calamity itself, and not the mere risk of it."[162] Richard Rorty, elaborating upon Ryle's thought in the article mentioned earlier, writes that

> awkward attempts to make a new question fit an old canon remind us . . . that new doxographies usually start off as fresh, brave, revisionist attempts to dispel the dullness of the previous doxographic tradition, attempts inspired by the conviction that the true problematic of philosophy has finally been discovered. So the real trouble with doxography is that it is a *half-hearted* attempt to tell a new story of intellectual progress by describing all texts in the light of recent discoveries. It is half-hearted because it lacks the courage to readjust the canon to suit the new discoveries.[163]

In part, Rorty's words appear apt for the case we have been considering, though, by the relatively conservative standards of Tibetan Buddhist scholasticism, Dölpopa and his successors may strike some as having remarkably sought "to readjust the canon," by however small a degree. That their efforts seem to us more successful in the delineation of a philosophical standpoint than in the revision of Buddhist historiography, however, discredits them no more than, as Rorty reminds us, the doxographic history of philosophy in other settings. We should not lose sight of the fact that, by making the history of Buddhist philosophy itself a field of contestation, Dölpopa may have to some degree actually encouraged the development of the traditions of Tibetan Buddhist historiography that flowered in the writings of his successors, Tāranātha above all.

Contestation and Self-representation

Those conversant with some of the varieties of Tibetan Buddhist discourse may object that I have loaded the dice in this chapter: though there are certainly important stylistic and substantive differences among doctrinal authors, they are not, by and large, so profoundly divided as the presentation here seems to suggest. With this I would agree. To illustrate the point, we may note that Sakya Paṇḍita, in writing on Madhyamaka philosophy, does countenance some place for skeptical argument,[164] while Karma Pakshi, as we know, wrote his own treatise on epistemology.[165] Dölpopa, for his part, was educated by and enjoyed warm relations with the successors of both and left his own mark on later Sakyapas and Kagyüpas.[166]

There can be no question but that the relationships among differing schools and approaches to doctrine were often fluid, and that Tibetan Buddhist thought permitted and sometimes even encouraged a remarkable degree of mutual exchange. Nevertheless, I am certain that anyone who has read these authors, among many others, with some care, cannot but conclude that, regardless of significant areas of overlap, there remain striking differences of approach and of content among them. The individuality of the major Tibetan thinkers is unmistakeable, whatever the difficulties involved in attempting to convey that difference through a non-Tibetan medium.[167]

In a polemical work written in the early nineteenth century, the great poet and mystic Zhabkar Tshokdruk Rangdröl (1781–1850), after reviewing some of the disputes that had erupted in the history of Buddhism in Tibet, concludes that if a dialectician is skillful enough, he may prove anything at all.[168] Indeed, in the monastic debate courts of Tibet, the ability to mount a successful defense for what was generally regarded as the weaker position was a much admired achievement.[169] It should be no surprise, then, that dialectical virtuosity could easily pass into sophistry. Argument alone was regarded in some circles with suspicion and seldom supplanted the authority of tradition when it came to matters of practice. In the world of Tibetan Buddhism, as for Indian religious traditions more generally, orthopraxy was crucial, orthodoxy less so. The famous claim of the Buddhist logicians that the only two valid criteria for knowledge were direct perception and inference tended to represent an ideal; a Buddhism of "reason alone" was never realized, except perhaps in the imaginations of small numbers of monk-scholars.

There are, however, other dimensions of intellectual contestation in the Tibetan world that in some respects may be of greater importance than the very interesting questions surrounding the soundness and validity of arguments. Janet Gyatso, in her fine recent study of the secret autobiographies of the "treasure-revealer" Jikme Lingpa

(1730–1798), examines in depth the general problem posed by the remarkable production of an abundant autobiographical literature in Tibet. Some of her conclusions warrant consideration here as well:

> Compelling reasons for self-assertion and distinction can be traced to the dawn of the hegemony of Buddhism in Tibet, which produced a competitive climate in which the personal accomplishments of the individual religious master became a centerpiece in the struggle to establish a lineage and eventually an institution and a power base. . . . The comparative absence of culture and traditional authority in the wake of the collapsed empire gave the individual religious entrepreneur considerable leeway for self-assertion . . . religious power and prestige were based upon ability and personal achievements.[170]

Something similar, I think, is at work in the articulations of doctrine we have been considering here. In the contest for authority within the Tibetan religious world, the crafting of a distinctive vision that at once established both the personal virtuosity of the author and his (or in rare cases, her)[171] mastery of what was sanctioned by tradition became a fundamental means of self-representation. This helps us to understand, for instance, the apparent paradox of Sakya Paṇḍita's *Eight Ego Poem*, which I have considered in greater detail elsewhere but which bears repetition here:

> *I* am the grammarian. *I* am the dialectician.
> Among vanquishers of sophists, peerless am *I*.
> *I* am learned in metrics. *I* stand alone in poetics.
> In explaining synonymics, unrivaled am *I*.
> *I* know celestial calculations. In exo- and esoteric science
> *I* have a discerning intellect equaled by none.
> Who can this be? Sakya alone!
> Other scholars are my reflected forms.[172]

We must recall that this bit of doggerel was authored by a prominent Buddhist monk, an exponent of the teaching of the selflessness of persons.

It is in this context, too, that we should also recall the assertion with which Karma Pakshi began his autobiography:

> I am Rangjung Dorje,
> The vajra-king, one of great might. . . .

Further, Dölpopa's identification with the kings of mythical Shambhala, and his tacit reliance on this identification as one of the warrants for his doctrinal speculations, must, I think, be seen in the same light.

This is not to say, of course, that reason and argument were wholly subservient to other interests, which they effectively masked. Doctrinal claims were only a single element in a larger field of contestation, in which many means of self-assertion might also be deployed. One result, which I have tried to illustrate in this chapter, was the great diversity and creativity of Tibetan Buddhist thinkers and visionaries, particularly prior to the fifteenth century, after which time the emerging dominance of the Gelukpa sect began gradually to narrow the range of scholastic thought.[173] As we shall see in the following chapter, however, there was still much left to debate, even under the Gelukpa's ascendant star.

7

The Purificatory Gem and Its Cleansing

A Late Polemical Discussion of Apocryphal Texts

Our Notions of Buddhist Canon and Apocrypha

When we first entertain the notion of Buddhist apocrypha, it may seem that the questions to be addressed are entirely straightforward ones: which Buddhist texts are to be considered apocryphal? what are their sources? how are they regarded within the Buddhist world? Indeed, it seems that such terms as "canon" and "apocrypha" have well-established and clearly defined positions within the field of contemporary Buddhist studies, and that as students of Buddhism we know just what it is of which we speak whenever we employ these terms.[1] Some scrutiny, however, reveals our usage to be equivocal: works termed "canonical" with reference to one traditional Buddhist context must be labeled "apocryphal" with reference to another, for instance, the entire corpus of Mahāyāna sūtras;[2] and texts that may be said to exemplify canonical scripture for the devotees of a given tradition are held to be apocryphal according to the canons of traditional or contemporary scholarship, for example, the Chinese *Śūraṃgama-sūtra* (The Sūtra of the Hero's March).[3] It is evident that for students of Buddhism the terms "canon" and "apocrypha" are not closely similar to the same terms used by, say, contemporary writers on Protestantism, who have well-defined sets of scripture in mind whenever they employ them. Thus, before proceeding to the main subject matter of this chapter—the problem of the revealed "treasures" (*gter-ma*) as treated in Tibetan polemical writings of the eighteenth century—we must first clarify the concepts we ourselves introduce into the discussion.

Let us begin with the notion of "canon." The term itself, with its meanings of "measure, model, norm, standard,"[4] is prima facie suggestive of our Buddhist term *sūtra*—"thread, measuring line, plan, aphoristic rule"[5]—and by extension carries some of the import with which Buddhists endow the terms *buddhavacana* ("Buddha-speech"), *buddhabhāṣita* ("spoken by the Buddha"), and *saddharma* ("True Dharma"). What a given Buddhist community considers to be *buddhavacana*, et cetera, is what, or at least is part of what, we would say it holds to be canonical, that is to say, representative of the ultimate scriptural authority to which it adheres. The important point to note is that "being canonical" is here not a one-term predicate of which the variable term is a given literary corpus, as it is in the sentence "The Pali Tipiṭaka is canonical." Rather it is a two-term predicate of which the relata are a literary corpus on the one hand and a religious community on the other, as in "The Pali Tipiṭaka *is canonical for* Theravāda Buddhists." When an individual representing a given religious community employs the concept of canonicity, or some analogous concept, he usually does intend the one-term predicate, as when, for instance, a Thera argues for the unique authenticity of the Pali Tipiṭaka, and the inauthenticity of other Buddhist scriptural collections. He is saying, in effect, that canonicity is a property uniquely exemplified by the Pali Tipiṭaka. But this is not how contemporary scholars in the field of Buddhist Studies usually employ the concept. We instead intend the two-term relationship "being canonical for," as it is only in this way that we can avoid absurdity in our discussions of the various canons: Pali, Tibetan, Chinese, and so on. In this sense, we may surely speak of the Mahāyāna sūtras in general, or the Chinese *Śūraṃgama-sūtra* in particular, as canonical texts, whatever may be decided regarding their origins.[6]

Our second key term is "apocrypha." As used in contemporary Buddhist Studies circles, this word often seems to mean "a text or group of texts regarded as canonical within some Buddhist community, but whose origins are somehow other than they are supposed to be."[7] It is in this sense that we may speak of the Mahāyāna sūtras as apocryphal. As such, a text is called "apocryphal" not so much in virtue of its being so regarded within the tradition in whose scripture it is found, but rather in virtue of the scholar's judgement. If we ride this concept of apocrypha too hard, we may find ourselves left with very little Buddhist scripture that we can unequivocally hold to be nonapocryphal. Like the pilgrims of *The Journey to the West*, we may arrive at the end of our search to discover only blank scrolls where we thought we would uncover the Buddha's original teaching. The whole notion of Buddhist Apocrypha thus becomes too meaningless to be of scientific value, though it may still be of use in the formulation of a new koan, to be used in the instruction of those among us whose philological meanderings have led them far from the true path.

The use of the term "apocrypha" to refer only to supposed inauthenticity of origin is, of course, in some respects dissimilar to its use in Jewish and Christian contexts, in which, after all, the concept evolved. Schneemelcher, for instance, considers New Testament Apocrypha to be "writings which have not been received into the canon, but which by title and other statements lay claim to be in the same class with the writings of the canon. . . ."[8] Most of what we regard as Buddhist Apocrypha are, on the other hand, texts that have indeed been "received into the canon" of one Buddhist tradition or another. The traditions that cast doubts upon their authenticity often discount them altogether as worthless deception.[9] In short, it is not at all evident that there is any such thing as "Buddhist Apocrypha," if by that we mean to refer to a scriptural corpus that plays a role within some given Buddhist community analogous to that played by the apocryphal literature of the Jewish and Christian traditions. A close approximation would be the "spiritual treasures" (*gter-ma*) of the Tibetan Nyingmapa tradition, extracanonical works that are regarded by their adherents as having a quasi-canonical status and by their opponents as being pseudepigraphical and anathematic. So there may be some similarity here with the *bíbloi apókryphoi* of the Gnostics.[10] The analogy, however, is not sufficiently strong to provide a basis for the regular use of the phrase "Buddhist Apocrypha" except in the sense first defined, that which refers to texts whose origins, when scrutinized from a philological standpoint, are deemed suspect. As such, there would appear to be no harm in retaining the phrase, so long as we maintain a cautious awareness that it embodies certain concepts that we may impute to traditional Buddhist discourse but that may not be truly represented therein.[11]

In the light of the foregoing remarks it can be said that this chapter concerns the problem of canonicity as conceived by two Gelukpa polemicists, and in particular their opinions of apocryphal traditions. At issue are their views regarding which textual traditions are to be taken as embodying the ideal norms or standards of Buddhist religious discourse and which are to be seen as failing to embody those ideals owing to supposed inauthenticity of origin. No attempt will be made here to establish a normative concept of the Tibetan Buddhist canon to which to relate the opinions of these authors; my only concern will be to elucidate those opinions and the reasons for which they were held. Before addressing this directly, however, it will be necessary to summarize some of the important elements of the canonicity debate that the Tibetans borrowed from India, and that inform the broadsides of Sumpa Khenpo Yeshe Peljor (1704–1787) and Thuken Chöki Dorje (1737–1802).

Realism, Idealism, and Scriptural Authenticity

The early schools of Buddhism may be characterized as having sought to embrace, in varying ways and to varying degrees, a naive metaphysical realism. Apparent wholes were to be analyzed into their parts, but the parts were real. Moreover, there was a strong tendency to temporal realism running throughout the abhidharma literature and made fully explicit in the Sarvāstivāda school and its branches. The world was thus constituted for the early traditions much as it is for the untutored imagination, that is, of real things obtaining at determinate locations in space and time. Adhering to such a view, we should want *buddhavacana*, the Buddha's utterances, to be just that, the actual speech sounds produced at given places and times by Śākyamuni himself. There is some reason to believe that the early schools did, in fact, wish to affirm such a view.[12]

Disregarding, however, the question of how consistently the assertion that the realistic orientation of early Buddhism carried over into its historical presuppositions can be maintained, it is certain that this was just what was asserted by thinkers within the Tibetan scholastic traditions. Sabzang Mati Paṇchen (1294–1376), perhaps the greatest Tibetan Sanskritist of the fourteenth century, for instance, while commenting on *Bodhicaryāvatāra*, chapter nine, verse 42, expounds the position of the *śrāvakas* as follows:

> The *śrāvakas* say: "[T]hose texts of the Mahāyāna are not the declarations spoken by the Buddha, because they were not heard by the great *śrāvakas* who were always in the [Buddha Śākyamuni's] following when he dwelt in the locations spoken of in the *Mahāvibhāṣa*:
>
> > 'The site of the doctrinal wheel, Vaiśālī,
> > Pāṇḍara, the realm of the gods. . . .'"[13]

The rigid adherence to such a view, if unqualified in any way, has the undesirable entailment that *buddhavacana*, in the strict and literal sense, came into being with the first turning of the wheel at Ṛṣipatana and ceased to be with the *parinirvāṇa* at Kuśinagarī. Hence, in the strict and literal sense, there has been no authentic *buddhavacana* in the world since the Buddha's decease. There is no evidence to suggest, however, that anyone within the Buddhist tradition ever actually held such a rigid position; the view must be softened in order to admit into the class of *buddhavacana* not the spatiotemporally determinate speech acts of Śākyamuni alone, but all speech acts and written symbols that are in some sense the same as the speech acts of the Buddha himself. The problem is: in just what sense?

The various attempts to define suitable criteria whereby *buddhavacana* might be distinguished from its opposites have been surveyed in some detail by R. M. Davidson in his fine article on this topic and so need not be repeated here.[14] The definitions elaborated for this purpose, depending as they do on concepts of consensus, doctrinal content, accord with manifest reality, and so on, all involve a weakening of the view suggested by a strict historical realism. That the early schools indeed departed from that view was well known to learned Tibetan circles through, for instance, Vasubandhu's assertion that to say that a text handed down in all the other *nikāyas* (here referring to the early Buddhist orders) and contradicting neither sūtra nor reality is not *buddhavacana*, merely because one's own *nikāya* does not recite it, is mere recklessness.[15]

Buddhavacana then can be recognized owing to the coherence of a certain body of tradition and doctrine, and owing to the coherence of these with the way the world happens to be, as is revealed to us in immediate experience. While this view suggests a modification of the realist position, it does not yet constitute a complete abandonment of realism; for the concepts of *buddhavacana* consisting of the actual speech acts of the Buddha and of its being a coherent body of texts as determined by certain patterns of consensus and the fulfillment of explicit doctrinal criteria are in no way to be taken as contradictory, but must be seen to be complementary. The claim that must be made in order to assert without absurdity that the former is *buddhavacana* in the strict and literal sense while the latter is *buddhavacana* nonetheless is simply that the textual traditions held to represent the authentic teaching of the Buddha are systematically correlated to the speech acts of Śākyamuni. The various attempts to define criteria for *buddhavacana* may thus be seen as efforts to pinpoint the relevant systematic correlations. These efforts failed in part, no doubt, because the exclusively oral transmission of the dharma during the first centuries of the Buddhist era precluded there being any simple and straightforward set of verifiable correlations.[16] And a critique of oral tradition in the manner of that suggested by early Greek historiography was unthinkable, for that would have involved tacitly acknowledging (though here perhaps falsely) that very little reliable could be known of the Buddha's teaching.[17]

Tibetan scholasticism inherited from this state of affairs the full tension between the impulse to affirm that in fact there was some set of determinate correlations linking the original *buddhavacana* to its present instances, and the impossibility of ever discovering decisively what these correlations might be. For this reason, as will be seen, it was never successful in its attempts to elaborate from the standpoint of a historical realism a satisfactory set of criteria for scriptural authenticity. In addition to the conflicts inherent in the realist approaches to canonicity, however, the Tibetans also derived several alternative orientations, all involving the rejection of the earlier realism.

Confronted with the defects of the early criteria, one possible reaction was simply to adopt those criteria for one's own purposes, while ignoring their historical presuppositions. The concepts of accord with sūtras and with perceived reality, et cetera, were sufficiently imprecise to be applied not only to the scriptures of the eighteen schools, but to the Mahāyāna scriptures as well. The step half taken in the *nikāyas* can now be completed, namely, to turn the question of scriptural authenticity from a historical problem into a hermeneutical one, as do the *Mahāyānasūtrālaṃkara* (Ornament of the Mahāyāna sūtras) and Śāntideva's *Bodhicaryāvatāra*.[18] Still, this need not involve an unqualified rejection of the realist position. Indeed, a realist reading of the relevant texts places in high relief the conclusion that, though it may seem strange to certain modern sensibilities, figured prominently in Mahāyāna attitudes to scripture throughout Central and East Asia right down to the present day: any text meeting the normative doctrinal criteria for *buddhavacana* must be genuine *buddhavacana* taught by the historical Buddha Śākyamuni himself.[19]

Another reaction to the problem, inspired by the luxuriant cosmologies, idealist metaphysics, and numinous buddhology of the Mahāyāna sūtras of the "third turning of the wheel," in particular, involved a complete overthrow of the realist program. This approach, already apparent in the *Ghanavyūhasūtra* (Sūtra of the Dense Array) and others among those discussed by Davidson,[20] influenced Tibetan thought above all through the exquisite teaching of the *Ratnagotravibhāga* (Discrimination of the [Three] Jewels and the Family [of Buddha-Nature]), which elaborates a theory of Buddha-activity, inclusive of the Buddha's speech, in which the Conqueror figures, for all intents and purposes, as the first principle and final cause of the spiritual lives of all beings.[21] For fortunate beings hear the Buddha's message without any effort on the part of the Sage himself, like the spheres that revolve through the effortless agency of the unmoved mover:

> Just as among the gods,
> perforce of the gods' ancient virtues,
> Without effort, locus, intellectual form,
> or conceptualization,
> The carefree gods are repeatedly roused
> by the drumbeat of the doctrine,
> With a proclamation of impermanence and pain,
> of selflessness and of peace;
> Just so it is that the Lord
> without effort embraces all beings
> With the speech of the Buddha and teaches
> the doctrine to those of good fortune.
> As the divine drumbeat among the gods,
> is born from their own actions,
> So the Sage's spoken doctrine among worldlings
> is born from their own actions.[22]

In the predominantly idealist milieu in which we now find ourselves, some criteria are still required in order to distinguish *buddhavacana* from whatever happens to come to mind. This problem, however, is a purely hermeneutical one. The manner in which it was treated is best indicated by an oft quoted verse from the *Ratnagotravibhāga*, the author of which, one fancies, must have greatly enjoyed turning the diction of the classical *śrāvakayāna* to such good use:

> Meaningful speech, associated with doctrinal phrases,
> Causing abandonment of the three realms' utter defilement,
> And demonstrating the advantages of peace:
> Such is the ṛṣi's speech; others are its opposites.[23]

In one sense, then, *buddhavacana* is exactly what we always imagined it to have been; only its metaphysical ground and etiology are regarded differently. In Tibet, the line of speculation represented here found its richest expression in the works of Dölpopa and his successors, the proponents of the extrinsic emptiness (*gzhan-stong*) of the absolute. Aspects of these developments have been considered in the preceding chapter; their peculiar implications for the question of scriptural authenticity may be illustrated by the virtually Platonic view of the Buddha's speech (one wonders if *lógos* might not be the better word to use here) propounded by Jamgön Kongtrül Lodrö Thaye (1813–1899/1900):

> If one examines such a text [in this case the *Ratnagotravibhāga*] carefully, there are three [aspects of it]: (1) first, it is the self-manifest speech-resonance of the Buddha, the absolute aspect of the Mahāyāna sūtras which is included within the nondual cognition that has arisen as all things—as such it is essentially identical with what is naturally pure, or the body of reality (*dharmakāya*) that results from separation [from fortuitous obscuration]; (2) second, it is the Mahāyāna sūtra endowed with groups of words, phrases, and phonemes that has arisen in the minds of exalted and ordinary persons in the form of universal expressions; and (3) third, it is the words and phrases uttered in conformity with that, which are termed the text, the sūtra or tantra of the definitive meaning of the Mahāyāna. These last two are essentially completely different from the trio of nature, fruit, and path; but they have arisen from the aspirations of Buddhas, substantially accord with the body of reality, and have the power to bring about the abandonment of the two obscurations. Therefore, know them to be included among the uncorrupted principles (*anāsravadharma*), the utterly refined objectives (*vaiyavadānikālambana*), and the entirely real (*pariniṣpanna*).[24]

The Purificatory Gem and Its Cleansing: Historical Background

By 1782, in which year Sumpa Khenpo authored the *Gsung-rab rnam-dag chu'i dri-ma sel-byed nor-bu ke-ta-ka* (The Purificatory Gem Which Removes Filth from the Pure Water of Scripture)[25] and Thuken penned his reply, entitled *Nor-bu ke-ta-ka'i byi-dor* (The Cleansing of the Purificatory Gem),[26] the question of scriptural authenticity had been debated in Tibet, with various degrees of acrimony, for the better part of a millenium. The problem had some of its roots, for the Tibetans as for the Chinese, in the fact that Indian Buddhism, especially the Mahāyāna and Vajrayāna schools, had never redacted a closed canon: it was well known, for instance, that the

Kālacakratantra, a work of much authority in Tibet following the promulgation there of its great commentary the *Vimalaprabhā* (Taintless Light), an event traditionally dated to 1027, had only made its appearance in India half a century before and yet was widely regarded as an authentic tantra.[27] Was one to adopt the extreme conclusion that anything claiming authenticity as a Buddhist scripture was to be so received without question?

The first occasion for the Tibetans to discuss these issues explicitly came as early as the closing years of the eighth century, when Indian Buddhism vied with Chinese Buddhist schools for spiritual paramouncy in Tibet.[28] It seems likely that, although the Indians had never formulated a closed canon, thinkers of such stature as Śāntarakṣita (fl. mid–eighth century) and his disciple Kamalaśīla, once engaged in the conversion of a non-Indian people, took a profound interest in just what notions of *buddhadharma* were being spread abroad.[29] In the end, the result, as we have seen, was the resolution attributed to the king Trhi Songdetsen (r. 755–797) to recognize Indian Buddhism uniquely to be the genuine article, a decision ironically like that taken in China itself in sorting out the difficulties surrounding the proliferation in that land of a great many "spurious" sūtras.[30] Of course, this solution to the problem was no solution at all: the criterion of Indian origin found no support in the sūtras and tantras of bona fide Indian origin, and no basis for the critical appraisal of possibly spurious Indian works could be derived from it. It should not surprise us then to discover, as we did in chapter 5, that there were Tibetan Buddhists who simply ignored this decision and continued to study eclectically traditions stemming from both India and China.

It was the restoration of monastic Buddhism in western Tibet, from the late tenth century onwards, that provided the ground for the next great eruption of controversy over matters of authenticity. Samten Karmay, in a series of important articles, has begun to assemble the materials needed for a thorough documentation of the sporadic debates of the period, known as that of the "later spread of the Teaching" (*bstan-pa phyi-dar*).[31] Two issues figure prominently in the known polemics: under the broad mantle of Vajrayāna, morally repugnant practices were spreading among the Tibetans; and many of the texts that were finding favor were suspected of being Tibetan forgeries rather than authentic Indian Buddhist works. It is the second of these issues that is of interest to us here.

Under fire were works teaching the Great Perfection doctrine and a miscellaneous assortment of Vajrayāna texts supposed to have been transmitted in Tibet during the imperial period, but now seemingly unknown in India. The situation became increasingly complex from the eleventh century onwards with the appearance of "spiritual treasure" (*gter-ma*), texts said to have been concealed by Padmasambhava and other ancient masters and now rediscovered for the timely edification of receptive individuals. Tibetan Buddhist masters adopted a whole range of positions with respect to such texts: some, not desiring to be burdened with the sin of blaspheming the Dharma, wished to affirm the authenticity of all that seemed to have some spiritual value; others, seeking to gain the merit of revealing false paths to be false, urged the rejection of any and all questionable works; and still others preferred to adopt a middle position, accepting some among the contested scriptures while rejecting others. As Tibetan sectarian trends ossified, from the twelfth through the seventeenth centuries, the first of these three positions came to characterize the Nyingmapa school and its sympathizers, the second became predominant among the Gelukpas and the Ngorpa branch of the Sakyapa school, and the middle positions came to be occupied primarily by the various Kagyüpa lineages and by the remaining Sakyapa traditions.[32] The formulation of standard polemical defenses for the position taken by one's own school and assaults on the positions of others went hand in hand with the formulation of the great scholastic commentarial traditions, and the leading polemicists are in most cases famed exegetes: Sakya Paṇḍita Künga Gyeltshen (1182–1251),[33] Comden Rikpei Reldri (fl. 1311–1320),[34] Butön Rinchendrub (1290–1364),[35] Longchen Rabjampa Drime Özer (1308–1363),[36] Terchen Ratna Lingpa (1403–1478),[37] Serdok Paṇchen Shākya Chokden (1428–1507),[38] Gorampa Sonam Sengge (1429–1489),[39] Karmapa VIII Mikyö Dorje (1507–1554),[40] and Sokdokpa Lodrö Gyeltshen (b. 1552)[41] being foremost among them. It is quite certain that there has been little, if any, methodological refinement in the contributions to the debate made by writers following the age of the figure last mentioned. The polemics of recent decades differ in few significant features from those of three centuries ago,[42] and, owing perhaps to its growing anachronism, recent sectarian invective often seems coarser than the debates of previous generations. This is no doubt due in part to the heightened political factiousness of Tibetans in the wake of the disaster of 1959, and all that has since followed.[43] Prior to the twentieth century, Tibet never seems to have produced an analogue to the Japanese thinker Tominaga Nakamoto (1715–1746), one who would shake the fundamental presuppositions of the entire scriptural authenticity question and in so doing open the way for the emergence of a new scholarship.[44]

In the light of these considerations, I have chosen the debate between Sumpa Khenpo and Thuken Rinpoche as a paradigmatic case. Coming relatively late, it illustrates both the content and the method of the traditional problem and its traditional solutions in all their main aspects, and, at the same time, it represents a scholasticism that has not yet died the death of stagnation. Also governing my choice is the fact that Tibetanists have previously called attention to facets of Sumpa Khenpo's polemic and in so doing have, I think, sometimes misinterpreted both its intent and its method. I shall return to this last point below.

The Texts and Why They Were Written

Sumpa Khenpo's *Purificatory Gem* is a product of the author's old age. It was written when he was in his seventy-ninth year[45] and xylographically published immediately thereafter under the author's supervision.[46] The first Western scholar to have called attention to it appears to have been A. I. Vostrikov, who describes it as a "small but highly interesting critical and bibliographical work"[47] and evidently found it most valuable, to judge from his many references to it.[48] More recently, Ariane Macdonald, Samten Karmay, and Eva Dargyay have all referred to Sumpa Khenpo's polemical writings—usually not to the work under consideration here but to passages from his *Dpag-bsam ljon-bzang* (The Wishing Tree, his history of Buddhism)—which are, in any case, similar in content to parts of the *Purificatory Gem*.[49]

The ostensible purpose of the *Purificatory Gem* is to distinguish between authentic and inauthentic scripture (*gsung-rab dag-ma-dag*).[50] The reasons for undertaking this exercise are firmly grounded in Buddhist soteriology:

> An intelligent person who carefully examines what is or is not the Conqueror's declaration, doing so with a mind subtle in respect to word and meaning owing to [the knowledge of] scriptural authority and reason, correctly distinguishes between the authentic and the inauthentic. Having done this, he rejects those which are inauthentic and adulterated and doubtful, and he honors, respects, worships, and praises even a small volume of authentic scripture. If he strives to listen to, read, recite, write, publish, and teach to others its words, and to cultivate meditatively its meaning for himself, he will easily attain all perfect spiritual and temporal goals.[51]

Accordingly, the main portions of Sumpa Khenpo's work are devoted to the consideration of what constitutes authentic Scripture,[52] and what inauthentic.[53] The second, much longer, part has three subsections, each questioning the authenticity of various texts: several contained in the *Gzungs-'dus* (Collected Dhāraṇīs), a popular scriptural collection;[54] the three-volume selection of tantras of the Nyingmapa school that is appended to the Kanjur;[55] and sundry texts including *gter-ma* and the works of the Bonpo tradition (900.7–904.1). The critique of inauthentic scripture then closes with a final summary and statement of conclusions.[56]

In contrast to the *Purificatory Gem*, Thuken's *Cleansing of the Purificatory Gem* has been overlooked in the Tibetological literature. It was composed, according to the colophon,[57] by Dharmavajra (= Chos-kyi-rdo-rje) in 1782 in response to the tract of his own guru, Sumpa Khenpo, and constitutes virtually a point-by-point critique of that work. It was most unusual in Tibet to launch a broadside against one's own master, and Thuken goes to obvious pains to excuse himself.[58] The irregularity of a work of this type, however, coupled with the fact that it is not to be found in Thuken's published *Collected Works*,[59] may lead to the suspicion that the *Cleansing of the Purificatory Gem* is a forgery. Nonetheless, there can be little doubt that in this case the attribution is a true one: this is not the sole instance in which he showed strong interest in traditions subject to the disapproval of some segments of Gelukpa orthodoxy.[60] There is really no aspect of the *Cleansing of the Purificatory Gem*, whether of style or of content, that strikes one as being too inconsistent with Thuken's known literary work. While it was cited in polemical writings in Amdo no later than the middle part of the nineteenth century, there seems to be no instance of any polemicist denying its authorship.[61] Finally, it should not be forgotten that Thuken was undoubtedly something of a Nyingmapa sympathizer.[62] This, however, only partially accounts for his decision to criticize the *Purificatory Gem* of Sumpa Khenpo. To understand the underlying difference of outlook between master and disciple in this case, we must look to the political circumstances that contributed to the shaping of their respective careers.

Sumpa Khenpo, as a young Gelukpa monastic scholar and official in Central Tibet beginning in the mid-1720s, was intimately familiar with the civil upheavals of the early eighteenth century.[63] The strife had its immediate roots in the sectarian-cum-regional rivalries of the preceding century, whose outcome had been decided primarily through the intercession of the Khoshot Mongols on behalf of the Gelukpas and their patrons in the central province of Ü, united under the leadership of the Fifth Dalai Lama. In the wake of the rule of the Great Fifth, Ngawang Lozang Gyamtsho (1617–1682), and of his regent Desi Sanggye Gyamtsho (1653–1705), the embers of factionalism burst into flame once more. In 1717 the Mongols of the Dzungar tribe took full advantage of the situation: they looted and plundered the monasteries of the Gelukpas' opponents and even murdered a number of leading hierarchs.[64] All of this was certainly deplorable, but for one of Sumpa Khenpo's background—he was, after all, a Monguor tribesman who in his early twenties had been a student at Gomang College, seat of the Dzungars' guru, Lozang Phüntshok—the Dzungars had merely helped the Tibetans do what they could not do themselves, namely, put their own house in order.[65] Though Sumpa's later years were to be spent enjoying the fruits of the Manchu-Gelukpa alliance, his formative years were thus spent in the crucible of bitter sectarian conflict, so that, for all his intellectual gifts and real curiosity, he was probably never capable of regarding sects other than his own from a truly unbiased perspective.[66]

Thuken, on the other hand, had a rather different experience, in which Central Tibet and its affairs were not to figure as the determining influences on his development overall. Like his teacher, he was a native of Amdo, and one of Tibetanized Mongol ancestry, too. But Lhasa was not the political center that drew him into its orbit.[67] Peking was. In this, he had more in common with another of his masters, the great Cangkya II Rölpe Dorje (1717–1786), than with Sumpa. He was one of a generation of clergymen from Amdo whose spiritual loyalties were unmistakably Gelukpa, but who allied themselves politically with the Qing court.[68] The worldview of these churchmen bore a strange resemblence to that of medieval Latin Christendom, with the Manchus filling the role of Imperial Rome and the Gelukpa hierarchy that of the Catholic Church. These were not the products of a denomination under fire but rather represented the synthesis of a peerless salvific vehicle with a universal temporal order. Not personally threatened by the Central Tibetan feuds, they could afford to regard the situation there only with equanimous compassion. Their intellectual curiosity could be given free rein to explore their own and other traditions impartially. Within their own domains, they were capable of regarding adherents of the other schools of Tibetan Buddhism with paternal kindness. Considering this and considering, too, that among the Amdo laity the Nyingmapa and Bönpo traditions commanded great devotion indeed,[69] the motivation underlying the *Cleansing of the Purificatory Gem* becomes clear: Thuken wishes his flock to know that his master's rhetoric represents merely the sectarian sympathies of an earlier generation that have no longer any useful role to play, and that he, for one, will not stand for a rebirth of intolerance and hostility among them. This, at any rate, is what we must take Thuken to mean when he tells us that one reason he is challenging Sumpa Khenpo is to insure that "contemporary persons who prattle without understanding what is essential will not come to amass sinful deeds in the name of the doctrine."[70] That Thuken does impute a measure of bigotry to his teacher is confirmed by his assertion that Sumpa Khenpo's purpose in writing the *Purificatory Gem* was "to obstruct the way of those persons who desire liberation on the basis of some rites of the Nyingmapa and Bönpo, which are widespread in these parts."[71]

It appears, then, that in addition to the conceptual parameters described earlier in this chapter, another set of factors restricted the scope of the traditional Tibetan discussion of canonicity, namely, political and sectarian convictions.[72] For this if for no other reason, the traditional scholarship, despite its excellent achievements in elaborating the Buddhist scholastic curricula, was incapable of giving rise to a wholly critical method of textual research analogous to that which developed in the West after the Renaissance. To see just what was at stake we must now review the arguments presented in the texts themselves.

The Question of Spiritual Treasures

What constitutes authentic scripture? We have seen that the various Buddhist traditions elaborated a whole range of answers to this question. The answer supplied by Sumpa Khenpo in the *Purificatory Gem* involves a curious mixture of themes that represent no single source in particular. He begins:

> Each and every aspect of what was spoken in a single instant in Jambudvīpa by the Transcendent Lord of the Ikṣvāku clan bestowed on numberless fortunate beings in need of training a limitless mass of doctrine. Among what remained [of that mass], at the time of the third council that which was retained in the minds of those of infallible retention was set down in writing. Most was preserved in the three doctrinal spires of Nālandā monastery, and, though most of that was damaged when later enemies thrice threatened the teaching, some part of what remained was translated in earlier and later times into Tibetan by translators who were like the eyes of the snowy land. That is what is renowned as the Kanjur.[73]

This account probably has to be read as elliptical for the detailed narratives of the emergence of the doctrine found in, for instance, Sumpa's own *History*.[74] What is remarkable is his assertion that, on the one hand, every aspect of the Buddha's speech refracted in unlimited ways among those who heard the Sage, but that, on the other, only a limited, determinate number of such refractions that are "utterly pure, unadulterated by later fools,"[75] are available to us today, that is, that the canon is a closed one. To know which texts belong to that canon, he continues, we must study the descriptive catalogues prepared at the order of the ancient kings or under the authority of the patrons of the various editions of the Kanjur and repeat the titles recorded therein.[76] Among the many catalogues, the one compiled by Butön is to be regarded as particularly useful for this purpose, as is the briefer inventory found in Khedrub Je's (1385–1438) *Rgyud-sde spyi-rnam* (General Dissertation on the Tantras).[77]

What this seems to amount to is an argument from authority: the authoritative doctrinal histories and textual catalogues alone tell us what is authentic. Sumpa Khenpo never raises the question of why it is that we are to accept this or that particular history or catalogue as being authoritative, and so he never answers it. Having made clear just who his authorities are, there is apparently no need to justify his preferences, beyond an appeal to Gelukpa orthodoxy. With the contents of the canon thus established, we may turn to the rejection of apocryphal traditions.

Of the three main catagories of suspect text with which Sumpa Khenpo is concerned, the treasures (*gter-ma*) fall into the very last. Before reviewing his argument for their rejection, it must be said in all fairness that, from a critical point of view, this is not the best section of the *Purificatory Gem*. Its interest is to be found in its subject matter, rather than in the virtues of the argument. Sumpa's finest argumentation, however, occurs in his attempt to identify spurious texts in the *Collected Dhāraṇīs*. It is there that he proceeds on a case-by-case basis, noting specific features of vocabulary and style that he thinks count against the authenticity of those texts. While his effort is certainly flawed, it does reveal the author's intention to elaborate precise, philologically significant criteria for scriptural authenticity. This in itself was no mean achievement and must be taken into account in assessing Sumpa Khenpo's contribution overall.[78]

Sumpa's critique of "spiritual treasures" (*gter-ma*) is already well known to Tibetologists through Vostrikov's work.[79] The essence of the argument is as follows:

> Though there appears to be no report that the mahāsiddha Padmasambhava composed many śāstras in the snowy land when he arrived at the time of the first building of Tibet's Samye temple, even if the so-called *Padma thang-yig* (The Testimonial Record of Padmasambhava)[80] and *Thang-yig sde-lnga* (The Five Testimonial Records)[81] happened [to be written] at that time I have doubts as to whether or not there are corruptions in their present texts. Moreover, it is easy to tell that they [i.e., Padmasambhava and the other masters of the imperial period] did not compose even a fraction of the many current "ancient doctrines" (*rnying-chos*) which cover the snowy land, including the *Maṇi bka'-'bum* (Maṇi Kambum),[82] *Bar-do thos-grol* (The Liberation-by-Hearing in the Intermediate State),[83] and the *Nyes-pa kun-sel* (The Removal of All Ills), *Rnga-sgra* (The Drumbeat), *Ngan-sngags phyir-bzlog 'khor-lo* (The Discus Repelling Evil Spells), and others which are found in the aforementioned *Collected Dhāraṇīs*.[84] Those "ancient doctrines" were later attributed to Orgyen Padma[sambhava] and, moreover, the famed "transmitted precepts" (*bka'-ma*) and "spiritual treasures" (*gter-ma*) were composed by numerous frauds, who mixed them with some words of the Conqueror as they wished. Any learned person who looks at them can know this easily.[85]

It is of course the case that, with reference to some of the texts mentioned, contemporary Tibetologists have arrived at much the same conclusion as did Sumpa Khenpo.[86] But we should not lose sight of the fact that scholarship consists not of merely arriving at conclusions, but also of justifying them. Sumpa Khenpo doubts the authenticity of the *Testimonial Record of Padmasambhava* and of the *Maṇi Kambum*, but never does he give us a detailed and critical account of his reasons for harboring those doubts. This being so, the correctness of his position is anything but self-evident. Given that he wishes his readers not merely to question the historical credentials of the popular works concerned, but to reject them spiritually as well, it should be no cause for astonishment that his opinion here met fierce opposition. Thuken's rebuttal is a classic defense of the entire Tibetan revelatory tradition:

> Again, in the *Purificatory Gem* a general declaration is made, beginning, "whatever are well known as 'profound doctrines, authoritatively sealed' (*zab-chos bka'-rgya-can*), 'earth doctrines' (*sa-chos*), 'stone doctrines' (*rdo-chos*), 'celestial doctrines' (*gnam-chos*), and 'treasure doctrines' (*gter-chos*), have been forged by deceitful frauds. . . ." [and ending:] "[O]ne must not unhesitatingly take up whatever one runs into, be it pure or impure, as a hungry dog takes up whatever it runs into, be it edible or inedible."[87]
>
> To this we pray to respond: "profound doctines, authoritatively sealed" are common to the Gelukpa, Sakyapa, and Kagyüpa. Because there are a great many profound doctrines which have been authoritatively sealed by the Conqueror Vajradhāra himself, I believe your declaration leads to great absurdity.[88]
>
> If all "celestial doctrines" were forgeries, nonetheless the *Dpang-skong phyag-rgya* (The Gesture of Contrition, *T* 267), a celestial doctine which fell from the heavens in the time of Lha-tho-tho-ri, is classified in your text as being pure.[89] Now, if the prime example of that which is defined as a "celestial doctrine" is classed as pure, then, were you to seek for a century, you would not find some other impure celestial doctrine.[90]

The appellations "earth doctrine" and "stone doctrine" are not familiar to anyone. There are those said to be "drawn forth from the earth" and "drawn forth from the rocks," but, as they are all "treasure doctrines," there is no need to discuss them separately. It is not certain that they were all forged by frauds, for there is a prophetic declaration in the *Mañjuśrīmūlatantra* (The Root Tantra of Mañjuśrī, *T* 543):

> Afterwards at that time
> A bhikṣu known as an arhat. . .
> Will by great austerities bring forth
> At that time, from a vase,
> Sūtras of the Mahāyāna,
> Which I had expounded in the past.
> Having studied that volume,
> He will recite such mantras. . . .[91]

Just so, the tale of the bhikṣu famed as an arhat, who brought forth from an auspicious vase whatever doctrines, including sūtras, he desired, and then attained practical experience of them, is found in many doctrinal histories. In the *Damomūrkhasūtra* (The Sūtra of the Wise and the Foolish, *T* 341), too, a tale appears in which a householder brings forth from his home's pillar a ritual describing the eightfold fast.

For those who are fortunate, the nectar of the true doctrine will emerge even from earth, stone, mountain, or rock; for it says in the *Sarvapuṇyasañcayasamādhi-sūtra* (The Sūtra of Concentration Which Gathers All Merits, *T* 134):

> O! Vimalatejas! those bodhisattvas, mahāsattvas who desire the doctrine, and who are endowed with a respectful and perfect attitude, though they dwell even in other world systems, even then will the Buddhas, transcendent lords, reveal their countenances to them, and they will hear the doctrine as well. O! Vimalatejas! there are doctrinal treasures for bodhisattvas, mahāsattvas desirous of the doctrine, which have been secreted in mountains, ravines, and woods. Dhāraṇīs and limitless doctrinal gates which have been made into volumes will also come into their hands.[92]

It is a bit coarse to declare that all treasure-doctrines were perpetrated by frauds. Not only the Nyingmapa, but all the Indian and Tibetan schools (*grub-mtha'*) have them. As examples: the tantras of Pacification (*Zhi-byed*) were brought forth by Phadampa from the Charnel Ground of Delight in the Glorious Tantric Cycles;[93] the *Mahāmāyatantra* (The Tantra of Great Illusion) was revealed in the land of Oḍḍiyāṇa by Kukuripa;[94] [the precepts of] the stage of perfection (*rdzogs-rim*) [entitled] *Rlung-sems dbyer-med* (The Indivisible Union of Vital Energy and Mind) were revealed by Marpa in Vajrāsana;[95] the *Seng-gdong sgrub-skor* (Cycle for the Attainment of Siṃhamukhā) was revealed by Guru Vajrāsana-pāda and by Bari Lotsāwa from beneath a yaklike boulder to the east of Vajrāsana;[96] some of the *Kurukulla'i sgrub-skor* (Cycles for the Attainment of Kurukullā) were revealed by the Lama Shenyen Lotsāwa, to whom Tārā had prophetically declared that they were to be found within the teat [of an image] of Devī Dhūmavatī to the north of Vajrāsana;[97] the *Lha-sa'i dkar-chag* (Guidebook to Lhasa) was revealed by Atiśa at the "vase-pillar" (*kwa-ba bum-pa-can*);[98] some cycles concerning beneficial and harmful rites (*phan-gnod las-tshogs*), which were in the "leaf-pillar" (*kwa-ba shing-lo-can*), "serpent-headed pillar" (*sbrul-mgo-can*), and "lion-headed pillar" (*seng-mgo-can*) were revealed to some extent by both Lama Zhang and Joden Könchok-trak;[99] the *Ro-snyoms skor-drug* (Six Cycles of the Even Savor) were concealed by Rechungpa in accord with the prophetic declaration of Tiphupa and then later extracted from their treasury by the lord of beings Tsangpa Gyare;[100] the *Sems-khrid yid-bzhin nor-bu* (Wish-Granting Gem of Psychological Guidance) was concealed as a treasure in the Black Maṇḍal Lake[101] by the venerable master Dakpo Rinpoche (Gampopa) and his disciple Kyebu Yeshe Dorje, and it was extracted from its treasury by Dungtsho Repa Rinchen Zangpo of the Dakpo lineage;[102] some of the *Rnam-sras-kyi sgrub-skor* (Cycles for the Attainment of Vaiśravaṇa) were revealed at Vulture Valley by Nyelwa Nyima Sherap;[103] and the *Putra ming-sring-gi sgrub-skor* (Cycle for the Attainment of Putra, Brother and Sister) were extracted from Samye by Lhatsün Changchup-ö.[104]

Even among our own virtuous sect,[105] Gyüchen Sanggye Gyamtsho revealed some rites of Dharmarāja (*Chos-rgyal-gyi las-tshogs*), which had been concealed as treasures in the shrine of the protectors (*mgon-khang*) of Segyü (*Sre-rgyud*) by Dülnakpa Pelden Zangpo,[106] and even the all-knowing Jamyang Zhepa seems to have intended to acquire the prophetic declaration (*lung-bstan*) and treasure-sacraments (*gter-rdzas*) of Macik in accord with a prophecy from a treasure (*gter-lung*).[107] In a dream which came to Trhichen Ngawang Chokdenpa, he received, from the venerable and great Tsongkhapa, who appeared about fifteen years of age, wearing garments of fine silk (*rgya-ras*), an injunction concerning the existence of some treasures which were to be revealed atop the stūpa at Changcup monastery (*Byang-chub dgon-pa*), but because the Khri-chen never traveled to the eastern provinces (*Mdo-khams*), the opportunity to obtain the treasures did not come about.[108]

Moreover, it says in the *Dam-chos mchog-gi rgyud* (The Tantra of the Supreme Holy Doctrine, unidentified):

O! Vajrapāṇi! may you bring forth
From treasure after treasure
All of the tantras and kingly tantras.

Thus, there would seem to be no purpose [in asserting] that all treasure-doctrines are Nyingmapa doctrines, or that all revealers of treasure-doctrines are deceitful frauds.[109]

Thuken's most powerful arguments against Sumpa Khenpo are clearly those that involve widely accepted counterexamples (for instance, that of the *Gesture of Contrition*) or those that are ad hominem (for instance, the arguments concerning revelations within the Gelukpa sect). There can be no doubt that from a strictly formal point of view he is entirely correct here: Sumpa Khenpo does condemn works that meet just the same criteria as certain widely accepted "canonical texts," and his own position requires him to assert the validity of traditions that do not meet those criteria. The problem for the latter is that he seems to lean towards the affirmation of a conception of canon based on a historical view similar to that of early Buddhism, but imperfectly adhered to. The result is that he allows the canonicity of works that, from the perspective of the traditional scholarship, cannot be satisfactorily distinguished from works he wishes to exclude from the canon.

I remarked earlier that it seemed that the references to Sumpa Khenpo's polemic found in the Tibetological literature suggest some misinterpretation of his intent and method. It is clear that there has been some temptation to characterize Sumpa's work as "critical scholarship," suggesting that it reveals some affinity with the text critical scholarship that has flourished in the West since the Enlightenment. Unquestionably, the analogy can be a misleading one, for Sumpa's biases did not allow him to develop a methodology that he could apply relatively impartially to the entire mass of scripture with which he was familiar: critical scholarship bears solely upon the works of his enemies. More satisfactory Western analogies to the Tibetan debates on scriptural authenticity might be found in the medieval polemics exchanged among Jewish, Christian, and Muslim thinkers,[110] although Sumpa Khenpo and his predecessors and contemporaries did certainly refine their discussions of textual traditions to a degree that in the West is more characteristic of the late Middle Ages, perhaps, for instance, the work of Nicholas of Cusa.[111] If this analogy is appropriate, then it would seem that while the Tibetan discussions of canon and apocrypha never succeeded in resolving the many difficulties inherited from the Indian tradition, they did represent the beginnings of the development of a consciousness of text-critical issues and, as such, merit careful attention. If a critical tradition similar to that of the post-Rennaissance West never blossomed, one reason can perhaps be seen in the ancient rejection of the historical realism that is methodologically required for historical philology (even if in the end it is to be overturned), and the concomitant failure to determine suitable criteria for the historical authenticity of the Buddha's word.

The apocryphal traditions of Tibetan Buddhism—the traditions whose historical credentials seemed dubious, but whose spiritual credentials seemed to some, at least, impeccable—occupied an uneasy position between two opposing tendencies: the tendency to anathematize and the tendency to canonize. The former was supported by elements of a realistic historical orientation, but above all by the conviction that the canon was closed and that its contents were known. The latter, by contrast, drew its strength from the belief that the canon could be held to be closed only on pain of self-contradiction, and from a fundamentally idealist vision of the Buddhist world. The rift was intensified, finally, by purely political considerations whose perverse alchemy transformed the gold of religious vision into the base metal of violent sectarianism. Once this had occurred, the conditions favoring the further development of a critical approach to the problems surrounding scriptural authenticity were lost, for the disputants' stakes were now too high to permit reasonably impartial and progressive scholarship. As will be seen in the following chapter, one well-known traditional scholar, the great historian and tantric master Tāranātha (1575–1634), did articulate the possibility of establishing something approximating a middle ground here, by affirming that while at least some of the treasures were genuinely based upon early materials, they were at the same time, nevertheless, elaborated by their "discoverers." In this formulation alone do we find the possibility of an alternative to the aporia of unimpeachable authenticity versus willful fraud.

During the mid-1980s, I expected that we would soon see new developments in traditional approaches to these matters, catalyzed by the encounter with contemporary methodologies of textual criticism. I could not have anticipated, however, that European and American scholars of Tibetan Buddhism would find themselves defending or condemning the "treasures" in a manner that closely recapitulates the polarities of the old Tibetan disputes.[112] In this regard, an interesting paradox comes to light in the late Michael Aris's important contribution to the discussion, *Hidden*

Treasures and Secret Lives, and points directly, I think, to the heart of the problem. Aris, who considered the famous Bhutanese treasure-finder Pemalingpa (1450–1521) to have been clearly a charlatan, writes:

> There is a peculiar reluctance on the part of many modern scholars to recognize the entirely fabricated nature of the Tibetan "treasure-texts." It is as if their enthusiasm for things Tibetan and Himalayan has blinded them to an obvious truth. There is no evidence whatsoever to support the claim that any of the "rediscovered" texts actually date from the period claimed for them. . . .
>
> To recognize that the whole cult depended on conscious pretence and fraud does not mean that we should therefore take an unsympathetic view of its prime members or of its ultimate purpose. . . . Apart from Pemalingpa's endearingly human weaknesses . . . there is the undoubted fact that his activities as a whole greatly enriched the cultural and spiritual life of his homeland and the regions beyond. The texts he produced, the dances he composed and the works of art he commissioned are among the real cultural treasures of Bhutan to this day. Moreover, if on the one hand the authenticity which is claimed for the origin of these treasures is entirely suspect, on the other hand and on a different level surely they carry their own authenticity as the genuine product of an inspired and highly imaginative character, rogue though he was.[113]

It is the apparent paradox of the fraud who is nonetheless genuinely inspired, and so becomes a *real* creator of culture, that interests me here. The question that we must ask, I think, is not so much whether the "treasures" were real or fake, but rather why it was that, in traditional Tibet, creativity so often masked itself as the retrieval of the past. Of course, this is not an entirely novel phenomenon in the history of highly conservative religious traditions: the elaboration of the Hermetic corpus, the formation of the Kabbalistic scriptures and above all of the Zohar, the revelations that contributed to the creation of the Taoist canon, and perhaps also the establishment of the Mormon faith—all suggest parallel developments in a wide range of religious cultures.

A variety of factors may be variously at work in these differing settings. In all cases, the authoritative weight of the past, the conception that paradigmatic excellence is to be found in antiquity and that history is a system of entropy encourage a valuation of retrieval over invention or progressive discovery. In some cases, too, there is perhaps a need felt to reassert past tradition in the face of foreign novelty, while at the same time selectively appropriating what is novel and alien under the description of what is native and past: Taoism in its relation to the advent of Buddhism in China, and the older traditions of Tibetan Buddhism and Bön in their relation to the post-tenth century influx of new teachings from India may be seen in this way.

I suspect as well that the argument of Plato's *Meno* has been tacitly presupposed more often than its explicit occurrences would lead us to believe. There, let us recall, Socrates' questioning leads the untutored slave boy Meno to articulate a geometric proof, and so the philosopher demonstrates to his interlocutors that, prior to this lifetime, knowledge of geometry had somehow been impressed upon Meno's soul. According to such reasoning, the knowing or creative individual must have been previously exposed to what he now knows or makes, and the same argument must of course be true in the first person: if I find myself to be endowed with some talent, it can only be because I acquired it long ago. Given the Buddhist affirmation of rebirth, and the special force it acquired in Tibet, it becomes axiomatic that "authenticity as the genuine product of an inspired and highly imaginative character" and "the authenticity which is claimed for the origin of these treasures" cannot be entirely different, even if a present act of manufacture is involved. The argument may appear to us to be sophistical, but this is just because we really don't buy into the concept of rebirth, and our culture's understanding and evaluation of individual creativity are so radically unlike traditional Tibetan conceptions.

We must fundamentally rethink, therefore, the problem of the rediscovered treasures in the history of Tibetan religions. The treasures are not exactly what they pretend to be, and yet they flow inexorably from the depths of the Tibetan cultural and religious system. Every discovery is also a memory. The treasures are exactly what they pretend to be.

PART III

MYTH, MEMORY, REVELATION

8

The Imaginal Persistence of the Empire

Even a man who is fond of myths is in a way a philosopher, since a myth is made up of wonders.
Aristotle, *Metaphysics*, I.2.

The Truth of Myth

Throughout this book I have steered a shifting course, tacking between systematic and narrative thought,[1] or, to put it differently, between philosophy and myth. In this final section I shall follow the same route once again, beginning in this and the following chapter with some of the mythic aspects of the rediscovered treasures and related texts, but turning later to aspects of systematic thought which they embody as well.

The relationship between philosophical and mythic modes of thought often seems problematic, and one may feel that the question "What is the relationship between philosophy and myth?" if not actually ill formed, is somehow fishy.[2] That there does sometimes appear to be a peculiar relationship between myth and philosophical or scientific reason, however, is underscored when we turn to some now generally discredited theories of myth, for instance, Sir James Frazer's view that myth is "false science." Many, probably most, contemporary folklorists would insist that, regardless of the actual truth or falsehood of a myth, assuming that to be capable of determination even in principle, the community in which a myth is transmitted traditionally regards it to be in some sense true. Given Frazer's assumptions, we can only conclude that myths are false explanations that are nonetheless taken to be true, for if they were thought to be false they would no longer be myths. Indeed, this explains quite well a very common use of the term "myth" in contemporary English: for instance, if one says, "It's a myth that you can get AIDS from a handshake."[3]

While Frazer's view of myth as false explanation is no longer much adhered to by those who make it their business to specialize in the study of myth, there are nevertheless two points made in this connection that I think should be underscored here: first, that what we term "myth" may often have a special relationship to reason, above all to reasoned explanation, that neither legend nor folktale generally has; second, that we should attend carefully to the question of the truth-value of myths. An additional point that I shall seek to emphasize in this and the following chapters relates to the common characterization of myths as narratives concerned with sacred history.

In its explanatory dimension, myth engages reason by disclosing as intelligible what had otherwise seemed mysterious, and by motivating appropriate human behavior in the light of what is thus explained, at least whenever the proper ordering of human agency is part of the mystery to be made intelligible, as it is in many important myths. For example, what we may term the "myth of our technological hubris" tells a certain community of believers among us that the mystery of much human misery may be understood with reference to humanity's overreaching itself and sacrificing an essential, vitalizing harmony with nature in the course of a self-defeating and obsessive drive to attain control of nature. Apart from the truth or falsehood of any particular claims advanced in this connection, the believer may assert that, in the light of this myth, much of human misery is revealed to be an intelligible phenomenon, and so he or she may be motivated to contribute to the alleviation of suffering by assisting in the effort to refrain from and limit our abuse of nature through technology. This, in turn, may or may not require that the believer master certain specific information about history or physical science.[4]

The same points might just as well be made with reference to traditional myth narratives. Consider, for example, one of the myths that is told in connection with the cult of Bhāṭbhaṭinī, a deified minstrel couple widely worshipped by the Newars of the Kathmandu Valley in Nepal:

> Bhaṭinī, like Hāritī, had a taste for human flesh. But Viṣṇu, by means of Garuḍa, seized one of Bhaṭinī's own beloved brood, restoring it only on the ogress' promise to foreswear human flesh and to become instead a protector of children. It is apparently in this role that the blessing of Bhāṭbhaṭinī is invoked by parents of children thought to be bewitched or to be suffering from mental or physical disease.[5]

So long as there is a community affirming the authority of this myth, its members will continue to propitiate the minstrel couple to alleviate the illnesses of their children, and they will do so reasonably so long as the myth is not falsified for them in practice, as it might be if *they* were to conclude, for instance, that recovery of health was notably less likely for children of Bhāṭbhaṭinī worshipers than among the children of other Kathmandu Newars. But this would likely be the case only if their worship precluded their recourse to other treatment, whereas in fact it may just as well motivate the search for alternatives; the discovery of the right doctor may be taken as a token of the deity's blessing no less than a miracle cure.

Reflection upon such relationships between mythic explanation and motivated action further calls into question the truth of myths. It may seem that in a certain sense this shows truth to be essentially irrelevant here, that the open-ended potentialities for artful interpretation render myth unfalsifiable. The myths that a given community considers authoritative need not be thought to be true in the sense that they convey demonstrably true "factual" information: mythic matters seem to be more subtle than the facts of the matter, so that the truth in myth may be thought to be expressed allegorically, metaphorically or approximatively; or myth may be thought just to orient us towards truth so buried in mystery that no human discourse can disclose it directly. The truth in myth is thus conceived as veiled and obscure truth, and this, of course, reinforces for some the conclusion that myths somehow stand outside of the domain of truth-value altogether.

That conclusion, however, I believe to be wrong. For myth-truth, while not factual truth, is perhaps allied to pragmatic truth in something approaching a Jamesian sense.[6] A myth is felt to be true whenever it functions in the discourse of a community to ground action that is itself felt to bring about the success of that community, or of its individual members. It may thus be said to be true to the extent that it is felt by those who yield to its authority to promote ends that are not self-defeating. This is very well illustrated by some aspects of the recent disputes within the Tibetan community concerning the status of the protective divinity Dorje Shugden, whose cult the Dalai Lama in recent years has sought to ban.[7]

Among the members of the Tibetan business community in Kathmandu, Dorje Shugden is widely propitiated as a divine bestower of wealth. Because Tibetans in Kathmandu have in fact flourished during the past couple of decades, growing rich through success in the tourist and crafts-export trades, the Dalai Lama's calls to abandon the Shugden cult have caused no small degree of consternation: the deity, after all, appears to be promoting the ends for which he is propitiated. The Dalai Lama, however, regarding matters from a clerical perspective, is more focused upon the role of Shugden as a militantly sectarian protector of the Gelukpa order, and the harm that has been done to Tibetan sectarian relations by the cult's more vociferous proponents. As sectarian strife appears to undermine the interests of the Tibetan community at large, the Dalai Lama and those who perceive the issue as he does have concluded that the cult is now a self-defeating one, and that it should therefore be set aside. This, of course, leaves some of the businesspeople who are supporters of the Dalai Lama in a position of inner conflict: their loyalty to their leader requires them to obey him, but at the same time, because they have prospered while worshiping Shugden, they find it difficult to accept that this practice has been in any sense self-defeating.

Because it is probably impossible to remove the determination of human ends and their successful fulfillment entirely from the domain of appearances, myth-truth cannot itself be more than a matter of seeming, but to say this is not to say that truth-value is irrelevant here; for the possibility of self-defeat entails that a myth may be in the course of a community's history revealed to be false to the very community that, at an earlier time, had affirmed it. And, as we have now seen, if differing factions within the same community arrive at opposing conclusions about this, the assessment of myth may become a cause for sharp division.

The truth of myth, then, is essentially tied to a community's history, and successful mythmakers may be said to know this. For even when, as is the case of the materials we shall examine in chapters 9 and 10, the time in which the events narrated in myth stand outside of historical time, it is nonetheless historical and lived time—whether some of its particular features or the whole thereof—that is explained and interpreted through myth. Myth is in this respect metahistorical discourse and so may sometimes emerge as a powerful medium for philosophical and scientific thought: consider here the myths of the state of nature and the social contract in political philosophy since Hobbes, or that of the primal horde in the thought of Freud.[8]

Myths, therefore, engage our thinking in reason, truth, and history, and so they express and constitute the thinker's vision of these domains, and of the manner in which they are related to one another. For this reason, it seems to me to be an error to associate mythical thinking too strongly with the "primitive" or the "archaic." Mythic discourse, as I understand it here, is part of the essential constitution of human discourse, though its precise role and value, and above all the specific manner of its articulation, may vary from one cultural-historical setting to another.

Of course, "myth," as I am using the word here, refers not exclusively to a particular discourse genre, but rather to any discourse that performs functions closely similar to those of the paradigmatic myths that do represent a type of narrative. This is a derivative way of using the term "myth," and one that I shall continue to employ from time to time, though it should not be conflated with the more primary signification of the term, which refers to a particular narrative category. In the two cases studied in the present chapter—the religious traditions that evolved in part from the earlier historical accounts of the great emperors Songtsen Gampo (c. 617–649/650) and Trhi Songdetsen (742–c. 797)—epic narratives buttressed a vast corpus of nonnarrative literature. These included works on morals, meditation, all sorts of ritual, and Buddhist doctrine, that in turn contributed to the ongoing elaborations of the mythic constructions to which they belonged.

The Most Compassionate King

The *Maṇi bka'-'bum* (Maṇi Kambum),[9] a heterogeneous collection of texts ascribed to King Songtsen Gampo and primarily concerned with the cult of the bodhisattva Mahākāruṇika-Avalokiteśvara, the "Great Compassionate Avalokiteśvara,"[10] has enjoyed a singularly long history of study in the West.[11] As early as 1801, P. S. Pallas had published an account of its first chapters, and, in 1838, the intrepid Magyar scholar Alexander Csoma de Kőrös mentioned it by name among Tibetan historical works, thereby creating the false impression that the Maṇi Kambum might be regarded as such.[12] A. I. Vostrikov, writing some one hundred years later, sought to provide a more accurate assessment of the Maṇi Kambum, saying that it

> contains much interesting material from the point of view of literature and folklore. Its fairly frequent deviations from the dominant views of Tibetan Buddhism are of great interest. As a historical source, however, it is of absolutely no value and cannot be classed under historical works.[13]

More recently, Ariane Macdonald has reported briefly on her investigations concerning the contents and compilation of the Maṇi Kambum as a prelude to the study of the legendary biographies of Songtsen Gampo found therein, for, as she observes, it is the historico-legendary aspect of the Maṇi Kambum that has held the attention of occidental scholars.[14] These aspects of the Maṇi Kambum have continued to be examined by Michael Aris and others, and traditions concerning one of the key figures involved in its early compilation, by Anne-Marie Blondeau.[15] In the present survey of the Maṇi Kambum and its allied literature, I emphasize three aspects of this important body of material: the history of the Maṇi Kambum's compilation; its significance for the development of a Tibetan worldview; and its peculiar approach to the problems of Buddhist theory and practice.

Compiling the Treasures

The Maṇi Kambum is usually divided into three "cycles" (*skor*):

1. *The Cycle of Sūtras* (*mdo-skor*), which includes various legendary accounts of the exploits of Avalokiteśvara and of King Songtsen Gampo;
2. *The Cycle of Attainment* (*sgrub-skor*), which contains the meditational "means for attainment" (*sgrub-thabs*, Skt. *sādhana*) of Avalokiteśvara in various aspects; and
3. *The Cycle of Precepts* (*zhal-gdams-kyi skor*), containing some 150 short texts treating a wide variety of topics, most of which are connected in some way with the systems of meditation focusing upon Mahākāruṇika.[16]

Further, there is a small collection of texts, sometimes referred to as the *Cycle of the Disclosure of the Hidden* (*gab-pa mngon-phyung gi skor*)—after the most renowned of the works found therein—which in some redactions of the Maṇi Kambum is appended to the *Cycle of Precepts*, and in others forms by itself a fourth cycle, an appendix to the entire collection.[17]

This entire mass of material—usually assembled in two volumes containing about 700 folios in all—was discovered as textual treasure (*gter-ma*) by some three treasure-revealers (*gter-ston*) over a period lasting approximately one century, beginning, it appears, in the middle of the twelfth. The Fifth Dalai Lama, Ngawang Lozang Gyatso (1617–1682), himself a great contributor to the tradition of revealed treasures,[18] has summarized its compilation in these words:

> The dharma-protecting king Songtsen Gampo taught the doctrinal cycles (*chos-skor*) of Mahākāruṇika to disciples endowed with [appropriate propensities owing to their own past] actions and fortunate circumstances[19] and had the cycles set down in writing. The *Great Chronicle* (*Lo-rgyus chen-mo*), which comes from the *Cycle of Sūtras*, was concealed together with the *Cycle of Attainment* and the *Cycle of Precepts* beneath the feet of Hayagrīva, in the northern quarter of the central hall [in the Lhasa Jo-khang temple].[20] Some, including the *Disclosure of the Hidden* and [the remaining portions of] the *Cycle of Sūtras*, were concealed in the right thigh of the *yakṣa* Nāga-Kubera, beneath the hem of his gown.[21] The glorious and great Orgyen [Padmasambhava] clearly revealed them to Lord Trhi Songdetsen, saying, "Your own ancestor Songtsen Gampo has concealed such treasures in Ra-sa [Lhasa]." Thereupon, [the king] gained faith and made the *Means for the Attainment of the Thousand-fold Mahākāruṇika*, the *Disclosure of the Hidden*, the *Creation and Consummation of the Thousand Buddhas*, the *Benefits of Beholding* [*Songtsen Gampo's*] *Spiritual Bond* [that is, the Jowo Śākyamuni image of Lhasa], and *Songtsen's Last Testament* into [his own] spiritual bonds.[22]
>
> Later, the siddha Ngödrup—a yogin who was taken into the following of Mahākāruṇika [by the deity himself],[23] and who lived in the human world for about 300 years—drew forth the *Cycle of Attainment* from beneath the feet of the Hayagrīva in the northern quarter of the central hall and transmitted it to Lord Nyang[rel Nyima Özer, 1124–1192],[24] the incarnation of Tshangpa Lheimetog [King Trhi Songdetsen]. Lord [Nyang] brought the *Cycle of Precepts* out from beneath the feet of Hayagrīva. Shākyawö, [who is also known as Shākya] Zangpo, a teacher from Lhasa in the central province, [later] brought forth the *Cycle of Sūtras*, as well as the *Disclosure of the Hidden* and so on, from the *yakṣa*-shrine. So it was that this doctrinal cycle had

> three discoverers. Nonetheless, it is renowned as the treasure of the venerable siddha Ngödrup, for he was foremost [among them]. For that reason, I have not here written [about the Maṇi Kambum] in the sections devoted to the doctrinal cycles of the other two treasure-discoverers but have placed [all their discoveries belonging to the Maṇi Kambum] together at this juncture.[25]

The Great Fifth later reinforces his case for insisting upon the preeminence of the siddha Ngödrup among the revealers of the Maṇi Kambum. Speaking of the *Great Chronicle* he tells us that the location in which it was concealed (*gter-gnas*, that is, under the feet of the Hayagrīva image) suggests it to have been among the treasures discovered by Ngödrup.[26] The attribution of the *Cycle of Sūtras* to Shākyawö, then, must refer to only four of the remaining texts in that section.[27] The Dalai Lama does not mention that one of the texts forming the Maṇi Kambum, the *Great Explanatory Commentary*, the colophon of which clearly attributes its discovery to Ngödrup and which belongs to the *Cycle of Attainment*, also refers explicitly to the *Great Chronicle*.[28] His hypothesis that the discovery of this latter text, or perhaps an earlier version thereof, preceded Shākyawö's discoveries may be cautiously accepted.

In sum, then, the siddha Ngödrup would seem to have discovered the original kernel of the Maṇi Kambum, consisting of a version of the *Great Chronicle*, the *Great Explanatory Commentary*, and at least three other texts included in the *Cycle of Attainment*, which are explicitly referred to in the *Commentary*.[29] It is by no means improbable that this treasure-revealer also disclosed at least some of the remaining works of the *Cycle of Attainment* as well, though the evidence on this point is inconclusive.

There is perhaps no reason to contradict the tradition that Nyangrel Nyima Özer increased this original body of material with the discovery of the *Cycle of Precepts*.[30] More problematic, however, is the contribution of Shākyawö, who, as a student of Nyang's disciple Mikyö Dorje of Latö, probably belongs to the early or mid-thirteenth century.[31] One text from the *Cycle of the Disclosure of the Hidden* is clearly attributed to him, the colophon of which states that it is but one of several works discovered together.[32] The opinion of the Great Fifth concerning his contribution to the *Cycle of Sūtras* has already been referred to here. Beyond that, I can only note that I have so far found no evidence that would render it impossible to ascribe the entire *Cycle of the Disclosure of the Hidden*, as well as the four works in the *Cycle of Sūtras* mentioned by the Fifth Dalai Lama, to the age of Shākyawö. It is certainly possible that the great majority of the texts presently included in the Maṇi Kambum were in existence by about 1250, though their present arrangement, in the form of a single collection, may still be the product of a later generation.[33]

The tale of the recovery of the works forming the Maṇi Kambum has few variations, reflecting the fact that most of the Tibetan historians who wrote on this topic probably did so with one and the same catalogue (*dkar-chag*) before them.[34] The most significant variation I have encountered is found in the writings of the learned Jonang Jetsün Tāranātha (1575–1634), who states:

> The means for the attainment of the deity[35] [found in] the *Collected Works of the King* [*Rgyal-po bka'-'bum*] and the roots of the precepts[36] appear, certainly, to have been composed by the religious-king Songtsen Gampo. Therefore, they are the actual words of Ārya Avalokita[37] and are really the ancient ancestral religion[38] of Tibet itself. It is

> well known that they were concealed as treasures by master Padma[sambhava]. Moreover, the history and most of the ancillary texts were composed by the treasure-discoverer, siddha Ngödrup, by Nyangrel, and by others.[39]

While this statement is of great interest for its critical, but not condemnatory, view of the Maṇi Kambum as revealed treasure—as for its assertion that it was Padmasambhava, and not Songtsen Gampo, who concealed the portions Tāranātha regards as being indeed ancient—it does not otherwise alter our conception of the history of the Maṇi Kambum's compilation as outlined earlier.[40]

Finally, we should note that it is not exactly clear when it was that this collection received the name Maṇi Kambum, save that it was universally known as such no later than the seventeenth century.[41] Elsewhere, it is entitled the *Collected Works of the Dharma Protecting King Songtsen Gampo*,[42] and even the *Doctrinal Cycle Concerning the Six-Syllable* [*mantra*] *of Mahākāruṇika*.[43] The meditational system it embodies is usually referred to as that of *Avalokiteśvara According to the System of the King*,[44] a phrase attested as early as the first half of the fourteenth century, when we find Karmapa III Rangjung Dorje (1284–1339) conferring its empowerment on the great Nyingmapa master, Longchen Rabjampa (1308–1363).[45]

Cosmology and Myth

The mythical portions of the Maṇi Kambum develop a distinctive view of Tibet, its history, and its place in the world. Three elements that inform this view are outstanding: the belief that Avalokiteśvara was the patron deity of Tibet; the legend of King Songtsen Gampo and his court, in which the king is represented as being the very embodiment of Avalokiteśvara, the founder of the Buddha's way in his formerly barbarian realm; and the cosmological vision of the Tibetan Avalokiteśvara cult, whereby the king's divinity, and the divinity's regard for Tibet, are seen not as matters of historic accident, but as matters grounded in the very nature of the world. Though all were, at least in rough versions, current by the time the Maṇi Kambum made its appearance, they were much elaborated and achieved their definite articulation within the Maṇi Kambum itself.

1. Following the Maṇi Kambum and related sources, later Tibetan historians have tended to assign the inception of the Avalokiteśvara cult in Tibet to the reign of Songtsen Gampo.[46] Thus, for example, one of the Gelukpa masters we met in the preceding chapter, Thuken Chöki Nyima (1737–1802):

> At first, the religious king Songtsen Gampo taught the *Creation and Consummation of Mahākāruṇika* (*Thugs-rje-chen-po'i bskyed-rdzogs*) and other precepts at length, and there were many who practiced them, too. It was at first from this, that [the custom] spread throughout Tibet and Kham of praying to Ārya Avalokita and reciting the six-syllable [mantra *Oṃ Maṇipadme Hūṃ*].[47]

In addition to acting as a teacher in his own right, the king is said to have encouraged and sponsored the establishment of shrines and images, as well as the translation into Tibetan of the fundamental texts of the Indian Avalokiteśvara tradition. The spiritual activity begun by Songtsen Gampo was then continued on a vast scale by his descendant Trhi Songdetsen.[48]

Contemporary Tibetanists have tended to be skeptical about such traditions. They point to the inconclusive evidence within the most ancient historical sources on the subject of Songtsen Gampo's actual commitment to Buddhism, and the near absence of manuscript evidence from Dunhuang of a widespread cult of Avalokiteśvara in Tibet prior to the eleventh century.[49] At the same time, the known history of the translation of Sanskrit and Chinese Buddhism into Tibetan does establish that canonical texts of fundamental importance for this cult were available in Tibetan by 812 or 824, the probable years of the compilation of the Denkar catalogue (*Ldan-kar-ma*) of Buddhist texts.[50] One may note, too, that the "oral precept" tradition (*Gsung bka'-ma*) of the Nyingmapa school, which purports to represent an unbroken lineage transmitting teachings that were introduced into Tibet primarily during the reign of Trhi Songdetsen and which likely does include some authentically ancient material, accords scant attention to Avalokiteśvara. It is, rather, with the recovery of the revealed treasure texts, above all the Maṇi Kambum, that the great bodhisattva assumes a role of considerable importance for the Nyingmapas.[51] Finally, we should remark that, even among those Tibetan historians who are inclined to accept the validity of the Maṇi Kambum and related traditions, there are those who see evidence in it not of a flourishing Avalokiteśvara cult in ancient Tibet, but rather of a secret transmission from Songtsen Gampo to a small number of worthy adepts, family members, and courtiers, who did not, in turn, transmit the king's teachings to a subsequent generation.[52] In short, the available evidence powerfully suggests that, while early medieval Tibet had some familiarity with the bodhisattva, the cult of Avalokiteśvara, as known to a later age, is a product not of the imperial period but of the "later spread of the doctrine" (*bstan-pa phyi-dar*) that began in the late tenth century.

There can be little doubt that the first great figure to actively promote the practice of meditational techniques focusing on Avalokiteśvara was Dīpaṃkara-Srījñāna, better known as Atiśa (982–1054, and in Tibet from 1042 onwards). Three major systems of instruction (*khrid*) on the rites and meditations of Avalokiteśvara may be traced back to this Bengali master.[53] During the latter part of the eleventh century and the beginning of the twelfth, several other systems were propounded by Bari Lotsawa (b. 1040), by the siddhas Candradhvaja and Tshembupa, and by Milarepa's famous disciple Rechung Dorjetrak (b. 1084).[54] The works familiar to me that relate to these systems do not make it clear whether or not these masters regarded Tibet to be Avalokiteśvara's special field. But the following passage, attributed to the emanation of the Great Mother, Macik Labdrön (1055–1145 or 1153), and thus possibly belonging to the very period we are considering, is of much interest in this connection:

> I have made both Avalokiteśvara and Bhaṭṭārikā-Tārā into special doctrines that are universally renowned. It also appears that the two are our common Tibetan ancestors, and in that they are certainly our "divine portion" (*lha-skal*), infants learn to recite the six syllables at the very same time that they are beginning to speak; this is a sign that the Exalted One has actually blessed their spirits. Thus, it is truly right for us all to make of the Exalted One our "divine portion."[55]

The tone of advocacy here is noteworthy. Are we reading too much between the lines if we see here a slight suggestion that Tibetans during the early twelfth century still required arguments that they did, indeed, have a special relationship with the ever compassionate Avalokiteśvara? During the later part of the same century, the *Great Chronicle* of the Maṇi Kambum is able to state the case with far greater assurance—as in this passage, addressed to Avalokiteśvara by the dying Buddha Śākyamuni:

> There are none left to be trained by me. Because there are none for me to train I will demonstrate the way of nirvāṇa to inspire those who are slothful to the doctrine and to demonstrate that what is compounded is impermanent. The snowy domain to the north [Tibet] is presently a domain of animals, so even the word "human being" does not exist there—it is a vast darkness. And all who die there turn not upwards but, like snowflakes falling on a lake, drop into the world of evil destinies. At some future time, when that doctrine declines, you, O bodhisattva, will train them. First, the incarnation of a bodhisattva will generate human beings who will require training. Then, they will be brought together [as disciples] by material goods [*zang-zing*]. After that, bring them together through the doctrine! It will be for the welfare of living beings![56]

So there can be no longer any doubt that the bodhisattva has been assigned to Tibet by the Buddha himself. To the assertion that the Snowy Land is Avalokiteśvara's special field, the Maṇi Kambum has lent a semblance of canonical authority.

2. Let us turn now to the legend of King Songtsen Gampo's having been an incarnation of Avalokiteśvara. Ariane Macdonald, in her superb study of the royal religion of this king, has argued that his religion, based in large measure on indigenous Tibetan beliefs, was most certainly not Buddhism.[57] The belief that the king was, in fact, the bodhisattva seems then to reflect the opinion of a later age, no doubt one in which the growing community of Tibetan Buddhists sought to reinforce the precedent for its own presence in the Land of Snows.[58] In this, of course, it goes hand in hand with the myth of the bodhisattva's role as Tibet's spiritual patron. Like this latter myth, the time of the former's origin cannot be established with great precision; when it makes its first datable appearance in 1167—which is probably close to the time of its appearance in the *Great Chronicle* as well—it is presented without reservations as established history.[59]

It is in the narrative portions of the Maṇi Kambum that the simple tale of the incarnate king is richly developed, so that his court becomes a veritable Tibetan Camelot. Further, it is in the form of an elaborate romance that the legend of Songtsen Gampo is restated repeatedly, in works like the apocryphal *Bka'-chems ka-khol-ma* (The Testament Drawn from a Pillar) and the semihistorical *Rgyal-rabs gsal-ba'i me-long* (The Mirror Clarifying the Royal Geneology).[60] In this literature, including the Maṇi Kambum, in which the myth of Avalokiteśvara's guiding role throughout the course of Tibetan history is developed, a distinct unifying theme emerges: the bodhisattva now functions as a deus ex machina of sorts, making benign incursions onto the Tibetan landscape at various critical junctures. As such, he may be projected into present and future situations, too, whenever the need for his assistance becomes known. So it is that the *Great Chronicle* of the Maṇi Kambum—looking back on the age of imperial greatness from the vantage point of twelfth century chaos and uncertainty—closes with this prophetic declaration concerning, one may safely assume, the era of its own discovery, when

> demons (*bdud*) will enter the hearts of religious teachers (*ston-pa*) and cause them to blaspheme one another and to quarrel. *Damsi* (*dam-sri*) spirits will enter the hearts of the mantra-adepts (*sngags-pa*) and cause them to cast great spells against one another. *Gongpo* (*'gong-po*) spirits will enter the hearts of men and cause them to defile themselves (*dme-byed*) and to fight with one another. Demonesses (*'dre-mo*) will enter the hearts of women and cause them to argue with their husbands and to take their own lives. *Therang* (*the-brang*, = *the'u-rang*) spirits will enter the hearts of youths and cause them to act perversely. The gods, nāgas, and *nyenpo* (*gnyan-po*) divinities will be disturbed, and the rains will not come during appropriate seasons. Sometimes there will be famine. A time will come when people's merits will decline. So, at that time, if you wish to amass happiness, then pray to Mahākāruṇika-Avalokiteśvara! Recite these six heart-syllables (*snying-po yi-ge drug-pa*): *Oṃ Maṇipadme Hūṃ!* Because all the happiness and requirements of this lifetime come forth from this, it is like praying to the [wish-fulfilling] gem. There can be no doubt that in future lives your obscurations will be removed and that you will attain enlightenment. Harbor not divided thoughts about it! Meditatively cultivate Mahākāruṇika! Attain it! Teach it! Expound it! Propagate and spread it! [In this way], the presence of the Buddha is established. The doctrinal foundation is established.[61]

It was during this same period that the custom of propagating the cult of Avalokiteśvara at public assemblies (*khrom-chos*) seems to have begun, for by the second half of the thirteenth century no less a hierarch than the renowned Karma Pakshi (see chapter 6) composed a rite for just that purpose.[62]

What was the result of Avalokiteśvara's ascension to a position of such central importance in the Tibetan world, particularly during a period of grave political unrest?[63] There can be little doubt that the myth of the religious king did much to support the notion that worldly affairs might best be placed in the hands of essentially spiritual leaders. And it is possible, too, that the Tibetan people came to expect their temporal woes to be set aright as before, by the timely intercession of the great bodhisattva. Can it be any wonder, then, that when Tibet finally achieved some measure of real unity during the seventeenth century—after almost eight centuries of intermittent strife—it did so under the leadership of a latter-day emanation of Mahākāruṇika residing in the ancient capital of Lhasa, and constructing for himself a hilltop palace named after the divine Mount Potalaka? It seems we are in the presence of a Tibetan twist on the Arthurian legend, whereby the once and future king becomes at long last the king, once and present.

3. The Maṇi Kambum's view of Avalokiteśvara's role in Tibetan history and, in particular, his manifestation as Songtsen Gampo, develops, as we have seen, themes whose general features had been well defined by the time the first sections of the collection appeared. More eclectic in their formation, and thus more resistant to efforts to understand their evolution, are the cosmology and theogony of the Maṇi Kambum.

The notion that Avalokiteśvara might be regarded as the primordial deity, the point of departure for a unique theogony, was introduced into Tibet no later than the ninth century with the translation into Tibetan of the *Karaṇḍavyūha-sūtra* (The Sūtra of the Cornucopia of Avalokiteśvara's Attributes), though the theogonic theme is but slightly developed therein.[64] The same sūtra presents also a vision of Avalokiteśvara in which each pore of the bodhisattva's body is seen to embrace whole world systems, a vision that was later said to have been taught by Atiśa in connection with the precepts of the *Four Gods of the Kadampas* (*Bka'-gdams lha-bzhi*).[65]

In the *Great Chronicle*, Avalokiteśvara undergoes a tremendous evolution. Though presented there as the emanation of the Buddha Amitābha, it is the bodhisattva whose own body gives rise to the thousand cakravartin kings and the thousand Buddhas of the Bhadrakalpa, just as the body of the Avalokiteśvara of the *Karaṇḍavyūha-sūtra* had given birth to the brahmāṇical pantheon.[66] Moreover, the *Karaṇḍavyūha*'s vision of the deity is now amplified by a cosmological vision widely associated in Tibet with the *Avataṃsakasūtra* (The Sūtra of the Bounteousness of the Buddhas), but with Avalokiteśvara here occupying a position even prior to that of the cosmic Buddha Vairocana.[67] It is, moreover, a novel sense of Tibet's station in the universe that constitutes the most striking innovation:

> [After Amitābha] had empowered the best of bodhisattvas, Ārya Avalokiteśvara, to benefit living beings, an inconceivable and immeasurable light radiated forth from his body and magically created (*sprul*) many fields of the buddhas' body of rapture (*sambhogakāya*) in which he magically created many buddhas of the body of rapture. So it was that he benefited many sentient beings.
>
> And from the hearts of those bodies of rapture, there radiated forth inconceivably many fields of emanational bodies (*nirmāṇakāya*) in which were magically created many emanationally embodied buddhas; and from the hearts of those emanational bodies, light radiated forth, which was ineffable and beyond being ineffable.[68] From that light Ārya Avalokiteśvaras, Bhṛkuṭīs, and Tārās were magically created equal to the number of sentient beings. So, too, did he benefit living creatures.
>
> Again, light emanated from his body and he magically created many world systems, as many as there are atoms in the substance of the world system that is the "middle array."[69] And in them the innumerable Tathāgatas magically emanated forth to an equal number, whereby he again benefited sentient beings.
>
> Then from their bodies, there radiated forth light rays, which were immeasurable and beyond being immeasurable.[70] At [the tip of] each one there was magically created a Jambudvīpa, in each of which was a Vajrāsana. To the north of each Vajrāsana there was a land beyond the pale, which was a Land of Snows, [and in each of these there was] a supreme horse who was a destroyer of armies,[71] an eleven-faced Avalokiteśvara, and a Tārā, and a Bhṛkuṭī. In each one, King Songtsen Gampo and the venerable ladies, white and green, were magically created.[72] Ineffable light rays poured forth from their bodies and they magically created Mahākāruṇikas and six-syllable mantras equal to the number of sentient beings. Thus they benefited living creatures.[73]

The enlightened activity of Avalokiteśvara, his incursion into Tibetan history in the form of King Songtsen Gampo, is no longer an event occurring within the Tibetan historical framework. Rather, Tibet itself is now an aspect of the bodhisattva's all-pervading creative activity. How could the Buddha's teaching have been artificially implanted in such a realm, the very existence of which is evidence of the Buddha's compassionate engagement in the world? That Tibet is here referred to as being "beyond the pale" (*mtha'-'khob*) is the fortuitous survival of an outmoded turn of phrase,

Figure 8.1 Avalokiteśvara emanates worlds. Nineteenth century (after *Bod-kyi thang-ga*).

for it is clear that the Maṇi Kambum regards the Land of Snows as no less part of the Buddhist universe than the sacred land of India itself.

The Teaching of Supreme Compassion

To what end has the Maṇi Kambum elaborated its peculiar worldview, with its broad ramifications for cosmology, theogony, and history? It is clear that the impulse to explain events in the external world is a consideration of but little importance here. The aim of the Maṇi Kambum's cosmology is, rather, to propagate the cult of Mahākāruṇika and his six-syllable mantra—to demonstrate that this is the most efficacious spiritual practice in this debased age, particularly for the Tibetan people. It is a measure of the emphasis of the Maṇi Kambum that merely one-third of its total volume is concerned with the themes we have been considering thus far, the remaining two-thirds being wholly devoted to the exposition of a unique system of meditation, which is developed throughout the *Cycle of Attainment*, the *Cycle of Precepts*, and the *Cycle of the Disclosure of the Hidden*. While many aspects of Buddhist metaphysics, psychology, and ritual are referred to and commented upon in these cycles, the Maṇi Kambum by and large eschews speculative philosophy and the elaboration of a systematic psychology. Hence, with the exception of the formal rites for the worship of and meditation upon the deity (*sādhana*, *sgrub-thabs*), which are accorded a fairly well-established pattern of exposition such as is required by the structure of sādhana itself, the doctrinal portions of the Maṇi Kambum exhibit much freedom in their development. Not confined by a single system, the Maṇi Kambum utilizes a variety of systems, calling upon them when they are needed to advance a teaching that, we are told, lies beyond them all.[74] These instructions that are placed in the mouth of Songtsen Gampo touch upon such diverse topics as the nine successive vehicles,[75] the two truths,[76] the Great Seal, or Mahāmudrā,[77] Great Perfection,[78] the sequence of the path,[79] the trio of ground, path, and result,[80] the trio of view, meditation, and action,[81] the three bodies of buddhahood,[82] et cetera. But none of these topics is ever allowed to ascend to the position of becoming a central leitmotif that would unify, to some extent, the Maṇi Kambum's diverse contents. Of this, the Maṇi Kambum is itself conscious. The catalogue of contents (*dkar-chag*) tells us that these precepts "are not all dependent on one another. They are 'magical fragments of instruction'[83]—each one benefits a particular individual."[84]

The peculiar term "magical fragment," which so appropriately describes the Maṇi Kambum's many short precepts, is itself the subject of a detailed definition found in the *Great Explanatory Commentary*:

> "Magical fragments" are so called because, just as magic appears variously but is without substantial existence (*rang-bzhin med-pa*), so too this doctrine of Mahākāruṇika is explained and taught by various means and in various aspects (*thabs yan-lag sna-tshogs-su bshad*) but nonetheless remains the same in that it is an indivisible union of emptiness and compassion. "Fragment" means that each particular division of the doctrine suffices as the occasion for the particular development of [spiritual] experience [by a given] individual.[85]

So the many doctrines referred to by the Maṇi Kambum all serve to illustrate the single doctrine of Mahākāruṇika and are thus the basis for an exposition of the central doctrines of the Mahāyāna, those of compassion and emptiness, which, though they are indivisible as aspects of the play of enlightened awareness, must nonetheless be distinguished conventionally. It is from such a perspective that the catalogue of contents endeavors to summarize the teaching of the Maṇi Kambum:

> [H]owever many precepts associated with the doctrines of provisional meaning (*drang-don-gyi chos-kyi zhal-gdams*) are expounded, they are not the doctrines of Mahākāruṇika unless you have deliberately taken up sentient beings, having seized the ground with loving kindness and compassion. If, because you fear the sufferings of saṃsāra, you desire freedom, desire bliss, desire liberation for yourself alone and thus cannot create an enlightened attitude for the sake of sentient beings, then these are not the doctrines of the bodhisattva Avalokita. If you do not practice for the sake of all living beings, you will not realize Avalokiteśvara. . . .
>
> However many doctrines of definitive meaning (*nges-don gyi chos*) are expounded, you must recognize the true Mahākāruṇika, Reality itself (*chos-nyid-don-gyi thugs-rje chen-po*), mind-as-such, which is empty and is the buddhas' body of reality (*dharmakāya*), to be within yourself (*rang-la yod-pa*). Cultivate it! Familiarize yourself with

> it! Grow firm in it! If you desire to attain some Mahākāruṇika who "dwells in his proper abode,"[86] or desire to behold his visage, or to attain the accomplishments (*siddhi, dngos-grub*), you will be granted the common accomplishments but will stray far from the supreme accomplishment, buddhahood.[87]

It appears that, in its emphasis on the union of compassion and emptiness, the teaching of the Maṇi Kambum is inspired by the eleventh-century renewal of interest in the path of the Mahāyāna sūtras, particularly as developed in the instructions of the Kadampa school.[88] But in its discussion of "the true Mahākāruṇika, Reality itself," that is, in its discussion of "doctrines of definitive meaning," the diction of the Maṇi Kambum becomes decidedly that of the Nyingmapa tradition—for example, in its identification of Mahākāruṇika, Supreme Compassion, with "the play of intuitive awareness and continuous, fresh gnosis."[89] These doctrinal orientations may be illustrated by a short collection of instructions, taught by the king to his daughter Trhompagyen, the "adornment of the town":

> The *view* of Supreme Compassion is the indivisible union of appearance and emptiness, and is like the sky.
> External appearances, the incessant appearing of whatever may be, are nonetheless the appearance of mind, self-manifest.
> The essential character of mind is that it is empty.
> And the essential character of appearance is that it is empty; for it is apparent, but without substantial existence.
>
> The *meditation* of Supreme Compassion is like the indivisible union of clarity and emptiness and is like a rainbow appearing in the sky.
> You must cultivate the realization that the essential character of mind, which is clear and unobscured, and which emerges by itself, arises by itself, is that it is empty.
> The *action* of Supreme Compassion is the indivisible union of awareness and emptiness, and is like the sun rising in the sky.
> Action is freedom from hankering after whatever there is that arises incessantly in mind, whose nature is pure awareness.
> Though you act, you act in emptiness, not grasping at entities as real.
>
> The *fruit* of Supreme Compassion is the indivisible union of bliss and emptiness.
> Mind itself, without contrivances, is blissful within the expanse that is the foundation of all that is real.
> Being empty and free from grasping, it is like the moon reflected in water.
> Being free from all superimposed limits, it is without features that serve to define it.
> And because it has ever been present within you, it cannot be achieved.
>
> The *spiritual commitment* of Supreme Compassion
> Is emptiness whose core is compassion.
> Its characteristic being just that,
> You'll grasp all living beings in all three realms
> With unqualified compassion.
> Being equal, you will act without "levels."

The *enlightened activity* of Supreme Compassion
Grasps beings with a snare of compassion in which
Buddhas and sentient beings are no different.
It slaughters their pain with the weapon of emptiness,
And draws sentient beings to the level of bliss supreme.[90]

While the great variety of the Maṇi Kambum's teachings of doctrine and ritual and the unsystematic way in which these topics are, for the most part, presented, do not permit us to define too strictly a "central doctrine" in this case, the teaching of the Maṇi Kambum represents, by and large, a syncretic approach to the doctrines of the Nyingmapas and those of the Avalokiteśvara traditions of the new translation schools, particularly the Kadampa, with its emphasis upon "emptiness imbued with compassion."[91] Further, through the instructions on the visualization and mantra of Avalokiteśvara transmitted by masters of all the major Tibetan Buddhist schools, as well as by lay tantric adepts and itinerant *maṇi-pas*—"Oṃmaṇipadmehūṃists"—who preached the bodhisattva's cult far and wide, it was this syncretic teaching that became, for all intents and purposes, Tibet's devotional norm.[92]

The Advent of the Lotus Guru

If there is a figure in the Tibetan pantheon whose popularity rivals the ubiquitous cult of Avalokiteśvara, surely it is Padmasambhava, the Lotus-Born Precious Guru (Guru Rinpoche). Indeed, the two in many respects have tended to reinforce one another and may be considered virtual twins. Padmasambhava, like Avalokiteśvara, is an emanation of the buddha Amitābha, and Tibet is his special field. Both are strongly associated with Tibet's glory days under the old empire. The tales of their compassionate intercession in the Tibetan world are elaborated in epic narratives that were discovered as revealed treasures (*gter-ma*), and in the early development of this literature the twelfth-century treasure-finder Nyangrel Nyima Özer and his successor, Guru Chöwang (1212–1270), emerge as central figures for the formation of both cults.[93] The most striking disanalogy between the two (besides the fact that one is supposed to be a cosmic bodhisattva and the other an historical individual), is that whereas we know that Avalokiteśvara was an important figure in the Indian Buddhist pantheon, whose following had come to extend throughout much of Asia long before Buddhism ever became established in Tibet, nothing similar can be said of Padmasambhava. Indeed, the evidence for him prior to his twelfth-century apotheosis in the *gter-ma* traditions is so thin that some have been inclined to regard him as a rather late Tibetan invention.[94] We shall therefore retrace here some of the ground we have already covered, following now the course whereby the Lotus Guru emerged from the margins of the old Tibetan empire to become, in effect, the royal master of the Tibetan people as a whole.[95]

According to the tradition of the *Testament of Ba*, repeated with considerable elaboration in later histories, the local deities and spirits of Tibet so obstructed the foundation of the temple at Samye that the intervention of occult power in the service of Buddhism was deemed essential. At the recommendation of Śāntarakṣita, a master of mantras named Padmasambhava was summoned, who visited Tibet briefly in order

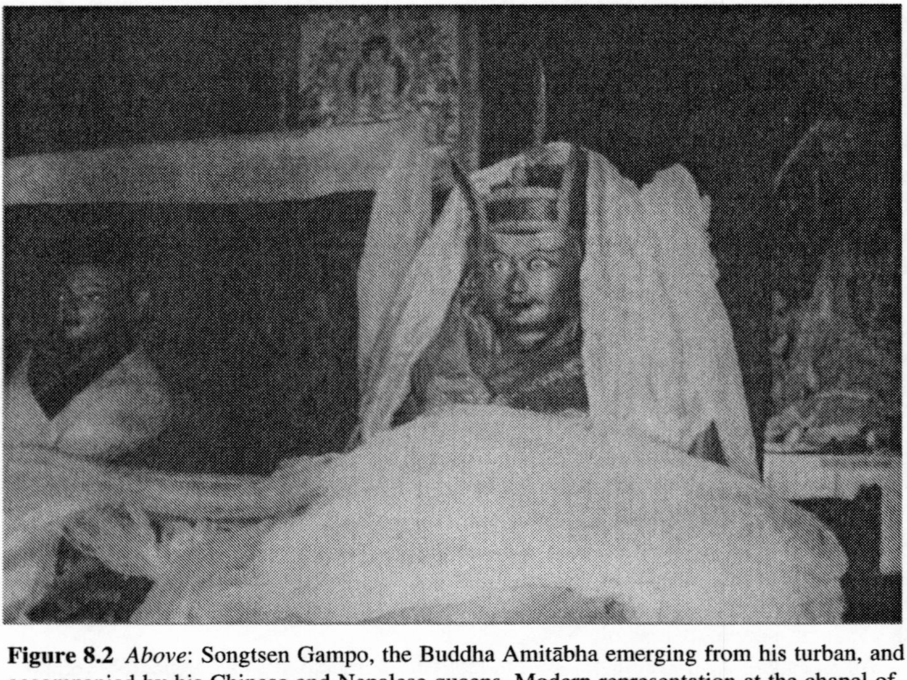

Figure 8.2 *Above*: Songtsen Gampo, the Buddha Amitābha emerging from his turban, and accompanied by his Chinese and Nepalese queens. Modern representation at the chapel of Songtsen's mausoleum in Yarlung valley. *Below*: Padmasambhava in the revered image from Yarlung Sheldrak, the Crystal Peak of Yarlung, where the treasures of Orgyen Lingpa were recovered (see chapter 9).

to suppress and place under oath the restless demonic forces. Towards the end of his visit, we are told:

> At the bamboo grove of Drakmar, having expounded the *Man-ngag lta-ba'i phreng-ba* (The Garland of Views: An Esoteric Precept)[96] to twenty-one, including the Tsenpo and his retainers, he said, "Great king! these secret mantras of mine conform with the Dharmakāya in respect to their view and conform with the factors of enlightenment in respect to their conduct. Do not allow conduct to slip into the sphere of the view, for, if you do, it will become antinomian [lit. 'no virtue, no sin']. That nihilistic view having arisen, there's no correcting it. But if you permit the view to follow in the way of conduct, becoming bound up in superficialities, you'll not be liberated. These mantras of mine, which are allied to the mind (*sems-phyogs*), are very great in respect to their view. In the future, there will be many who will be confident about the words but will not have acquired confidence in the application of that view to the mind-stream, and they will descend to infernal births. Some exceptional persons, however, who will not have broken up view and conduct, will come to benefit many beings. But because, owing to the contrivances of ordinary persons, there will be many variations, the blessing will decline and there will be few who are realized. So if I conceal all these that are not corrupted, in the future they will serve well some who have a karmic connection." Saying this, he hid many books in a clay pot. Having bestowed upon the Tsenpo the sequence of empowerment, he granted the transmission of the secret mantras of the Mahāyāna. After explaining the *Phur-bu 'bum-sde* (The Hundred Thousand [Verse] Tantra of Vajrakīla),[97] he placed the other esoteric precepts, with prayers, in the Akaniṣṭha heaven:
>
> "I pray that I and my patrons, whosoever,
> In this lifetime and wherever we are born,
> Practice the fruitional Mahāyāna of Yoga,
> In that sacred realm called Akaniṣṭha."
>
> Having so spoken, he departed without completing what remained of the *homa*-ritual [that had been begun earlier].[98]

Towards the end of the *Testament of Ba*, when Trhi Songdetsen enters into retirement, the master Vimalamitra arrives in Tibet and the emperor receives from him the remaining teachings of Padmasambhava that he had not obtained earlier. These he practices as his personal way of meditation.[99]

The account that we find here represents, no doubt, a version of the tale of Padmasambhava's visit to the king, developed in the century or so after the events it recounts but prior to the massive elaborations of the twelfth century and after; these elaborations begin, so far as we now know, primarily in works authored or rediscovered by Nyangrel Nyima Özer.[100] Given the fact that the *Garland of Views* was certainly in circulation and accepted by some as a genuine work of Padmasambhava before the mid-eleventh century,[101] we may posit that the great guru's cult began its ascent during the obscure period between the fall of the empire and the late-tenth-century renaissance. This finds some support in the couple of references to Padmasambhava known from the pre-eleventh-century documents found at Dunhuang, both of which may well date to the postimperial period.[102]

An important tantric cycle of the Nyingmapa school that came under fire in later times is that of the wrathful deity Vajrakīla (*Rdo-rje phur-pa*), the Vajra Spike or Dagger. Vajrakīla embodies the ritual tent peg or spike (*kīla*, often referred to in

English as a "magic dagger") through whose power the place of practice is, literally or metaphorically, staked out and so rendered safe from harmful interference and obstacles.[103] For the later Nyingmapa traditions, including those handed down within the Khön family, which in the eleventh century founded the Sakyapa school, this was to be one of the most popular and widespread cults, generating an enormous ritual and exegetical literature, together with elaborate rites of dance, exorcism, yoga, et cetera.[104]

The ritual traditions of Vajrakīla are represented in the Dunhuang documents in *PT* 44, a small manuscript preserved at the Bibliothèque nationale in Paris, and in several smaller fragments.[105] The manuscript *PT* 44 is in most respects rather crude, and one can well imagine that it emanates from a source outside of monastic orthodoxy. There is no positive indication of its source of origin, however, or of the date of its production.[106] Its opening chapter reads as follows:

> At first, there was the journey from Yang-la-shod in Nepal to the temple of Nālandā in India in order to fetch the *Phur-bu'i 'bum-sde* (The Hundred Thousand [Verse] Tantra of Vajrakīla): when the Nepali porters Shag-kya-spur and I-so were hired and sent off, there was a tetrad of *Bse* goddesses who, at about nightfall, killed everyone and stole their breath. Padmasambhava became short-tempered, made as if to steal [their] breath, and caught them as they were wondering where to flee. Then he put them in his hat and departed. Arriving at Nālandā, he opened his hat and an exceedingly pretty woman appeared in the flesh. When she vowed to be a protectrice for the practice of the Kīla, he empowered her as its protectrice. Because the prognostications were fine, he laughed, offered up a whole handful of gold dust, and then brought forth the *Hundred Thousand* [*Verse*] *Tantra of Vajrakīla.* After arriving at Yang[-la]-shod in Nepal [with it] he performed the practices belonging [to all the classes of yoga] from the general Kriyā up through Atiyoga. He proclaimed each and every transmission of the Kīla, for the purposes of all the vehicles, from the *Hundred Thousand* [*Verse*] *Tantra of Vajrakīla*, as [is affirmed] in all the secret tantras. In that way, having definitively established the transmissions concerning attainment, and having again escorted the *Hundred Thousand* [back to Nepal], Ācārya Sambhava then performed the rites of attainment in the Asura cave with the Newari Ser-po, Indra-shu-gu-ta, Pra-be-se, and others. And thus he performed the rites, impelling the four *Bse* goddesses, whose embodied forms had not passed away. He named them Great Sorceress of Outer Splendor, Miraculous Nourisher, Great Witch Bestowing Glory, and Life-Granting Conjuress. Having performed the great attainment for seven days, he manifestly beheld the visage of Vajrakumāra [the Adamant Youth, an epithet of Vajrakīla].
>
> Having acquired the accomplishment of the Kīla, concerning [his attainment of] the signs, Padmasambhava, having set a limitless forest ablaze, thrust [the Kīla] at the blaze. Śrīgupta, having struck it at the rock in the region of the frontier forest of India, broke the rock into four fragments and thus "thrust it at stone." The Newari Ser-po thrust it at water and so reversed the water's course, thereby establishing Nepal itself as a mercantile center. Such were the miraculous abilities and powers that emerged.[107]
>
> In Tibet Ācārya Sambhava explained it to Pagor Vairocana and Tse Jñānasukha. Later Dre Tathāgata and Buna Ana heard it and practiced at the cave of Samye Rock at Drakmar. Dre Tathagata thrust it at fire. Buna thrust it at the Rock of Hepo. Then the glory of the Kīla came to Chim Śākya and Nanam Zhang Dorje-nyen. Then it was explained to Jin Yeshe-tsek.

> The trio of Yeshe-tsek, Nyen Nyiwa Tsenbapel, and Demen Gyeltshen successfully practiced at Nyengong in Lhodrak. The preceptor thrust [the Kīla], having set the rock of Bumthang ablaze. Nyiwa and Demen thrust it into wood and stone. Thrusting it thus, and displaying the signs, they attained it while maintaining the appearance of secrecy. Teaching it as a method for those who would follow, they conferred the mantra and transmission together.[108]

This text offers little hint of the later destiny of the cult it describes, for Vajrakīla certainly ranks among the most widely propitiated of the tutelary divinities. Nevertheless, it seems continuous with later tradition in a number of highly suggestive ways. These include its emphasis on the role of Padmasambhava and the assignment of the inception of his involvement in the Vajrakīla cult to the period of his meditation in the cave of Yangleshö, near modern Pharping, a town to the south of the Kathmandu Valley.[109] Its tale of four goddesses, Padmasambhava's scattering of gold dust, the episode of the porterage of the texts relating to Vajrakīla from India, and the marvelous powers attributed to its adepts—all are among the features of the account that, in one form or another, are preserved in the later traditions as well.[110]

What do these relatively early texts tell us of the beginnings of the cult of Padmasambhava? I believe that, if we accept in general the historical veracity of only the most plausible of the circumstances recounted in these tales, matters begin to come into focus. The two elements I should like to emphasize are: first, that part of the tradition of the *Testament of Ba*, according to which Padmasambhava did visit central Tibet at the time of the foundation of Samye, perhaps meeting there with the king, whether or not he actually instructed him;[111] second, the affirmations of the Vajrakīla manuscript to the effect that Padmasambhava was a charismatic tantric master with a following in Nepal and a growing group of disciples in southern Tibet, that is, in the regions of Drakmar and Lhodrak, down to Bumthang in what is today Bhutan. In short, in the early legends of Padmasambhava we may perhaps discern the recollection of a popular eighth-century guru who met with a king, rather like those among contemporary Buddhist teachers who have attracted large followings and on one occasion or another have met with leading political figures. From this perspective it becomes possible to imagine that the several lineages of lay tantric practitioners that during the late tenth and early eleventh centuries traced their antecedents back to Padmasambhava, and that were devoted to the cult of Vajrakīla, would have laid great stress upon the royal meeting, whatever the facts of the matter may have been, as this no doubt strengthened their sense of legitimacy and authority. Once these older tantric lineages started to come under attack by proponents of the newer lines of tantrism being introduced from India from the late tenth century onwards, the tendency would have been to insist increasingly upon recollections of Padmasambhava's imperial connection, thereby reinforcing the ancient tradition against the upstart claims of the new teachings. Padmasambhava, a marginal Dharma master of the eighth century, in this way reemerged two centuries later as an emblem of Tibet's imperial greatness, and a hero to a wide network of tantric cults that had taken root and flourished during this time.[112]

In the preceding chapter, I argued that the phenomenon of the rediscovered treasures in Tibet must be understood in terms of the authority of the past, the conception of a lost golden age whose retrieval came to be valued over progressive discovery. Beyond this, there was at the same time a need felt to reassert past tradition in the face of foreign novelty, while appropriating innovation under the description of what was past. The apotheosis of Padmasambhava must be seen in this light, for he was at once ancient hero and foreign presence. However indistinctly, we may thus begin to discern how it was that he became the definitive signifier of the entire treasure phenomenon.

Hierarchy and Universality

The Tibetan cults of Avalokiteśvara and Padmasambhava, and indeed the entire treasure tradition with which they are intertwined, are in interesting respects at once both hierarchical and antihierarchical. The dialectic between these two apparently opposed tendencies offers, I think, a valuable key to their interpretation. They explicitly share a common allegiance to the hierarchical order of the Tibetan empire of the seventh to the ninth centuries,[113] and thus implicitly, and sometimes explicity as well, they call into question the credentials of the various hegemonic orders that arose in Tibet during the postimperial period. Both can be strikingly egalitarian, above all when compared with the self-conscious elitism of much of Buddhist esotericism, in that their cults are addressed to the Tibetan people as a whole, as if to one extended family. In this respect they perhaps recall that the old Tibetan empire, though hierarchical, had also staked a claim to being a universal order. The universalist dimension of the Padmasambhava cult is in evidence, for instance, in the introduction to a fourteenth-century treasure promulgating the benefits that accrue from the recitation of the guru's mantra:[114]

> I, the woman Yeshe Tshogyel, offered the vast inner and outer maṇḍalas and then prayed in this way: "Great Teacher! Padmasambhava! in the past there has been no one so gracious to us, the living beings of Tibet, as you yourself have been, by extensively fulfilling our needs in this and future lives; nor will one so gracious come forth in the future. You have bestowed upon us your own sādhana as the very essence [of your teaching]. Therefore, even though I am just a woman, I harbor no doubts. Nevertheless, in the future, beings will have much on their minds and will become extremely wild. They will look askance at the True Dharma and, in particular, they will come to blaspheme the unsurpassed doctrine of the esoteric mantras. When that occurs, disease, famine, and strife will spread among all creatures, and, above all, China, Tibet, and Mongolia will become like a ravaged ants' nest, so that the subjects of Tibet will have fallen on hard times. Though many remedies for that have been spoken of, individuals in the future will not have occasion to practice; and even those who wish to practice a little will confront formidable obstacles. Beings will be argumentative, and their thoughts and actions will not be harmonious. Because such bad times will be most difficult to avert, what would be the benefits, during such times, of relying solely on your own sādhana, the Vajraguru mantra?[115] I pray that you speak of this for the sake of the base-minded ones of the future."

Padmasambhava's response to her request powerfully affirms the universal presence and applicability of his teaching, and its availability to devoted persons throughout the Tibetan world:

> "Faithful girl! your prayer is most truthful. At such a time in the future, it will certainly benefit beings, both temporally and ultimately. I have concealed innumerable instructions and sādhanas as treasures in the earth, treasures in the waters, treasures in

the rocks, and treasures in the sky. But in those bad times, it will become exceedingly difficult for fortunate ones to find the means, the auspicious occasion [for their discovery]. This will be a sign that the merits of beings are exhausted. Nevertheless, even then the essential Vajraguru mantra will have inconceivable benefits and powers if it is recited at great places of pilgrimage, places of retreat, mountain peaks, the banks of great rivers, or in craggy places and ravines inhabited by deities, ogres, and spirits, or elsewhere, by adepts adhering to the spiritual commitments of the tantras, members of the saṃgha adhering to their vows, faithful men, suitable women, or others, who with the vast inspiration of bodhisattvas, recite it one hundred, one thousand, ten thousand, one hundred thousand or more times. Then, all disease, famine, and strife, as well as war, crop failure, evil omens, and magical calamities will be averted everywhere; and the rains will fall and the country will prosper. In this and in future lives, and in the abyss of the intermediate state, the greatest adepts will meet me repeatedly in person, those of moderate calibre in visions, and even the least in dreams. Have no doubt about it! such persons will perfect the sequence of spiritual stages and paths and will enter the company of the male and female knowledge-holders on Cāmara Isle. One who recites my mantra one hundred times daily will be well thought of by others and will obtain food, wealth, and enjoyments without effort."

Moreover, it is stressed that the treasures have been concealed throughout the land of Tibet, so that there is no particular locality, and therefore no local hegemony, that can claim unique authority with respect to them or to the source of their authority, which must be identified with the continuing spiritual power of the old empire. As a famous passage from a fifteenth-century treasure declares:

Because, generally, I harbour great compassion
For the Tibetans, who love what is new,
And for creatures of this defiled age,
I have filled the frontier and centre with treasures. . . .[116]

The emerging cults of Avalokiteśvara and Padmasambhava from the twelfth century onwards thus both engendered a mythical reconstruction of the Tibetan world and set forth in their sādhanas and precepts the means by which one might live in the world thus created, a way which affirmed that the same creative, spiritual ground from which the empire drew its power might be actualized within every individual. We must resist, however, the temptation to place too much emphasis upon the apparently antihierarchical dimensions of this description. Though there is some reason to suppose that there may be a correlation between these cults and the relatively egalitarian communities thriving outside of the political realm dominated by the Central Tibetan estate system,[117] we must also recall that the treasure traditions did establish their own local hierarchies, which focused upon the figure of the treasure-discoverer himself, who was thought always to be Padmasambhava's direct representative.[118] This is very much in evidence in Aris's study of Pemalingpa, of whose legacy in Bhutan he writes:

So prestigious was Pemalingpa's name that his sons, grandsons, and great-grandsons became highly sought after as husbands throughout the area. . . . Thus at least ten of the most important houses headed by religious hierarchs . . . trace their descent from three of Pemalingpa's sons . . . This new aristocracy more or less supplanted the earlier one into which it had married.[119]

The phenomenon that we see at work here drew its strength in large measure from the persisting presence of the old empire and from the continuing felt allegiance to it, rather than to the new and strictly local hegemons who rarely commanded much loyalty outside of their own narrow domains. Once more, it was the Fifth Dalai Lama who clearly understood this, and who systematically deployed the authority of the treasures to underpin the authority of his own regime.[120] It is perhaps not too great an exaggeration to hold, therefore, that it is in the writings and rediscoveries of the twelfth-century treasure-finder Nyangrel Nyima Özer that we find the clearest blueprint for the later Tibetan religiopolitical construction.

9

Samantabhadra and Rudra

Myths of Innate Enlightenment and Radical Evil

Fragments from a Myth of Tibet

I do not propose to examine the historical origins of the myths of Samantabhadra and Rudra in the compass of the present chapter. Even limiting one's field solely to Buddhist materials, it would be essential to consider an extensive body of Indian literature—above all, the many Buddhist tantras—even before seeking to elaborate peculiarly Tibetan developments. And in Tibet itself, we would have to investigate the manner in which the Indian versions of these myths were variously assimilated and transformed through the historical ramification of Tibetan Buddhism into a great number of distinct lineages and schools.[1]

My concern here, therefore, will be solely with the best-known versions of these myths as transmitted in the Nyingmapa tradition of Tibetan Buddhism, for which they have a special importance. I believe that some puzzling aspects of Nyingmapa thought and practice become more readily understandable when we grasp something of the manner in which these myths are employed within that tradition.

The Nyingmapa stand in a distinctive relationship to all other religious traditions of Tibet. As their name, which literally means the "Ancients," suggests, the school maintains that it uniquely represents the ancient Buddhism of Tibet, introduced during the reigns of the great kings of Tibet's imperial age, in the seventh to the ninth centuries C.E. In contradistinction to the organized Bön religion, it identifies itself as a purely Buddhist school, whereas, over and against the other Tibetan Buddhist schools and in harmony with the Bön, it insists upon the value of an autochthonous Tibetan religious tradition, expressed and exalted within a unique and continuing revelation of the Buddha's doctrine in Tibet, often in the form of "treasures" (*gter*). Certain features of Nyingmapa Buddhism are particularly noteworthy in connection with the present discussion. The primordial Buddha Samantabhadra (Tib. *Kun-tu bzang-po*, the "Omnibeneficent"), iconographically most often depicted as celestial blue and naked, is regarded as the supreme embodiment of Buddhahood (shared with Bön). The highest expression of and vehicle for attaining that Buddha's enlightenment (which is equivalent to the enlightenment of all Buddhas) is the teaching of the

"Great Perfection" (*Rdzogs-chen*, shared with Bön). The paradigmatic exponent of this teaching, and indeed of all matters bearing on the spiritual and temporal well-being of the Tibetan people, is the immortal Guru Padmasambhava, who is the apotheosis of the Indian tantric master remembered for playing a leading role in Tibet's conversion to Buddhism during the eighth century, and who is always present to intercede on behalf of his devotees (distinctively Nyingmapa, though the cult of Padmasambhava claims many adherents who are not otherwise Nyingmapa). Moreover, the teachings of the latter are continually renewed in forms suitable to the devotee's time, place, and circumstances, the agents for such renewal being "discoverers of spiritual treasure" (*gter-ston/-bton*), thought to be embodiments of, or regents acting on behalf of, Padmasambhava (in this form, the tradition of "spiritual treasure," *gter-ma*, is distinctly Nyingmapa, though non-Nyingmapa *gter-ma* are known, particularly among the Bönpo).

While the Nyingmapa adhere, as do other Tibetan Buddhists, to tantric forms of ritual and contemplative practice, their tantric canon is altogether distinctive, incorporating a great quantity of literature whose "authenticity" is challenged, as we have seen, by many adherents of the other Tibetan Buddhist schools, as is the authenticity of their special teaching of the Great Perfection.[2] Hence, from relatively early times, their unique standpoint created for the Nyingmapas a remarkable justificatory problem, which has generated an elaborate apologetical literature, much of which is historical in character. Moreover, the peculiar Nyingmapa emphasis on a way of practice that combines elaborate tantric ritualism, including a vast body of regulations and precepts, with the apparent antinomianism of the Great Perfection may appear to embody a remarkable contradiction. It is just this contradiction, in fact, that is both intensified and resolved by the conjunction of the myths considered here. The myths, therefore, may be regarded as part of the justificatory apparatus of the Nyingmapa school.

In their thinking about the history of their own tradition, the Nyingmapas have come to identify three phases in the lineage through which their special doctrines have been transmitted: the "lineage of the Conquerors' intention" (*rgyal-ba dgongs-brgyud*); the "symbolic lineage of the awareness holders" (*rig-'dzin brda-brgyud*); and the "aural lineage of human individuals" (*gang-zag snyan-brgyud*).[3] The first of the "three lineages" is related to the primordial origination and disclosure, in the domain of the Buddha's enlightenment, of the doctrine in question, in this case the Great Perfection teaching. The third concerns the successive transmission of that doctrine through a line of human individuals, related each to the next as master to disciple, and always thought to be placeable, datable persons, though the specifics may be much debated. The second lineage explains the beginnings of the transmission in the human world, the stages whereby a doctrine belonging to the timeless, inexpressible realm of awakening came to be expressed in time. While the conception of the three lineages in this way establishes a context in which some of what we would regard as purely mythic material is systematically distinguished from legend and history, the distinction is made here in terms of a specific narrative content, rather than in terms of narrative genre taken generally.

Of the myths to be considered here, that of Samantabhadra concerns only the "lineage of the Conquerors' intention," while the myth of Rudra sets the stage for the arising of the "symbolic lineage of awareness holders." The latter may thus be placed, liminally, at the boundary of myth and legend, a characterization that seems in several respects to be appropriate. Some writers, for instance, do suggest that it is in principle possible to calculate the date of Rudra's subjugation,[4] but Samantabhadra is everywhere acknowledged to stand outside of ordinary temporal determinations.

Because it is possible to trace out a long incremental development of these myths, extending far back in Indian Buddhist literature—in the case of the myth of Rudra, the eighteenth-century Tibetan author Lelung Zhepei Dorje has in fact assembled much of the required background[5]—there is no more reason to associate them particularly with the authors whose versions I consider here than there is to associate the Christian Hell-Purgatory-Heaven cosmology particularly with Dante, or Satan's fall particularly with Milton. Nevertheless, there is also not much less reason to do so. If I risk overemphasizing here Longchenpa's association with the myth of Samantabhadra, or Orgyen Lingpa's with that of Rudra, it is nonetheless fair to say that these writers are particularly closely associated with the myths in question by Tibetans themselves.

Longchen Rabjampa (1308–1363) and Yarje Orgyen Lingpa (b. 1323) belong to a critical period in Tibetan history, during which, in conjunction with the weakening and final collapse of Mongol power in China (1368), the Sakyapa hegemony (1260–1358), which had successfully protected Tibet from outright Mongol invasion, grew feeble. As a result, Tibet was engulfed in a civil war from which the Phakmodrupa hierarchs eventually emerged victorious.[6] Loyalties shifted rapidly, and Central Tibet found itself adrift in uncertainty. The formative tendencies of the Nyingmapa school, already evident in the work of earlier writers,[7] now resurfaced as a powerful polemic, upholding the spiritual and temporal magnificence of Tibet's imperial past against the decadence and factiousness of contemporary hegemonic leadership. While both Longchenpa and Orgyen Lingpa must be understood in the context of the historical setting in which they lived and worked, and despite their common sectarian affiliation, they appear as altogether distinctive personalities, expressing their common affirmation of the Nyingmapa vision of the Buddhist enlightenment from fundamentally different perspectives.

Longchenpa, to begin, had enjoyed a thorough Buddhist scholastic education; there are suggestions that during his youth he had something of the reputation of a brilliant dilettante.[8] Little of the large corpus of poetry and works on poetics attributed to him, and probably belonging to his earlier years, is now available, but the colophons of such poetical works as have come down to us make clear that he was exceedingly proud of his accomplishments in refined Tibetan composition modeled on Sanskrit *kāvya*.[9] Stylistic elegance would continue to characterize his writing, right down to his final testament. None of the philosophical writings (mostly commentaries) attributed to his early career appear to be currently available,[10] though his command of the major traditions of Indian Buddhist philosophy known in Tibet is evident throughout his later expository writing on the Great Perfection.

When he was in his midtwenties, Longchenpa became disgusted with what he had come to regard as the pretensions of learning in the monastic colleges of Central Tibet, and he decided to seek his enlightenment among the itinerant yogins who dwelt in the isolated hermitages of the Tibetan wilderness. It was here that he came to encounter Kumārarāja (1266–1343), a renowned and saintly adept who specialized in the Nyingmapa tradition of the Great Perfection. The inspiration derived from this teaching would motivate the entire course of Longchenpa's later career, and the volume of his literary work devoted to it is enormous. Though he apparently sought to live as an exemplary yogin and teacher of the Great Perfection tradition, he was not able to avoid political entanglement completely and spent some years in exile in what is today Bhutan. His biography, by one of his disciples, however, provides little detail concerning the charges brought against him and the manner of their resolution, save to indicate that he had been falsely accused of being a partisan of a faction rivaling the Phakmodrupas.

The corpus of Longchenpa's writings on the Great Perfection may be divided into two broad categories: there is his contribution, as final redactor, to the eleven-volume collection of precepts, meditation texts, and ritual manuals known as the *Fourfold Innermost Spirituality* (*Snying-thig ya-bzhi*), this being a particular system (or rather a group of closely related systems) of Great Perfection practice; and there are his numerous original treatises on the theory and practice of the Great Perfection.[11] The works making up the latter category reveal an extraordinarily rich blend of materials and genres—all branches of Indian and Tibetan Buddhist literature are drawn into his discussions, and he moves freely among allegory, rigorous philosophical argument, history, didactic poetry, and so on, as his discourses concerning the Great Perfection progress. So completely does the Nyingmapa tradition regard him as epitomizing this teaching that Longchenpa is called the "Second Samantabhadra"—hence my belief that his formulation of the myth of Samantabhadra may be justly thought to be paradigmatic.

Of Orgyen Lingpa almost nothing reliable is known; the available hagiographies—which make him out to have been, like Longchenpa, the object of some persecution at the hands of the Phakmodrupas—are all quite late.[12] However, the major works attributed to him are the products of an unusual tour de force and so do permit us to adduce a few generalities regarding their author.

All of Orgyen Lingpa's known writings belong to the class of texts known as "treasures," said to have been set down and then concealed by Padmasambhava and his immediate disciples during the eighth or ninth century. Orgyen Lingpa is presented as being merely their rediscoverer. Though "treasures" of various kinds are attributed to him, those for which he is best known are six "historical" works relating the legends of Padmasambhava and of Tibet under the reign of Padmasambhava's royal patron, King Trhi Songdetsen (reigned until 797). These six texts are always thought to form a pair: the *Testimonial Record of Padmasambhava* (*Padma bka'-thang*) and the *Fivefold Collection of Testimonial Records* (*Bka'-thang sde-lnga*). The first is a verse epic, in 108 cantos, telling of the coming of Padmasambhava and his conversion of Tibet to Buddhism during Trhi Songdetsen's reign.[13] The five texts forming the second member of the pair develop aspects of the same story from separate perspectives as documents concerning (1) the indigenous Tibetan gods and demons, (2) the Tibetan kings, (3) the queens, (4) the ministers, and (5) the scholars.[14] Taken together, these works elaborate a powerful vision of Tibet and its historically unique station in the Buddhist universe. Their "prophetic" passages explicitly comment on the political situation in mid-fourteenth-century Tibet, so that the hagiographers' assertions that Orgyen Lingpa became the object of political persecution seem not at all implausible.[15]

The extraordinary body of tradition that finds its way into Orgyen Lingpa's *Testimonial Records* makes it clear that their author was greatly learned in a certain sense, but also that he was not the product of the same refined scholastic upbringing that we know Longchenpa to have enjoyed. His writing is vigorous, but coarse; stylistic fine points were of no interest to him, and this lends his work a peculiar raw power. If Longchenpa's harmonious marriage of poetic elegance and ethereal spirituality suggests at times a Tibetan smiled on by Dante's Beatrice, then Orgyen Lingpa's pen would appear to have been blessed by Chaucer's Wife of Bath.

What I wish to stress here, however, are some assumptions that seem common to them both, which may be summarized briefly: our world is such that the full enlightenment of a Buddha is both a desirable and realizable end for human beings; Tibet has historically become the guardian of the Buddha's doctrine, in which the means to realize that enlightenment are disclosed; and it is the ancient Nyingmapa tradition alone that possesses the quintessential revelation of that doctrine. The myths under consideration here are both concerned to underwrite the first and last of these points in particular.

Before I close this section, it occurs to me that some may wish to know something about the tradition of teaching I've been referring to throughout this book as the Great Perfection (*Rdzogs-pa chen-po*). This is a very difficult question, to which I shall return in the following chapter.[16] Suffice it for the moment to provide some remarks on this topic by Longchen Rabjampa himself, though I recognize that, without further commentary, the terse discussion found here is bound to remain somewhat obscure:

> The unsurpassed vehicle is the supremely esoteric Great Perfection, which brings about real union with the spontaneously present expanse [of reality, *dharmadhātu*]. In the unchanging expanse of the ground, similar to space, the qualities of enlightenment are spontaneously present, like the sun, moon, planets, and stars. Because they are spontaneously present from the very beginning, without having been sought out, the path is one of natural direct perception, without tiresome exertion. Its intention is equivalent to that of the Dharmakāya, self-abiding as the unconditioned maṇḍala of the expanse of inner radiance, and it is the supreme view of the abiding nature of reality that brings about [its] realization. Ephemeral obscurations are clouds in the expanse of purity: in the minds of beings, bewildering appearances become manifest without veridical existence. . . . It is by knowing the nature of bewilderment as the appearance of what is not that one is freed. . . .
>
> Whatever consciousness arises is the self-liberated play of the body of reality, like water and waves, a single undulation in the body of reality. This is the intention of ultimate truth, the uppermost pinnacle among views; this is the Great Perfection.[17]

The Myth of Samantabhadra

Buddhist doctrine has generally affirmed the world to be entirely lawlike; there is a final and ultimate principle (or body of principles), even though, at a certain point in the rarified atmosphere of Buddhist discourse, this may become impossible to grasp in thought or in words. The attempt to analyze the principles underlying apparent reality, and to pursue the course of analysis until no further analysis is possible, has given much of classical Buddhist thought a markedly "metaphysical" character, so that here, perhaps more than in many other instances where a stream of thought not flowing from the Greek spring is termed "philosophical," we may retain this convention unapologetically.

A key problem for Buddhist philosophical thought, throughout its long history, has been this: how can we resolve the triple tension arising from the fundamental assumptions that: (1) the world is lawlike through and through; (2) the world is such that there are ignorant beings who are subject to a continual round of trouble due to their ignorance; and (3) the world is such that these beings may possibly overcome their ignorance and the pain that it brings, thus attaining nirvāṇa? Tension arises here, because it may be thought that (1) determines (2), and so precludes (3); or that (1) determines (3), and so neutralizes (2); or that (2) and (3) jointly entail that (1) be weakened, that is, that the world is almost nomic, but not quite. This is perhaps the Buddhist analogue to the West's headache concerning free will and determinism. The myth of Samantabhadra represents the formulation in Nyingmapa Buddhism of a peculiar way of expressing the mystery of these three fundamental assumptions and their interrelationships.

Corresponding to the three assumptions, what I am terming the "myth of Samantabhadra" (the closest equivalent Nyingmapa phrase is (ii) just below), actually consists of three topics:[18] (i) how the ground became manifest in spontaneous presence (*lhun-grub gzhi-snang-gi shar-tshul*); (ii) how Samantabhadra was liberated (*kun-tu bzang-po'i grol-tshul*); and (iii) how ignorant sentient beings became bewildered (*ma-rig sems-can-gyi 'khrul-tshul*). In form, then, what we have here is a creation myth[19] that explains certain broad features of our world, how it came into being as the peculiar sort of world that it is, and why things are such that it could be no other way. But it is a myth elaborated with a specific philosophical purpose, namely, through topics (i), (ii), and (iii) to make three fundamental but not clearly compatible assumptions of Buddhist thought somehow co-intelligible.

Longchen Rabjampa repeats the myth of Samantabhadra, with or without detailed exposition, at many points scattered throughout his writings. I shall discuss here only the versions found in his massive summation of the peculiar doctrines of the Great Perfection tradition, the *Jewel Treasury of the Supreme Vehicle* (*Theg-mchog rin-po-che'i mdzod*). Here the myth of Samantabhadra is summarized briefly at the very beginning of the text, to introduce the manner in which the Great Perfection teaching originated in the world. It is in this context that Nyingmapas sometimes speak of the myth as representing the "lineage of the Conqueror's intention." Later in the same treatise, the myth is made the subject of a very detailed discussion constituting the whole of the ninth chapter, upon which the discussion that follows here will partially be based. The initial short version is as follows:

> Prior to everything, saṃsāra and nirvāṇa being not divided, nor dividing, nor to be divided, Samantabhadra, the teacher whose dominion is perfect, arose from the primordial ground—the expanse that is self-emergent pristine gnosis, the nucleus of the Sugata—as the manifestation of the ground. In the instant that he emerged from the ground, because he recognized this to be self-manifest, then owing to the three self-emergent principles he seized his imperial realm in the spontaneously present precious enclosure, the great primordial purity that is the original site of exhaustion, the field of the vase-body of youth. The enlightened attributes of renunciation and realization being perfected, he achieved buddhahood in the manner of the dharmakāya, and abides thus inwardly clarified. . . . Subsequently, from the expressive play that arises from

> the original ground as the manifestation of the ground, mundane creatures appeared as if bewildered without cause for bewilderment, as in a dream. Seeing them thus disturbed, his compassionate excellence was aroused. . . .[20]

The original ground (*gdod-ma'i gzhi*) stands wholly removed from the three temporal determinations of past, present, and future. For this reason, it is sometimes spoken of in Nyingmapa thought as being atemporal (*dus-med*), or as being an "indeterminate time" (*ma-nges-pa'i dus*), or a "fourth time" (*dus bzhi-pa*). The ground is pure potency, possible manifest as anything whatsoever (*chos ci-yang 'char-ba, ci-yang snang-ba*). Its faculty for the actualization of its potencies is termed "expressive power" (*rtsal*), and this is intrinsically noetic. The ground in its indeterminacy is essentially empty (*ngo-bo stong*); in its unlimited potency is characteristically open, or limpid (*rang-bzhin gsal*); and in its expressive power is unimpeded spirituality (lit. "compassion," *thugs-rje ma-'gags-pa*). In virtue of these three principles, it is the ground of primordial buddhahood, embodying the attributes of the three "bodies" (*sku-gsum*) of reality (*chos-sku*), rapture (*longs-sku*), and emanation (*sprul-sku*). The expressive power of the ground, being intrinsically noetic, is possibly aware that it is itself the expressive power of the ground—it may "recognize" itself (*rang-ngo-shes*). Because the self-recognition of a timeless ground must belong to the ground in its timelessness, its self-recognition is uniquely characterized as the attainment of buddhahood by the primordial Buddha Samantabhadra. Whereas such self-recognition is a possibility of the noetic aspect of expressive power, that power has also primordially actualized non-self-recognizing cognition, which, alienated from the ground from which it is no other, by virtue of its non-self-recognition, has become "bewildered" (*'khrul-pa*) and so has fallen into multiplicity, projecting itself forward temporally. In this aspect, the expressive power of the ground is "limitless sentient beings." In the *Bkra-shis mdzes-ldan chen-po'i rgyud* (The Great Auspicious and Beauteous Tantra), cited by Longchenpa, the primordial Buddha is made to speak as follows:

> Though I am free from bewilderment, bewilderment has emerged from my expressive power. Though I do not come into being as ground, my nature having arisen without impediment, unawareness has spontaneously emerged from my spirituality that is without determination. Just as clouds do not intrinsically exist in the sky, but emerge fortuitously, so there is no unawareness at all that belongs to the ground. . . .[21]

The passage from the indeterminacy and atemporality of the ground to the temporal projection of numberless sentient beings, without implying that the primordial Buddha must himself fall from his primordial enlightenment, is one that perhaps cannot be made without some element of apparent paradox. My concern is not, however, to elaborate here a suitably purified Nyingmapa cosmogony, but rather to illustrate the manner in which the fundamental Nyingmapa cosmogonic myth is itself constructed as an expression of Nyingmapa speculative thought. What is crucial for the Nyingmapa is that this account establish an essential relationship between the primordial Buddha and sentient beings, such that it be possible for us to recover the ground of our being and thus to participate in Samantabhadra's beginningless enlightenment.

The path of practice by means of which our recovery of Samantabhadra's enlightenment is to take place is, of course, the path of the Great Perfection, whose skillful means are intended precisely to introduce sentient beings directly to their affinity

Figure 9.1 Samantabhadra in the form of the body of rapture (*Sambhogakāya*). A modern statue at Mindröling. The iconography merits comparison with that of the imperial-period Vairocana (see fig., p. 64).

with Samantabhadra. When such an introduction takes place, the goal of the path may be realized almost immediately. As the Tibetan poet-saint Milarepa (1040–1123) was told by his Nyingmapa teacher Rongtön Lhaga:

> "This teaching of the Great Perfection leads one to triumph at the root, to triumph at the summit, and to triumph in the fruits of achievement. To meditate on it by day is to be Buddha in one day. To meditate on it by night is to be Buddha in one night."[22]

But what is one to do who is so bewildered by obscuration that he simply cannot perceive that to which he is to be introduced by the teaching of the Great Perfection? That was Milarepa's problem; perhaps it is also my problem; and it is possibly your problem, too. The myth of Rudra offers the Nyingmapa response to this dilemma.

The Matricide Rudra

In the Rudra episode of the *Testimonial Record of Padmasambhava*, the raw energy of Orgyen Lingpa's verse reaches one of its several pinnacles. The episode occurs early on and belongs to the section of the work treating the cosmological background for, and past lives preceding, the actual birth of Padmasambhava. In its earliest versions, in Indian Buddhist tantric literature, the myth concerns the defeat of Śiva by the Buddha, and the manner in which their battle necessitated and prepared the ground for the appearance in the world of the tantras taught by the Buddha.[23] Perhaps an antecedant can even be detected in the Buddha's confrontation with Māra.[24] In one of the peculiarly Nyingmapa tantras, the *Mdo dgongs-pa 'dus-pa* (The Sūtra Gathering All Intentions), the myth is enormously expanded and becomes the organizing metaphor for the text as a whole.[25] It is this tradition that Orgyen Lingpa incorporates into his own work, where the fifth canto tells of Rudra's appearance in the world, and the sixth of his final subjugation.[26] The translated text of the opening of the fifth relates Rudra's past life as the wayward monk Tharpa Nakpo ("Black Liberation"):

After the teaching of Samantabhadra,
In the land called Dujongtsham,
There was the householder Koukāla,
Who had a son named Kouküntri
And a servant, Pramadeva.
The two were seen to be fit to be trained by the two teachings.[27]
To prevent the decline of the emanational body's teaching,
[The master] took birth as the monk Thupka Zhönu.
To prevent the decline of the secret mantras, the teaching of the body of
rapture,
He took birth as a great householder, a "family-maintainer."
All men were exceptionally devoted to that monk,
Known as one with one body but two names.[28]
Taking up the great path of five yogas,[29] he practiced,
And saw the skandhas' abode to be empty.
At that time Kouküntri grew faithful,
And his doubts were resolved, whoever he asked:
"What manner of teacher is Thupka Zhönu?
Does he teach the doctrine that without attaining enlightenment,
Without abandoning affliction, you may practice just as you please?"
"The monk teaches just that," they said,
"To remove ignorance and realize nirvāṇa,
Thupka Zhönu is the best."
Kouküntri and Pramadeva
Went to Thupka Zhönu's abode.
"May you, skillful in means, accept us
To receive the mantras' intention, to behold the exalted truth
In yoga by practicing as one pleases,
Retaining doubts and the three afflictions."
Praying thus, they bowed their heads to his feet.
The teacher said, "So it is! Certainly! Fine!
Men say that while the round of saṃsāra persists,
The jewel of the saṃgha is best!"
Then both master and servant came forth as monks,

Ordained as Tharpa Nakpo and Denphak by name.
Denphak was elected to grasp the occasion for his liberation.
At that time the monk Tharpa Nakpo
Petitioned Thupka Zhönu in these words:
"O mantra guardian, great holder of spells!
What is the path that causes release
From all extreme sufferings?"
The teacher, with radiant smile, responded:
"In what is as it is there's no contrivance.
Though you live practicing the four evil matters,[30]
They are just like clouds in the sky.
This is the path of genuine yoga.
If you don't realize this, then throughout the three realms
No further stage among views will be found!"
So he taught well the investigation of mind.
Tharpa and his servant rejoiced,
And worshiped him with offerings of devotion.
Singing his praises they went home.
Tharpa practiced the doctrine literally;
Not realizing the definitive meaning, his afflictions were inflamed.
Engrossed in the four evil matters,
He maintained a religious deportment in body, while his mind became foul.
The servant Denphak realized the definitive meaning:
His intelligence grew while he practiced correctly.
Unengrossed, he knew to uphold just what the teacher had taught.
He maintained a deteriorating deportment in body,
While his mind, journeying on the certain path, deviated not in its view.
After some time had passed, master and servant,
Discordant in theory and practice, had occasion to quarrel.
The monk Tharpa Nakpo expressed his opinion:
"The two of us met with one single master.
How is it that we disagree on the meaning
And experiential cultivation of one phrase?"
Denphak gave Tharpa Nakpo this answer:
"I understand only confident meditation
Based on perfect equipoise."
Tharpa Nakpo responded:
"I have also practiced quite certainly,
So that my practice of secret mantras accords with the doctrine."
And Tharpa Nakpo added in arrogance:
"Denphak, your theory and practice are wrong!
Affliction and pristine noesis
have only a single basis.
By relative, tiresome virtues
one achieves enlightenment not.
I am established in an absolute, effortless condition!"
To that Denphak made his reply:

"Consciousness purified of obsessive attachment is pristine gnosis.
What is as it is, uncontrived, is the mantra-path.
Afflictions, like clouds, dissolve in the expanse.
One must strive, maintaining the three superior practices.[31]
This is teacher Thupka's intention."
When he said this, Tharpa Nakpo was enraged:
"Master Thupka Zhönu, without contrivance,
Is no deceiver, but upright and honest!
Let's go—get up quickly!—to ask that great sage,
The world's doctrinal king, just what's what!"
Master and servant both went and asked.
The teacher, discerning the difference, said, "Denphak's right."
Tharpa Nakpo's mind flew into a rage of resentment:
"One master with two dissimilar viewpoints!
His entire teaching is perverse,
And always involves self-contradiction!"
With verbal abuse he fired his servant Denphak,
And, it being his way to wander down all evil paths,
Accusing him harshly, banished him to distant abodes.
"Like the disciple, the master's a common man.
Not just saying that we two were similar,
Teaching error, he really rebuked me.
That biased one, not allowed to live here,
Must be expelled. I'll seize the realm!" So he thought.
He expelled him to the farthest frontier,
  and abandoned him someplace far away.

The apostate Tharpa Nakpo now becomes increasingly vile—a murderer, drunkard, and whoremonger. His path becomes a descending spiral, traced through numberless lives, born in forms ever more despicable, until he falls to the abysmal Vajra Hell. Aeons pass and he is released, only to be reborn among goblins and vermin for 20,000 more lifetimes. And then:

After Buddha Dīpaṃkara's teaching,
Before Śākyamuni's teaching appeared,
Was an interval of many years without teaching.
In the demon-land called Laṅkāpurṇa,
There was a whore named "Wanders About."
In the evening she slept with a devil, at midnight with a king,
And at dawn with a god.
  In her womb he was conceived.
Because there were three fathers—god, devil, and man—
After eight months a three-headed son was born.
He had six arms and four legs;
Spontaneously two wings burst from his body.
Each head had three eyes, nine in all.
His attributes were many and varied.
When he was born, evil omens appeared:

Ills of all kinds filled Laṅkā;
The whole mass of merit declined;
All auspicious portents fell away;
Famine, plague, and the pox all spread;
As in nightmares, the host of ghosts gathered.
After his birth, in the ninth month, the childbirth illness returned,
And Wanders About herself passed away.
The locals said, "This evil bastard
Should be returned to his mother's womb!"
To the root of the charnel tree Fornication,
Where there sleeps Ignorance, the black charnel pig,
Where the poison snake Hatred coils the trunk,
Where the charnel bird Passion makes its topmost nest,
All dead demons were carried there.
Tigers and elephants made their abodes there,
And there all venomous snakes were entwined.
Ḍākinīs brought human corpses there.
At the root, the demons built their charnel house.
The mother's corpse, with her son, was hauled out
on a stretcher and left there.

The demon-child survives by devouring his deceased mother's body, eventually emerging from the charnel ground as a monster of extraordinary power. His conquests engulf the subterranean and terrestrial realms, until he seeks to bring even the domain of the gods under his sway, challenging all to do battle with him. The name by which he is feared is "Matricide Rudra." The Buddhas and bodhisattvas of all times and places, responding to the terrified supplications of the gods, assemble to determine the means whereby this demonic force that threatens to engulf all saṃsāra might be at last defeated. Prominent among the Buddhas is Vajrasattva, the Adamantine Being, who, it so happens, is none other than Thupka Zhönu, the banished master of Rudra's past life as the apostate Tharpa Nakpo, while his former servant Denphak is now Vajrapāṇi, the Holder of the Adamantine Sceptre. They are ordained by those assembled to assume the forms of Avalokiteśvara, the bodhisattva of compassion, and his consort, the saviouress Tārā, who are then consecrated as the ferocious couple Hayagrīva, "Horse Neck," and Vajravārāhī, "Adamantine Sow," to do battle with Rudra. Hayagrīva, making himself minute, enters Rudra's "lower gate," the anus, and then explodes to tremendous proportion within his body. The demon, vanquished, vows to serve the Buddha's teaching as a powerful protector, and the elements of his broken body are transubstantiated to become the sacraments of tantric Buddhism. For this reason, Hayagrīva, as Avalokiteśvara's wrathful counterpart, is depicted as demonic in outer form, with a small horse's head emerging from the crown of the demon's skull; he is thus always garbed in the body of Rudra.

In Orgyen Lingpa's telling of it, the myth of Rudra is exceptionally complex, and the would-be interpreter of it must be wary of the seductions of possible reductionist readings. Robert Paul, among the most perceptive interpreters of this myth to date, has focused primarily on those themes that can be clearly related to his overriding concern with exploring the structural problems posed by the continuity of genera-

Figure 9.2 The wrathful Hayagrīva, a small horse's head protruding within his flaming hair. A recent *thang-ka* painting.

tions in Sherpa and Tibetan society. Fraternal rivalry (= the rivalry of codisciples), antagonism between father and son (= master and disciple), matricide, and homosexual anal rape are among the key motifs in Paul's reading, which is markedly influenced by the psychoanalytic work of Géza Róheim.[32] It is not my concern here to attempt to assess Paul's interpretations in general, and, indeed, I think that Paul has suggested and begun to develop a powerful hermeneutic. At the same time, however, he has necessarily bracketed those elements of the tale that have no apparent bearing on the proposed interpretation. What I should like to do, then, is to turn to some of the other aspects of Orgyen Lingpa's version of the myth, without attempting an overarching interpretation. In accord with my primary focus on the character of Tibetan Buddhist thought, I wish to concentrate on the apparently "philosophical" aspects of the first section of the Rudra tale just translated. Paul dismisses this entire passage in a single and, to my mind, misleading sentence:

> Whereas Evil Pig [= Denphak in my translation here. Paul is following Toussaint's problematic reading of the name as Ngan-phag.] understood and accepted the master's teaching, Universal Misery, or Black Deliverance [= Tharpa Nakpo], failed to see the

value of a doctrine which preaches the vanity of this world and nonattachment to all things.[33]

Clearly, Orgyen Lingpa's narration of the episode attaches more weight than this to the "bad disciple's" failure of understanding: if Tharpa Nakpo's response to the teaching is to be summed up as a shrugged "I don't get it," then it becomes very difficult to see how this long segment of the story should be related to the brutal events that follow.

Let us return then to the beginning of the tale, to the assertion that the events to be recounted take place after the teaching of Samantabhadra. We have seen already how the Samantabhadra myth attempts to bridge the gulf between time and eternity, between primordial enlightenment and the bewilderment of sentient beings. The Rudra episode, by opening with reference to this, begins by indexing itself in relation to the temporal projection of mundane being that unfolds when the expressive power of the ground has passed into bewilderment. All of the events that follow are thus circumscribed by bewilderment.

As sentient beings, we have all already failed to see what Thupka Zhönu sought to reveal to his two disciples. Because we have all thus failed in primordial time, it would be odd to regard that to be the particular point Orgyen Lingpa is seeking to drive home here; for it has already been driven home by placing the entire episode outside the domain of Samantabhadra's teaching. What I think we should attend to, rather, is the relationship delineated among simple failure to understand, egocentric rebellion of the will, and radical evil. Saṃsāra is not merely bewildering (after all, couldn't one be eternally subject to pleasant bewilderment?), but it's downright vicious, and to see why this is so, we must trace the temporal projection of saṃsāric being from the primordial origination of bewilderment to the point at which that bewilderment generates pride—it is not just error, but rather arrogant error, that condemns us to the round of meaningless pain. The myth of Rudra is Buddhism's closest approach to a myth of original sin.[34]

The myth of Rudra "explains" the origins of tantricism, in part because Rudrahood characterizes our nature as embodied persons who are constitutionally disposed to lust and self-protection, to arrogance and rage. Tantricism, or something like it, is soteriologically necessitated by our being what we are, by our world's being as it is. So it is that the Nyingmapa practitioner, on days when penitential rites are required, recites a confessional litany entitled *Rudra's Lamentation*.[35]

Must the Message Be Mythic?

If the "philosophical" readings of the myths of Samantabhadra and Rudra that I've begun to sketch out here (and, admittedly, much remains to be filled in) reflect in part the manner in which these myths are understood within the Nyingmapa tradition, then they will contribute to the formation of a contextualizing myth about Nyingmapa Buddhism, in relation to which other features of Nyingmapa practice and thought will be more intelligible to us than they might have been otherwise. I believe that this is in fact the case, that the peculiar Nyingmapa synthesis of the Great Perfection teaching of the intrinsic enlightenment of all beings—a teaching that, like certain aspects of Chan, seems irreducibly subitist and antinomian—with the gradualist esotericism of the tantras, may be now seen as something more than jumbled eclecticism. For the combined argument of the two myths generates a view of the human condition according to which our inherent identity with the Omnibeneficent Buddha is concealed not only by the veil of unknowing, but further by a profound and eminently evil act of rebellion—some may recognize here an intensified reformulation of the classical Buddhist doctrine of the "two obscurations."[36] It is therefore only the violent inversion of the soul, catalyzed by the powerful means taught in the tantras, that can create within us the essential clearing in which the truth of the Great Perfection may be disclosed.

The myth of Samantabhadra as told by Longchen Rabjampa, and that of Rudra as told by Orgyen Lingpa, are thus seen to be constructed so as to convey, among other things, a number of apparently philosophical messages concerning eternity and temporality, enlightenment and bewilderment, understanding and the rebellion of the will in ignorance. It is clear that both of these authors have deliberately incorporated these messages into their mythmaking; these are not cases in which apparent philosophical messages are discovered in "primitive" myths thanks only to the learned interpretations of contemporary readers. It is equally clear that the messages in question can in some respects be separated from the myths in which they are found—not only our analysis, but the commentarial tradition of Nyingmapa Buddhism confirms that in practice.[37] Why, then, continue to tell the myths at all? Because they are more entertaining than cold, dry philosophy? Because they give the messages in question extra oomph? Or is there some essential element that is unavoidably left out whenever the philosophical message is removed from the tale in which it is told?

Human thought, to repeat what an ancient and hallowed tradition tells us, is forever oscillating between two poles, and finding a lasting home for itself in neither: at one extreme it follows Plato into his heavens and takes up its dwelling among eternal and unchanging objects; at the other it steps into the stream with Heraclitus, to be inundated by the surging flood of change. The abiding truths of the human condition, however, disclose themselves to us, if ever they do, precisely in the midst of the stream. For this reason we cannot desist from being tellers of tales: our fall and redemption are played out only in time. The philosopher who knows well to bathe in the Heraclitean stream, to warm his head beneath Plato's sun, will be content that both are present in the landscape of thought and recognize in narrative a path between them. Sometimes he will find philosophy progressing along it, seeking out a fertile spot, trying to find the perfect balance of moisture and warmth.

So long as philosophy remains anchored in our common experience, it will have need of plentiful tales, and some of these tales will be myths. For these, indeed, are its anchor. Must the message be mythic? From the vantage point we've reached here, it becomes difficult to see how it could be otherwise.

10

The Amnesic Monarch and the Five Mnemic Men

"Memory" in the Great Perfection Tradition

Preliminary Orientations

In the literature of the Great Perfection (rdzogs-chen) traditions of the Nyingmapa school of Tibetan Buddhism, the words *dran-pa,* "memory" (= Skt. *smṛti, smaraṇa*), and *dran-med,* "freedom from or loss of memory, unconsciousness, inattentiveness" (= Skt. *vismṛti, asmṛti*), are very frequently encountered, among other terms formed on the lexeme *dran-,* "to remember."[1] Though no systematic exegesis of the use of these terms within the tradition itself has yet come to my attention, it appears nonetheless possible to attempt a tentative account of the role of certain basic terms relating to memory in a few distinctive contexts.[2]

Something must be said at the outset of the way in which "distinctive context" is to be understood here. The literature of the Great Perfection developed in some respects in a fluid relationship with other branches of Tibetan religion and culture:[3] on the one hand, for instance, we find the colloquializing tendencies of Tibetan biographical and popular literature informing the diction of those writing on the Great Perfection; while on the other, normative uses of Indian Buddhist scholastic materials are also well represented. Thus such monumental products of doctrinal speculation and systematization as the *Yid-bzhin mdzod* (The Wish-Fulfilling Treasury) or the *Shing-rta chen-mo* (Great Chariot) of Longchen Rabjampa (1308–1363) involve the deliberate effort to disclose the Great Perfection as fully harmonized with, in fact the culmination of, the Indian Buddhist inheritance of theory and practice.[4] To survey the occurrences of *dran-* derivatives in such works would require the repetition of a great amount of material gleaned from Indian Abhidharma and Yogācāra sources, which are not among our present concerns.[5]

Nonetheless, the superabundance of texts of the Great Perfection traditions that have become available during the past two decades do reveal a unique system, a substantial portion of whose technical terminology is not shared by other Buddhist schools, for example, *rtsal*, "expressive power," *ka-dag*, "primordial purity," *cog-bzhag*, "total presence," and so forth. And many terms that are common elsewhere are also found in Great Perfection writings, used in special senses or with peculiar connotations, for instance, *rig-pa*, "awareness," *rol-pa*, "(dis)play," or *thugs-rje*, "compassion/spirituality."[6] The question we should ask about *dran-* derivatives then is: in those texts that are not especially concerned to harmonize the Great Perfection with scholastic norms, but instead to present it as a distinctive way of thought and practice, do we find evidence to suggest that these terms were regularly used in a peculiar manner, which possibly extends beyond the parameters of normal Tibetan colloquial and Buddhist technical usage?

It is clear that this question must be answered affirmatively, though the volume of extant Great Perfection texts precludes a thorough survey of the relevant material at the present time. My discussion will therefore concern selected themes in just one well-defined group of texts whose authority within the tradition provides some assurance that the conclusions reached will characterize the perspective of the Great Perfection traditions more broadly than such a narrow sampling might otherwise suggest.

The texts chosen for consideration here are all drawn from the rediscovered "treasures" (*gter-ma*) of Rikdzin Gödem (1337–1408), founder of the important Nyingmapa suborder of the Northern Treasure (*byang-gter*), so called because the original site of these treasures' revelation was Zangzang Lhadrag, a sacred mountain in the wilds of Tibet's Northern Plain (*byang-thang*).[7] Among the many treasures forming the corpus of Rikdzin Gödem's rediscoveries, the Great Perfection is expansively treated in the two closely related cycles of the *Kun-tu bzang-po'i dgongs-pa zang-thal* (The Penetration of the Intention of Samantabhadra) and the *Ka-dag rang-byung rang-shar* (Primordial Purity, Self-Emergent and Self-Arisen), which in fact are often transmitted as a single corpus.[8] They are marked by an unusual clarity and precision of diction, in which it may be possible to detect some affinity with the Great Perfection writings of Longchen Rabjampa. And—what makes them most suitable for present purposes—*dran-* derivatives seem to receive a remarkable degree of emphasis throughout.

In the discussion that follows, I shall set forth a preliminary analysis of the use of words generated from the lexeme *dran-* as they occur in a single text of the *Primordial Purity, Self-Emergent and Self-Arisen* collection, the *Sangs-rgyas rdo-rje sems-dpa'i dgongs-pa: kun-grol yangs-pa'i rgyud* (The Intention of Buddha Vajrasattva, the Wide-Open Tantra of Universal Liberation).[9] So as to bracket out irrelevant connotations that stem from the use of the English words "memory," "recollection," "forgetting," and so on, I shall use derivatives of the Greek root *mnā*, "to remember, be mindful" (= Skt. *smṛ*) for all Tibetan terms formed on *dran-*. Thus, for *dran-pa*, I shall use the phrase "mnemic engagement"; for *dran-med*, "amnesis"; for *dran-rig*, "mnemic awareness" (i.e., acts of awareness involving mnemic engagement); and for *dran-pa'i mi*, "mnemic man" (the sense of this allegorical phrase will become clear later). Where *dran-* is best treated as a verb, it will unfortunately be necessary to employ some wordy constructions, for instance, "to practice mnemic engagement," but this still seems preferable to the introduction of English verbs whose connotations might sometimes be even more misleading. For "memory" and "remembering" seem to be for us terms preeminently referring to the representation of the past, so that our preunderstanding as determined by them may sometimes obscure the significance of *dran-* in the present discussion.[10]

While the preliminary analysis of the concept of mnemic engagement in Great Perfection thought will have a markedly phenomenological coloring to it, it would be an error to suggest, as some recent writers have perhaps done, that the tradition of thought and practice here considered is to be distinguished as a sort of phenomenology par excellence. This is plainly incorrect. Indeed, it will be precisely to avoid this misapprehension that we shall turn, in later sections of this chapter, to study the doctrines considered here as they are employed within the cycle of the *Penetration of the Intention of Samantabhadra* in allegory and in the practice of prayer. The issue of paramount concern for the Great Perfection thinker is salvific praxis, praxis that must open up a passageway mediating between "ordinary" experience and the rich domain of symbolic forms, the *mundus imaginalis,*[11] and between the latter and that primordial reality that stands in the final analysis beyond temporality and symbolic mediation. Our discussion, accordingly, will seek broadly to introduce the theme of mnemic engagement as it pertains to each of these three worlds, proceeding from its function in "introducing" the timeless realm of the *dharmakāya,* to its symbolic representation in allegory, to its role in the transfiguration of the ordinary through the ritual practice of prayer.[12]

Mnemic Engagement in the *Wide-Open Tantra of Universal Liberation*

The *Wide-Open Tantra of Universal Liberation* does not use all of the terms just listed. So as to comprehend more clearly the contextual background for the occurrences of *dran-* we do find there, it will be useful to have some conception of the text overall, as this will supply a brief Baedeker to the particular system of the Great Perfection involved here. A short work of nine chapters, its first treats the nature of the primordial ground, and the manner in which the original Buddha Samantabhadra and bewildered sentient beings have both arisen from it.[13] The second chapter concerns the characteristics of bewilderment, which obstructs the potential to encounter and realize the teachings whereby the freedom of buddhahood may be achieved. This is followed by "The Introduction to Awareness as the Dharmakāya." "Introduction" (*ngo-sprod/-sprad*), as used in this third chapter in its technical sense, refers to instruction that, if skillfully delivered to an appropriately receptive disciple by an appropriately qualified master, catalyzes an immediate intuitive grasp of the instruction's content. This need not be so mysterious as it may seem: when a tennis pro points out what's wrong with your serve with the result that there is a flash of recognition, you exclaim, "Got it!" and then deliver one that screams past Martina, you've just become the fortunate recipient of an "introduction." But here we're concerned not with the contact of racket and ball, but with the primordial relationship between the essential nature of mind and the ground of its origination. It is this third chapter that first uses *dran-*, though elsewhere Gödem does use it in connection with subject matter similar to that of the earlier chapters of the text, for example, in the *Prayer of Great Power* (translated in the book's appendix).

The fourth and fifth chapters survey, respectively, false assumptions about the nature of apparent reality and the manner in which these generate continued bewilderment, and the essential elements of practical instruction on meditation that accord with the teachings given in the preceding chapters. For the purposes of the present discussion, it is the sixth chapter that is perhaps the most important: "On Circumstantial Proximity to the Dharmakāya." This describes the recovery of the realization of the dharmakāya under the varied circumstances to which ordinary experience subjects us, such as birth and death, waking consciousness, sleep and dream.

The two following chapters conclude the actual teaching of the *Wide-Open Tantra of Universal Liberation* by providing practical details regarding the appropriate times at which the various meditational practices of the Great Perfection are to be undertaken, and the means whereby buddhahood may be realized during the intermediate state following death. Because this is a "rediscovered treasure" (*gter-ma*), the ninth and final chapter presents a discourse on the concealment of the text, with prophecies of its recovery.[14]

In its small span of ten folios, then, the *Wide-Open Tantra of Universal Liberation* provides a remarkably thorough account of the central features of Great Perfection cosmology, phenomenology, and soteriology, describing the most essential elements of both theory and practice. The fact that a given term does not occur in a particular context, of course, should not be taken as evidence that the term does not elsewhere so occur. But the very brevity of the text permits, at least, the isolation of a relatively small range of characteristic occurrences of the technical terms found therein. The instances of *dran-* occurring in the *Wide-Open Tantra of Universal Liberation* are given here in full, beneath the headings of the chapters in which they are found and in the order of their occurrence:

Chapter 3: The Introduction to Awareness As the Dharmakāya

(137.5) "One ought to attend to the example and its significance, with unwavering mnemic engagement."[15] This occurs in the beginning of the chapter and is offered as an injunction preceding the "introduction" itself. "Mnemic engagement" in this instance means, roughly, "mindful attentiveness," that is, to the content of the teachings about to be conferred.

(138.3) "Concerning this mind that is bewildered at present, from the time of one's birth until now, mnemic engagement [reflecting] whatever one's done [has been and] is [karmic] residue."[16] The topic under discussion is the bewilderment arising from the universal ground in its conditional aspect (*sbyor-ba rkyen-gyi kun-gzhi*). Here, "mnemic engagement" is a determination of the "bewildered mind," referring to my continuously renewed construction of my past, and to the particular acts of consciousness that inform that construction. It is not uncommon, in similar contexts, to see it closely related to *bag-chags* (Skt. *vāsanā*), residual dispositions generated by previous action, *karman.*

(138.6–139.1) "Just that is the self-presenting awareness that is the dharmakāya. By continuous mnemic engagement in it, one thoroughly investigates and establishes it."[17] This passage concludes the "introduction" given in chapter three. Reference to "mnemic engagement" here involves a double entendre: on the one hand, the "it" (*de*) that in the second sentence indicates the object of the act in question may refer to the propositional content of the teaching just given (namely, that "thus-and-such is the self-presenting awareness that is the dharmakāya."). In this case, "mnemic engagement" must mean, roughly, "mindful attentiveness" that is directed upon that teaching. On the other hand, the object must also be understood to be the "self-presenting awareness that is the dharmakāya," so that "mnemic engagement" must also refer to the reflexive disclosure of that awareness to the meditator who has grasped the point of the teaching, who has genuinely realized the "introduction." "Investigation" in this case cannot be the discursive analysis of ideas or their contents. Rather, it is the self-disclosure of the meditator's awareness *qua* dharmakāya. The double entendre here is, I think, deliberate, precisely marking the passage from a preliminary intentional relationship between the disciple's thought and the content of the "introduction" she has been granted, to the disciple's nonintentional, reflexive recovery of the self-presenting awareness that is the dharmakāya. This act of recovery is in a sense the objective of a secondary intention, for it is the intention of the teaching whose content is the intention of initial reflection. In the terminology of normative scholastic Buddhism, this passage would be analogous to the movement from "discernment born of thought" (*cintāmayī prajñā*) to "discernment born of meditative cultivation" (*bhāvanāmayī prajñā*).[18]

Chapter 5: The Teaching of the Conduct of the Path

(141.2–3) "At that time, when one is in meditative equipoise, then, neither passing into amnesis, which follows after [the discursive thoughts, imaginings, and so forth, that] proceed one after the next, nor passing, withdrawn, into sleep and oblivion, awareness is essentially self-clarifying."[19] "Amnesis" is here the engagement in discursive thought that militates against those forms of "mnemic engagement" that favor or are constitutive of the realization of the goals of the path. A few lines later the latter conception is further elaborated:

(141.3–4) "The wide-open universal ground is dharmakāya-as-mother, and uncontrived awareness is dharmakāya-as-son. If the son's mnemic engagement is not lost, then, meeting with the mother, bliss is won."[20] And later in the same chapter we are told:

(142.6) "When the five poisons [stupidity, passion, hate, envy, and pride] adventitiously arise, the least [of disciples] looks to the essence of beginning-and-end [that is, determines the emptiness of the 'poisons' in terms of their coming-into-being, abiding, and perishing], the middling [disciple] looks to the appearance of objects as apparition, and the best, through mnemic engagement, looks to self-presenting awareness."[21] The continued use of the verb "to look/gaze/perceive" (*lta*) throughout this passage, which accords with the Tibetan stylistic love of verbal parallelism, should not obscure the nonintentional character of the practice attributed to the best disciple here, as contrasted with the two preceding (though it must also be noted that the Great Perfection traditions make abundant use of ocular imagery). To clarify somewhat the notion of nonintentional presentation, consider those instances in which we have a "sense-memory" or the memory of a mood, not in the propositional sense of remembering that we were once in the mood in question, but in the sense of being in a certain mood and re-cognizing it, as part of that experienced state of being. "Memory," in such cases, is the palpable recovery of a state of being or affect, and thus in a peculiar sense is no more intentional in its phenomenological character than were the apparently recovered experiences when they originally occurred. It is a secondary act of awareness that determines that the act in question is a memory of a prior experience, and this secondary act is, of course, an intentional one. It is, however, an act of awareness that one is experiencing a type of memory and not the memory itself.

Chapter 6: On Circumstantial Proximity to the Dharmakāya

This chapter makes plentiful use of *dran-*, and, most significantly, closes by making explicit a distinction of usage that has been presupposed throughout the preceding discussion. Rather than enumerate each occurrence in this chapter separately, it will be clearer to present them in two groups, abridging the text somewhat in the first instance.

(144.3–6) "This arising of awareness as anything whatever, by dissolving into the dharmakāya itself, [results in] sleep's being a self-emergent immobility. When dream-appearances arise, suffering fades away immediately following mnemic engagement. . . . Thus, the many bewildering appearances of dream are just mind's own light: manifesting shimmeringly, they dissolve into [that] itself. By mnemic engagement alone, [the dualistic modes of] apprehended object and apprehender are released. Therefore, swiftness of mnemic engagement is supreme."[22] The modes of mnemic engagement involved in the meditational discipline of the dream-state appear to be essentially similar to those already considered: there may be a mindful attentiveness to the content of received teaching, leading to an immediate "fading away" of phenomenal suffering, or the nonintentional recovery of mind's ground, aroused by the recognition that the "bewildered appearances of dream are just mind's own light," and involving the "release" of subject and object.

(145.1–4) "The trio of womb, sleep, and the intermediate state, are envisioned as one in essence: this is repeatedly envisioned [through] mnemic engagement, in which the succession of discursive thought has not arisen. If one thinks that mnemic engagement becomes discursive thought,[23] then [in response to that objection it may be affirmed that] discursive thought is that successive mnemic engagement that pursues external objects. The genuine mnemic engagement associated with the dharmakāya is not lost in succession and is free from obsessive attachment. It is self-emergent and is pristine gnosis, the view of the equanimity of the dharmakāya, awareness that is self-clarifying pristine gnosis."[24]

Chapter 7: The Teaching of the Time of Realization

(146.2) "Even if a bewildered mind does arise with respect to appearances, it is reined in immediately by mnemic engagement. The self-emergent body of essential reality (= Skt. *svābhāvikakāya*) being comprehended, realization is at hand when objects arise."[25] The reflexive mnemic engagement of mind in its ground is not to be construed as a sort of trance-like oblivion. Emergent objects are neither forgotten nor forsaken, but now are revalued as reminders, signaling mind's potential straying into bewilderment to mind itself, and thus continually arousing its capacity for genuine mnemic engagement.

Chapter 8: The Attainment of Buddhahood during the Intermediate State

(147.2–3) "As soon as you part from this physical body, then just as darkness is dispelled at dawn, you become mnemically engaged in the esoteric precepts of the three temporal phases of the intermediate state. Attaining stability in the appearance of pristine gnosis, visionary clarity emerges in the self-presenting awareness that is dharmakāya."[26] *Dran-* here operates much as it had the earlier in passages 137.5 and 138.6–139.1, though the occasion is now the intermediate state (*bar-do*) intervening between death and rebirth, and not the state of ordinary waking consciousness.[27]

The foregoing survey provides, I believe, sufficient evidence to suggest that, in the doctrines of the Great Perfection as represented by Rikdzin Gödem, *dran-* derivatives are used in some clearly delineated senses, which will be found to occur with remarkable consistency throughout the textual corpus under consideration, despite the genre differences of particular texts. In the absence of a formal treatise explicitly devoted to *dran-*, we are nevertheless entitled to maintain that the texts under consideration do present a relatively well-formed doctrine of "memory." The occurrences of *dran-* found here may be gathered into four primary categories, which I have summarized, enumerating the passages that I believe represent the uses in question. The first of these categories is quite general. Passages listed under more than one heading either include several distinctive occurrences of the terms under consideration, or, in a few instances involving uses B and C, seem reasonably subject to either interpretation:

A. Mnemic engagement (*dran-pa*) = mnemic acts (i.e., memory, recollection, recognition, etc.) that are determinations of the domain of mundane possibilities, or saṃsāra: 138.3, 145.1–4.
B. Mnemic engagement (*dran-pa*) = mindful attentiveness (directed upon whatever contributes to advancement on the path): 137.5, 138.6–139.1, 141.3–4, 144.3–6, 145.1–4, 147.2–3.
C. Mnemic engagement (*dran-pa*) = immediate recovery of the self-presenting awareness of the dharmakāya: 138.6–139.1, 141.3–4, 142.6, 144.3–6, 145.1–4, 146.2.
D. Amnesis (*dran-med*) = negatively valued engagement in discursive thought, oblivion with respect to primordial awareness. (Let us note that *dran-med*, as the negation of B. and especially of C., refers to discursive engagement constituting the bewilderment of saṃsāra, so that in one sense D. *dran-med*, is equivalent to A. *dran-pa*. As the *Prayer of Great Power* also makes clear, amnesis marks a drifting away from the original ground of awareness on the part of sentient beings.]: 141.2–3.

We may note too that in some contexts *dran-med* may be said, quite oppositely, to characterize the practice of the path, referring in this case, it seems, to contemplative "oblivion" marked by freedom from discursive thought (i.e., freedom from A. *dran-pa*). Gödem in fact uses *dran-med* in this fashion in several passages I've located, though not in the tantra considered here.[28] We shall refer to this as:

E. amnesis (*dran-med*). (Because this is not much emphasized in the texts we are considering, it is bracketed in table 2.)

In elaborating our account further, it seems essential that we address at once an important objection, for we have not yet shown that the various significations of the *dran-* derivatives found here do indeed have some common semantic or conceptual core. Some might object that we are dealing not with a unified concept, but with the use of a single lexeme to refer to a number of genuinely distinct concepts that, for one reason or another, are often accidentally associated with one another. The association of both memory and mindfulness with the Sanskrit root *smṛ-* is often thought of as an instance of just such a phenomenon. I believe that, in this instance, the objection will not hold; *dran-* in Great Perfection thought represents a univocal but highly abstract concept, with reference to which the various *dran-* derivatives surveyed here may all be understood.

To see how this is so, let us consider the three fundamental significations of *dran-pa* just noted, and the two of *dran-med*, in their relationships to one another and to the categories of ground (*gzhi*), path (*lam*), and result (*'bras-bu*). We may further distinguish between two process categories, termed cosmogonic and soteriological. Cosmogonic process embraces, in classical Buddhist terms, the truths of suffering and its origin, while soteriological process pertains to the extinction of suffering, nirvāṇa, and the path whereby that is achieved. The interrelationships among the terms and categories with which we are concerned may be illustrated schematically (tab. 2).

The arrow indicates a weak relationship of conditionality: "A → B" means here, roughly, that "A is generally a necessary condition for the occurrence or realization of B." Of course, in some cases, a stronger relationship may also be affirmed: the primordial awareness of the ground is the condition sine qua non for all modes of awareness, for example; and A. *dran-pa*, is certainly a necessary condition for B. *dran-pa*, which is to say only that there must be some mnemic intentions present if there are to be any soteriologically valuable mnemic intentions. The relationship of conditionality presupposed here is useful in that it permits one to plot out a sequential ordering of the cosmogonic and soteriological processes—the ways of bewilderment and liberation (*sems-can 'khrul-lugs, sangs-rgyas grol-lugs*)—that well accords with what is in fact set forth in traditional expositions. This is first and foremost a matter of exegetical convenience, providing a generalized and idealized map of the path.

The proposed schematization, whatever its other defects may be, does suggest an observation of some consequence here, emphasizing what we may designate the primacy of amnesis. Amnesis (D. *dran-med*), as the loss of, or deviation from, the primordial awareness of the ground, must be regarded as the first of all mnemic phenomena. This determines a proper understanding of mnemic engagement (*dran-pa*), for we must now say that all acts of mnemic engagement involve the apparent recovery or retention, that is to say nonloss, of a causally or temporally precedent psychic or experiential condition by an act of awareness. Memory, for instance, is now determined to be the mind's recovery or retention of, and is presumed to be causally related to, the content of prior experience; recognition, the cognition that one has recovered the object of prior perception; recollection, the recovery of knowledge acquired earlier; memorization, the deliberate retention of knowledge; mindfulness, the retention of awareness's specifically appropriate engagement in a given act or experience. (In this last case, what counts as "specifically appropriate" will necessarily vary according to the nature of the act or experience concerned: a chainsaw operator's mindfulness will involve a rather differently specified sort of engagement than will that of a practitioner of *ikibana.*)

"Recovery," "retention," and "loss" are here, admittedly, metaphorical terms, but this seems not to present grave difficulties in the present context. "Loss" may be understood phenomenologically as the alienation of the subject from any of its ap-

Table 2. Mnemic Process and Praxis

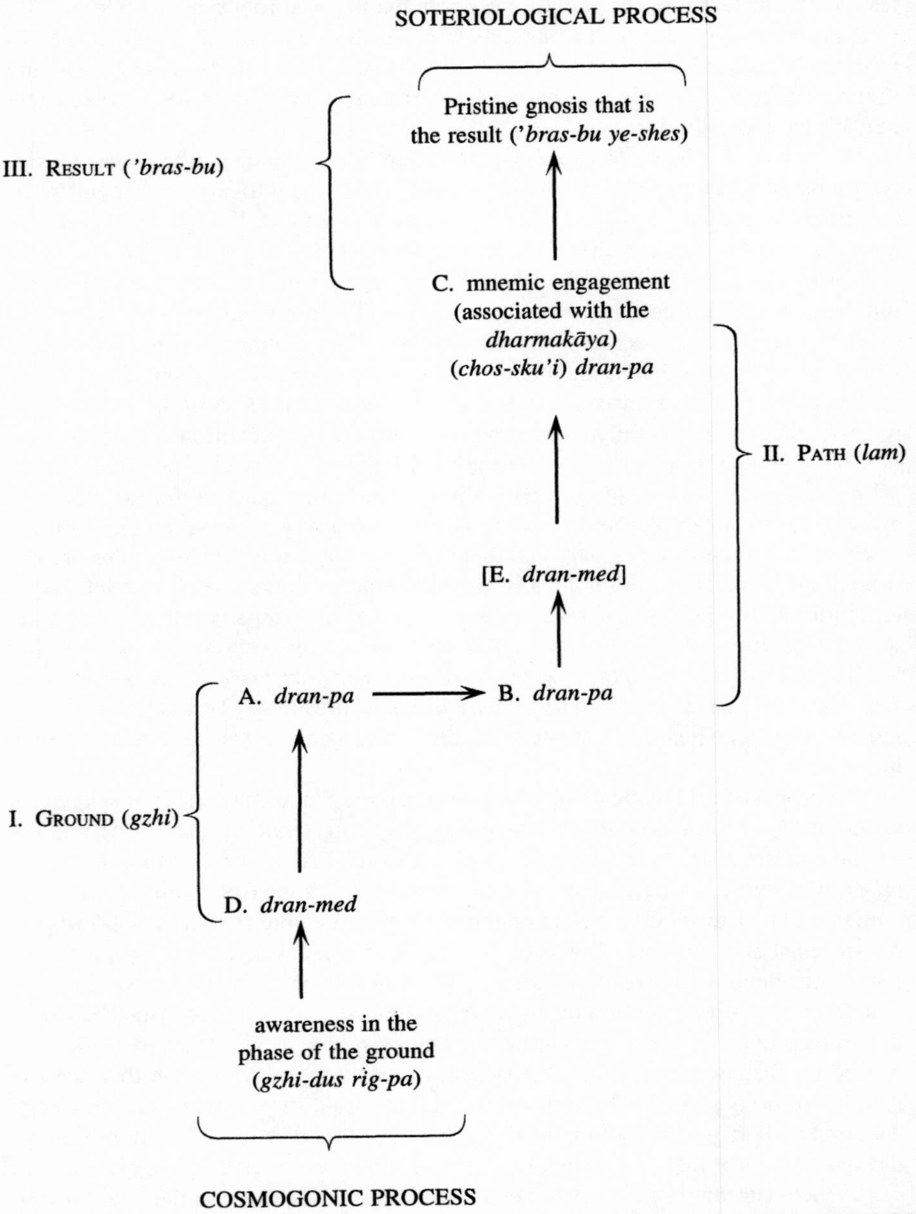

parent properties, and "recovery" and "retention" together determine its contradictory. Regarded in this way, it appears not at all strange that "memory" and "mindfulness" have often been gathered together under a single lexical head—e.g., *mnā-*, *smṛ-*, or *dran-* —and rather odd that this convention has sometimes been thought problematic. Although the normal temporal reference of memory to the past is sometimes not a feature of the codesignated phenomena in question, we nonetheless find in these cases a relatively straightforward analogy of intention.

To the foregoing considerations, our sources further suggest that when awareness turns not to the ground of any particular act, but to the ground of all possible acts of awareness, it reaches its end in the reflexive recovery of the pristine gnosis of the ground-of-all (*kun-gzhi'i ye-shes*) that is the dharmakāya in its noetic aspect. Here the analogy with "memory" as we ordinarily conceive of it is found solely in the phenomenon of recovery, but the character of the act in question has neither the temporal nor the intentional properties of the quotidian concept. In its most characteristic sense, then, *dran-* in Great Perfection thought as represented by Rikdzin Gödem refers to awareness *qua* awareness orienting itself to its proper ground. Its primary "referent," the "object" of this act of retention/recovery, is the self-presentation of awareness as dharmakāya; and it is by analogy that all mnemic acts, by virtue of their orientation to their proper ground or some part thereof, counteracting "loss" or "deviation," are equally *dran-pa*.

An Allegorical Re-presentation

The *Penetration of Samantabhadra's Intention* and its allied literature are, on the surface at least, extremely repetitive compilations; the topics we've seen surveyed in the brief tantra just discussed are variously restated, with more or less elaboration, in many of the texts forming the corpus of the *Penetration of Samantabhadra's Intention*. The repetitiveness of these works, however, betokens no want of ingenuity on the part of the redactor; for this represents in part a carefully crafted effort to clarify and reinforce the vision of the Great Perfection. Repetition, in short, functions mnemotechnically.[29] As the preceding section makes clear, it is part of the soteriological strategy of the Great Perfection to arouse mnemic engagement of a type that, indirectly or immediately, re-calls, calls one back to an object of loss, the revelation of the dharmakāya *qua* self-presenting awareness. The mnemotechnics of the literature and practice of the Great Perfection must be seen as contributing to the formation of such soteriologically valued mnemic engagement. In this and the section which follows, we shall examine two aspects of the mnemotechnic strategies that are employed here: allegorization and ritualization.

The *Wide Open Tantra of Universal Liberation* exemplifies the character of much abstract Great Perfection discourse: like certain aspects of Indian Buddhist abhidharma, it employs what in many respects is a sort of phenomenological language whose operating terms are to be understood as signifying empirical phenomena that are revealed and clarified only when one becomes engaged in appropriate types of contemplative abstraction.[30] One of the functions of allegory, of course, is to render an abstract message more memorable by recasting it in terms of the concrete relationships portrayed as holding among fictitious agents.[31] Allegorical narrative, like mythic and historical narrative, may seek to overcome the atemporal character of more highly abstracted modes of discourse, disclosing to us what that discourse had situated outside of time in an abode phenomenologically rather like that of human temporal experience. Ironically, therefore, allegorical narrative ("the figure of false semblance," as it was known to the Renaissance) may be employed as a corrective to a distortion inseparable from much philosophical language—we may say, to a lie of philosophical language, the lie of timelessness.

The teaching of the *Penetration of Samantabhadra's Intention* is given allegorical expression in the sixth chapter of a tantra entitled the *'Khrul-pa rtsad-gcod-kyi rgyud* (The Tantra of the Eradication of Bewilderment), whose importance in the corpus as a whole is signaled by the description of the text as "the first of all tantras of the esoteric instructions of the Great Perfection."[32] The chapter that interests us here is called "The Symbolic [i.e., Allegorical] Teaching of the Authentic and Real Introduction to the Abiding Nature of Mind and the Approach to the Path of Purification."[33] Because, for reasons argued earlier, the attempt to separate the particular symbolic figures met here from their narrative context would necessarily miss the very point of their employment in narrative, the chapter is presented in its entirety. Readers may find this text to be confusing in parts, but, bewilderment being precisely an aspect of experience that it seeks to underscore, it would be, I think, in some respects misleading to attempt to clarify it through editorial abridgement or alteration.[34]

> The Lord of Secrets petitioned the Teacher Vajrasattva: "O Body of Perfect Rapture! Teacher Vajrasattva! Concerning the so-called 'mind of sentient being,' is it the case that, even though other names be attributed to it, it comes into being from the ground of arising because of varied agitations? And is it the case that there is a difference between the mind autonomously engaged in the afflicted states and the mind of the individual who has embarked on the path of the bodhisattva?"
>
> In response, [Vajrasattva] declared: "This so-called mind is most exceedingly miraculous! Its potencies and enumerations are inconceivable, beyond speech. Nonetheless, this so-called mind is spontaneously present, though of indeterminate material cause. The contributory condition is ignorance. Its essential characteristic is such that it can become anything. At first, when the appearance of twofold apprehension [of subject and object] is vaguely set in motion, one may speak of 'precedent intellectual cognition,' or 'doubtful thought,' or 'pride-generating sensation.' Then, when that has coarsened, there is the bifurcation of outer and inner, the vessel [of the world] and its contents [that is, sentient beings]. When the residues have extensively developed, one may speak of 'the intermediate state of imaginative cognition,' 'dualistic bewilderment,' or 'the ramification of the residues of action.' Thence proceeds saṃsāra. When the body of a sentient being is acquired, one speaks of 'the mind that constructs all bewildered appearance.' It is that which apprehends bewildered appearance as an autonomous continuum. That is the King of All Bewilderment.
>
> "Though he performs many deeds, without associates he remains at leisure. He has five ministers, the greatest of whom is stubborn, speaks indistinctly, is derisive towards all, and obscure. His name is Stupidity. When that minister and the king enter into consultation, the whole country is thrown into blackness. Following him, there is one [characterized by] clear mnemic engagement, who rushes about to and fro. Evilly motivated, he's a clever talker. His name is Desire. When that minister and the king

enter into consultation, he teaches deceit towards all, ensnarement through the appearance of truth. Following him, there's one who looks after himself, not others, and ruins both. He holds himself dear but has no thought for any other. His name is Hatred. When he and the king enter into consultation, they wreck everything they see, touch, or otherwise handle. Following him, there's one with great words and little skill. He brings about self-regard and blame of others. His name is Pride. When he and the king enter into consultation, disregarding subjects and property, there's only self-regard. The last causes only selfish desire. He takes everything he sees to be an enemy and accords with no one. His name is Envy. When he and the king enter into consultation, everyone becomes an enemy. Those are the five afflictions. Serving under those five ministers are eighty-four thousand slaves who conform with them. They are called 'the host of adventitious afflicted thoughts.' They emanate from the mind that is an autonomous continuum of affliction.

"Now, if a fortunate individual emerges who enters into [the cultivation of] the enlightened mind, then the so-called inception of pure pristine gnosis occurs:

"At some interval, when the five ministers are not in the presence of the Omnicreative King of Mind, a man may come forth to teach in symbols the purification of mnemic engagement [that pertains to] desire for and subjective apprehension of what may be [*srid-pa chags-'dzin dran-pa'i dag-pa*], saying, 'You, king, were alone even before the first origins of what may be. When you fell asleep and became bewildered you met with associates [who arrived] from here and there. They altered your mind, making the king as you are today, by affirming the being of what is not. Therefore, through the power of deeds, you've been made to consult with the five ruinous ministers. Now, many incompetent functionaries have assembled, one such as yourself is present, and these evil courtiers have transformed you, so that you've fallen, without autonomy, into unbearable suffering. You must wake up! Being deceived by me, you must go off without associates. What can you do with a retinue like this? If you listen to me, you'll just abandon this ruinous retinue. There's the one called the Friend who is a Pure Antidote, into association with whom I'll place you. Joining forces with him, without separation, run off with your thoughts bent on the Three Gems Blazing with Light that are found in the upper valley. That way, O king, you'll be happy both immediately and ultimately. Then waking up, you'll come to be undeceived.'—So he spoke.

"Then the king, freeing his mind, renounced all the retinue and his ministers, and, undetected by anyone, joined together with the Friend who is a Pure Antidote. Directing his thoughts to the Gems at the head of the valley, he fled and, though pursued by his servants and ministers, escaped in an instant. Such is the entranceway according to the lower vehicle. So it is that in the lower vehicle, the king whose mind has given birth to an attitude of renunciation has only the single friend, Pure Antidote.

"In entering upon the path of the higher vehicle, there are, just as described above, the king of the mental continuum, with his servants and ministers. At some time an adviser comes forth and addresses him as follows: 'O king, listen to me. Formerly, in the city of Vaiśālī, the universal ground, there was a prince called Luminous Essence. He had a wish-fulfilling gem from which all desired qualities naturally emerged. At some point that great city was destroyed, there was the terrifying roar of a thousand thunders, and all was scattered to the wind. The tornado that demolished the palace took the form of a brilliant conflagration and the prince became senseless, lost his composure, and, terrified, fled in a state of oblivion. Arriving in a district in a neighboring land, he met an old woman with cataracts. The old woman took the prince to her home and dressed him in thick garments. The prince, exhausted, fell asleep, and the old woman stole the precious gem that he wore beneath his shirt. That thief then fled into the darkness, where she met up with five men. The old woman got to talking with them and lost the gem to those five men, who couldn't hold on to it either and so sold it in the six cities of deeds. There, in the desire to worship the gem without the prince, the six cities shared it; but when the desired objects failed to appear in [those] six dungeons, it was abandoned.

"'At that time the prince awoke and, the old woman not having returned, he was amazed and ran out the door. [On his meeting] a man named "Self-Manifest Bewilderment," the two conversed. [The prince's] mind, unaccustomed [to the condition in which he found himself], entered into dualistic apprehension, whereupon many motivational bandits arrived and kidnapped the prince. They sold him in a city of perversity, which was princeless, and the prince was appointed lord of that land. At that, one adviser came forth and said, "I've come to give you a message, for I've heard about your incessant suffering, due to the five ministers who ruined everything, along with the eighty-four thousand subjects who created meaningless pain. At that time you were the king. Now, what is it that you're doing?"

"'The prince made his previous pain an object of mnemic engagement and wept until he was exhausted. "Alas, alas! I have no friends," he cried. At that the adviser said, "At first you were the owner of the precious gem. So it's impossible that you're without a pouch for the gem, or perhaps some garment that came into contact with the gem. Examine your body!"

"'The prince found that there was a cord for the gem around his neck that reached his heart. Cutting it into five pieces, he made the gem an object of mnemic engagement and prayed to it, whereupon, by the blessing of the gem, five heartlike men came forth. The adviser spoke as follows: "The eldest of the five men should be appointed to be the Guardian of Inseparable Mnemic Engagement (*dran-pa 'bral-med-kyi so-pa*). Without separation from him, whatever you do will be easy. Next, there is one called Impermanence That Reveals the Fault of the Round (*'khor-ba'i mtshang-'don-gyi mi-rtag-pa*). Without separation from him, you needn't wander in evil abodes. This next one is called the Person Who Is the Self-clarification of Cognition (*shes-pa rang-gsal-gyi skyes-bu*). Without separation from him, whatever you do is delightful to the mind. The next one is called the Sentinel of Mnemic Engagement and Mindfulness with Respect to the Manifest Fluctuations of One's Evil Residues (*bag-chags ngan-pa'i yo-lang 'don-pa-la dran-pa shes-bzhin-gyi byar-ba*). Without separation from him, whatever you do will come out well. The youngest one is called the Messenger of the Connection Between Saṃsāra and Nirvāṇa (*'khor-'das mtshams-sbyor-gyi phrin-pa*). Without separation from him, you and I will meet repeatedly. Never let yourself be separated from these five mnemic men! Now you must change your name. You have parted ways with the retinue of ruin. As for the manner in which misery arose so long as you were alienated from your original homeland, you must continually practice mnemic engagement with respect to the heartfelt advice I've now given to you. May you bear the name 'Youth of Awareness!'"

"'When he had spoken thus, the youth and the five mnemic men became constant companions. They captured the five thieves and imprisoned them. They vanquished all the retinue and subjects. They demolished the six cities and stole back the gem. They killed the old woman with cataracts. Having returned to his former land, the prince, together with the five mnemic men, were united with the precious gem. In the pinnacle of the castle the first of the five mnemic men was appointed watchman.

The next was appointed guard at the door of the royal apartments. The next one, accompanying the prince and the gem, was appointed to reside at the center of the fortress and became inseparable from them. The next was assigned to be a hero, a tamer of enemies. The next was assigned to be a fleet-footed messenger, incessantly arranging for princely audiences with the gracious adviser. So it was that the prince's land achieved a stable ground, and the various desires were fulfilled.

"'It is said that afterwards there was nothing to fear in that land. And it is said that sometimes messengers were dispatched, to guide men who wished to reach that land on the path.'

"That is the manner of entry into the higher vehicle. Such is the allegory concerning the need of the Youth of Self-presenting Awareness for the five self-emergent associates who are mnemic engagement." So he said.

Thus the sixth chapter of the tantra of bewilderment and mind, which teaches as an allegory the genuinely meaningful introduction to the abiding nature of mind, and the manner of entry into the pure path.

The allegory in its two versions, pertaining to the "lower" and "higher" vehicles,[35] involves considerable complexity of detail, so that remarks here must be limited to addressing only a few elements that are especially pertinent in the present context. The *Prayer of Great Power*, translated in the appendix to this chapter, will provide a key that, I believe, together with some knowledge of the classical Buddhist doctrine of dependent origination (*rten-cing 'brel-bar 'byung-ba, pratītyasamutpāda*) and the material presented in the section above on the *Wide-Open Tantra of Universal Liberation*, will help the reader to decipher many of the particular symbolic allusions.

Both versions of the allegory emphasize a reorientation involving mnemic engagement, a reorientation aroused by the appearance of a benevolent adviser at the decisive turning point of the monarch's troubled career: starting here, the increasingly ramified network of affliction begins to come undone. The narrative fulcrum of the allegories is thus found at the point at which soteriologically valuable mnemic engagement (B. *dran-pa*) is born within the obscure domain of bewilderment (*'khrul-pa*). Deception, as these allegories clearly illustrate, must therefore be part of the inception and development of the path. The notion of deception (*bslu-ba*) that we find here is notably similar to the concept of *upāyakauśalya,* "skillful means," famously revealed in the Lotus Sūtra's "Parable of the Burning House."[36]

Given the essential constitution of the round of saṃsāra as bewilderment, determined throughout by amnesis, it seems clear that this concession to deception is in fact required: honest recognition of the limitations of ordinary discourse, as that is conceived here, and not cynical manipulation of the faithful, demands such a concession. With this in mind, the purpose of the apparently strange *emboîtement* of several speakers' discourses in the second allegory becomes clear; for, without explicit reference to deception, the inclusion of allegory within allegory self-referentially betokens the text's own deceptiveness, so that one need be no longer deceived by it.[37] The technique of allegorical *emboîtement,* generating the functional equivalent of a metalanguage, permits the disclosure of deception to take place without its involving the obvious circularity of the liar paradox. The narrative's allegorized self-reference further reinforces the allegorical passage from lower to higher vehicle, in which the self-referentiality of awareness is itself disclosed and characterized as the inalienable possession of mnemic engagement, embodied now as the Self-Clarification of Cognition, third (and so central) among the mnemic men. Thus, allegory recapitulates the course we have previously traversed in preeminently doctrinal terms, and in so doing it reminds us that the actual path will be disclosed symbolically; for the intentional character of symbolic discourse is at once the mark of bewilderment and the conveyance of the antidote for it.

Before leaving the allegory of the amnesic monarch, it may be worth noting the striking resemblance that it bears to the celebrated Gnostic text "The Hymn of the Pearl."[38] The narrator of the hymn is a prince, sent by his royal parents to Egypt to "bring back the One Pearl which lies in the middle of the sea." Arriving in Egypt, he is treated rather badly:

> [S]omehow they learned
> I was not their countryman,
> and they dealt with me cunningly
> and gave me their food to eat.
> I forgot that I was the son of kings,
> and served their king.
> I forgot the pearl
> for which my parents had sent me.
> Through the heaviness of their food
> I fell into a deep sleep.[39]

Recognizing the prince's plight, his parents and "the kings and princes of Parthia" send a collective letter to him, which reads in part:

> Awake and rise from your sleep
> and hear the words of our letter!
> Remember that you are a son of Kings
> and see the slavery of your life.
> Remember the pearl
> for which you went into Egypt![40]

The prince, once awakened, defeats the terrible serpent who guards the pearl, seizes it, and frees himself from the impure garments of the Egyptians, thereby achieving the glory of gnosis.

Is the apparent parallelism of these two allegories of awakening a fortuitous accident, or the result of the transmission of gnostic lore, of "Gnosis on the Silk Road," to borrow Klimkeit's phrase? Herbert Guenther, investigating seemingly gnostic elements in several Great Perfection allegorical texts, has recently advanced the latter alternative, while insisting nevertheless upon "not only the close connection, but also the tremendous difference that existed between early rDzogs-chen thought and Hellenistic-Gnostic ideas." This difference, he argues, lies in part in the "dualism that reflected [the Gnostic's] restrictively rational approach to the question of Being. By contrast, the rDzogs-chen thinkers . . . being process-oriented in their thinking could not but conceive of the origin of the world as a self-organizing process whose success or failure was a matter of comprehension or incomprehension on the part of the experiencer as an integral aspect of this process."[41]

As tantalizing as indeed it is to find suggestions of a religious dialogue unfolding between two greatly differing traditions supposed to have been nevertheless interacting to some extent in late antiquity, the historical framework for such exchange remains largely a matter of speculation.[42] Still, given what we have said earlier regarding Tibet's far-flung cultural relationships, we would be rash to discount such possibilities altogether.

Mnemic Engagement in the Practice of Prayer

While the study and practice of the Great Perfection traditions emanating from Rikdzin Gödem have been traditionally maintained among lineages of highly trained religious specialists within particular branches of the Nyingmapa sect, including both laypersons and celibate clergy, there is one short litany derived from the *Penetration of Samantabhadra's Intention* that is known and practiced throughout the Tibetan Buddhist world. This is the *Smon-lam stobs-po-che* (The Prayer of Great Power), a text without parallel in Tibetan Buddhist literature, whose peculiar popularity was perhaps from the beginning part of its intention. The text, translated in the appendix to this chapter, aims to reveal the manner in which the awakened intention of the original buddha Samantabhadra literally penetrates the universe of sentient beings, and in its original context the *Prayer of Great Power* occurs not as a self-contained work, but rather as the penultimate (and so possibly culminating) chapter of a very extensive tantra.[43] The title of the chapter in which it is given is "The Teaching of the Inability of Sentient Beings Not to Become Buddhas, on Reciting the *Prayer of Great Power*."[44]

The *Prayer of Great Power* is of interest in part because it recasts several of the fundamental elements commonly attributed to prayer, while at the same time conforming to normative conventions in important respects. How this is so may be made clear with reference to the brief phenomenology of prayer suggested by Gerardus van der Leeuw,[45] who begins his account by considering the relationship between prayer and magical formulae, the efficacious recitation of which always demands that they be repeated with perfect accuracy. Their power may be enhanced by additional factors, too, especially by the introduction of what van der Leeuw terms the "magical antecedent," often a mythical narrative invoking the past efficacy of the formula concerned. Again, we find incorporated in prayer exclamations that originally served to summon the deity, or "to remind the god of the pact that had been concluded," and even to "compel the presence of divine Power."

Prayer, properly speaking, emerges "[w]hen man recognizes first of all Form, and later Will, within Power." These are among the key terms of van der Leeuw's phenomenology of religion, and elsewhere he explains that "in the three terms Power, Will and Form, there lies practically the entire concept of the the Object of Religion," that is to say, whatever object is deemed "sacred."[46] The recognition of Form and Will here gives rises to the characteristically dialogic aspect of prayer: "it is an address from man to the Will which he knows to be above him, and the reply of this Will." Finally, in mystical faith, prayer may lose its dialogic character and become "a monologue saturated with religious energy," a "merging in God." "[P]rayer attains its highest form in submersion, while the dialogue type of supplication, on the other hand, always remains word and entreaty, practical demonstration of Will to will, even when it prays in its highest form: 'not my will, but thine, be done.'"

It will be seen at once that the phenomena of prayer are thoroughly bound up with mnemonics: perfect accuracy of recitation necessitates perfect recall; the "magical antecedent" involves the recollection of past events; the exclamatory summoning of the deity requires both summoner and summoned to remember their compact; dialogic prayer presupposes the petitioner's recollection of the object of faith; and mystical prayer presupposes the exercise of mindful self-collection. In the *Prayer of Great Power*, all of these elements, with interesting variations, are in evidence. Moreover, the prayer traces a path through the cosmogony and soteriology of amnesis and mnemic engagement.

The relationship of the prayer we are considering to magical power is made explicit even in its title and is further asserted in its concluding passage, in which the most propitious times for recital are described. The "magical antecedent," a remembrance of mythical events, is incorporated into the main body of the text itself, which details the manner in which the awakening of the primordial Buddha and the amnesis of sentient beings have orginated in a common ground. The exclamations *ho!* and *aho!* used throughout Tibetan religious poetry and prayer are intended always to recall a sense of awe and wonderment, and the ejaculation *tsitta ā!* with which this prayer is introduced uniquely recalls the primordial purity (*ka-dag*) of the Great Perfection.

Where the *Prayer of Great Power* curiously departs from the examples examined by van der Leeuw, however, is in its remarkable simultaneous instantiation of both dialogic and mystical paradigms: the petitioner reestablishes a primordial relationship with the buddha Samantabhadra by becoming Samantabhadra. The mnemonics of prayer are thus called upon to reawaken one's original affinity with the dharmakāya, that is to say, to arouse the reflexive mnemic engagement of the dharmakāya, to introduce a convergence of will and Will. According to its own logic, then, all beings are indeed powerless not to become buddhas upon reciting this prayer; and *that* is its magic and power.

By Way of Conclusion

The foregoing reflections on *dran-pa* in Great Perfection thought suggest that we indeed find here a distinctive doctrine of "memory" that is by no means a simple reiteration of classical Indian Buddhist materials. It is equally clear, however, that this doctrine does not represent a decisive break with the earlier tradition. In this respect, the Great Perfection treatment of *dran-pa* is consistent with many of the other elements incorporated into Great Perfection thought: the resonances of Indian Buddhist teachings are deliberately appropriated, while particular nuances are carefully refined, but in such a manner that the passage from normative Buddhist sources to the peculiar realm of the Great Perfection is rendered quite seamless. It is precisely in virtue of this strategy that the various attempts to forge a scholastic synthesis founded on the Great Perfection tradition, for instance, in the writings of Karma Pakshi and Longchen Rabjampa, are synthetic achievements and not mere eclecticism.[47] To this, however, the adherents of the Great Perfection would add that their strategy works so well precisely because Great Perfection thought gets us closer to the bedrock of

Buddhist insight than do its competitors, and so best comprehends the genuine insights of particular Buddhist traditions.

It remains a peculiar feature of the Great Perfection approach to "memory" that it emphasizes above all a type of psychological act that stands quite apart from both the intentional character and the temporal reference we usually attribute to memory. And this, we have seen, goes far beyond the appropriation of mindfulness to memory terms, for in such cases the analogical rapport of the intentionality of the former act with that of properly mnemic phenomena seems relatively clear. The puzzlement that is occasioned for us by the Great Perfection transposition of the phenomenological heart of the mnemic act to the reflexivity of awareness is deepened, perhaps, when we remark that the Great Perfection tradition has not been alone in its execution of this striking maneuver.[48] Consider in this respect the argument of Augustine:

> But some one will say, That is not memory by which the mind, which is ever present to itself, is affirmed to remember itself; for memory is of things past, not of things present. For there are some, and among them Cicero, who, in treating of the virtues, have divided prudence into these three—memory, understanding, forethought: to wit, assigning memory to things past, understanding to things present, forethought to things future; which last is certain only in the case of those who are prescient of the future; and this is no gift of men, unless it be granted from above, as to the prophets. And hence the book of Wisdom speaking of men, "The thoughts of mortals," it says, "are fearful, and our forethought uncertain." But memory of things past, and understanding of things present, are certain: certain, I mean, respecting things incorporeal, which are present; for things corporeal are present to the sight of the corporeal eyes. But let any one who denies that there is any memory of things present, attend to the language used even in profane literature, where exactness of words was more looked for than truth of things, "Nor did Ulysses suffer such things, nor did the Ithacan forget himself in so great a peril." For when Virgil said that Ulysses did not forget himself, what else did he mean, except that he remembered himself? And since he was present to himself, he could not possibly remember himself, unless memory pertained to things present. And, therefore, as that which is called memory in things past which makes it possible to recall and remember them; so in a thing present, as the mind is to itself, that is not unreasonably to be called memory, which makes the mind at hand to itself, so that it can be understood by its own thought, and then both be joined together by love of itself.[49]

And a contemporary Augustine scholar comments:

> Augustine extends the scope of *memoria* so as to include all that we are capable of getting to know explicitly that does not come to us through sense-experience. This includes, for Augustine, knowledge of self, of the truths of reason, of moral and other values, of God. Hence *memoria* loses all reference to the past, except in the case of knowledge derived from sense experience, since the content of this is only in the mind if the experience has in fact occurred at some previous time; otherwise, *memoria* is not confined to past experience but embraces all that is latent and *present* as such in the mind. (Emphasis in original.)[50]

The redescription of memory as all that is present as such in the mind, or as the mnemic engagement of the dharmakāya and thus standing outside of time, despite the manifold differences between Augustinian thought and that of the Great Perfection traditions with respect to perhaps most matters of "theology,"[51] serves in each case to ground the role of "memory" in a religious epistemology, in part by short circuiting the doubts frequently raised about the relationship between memory and knowledge: memory is here revealed to be *the most natural thing in the world* and, hence, absolutely authoritative. One may well be tempted to suppose that Augustine and the masters of Great Perfection were indeed on to something here, that their assertion that memory is so very much more than a doubtful relationship between an evanescent present and a forever lost past is a real insight, in fact, a discovery. I am inclined to think that it is plausible to view matters in this way; but, still, philosophical scruples require that the most skeptical objections be heard. Let us consider the terrible words of Nietzsche on the subject of memory:

> [P]erhaps indeed there was nothing more fearful and uncanny in the whole prehistory of man than his mnemotechnics. . . . Man could never do without blood, torture, and sacrifices when he felt the need to create a memory for himself; the most dreadful sacrifices and pledges (sacrifices of the first-born among them), the most repulsive mutilations (castration, for example), the cruelest rites of all the religious cults (and all religions are at the deepest levels systems of cruelties)—all this has its origin in the instinct that realized that pain is the most powerful aid to mnemonics.
>
> In a certain sense, *the whole of asceticism belongs here:* a few ideas are to be rendered inextinguishable, ever-present, unforgettable, "fixed," with the aim of hypnotising the entire nervous and intellectual system with these "fixed ideas"—and ascetic procedures and modes of life are means of freeing these ideas from the competition of all other ideas, so as to make them "unforgettable."(Emphasis added.)[52]

Nietzsche perhaps did not perceive the highest degree of subtlety to which mnemotechnics have aspired: with the insight that memory is the most natural thing in the world, we may dispense with all mnemonic torture; the bond linking pain and memory may at last be severed.

A genuine discovery, then, or the most exquisite possible refinement of ascesis? According to what principle is this puzzle to be resolved? I shall have to leave it for the reader to ponder; possibly this will serve as an invitation to *memoria,* to genuine *dran-pa.*

Appendix

The Prayer of Great Power

Tsitta Ā! [Heart-mind Ā!]

Then the original buddha Samantabhadra recited this special prayer, concerning the powerlessness of sentient beings in the round not to become buddhas:

Ho! All phenomenal possibilities—the round and transcendence—
One ground, two paths, two results—
A miracle of awareness and unawareness!
By the aspiration of the Omnibeneficent
May the buddhahood of all be perfectly disclosed
In the fortress of reality's expanse!

The ground-of-all is unconditioned,
A self-emergent, open expanse, ineffable,
Without even the names of either "round" or "transcendence."
Being aware of just that is buddhahood,
While sentient beings, unaware, wander the round.
May all sentient beings of the three realms
Be aware of the ineffable significance of the ground.

For I, the Omnibeneficent,
Am the significance of the ground,
without cause or condition.
Awareness, self-emerging from the ground that's just that,
Imputes no fault, outer or inner,
by exaggeration or depreciation.
It is free from the dark taint of amnesis,
And so unsullied by self-manifest fault.
In abiding in self-presenting awareness,
There is no terror though the three worlds be afraid;
There is no desire for the five sensual pleasures.

In nonconceptual cognition, self-emergent,
There are neither concrete forms nor the five colors.
The unimpeded radiant aspect of awareness
Has five modes of pristine gnosis in its sole essence.
As these five modes of gnosis mature,
The original buddhas of five families emerge.
The horizon of pristine gnosis expanding thereafter,
Forty-two buddhas emerge.
The expressive power of the five modes of gnosis arises,
And the sixty blood-drinkers emerge.
So the ground-awareness experiences no error.

Because I am the original buddha,
By reciting my aspiration,
May the sentient beings of the round's three realms
Know the face of self-emergent awareness
And expand the horizon of great pristine gnosis.
My emanations are incessant,
Radiating inconceivably by hundreds of millions,
Variously revealing how each is trained according to need.
By the aspiration of my compassion,
May all sentient beings in the round's three realms
Be set free from the six classes' abodes.

At first, sentient beings, in error,
Awareness of the ground not arising,
Suffer total amnesis and oblivion.
Just that is unawareness, the cause of error,
Overcome by which, as in a faint,
Cognition, in terror, wanders intoxicated.
Thus dividing self and other, enmity is born.
As its residues develop by stages,
The round emerges in evolutionary sequence;
The five poisonous afflictions expand therefrom;
The activity of the five poisons is incessant.
Therefore, because error's ground within sentient beings
Is amnesic unawareness,
By my aspiration as a buddha,
May all sentient beings of the three realms
All know by themselves their own awareness.

Coemergent unawareness
Is cognition in amnesic oblivion.
Imputative unawareness
Is the apprehension of self and other as two.
Coemergent and imputative unawareness together
Form error's ground for all sentient beings.

By my aspiration as a buddha,
May all sentient beings in the round
Find the thick darkness of amnesis dispelled,
Dualistic cognition removed,
And then know the proper face of awareness.

Dualistic intellect is doubt.
When subtle obsessive attachment arises,
Its residues densely ramify in sequence.
Food, wealth, clothing, abode, and friends,
The five sensuous objects and loving relations—
You are tormented by passionate desire for what pleases.
These are worldly errors;
Apprehended, apprehender, and act have no final end.
When the fruit of obsessive attachment matures,
Embodied as a ghost wracked by craving,
You are born to terrible hunger and thirst.
By my aspiration as a buddha,
May sentient beings engaged in desire and obsessive attachment
Neither renounce the torment of desire,
Nor adhere to desire and obsessive attachment,
But, by letting cognition relax in its proper domain,
May they seize the proper domain of awareness,
And acquire all-comprehending pristine gnosis.

Directed to the appearance of outer objects
There proceeds a subtle, frightened cognition;
When the residues of hatred spread forth,
Coarse enmity and violence are born.
When anger's result has matured,
You suffer in the inferno of hell.
By the power of my aspiration as a buddha,
May all sentient beings of the six destinies,
Whenever fierce anger is born,
Neither adhere to nor reject it,
  but relax in their proper domain,
And by seizing the proper domain of awareness,
May they acquire clarifying pristine gnosis.

When your mind becomes inflated,
There's the thought to debase, in competition with others.
The thought of fierce pride being born,
You suffer combat between self and other.
When the result of that action matures,
Born a god, you are liable to fall and to die.
By my aspiration as a buddha,
May self-inflated sentient beings

Relax cognition in its proper domain,
And by seizing the proper domain of awareness
Acquire equanimity's pristine gnosis.

Owing to ramified residues of dualistic grasping,
There are tortured deeds of self-praise, blame of others;
Violent competitiveness develops
And you are born in the murderous antigods' abode:
The result, a fall into hellish abodes.
By the power of my prayer as a buddha,
May those born competitive and violent
Not engage in enmity, but relax in their proper domains,
And by seizing the proper domain of awareness
Realize the pristine gnosis of unimpeded enlightened activity.

The result of amnesis, apathy, and distraction,
Oblivion, dullness, forgetfulness,
Unconsciousness, laziness, and stupidity
Is to roam as an unprotected beast.
By my aspiration as a buddha
May the lustre of mnemic clarification arise
In the darkness of insensate stupidity,
And bring acquisition of nonconceptual pristine gnosis.

For all the sentient beings of the three realms
Are equal to me, the buddha of the universal ground.
Amnesic, they've drifted into bewilderment's ground,
And so now are engaged in meaningless deeds:
The six deeds are like the bewilderment of dreams.
I am the original buddha:
To train the six destinies by my emanations,
By my aspiration as the Omnibeneficent,
May all sentient beings, none excepted,
Become buddhas in reality's expanse!

Aho!
In the future a powerful yogin,
With unbewildered awareness, self-clarified,
Will recite this powerful prayer,
And all sentient beings who hear it
Will disclose buddhahood within three lives.
During solar or lunar eclipse,
At times of thunder or earthquake,
During the solstices or at New Years,
He will recreate himself as Samantabhadra.
If this is uttered so that all may hear,
Then all the sentient beings of the three realms,
Because of that yogin's prayer,

Will be successively released from suffering
And swiftly attain buddhahood!

(From the *Tantra Which Teaches the Great Perfection, the Penetration of Samantabhadra's Intention,* the nineteenth chapter, which teaches the powerlessness of sentient beings not to become buddhas, on reciting the *Prayer of Great Power.*)

Notes

Abbreviations

AA	*Acta Asiatica*
ArtsA	*Arts Asiatique*
AOH	*Acta Orientalia (Hungarica)*
BA	G. N. Roerich, trans. *The Blue Annals*. Delhi: Motilal Banarsidass, 1976.
BEFEO	*Bulletin de l'École Française d'Extrême-Orient*
BM	British Museum
BST	Buddhist Sanskrit Texts Series. Darbhanga: Mithila Institute.
BT	*Bulletin of Tibetology* (Gangtok)
CDT I	Ariane Macdonald and Yoshiro Imaeda, *Choix de documents tibétains*, vol. I. Paris: Bibliothèque Nationale, 1978.
CDT II	Ariane Spanien and Yoshiro Imaeda, *Choix de documents tibétains*, vol. II. Paris: Bibliothèque Nationale, 1979.
CTBRP	Steinkellner, Ernst, and Helmut Tauscher, eds. *Contributions on Tibetan and Buddhist Religion and Philosophy*. Proceedings of the Csoma de Kőrös Symposium held at Velm-Vienna, Austria. Vol. 2. Vienna: Arbeitskreis fur Tibetische und Buddhistische Studien Universität Wien, 1983.
CTLHC	Steinkellner, Ernst, and Helmut Tauscher, eds. *Contributions on Tibetan Language, History, and Culture*. Proceedings of the Csoma de Kőrös Symposium held at Velm-Vienna, Austria. Vol. 1. Vienna: Arbeitskreis fur Tibetische und Buddhistische Studien Universität Wien, 1983.
EAA	*Estudios de Asia y Africa*
ECCT	Lancaster, Lewis and Whalen Lai, eds. *Early Ch'an in China and Tibet*. Berkeley Buddhist Studies Series 5. Berkeley, Calif.: Asian Humanities Press, 1983.
ET	Macdonald, Ariane, ed. *Études tibétaines dédiées à la mémoire de Marcelle Lalou*. Paris: Adrien Maisonneuve, 1971.
GCRDz	*Gangs-can rig-mdzod* Series. Lhasa: Bod-ljongs bod-yig dpe-rnying dpe-skrun-khang.
IO	*India Office Library*
IO Cat.	La Vallée Poussin, Louis de. *Catalogue of the Tibetan Manuscripts from Tun-huang in the India Office Library*. Oxford University Press, 1962.
JA	*Journal Asiatique*

JAOS	*Journal of the American Oriental Society*
JIABS	*Journal of the International Association of Buddhist Studies*
OTA	*Old Tibetan Annals. PT* 1288, *IO* 750, *BM* 8212. First edited and translated in Bacot, Thomas and Toussaint, 1940. Published in facsimile in *CDT II*. Edited, with modern Tibetan annotations, Chinese translation, and facsimile of the original manuscripts in Dbang-rgyal [= Wang Yao] and Bsod-nams-skyid, *Tun hong nas thon pa'i bod kyi lo rgyus yig cha*. Beijing: Mi rigs dpe skrun khang, 1992.
OTC	*Old Tibetan Chronicle. PT* 1287. Published together with *OTA*.
OTG	*Old Tibetan Geneology. PT* 1286. Published together with *OTA*.
P	Suzuki, Daisetz T., ed. *The Tibetan Tripitika: Peking Edition, Kept in the Library of the Otani University, Kyoto*. Tokyo/Kyoto: Tibetan Tripitika Research Institute, 1961.
PT	*Pelliot tibétain*
PT Cat.	Marcelle Lalou, *Inventaire des Manuscrits tibétains de Touen-houang conservés à la Bibliothèque Nationale*. Vol. 1. Paris: Adrien-Maisonneuve, 1939. Vol. 2. Paris: Bibliothèque Nationale, 1950. Vol. 3. Paris: Bibliothèque Nationale, 1956.
SCH	Gimello, Robert M., and Peter N. Gregory, eds. *Studies in Ch'an and Hua-yen*. Studies in East Asian Buddhism 1. Honolulu: University of Hawaii Press, 1983.
SG	Gregory, Peter N., ed. *Sudden and Gradual: Approaches to Enlightenment in Chinese Thought*. Studies in East Asian Buddhism 5. Honolulu: University of Hawaii Press, 1987.
STC	Aziz, Barbara Nimri, and Matthew Kapstein, eds. *Sounding in Tibetan Civilization*. New Delhi: Manohar, 1985.
T	Ui, Hakuju, Munetada Suzuki, Yenshô Kanakura, and Tôkan Tada, eds. *A Complete Catalogue of the Tibetan Buddhist Canons (Bkaḥ-ḥgyur and Bstan-ḥgyur)*. Sendai: Tôhoku Imperial University, 1934.
TBS	Ligeti, Louis, ed. *Tibetan and Buddhist Studies Commemorating the 200th Anniversary of the Birth of Alexander Csoma de Kőrös*. 2 vols. Budapest: Akadémiai Kiadó, 1984.
TS	Kværne, Per, ed. *Tibetan Studies*. 2 vols. Oslo: Institute for Comparative Research in Human Culture, 1994.
TSHHR	Aris, Michael, and Aung San Suu Kyi, eds. *Tibetan Studies in Honour of Hugh Richardson*. Warminster: Aris and Phillips, 1980.

Where the date of publication is followed by an earlier date in brackets—for example, Richardson 1998 [1980]—the bracketed entry refers to the original date of publication of the chapter in question.

Chapter 1

1. For summaries see Stein 1972a, pp. 191–229; Tucci 1980, ch. 6; Samuel 1993, ch. 10. A broad range of representative texts, relating to both Tibetan Buddhism and indigenous traditions, may be found in Lopez 1997.

2. Detailed references will be found below, ch. 2, n. 50, and ch. 4, nn. 45–50.

3. For instance, Reynolds and Tracy 1990, 1992; Collins 1998. For investigations of related issues in the history of Western thought, see Taylor 1989; Hatab 1990; Nussbaum 1990.

4. Scharfstein 1989 offers a perceptive essay on this question.

5. As Lopez rightly argues (1998, p. 4): "the play of opposites has been both extreme and volatile in the case of Tibet, and it remains at work in contemporary attitudes toward Tibet and Tibetan Buddhism."

6. Tenzin Gyatso 1975, pp. 21–22, states this unequivocally: "Thus, the Buddhist teaching that spread to Tibet is just the stainless teaching of India and nothing else. The Tibetan lamas neither altered it nor mixed it with another religion." H. H. the Dalai Lama's perspective is, of course, precisely the normative viewpoint among those educated within the tradition.

7. Thus *rang-bzo*, literally "personal invention," is almost always mentioned as a negative quality. A commentator assures his readers of the reliability and authority of his work by proclaiming it to be *rang-bzo-med-pa*, "without personal invention."

8. During the 19th century, this was the view commonly held with regard to "lamaism," a designation that accentuated the notion that Tibetan Buddhism had moved so far from Buddhism's sources that it was no longer really Buddhism at all. Lopez 1998, ch. 1, reviews the history of the idea of "lamaism" in depth.

9. This is not to say that there were no Tibetans who invented the teachings or texts they were said to have transmitted. The problem comes to the fore in the study of the revealed scriptural "treasures" (*gter-ma*), on which see ch. 7, 8.

10. Thus Samuel 1993, p. 446, holds that there was an "accommodation between Buddhism and shamanic religion. Buddhism was acceptable as a new improved shamanic technique, which would maintain the good fortune and welfare of the country without threatening the established order laid down in the past."

11. Tucci 1950, 1973; Lalou 1952; Haarh 1969, ch. 15, 16; Stein 1970; Chu 1991; Chayet 1994, ch. 2; Richardson 1998, pp. 219–233 ("Early Burial Grounds in Tibet," first published in 1963). For a thorough survey of recent Chinese archaeological research, see now Huo Wei, *Xizang gudai muzang zhidu shi*. I am grateful to the author for his presentation to me of this useful work. On the development of mortuary rites within the Bon-po tradition, see Kværne 1985.

12. *OTC*, lines 45–49: *btsan po rje dbyal zhig nongs na/ thor to 'phren mo ni bcings/ ngo la mtshal gyis byugs . . . zas la nï za 'thung . . . gyang to bla 'bubs kyi mgur du bang so brtsigso/* The entire passage from which these extracts are taken includes a number of points of difficulty, about the interpretation of which there is no firm consensus.

13. Lalou 1952; Chu 1991.

14. *OTA*, *passim*. The relevant passages are compared in Haarh 1969, pp. 357–360.

15. An exceptionally clear example is *Mkhas-pa Lde'u*, pp. 376–380, which gathers these traditions together.

16. They are duly noted, for example, in the influential pilgrimage guide of 'Jam-dbyangs Mkhyen-brtse (1820–1892): Ferrari 1958, pp. 13–14 (text), 52–53 (trans.).

17. For instance, in the tale of the first mortal king, Gri-gum btsan-po, as given in *OTC*, ch. 1, it is clear that his violent death creates a grave problem that is related to the question of the proper disposal of his corpse, which seems to exist in a sort of limbo until last rites are correctly performed. But there is no description here of the condition of his soul following his death, either before or after the last rites are achieved. The problem of the dead is here one for the descendants and others who remain.

18. Blondeau 1997.

19. The comments of E. G. Smith 1968 on the emergence of the institution of rebirth as a preeminent means of monastic succession remain seminal here. He argues that it was in fact only in the fifteenth and sixteenth centuries that lineages of rebirth achieved priority "over familial claims in the transmission of accumulated religious prestige and wealth." Though we do find evidence that religious figures as early as the eleventh century were sometimes thought to be the incarnations of earlier masters—see, for example, Dudjom 1991, vol. 1, pp. 703–709, on Rong-zom-pa; Kapstein 1997b on Khyung-po Rnal-'byor; Kapstein in press on 'Brom-ston Rgyal-ba'i 'byung-gnas—the crucial shift that later takes place is the application of such identifications to actual questions of inheritance.

20. *'Od-'bar-rgyal*. The name appears to be modeled on that of the god Vimalatejaḥprabha (Pure Splendrous Light), whose death is the point of departure for the *Sarvadurgatipariśodhanatantra* (edited in Skorupski 1983). The probable influence of the latter on the *Cycle of Birth and Death* is discussed in Kapstein in press.

21. The name is given as *Rin-chen-lag[s]*, which may be equivalent to Sanskrit *Ratnapāṇi, "Jewel-in-hand." Stein 1983, however, has argued with some plausibility that the Tibetan should probably be *Rin-chen-legs*, in which case this is likely a translation of the *Chinese* rendering of the name Sudhana, the hero of the *Gaṇḍavyūhasūtra*, which in Tibetan translations from the Sanskrit is *Nor-bzang*. As Imaeda has shown, the *Cycle of Birth and Death* is very much influenced by the *Gaṇḍavyūha*.

22. Translated following the text as given in Imaeda 1981b, pp. 87–90.

23. Collins 1982, ch. 1.

24. Imaeda 1981b, pp. 68–73.

25. *PT* 239, reproduced in *CDT I*.

26. These passages are examined in Stein 1970.

27. Yoshiro Imaeda, *"Bar do thos grol*, 'Le livre des morts': le bouddhisme tibétisé ou le Tibet bouddhisé." I wish to thank the author for sharing this unpublished paper with me. It was presented at the Colloque Franco-Japonais, "l'adaptation du bouddhismes aux cultures locales," at the Collège de France, Paris, in September 1991.

28. *PT* 239, plates 2–8.

29. This is particularly suggestive in the light of Collins 1998, on nirvāṇa and other "felicities," such as the heavens, in the Theravāda traditions.

30. The progression of the deceased from the peaceful realm of Indra to the wrathful domain of Vajrapāṇi perhaps offers a precedent to the visionary encounters with peaceful and wrathful deities that become a central motif in the *Bar-do thos-grol*.

31. *PT* 239, plates 14–19.

32. For translations, see Evans-Wentz 1960 (originally published in 1927), and Freemantle and Trungpa 1987. Relevant studies include Lauf 1977; Pommaret 1989; Blezer 1997; and Lopez 1997, pp. 421–510. Lopez 1998, ch. 2, provides an interesting and thorough account of the history of the reception of the "Tibetan Book of the Dead" in the West. He argues (p. 49), however, that "the Tibetan text upon which it is based, the *Bar do thos grol*, would have been familiar to scholars who knew the literature of the Nyingma sect; they would have recognized it as the name of a large genre of mortuary texts used by Nyingma lamas." This, however, is misleading: the Tibetan title in question is preeminently associated with a particular book "discovered" in the fourteenth century by Karma-gling-pa. Though it is indeed a Rnyingma text, its transmission and employment were very widespread in the other sects as well, particularly among the Bka'-brgyud. Its unusually wide distribution made it something of a cultural phenomenon, and this was well-recognized in traditional historiography, for instance, Dudjom Rinpoche 1991, vol. 1, p. 801.

33. Kapstein 1980, 1992b, 1997b.

34. *Bar-do'i gdams-pa*.

35. Thus, for instance, Evans-Wentz 1960, p. 183: "perseverance in the reading of the Great *Bardo Thödol* for forty-nine days is of the utmost importance." In China, the funerary ritual period of seven weeks was common to Taoism as well as Buddhism; see Schipper 1993, p. 75.

36. The relevant doctrinal background is surveyed in Snellgrove 1987, vol. 1.

37. *Bar-do'i gdams-pa*, plates 163–165.

38. Of course, as recent ethnographical research in Tibetan and Himalayan communities confirms, mortuary rites continue to be informed by many concerns and themes only tangentially related to normative Buddhist aspirations for the highest enlightenment. Issues such as the fear of the deceased's return as a zombie or harmful ghost are only partially addressed by

the attempt to guide the departed to liberation and so must sometimes be addressed by special rituals.

39. The period is in many respects a puzzling one for traditional historiography. An interesting attempt to assemble the available data may be found in *Shel-dkar phreng-ba.*

40. Uebach 1987, pp. 120–153, supplies the text and a translation of one of the most thorough traditional accounts of the revival of Central Tibetan monasticism during the tenth century, that of Nel-pa Paṇḍita.

41. *Zhe-chen chos-'byung*, pp. 68–72, summarizes the traditional accounts of the survival of these branches of learning in Khams.

42. It will require greater progress than we have seen to date in the investigation of Tibetan historical linguistics to clarify these matters adequately. Nevertheless, I think that my remarks accord with widespead impressions of the history of literary Tibetan. For instance, Miller 1976, p. 103, writes: "Classical Tibetan [is] the language of the Tibetan translations of the Mahāyāna Buddhist canon as well as of other original texts, chiefly on religious, medical, historical, and grammatical subjects. . . . It was based upon Old Church Tibetan, which was a variety of Old Tibetan and the language of earlier Buddhist texts. . . ."

43. It seems absurd to hold that when the translation of Sanskrit was resumed by Rin-chen-bzang-po (958–1054), he had to reinvent the entire system of Sanskrit-Tibetan lexicography. We must assume, I think, that basic knowledge along these lines was available all along. The earliest known version of Rin-chen-bzang-po's biography relates that he studied Śākyaprabha's Vinaya treatise, the *Triśatakārikā*, and its commentary, in Tibetan as a teenager and at seventeen was inspired to take up translation after seeing an Indian book in the possession of a paṇḍita from Uḍḍiyāna (Snellgrove and Skorupski 1977–1980, vol. 2, p. 102). In their translation of this passage (p. 86) Snellgrove and Skorupski say that Rin-chen-bzang-po saw the book after "receiving some small hospitality from the wife of a paṇḍita who had come from Uḍḍiyāna," but I think it is perhaps better to read: "a paṇḍita who had come from Uḍḍiyāna received some small hospitality from [Rin-chen-bzang-po's] mother (*yum*), and, after eating, left behind a nice little Indian book."

Another interesting datum from this period is *PT* 849, a manuscript first studied in Hackin 1924, which dates, roughly, to 1000. It includes a small Sanskrit-Tibetan word list, with the Sanskrit rendered according to a very rough phonetic system, rather than the standard equivalencies invented for exact transcription. Thus, one reads, for instance, *'bu-tha* for *buddha.* Perhaps this is indicative of an interest in the basic Indian Buddhist vocabulary even among Tibetan Buddhists who had little or no specialized concern with translation, just as one finds in contemporary nonacademic writing on Buddhism a rudimentary knowledge of Sanskrit or Pali vocabulary, though often in vulgar transcription.

44. The evidence is reviewed by Samten Karmay (1981) and in Karmay's *Btsan-po Dar-ma.* Yamaguchi 1996 shows that a Madhyamaka treatise mentioned by Bu-ston may even be attributed to Dar-ma's authorship (under his actual regnal title, 'U'i-dum-btsan). Both Karmay and Yamaguchi also take note of *PT* 134, a dedicatory prayer in honor of this same king, found at Dunhuang. This, however, strikes me as an inconclusive element of the argument: with the change of kings the clergy may have been expected to perform dedications on behalf of the new monarch ("the king is dead, long live the king!"), even before knowing anything of his actual policies.

45. *PT* 849, lines 116–121.

46. As the politics of funding for the arts and humanities in our own times demonstrate, it is by no means unusual to find fiscal austerity described, by those who must bear the brunt of it, as oppression of one sort or another.

47. Dudjom 1991, vol. 1, pp. 610–612, supplies the traditional, much mythologized account of Glang Dar-ma's decision not to persecute lay tantric adepts. In this case, however, the myth is certainly based on the indisputable evidence of continuous lay tantric activity during

the period following the empire's decline. A good example is the early history of the 'Khon family, which in the eleventh century founded the Sa-skya-pa order: *Sa-skya'i gdung-rabs*, pp. 10–16.

48. Stein 1988 makes a similar argument with respect to the Dunhuang documents that are connected with Bon-po developments. The oft-held assumption that Tibetan writings found at Dunhuang generally date to the period of the Tibetan occupation of the late eighth and early ninth centuries is a bad one. As Takata 1994 shows, the Tibetan script was being used at Dunhuang even to write Chinese as late as the tenth century.

49. See, in particular, Davidson 1994; Karmay 1975a, 1980a, 1980b; Ruegg 1984; Snellgrove 1987, vol. 2, pp. 451–484.

50. Hakeda 1972, p. 3: "Kūkai did not actually invent the *kana* syllabary, but its emergence owed much to his introduction of Sanskrit studies, for the *kana* system is formed on the basis of the Sanskrit alphabet." Kūkai himself, however, makes perfectly clear that his own interest in Sanskrit is primarily related to the phonology of the mantras: "The mantras, however, are mysterious and each word is profound in meaning. When they are transliterated into Chinese, the original meanings are modified and the long and short vowels confused. In the end we can get roughly similar sounds but not precisely the same ones. Unless we use Sanskrit, it is hardly possible to differentiate the long and short sounds. The purpose of retaining the source materials, indeed, lies here" (p. 144).

51. As Richardson 1998 [1990], p. 178, shows, Dpal-'khor-btsan, who reigned towards the beginning of the tenth century, constructed the temple of Bya-sa, which formerly housed a celebrated image of Vairocana. The great Sa-skya-pa master Bsod-nams-rtse-mo (1142–1182), writing in 1167 (*Sa-skya bka'-'bum*, vol. NGA, *Chos-la 'jug-pa'i sgo*, folios 53–55), provides a continuous account of calendrical calculation from the period of the empire down to his own time. The king just mentioned, Dpal-'khor-btsan, is again noted as having completed his father's last rites in a wood female ox year, probably 905.

52. See esp. Iwasaki 1993.

53. Snellgrove 1967b, p. 20: "The *bon* were just one class of priests among others, whose practices and beliefs are covered by the general term of *lha-chos*, which may be translated perhaps as 'sacred conventions'. The term BON, as referring to a whole set of religious practices, would seem to have come into use at a later stage in deliberate opposition to the new use of CHOS which now had the meaning of Sanskrit *dharma* limited specifically to the religion of *Śākyamuni*. Thus there is probably no such thing as pre-Buddhist BON. . . ." See also Stein 1988. Kværne 1995, introduction, provides a judicious survey of the varied senses of the term *bon*, and of contemporary Bon-po self-understanding in this regard.

54. See, for example, Karmay 1975b; Kværne 1987; Martin 1994.

55. An international project directed by Per Kværne (Oslo) has compiled the materials for the first detailed catalogue of a version of the Bon-po *Bka'-'gyur*, published in Sichuan. The publication of their results will be an important step in making this material accessible to contemporary research. In addition to the *Bka'-'gyur*, an edition of the Bon-po *Bstan-'gyur* in over 300 volumes has now been published in Lhasa.

56. These scriptures are among those studied in Rossi in press.

57. Stein 1988.

58. Much of the material to be discussed here has been used previously for comparative purposes by Karmay 1988a, pp. 172–174, and, esp., Mimaki 1994. Compare also Snellgrove 1987, vol. 2, p. 407.

59. The notion of the *yāna* is developed in so many Indian Buddhist sūtras and śāstras that it probably makes little sense to seek to identify too narrowly the likely sources of Tibetan inspiration in this regard. One work, however, that certainly does merit particularly careful scrutiny is the *Laṅkāvatāra*, which propounds a theory of five vehicles, that is explicitly capable of indefinite expansion, in ch. 2, verses 201–202ab: *devayānaṃ brahmayānaṃ*

śrāvakīyaṃ tathaiva ca/ tāthāgataṃ ca pratyekaṃ yānān etān vadāmy ahaṃ// yānānāṃ nāsti vai niṣṭhā yāvac cittaṃ pravartate/ "I speak of these vehicles: the vehicle of gods, the vehicle of Brahmā, that of the Śrāvakas, of the Tathāgatas, and of the Pratyekabuddhas. There is no end of vehicles, so long as mind extends." The *Laṅkāvatāra* was certainly well known to Rnying-ma-pa authors for its teaching of the vehicles; see, e.g., Dudjom 1991, vol. 1, pp. 60–61, 80–81.

60. *PT* 849, lines 14–16: *theg pa rim pa dgu gang la bya zhe na/ /myi'i theg pa dang/ /lha'i theg pa dang/ nyan thos kyi theg pa dang/ /rang sang rgyas kyi theg pa dang/ /mdo sde'i theg pa dang/ byang chub sems pa'i theg pa dang/ /mdzo ga dang/ kyïr yā dang/ u pa ya dang/ de rnams ni theg pa rim pa dgu la bya*. The text goes on to enumerate various subdivisions of the last three vehicles, of which Yoga is divided into the four branches of Yoga, Mahāyoga, Anuyoga, and Atiyoga. It is not clear, however, that these have here the same sense that they do in the Rnying-ma-pa systems of nine vehicles.

61. Karmay 1988a, ch. 6, provides the most thorough study of this text to date and discusses its probable antiquity on pp. 142–144. He concludes that it must have been in existence during the tenth century at the latest.

62. *Man-ngag lta-phreng*, pp. 2–6; Karmay 1988a, pp. 163–165 (text), 152–155 (translation).

63. *Theg-rim*. The text was rediscovered as treasure (*gter-ma*) by the Ban-dhe mi-gsum (the "three Buddhist monks"), whose exact dates are not known, but who appear to have been active perhaps in the early eleventh century. It may, however, be in fact a somewhat later work. I am indebted to the great contemporary Bon-po master, Slob-dpon Bstan-'dzin Rnam-dag (Lopön Tenzin Namdak), for having first introduced me to it.

64. This is Ston-pa Gshen-rab Mi-bo-che, revered by the Bon-po as the Buddha of our world age.

65. *Theg-rim*, folios 1b–3a. The names of the nine vehicles in Tibetan are: (1) *lha mi gzhan brten theg pa*, (2) *rang rtogs gshen rab theg pa*, (3) *thugs rje sems dpa'i theg pa*, (4) *g.yung drung sems dpa'i theg pa*, (5) *bya ba gtsang spyod ye bon theg pa*, (6) *rnam pa kun ldan mngon shes theg pa*, (7) *dngos bskyed thugs rje rol ba'i theg pa*, (8) *shin tu don ldan kun rdzogs theg pa*, (9) *ye nas rdzogs chen yang rtse bla med theg pa*.

66. It must be noted that there were several other Bon-po nine-vehicle systems, and that the one we have examined here, that of the "Central Treasure" (*dbus-gter*), which is attributed to Vairocana, most closely corresponds to the Buddhist versions. Snellgrove 1967a provides a detailed account of a rather different system, according to the "Southern Treasure" (*lho-gter*), whose first four vehicles focus upon medicine, divination, and other mundane arts. In addition there is the system of the "Northern Treasure" (*byang-gter*), which remains so far unstudied. For the classifications of these systems, see *Bon-gyi bstan-'byung*, p. 142.

67. The Sanskrit text may be found, for instance, in *Sarvadarśanasaṃgraha*, p. 2: *yāvaj jīvet sukhaṃ jīved nāsti mṛtyor agocaraḥ/ bhasmībhūtasya dehasya punarāgamanaṃ kutaḥ//*

68. Klein and Wangyal 1995 offers an excellent example.

69. Blondeau 1971 demonstrates this. Kværne 1980 illustrates the complexity of the entire question of borrowings between Buddhists and Bon-po.

70. The cuckoo's warble was an important metaphor in early works on Rdzogs-chen. See Karmay 1985, 1988a, pp. 41–59.

71. *Gal-mdo*, pp. 192–193. The text cited here is said to be a treasure of Khu-tsha zla-'od (twelfth century), commenting upon an earlier text discovered by Gshen-chen klu-dga' (996–1035).

72. The best example is Vasubandhu's *Vyākhyāyukti*, which was available in Tibetan together with the commentary of Guṇamati by the early ninth century (Lalou 1953, nos. 649–650). This important text has been little studied as yet. A useful beginning may be found in Cabezón 1992.

73. *OTG*, lines 32–33: "[When Nyag-khri btsan-po] arrived at the divine mountain Gyang-do, even Mount Meru bowed in submission, the trees hastened forth, the springs ran clear and cool."

74. *OTC*, ch. 1, on the first mortal king, Gri-gum btsan-po, offers one of the finest examples from the Dunhuang documents. Stein 1959, ch. 10, analyzes the character of the hero in the Gesar narratives.

75. Stein 1981.

76. *Shangs-pa bla-rabs*, pp. 5–6.

77. Dudjom 1991, vol. 1, p. 624.

78. Samuel 1993, ch. 1. Samuel 1990 provides the theoretical background for Samuel's elaboration of the categories "shamanic" and "clerical" and helps to dispel some of the misunderstandings that may arise owing to the associations of the former term in particular.

79. In the interest of full disclosure, I should note that in Kapstein 1992b I have also spoken of a Tibetan tantric seeker in India as one embarked upon a "shamanic vision quest." Despite my present misgivings about the term in question, I still believe that my argument there was essentially correct, and I am not sure that there is another term available that would do the same work as "shamanic" in the context in which I chose to employ it.

80. This is particularly true of the tendencies described in Lopez 1998, ch. 6.

81. Among anthropologists who have considered relations between elite and nonelite religious practice in Tibetan and Himalayan communities, one may refer to Ortner 1989; Mumford 1989; Samuel 1993.

82. A good example is the popular opera *Rgya-bza' bal-bza'* (Chinese Bride, Nepalese Bride), based on the legends of King Srong-btsan-sgam-po's court. The monastic sacred dances (*'cham*) also often dramatized elements of the story of Tibet's adoption of Buddhism. Historical lore was also widely transmitted in connection with pilgrimage. See Huber in Lopez 1997, pp. 120–134; Kapstein 1997c, 1998. See now also Huber 1999.

83. As Goldstein, in Goldstein and Kapstein 1998, p. 22, remarks: "Tales abound in Drepung of famous scholar monks so poor that they had to eat the staple food—*tsamba* (parched barley flour)—with water rather than tea, or worse, who had to eat the leftover dough from ritual offerings (*torma*)." This refers primarily to their early years of study; once established as teachers in their own right, noted monastic scholars often received sufficient support from patrons to permit them to escape such abject poverty.

84. Karma Chags-med (ca. 1600–1666), Gung-thang Bstan-pa'i sgron-me (1762–1823), Zhabs-dkar Tshogs-drug-rang-grol (1781–1850), and Rdza Dpal-sprul Rin-po-che (1808–1887) offer some of the best examples. Their lives and writings supply ample evidence of sustained involvement in teaching to the laity.

Chapter 2

1. Fletcher 1997, writing on the Christian conversion of pagan Europe, discusses the "Christianization of time" (pp. 255–258) and the effects of this upon medieval historians: "Could a pagan past be permitted for the legatees of the western Roman empire? . . . For [Bede] the pre-Christian past of the English scarcely existed. . . . Isidore of Seville, whose *History of the Goths* was composed in about 620, preferred to provide them with a biblical ancestry. The Goths were descended from Magog son of Japheth son of Noah."

2. Though I speak here of a Tibetan "conversion," or "adoption of Buddhism," it is important to remember throughout that this was neither complete nor universal. For the early period with which we are concerned, in particular, we have little evidence that allows us to determine just how successful Buddhism may or may not have been, outside of the specific royal and monastic circles we know to have been actively involved in the promotion of the new religion.

3. There is no consensus regarding the proper designation of the dynasty of the Btsan-po-s who ruled Tibet. Following Haarh 1969, some refer to the "Yar-lung dynasty," a phrase derived from the name of the valley to the southeast of Lhasa, which was the region in which the Btsan-po-s had first established their rule. This usage, however, is unknown to Tibetan sources. The early inscriptions and chronicles often designate the ruler as the Spu-rgyal (Beckwith 1987, pp. 8, 17), and sometimes this seems a dynastic title. To refer to Tibet during the period of consolidation and expansion of the empire until its decline in the mid-ninth century, some scholars speak of "imperial" or "dynastic" Tibet. When referring to this historical period here, "early medieval Tibet," following Beckwith 1987, is preferred to the inaccurate "ancient Tibet" one finds in many popular books. Indeed, some even describe fourteenth-century Tibet as "ancient," for it is the allure of antiquity that engages the contemporary imagination when it comes to Tibet, and not at all the question of historical periodization.

4. As Tucci put it in his pioneering essay "The Validity of the Tibetan Historical Tradition" (1947): "we can accept as well founded the traditional account of Tibetan history . . . without of course taking into consideration the legends and myths which later on were circulated and grew up concealing, as it were, the authentical kernel of the ancient chronicles" (1971b, vol. 2, p. 462).

5. Beckwith 1987, p. viii: "In early medieval Oriental history [there] are not technically primary sources at all: they are mainly the surviving narrative accounts, written long after the fact. . . ."

6. Collingwood 1956. Refer esp. to the Epilegomena.

7. A popular introduction to the discovery of the "hidden library" of Dunhuang may be found in Hopkirk 1984, ch. 12. For an account of Aurel Stein's finds there in particular, see Stein 1933, ch. 12–14; Mirsky 1977, ch. 14. The India Office Library holdings of Tibetan manuscripts brought to England by Stein are catalogued in *IO Cat.* and Yamaguchi 1977–1988. *PT Cat.* supplies an inventory of the Paris collections gathered by Pelliot. Selections from the Tibetan Dunhuang documents have been reproduced in *CDT I* and *CDT II,* which include introductory essays with references to earlier studies of these texts. Many of these same documents are edited with notes in *Tun-hong bod-yig shog-dril* and Wang Yao and Chen Jian, eds., *Dunhuang Tubowen Shulun Wenji.* Refer also to *OTA, OTC,* and *OTG,* and, concerning these same texts, Beckwith 1987.

Bod-kyi rdo-ring, Richardson 1985, and Li and Coblin 1987 provide useful editions of the inscriptions dating to the period of the empire (though a number of previously unknown inscriptions have also appeared in recent years, to some of which reference will be made at appropriate points). Richardson's many studies of particular topics in early medieval Tibetan history are now gathered together in Richardson 1998, Pt. 1. For additional studies of particular Dunhuang Tibetan documents, especially those by Imaeda, Lalou, Stein, and Uray, refer to the bibliography. For a recent bibliography of Dunhuang studies in Western languages, unfortunately limited to Sinological work and thus effacing the international character of the Dunhuang finds, see Bussotti and Drège 1996.

8. L. W. J. van der Kuijp, "Tibetan Historiography," in Jackson and Cabezón 1995, pp. 39–56, offers a fine point of departure for the study of the formation of Tibetan traditions of historical writing. Vostrikov 1970 remains a magisterial introduction to Tibetan historical writing, all the more remarkable for having been written in the 1930s, though it remained for many years unpublished following the author's untimely death at the age of thirty-three. Martin 1997 now provides a very thorough bibliographical survey of the field of Tibetan historical writing. The "historical myths of the early empire" to which I refer are reviewed in chapter 8 of the present volume.

9. Martin 1997, in fact, orders the vast majority of the texts he lists chronologically, in many instances giving exact dates of composition. Though in some instances, his conclu-

sions in this regard may be questioned, most Tibetanists will concur with him in the large majority of cases.

10. Uray 1975, 1992.

11. The *Sba-bzhed* is now known to us through two differing redactions of the text, each incorporating readings from several manuscripts: Stein 1961 and *Sba-bzhed.* (The text published by Stein was reprinted in 1968 in a typeset edition at the Tibetan Educational Printing Press in Dharmasala, India, incorporating some readings from a manuscript in the possession of Burmiak Densapa of Gangtok, Sikkim. This edition, however, contains many misprints, which makes it difficult to identify precisely actual variant readings, and so will not be referred to herein.) In addition, as the present book was nearing completion, a manuscript was discovered in Tibet of a work entitled *Dba'-bzhed,* which is an older version of the same or a similar text, perhaps its very original. (*Dba'* here is the archaic spelling of the clan name that later came to be rendered *Sba.*) While the discovery of the *Dba'-bzhed* does not cause me to substantially alter the conclusions for which I argue in this and the following two chapters, I have added to the end of this note a paragraph discussing its implications, so far as I can adduce them in advance of the publication of the manuscript itself, and have added occasional brief remarks about the *Dba'-bzhed* as seems relevant elsewhere as well.

Extensive quotations in the *Mkhas-pa'i dga'-ston* of Dpa'-bo Gtsug-lag-phreng-ba provide considerable evidence of the *Sba-bzhed* in a version that was known to Tibetan scholars of the sixteenth century; direct references, as well as obvious paraphrases and allusions, in the writings of Nyang-ral Nyi-ma-'od-zer (1124–1196), Sa-skya Paṇḍita Kun-dga'-rgyal-mtshan (1181–1251), and Bu-ston Rin-chen-grub (1290–1364), among many others, all contribute to the conclusion that, excepting perhaps for variant spellings and other like points of detail, the portions of the *Sba-bzhed* dealing with the confrontation between Chinese and Indian Buddhism in Tibet during the reign of Khri Srong-lde'u-btsan were, as early as the twelfth century, substantially similar to what we have today. Indeed, even in Nyang-ral's day, to judge from his paraphrases, which tend often to bring the text into accord with "standard" literary Tibetan, the *Sba-bzhed* must have seemed archaic and often difficult to understand. It comes as no great surprise, then, that Tibetan historical tradition frequently considers the author of the early sections of the *Sba-bzhed* to have been a direct witness to the late eighth-century and early ninth-century events narrated therein. And contemporary Tibetanists, while unwilling to affirm this without much qualification and expressing a degree of puzzlement about it, clearly regard the *Sba-bzhed* as an authentically ancient source, or at least a direct derivative of such sources. Despite the awareness of and interest in the *Sba-bzhed* on the part of leading Tibetanists, however, questions regarding its origins and the precise nature of its contribution to our understanding of eighth- and ninth-century Tibetan history and to the later formation of Tibetan religious historiography remain mostly unresolved.

The *Sba-bzhed* first became available to contemporary scholarship through manuscript copies that were independently collected in Lhasa during the 1940s by Hugh Richardson and Giuseppe Tucci. A collation of these manuscripts—both of which represent the so-called "*Sba-bzhed* with supplement" (*Sba-bzhed zhabs-btags-ma*)—was prepared and published in 1961 by Rolf Stein. In his introduction, Stein notes that this version with supplement had been estimated by Richardson to date to the fourteenth century, and by Roerich to the twelfth or thirteenth. Yoshiro Imaeda (1975) lent his support to Richardson's estimate, while Stein himself characteristically withheld judgement about this.

That the supplemented version could not be assigned to a period prior to the twelfth century, or the last decades of the eleventh at the very earliest, was established by the supplement itself, which concerns events following the fall of the imperial dynasty during the mid-ninth century, continuing down to Atiśa's mission in Tibet in the mid-eleventh. The fourteenth-century date assigned to the supplemented *Sba-bzhed* by Richardson and Imaeda is supported by a single reference within it (Stein 1961, p. 54) to the 1322 history by Bu-ston

(*Gsung-rab rin-po-che'i bang mdzod* = *Bu-ston chos-'byung*, translated in Obermiller 1931–1932). The sentence in which this occurs, however, may not be an integral part of the text; if, as I suspect is the case, this is really a reader's annotation (*mchan-bu*) that has been copied by a later scribe as if integral, then the major objection to Roerich's estimate is answered.

However this may be, it was also clear that the supplemented *Sba-bzhed* was based at least in part on uncontestably ancient sources. One example that demonstrates its antiquity is discussed in chapter 5, namely, the highly interesting references found within the *Sba-bzhed* to the Korean Chan master Kim Hwasang (Ch. Jin Heshang), also known as Wuxiang. None of this would likely have been familiar to later Tibetan historians were it not for the testimony of the *Sba-bzhed*, the author of which, accordingly, must be thought to have at least had access to some very old documents.

The 1980 edition of the Nationalities Publishing House in Beijing differs in certain respects from the Richardson-Stein text, though in its general outlines it is closely similar to the first sixty-five pages of that edition, that is to say, to the section that the colophon of the Richardson-Stein edition specifies to be the "real original" (*rang-gi ngo-bo*) of the text (Stein 1961, p. 92). The colophon of the Beijing edition (which is not found in the Richardson-Stein text) closes with the comment (*Sba-bzhed*, p. 82) that the text was prepared by a scribe called Snyas-kyi btsun-pa Ldum-bu Ma-ṇi Arga Sidhi. I assume that "Arga" is a transcription or typographical error for "Artha," in which case the scribe's proper name should be: Ldum-bu Nor-bu-don-grub, the venerable monk (*btsun-pa* = Skt. *bhadanta*) of Snyas. Now, this is very interesting, because this name is suspiciously similar to that of Ldum-bu Don-grub-dbang-rgyal, considered to have been "the greatest scholar in astrology, astronomy and calendrical calculations to appear in Tibet during the 17th century" and one of the Fifth Dalai Lama's inner circle (Smith 1970, p 18, n. 36). If this supposition proves to be correct, then, because the Great Fifth's intense interest in the *Sba-bzhed* is well known, we might surmise that the Beijing edition in fact represents a version of the text, if not *the* version of the text, prepared for or at least available to the Fifth Dalai Lama himself. In other words, it is possible that the Beijing edition represents what was thought to be the most authentic version of the *Sba-bzhed* still to be found during the seventeenth century. Because the *Mkhas-pa'i dga'-ston* of Dpa'-bo Gtsug-lag-phreng-ba, a scholar well known for his antiquarian interests and access to genuinely old documents, seems also to suggest that he regarded as authoritative a version of the text closely similar to this one, we must further entertain the possibility that the Beijing edition represents a relatively early redaction of the *Sba-bzhed* indeed. But even if we now accept the age of Nyang-ral in the twelfth century as an approximate *terminus ad quem*, the question remains: just how old is it?

Ruegg 1989 has commented on the probable antiquity of the *Sba-bzhed* in the light of the Beijing edition. His primary concern there is the confrontation between Chinese and Indian Buddhism in Tibet that the *Sba-bzhed* describes, and he writes:

> In sum, despite the fact that the Supplemented Version of the *sBa bźed* published by Stein must for the reasons mentioned above be considered as a whole to be much later than the eighth century, and although the recensions of the *sBa bźed* now available to us differ in wording and in many details, there would nevertheless seem to exist no compelling reason to reject as completely spurious and unreliable the matter on which the recensions agree in substance. And there is reason to think that both these recensions contain ancient records or traditions (*bźed lugs*) that could go back to members of the sBa family which played so important a rôle at the time of the foundation of bSam yas and the controversy between the "Gradualists" and "Simultaneists" in late eighth-century Tibet, and that we thus have reflected (however indirectly) in our texts of the *sBa bźed* the views of major participants in these events. (Ruegg 1989, p. 71)

Though Ruegg's assessment seems generally reasonable, his argument is in one important respect flawed: as will be made clear later in this chapter, we can demonstrate instances in which the two versions of the *Sba-bzhed* are in perfect agreement about matters concerning which they can both be shown to be false. Their mere convergence, therefore, provides no sure ground for judgements of probable veracity. The reason for this is not hard to adduce: if, as seems most likely, the expanded redaction represented by the Richardson-Stein text had in its ancestry a text closely resembling the Beijing edition, then their agreements, as well as the evidential weakness of some of these agreements, are adequately explained.

One additional, curious bit of evidence has been brought to the attention of Tibetanists by Eimer 1991: an eleventh- or early twelfth-century work of the Bka'-gdams-pa tradition, the *Be'u-bum sngon-po* of Dge-bshes Dol-pa (1059–1131), a disciple of Po-to-ba (1027–1105), with its commentary by Lha-'bri-sgang-pa (early twelfth century), offers a brief account of the Bsam-yas debate, in terms that mostly match those of the *Sba-bzhed* verbatim, an abridgement (if, indeed, abridgement is what is involved here) that usually avoids archaic turns of phrase. Moreover, the *Be'u-bum sngon-po* specifies that Po-to-ba himself learned of the debate from one Jo-bo Se-btsun, a rather obscure figure from eastern Tibet (Khams) who, however, is also known to have been an early teacher of Atiśa's most renowned Tibetan disciple, the great 'Brom-ston Rgyal-ba'i 'byung-gnas (1004–1064). The information we derive from this source explicitly confirms that there was indeed some sort of ongoing transmission of a system of "sudden enlightenment meditation" that was described as just that, continuing at least into the early part of the eleventh century, a circumstance that lends some plausibility to the contention of Sa-skya Paṇḍita and others that Chinese sudden meditation techniques became mixed up with the teachings of the eleventh- and twelfth-century Tibetan meditation schools. (On this, see ch. 5.) And Se-btsun's own preference for the Kamalaśīla tradition of gradualism, articulated in a manner that so closely corresponds to what we find in the *Sba-bzhed*, does much to strengthen the supposition that some version of the *Sba-bzhed*'s account was already in circulation before Atiśa arrived in Tibet in 1042, whether or not it was known by that title.

The recent discovery in Lhasa of an old manuscript of a work called the *Dba'-bzhed* now suggests that the suppositions just outlined are largely correct. The manuscript, which is the object of a collaborative research project involving the Tibet Academy of Social Science (Lhasa) and the Austrian Academy of Science (Vienna), has been described in reports by Pa-sangs-dbang-'dus (Lhasa) and Hildegard Diemberger (Vienna) to the International Association of Tibetan Studies during its 1998 seminar at Bloomington, Indiana. I am further grateful to Pa-sangs-dbang-'dus for informative conversations about this manuscript during my visit to Lhasa in August 1998. The *Dba'-bzhed,* on which we now see the publication referred to in n. 15 below, confirming the hypotheses offered in this book, does not include the episode discussed in the present chapter and does have a version of the story analyzed in chapter 3. In its description of the confrontation between Chan and Indian Buddhism, it accords more closely with the Chinese account studied in Demiéville 1952, and this perhaps confirms the argument given later in this chapter, that the text is the work of an author (or authors) largely sympathetic to the activities of Chinese Buddhists in eighth-century Tibet.

12. *OTA* reports this in the entry for the year 762; *OTC,* line 377; Pelliot 1961, p. 30; Beckwith 1987, p. 146.

13. On early medieval Tibetan historiography, see especially Uray 1975, 1979, 1992.

14. Stein 1980, p. 329, n. 2: "C'est un récit romancé, relativement ancien, des événements du VIIIe siècle. Il a visiblement été manipulé, mais contient des éléments historiques vérifiés par des sources indépendantes et anciennes."

15. See now Pasang Wangdu and Hildegard Diemberger, *dBa' bzhed: The Royal Narrative Concerning the Bringing of the Buddha's Doctrine to Tibet* (Vienna: Austrian Academy of Science, 2000).

16. *Sba-bzhed,* p. 1: *nga'i dbon sras kyi ring la rgyal po lde zhes bya ba'i ring la dam pa'i lha chos 'byung ste de bzhin gshegs pa'i rjes su rab tu byung ba dbu reg dang zhabs rjen/ sku la ngur smrïg gi rgyal mtshan gsol ba/ lha dang mi'i mchod gnas kyang mang du 'byung. . . .* Stein 1961, p. 1.

17. Bran-ka Mu-le-ko is mentioned in later Rnying-ma-pa sources in connection with Buddhagupta's transmission of materials relating to the *Guhyagarbhatantra* (*Rgyud gsang ba snying po*) (Dudjom 1991, vol. 1, p. 533). Gnyags Jñānakumāra is a figure celebrated in later Rnying-ma-pa tradition as a great master of the rites of Vajrakīla, and above all of the wrathful powers of sorcery derived from those rites (Dudjom 1991, vol. 1, pp. 601–605).

18. On Buddhagupta see ch. 4, nn. 68–72.

19. *OTC,* lines 354 and 358, does use the phrase *chos-bzang* in a song attributed to Khri Lde-gtsug-btsan and his court, but this appears to mean "fine customs" in this context, and not "excellent dharma." The early ninth-century inscription at Skar-chung, however, does ascribe the construction of some temples, including one at Mchims-phu (Mching-phu), to him (Richardson 1985, pp. 74–75, lines 10–12).

20. Ljang is commonly used to designate the kingdom of Nanzhao, in modern Yunnan, which was subjugated by the Tibetans in 703, according to *OTA.* So it is plausible to hold, concurring with Backus 1981 and Beckwith 1983, that Queen Khri-btsun was from Nanzhao. Stein 1983, p. 216, however, shows that Ljang may sometimes have other significations in Old Tibetan, so that its exact reference here is somewhat uncertain. Backus, pp. 44–45, misreads Thomas 1951, p. 107, in asserting that there is inscriptional evidence concerning Ljang-tsha Lha-dbon. For more on Nanzhao in relation to early Tibet, see Ecsedy 1984.

21. This is a relatively early reference to this well-known myth, which is already well developed in the eleventh or twelfth century (*Bka'-chems,* pp. 48–57).

22. This also seems to be an early mention of a popular myth, on the evolution of which see ch. 4 and 8, and Stein 1986a.

23. The "names" of the Chinese princesses who were sent to Tibet—Wencheng Gongzhu and Jincheng Gongzhu—are of course not proper names at all, but the formal titles connected with their appanages.

24. The practice of sorcery by mantra-adepts becomes a major theme in Tibetan tantric literature from the eleventh century onwards. This perhaps also points to the period in which the *Sba-bzhed* was redacted on the basis of earlier materials.

25. Richardson 1998 [1997], pp. 207–215, "Two Chinese Princesses in Tibet," provides a useful summary of evidence concerning the Wencheng Gongzhu (Tib. Mun-sheng Kong-co) and the Jincheng Gongzhu (Tib. Kim-sheng Kong-co).

26. *Tshe* in this case is evidently not the familiar Tibetan word meaning "life" or "longevity" but probably transcribes the Chinese *zhāi,* "a fast of abstinence." See ch. 3.

27. Brag-dmar included the north bank of the Gtsang-po in and around the region in which Bsam-yas was founded (Chan 1994, p. 628ff).

28. *Sba-bzhed,* pp. 4–5: *khri srong lde btsan rgya tsha lags, sna nam zhang gi ci bgyi 'tshal?*

29. For instance: *Klong-chen chos-'byung,* pp. 225–227; *Mkhas-pa Lde'u,* p. 300; *Mkhas-pa'i dga'-ston,* vol. 1, pp. 297–298; *Rgya-bod yig-tshang,* p. 178; *Rgyal-rabs gsal-me,* pp. 199–200; *Nyang-ral,* p.272; *Deb-dmar,* p. 36; *Deb-dmar gsar-ma,* pp. 22–23 ; *Ne'u Paṇḍita,* p. 20 (where the tale is given in an annotation); *Dpag-bsam ljon-bzang,* p. 151; *Bu-ston chos-'byung,* pp. 183–184; *Bod-kyi deb-ther,* p. 51; *Yar-lung chos-'byung,* p. 59. This much should suffice to indicate the very wide distribution of the story, and the extent to which it was traditionally accepted as true.

30. Compare, however, Bu-ston's account (Obermiller 1932, p. 186), where the abduction takes place but not the recovery of the child, so that Khri Srong-lde-btsan is in fact brought up as a Sna-nam-pa on his mother's side.

31. Obermiller 1932, p. 186.

32. Demiéville 1952, p. 1, n. 2, which concludes on p. 9.

33. *OTA,* lines 231, 236–237, 240–241.

34. Demiéville 1952, p. 7, notes that the date of her death is given in the Chinese sources as November or December 740, and that a Tibetan embassy arrived in Chang'an in early 741.

35. *OTG,* lines 66–67.

36. Demiéville 1952, p. 9: "[D]e toutes ces traditions selon lesquelles le Roi Khri-sroṅ-lde-bcan aurait été le fils de la princesse de Kin-tch'eng, il n'y a en réalité rien à retenir. Elles ont contre elles les nombreaux indices du fait que, lors du concile de Lhasa, le Roi était du côté des Indiens et ne favorisait pas le parti pro-chinois. . . ."

37. Thus Bu-ston's account (see n. 30, above) is an attempt to reconcile conflicting sources.

38. Yamaguchi 1996.

39. Beckwith 1983.

40. Beckwith 1983, in fact, concurs with this second point, but, as will be seen in the following note, we differ in some respects in our interpretations of its implications.

41. Beckwith 1983 is not primarily concerned with our present conundrum, so it will not be necessary for our purposes here to survey all the many issues that are at stake, but, together with some additional background, it will be useful at the least to be familiar with his major conclusions.

According to *OTA*, King Khri 'Dus-srong died in 704, and in 705 his eldest son, Lha Bal-pho, was deposed, apparently by the late monarch's mother, the dowager empress Khri Ma-lod, who established the younger son, the year-old infant Rgyal Rtsug-ru, as monarch. (On Khri Ma-lod, see now Uebach 1997, pp. 55–56.) In 712, Khri Ma-lod dies and the eight-year-old monarch assumes the title by which he would henceforth be officially known, Khri Lde-gtsug-rtsan. The *Jiu Tangshu* notes that the request for a Chinese princess to marry the Tibetan monarch was first issued in 702/703, that is, prior to the birth of Rgyal Gtsug-ru in 704, and was followed by a repeated request from the Tibetan empress, the monarch's grandmother, in 705. Both the *OTA* and the *Tangshu* place the arrival of the Jincheng Gongzhu in Tibet in 710. It would, of course, be a great pity if the six-year-old monarch had at that time already become a "Bearded Ancestor" (but, as his brother's fate makes clear, life at the top can be hard!). Now, Beckwith supposes that the monarch's deposed elder brother, Lha Bal-pho, is none other than the Ljang-tsha Lha-dbon of the later histories, and that this person is further to be identified with the Sras Lhas-bon who dies in 739, the same death year as that of the Chinese princess, and whose last rites are recorded together with hers as falling in 741. Beckwith suggests further that the princess may have really been married to this person, for whom, clearly, she was first intended, and that her marriage to the king Khri Lde-gtsug-btsan was a fiction. Beckwith argues that the empress Khri Ma-lod's deposition of the rightful monarch may have amounted to a palace coup that created a real crisis of legitimation for the child she placed on the throne, and by extension for his successors. (In any event, there seems certainly to have been some sort of ministerial rebellion in 704.) This would help to explain, he argues, why some of the ministers, in 755, revived the ancient custom of murdering the old, and in this case possibly illegitimate, king, intending Khri Lde-gtsug-btsan to be succeeded by his thirteen-year-old son, Khri Srong-lde'u-btsan. The assassination is asserted by the Stag-sgra Klu-khong inscription in Lhasa (Richardson 1985, pp. 6–7, lines 5–10) and indirectly supported by the continuation of *OTA* (*BM* 8212), as well as by later histories that report the banishment of the ministers named as the assassins in that inscription. (The later histories usually have the king die in a riding accident.) Beckwith reasons that the problem of legitimation was not dispelled by the old king's blood, however: his son's promotion of a universal religion, construction of the Bsam-yas monastery with what Beckwith terms its "kosmokrator symbolism," and the later attribution to him of maternal descent from the Chinese imperial line may all be seen as part of an effort to restore the dynasty's shaken credibility. It should be noted that Beckwith takes great care to emphasize that he offers this as hypothesis only, an effort to make sense of a deeply perplexing record.

While the evidence is not so decisive as to enable us to assess Beckwith's suppositions with any assurance, some points, it seems to me, require extreme caution. Not long after Beckwith's article was published, two related, previously unknown histories made their appearance in Lhasa: *Mkhas-pa Lde'u* and *Lde'u Jo-sras*. These were attributed by the editors of *Mkhas-pa Lde'u* to a pair of relatively obscure twelfth- and early thirteenth-century Buddhist teachers affiliated with the Rnying-ma-pa and Bka'-gdams-pa traditions. (On the question of authorship and provenance see Kuijp 1992.) These works seem often to make use of genuinely ancient and now otherwise unavailable sources, and this accords well with the assumption that their provenance is one of the southern Tibetan districts of Lho-kha, neighboring Lho-brag, or an immediately adjacent region (oral tradition sometimes attributes them to Spo-bo), for there is much evidence that authentic documents of the imperial period survived for centuries in just these places. See now, for instance, Huang 1989.

With regard to Khri Lde-gtsug-btsan and his succession, the two histories just mentioned, though very obscure in places, offer several interesting indications. Of course, I am not suggesting that these be accepted outright, only that, in the light of these works, alternative interpretations of the evidence may be put forward. In the first place, *Lde'u Jo-sras,* pp. 120–121, states that Khri Lde-gtsug-btsan had an elder brother Pa-tshab-tsha Lha Bal-po, a younger brother Lod Ma-lod, and a son Ljang-tsha Lha-dbon, who died before his Chinese bride arrived in Tibet. The "younger brother Lod Ma-lod" is almost certainly a badly mangled record of the name of the grandmother Khri Ma-lod, the dowager empress. Lha Bal-po and Lha-dbon are here explicitly not the same man, and, what is more, the likelihood of their identity is diminished by the assertion that their maternal lines were altogether different: the former was born to a mother of the Central Tibetan Pa-tshab clan, while the latter, as Beckwith has emphasized, may have been born to the Tibetan king's Nanzhao bride, for 'Jang/Ljang is the old Tibetan designation of Nanzhao, though it was not exclusively so used. (See n. 20 in this chapter. Nanzhao, according to *OTA,* was defeated by the Tibetans in 703 and fell intermittently under Tibetan sway throughout the eighth century, so that marriages between the royal families may well have taken place.) Given the apparent distortion of the dowager empress's name, however, we must be very cautious about assigning too much weight to the testimony of this passage.

Nevertheless, there is one additional piece of evidence from the *OTA* themselves, which, given the account of *Lde'u Jo-sras,* probably should be weighed more heavily than Beckwith has allowed: the mention of the monarch's deposed brother in 705 calls him Btsan-po *gcen* Lha Bal-pho, "the monarch's *elder brother,* Lha Bal-pho," whereas the figure whose death in 739 and funeral in 741 are mentioned together with those of the Chinese princess is referred to as Btsan-po *sras* Lhas-bon, "the monarch's *son,* Lhas-bon." Certainly Lhas-bon is equivalent to the classical Lha-dbon, the name meaning literally "divine or royal heir-nephew," which the *Sba-bzhed* takes to refer to the prince's godlike good looks. It seems possible that the Chinese princess, whom other sources specify to have been a victim of plague, died close to the birth of the unnamed heir she bore, who was taken by the same illness. However this may have been, it seems certain that *OTA* cannot not be naming one individual as *both* the brother and son of *the present monarch,* i.e., Khri Lde-gtsug-btsan; and, though it is not impossible, it seems very improbable that, in identifying a single individual, "Btsan-po" should refer to "the present monarch," Khri Lde-gtsug-btsan, in 705 but to "the previous monarch," Khri Lde-gtsug-btsan's father, Khri 'Dus-srong, in 741.

The plot, however, grows thicker still: *Mkhas-pa Lde'u,* p. 300, while not mentioning Khri Lde-gtsug-btsan's brother at all, has something curious to say about his first son, Ljang-tsha Lha-dbon. It tells us that the Chinese princess was invited to be his bride, that the omens were good, but that when she arrived in Tibet those prognostications were defeated because the prince had become demented, for which reason she married the old king instead.

Now, I have two hypotheses to offer in connection with all this, and following Beckwith's lead, I must emphasize once more that these are only hypotheses; the evidence simply does not permit one to draw very strong conclusions:

(1) The deposition of Khri Lde-gtsug-btsan's elder brother in 705 remains still very much a mystery. We really have no certain evidence establishing there to have been a palace coup, though we have no way of ruling this out as a possibility either, especially given the evidence we do possess of a ministerial rebellion. Now, let us suppose that the mention of princely dementia applies, not to Ljang-tsha Lha-dbon, but to the deposed Lha Bal-pho. If something like that were the case, we can well imagine that an alteration of the order of royal succession would have been perceived as necessary, without at the same time devastating the dynasty's claim of legitimacy. Indeed, given the normal violence of dynastic succession in imperial (and even in postimperial!) Tibet, a phenomenon to which the author of *Mkhas-pa Lde'u* even devotes a special section of his book (pp. 375–376), it is difficult to see why Beckwith regards the events of 705, whatever they may have been, to have created in this instance a special legitimation crisis extending even to the following generation.

(2) If the Chinese princess were indeed the mother of an heir apparent who died at or near birth together with his mother, and if the Chinese princess had been, as tradition maintains, a much admired figure among certain later circles in Tibet, then the Sna-nam queen, who was Khri Srong-lde'u-btsan's real mother according to *OTG*, may have come to be regarded metaphorically as the thief of the rightful crown prince, and the dead prince may have then been attributed in legend to the otherwise unknown Nanzhao queen. It is, moreover, most probable that there was considerable confusion about Khri Srong-lde'u-btsan's maternal line even at a relatively early date, for the *OTA*, line 241, informs us that his mother, Mang-mo-rje—this being specified in *OTG* as a name of the Sna-nam queen—died, not in childbirth, but before a year was out.

Thus, we see that an alternative construction of the record is available to us. The crucial point is this: in the light of what has been said so far, it becomes very difficult to imagine—even if Beckwith were in large measure correct—that the attribution of birth to a Chinese princess would have importantly contributed to the conception of Khri Srong-lde'u-btsan's legitimate kingship. Why, for instance, did the Dunhuang annalist, who has no apparent reservations over the issue of legitimacy, and who, as Uray has cogently argued, almost certainly reflects the official historical record of the old Tibetan state, preserve the opposing account? Why would later Buddhist historians have then grown so uncomfortable over the question of legitimacy that they felt the need to relate the king to the Chinese royal line, centuries after the fact?

42. I do not take account here of the long appendix added sometime after the eleventh century to the *Zhabs-btags-ma* version of the text (see Stein 1961, p. 65, line 15, through p. 92).

43. See ch. 5.

44. Takeuchi 1985.

45. Kværne 1980.

46. *Yar-lung chos-'byung,* p. 36. I am grateful to Heather Stoddard (Paris) for bringing this passage to my attention. The Western Xia are known in Tibetan as Mi-nyag and are frequently referred to in the West by the Mongolian designation Tangut. On their history and culture, with much reference to relations with Tibet and with the Buddhist religion, see now Piotrovsky 1993; Dunnell 1996.

47. Dudjom 1991, vol. 1, pp. 490–494.

48. Beckwith 1987, ch. 5, recounts the role of the Tibetans in early 8th-century Arab-Chinese relations, culminating in the battle of Aṭlakh in 751.

49. Messina 1947 supplies a still useful introduction to the areas in which Buddhism, Christianity, and Manichaeism intersected and perhaps interacted. Moffett 1992 surveys Christian traditions in Asia. Klimkeit 1993 usefully introduces Manichaean and Gnostic traditions in Central Asia. Recently, M. A. Williams 1996 argues cogently that "gnosticism" as a category should be "dismantled." The likelihood that "gnosticism" is more a modern academic construct than an actual movement in Hellenistic religion, however, has few ramifications for the small number of instances in which I refer in this book to it. What is at stake in these cases is the particular text or idea mentioned, and not the larger construct into which it may have been bundled.

50. Tucci 1980, p. 214, referring to the Bon religion, remarks that "older elements indicate perceptible influences of Iranian beliefs, especially, it would seem, those of Zurvanism." In a note to this sentence, Tucci adds, "These came about either through contacts with Central Asiatic peoples, through the intermediary of Manichaeism . . . or, later on, through the influence of the Uighurs" (p. 271, n. 5). In Tucci 1973, p. 39, he discusses finds of Nestorian crosses in Tibet but suggests they may be rather late, dating to the Yuan period. See, further, Stein 1980; Uray 1983; Kværne 1987.

51. Stein 1980.

52. Saeki 1916, p. 180.

53. Huc, 1897, vol. 1, p. 195, quoting Rubruk: "The Nestorians do possess the Holy Scriptures in the Syriac tongue, but they scarcely understand anything of them. They chant like our ignorant monks who do not know Latin, and thence it comes that they are mostly corrupt and wicked, and especially great userers and drunkards."

54. Boris Marshak, "L'Iran, la Sogdiane et l'art sérindien," unpublished paper presented 13 February 1996 at the conference "La Sérinde," Paris.

55. *Sgra-sbyor bam-po gnyis-pa,* in Ishikawa 1990, p. 1, describes the Karluk envoys as rendering homage before the early ninth-century Tibetan monarch Khri Lde-srong-btsan. Refer to Vitali 1996, pp. 281–291, on eleventh-century, and pp. 347–353 on early twelfth-century hostilities between the Karluk and the kingdoms of West Tibet.

56. Klimkeit 1993, p. 2; Reeves 1992. I am grateful to Alan Segal (Barnard College, New York) for referring me to Reeves's work.

57. Margoliouth 1907.

58. The text is most recently studied in Wu Chi-yu 1996. For a general description, see Michel Garel's entry in Giès and Cohen 1995, pp. 78–79.

59. Goitein 1971 provides ample evidence along these lines; refer to ch. 6 on education in general, and for the situation in the communities most likely connected to the Inner Asian trade, p. 201: "During the eighth through the tenth centuries, the period in which the Jewish ecumenical seats of learning prospered most, Iraq and Iran were among the richest countries of the world. They contained a very large Jewish population, which was able to maintain hundreds and even thousands of scholars as community officials or as part-time students."

60. Benjamin of Tudela, who journeyed in the Middle East in 1165–1173, and whose record of his travels became widely known in Latin translation, was perhaps the first author read in Western Europe to mention Tibet. He writes that "[the Caliph] is accompanied by . . . the princes of the land of Tibet, which is three months journey distant, and westward of which lies the land of Samarkand" (Adler 1987, p. 45).

61. Ibn-Khordâdhbeh, writing c. 817, says of Jewish traders in Inner Asia that "on their return from China they carry back musk. . . ." (Adler 1987, p. 2).

62. Hoffman 1969, 1972.

63. Momigliano 1990, p. 16.

64. Butterfield 1981, pp. 104–105.

65. Here are a few of the points at which karma and rebirth are emphasized:

When the Jincheng Gongzhu finds that her original bridegroom, prince Ljang-tsha Lha-dbon, has died, she concludes that it is because "his karma did not accord with my own" (*Sba-bzhed,* p. 3). Afterwards, she institutes last rites (*tshe/zhāi*) for the departed ministers, moved by compassion for their fate after death.

When the four-year-old Khri Srong-lde'u-btsan is playing in a pond with his pals, they hear that the father of one of them is said to have committed a great sin by killing some pigeons. The children begin to debate whether they would also become sinners were they to harm the bugs and worms in the sand beneath their feet. One of the playmates, a Chinese boy who seems to be none other than the young Sba Shan-shi, invokes a Chinese scripture called *Hur* (< Ch. *fó* < Skt. *buddha*), which teaches the doctrine of moral virtue, *kuśalakarma*. It is the little prince's delight about this that arouses ministerial suspicions that he will come to favor the Dharma (*Sba-bzhed,* p. 5.)

Later, when Kim Hwasang relates to Sba Shan-shi his prophecy of Khri Srong-lde'u-btsan's eventual conversion (pp. 7–8), he transmits to him three volumes that will promote the king's faith; the first among them, as it turns out, again concerns the teaching of the ten virtues (*Sba-bzhed,* p. 15).

Before the king attains his majority, however, and following the decease of Khri Lde-gtsug-btsan, a clique among the ministers succeeds in suppressing Buddhism and banning the funerary rites instituted by the Chinese princess. It is at this time that the episode to be examined in detail in chapter 3 occurs (*Sba-bzhed,* p.10).

Sba Gsal-snang travels to Nepal to meet Śāntarakṣita, setting the stage for the latter's eventual mission to Tibet. On their first meeting, the Indian master discloses that their connection was one formed over many lifetimes (*Sba-bzhed,* p. 12).

One might go on at far greater length in this vein, but this much should be sufficient to suggest that the *Sba-bzhed* is well aware that karma and rebirth had been in some respect contested notions, and that it seeks not only to report this controversy, but to take a standpoint of active advocacy with respect to it. And to this we must add that the intense opposition to the teaching of Heshang Moheyan and his followers that it attributes to Khri Srong-lde'u-btsan appears to stem primarily from the conviction that such teaching threatens to undermine the well-ordered "kammatic" universe.

66. See ch. 3, pp. 42–46.

67. The early *Dba'-bzhed* text, described by Hildegard Diemberger in her presentation to the July 1998 seminar of the International Association for Tibetan Studies, at Bloomington (n. 11 above), includes an account of a debate, following the death of Khri Srong-lde'u-btsan, between ministers favoring Bon-po last rites and those supporting Buddhism. Though not found in the *Sba-bzhed,* this comports very well with my emphasis here on the role of controversy about cosmology, for Buddhist cosmology represents in this context the ideological dimension of the practical problem of how best to address the fate of the dead.

68. See n. 22.

69. *Sba-bzhed,* p. 4; Stein 1961, p. 4.

70. This becomes an important motif in the later legends of the great stūpa of Bodh Nāth, Nepal, in particular. See Blondeau 1994.

71. The literature on the "council of Tibet" has grown very large since the debate first became known to contemporary researchers through the translation of Bu-ston's account in Obermiller 1932, pp. 191–196. More recent contributions include: Demiéville 1952; Tucci 1956–1958; Imaeda 1975; and Houston 1980. This last mentioned work, however, being based on late sources, is of rather limited utility and should now be supplemented by: R. Jackson 1982; van der Kuijp 1984, 1986; Stein 1987; D. Jackson 1990, 1994; Eimer 1991; and, above all, Ruegg 1989. Note, too, Gómez 1983a for extensive references to relevant secondary studies on the sudden-gradual controversy in Tibet. Research on Tibetan Chan sources from Dunhuang will be surveyed in greater detail in chapter 5, nn. 7–8.

72. *Sba-bzhed,* p. 75.

73. The Jincheng Gongzhu, Sba Shan-shi (who, let us recall, is described here as being of Chinese origins), Kim Hwasang, the Heshang who declares Khri Srong-lde'u-btsan to be a bodhisattva, and the Heshang who secures Sba Gsal-snang's faith in rebirth—all of these figures, without qualification, are positively valued by the author of the *Sba-bzhed.*

74. According to Pasang Wangdu (Lhasa, August 1998), the recently discovered *Dba'-bzhed* (n. 15 above) approximates the Chinese sources studied in Demieville 1952. Moheyan is here defeated in debate (fol. 24b), but without the condemnation reported in *Sba-bzhed.*

75. The text has been published many times with translation and commentary. Recent editions, with references to earlier studies, include: Richardson 1985, pp. 106–143; Li and Coblin 1987, pp. 34–137; *Bod-kyi rdo-ring,* pp. 21–58. *Dbon-zhang rdo-ring* offers a detailed reading of the inscription in its historical context.

76. East Inscription, lines 29–30: *bar 'ga' phan tshun gyi so'i blon pos gnod pa dag rngul gyis kyang.* (On the verb *rngul,* see Richardson 1985, p. 115, n. 5.)

77. It is of interest to speculate that the uncle-nephew relationship may have had very different cultural connotations in Tibet and China, and that this, unfortunately, has contributed to the long history of Sino-Tibetan misunderstanding. Chinese sources seem clearly to regard the relationship as implying Tibet's status as a tributary state, the junior party enjoying the protection of the avuncular Chinese empire. In Tibet, however, where the Btsan-po had traditionally required the support of the leading aristocratic clans to maintain his rule, the relationship perhaps involved another symbolic code: the heads of the clans that had entered into marital relations with the Btsan-po became his fathers-in-law, "uncles" by marriage, and this was reflected in the title "uncle minister" (*zhang-blon*). In other words, a familial designation of seniority was in effect exchanged for a subsidiary political position; real power was alienated for a gain in symbolic prestige. Thus, there is nothing in the 822 treaty inscription to suggest that by referring to himself as the "nephew" of the Chinese emperor, Khri Lde-gtsug-btsan considered himself to be a political inferior. From the Chinese perspective, the Tibetans were a subsidiary power, but from the Tibetan perspective, the familial relationship may have implied the Chinese acceptance of their lack of real political authority in Tibet.

78. East Inscription, lines 31–34; Richardson 1985, pp. 112–113.

79. Andersen 1917, pp. 58–59. Katz 1994, pp. 47–49, compares the Pali and biblical tales but seems not aware of the Tibetan versions.

80. Schiefner 1905, p. 121, in the tale of Viśākhā. For the Sanskrit text, found in the *Cīvaravastu* section of the *Mūlasarvāstivāda Vinayavastu,* see Dutt 1942, pp. 65–66.

81. Lalou 1953, no. 483. *Sba-bzhed,* p. 61, shows that the author was well aware that the *Mūlasarvāstivāda Vinayavastu* had been translated into Tibetan at that time.

82. Taylor 1989, pp. 50–51.

83. Or as Ernest Renan trenchantly put it: "Getting its history wrong is part of being a nation" (quoted in Hobsbawm 1992, p. 12).

84. Uray 1975.

Chapter 3

1. *Sba-bzhed,* p. 10; Stein 1961, p. 9.

2. Stein 1980, p. 329.

3. *Sba-bzhed,* p. 10. The monk is said to reside at the *hen-khang,* no doubt derived from Ch. *fàn,* "Brahman, Buddhist" + Tib. *khang,* "house," i.e., a Buddhist temple.

4. The precise significance of *bon* in early texts has been subject to much discussion, and it is generally agreed that it does not yet designate the organized religion of that name as it is known from roughly the late tenth century onwards. Nevertheless, as the evidence gath-

ered in Stein 1988 demonstrates, the antecedents of organized Bon are already well-represented in the documents discovered at Dunhuang. One point that seems clear, and of considerable interest in connection with our present text, is that *bon* seems often to be used in connection with funeral rites and the specialized officiants who performed such rites, as is the case in the important manuscript first studied in Lalou 1952.

5. Schopen 1997, esp. ch. 6–8, demonstrates the steps whereby, in Indian monastic Buddhism, *śarira,* "the body," came to mean "relics." In our present text the Sanskrit term itself is transcribed and the Tibetan translation term, *ring-bsrel,* is not used.

6. In the episode itself, the gender of the reborn daughter is unclear, but near its end, the *Sba-bzhed,* p. 78, speaks of a daughter of Sba Gsal-snang named Spyan-ras-gzigs (= Skt. Avalokiteśvara), who may be the same person. That the daughter was named for Avalokiteśvara, who as Guanyin in China became a female bodhisattva, is of great interest in the light of her birth's connection with a Chinese Buddhist monk. See also Stein 1986b.

7. Blondeau 1997.

8. Blondeau 1997, p. 202.

9. Blondeau 1997, pp. 197–198.

10. Jonas 1963, ch. 5.

11. Klimkeit 1993, p. 110ff.

12. Parfionovitch, Dorje, and Meyer 1992, plate 5, illustrates later Tibetan embryological theories, which were in large part inspired by Indian medical sources.

13. Williams 1941, p. 138, gives the following anecdote: "A Minister of State—Chi Liang, Marquis of Sui—walking abroad on a certain occasion, found a wounded snake, to which he gave medicine and saved its life. Afterwards, when he was again abroad in the evening, he saw the snake holding a brilliant pearl in its mouth, and as he approached it, the snake is said to have addressed him thus: 'I am the son of His Majesty the Dragon, and while recreating myself was wounded; to you, Sir, I am indebted for the preservation of my life, and have brought this pearl to recompense you for your kindness.' The Minister accepted the pearl and presented it to his Sovereign, who placed it in his hall, where by its influence the night became as day." And on p. 320, Williams notes: "The offspring of aged parents is compared to a pearl produced by an old oyster." See also Schipper 1993, p. 21, on the pearl that adorns the roof of Taoist temples.

14. Lamasse 1984 (originally published in 1920), where the source is *Xīn gúo wēn,* originally published by the Commercial Press of Shanghai, c. 1904. The same story is given in Brandt 1954 (originally published during the 1920s), pp. 50–54.

15. Here and in the following paragraph, my comments on the composition of Chinese characters are indifferent with respect to their actual etymologies, Chinese etymology being a field entirely beyond my competence. Popular or folkloric etymologies are all that are at stake in the present context, for I am concerned only with associations, not the true histories, of words.

16. Laufer 1912, pp. 294–305, "Jade Amulets of the Dead." However, Eberhard 1986, p. 230, asserts that "[i]n ancient times, a pearl was laid in the mouth of a dead person," and he further connects this with its symbolic associations with fertility. Groot 1892, pp. 269–279, discusses "Placing Precious Objects in the Mouth of the Dead" in some detail and writes (277): "During the Han dynasty pearls also occupied a place among the objects which were introduced in to the mouth of the dead. . . . The same reasons why gold and jade were used for stuffing the mouth of the dead hold good for the use of pearls in this connection; indeed, the latter are also very frequently alluded to in Chinese literature as depositories of Yang matter, and as such ranked amongst the bearers of vitality. . . . [Medical works] say that pearls can be useful for recalling to life those who have expired or are at the point of dying." See, further, Schafer 1963, pp. 242–245 ("pearls"), and 237–239 ("fire orbs").

17. This is clear, for instance, in its fanciful explanations for the terms *brtse-min-pa* and *ston-min-pa,* reading them as if they were Tibetan words (*Sba-bzhed,* p. 64; Stein 1961,

p. 54). The former, a transcription of the Chinese for "gradual entrance sect" (*jiànménpài*), is explained there to refer to "one who is loveless," while the latter, meaning "sudden entrance sect" (*dùnménpài*), is taken to refer to "one who is not a teacher," with suitable anecdotes presented to account for these odd ways of denoting the two factions. As Tibetan writers seem usually to be well aware that these are in fact Chinese words and aware too of their actual significance (for instance, Bu-ston, in Obermiller 1932, p. 196), we must assume, I think, that the redactor of the *Sba-bzhed* was enjoying some coarse wordplay here.

18. Maspero, 1971, p. 381.

19. Snellgrove 1987, vol. 2, pp. 418–419; Richardson 1998 [1997], p. 208.

20. Pelliot 1961, p. 80.

21. Pelliot 1961, p. 83; see also the remarks of Richardson 1998 [1997], p. 208.

22. *OTC*, lines 45–46: *btsan po rje dbyal zhig nongs na . . . ngo la mtshal gyis byugs.*

23. Thomas 1951, pp. 85–87; Karmay 1988a, pp. 76–80; Uebach 1990, pp. 407–413.

24. *Sba-bzhed*, pp. 11–12, 59; Stein 1961, pp. 11–12, 51.

25. Beckwith 1983.

26. Rockhill 1884, ch. 8; Thomas 1935; Emmerick 1967; Cannata 1990.

27. *PT* 960 in Emmerick 1967, pp. 84–85, lines 57–61.

28. Biraben and Le Goff 1969, p. 1497, confirm a series of outbreaks in the lands of the eastern Mediterranean during the 740s, so it is possible this was part of the same plague cycle that killed the princess of Jincheng. They describe the plague in question as "une vraie peste à bubons bien décrite," citing J. D. Tholozan, *Histoire de la peste bubonique en Mésopotamie* (Paris, 1874). Herlihy 1997, ch. 1, however, demonstrates that historical reports of buboes as a plague symptom do not alone permit a precise epidemiological identification of the disease in question in any given case. For a broad interpretation of the historical significance of plague cycles, see McNeill 1977, and ch. 3, in particular, for late antiquity and the early medieval period.

Commenting on the relationship between the 739 outbreak of plague in Tibet and the persecution of Buddhism, Beckwith 1983, p. 7, writes: "The foreign monks were blamed—no doubt justly—for having brought the plague with them. . . ." Assuming that the plague did spread from Inner Asia, however, and given Tibet's very extensive military and administrative presence in Inner Asia during this period, as is well documented in Beckwith 1987, it seems not warranted to conclude that the spread of Buddhism was specially linked to the spread of the disease. Military convoys were no less likely to have been accompanied by rats and fleas. What seems certain is that the presence of plague aroused fear of the alien, and that this sentiment, rather than precise knowledge of the illness's sources, provoked the anti-Buddhist reaction.

29. Beckwith 1983; *OTA*, line 230: *yos bu'ï lo* [= 739 C.E.] *la . . . sras lhas bon dron na bzhugs/ bzhugs pa las nongs . . . btsan mo kïm sheng khong co nongs par lo chig.*

30. Herlihy 1997, esp. pp. 73–81.

31. This section culminates in *Sba-bzhed*, pp. 14–16.

32. For instance, *Sba-bzhed*, p. 5, and Stein 1961, p. 5, where after the young prince is impressed by accounts of the ten cardinal virtues, the ministers express suspicion that he is partial to the Dharma.

33. *Sba-bzhed*, pp. 19–64.

34. *Sba-bzhed*, pp. 64–76. See Ruegg's analysis, 1989, ch. 2 and 3. The recently recovered *Dba'-bzhed* (see ch. 2, n. 15) is reported to treat the debate along lines more closely resembling the Chinese dossier given in Demiéville 1952 (Pa-sangs-dbang-'dus, oral communication).

35. *Sba-bzhed*, pp. 43–45. Chayet 1988.

36. *Sba-bzhed*, pp. 64–76. On the apparent antinomianism of Heshang Moheyan, see ch. 5, n. 34.

37. Beckwith 1990 attributes this threefold structure to Sa-skya Paṇḍita (1182–1251), though he rightly notes that there were Indian antecedents. The recent publication of the *Dbu-ma śar-gsum* of Phya-pa Chos-kyi-seng-ge (1109–1169) makes clear that the elements of this mode of analysis were well-established in Tibet before Sa-skya Paṇḍita's time, though without employing the latter's strict threefold outline.

38. Blondeau 1997, p. 213: "Pour dire l'essentiel, un individu est la réincarnation d'une âme issue d'un <<stock>> d'âmes, et son humanisation résulte de la jonction harmonieuse de cette âme avec la <<force de vie>>. . . ."

39. Steinkellner 1988, treating a Dunhuang Buddhist scholastic text that cffers a proof of the teaching of rebirth, suggests that such an argument was being promulgated in monastic circles, at least.

40. The relevant manuscripts are *PT* 37, 126, 640, 992, and 1284; and *IO* 285 and vol. 70, fol. 49.

41. These are explained in detail in *Shes-bya kun-khyab,* vol. 3, pp. 87–109. The four reversals are: to turn the mind from the interests of this life to that of future lives (*tshe 'di-las blo ldog-pa*); to turn the mind from interest in saṃsāra to freedom therefrom (*'khor-ba-las blo ldog-pa*); to turn the mind from the peace of individual nirvāṇa to the universal aspiration of the Mahāyāna (*zhi-bde-las blo ldog-pa*); and to turn the mind from dualistic apprehensions of subject and object (*gzung-'dzin-las blo ldog-pa*). Following works of popular instruction such as *Dwags-po thar-rgyan* and *Kun-bzang bla-ma,* however, the four are often thought to be the particular study topics of: the precious human birth (*dal-'byor rnyed-dka'*); death and impermanence (*'chi-ba mi-rtag-pa*); the defects of saṃsāra (*'khor-ba'i nyes-dmigs*); and karmic causation (*las rgyu-'bras*). In the earlier Bka'-gdams-pa sources, followed by Kong-sprul in *Shes-bya kun-khyab,* these topics are included in the first two "reversals of attitude."

42. *PT* 239, described in chapter 1. Stein 1970 has analyzed its polemical passages.

43. Steinkellner 1988.

44. This is especially evident in *PT* 16–*IO* 751, reproduced in *CDT I,* plates 7–16, the *IO* portion of which was first studied in Thomas 1951, pp. 92–109. Note, for example, the following in Thomas's translation (p. 102, and p. 96 for the text): "[M]ay the purpose in the mind of the prince Khri Gtsug-lde-brtsan have been accomplished; and the harm done to the enemy by the Great Councillor Uncle Khri-sum-rje and Great Uncle Lha-bzaṅ through great defeats of the hostile Chinese and Drug and other means great and small, and on the part of certain of the city of Mkhar-tsan, who, taking sides with the stubborn heroic people of Tibet and being foremost of heroes in winning two great victories in a single year, on behalf of the venture for dominion on the part of the lord and people of Tibet went forward with a will to harm animate creatures, so that wounds were needs afflicted, may those wounds likewise be healed so that not a scar remains!"

45. *OTC*, lines 374–375: *sangs rgyas kyï chos bla na myed pa brnyeste mdzad nas/ /dbus mtha' kun tu gtsug lag khang brtsigs te/ chos btsugs nas/ thams shad kyang snying rje la zhugs shïng dran bas skye shi las bsgral te/ g.yung drung du bton to.*

46. Tucci 1950; Ariane Macdonald 1971, pp. 308–309; Richardson 1998 [1980], pp. 89–99, "The First Tibetan *Chos-'byung*"; Stein 1986a.

47. *Sba-bzhed,* p. 82; Stein 1961, p. 65.

48. The text is given by Richardson 1998 [1980], p. 97. I differ here slightly from his translation, pp. 93–94. Cf. also Snellgrove 1987, vol. 2, p. 411.

49. Richardson 1998 [1980], pp. 89–99.

50. Previous investigations of this work may be found in Tucci 1956–1958, rprt. 1978, pp. 432–435; Ariane Macdonald 1971, pp. 367–368; Stein 1980; Steinkellner 1989.

51. Lalou 1953, no. 723; *Bu-ston chos-'byung,* p. 309.

52. *Bka' yang-dag tshad-ma,* p. 98 (65b7–8): *chos so cog gi dbang bgyid rigs pa'i rnam pa smos pa 'jig rten na rgyal po dag bdag gi rigs su ci 'dod pa ngag gi dbang gi 'grub pa*

bzhin du chos so cog la bdag gi phyogs su bzung ba yang ji ltar 'dod pa'i rigs pa'i dbang gis 'grub ste.

The parallel between religious and legislative reason was also affirmed in Western medieval political thought. Thus, in a similar vein, Kantorowicz 1957, p. 121, cites Accursius, writing in the thirteenth century: "Just as the priests minister and confection things holy, so do we, since the laws are most sacred. . . . And just as the priest, when imposing penitence, renders to each one what is his right, so do we when we judge."

53. It remains a question whether or not he is to be identified with the Dharmaghoṣaśānti of Za'ur praised by the Btsan-po as his guru in the introduction to the *Bka' yang-dag-pa'i tshad-ma.* As Steinkellner 1989 points out, the text follows the system of logic propounded in the *Saṃdhinirmocanasūtra,* which differs in important aspects from the tradition of Dharmakīrti with which Śāntarakṣita's logical writings are affiliated. Nevertheless, Śāntarakṣita's disciple Kamalaśīla does cite the *Saṃdhinirmocanasūtra* on occasion, for instance, in the first and third Bhāvanākrama (Tucci 1956–1958, rprt. 1978, pp. 515, 516, 538; 1971c, p. 22). I think it is therefore unwise to rule out the possibility that Śāntarakṣita may have taught on the basis of this sūtra in Tibet, particularly if it were already available in its Tibetan translation. As the *Ldan-dkar-ma* catalogue makes clear, the translation of neither Dharmakīrti's *Pramāṇavārttika* nor Śāntarakṣita's *Tattvasaṃgraha* had been completed even a decade or more after Khri Srong-lde'u-btsan's death (Lalou 1953, nos. 733, 736). Though other texts on logic were available by that time (Lalou 1953, nos. 695–722), it is by no means clear that this material would have been familiar when Śāntarakṣita was present in Tibet. In any event, Śāntarakṣita, like Dharmaghoṣaśānti, is usually said to have hailed from Za'ur, a toponym that has given rise to some puzzlement, and is variously placed in the east or west of India. I suspect that it transcribes Sauvīra, one of the old names for the region of Sindh. Interestingly, as Mitra 1971, p. 130 notes, there is evidence of the presence of monks from this region at Odantapurī monastery, near Nālandā in Bihar.

54. *Bka' yang-dag tshad-ma,* p. 109 (92a4–92b2): *so so'i skye bo rnams tshe'i 'du byed zad cing 'jig rten pha rol tu skye ba . . . gzugs med pa'i phung po rnam par shes par 'gro ste/ dper na rlung gi khams gzugs ltar mi snang ba ldang zhing 'gro ba me tog la sogs pa dri zhim po dang rul po la sogs pa dri nga ba gang dang phrad pa de'i dri khyer te mnar bar 'gyur ba rlung de'i gzugs kyang mi dmigs/ dri de'i gzugs kyang mi dmigs mod kyi rlung gi rgyun kyang mi 'chad la dri nga ba dang zhim po so so'i ro las kyang ma gyur par mnar par gyur ba dang 'dra ste/ rnam par shes pa dang las gnyis ka la yang gzugs med mod kyi/ gang gi rnam par smin pa ni de'i 'bras bu mngon pa dang 'dra ste/ gzhan du na las gang byas pa'i rgyus 'jig rten pha rol tu gzugs kyi rnam par skye ba ni me long gi nang du gzugs gang du bstan pa'i gzugs brnyan 'byung ba dang/ 'jim pa la rgya ci 'dra bas btab pa'i 'bur snang bar skye 'o zhes. . . .* This passage is largely based upon the *Bhadrapālaparipṛcchāsūtra.*

55. Typical of later Tibetan religious attitudes in this regard is *Kun-bzang bla-ma,* pp. 88–92, which introduces the problem of rebirth as given and so offers no argument whatever in support of this doctrine.

56. Bu-ston, in Obermiller 1931–1932, p. 187.

57. *Mkhas-pa'i dga'-ston,* vol. 1, pp. 304–306.

58. *Bod-kyi deb-ther,* p. 54.

59. Demiéville 1952, p. 33, mentions a maternal aunt of the Btsan-po, of the "Si-nang-nan" (= Tib. Sna-nam) clan, and "more than thirty wives of the great men of the land." *Sba-bzhed,* p. 67, mentions a certain "Lady Bodhi" (*Jo-mo Byang-chub*), among others.

60. Eastman 1983 provides a preliminary survey of this literature. The dating of many of these texts, and the nature of the communities which produced them, remain problematic.

61. Spiro 1982. Applying Spiro's categories to Tibet, Samuel 1993 speaks of a "karma orientation" and a "bodhi orientation."

62. Petech 1994 surveys the history of the empire's collapse. In *Shel-dkar phreng-ba,* Nor-brang O-rgyan assembles the Tibetan sources for the period.

63. Davidson 1994 provides a thoughtful account of aspects of this transition. Wylie 1977 offers interesting speculations on the meaning of the term *bla-ma,* but on this see now Lopez 1998, ch. 1. Pace Lopez, however, I am inclined to think that the term *bla-ma* does preserve some echo of the term *bla,* "vital soul." Refer to Kapstein 1992b. Oral tradition among masters of the Rnying-ma-pa school sometimes also invokes the concept of *bla* in this connection.

64. Traditional summaries of the history of this collection are given in Dudjom 1991, vol. 1, pp. 554–555, 580–588. Germano forthcoming offers a thorough investigation of the formation of the *Mkha'-'gro snying-thig* corpus.

65. The treasures (*gter-ma*) are discussed in chapters 7 through 10, with references to earlier research in the notes to those chapters.

66. *Mkha'-'gro snying-thig,* vol. 3, pp. 377–390. The story is repeated by Klong-chen-pa's disciple Bya-bral-pa Bzod-pa in *Mkha'-'gro snying-thig,* vol. 3, pp. 491–497.

67. This is evident in modern retellings, e.g., Dudjom 1991, vol. 1, pp. 512–521.

68. *Ba-dzra-gu-ru'i phan-yon,* a work probably dating to the fourteenth century (see ch. 8 here), for instance, declares: "[I]n the future, beings will have much on their minds and will become extremely wild. . . . When that occurs, disease, famine, and strife will spread among all creatures, and, above all, China, Tibet, and Mongolia will become like a ravaged ants' nest, so that the subjects of Tibet will fall on hard times."

69. Dudjom 1991, vol. 1, pp. 533–537.

70. Dudjom 1991, vol. 1, p. 517. It is possible, however, that the Rnying-ma-pa tradition is in fact preserving a recollection of the *Dba'-bzhed,* which according to Diemberger (ch. 2, n. 11), describes a "rather unsuccessful journey of Padmasambhava." See also ch. 8, below.

71. *Padma bka'-thang,* pp. 535–547.

Chapter 4

1. Again I remind the reader that the version of the *Sba-bzhed* referred to here is a post-tenth-century work based on an earlier text, perhaps the recently rediscovered *Dba'-bzhed* (see ch. 2, n. 11). The recent publication of the latter will no doubt contribute to the refinement of the arguments offered in the present chapter.

2. See especially Bogoslovskij 1972, pp. 52–66; Ariane Macdonald 1971; Richardson 1998, esp. pp. 89–99 [1980], "The First Tibetan *chos-'byung,*" and pp. 196–202 [1992], "Political Aspects of the *Snga-dar";* Samuel 1993, pp. 451–455; Snellgrove 1987, vol. 2, pp. 381–463; Stein 1986a; Tucci 1980, pp. 5–15. Of course, many of the other writings on aspects of early Tibetan religion and culture to which reference is made in this book also offer fundamental contributions to our understanding of the early adoption of Buddhism.

3. For instance, Harvey 1990, p. 202, writes: "Buddhism contributed to ending Asoka's warlike expansion of his empire and tamed the warlike Tibetans and Mongolians." As Lopez 1998, p. 7, rightly observes: "The history of Tibet was portrayed as . . . having turned, with the introduction of Buddhism in the seventh century, from a society that had been directed outward, to conquer the world, into one that directed all its energies inward, to conquer the mind." Demiéville, for one, clearly recognized the discrepancies between ideology and practice and so rightly remarked (1952, p. 223): "Ce n'est pas sans accrocs, déviations et entorses que s'actualisent dans l'histoire les principes des grandes doctrines religieuses et morales, et il serait aisé de montrer comment les préceptes antimilitaristes du bouddhisme furent copieusement et perpétuellement violés par les bouddhistes d'Extrême-Orient. . . ." See also Demiéville 1957.

4. The evidence is reviewed in Richardson 1998, pp. 140–148, "Great Monk Ministers of the Tibetan Kingdom," esp. pp. 143–144.

5. Simonsson 1957, pp. 239–241; *Btsan-po lo-rgyus*, p. 60; Ishikawa 1990, p. 1: *rta'i lo la btsan po khri lde srong btsan pho brang skyi'i 'on cang rdo na bzhugs/ stod smad kyi dmag rnying rjed dang rkun chen btul/ gar log gi pho nyas phyag btsal/ blon chen po*[*s*] . . . *rgya las gnang mang po bcad de/ rnga rta dang lang phal mo che phyag tu phul/ zhang blon man chad so sor bya dga' dga' stsal ba'i lan la* . . . *lo tsā ba mkhas par chud pa*[*s*] . . . *theg pa che chung las byung ba'i rgya gar gyi skad las bod kyi skad du bsgyur cing ming du btags pa dkar chag bris te* . . . *ces bka' stsal*. . . .

6. Renondeau 1957; Demiéville 1957; Forte 1976; and Ling 1979 offer some useful points of departure for reflection on the question of Buddhism's relation to political expediency. On Buddhism in its relation to modern Japanese nationalism, see now Heisig and Maraldo 1994, and, on the historical background of the current tragedy in Sri Lanka, Tambiah 1992. Concerning Tibet, particularly in recent centuries, Dawa Norbu 1985, p. 177, argues: "The very history of *chos-srid gñis-ldan* demonstrates that even if force is renounced in principle, it is still a necessary part of a state's existence. . . . This does not mean no force was used in Buddhist Tibet; one can recall three incidents of monastic participation in warfare in this century alone." Goldstein 1989 provides a detailed account of Tibetan political life, and the role of the clergy within it, during the period 1911–1950.

7. Even Tucci 1980, p. 12, writes: "The attitude of *Glang dar ma* was doubtless in part formed by the concern he must have felt at the growing economic power of the monasteries, at their privileges and their arrogance. The steady extension of the religious community brought the existence of the state into serious danger. In addition there was the monasteries' freedom from taxation, the continual increase of their property through the assignment to them of estates and pastures, and the growing proportion of the population working for them in agriculture or as herdsmen, and therefore exempted from military obligation and compulsory labour. Also, donations did not only go towards the building of a temple; in addition they had to support the monastic community belonging to the temple, so as to secure for all time the performance of the ceremonies directed by the donor or testator in accordance with his will. This development deprived the state of considerable resources in both men and revenue. . . ." Neat as this may seem, Tucci offers no documentation to support his assertions here. Though elements of his argument are no doubt correct, the fact remains that our knowledge of the economy of the old Tibetan empire remains too poor to permit us to affirm his broad conclusions regarding the implications of Buddhist monasticism for the old Tibetan state.

8. Thus, even in the tale of Tibet's first mortal king, Gri-gum-btsan-po, the king's death is brought about by rivalry with a retainer. Evidence of feuds involving the nobles and the court is found throughout *OTA* and *OTC*. See, for instance, Beckwith 1987, pp. 11–17; Beckwith 1983.

9. A similar boom-and-bust pattern may be discerned in the histories of many ancient and medieval empires. See, e.g., Finley 1973, pp. 175–176 on the decline of Rome.

10. Karmay 1972 offers a complete translation of an important Bon-po religious history; Kværne 1995 summarizes the Bon-po historical view in brief.

11. Cf. Tucci 1971b [1947], cited in ch. 2, n. 4 above.

12. This is not by any means to minimize the many advances that have already been made in these areas, especially in the contributions of Beckwith, Lalou, Petech, Richardson, Takeuchi, Thomas, Uebach, and Uray, among others (see bibliography). Despite this, a synthesis of the data that would offer a clear account of the economic conditions of the rise and decline of the Tibetan empire has not yet been achieved, though Bogoslovskij 1972 remains a pathbreaking effort in this regard.

13. The Eastern Tibetan Buddhicization of the Gesar epic illustrates this well (Stein 1956).

14. I concur here with Ariane Macdonald 1971, pp. 308–309, and Stein 1986a, that Tucci's emendation of *ma-lags* ("was not") in the first sentence to *ma-legs* ("was no good") is probably not warranted. Richardson 1998 [1980], pp. 93 (trans.) and 97 (text), and Snellgrove

1987, vol. 2, p. 411, follow Tucci in their translations of the text. The text is in all cases based upon that given in *Mkhas-pa'i dga'-ston,* vol. 1, p. 374.

15. As Samuel 1993, p. 446, puts it, "Buddhism was acceptable as a new, improved shamanic technique, which would maintain the good fortune and welfare of the country without threatening the established order laid down in the past." Without quibbling about the use of the term "shamanic," this seems generally correct. Nevertheless, it is equally clear that there were important factions in Tibet that did not find Buddhism acceptable in this or any other way and reacted sharply against its introduction. We should avoid placing too much emphasis upon apparent accommodation between Buddhism and other religious systems, at the expense of the evidence that suggests confrontation.

16. See the *Bka' yang-dag tshad-ma,* as cited in ch. 3, p. 45.

17. *Chos-skyong bka'-slob,* pp. 184–185. On this dispute, see ch. 7, n. 43.

18. One can point to other occasions on which worship of the protectors appears as a contentious issue. In a work connected with the germinal stage in the development of the Rnying-ma-pa tradition, the *Rdor-sems zhu-lan* of Gnyan Dpal-dbyangs, which evidence from Dunhuang demonstrates to have been in circulation no later than the early ninth century, we read:

> *Question:* If yogins worship the deities and mother-spirits of Tibet and Khams, does that accord with the texts of yoga or not?
> *Response:* According to the declarations of Samantabhadra-Vajrasattva,
> The worship of worldly gods and demons as superiors,
> Would be like a king's acting as a commoner.
> Do not beseech them for your provisions, for that would contradict the very point of yoga. (*P* 5082, p. 165 [138a–5])

This passage has been discussed in Eastman 1983. The entire text is translated in Kapstein forthcoming.

Similarly, writing in the thirteenth century, Sa-skya Paṇḍita enters into controversy regarding the appropriateness of taking refuge in the protectors. He concludes that if the protectors are Buddhas or bodhisattvas, then they are already included in the refuge in the Three Jewels, so that no special refuge in them is warranted, whereas if they are not, then by no means should one take refuge in them at all (*Sa-paṇ gsung-'bum,* vol. 1, p. 18).

19. Weber 1964.

20. Ch. 1, n. 11, and, in this chapter, n. 2.

21. For example, *btsan-sa* means "stronghold," and *btsan-thabs,* "forceful means."

22. Nebesky-Wojkowitz 1956, ch. 12. Phillippe Cornu, cited in Samuel 1993, p. 162, states that they are "all male, and are the spirits of past monks who have rejected their vows."

23. The Manchu emperors, however, did attempt to appropriate *btsan-po* as part of a proper title of their own, in the phrase *tshe-ring gnam-gyi she-mong btsan-pos sa-steng yongs-la mnga'-sgyur-ba,* "he who exercises his rule over the whole earth owing to the steadfast (*btsan-po*) power of long-living heaven," i.e., who rules by the mandate of heaven. This occurs in the Qing imperial proclamations published in *Bod-kyi yig-tshags,* beginning with no. 47, the Qianlong emperor's 1790 decree to the Eighth Dalai Lama. In earlier documents, however, the equivalent phrase was *tshe-ring gnam-gyi she-mong-gis da-lta yongs-la mnga'-bsgyur-ba,* "he who now exercises his rule over everything owing to the power of long-living heaven" (Document 43, reign of Qianlong, dated 1762), or similar expressions used at least as early as the Kangxi emperor's 1713 decree (no. 36) granting a title to the Fifth Paṇchen Lama. We can only speculate as to why *btsan-po* was added during the Qianlong reign, though the ancient resonances of the expression may well have played a determining role here. To the best of my knowledge, however, indigenous Tibetan sources never use *btsan-po* to describe the Manchu or other Chinese monarchs.

24. Pelliot 1961, p. 79. The Chinese chronicle clearly reflects, however, that *btsan* was more or less correctly understood to mean "hero," although it was left untranslated.

25. Tucci 1971b [1955–1956], vol. 2, pp. 569–583, "The sacral character of the kings of ancient Tibet"; Haarh 1969; Stein 1981. On this last mentioned, see also the remarks of Snellgrove 1987, vol. 2, p. 381.

26. A particularly clear formulation of these as three interrelated phases is found in *Bod-kyi deb-ther,* pp. 19–23.

27. The interpretation of the term *gtsug-lag* as it is used here has aroused considerable controversy, especially since the appearance of Ariane Macdonald 1971, where it was argued that this was the proper name of the pre-Buddhist imperial Tibetan religion. Stein 1985 very convincingly demonstrates that this cannot be maintained, and that the term refers broadly to what we might term "wisdom," particularly the worldly wisdom of good governance. Hahn 1997 has added to this an exceptionally insightful discussion of the possible etymology of the term.

28. *OTC,* lines 451–455.

29. Bogoslovskij 1972, ch. 4, describes some of the social transformations that appear to have accompanied the evolution of the empire's political organization during the seventh through the ninth centuries. As he remarks (p. 143) concerning the imperial legislation: "au droit traditionnel de l'époque des clans, se substitua un droit de société de classes. Le but essentiel de cette législation était le maintien et le renforcement des rapports de classes naissants, rapports d'exploitation de l'homme par l'homme."

30. Allan Grappard, in his paper "Ritual and the Economy of Power," presented to the Evans-Wentz Workshop at Stanford University in April 1997, has argued, on the basis of Sakaehara Towao's research's on Heian-period sūtra-copyists in Japan, that their lives were "as bad as that of any assembly-line worker today." He adds: "Analysis of the materials and styles of [their] clothes indicates that sūtra-copyists were treated like low-rank officials, below whom, still, were novices and servants. A far cry from the treatment accorded to prelates, and even more so from that of high-level officials who were granted free houses on large pieces of land in the capital and clothing made of expensive materials." Of course, we cannot by any means extrapolate from Heian Japan to contemporaneous Tibet, but we should be cautioned at least not to assume the condition of scribes to have been particularly exalted.

31. This seems to be reflected in the later legends of Srong-btsan's minister Thon-mi Saṃbhoṭa, which probably exaggerate the degree to which Indian linguistic science served as a model for the Tibetans as early as the seventh century. However, by the early ninth century, when the emperor Khri Lde-srong-btsan issued his preface to the *Sgra-sbyor-bam-gnyis* (Simonsson 1957; Ishikawa 1990), it is clear that the relevance of Indian linguistics to things Tibetan was now seriously considered. See also Verhagen 1992a; Kapstein in press.

32. Particularly intriguing in this regard is the role of the *Shujing,* fragments of the Tibetan paraphrase of which are preserved among the Dunhuang finds (*PT* 986). Refer to Coblin 1991; Stein 1983, esp. p. 201ff. and 210–212.

33. Despite whatever decline may have occurred in the Buddhism of Central Tibet during the century or so intervening between the collapse of the dynasty and the monastic revival of the mid–tenth century, it is striking that much of the Buddhist literature that had been translated by the imperial committees was preserved, as was the knowledge required to read and understand Buddhist canonical texts. It appears too that this included knowledge of the system of Tibetan-Sanskrit equivalencies that had been devised during the late eighth century. See ch. 1.

34. Again, the lexicons and catalogues of the early ninth century strongly suggest this to have been the case (Sakaki 1916–1925; Lalou 1953; Simonsson 1957; Ishikawa 1990).

35. I am not arguing, of course, that reason itself among the Tibetans was an outcome of the introduction of literacy among them. The creation of a literate culture no doubt encour-

ages and facilitates the rationalization of many social activities and probably also supports the development of second-order reflection on reason, but this is not to say that it engenders reason itself. My thesis, in short, is broadly compatible with Goody 1986, but probably not with Goody 1977. For a model study of literacy during the early medieval period that merits careful comparison with roughly contemporaneous Tibet, see McItterick 1989, supplemented by the articles on several aspects of early medieval literacy in Europe in McItterick 1990.

36. Stephen F. Teiser, "On the Idea of a Chinese Buddhist Canon," unpublished. I am grateful to the author for permitting me to refer to this work-in-progress. "Charisma" is not a word of his choosing, however; he speaks instead of "an ideal of power."

37. Uray 1972b; Stein 1986a; Richardson 1998 [1989], pp. 135–139, "Early Tibetan Law Concerning Dog-bite," [1990], pp. 149–166, "Hunting Accidents in early Tibet," and [1991], pp. 182–188, "An Early Judicial Document from Tibet." This last is of special interest in this context, as Buddhist monks were involved in the proceedings described. French 1995, 1996, follows Uray 1972b in attributing elements of Buddhist moral law to the legislation of Srong-btsan-sgam-po. Uray's work, however, was primarily an attempt to interpret the late record found in the sixteenth-century *Mkhas-pa'i dga'-ston.* The subsequent research cited tends to support the view we propose here, that the Buddhist elements were elaborated long after the fact by Buddhist chroniclers, though the process of creating a Buddhist gloss on the early history of Tibetan legislation no doubt began during the late imperial period.

38. Stein 1986a.

39. Richardson 1998, pp. 74–81, "'The Dharma That Came Down from Heaven'." A facsimile of the original manuscript was given in the first publication of the article (Richardson 1977). Stein 1986a.

40. *IO* 370 (5), lines 1–16, following the text as given by Richardson 1998, p. 75.

41. The Fifth Dalai Lama, for instance, writes in *Bod-kyi deb-ther,* p. 15, that "the royal line had arisen from the exceptional power of the blessing of absolute great compassion [= Avalokiteśvara in his absolute aspect]" (*don gyi thugs rje chen po'i byin rlabs kyi mthu phul du byung ba las bskrun pa'i rgyal rigs*).

42. Allan Grappard, "Ritual and the Economy of Power," n. 30 above, makes a similar point about medieval Japan and the role there of "fear of hell." Teiser 1988, p. 12, analagously notes the relationship in Tang China among "a Buddho-Taoist pantheon staffed by bureaucratic divinities; a systematized picture of the afterlife in heavens and hells; the involvement of Buddhist and Taoist monks as ritual specialists at critical junctures in the life of the individual and the community; and a comprehensive worldview in terms of which fate and retribution could be figured and the divinatory arts could be practiced." The promulgation of the Buddhist moral cosmology in early ninth-century Tibet is well in evidence in the first of the Ldan-ma-brag inscriptions, given in Heller 1994a, appendix, p. 12. Khri Srong-lde'u-btsan's edict, which we have cited elsewhere, (pp. 45, 53) offers further confirmation along these lines.

43. On the history of Tibetan expansion in these areas, see Beckwith 1987; Wang Xiaofu, *Tang Tufan Dasi zhengzhi guanxi shi.*

44. We have earlier seen (pp. 41–42) that the monks brought to Tibet by the princess of Jincheng were from Khotan. In the early ninth century, the *Sgra-'byor bam-gnyis* (Ishikawa 1990) specifies that the Buddhist preceptors active in the court were from *nyi-'og,* Skt. *aparāntaka,* the western regions—that is, countries to the northwest of India.

45. On the question of Khotanese influence in the development of Tibetan artistic traditions, refer to Vitali 1990, pp. 6–8, 11–15, 52–54, though, as Vitali argues in the last passage cited, *Li-lugs,* "Khotanese style," may in fact refer sometimes to the style of Xixia and not Khotan.

46. Watt and Wardwell 1997, pp. 34–37, offers the splendid example of a child's coat and pants made in part of Sogdian silk and preserved in Tibet.

47. Beckwith 1979.

48. See ch. 3, n. 26.

49. Bacot 1956; Moriyasu 1981; Ecsedy 1964; Szerb 1983.

50. Balbir 1963; Jong 1989; Kapstein in press.

51. See Zürcher 1962, map pages 8–9 ("The spread of Buddhism from the 5th till the 12th Centuries A.D.") and 10–11 ("Buddhism in Central Asia and China till the 13th Century A.D.").

52. A graphic example of this is fig. 4.1, the famous painting of a Tibetan king in the depiction of the Vimalakīrti story in Dunhuang cave 159: Dunhuang Wenwu Yanjiusuo, comp., *Dunhuang Mogaoku* 4, plate 91.

53. The development of Angkor Wat in the Khmer kingdom (ninth century), Barabuḍur in the Śailendra domains in Java (late eighth century), and Tōdai-ji in Heian Japan (eighth century) are all suggestively close to the period of Bsam-yas's foundation.

54. It is likely, however, that some Tibetans had already been receiving ordination in non-Tibetan monastic communities (Snellgrove 1987, vol. 2, p. 420).

55. Chayet 1988, 1990; Mémet 1988.

56. *Sba-bzhed,* pp. 42–45.

57. *Sba-bzhed,* pp. 43–44, for instance, speaks of the icons of Guhyasamāja according to the tradition of Buddhajñānapāda.

58. Richardson 1998 [1990], pp. 177–181, "The Cult of Vairocana in Early Tibet."

59. This association appears most clearly in the case of Tabo, founded by the late tenth-century West Tibetan ruler Ye-shes-'od and located in Himachal Pradesh; see now Klimberg-Salter 1998.

60. Thus, in the introduction to the *Sgra-'byor bam-gnyis,* Khri Lde-srong-btsan famously declares: "The tantras of secret mantra, according to the texts, are to be kept secret. It is also not appropriate to explain and to teach them to the unqualified. Still, in the meantime, though it has been permitted to translate and to practice them, there have been those who have not deciphered what is expounded allusively, and seizing upon literal understanding have practiced perversely. It is stipulated that, among the tantras of mantra, there have also been some haphazardly translated into the Tibetan language. This being so, hereafter it is not permitted to translate haphazardly the tantras of mantra and the mantra-terms except for those *dhāraṇīmantra*s and tantras whose translations have been enjoined on order from above" (Ishikawa 1990, p. 4).

61. Refer to the studies mentioned in ch. 1, n. 49.

62. See, for example, Bernard Frank 1991, pp. 163–185, "La réplique du maṇḍala sculpté du Tōji."

63. See Malandra 1993, pp. 71–90, on the development of the group of eight bodhisattvas in India, in particular in the iconography of the Ellora caves. Heller 1994b surveys ninth-century representations of Vairocana known from eastern Tibet and adjacent areas, several of which are also surrounded by the eight bodhisattvas. Despite my reference here to the *Mahāvairocanābhisambodhi,* we must be very cautious about interpreting the precise relations between texts and icons until we have achieved a better understanding of the rituals involving these deities that were promulgated in the times and places under consideration. As Kuo Li-ying 1994, pp. 152 and 158, suggests, any number of differing liturgical traditions may be involved. The occurrence in Kuo's work of the eight bodhisattvas in a confessional context is also of much interest, given that at Ldan-ma-brag they are depicted accompanied by an inscription concerning karma and rebirth (see n. 42 in this chapter).

64. Evidence of this may be also seen in the liturgy for the seven tathāgatas authored by Śāntarakṣita on behalf of the Tibetan king (*P* 3953, in vol. 80, pp. 38–52), where the colophon (p. 52, plate 5) specifies that the composition is intended to "promote the longevity of the divine Tsenpo, the son of the gods, Khri Srong-lde'u-btsan, and to make firm his crown,

elevate his royal authority, purify his karmic obscurations, and increase his provisions [of merit and gnosis]. . . ." (*dpal lha btsan po lha sras khri srong lde'u btsan gyi sku tshe bsring ba dang/ dbu rmog brtsan pa dang/ chab srid mtho ba dang/ las sgrib sbyang ba dang/ tshogs gnyis spel ba'i ched du. . . .*). I am grateful to Leonard van der Kuijp for this reference. The genuine antiquity of the text in question is verified by its inclusion in the Ldan-kar-ma catalogue (Lalou 1953, no. 147).

65. Refer to the argument of Richardson 1998 [1977], p. 67, concerning the year of Bsam-yas's foundation.

66. *Bka' yang-dag tshad-ma,* p. 98 (64b6–8): *khams gsum rnam rgyal dpa' bas mgon mdzad pa// brjid kyi 'dul la gus par phyag 'tshal te// srid pa gsum gyi log lta thams cad las// rnam par rgyal ba nges par bsgrub par bya// 'phags pa mi g.yo g.yo ba kun mi brten// ri rab mthu bas brtan la phyag 'tshal te// bdud dang phas kyi rgol ba'i 'jig rten gyis// nam yang sus kyang mi g.yo bsgrub par bya//*

67. Bernard Frank 1991, p. 180: "Leur rôle est de subjuger, briser, brûler les forces, les pechants opiniâtrement mauvais."

68. Tradition attributes to him a lengthy letter addressed to Khri Srong-lde'u-btsan (Dietz 1984, pp. 79–84 [introduction] and 358–400 [text and translation]; Snellgrove 1987, vol. 2, pp. 446–449). I am inclined to regard this text, at least in the form in which it is preserved, as pseudepigraphic, though it may be based in part upon an authentic early work.

69. Karmay 1988a, pp. 59–76; *Sbas-pa'i rgum-chung.*

70. Lalou 1953, nos. 322, 324, 326, 328.

71. Lalou 1953, nos. 322, 324.

72. Skorupski 1983.

73. Among the problems we face here, one of the foremost remains the precise identification of the works that can be securely attributed to the eighth-century author Buddhagupta. For instance, though Lalou 1953, no. 322, is the sole commentary on the *Mahāvairocanābhisambodhi* attributed to this master in the *Ldan-kar-ma* catalogue, the Peking edition of the Tanjur lists three commentaries on the same text by this author: *P* 3486, 3487, and 3490. (Though "Buddhaguhya" is the form of the name used in *P*, "Buddhagupta" is consistently used in the *Ldan-kar-ma.*) [N.B. As this book goes to press it has been announced that Stephen Hodge has translated, and is due to publish shortly, one of these commentaries by Buddhaguhya.]

74. The iconographic resemblance by itself, of course, does not confirm that the same texts and liturgies are involved.

75. Heller 1994a, 1994b, 1997a, 1997b.

76. See Richardson, cited in Heller 1994a; the Dunhuang manuscript in question is *PT* 996, first studied in Lalou 1939.

77. Richardson 1998 [1997], pp. 207–215, is inclined to draw skeptical conclusions regarding the Wencheng princess's actual influence. He writes (p. 212) that she was "a dim figure . . . who made no mark on either Tibetan or Chinese history in the remaining thirty years of her life [following Srong-btsan sgam-po's death], and whose religious affiliation is uncertain. . . ."

78. Dunhuang Yanjiusuo, comp., *Anxi Yulinku,* plate 39.

79. Dunhuang Wenwu Yanjiusuo, comp., *Dunhuang Mogaoku* 4, plate 169. In addition to these images, a unique gilt bronze statue has appeared on the international art market depicting exactly the same icon. The quality is very fine, and the statue is stylistically unlike anything else known so far, though it resembles the reliefs and murals just mentioned in many telling points of detail, e.g., the pattern in the textiles of the Buddha's robes. It seems plausible, though given the object's uniqueness this remains uncertain, that it is indeed an authentic imperial Tibetan bronze, and if it is, then it is surely significant that it represents the figure that I have begun to think of as the Tibetan Imperial Vairocana.

80. Beckwith 1987, pp. 173–196.

81. Strong 1983, p. 117.

82. Strong 1983, p. 119.

83. *OTC,* cited here in ch. 3, n. 45, and the documents studied in Uebach 1990 exemplify this well.

84. China, of course, had already pioneered the political exploitation of Buddhist cosmology and symbolism under the Empress Wu (reigned 690–705), to mention only one of the most prominent examples that may well have been known in Tibet. Refer to Forte 1976.

85. James 1987.

86. Hobsbawm 1992 demonstrates that the concept of the "nation" is in fact of recent origin and, strictly speaking, is inapplicable to the period with which we are here concerned. "National identity," in this context, I use to refer to what Hobsbawm terms "popular proto-nationalism." On the application of these concepts to premodern Tibet, see further Dreyfus 1994; Kapstein in Goldstein and Kapstein 1998, ch. 6.

87. *bstan-pa snga-dar, bstan-pa phyi-dar.*

Chapter 5

The present chapter was originally presented at the conference "Korea's Place in the East Asian Buddhist Tradition," organized by Robert Buswell at the University of California at Los Angeles in September 1995. I am grateful to the organizer and to the other participants for their suggestions contributing to the present revision.

1. Tibetan ethnonyms are frequently multivalent and must be interpreted with caution according to context. Tibetanists may wish to ponder in this regard such common designations as *sog-po* ("Mongolian," but no doubt originally "Sogdian"), *hor-pa* (referring to any number of Turkic and Mongolian peoples, or Tibetanized peoples possibly of Turkic or Mongolian extraction, and probably derived from "Uighur"), *mon-pa* (used for many peoples of Tibet's southern frontiers, including, in earlier times, the people of present-day Bhutan), etc. Even *bod-pa,* "Tibetan," in some contexts refers restrictively to the people of Central Tibet in contrast to eastern Tibetans. The fluid use of ethnonyms we find in Tibet is by no means an uncommon phenomenon elsewhere in Inner Asia.

2. *Deb-dmar,* p. 18, n. 138, for instance, mentions *ka'u-hi(< ka'u-li).* The work in question was written during the period 1346–1363. Joachim Karsten and Leonard van der Kuijp have indicated to me that they have located other, similar references in works of the Yuan and early Ming. On the other hand, the earliest Korean references to Tibet date to the Tang period: the pilgrim Hye Ch'o, who traveled to India during the early part of the eighth century, mentions Tibet on several occasions (Yang Han-sung et al., pp. 44, 47, 48) and significantly remarks, "The king and the common people do not know Buddhism. There are no monasteries. . . ." Koreans also gained some familiarity with Tibet under the Mongols; the retired king Ch'ungsŏn was in fact exiled to Tibet during the third decade of the fourteenth century (Sohn, Kim, and Hong 1970, p. 118). H. Sørensen 1993 complements the present discussion by surveying East Asian reports of Tibetan lamas who visited the Korean peninsula.

3. *'Dzam-gling spyi-bshad,* p. 28.

4. *'Dzam-gling spyi-bshad,* p. 34.

5. *'Dzam-gling rgyas-bshad.* On this work, see also Wylie 1958, 1962.

6. *'Dzam-gling rgyas-bshad,* p. 162: *rgya nag gi yul nas man 'ju'i yul brgal te shar phyogs su song ba na kwo le'am rgya gar ser sogs kyis ko ri ya zer ba dag gi yul khro zhang zer ba yod/ yul de'i mi rnams gzugs byad bzang la/ tshul lugs zab pa/ cha lugs dang yi ge sogs sngon gyi rgya nag dang 'dra yang skad rigs mi 'dra/ yul de'i bud med rnams rang gi pha ma dang/ khyo po dang/ bu sogs las gzhan pa'i mi rnams yang mthong ba'i skabs med zer/* John Jorgensen, at the conference mentioned in the introduction to this chapter's notes, remarked

that this seems more a reflection of Qing official opinion than evidence of direct familiarity with things Korean.

7. In addition to the articles referred to in the following note, see Eastman 1983; Gómez 1983a, 1983b, 1987; Imaeda 1975; Kimura 1981; McRae 1986; Mala and Kimura 1988; Yampolsky 1983; and Yanagida 1983a. See also ch. 2, n. 71.

8. Obata's researches are summarized in Demiéville 1979; Ueyama 1981, 1983; Broughton 1983.

9. *Sba-bzhed,* pp. 7–8; Stein 1961, pp. 6–7.

10. On this term, see ch. 4, n. 27.

11. Ba Sangshi is often described in the *Sba-bzhed* as *rgya-phrug gar-mkhan,* a "Chinese dancing child."

12. The precise significance of the text here is obscure. *Sba-bzhed*, p. 7, reads *pha bong mgron po,* while Stein 1961, p. 6, has *pha 'ong 'gron bu.*

13. *Sba-bzhed,* p. 7, and Stein 1961, p. 6, read *sbos grir,* which makes no sense to me. *Mkhas-pa'i dga'-ston,* vol. 1, p. 301, has *rbab grir,* defined in *Tshig-mdzod chen-mo,* vol. 2, p. 2010, as *gyen gzar nas thur du lhung ba'am, ri rdo thog bab tu phog pa'i shi rkyen,* "falling down a steep declivity, or death caused by the fall of stones from above." I have adopted the latter signification for my translation, though the former is equally feasible. The word *gri,* "knife," is frequently used in compounds to mean "fatal danger of . . . ," e.g., *ltog-gri,* "starvation," *skom-gri,* "dying of thirst."

14. Stein 1961, p. 6, reads *nyi ma hā shang.*

15. In Stein 1961, p. 6, this is abridged slightly.

16. See ch. 2, n. 27.

17. *Mu-stegs rig-byed-kyi chos.* Stein 1961, p. 7, reads *mu-stegs-byed-kyi chos,* "doctrines of non-Buddhists."

18. *Sba-bzhed,* pp. 7–8.

19. *Sba-bzhed,* p. 8.

20. Demiéville 1979, p. 4. Kalgren's reconstructions have been surpassed by more recent refinements in Chinese historical linguistics but are nevertheless adequate for our present, modest purposes.

21. Master Kim is better known in the Chinese Chan tradition by his ordination name, Wuxiang (Musang in Korean). The hagiography drawn from the *Lidai fabao ji* is translated in Lee 1993, pp. 221–222. It is perhaps significant, in the light of the Tibetan account, that he is described there as living "at the foot of a boulder on Mount T'ien-ku. . . . Even savage beasts were moved [by his austerities] and protected him." He later moves to the Jingchuan Monastery in Chengdu, where he teaches "the people the path of conversion." The hagiography further mentions that, during the twelfth and first month of every year, he granted public meditation instruction. The phrase used in the Tibetan account, which I have translated literally as "meditation transmission" (*sgom-lung*), would be an appropriate term to use to describe a public teaching of this type.

22. Beckwith 1983.

23. See ch. 2, n. 15, on the recently discovered *Dba'-bzhed.* The episode involving master Kim is treated there on pp. 47–52 of the translation (text fols. 8b–10b).

24. As Broughton 1983, p. 7 and n. 29, notes, Obata holds it to be likely that the Tibetan envoys encountered not Kim, but rather the latter's soi-disant disciple Wuzhu, whose lineage claims the *Lidai fabao ji* underwrites. Wuzhu is himself frequently cited in the Tibetan Chan scroll *PT* 116, which clearly has the *Lidai fabao ji* in its background.

25. An introduction to, and partial edition and translation of, this singularly important manuscript may be found in Mala and Kimura 1988.

26. The Tibetan manuscript *PT* 116 consistently uses *bsam-gtan-gyi mdo,* which according to the standard conventions for Tibetan translations of Sanskrit would be *dhyānasūtra,*

i.e., **chánjīng* in Chinese. As the conventions for translating Chinese were not always identical with those used for Indian texts (Stein 1983), however, and as *lùn* and not *jīng* is the Chinese term used to designate the discourses attributed to the Chan masters, it is preferable to reconstruct **Chánlùn* in this context. We should note, too, that by the middle of the ninth century several other expressions were current in Chinese to denote the "recorded sayings" of Chan masters: see Yanagida 1983b.

27. Owing to the unexplained syllable *hu(n)*, Broughton 1983, p. 13, rightly expressed some reservations about this. *Shen-shi* (or *shan-shi* in some sources), occurring throughout the old Tibetan Chan literature, has already been interpreted by Tucci 1956–1958 and Demiéville 1952, 1979, as a transciption of *chánshī*, "Chan master." Yamaguchi, following the reading *shang shi ta* found in some sources, has argued that their interpretation is incorrect, but I am inclined to agree here with Tucci and Demiéville and to see *shang shi ta* as a late hypercorrection, perhaps influenced by Sanskrit *śaṃsita*, "praised." The occurrence in the present instance of *shen-shi* has caused us to read *Kim-hu(n)* as a bisyllabic name, which gives rise to some puzzlement; and this reading is reinforced by the Tibetan sources themselves, which sometimes give the name in this form alone, not followed by *shen-shi* (e.g., *PT* 116, plate 177.4). It is possible, however, that *hu(n)-shen-shi* was originally a single phrase, representing *héshangshī*, "master preceptor," that has been deformed by a Tibetan copyist who has written *shen-shi* so frequently that he has assimilated the former phrase to it. This being done, it became possible to drop the honorific phrase *shen-shi* altogether, leaving only *Kim-hu(n)*. If this is approximately correct, the identification with master Kim of the author to whom the passages in question are attributed no longer poses a great problem. A second possibility, suggested to me by John Jorgensen, is that Kim's association with tigers in fact does originate with Chinese traditions (see n. 21 in this chapter), in which case *Kim-hu* might mean "Tiger Kim."

28. Broughton 1983, p. 13, translates: "At the time that one is not possessed of the reality sphere in the mind, there is no understanding." But I think this misses the point here. The text is saying that one who has achieved genuine insight does not engage in further seeking and the hankering that involves, even at times when the experience of realization is not in the foreground.

29. *PT* 116, plates 174.2–175.1.

30. Tib. *tshor-ba*, translated here as "intuition," regularly represents Ch. *júe*, "awakening, enlightenment," in Tibetan Chan documents. In the Sanskrit Buddhist vocabulary, it stands for *vedanā*, "feeling, sensation."

31. *PT* 116, plates 177.3–178.2.

32. The hagiography found in the *Lidai fabao ji*, for instance, has this saying (Lee 1993, p. 222): "With the absence of thought, the mind is like a bright mirror that reflects all phenomena. The rise of thought is like the back of a mirror that cannot reflect anything."

33. Cf. Randall 1962, p. 119: "The Reformers made salvation a purely religious problem, not dependent upon human conduct at all. . . . Luther's mysticism led him to make religion non-moral, a matter of inner experience. . . ."

34. Gómez 1983b surveys the citations attibuted to Moheyan in Dunhuang Tibetan texts.

35. *Bsam-gtan mig-sgron*, pp. 119–120, 161. The name is transcribed here as Kin-hun and Kyin-hu. On this text in relation to the Tibetan sudden enlightenment traditions, see in particular Karmay 1988a, ch. 3.

36. Tucci 1956–1958, p. 383; citing *Blon-po bka'i thang-yig*, fol. 23a (= *Bka'-thang sde-lnga*, p. 460).

37. *Mkhas-pa'i dga'-ston*, vol. 1, pp. 301–302. The episode is also recounted summarily, without mentioning Kim by name, in *BA*, p. 41.

38. See p. 160, where Tibet, China, and Mongolia are compared to a teeming ants' nest.

39. Indeed, Kim already seems to have suffered erasure even in the pre-Yuan-period Tibetan histories that have so far become available. *Mkhas-pa Lde'u*, p. 302, for example, re-

tains only the tradition that Sba Khri-bzhir Sang-shi-ta brought three sūtras from China. Hence, Kim was to all intents and purposes forgotten long before any provocation of anti-Chinese sentiment under the Yuan.

40. On Padmasambhava, see ch. 8.

41. Petech 1994.

42. Davidson 1994.

43. Piotrovsky 1993; Dunnell 1996.

44. There are many objections to this suggestion, of course. Deities and religious heroes depicted as riding upon or accompanied by tigers are very widespread, so that it would be difficult to identify a unique source for a particular image. The heavenly-master tradition of Taoism in Sichuan, for example, depicts its founder, Zhang Daoling, riding upon a tiger, and the arhat Dharmatrāta is similarly represented. Tibet is replete with protective divinities known as *stag-zhon,* "tiger riders," as well. The motif of the Buddhist pilgrim (sometimes identified with Xuanzang) accompanied by a tiger is well known in paintings from Dunhuang; for example, in the Pelliot collection of the Musée Guimet, nos. 206, 207, and 208 in the catalogue of Nicolas-Vandier et al. 1974–1976. Though these considerations do diminish the prospects for finding an antecedent of Padmasambhava's *Rdo-rje gro-lod* form in master Kim, we must recall, too, that, as we have seen in ch. 3. Padmasambhava does appear to have absorbed aspects of some of the Chinese teachers mentioned in the *Sba-bzhed,* so the suggestion cannot quite be ruled out.

45. See especially Karmay 1988a; Ruegg 1989; D. Jackson 1994.

46. Lalou 1939; Heller 1994a. Heller credits Richardson with calling her attention to the identity of the names mentioned in the Ldan-ma-brag inscription with those found in Lalou 1939.

47. The Ldan-ma-brag inscription, studied in Heller 1994a, as we have seen in ch. 4, emphasizes karmic reward and retribution and is found in conjunction with a relief image of Buddha Vairocana and the eight major bodhisattvas. The continuing insistence on immediate and intuitive enlightment, however, is very much in evidence in *PT* 996, first studied in Lalou 1939.

48. Gómez 1983b, on surveying the Dunhuang fragments attributed to Moheyan, remarks (p. 89): "The total picture of Mo-ho-yen as a 'Dhyāna Master' that we can derive from these fragments does not contradict the generally held view that he espoused a radical sudden enlightenment position. . . ."

49. Eimer 1991; see also ch. 2, n. 11, in this volume.

50. On the Rdzogs-chen within the Rnying-ma-pa tradition, see now Guenther 1975–1976, 1983, 1984, 1994; Karmay 1988a; Ehrhard 1990; Dudjom 1991, vol. 1, pp. 294–345; Germano 1994, forthcoming; and, within the Bon-po tradition, Snellgrove 1967a; Kværne 1973, 1983; Karmay 1988; and Rossi 2000. See, further, ch. 9 and 10 in this volume.

51. D. Jackson 1994, pp. 22–24.

52. Buswell 1989 provides a thorough historical study and excellent translation of the *Vajrasamādhisūtra.*

53. Buswell 1989, esp. ch. 2.

54. Buswell 1989, p. 3: "Until the middle of this century, this scripture was thought to be a translation into Chinese of an Indian Buddhist text. . . ."

55. Buswell 1989, pp. 179–181.

56. Stein 1983.

57. Lalou 1953, no. 254.

58. Besides the citations in *PT* 116, to be discussed here, there is also an incomplete Dunhuang Tibetan manuscript, *PT* 623, on which see Stein 1983, p. 213.

59. In Buswell 1989, this passage is found translated on p. 192. As will be seen, my translations, based on the Tibetan citations, do not always correspond precisely with Buswell's

translation of the Chinese text. A careful comparison of the Chinese and Tibetan versions remains a desideratum.

60. *Bsam-gtan mig-sgron,* p. 139; Buswell 1989, p. 193.

61. D. Jackson 1994, pp. 17–24.

62. Guenther 1971, pp. 221–222.

63. Sgam-po-pa's teaching tradition is in fact frequently referred to as *bka'-phyag chu-bo gcig-'dres,* the "Bka'-gdams-pa teaching and the Mahāmudrā (*phyag-chen*) intermingled in a single stream."

64. R. Jackson 1982; D. Jackson 1990, 1994; but cf. ch. 7, n. 33.

65. *Man-ngag rin-chen spungs-pa,* p. 98: *ma rig pa nyid sems kyi phyi mo nas med na/ ma rig pa las byung ba'i 'du byed nas rga shi'i bar du lta smos kyang ci dgos/* This paraphrases the passage as we find it in the Tibetan canon, *P* 803, vol. 32, p. 156 (139b2): *sems kyi ngo bo nyid phyi mo nas skye shi med do/* "There is neither birth nor death [in] the nature of mind, from [its] original matrix." Buswell's translation (1989, p. 217), based upon the Chinese, differs slightly: "The natures of sentient beings are originally free from both production and extinction."

66. A brief biographical note on Lce-sgom-rdzong-pa may be found in the A-kya Yongs-'dzin's *Brda-bkrol don-gnyer yid-kyi dga'-ston,* pp. 518–519, in *Dpe-chos rin-chen spungs-pa.*

67. Indeed, the structure of Lce-sgom-rdzong-pa's work closely resembles that of the *Lam-mchog mthar-thug* of the controversial early Bka'-brgyud master, Bla-ma Zhang (1123–1193), for a translation of which see Martin 1992. Refer also to D. Jackson 1994, ch. 3.

68. The renowned Dge-lugs-pa encyclopedist Klong-rdol Ngag-dbang-blo-bzang (1719–1795), for example, refers favorably to Lce-sgom-rdzong-pa's work no less than three times: *Klong-rdol gsung-'bum,* vol. 2, pp. 112, 337, 498.

69. I am grateful to Geshe Sonam Rinchen of the Library of Tibetan Works and Archives, Dharmasala, for taking the time to meet regularly with me to discuss this and other texts throughout the spring of 1993.

70. The later Tibetan meditation manuals also derive many citations of well-known sūtras, such as the *Laṅkāvatāra* or the *Vajracchedikā,* from the earlier Chan compilations. However, because these may also be drawn from non-Sinitic traditions, compared to the quotations of the Chinese apocryphal scriptures, they are not of similar value for historical research. It is, for example, Lce-sgom-rdzong-pa's citation of the *Vajrasamādhi,* not the *Vajracchedikā,* that assures us that the Chan florilegia were indeed among his ultimate sources.

71. On this figure see Demiéville 1952, pp. 20–21; Inaba 1977; Ueyama 1983, n. 1; Verhagen 1992b.

72. *T* 4016; *P* 5517.

73. Large parts of the Chinese text, however, have survived: refer to Inaba 1977.

74. The manuscript or printed versions of the canon kept behind or surrounding the altars of Tibetan Buddhist temples serve a ritual function and represent the presence of the Precious Jewel of the Dharma as an object of refuge. Ritual interactions with the canon may include offering prostrations before it, or performing circumambulations while carrying several heavy volumes as an act of merit. (This last I have noticed particularly practiced by women of the Mongour [Ch. *Tuzu*] communities of Qinghai.) One ritual that does require some reading of the canon, or at least the rapid recitation of the first pages of each volume, is *Bka'-'gyur zhal-klog,* which involves the volumes only of the Kanjur, not of the Tanjur. In a similar vein, the ritual transmission of the canon, or *zhal-lung,* which is performed by a teacher reading aloud those portions of the text he has himself heard recited in this way from his teacher, continues to be practiced in connection with the entire Kanjur, but only about 20% of the Tanjur is still transmitted in this manner. (I am indebted to the late Dezhung Rinpoche for this information.)

75. I do not mean to suggest here that reading is a uniform practice in our own society. Reading is obviously multivalent, and just what we mean by "to read" differs according to

text, context, purpose, etc.; and this was also true in Tibet. Nevertheless, it is probably fair to say that the practice of reading in Tibet was restricted in ways with which we, in contemporary secular societies, are not very familiar, above and beyond the restrictions imposed by the physical limitations of manuscript and block-print reproduction. The late Kalu Rinpoche, for example, remarked to me on one occasion that whereas a Tibetan would seldom look further than the title of a tantric text into which she or he had not been initiated, he found that his Western students had few inhibitions along these lines. He did not mean this to be a compliment: his point in the conversation was that he found the ritual framework for textual study to be compromised outside of a traditional Tibetan setting. Tibetan reading practices, and the traditional educational practices through which they were formed, however, have yet to be well studied, and my comments about this subject are therefore somewhat impressionistic. On the question of religious reading in general, see now Griffiths 1999.

76. By referring to a "very small number of texts," I intend no slight: Tibetan monk-scholars pursued their education with a thoroughness we can scarcely imagine, combining memorization, discussion, and debate, until the key elements of the curriculum were mastered in detail, a process requiring fifteen or more years of rigorous study. Aspects of education at Bla-brang monastery in A-mdo are surveyed in Li An-che 1982, ch. 2. On the curriculum, see also Hopkins 1999, pp. 9–12. Goldstein, in Goldstein and Kapstein 1998, ch. 2, examines matters relating to the economy of education at 'Bras-spungs. For remarks on monastic education in relation to soteriological ends, see Dreyfus 1997b. Dreyfus is now engaged in detailed research on Tibetan monastic education, and his results will no doubt help to illuminate some of the issues raised here.

77. Nevertheless, it is important to stress that there was a tradition of bibliographical connoisseurship that often did focus upon rarely studied texts and traditions. This is evident, for instance, in bibliographical writings such as the *Dpe-rgyun dkon-pa tho-yig* (The Inventory of Rare Books) of A-khu Shes-rab-rgya-mtsho (1803–1875), among many others. However, it is striking that for the most part such bibliophilia was focused upon rare *Tibetan* books and authors, whose relevance for the living traditions of Tibetan Buddhism was relatively clear. The interest, during the late nineteenth and early twentieth centuries, among Rnying-ma-pa masters in eastern Tibet in recovering the *Mun-pa'i go-cha* and *Bsam-gtan mig-sgron* of the tenth-century adept Bsnubs-chen Sangs-rgyas-ye-shes is an instance in point. In the case of unstudied books in the canonical collections, however, the physical rarity of the texts was not particularly at issue; at issue was the motivation to delve into them at all.

78. Thurman 1984; Hopkins 1999.

79. Sparham 1993.

80. The extensive commentarial writings on Tsong-kha-pa's *Legs-bshad-snying-po* are studied in Hopkins 1999, where the commentarial tradition on the text is introduced in general, pp. 16–25. Hopkins remarks (p. 23, n. c) that he has so far collected twenty-six commentaries on Tsong-kha-pa's text. Only one, though, seems to be based in large measure on detailed examination of Wŏnch'ŭk's work itself, beyond the citations already given by Tsong-kha-pa. This is the altogether remarkable commentary of the recent A-mdo master 'Jigs-med-dam-chos-rgya-mtsho (1898–1946). (Hopkins's remarks on p. 24, though, suggest that Gung-thang Dkon-mchog-bstan-pa'i-sgron-me [1762–1823; Hopkins mistakenly gives 1728–1791] also may have made some independent use of Wŏnch'ŭk.)

81. Thurman 1984, p. 205, n. 50; Powers 1992.

82. We must recall in this context that Tsong-kha-pa was active during the early Ming period, when many Tibetan hierarchs had intensive dealings with the Chinese court, following the precedents for religious relations with the Mongol court established under the Yuan. As Franke 1996 makes very clear, there had been sufficient interaction so that learned Tibetans during the fourteenth century would have known much more of Chinese Buddhism than just the account of Moheyan.

83. Powers 1992, n. 10.

84. Of the Tibetanists who have considered Tsong-kha-pa's relation to Wŏnch'ŭk, it is so far only Hopkins 1999, p. 46, who rightly suggests that Tsong-kha-pa may have had predecessors who also drew upon the Korean commentator. The repeated emphasis that we find throughout Western writings on Tibetan Buddhism on describing Tsong-kha-pa as a "reformer," implying an analogy to Western Christian reformers such as Luther and Calvin, is deeply misleading and has wrongly skewed our understanding of Tsong-kha-pa. Even when considering relatively small points, such as his references to Wŏnch'ŭk, the tendency has been to presuppose novelty, and therefore not to examine carefully his relationship with earlier tradition. Many of the distinctive features of Tsong-kha-pa's approach to Buddhist teaching are clearly presaged, however, in the career of his Sa-skya-pa teacher Red-mda'-ba (1349–1412), for instance, his emphasis upon the Bka'-gdams-pa *Lam-rim* teachings, the insistence upon the primacy of Candrakīrti among Mādhyamikas, and the fundamental position of the *Guhyasamāja* in his approach to tantrism. It remains unclear, moreover, whether there is good evidence of the formation of a distinctive sectarian identity on the part of Tsong-kha-pa and his disciples during Tsong-kha-pa's own lifetime, though this seems to have emerged soon after his passing. It is true, however, that Tsong-kha-pa did elaborate a distinctive philosophical position, particularly in reference to Yogācāra and Madhyamaka thought, and that this early on became a matter of doctrinal controversy. Even this, however, in the context of early fifteenth-century Tibet, must be seen as controversy within the tradition, and not as part of a movement at all similar to the Reformation.

85. Thurman 1984, pp. 203–208, 352–353.

86. This was the lineage claimed in the Tibetan tradition for the "five doctrines of Maitreya" (*Byams-chos lnga*) and included the fundamental treatise on Buddha-nature, the *Ratnagotravibhāga-Mahāyānottatantraśāstra* (*Theg pa chen po rgyud bla ma'i bstan bcos*). See further ch. 6, on Dölpopa.

87. *Dbu-'jug 'grel-chen,* p. 4.

88. *Dbu-'jug 'grel-chen,* p. 6.

89. *Dbu-'jug 'grel-chen,* pp. 26–27.

90. Sparham 1993, pp. 155–156. Rig-pa'i-ral-gri's precise dates do not seem to be available, though it is certain that he was active during the reign of the fourth Yuan emperor Buyantu (Renzong, reigned 1311–1320). See Ruegg 1969, pp. 22–25; Mimaki 1982, p. 14.

91. Sparham 1993, pp. 153–156.

92. Kapstein 1992f, pp. 23–25; see also ch. 6, on Dölpopa, this volume.

93. *BA,* p. 337, attributes "about sixteen volumes of śāstras" to Bcom-ldan Rig-ral. The only work published to date is *Tshad-ma rgyan-gyi me-tog,* including two treatises on Pramāṇa. Leonard van der Kuijp has in recent years located a number of manuscripts of Bcom-ldan Rig-pa'i-ral-gri's writings in China and Tibet. The eventual publication of this material will fill a major gap in our knowledge of Tibetan scholastic history.

94. *BA,* p. 337; Mimaki 1982.

95. *Mdzod 'grel,* p. 767.

96. *Mdzod 'grel,* p. 53: *yang slob dpon yang dag bden pa ni de dag dang dri ma med pa'i yid dang dgu yin no zhes zer ro.* "Again, master Paramārtha says that together with those [eight aggregates of consciousness] the taintless mind makes nine."

97. Lcang-skya Rol-pa'i rdo-rje (1717–1786) is perhaps the best example. See Smith 1969, and here, ch. 7, n. 77.

98. Franke 1996, ch. 2 "Der Kanonkatalog der Chih-yüan-Zeit und seine Kompilatoren," pp. 69–124. The Tibetan version of this comparative catalogue was lost but was retranslated into Tibetan by Mgon-po-skyabs in the eighteenth century; parts of it make up his *Rgya-nag chos-'byung.*

99. The Korean king Ch'ungsŏn, after his abdication, retired to the Yuan capital during the reign of Buyantu, a curious coincidence in this context. He is also known to have been a

bibliophile. Later, he was in fact exiled to Tibet, though so far no evidence of his impact there has emerged. See Sohn, Kim, and Hong 1970, pp. 117–118. It is amusing to speculate, though of course there is no evidence to support it, that he and Mchims 'Jam-dbyangs might have crossed paths at some point!

100. This is very much in evidence in Sparham 1993 and Hopkins 1999.

101. A world-systems approach to the study of Central Asian history is elaborated in Andre Gunder Frank 1992.

102. Of course, in the examples we have considered, the only teaching actually formulated in Korea whose transmission reached Tibet was that of the *Vajrasamādhisūtra.* Master Kim and Wŏnch'ŭk, by contrast, though of Korean birth, both spent their careers in China.

103. Hobsbawm 1992.

104. Robert E. Buswell, Jr., at the conference "Korea's Place in the East Asian Buddhist Tradition" in his remarks entitled "Imagining 'Korean Buddhism': The Invention of a National Religious Tradition."

105. Cf. my remarks in Goldstein and Kapstein 1998, ch. 6.

106. Mair 1994, Pollock 1996.

107. Takata 1994 offers an excellent example. The Tibetan script was being used to write a number of other languages as well, for instance, the otherwise unknown language called *Nam* (see Thomas 1948).

108. Refer to n. 71 above.

Chapter 6

1. Refer to ch. 1, pp. 10–12.

2. Mar-pa's disaffection with the translator 'Brog-mi, and the long history of complex relations between the Bka'-brgyud-pa lineages (stemming from Mar-pa's teaching) and the Sa-skya-pas (stemming from 'Brog-mi's), offer much data meriting reflection in this regard. D. Jackson 1990, 1994, offer valuable points of departure, though perhaps Jackson minimizes to some degree the role played by material and political competition, in tandem with the more purely doctrinal contests that he excellently documents.

3. Cabezón 1994 examines the relationship between the Western notions of scholasticism and aspects of Dge-lugs-pa thought, while the essays in Cabezón 1998 explore scholasticism as a category in the comparative philosophy of religions. For the purposes of the present discussion, I have restricted my initial conception of scholasticism to one grounded in Western medieval thought, as defined and described, for instance, in Price 1992, ch. 6.

4. This distinction is made explicit by the use of the terms *rigs-pas rjes-su 'brangs-pa,* "rationalist," and *dad-pas rjes-su 'brangs-pa,* "fideist." A fine example of the distinction is found in the famous *Tshad-ma lam-rim* (The Progressive Path of Pramāṇa) of Lcang-skya Rol-pa'i rdo-rje, *Lcang-skya rnam-thar,* p. 636: "This *Pramāṇavārttika* is a superlative treatise! In those who strive for liberation and omniscience a faith in our teacher and teaching that reaches the depths must be born from the heart. About that, even though certainty brought forth by pure reason is not born in the fideists, though a faith involving conviction may well be born in them, it is hard [for them] to get beyond a conditional [sort of faith]. If certainty is born on the basis of genuine reason, it won't be turned back by conditions; a firm disposition is established."

5. Dreyfus 1997a.

6. *On Interpretation*, ch. 5, 6, in McKeon 1941, pp. 42, 43.

7. Dudjom 1991, vol. 1, p. 874.

8. *Posterior Analytics*, book 1, ch. 25, in McKeon 1941, pp. 150–152.

9. For a review of Sa-skya Paṇḍita's life, career, and contributions, with full references to earlier studies, see D. Jackson 1987. More recent contributions include D. Jackson 1990, 1994; Kapstein in press; Rhoton forthcoming.

10. As Shayegan 1990, pp. 52–53, explains: "Ce [monde de l'*imaginal*] a de multiples résonances tant au niveau de l'ontologie que de la cosmologie et de l'angélologie. Il fonde une métaphysique des Images où celles-ci acquièrent une valeur cognitive et noétique propre. Car les Images surgissent non pas de l'inconscient mais de la surconscience; elles sont donc de ce fait des Images intellectives. Pour les distinguer nettement de l'imaginaire qui en tant que <<folle du logis>> ne sécrète que du fictif et de l'irréel, Corbin forgea le terme d'*imaginal.* Le monde de l'Imaginal, *'âlam al-mithâl* est le monde où ont lieu les visions des prophètes, des mystiques et les événements de l'âme, événements aussi réels que ceux du monde sensible mais qui ont lieu à un autre niveau de l'Être." Corbin 1969, pt. 2, elaborates this conception at length; the English translation uses the phrase "world of Idea-Images."

11. A caveat is required here, for there is a sense in which the privileging of particular texts, doctrines, or practices is standard procedure in Tibetan Buddhist circles, and not at all a peculiarity of Dölpopa's approach. Nevertheless, I think that it is fair to say that Dölpopa's use of selected key texts and passages, as will be illustrated here, at the very least exemplifies with unusual sharpness the role of the proof text in Tibetan dogmatics.

12. On the historical background and the development of the tradition at Gsang-phu, see Kuijp 1983, 1989; D. Jackson 1987; Onoda 1990, 1992.

13. D. Jackson 1987, pp. 112–113.

14. On Sa-skya Paṇḍita in relation to the Gsang-phu school, see in particular D. Jackson 1987 and Dreyfus 1997a.

15. For a detailed topical analysis of the entire text, see Horváth 1984.

16. Alexius Meinong, "The Theory of Objects," in Chisholm 1960, p. 78.

17. *Abhidharmakośam,* vol. 1, p. 90 (ch. 1, verse 34ab).

18. *Tshad-ma rigs-gter,* pp. 43–44.

19. For these definitions, I follow one of Sa-skya Paṇḍita's leading commentators, Go-rams-pa Bsod-nams seng-ge (1429–1489), in his *Rigs-gter gsal-byed,* pp. 2–5.

20. In this paragraph, I follow the eighteenth-century commentator, Ngag-dbang-chos-grags, in his *Rigs-gter dgongs-don,* p. 20.

21. I concur here with the remarks of Dreyfus 1997a, ch. 14, who translates *don-spyi* as "object universal."

22. Nevertheless, there are strong tendencies to realism within certain of the Buddhist epistemological traditions, e.g., the Dge-lugs-pa, though I think that they would resist genuine Platonic realism. For an excellent review of this issue, refer to Dreyfus 1997a, pt. 2, esp. chs. 9–10.

23. In the symbolic notation of the predicate calculus this is: $(\exists x)$(Dechen wants x).

24. $(\exists x^1)(\exists x^2)\ldots(\exists x^n)$(Dechen wants $x^1 \vee x^2 \vee \ldots \vee x^n$).

25. $(\exists x)$(Rāma sees x).

26. *Tshad-ma rigs-gter,* p. 74, *tshad ma'i shes pa gnyis po yang, rang rig tshad ma kho nar 'dus;* and p. 47, *gzhal bya rang mtshan gcig kho na.* On the primacy of discrete self-presentations, cf. Kapstein 1988b, p. 158.

27. *Tshad-ma rigs-gter,* pp. 55–60.

28. *Tshad-ma rigs-gter,* p. 44: *yul yin na de 'dzin pa'i rtog pa . . . ma 'khrul par 'gyur.*

29. $(\exists x)$(Sonam takes x to be a snake).

30. $(\exists x)$(Sonam takes the rope to be x).

31. *Tshad-ma rigs-gter,* p. 44: *yul yod phyir ma 'khrul.*

32. *Tshad-ma rigs-gter,* p. 44: *don spyi dang med pa gsal ba gnyis shes pa las tha dad pa'i yul zhig yin na yul snang rung gcig na gnas pa'i gang zag gzhan gyis kyang mthong bar 'gyur.*

33. *Tshad-ma rigs-gter,* p. 45: *gnyis ka'i brjod bya thun mong ba go bar mi nus.*

34. *Tshad-ma rigs-gter,* p. 46: *don spyi rang rang gi yul tha dad yin yang 'khrul nas gcig tu 'dzin.*

35. Williams 1983b; Kapstein 1988b.
36. Russell 1919, pp. 169–170.
37. Grossmann 1974, pp. 41–42.
38. Grossmann 1974, p. 42.
39. Husserl, 1962, vol. 2, pt. 2, sec. 5, pp. 175–176.
40. The outer sciences (*phyi'i rig-pa*) are: the linguistic sciences, logic and epistemology, medicine, and the arts and crafts. Refer to Dudjom 1991, vol. 1, pp. 97–107.
41. Thus, for instance, in the third chapter of Sa-skya Paṇḍita's *Mkhas-'jug,* concerning logic and debate, he describes purposeful debate as that which "takes up truths that accord with the doctrine, while abandoning errors," and he extols such debate as "a cause of the teaching's increase" (text in Jackson 1987, p. 251, line 7, and p. 296, lines 7–8), but nowhere does he seem to suggest that mastery of Pramāṇa will conduce directly to enlightenment. The relationship between the study of Pramāṇa and Buddhism's soteriological ends was a contested issue in Tibet, and the interpretation of this matter has given rise to some confusion in contemporary scholarship, which often misleadingly treats it as a dispute between "secular" and "religious" understandings of Pramāṇa, though there is clearly no distinction made, in a traditional context, that closely conforms with the Western notions this involves. For a judicious survey of the question, see Dreyfus 1997a, ch. 27. Cf. also Kapstein 1988b.
42. *Āryabhadracaripraṇidhānarāja,* verses 39–40.
43. Karma-pa III, Rang-byung-rdo-rje's *Phal-chen zhing-bkod-kyi bstan-bcos,* is referred to in *Mkhas-pa'i dga'-ston,* II.938; *Karma-pa'i mdzad-rnam,* p. 128.
44. Unfortunately there is no available *dkar-chag* giving a complete list of the contents of the *Rgya-mtsho mtha'-yas*. While no complete set of *Rgya-mtsho mtha'-yas* has been located to date, some were in circulation in Tibet: the Rnying-ma-pa Bla-ma Bsod-nams stobs-rgyal, presently of Toronto, has told me of such a set that was kept at the home of an uncle in Khams Ri-bo-che. See Kapstein 1985, p. 359, n. 2, for remarks on the marginalia of the present manuscript.
45. The author refers to himself as Rang-byung rdo-rje at *Rgya-mtsho mtha'-yas*, I.29, 207, 435, 467, 637, II.453, and elsewhere; and as "Bla-ma Karma-pa" at I.637.
46. On Rang-byung rdo-rje's astronomical contributions, see Schuh 1973, pp. 34–36. Rang-byung rdo-rje's great work on yoga is the *Zab-mo nang-gi don,* a good modern xylographic edition of which is available at Rumtek Monastery, Sikkim. The autocommentary, though long unavailable, has recently reemerged: I am grateful to Ven. Rdzogs-chen Dpon-slob Rin-po-che for his efforts to make this text available to me. For examples of his contemplative works, see *Gdams-ngag mdzod,* vol. 6.
47. This is not found in the present edition of *Rgya-mtsho mtha'-yas*. It is referred to, however, at I.4, 207, II.53, and elsewhere.
48. Unavailable, but referred to at *Rgya-mtsho mtha'-yas*, I.207.
49. *Chags-med ri-chos,* fol. 217.b.5–218.b.3. This passage was dictated on the twenty-third of Bhādrapada (*Khrums-zla*) during a fire-horse year, i.e., September 21 or 22, 1666.
50. *Pakshi'i rang-rnam*, pp. 2–3.
51. It is perhaps noteworthy that this is the name by which he chooses to be propitiated in a prayer to the Bka'-brgyud lineage: *Pakshi'i rang-rnam*, p. 6.
52. E.g., *Pakshi'i rang-rnam*, pp. 12, 18; cf. the name given to him in infancy, according to *Mkhas-pa'i dga'-ston,* II.882, "Chos-'dzin."
53. The first occurrence of this name in *Pakshi'i rang-rnam* is on p. 16, line 1. Note that in addition to the names given here, Karma Pakshi also had the ordination name of "Chos-kyi-bla-ma," which he received from the Rnying-ma-pa hierarch Byams-pa-'bum of Kaḥ-thog (1179–1252), certainly the major source of his Rnying-ma-pa doctrinal background (Dudjom 1991, vol. 1, pp. 693–694). Kaḥ-thog appears to have specialized to some degree in the exegesis of the nine-vehicle system, and the work of Kaḥ-thog's founder, Dam-pa Bde-gshegs

(1122–1192; Dudjom 1991, vol. 1, pp. 688–691), on this, *Theg-pa spyi-bcings,* has recently become available. The study of this work may well help to clarify further Karma Pakshi's sources of inspiration.

54. See, for instance, *Pakshi'i rang-rnam*, pp. 21–22, 79–80. Significant in this regard is the remark made to me by the late Ven. Gnas-nang Dpa'-bo Rin-po-che in July 1981: "Rang-byung-rdo-rje is the name of *all* the Karma-pas." The Sems-dpa' Rang-byung-rdo-rje of Karma Pakshi's autobiography is a form of the bodhisattva Avalokiteśvara, who is thought to be the ground for the emanation (*sprul-gzhi*) of the Karma-pas.

55. *Mkhas-pa'i dga'-ston,* II.927; *Karma-pa'i mdzad-rnam,* p. 119.

56. Indeed, according to the account of O-rgyan-pa's recognition of the infant third Karma-pa given in *Mkhas-pa'i dga'-ston,* II.926–929, it is evident that some among Karma Pakshi's former disciples were extremely reticent, at least initially, to accept this as a valid succession. It must be emphasized that the notion of there being identifiable rebirths of deceased masters was not in itself an innovation; what was new was the effort to tie actual inheritance to such identification.

57. Following the passing of the sixteenth Karma-pa in 1981, two of his leading disciples, Tā'i Si-tu Rin-po-che and Zhwa-dmar Rin-po-che, recognized opposing candidates. The former's, O-rgyan Phrin-las, was installed as the seventeenth Karma-pa at the traditional seat of the order at Mtshur-phu monastery in Central Tibet, where he commands very broad allegiance in Tibet itself, and among important elements of the Tibetan communities in India and Nepal. The Zhwa-dmar's candidate, who resides in New Delhi, has a smaller following, which strongly insists, however, upon the unique legitimacy of his claim. In late 1999 O-rgyan Phrin-las left Tibet to continue his education in India.

58. See n. 53.

59. Dudjom 1991, vol. 1, pp. 688–699.

60. For convenient summaries, see Dudjom 1991, vol. 1, pp. 223–237, 346–372.

61. These are commonly referred to by the acronym *mdo-rgyud-sems-gsum,* "the trio of the sūtra, tantra, and mind." (The first two are named in reverse order for reasons of euphony.) The history of this tradition is the main topic of Dudjom 1991, vol. 1, book 2, pt. 5.

62. See n. 81.

63. Demiéville 1973; Douglas and White 1976; Karma Thinley 1978; Rossabi 1988, pp. 40–41; Petech 1990, pp. 14–16.

64. This is discussed in the seventh Karma-pa's *Rigs-gzhung rgya-mtsho,* vol. 1, p. 76ff.

65. *Pakshi'i rang-rnam,* p. 25. Of the available texts, three have titles that include the phrase *Limitless Ocean of the Teaching:* (1) *Bstan-pa rgya-mtsho mtha'-yas-kyi spyi-gzhung chen-mo rtogs-pa rab-'byams chos-dbyings ye-shes lnga-ldan,* = *Rgya-mtsho mtha'-yas,* I.25–208; (2) *Glegs-bam 'dir bstan-pa rgya-mtsho mtha'-yas-kyi bshad-pa phun-sum-tshogs-pa,* = *Rgya-mtsho mtha'-yas,* I.209–470; and (3) *Bstan-pa rgya-mtsho mtha'-yas byin-gyis-rlabs-pa'i bka'-chen,* = *Rgya-mtsho mtha'-yas,* I.471–601. Judging on the basis of the contents of these, my guess is that if the reference in the passage cited is not to *Rgya-mtsho mtha'-yas* as a whole, then it is to (1).

66. *Pakshi'i rang-rnam,* p. 86.

67. *Pakshi'i rang-rnam,* p. 84. It is not entirely clear whether *Ye-shes rgya-mtsho mtha'-yas* refers to a text, or to the enlightenment that is the goal of the *Rgya-mtsho mtha'-yas.*

68. For the name "Rang-byung rdo-rje," see *Mkhas-pa'i dga'-ston,* II.897, 904, 906, 910, etc.; and *Karma-pa'i mdzad-rnam,* pp. 83, 85, 101, etc. For the *Rgya-mtsho mtha'-yas,* see *Mkhas-pa'i dga'-ston,* II.885, 906; and *Karma-pa'i mdzad-rnam,* p. 85. Note, too, that *Mkhas-pa'i dga'-ston,* II.896ff. quotes *Pakshi'i rang-rnam* profusely. *Karma-pa'i mdzad-rnam,* pp. 107–108, mentions that there are six volumes of Karma Pakshi's writings presently in the "human world."

69. *Rgya-mtsho mtha'-yas,* I.603–637.

70. Presently unavailable.

71. *Rgya-mtsho mtha'-yas*, I.45.

72. The question here is whether the round of rebirth has a fixed stock of sentient creatures, or whether genuinely "new" beings are sometimes produced.

73. Contemporary Western logics generally hold that between any two entities, *a* and *b*, there must be some relationship or another that can be posited as a value for *R* in a statement of the form *Rab*, "*a* is *R*-related to *b*," as, for example, "the Potala *is very far from* (= *R*) Mars." Karma Pakshi, however, in referring to "connections" in this passage, means either of the two types of relation that Buddhist epistemologists considered significant: causal relations, and what Western philosophers sometimes term "internal relationships," i.e., relationships that are intrinsic to the relata (e.g., the relation of a pot to its materiality). Kapstein 1989c outlines the Dharmakīrti's theory of relations, with which Karma Pakshi was certainly familiar.

74. *Rgya-mtsho mtha'-yas*, I.611–613.

75. Sa-chen Kun-dga'-snying-po (1092–1158), in his *Rgyud-sde spyi'i rnam-gzhag chung-ngu* (in *Sa-skya bka'-'bum*, vol. 1, pp. 5–9), cites the same passage but understands *'dod-pa* in its more primary sense of "desire" and not "tenets."

76. *Rgya-mtsho mtha'-yas*, I.613–614.

77. Annas and Barnes 1985, pp. 151–171.

78. *Rgya-mtsho mtha'-yas*, I.625–626.

79. *Rgya-mtsho mtha'-yas*, I.634.

80. Popkin 1979.

81. *Rgya-mtsho mtha'-yas*, I.41. To assess Karma Pakshi's view of other religions, it is essential that we take account not merely of his doctrinal viewpoint, which was derived from Buddhist textual sources, but also of his practical dealings with the religious life of the Mongol empire. A number of interesting passages may be found in *Pakshi'i rang-rnam*, e.g., pp. 21–22, where he claims to have sponsored the restoration and new construction of non-Buddhist (*phyi-rol mu-stegs-pa*) shrines, and pp. 101–102, where he notes with approval an edict promulgated by Möngke Khan directing all to adhere to the vows of their own religions (*thams-cad rang-rang-gi grub-mtha' dang 'thun-par* [sic!] *sdom-pa srung-ba'i 'ja'-sa*). This latter reference occurs in connection with an assembly of the royal line at Sira-ordos during a dragon year (certainly = 1256; *'brug-gi lo-la zi-ra-'ur-rdor rgyal-rgyud thams-cad 'tshogs-pa'i dus*), at which Karma Pakshi also claims to have turned the Khan and his immediate circle away from other religions and to have converted them to Buddhism (*mu-stegs-kyi grub-mtha'-las rje-'bangs thams-cad bzlog-cing/ nang-pa sangs-rgyas pa'i-bstan-pa-la btsud. . . .*). One is tempted to associate all this with the famed Buddhist-Taoist controversy of 1255–1256. It has been hypothesized that Karma Pakshi is none other than the somewhat mysterious Lama Na-mo, though the evidence for this identification is not to be found in the present sources (see, e.g., Demiéville 1973, esp. pp. 205–209 and n. 29). Pakshi's fanciful etymologizing of *mu-stegs-pa* no doubt has its origin in earlier Rnying-ma-pa sources, and it reappears in later doxographical writing, as well. (*Tīrthika* in Sanskrit is derived from *tīrtha*, the ford of a river, and is used also for sacred places for ritual ablutions. The Tibetan coinage that was contrived to represent this foreign idea, *mu-stegs*, was no doubt intended to refer to a bathing platform [*stegs*] on the bank [*mu*] of a river. Though this was well known to scholars of the canonical commentaries, it is easy to see how it might also be taken to mean "approaching [*stegs*] the limit [*mu*]" and so give rise to more extravagant etymological speculations.) 'Jam-dbyangs-bzhad-pa, for instance, is sharply critical of Stag-tshang Lo-tsā-ba Shes-rab-rin-chen (b. 1405) for defining the term in this way (*Grub-mtha' chen-mo*, p. 80). At the same time, there are no authors known to me besides Karma Pakshi who actually sought to invoke this definition in a context in which it seems to have clear political entailments.

82. The mahāyoga system of the *Guhyagarbhatantra* is summarized in Dudjom 1991, vol. 1, pp. 275–283, 359–363. Guenther 1984 offers an interpretation of the *Guhyagarbhatantra* based upon the commentary of Klong-chen Rab-'byams-pa.

83. *dgongs pa 'dul ba gsang ba dang// ma rtogs pa dang log par rtogs// phyogs rtogs yang dag nyid ma rtogs// don dam 'di la the tsom za//* Cf., e.g., *Rgya-mtsho mtha'-yas*, I.26, 30, 210, 632–633, II.53, etc. Karma Pakshi himself refers to the source at I.210 as being the *Rgyud-kyi rgyal-po gsang-ba'i snying-po de-kho-na-nyid nges-par 'byung-ba.* The passage he is paraphrasing in this verse may be found on folio 30a of the Rumtek xylographic edition of that text.

84. According to Vilāsavajra's influential commentary on the *Guhyagarbha*, "non-realization" refers to ordinary mundane folk; "mistaken realization" to those who adhere to nihilism or eternalism, i.e., the non-Buddhists; "partial realization" to the Śrāvakas, Pratyekabuddhas, and adherents of the Vijñaptimātratāvāda; "not realizing what is genuine" to the Mādhyamikas; and "intention, discipline, and esotericism" to the followers of the lower tantras. See *Gsang-snying Rgyud-'grel,* vol. 1, pp. 160–161.

85. *Rong-zom gsung-btus,* p. 20. Rong-zom-pa's quotation agrees precisely with the tantra. On Rong-zom-pa (eleventh century), see Dudjom 1991, vol. 1, pp. 703–709.

86. *Rgya-mtsho mtha'-yas*, I.210.

87. The nine-yāna system is taught throughout Rnying-ma-pa tantric traditions but has a special association with the anuyoga teaching owing to the great emphasis it receives in the primary tantra of the anuyoga, the *Mdo dgongs-pa 'dus-pa,* in connection with which the nine-yānas form the basis for the initiatory progression of the rites of empowerment. This became a matter of some controversy, as it required the conferral of tantric empowerments for the nontantric yānas of the Śrāvakas, Pratyekabuddhas, and Bodhisattvas. On this, refer to Dudjom, vol. 1, pp. 911–913. For more on the teaching of the *Mdo dgongs-pa 'dus-pa,* see also ch. 9 in the present work.

88. *Sog-bzlog-pa,* vol. 2, p. 135. Though not referring to the *Rgya-mtsho mtha'-yas* by name, Sog-bzlog-pa does mention, among other works of Karma Pakshi, a *Dgongs-'dus-kyi don so-sor-dbye-ba.* This may be a reference to the lengthy anuyoga section (pp. 374–435) of the *Phun-sum-tshogs-pa rgya-mtsho mtha'-yas* (*Rgya-mtsho mtha'-yas*, I.209–470). See, in particular, the remarks introducing that section, on p. 376: *de-la Mdo dgongs-pa 'dus-pa lung thams-cad-kyi rtsa-ba yin . . . so-sor-'byed shes-par bya'o//* "The *Mdo dgongs-pa 'dus-pa* is the root of all transmitted doctrines. You should know how to analyze it. . . ."

89. *Rgya-mtsho mtha'-yas*, I.430–431.

90. The origin of Klong-chen Rab-'byams-pa's renowned epithet may be the group of Rdzogs-chen tantras called *Klong-chen rab-'byams-kyi rgyud.* Karma Pakshi, referring to these (*Rgya-mtsho mtha'-yas*, I.453), attributes to them the "ultimate view of the Great Perfection."

91. E.g., *Rgya-mtsho mtha'-yas*, I.27, 467, 637, etc.

92. See, in particular, *Rgya-mtsho mtha'-yas*, II.1–70, 235–453, the latter being wholly devoted to an exposition of the Gsar-ma tantras.

93. *Pakshi'i rang-rnam*, p. 86.

94. *Chags-med ri-chos,* 218b: "Pakshi's intention was the coalescence of the new and ancient [schools of the Vajrayāna], and his ultimate intention was the coalescence of Mahāmudrā and of Rdzogs-pa chen-po." See, too, his *Phyag-rdzogs-zung-'jug,* p. 9: "Karma Pakshi received the three cycles of the *Mdo dgongs-pa 'dus-pa, Guhyagarbha,* and *Rdzogs-chen sems-sde* (*Mdo-sgyu-sems-gsum*) from Byams-pa-'bum of Kaḥ-thog, and he became learned in them. Hence, his own doctrinal compositions concern the coalescence of Mahāmudrā and Rdzogs-pa chen-po."

95. See, for example, Goldstein and Kapstein 1998, ch. 4, on the 'Bri-gung Bka'-brgyud.

96. Two important works deserving attention in this regard are: Karma-pa VII Chos-grags rgya-mtsho's *Rigs-gzhung rgya-mtsho,* vol. 1, p. 76ff., which preserves extracts from Karma Pakshi's now unavailable *Tshad-ma rgya-mtsho mtha'-yas;* and Karma-pa VIII Mi-bskyod rdo-rje's extraordinary commentary on Pakshi's *Sku-gsum ngo-sprod* precepts, the *Sku-gsum rnam-bshad.*

97. The canonical teachings of the Prajñāpāramitā Sūtras and the Madhyamaka philosophy of Nāgārjuna of course employ a wide range of skeptical arguments, though the main lines of interpretation in Tibet sought to contextualize them so as to restrain the force of their skepticism. Skeptical argument is sometimes employed in connection with the meditational teachings of the Mahāmudrā and Rdzogs-chen, and this was sometimes castigated as a "nihilist" (*chad-lta*) tendency within these traditions. See, for instance, Takpo 1986, pp. 105–109; Dudjom 1991, vol. 1, pp. 896–910. A good example of the application of skeptical argument in a contemplative context may be found in Takpo 1986, p. 184ff., where it is a question of analytic meditation (*dpyad-bsgom*), systematically calling into question the assumptions and attributions through which one conceptualizes the mind. The author comments that the "meditator should therefore examine thoroughly with a persistence in the manner of an inquisitive person crushing a bone with a stone!"

98. This section is based on my unpublished article "A Golden Age of Understanding? Dol-po-pa on the Kṛtayuga and What Followed." In Stearns 1999, it is referred to as "Kapstein 1994."

99. Several versions of Dölpopa's biography have now become available. These have recently been studied with great care in Stearns 1999, which work should be consulted by those wishing to examine Dölpopa's life in depth. See also Kapstein 1992f.

100. See n. 56 above, and Kapstein in press.

101. This raises interesting questions concerning the possible relationships between 'Bri-gung Skyob-pa's distinctive *dgongs-gcig* ("single intention") doctrine and the *Rdzogs-ldan-lugs* ("Kṛtayuga tradition") of Dol-po-pa. One apparent affinity between them is noted below, n. 131. Both, of course, are castigated by their opponents as representatives of *Hwa-shang lta-ba,* "the views of Heshang Moheyan."

102. Refer to *BA,* book 10, and Tenzin Gyatso and Hopkins 1988.

103. On the Dol-po region, which is within the political boundaries of modern Nepal, see esp. Snellgrove 1957, 1967b, 1989; Jest 1974a, 1974b.

104. Dol-po-pa's own biography of his master is found in *Dol-po-pa,* no. 60.

105. The construction of the *caitya* is described in Kapstein 1992f, pp. 13–14; Stearns 1999, ch. 1, pt. 4. For further background see Tucci 1949, p. 189ff., and Vitali 1990, pp. 126–133. Cabezón 1998, pp. 141–158, offers interesting suggestions concerning the relationship between Tibetan religious thought and architecture.

106. As A. W. Macdonald 1984b, p. 70, remarks of the Sherpa scholar Sangs-rgyas-bstan-'dzin (1924–1990), his biography "shows us what can still be accomplished, even in these days, by a man of stubborn courage and solid faith."

107. The fourteenth century, however, was a period of distinctive doctrinal synthesis. Dol-po-pa's contemporaries—including Karma-pa Rang-byung-rdo-rje (1284–1339), Bu-ston Rin-chen-grub (1290–1364), and Kun-mkhyen Klong-chen Rab-'byams-pa (1308–1363)—all merit comparison in this regard.

108. *Dol-po-pa*, nos. 16, 39, 70.7, 70.8.

109. Stearns 1995, 1999, ch. 1, pt. 4–5.

110. "Doxography" has been more widely used in continental than in anglophone discourse on the history of philosophy; it refers to writings on philosophical doctrines and systems, for example, in standard histories of philosophy that summarize the key ideas of a succession of thinkers, often beginning with the "Presocratics." Refer to Rorty 1984. The term has become current in recent work on the Indian and Tibetan Buddhist *siddhānta* (*grub-mtha'*), "philosophical systems," lit. "limit [of what can be] proven." See, for instance, Hopkins in Jackson and Cabezón 1995, pp. 170–186; Mimaki 1994.

111. *Prasannapadā,* on *Madhyamakaśāstra,* ch. 1, verse 3, for instance, repeatedly cites Bhāvaviveka's criticisms of Buddhapālita, e.g.: *ācāryabuddhapālitas tu vyācaṣṭe . . . ācārya-*

bhāvaviveko dūṣaṇam āha, "Master Buddhapālita asserted . . . and Master Bhāvaviveka said in refutation. . . ."

112. *Abhisamayālaṃkārāloka,* ch. 1, verses 1–3, traces the commentarial succession of the Prajñāpāramitā from Maitreya, through Asaṅga and Vasubandhu, and thence to Ārya-Vimuktisena and Vimuktisena.

113. Refer to the introductory verses to the *Sphutārthā Vyākhyā* in *Abhidharmakośam,* vol. 1, pp. 1–2.

114. This has been affirmed to me by many of the traditionally trained scholars I have queried about the place of history in Tibetan scholasticism, including H. H. the Dalai Lama, when I interviewed him at his home in Dharamsala in the spring of 1993. Nevertheless, there have always been some who have taken a special interest in this area. Among my own teachers, for instance, H. H. Dudjom Rinpoche and Ven. Dezhung Rinpoche particularly encouraged the investigation of Tibetan historical writing, though this was never part of a formal scholastic curriculum. Indeed, the inherent perennialism of Tibetan scholastic traditions militated strongly against the independent value of historical research.

115. Dudjom 1991, vol. 1, p. 959, exemplifies prevailing opinion when he writes: "Although, in general, there have been many changes in the political life of Tibet during the past, as far as the doctrine is concerned, the veracity of the Teacher's own prophetic declaration that his teaching would increasingly spread northwards has been actualised. Due to the merits of those to be trained in Tibet, and by the power of the timely penetration of [the world by] the Conquerors' compassion, individuals who have held the teaching and have shown mastery in inconceivable careers of learning, dignity, and accomplishment, have successively appeared from the time of the teaching's inception in the past down to the present day. Because they preserved the most precious teaching and continue to preserve it, the continuity of the doctrine in Tibet has never been impaired."

116. This is perhaps best exemplified by the entire *Bka'-brgyud gser-phreng*—"golden rosary of the oral lineage"—genre. For an example in English translation, see Könchog Gyaltsen 1990 on the 'Bri-gung Bka'-brgyud.

117. Mimaki 1982, text fol. 2a–3a.

118. Rorty 1984.

119. See now, in particular, Collins 1998, ch. 3, "Nirvana, Time, and Narrative."

120. Buddhist prophecies of decline and their ramifications for Buddhism in East Asia are considered in detail in Nattier 1991.

121. Nattier 1991, pp. 136–139, on "Decline and Dispensationalism in Buddhist Thought and Practice."

122. van der Kuijp 1983; Tillemans and Tomabechi 1995; Dreyfus 1997a, pp. 383–385.

123. *Grub-mtha' lhun-po mdzes-rgyan,* pp. 2–9.

124. *Grub-mtha' lhun-po mdzes-rgyan,* p. 8: *snyigs ma las kyang ches snyigs ma'i// ngang tshul mngon par brtas gyur kyang// thub pa'i gsung gi gsang ba ni// da dung ma nyams 'di yi drin//*

125. The Rnying-ma-pa and Bon-po must be noted as having also formulated peculiar views of many aspects of doctrinal history, though we shall not consider them here. See, in particular, Karmay 1972; Dudjom 1991.

126. Ruegg 1963.

127. Smith 1970; Ruegg 1989; Hookham 1991; Thurman 1984; Dudjom 1991; Kapstein 1992f, 1997c; Hopkins 1999; Stearns 1999.

128. Lamotte 1935, p. 85 (Tibetan text) and pp. 206–207 (translation).

129. These topics and the previous researches relevant to their investigation are recently examined in Tauscher 1995. See also Kapstein 1997a, 1997c; Hopkins 1999, pp. 47–55.

130. *Dol-po-pa*, vol. 2, p. 228, line 3f.; *Dol-po-pa'i ri-chos*, p. 177, line 3f.

131. Thus, for instance, 'Bri-gung Skyobs-pa 'Jig-rten-mgon-po (1143–1217) in his *Dam-chos dgongs-pa gcig-pa'i rtsa-tshig:* "There are those who hold the promulgations of Madhyamaka and the promulgations of Mind Only to be different, but, according to the vajra-speech, the very same promulgations that teach Mind Only teach Madhyamaka" (*dbu-ma'i bka'-dang sems-tsam-pa'i bka' tha-dad-par 'dod-de; rdo-rje'i gsung sems-tsam ston-pa'i bka'-nyid dbu-ma ston-par bzhed*). From *Dgongs-gcig yig-cha,* vol. 1, pp. 157–158. It is perhaps not without significance that Dol-po-pa was regarded as an emanation of 'Bri-gung Skyobs-pa.

132. See, for example, Dudjom 1991, vol. 1, pp. 191–216, 243–256, 911–913.

133. The key technical terms here are: *tathāgatagarbha* (*de-bzhin-gshegs-pa'i snying-po*), *advayajñāna* (*gnyis-med ye-shes*), Mahāmudrā (*phyag-rgya chen-po*), and *pāramārthika-bodhicitta* (*don-dam-pa'i byang-chub-sems*).

134. *Śūnyatā* (*stong-pa-nyid*), *dharmatā* (*chos-nyid*), and Prajñāpāramitā (*shes-rab-kyi pha-rol-tu phyin-pa*).

135. I use "esotericism" here in the specific sense in which contemporary philosophers of religion understand it, that is, as referring to the assertion of a philosophical doctrine or intuition that, while not explicitly represented throughout the corpus being interpreted, is nevertheless held by its proponents to be present as the implicit or concealed message unifying the whole as its deepest or ultimate significance. In this sense, efforts to identify, say, Advaita Vedānta as the teaching underlying all Hinduism are similarly esoteric.

136. *Dol-po-pa,* nos. 7, 8, 9, 10, 12, 13. The commentaries on the three Prajñāpāramitā do not offer word-by-word explanations, of course, but rather detailed summaries, with glosses on selected topics, that attempt to illustrate the manner in which the *Abhisamayālaṃkāra* itself functions as a commentary on these sūtras.

137. *Dol-po-pa,* vol. 3, p. 76.

138. *Dol-po-pa,* vol. 3, p. 277, line 6f.

139. See n. 128.

140. *Dol-po-pa,* vol. 5, pp. 340–343; Kapstein 1992f, p. 40–43.

141. Nattier 1991, pp. 15–19.

142. "Third" here refers to the second age, and is called "third" because three was the second-best score in the Indian game of dice ("threes"). Similarly, "second" (*dvāpara*) is the Third World Age ("twos" in the dice game), while the worst and last is *kali* ("craps"). Contrary to the prevailing (Western) mythology, the name of the Kaliyuga has nothing whatever to do with the goddess Kālī. Refer to Nattier 1991, p. 17, n. 4.

143. The title is explained in *Dol-po-pa,* vol. 5, p. 328. See also Stearns 1999, where a complete translation of the root text will now be found.

144. This couplet paraphrases *Bodhicaryāvatāra,* ch. 9, verse 4ab: *bādhyante dhīviśeṣeṇa yogino 'py uttarottaraiḥ.* "[Inferior] adepts are refuted by ever superior ones, according to perspicacity."

145. *Dol-po-pa,* vol. 5, pp. 208–209.

146. *Dol-po-pa,* vol. 5, pp. 336–343; Kapstein 1992f, pp. 27–43.

147. *Dol-po-pa,* vol. 7, nos. 56, 58, 59, all related to the *Vajrāvalī* of Abhayākaragupta, the transmission lineage of which has been preserved by Dol-po-pa's successors in the Jo-nang-pa tradition. In fact, during my investigations of contemporary Jo-nang-pa communities in Sichuan (Kapstein 1991), I learned that only the initiation of Kālacakra as included within the *Vajrāvalī* is considered an acceptable substitute for the properly Jo-nang-pa Kālacakra *abhiṣeka.*

148. Compare Stearns 1999, ch. 3.

149. *Dol-po-pa,* vol. 5, p. 293.

150. *Vimalaprabhāṭīkā,* p. 74, on ch. 1, verse 22.

151. *Vimalaprabhāṭīkā,* pp. 255–271.

152. *Dol-po-pa,* vol. 1, pp. 190–201; see also Stearns 1999.

153. "Great Madhyamaka" is widely used by Rnying-ma-pa, Bka'-brgyud-pa, Sa-skya-pa, and Jo-nang-pa authors as a designation of the highest philosophical view, in many cases with the polemical intent of asserting a position which, like Dol-po-pa's, is thought to harmonize the traditions of Nāgārjuna and Asaṅga, while transcending both Cittamātra and Madhyamaka insofar as they are discursively accessible philosophical systems. See, e.g., Dudjom 1991, vol. 1, pp. 178–186.

154. For Haribhadra's text, see Amano 1975, p. 3.

155. *Dol-po-pa,* vol. 5, p. 339; Kapstein 1992f, p. 39.

156. *Mkhyen-brtse'i gsung-rtsom,* p. 222; *Shes-bya kun-khyab,* vol. 1, p. 403. On Tāranātha see n. 159.

157. *Jo-nang chos-'byung,* pp. 13–14.

158. *Gzhan-stong chen-mo,* p. 92.

159. Tāranātha does mention Avitarka (Chimpa and Chattopadhyaya 1980, p. 102) but only characterizes him generally as a teacher of the Mahāyāna.

160. Makransky 1997 now offers an excellent study of the main commentarial traditions on the *Abhisamayālaṃkāra,* devoting particular attention to Haribhadra in chapter 10, and in chapter 12 taking up the question of Tsong-kha-pa's debt to Haribhadra and, hence, his importance to the later Dge-lugs-pa school.

161. Examples include Buddhist works such as Bhāvaviveka's *Tarkajvālā,* and the *Jñānasārasamuccaya,* attributed to Āryadeva, as well as Brahmāṇical texts like the *Sarvasiddhāntasaṃgraha,* attributed to Śaṅkara, and Sāyaṇa Mādhava's *Sarvadarśanasaṃgraha.* There can be no doubt that, in India, Vasubandhu and Asaṅga were in fact widely associated with a form of idealism.

162. Rorty 1984, p. 62.

163. Rorty 1984, pp. 62–63.

164. It must be said, however, that Sa-skya Paṇḍita is remarkably restrained here. Thus, even in commenting on Śāntideva's (in)famous verse, "the absolute is not within the scope of intellect" (*buddher agocaras tattvaṃ, Bodhicaryāvatāra,* ch. 9, verse 2, cited in *Sa-paṇ gsung-'bum,* vol. 1, p. 131), he remarks that "this [refers to] the definiendum but not to the definiens" (*'di mtshan gzhi yin gyi mtshan nyid ma yin no*), which is to say that the skeptical view apparently articulated by Śāntideva in this passage bears upon the intellect's ability to refer directly to the absolute, but *not* upon its ability so to refer indirectly, through a mediating concept.

165. See nn. 64, 96.

166. Kapstein 1992f; Stearns 1999.

167. Hopkins 1999, p. 3, nicely describes the perspective that must characterize thoughtful interpretation of Tibetan religious discourse when he writes of his own fascination "with what seemed to be a cacophony of perspectives within the tradition."

168. *O-rgyan glegs-bam,* p. 489.

169. This may also be a point of some importance for the assessment of Tibetan philosophical writings. The great Rnying-ma-pa master, 'Jam-mgon 'Ju Mi-pham Rin-po-che (1846–1912), for instance, was the author of a short treatise in defense of the "extrinsic emptiness" doctrine, *Gzhan-stong khas-len.* In interviewing scholars trained in differing branches of Mi-pham's lineage, however, it became apparent that while some held this text to represent Mi-pham's real view of the matter, others maintained that Mi-pham dictated the *Gzhan-stong khas-len* only as an exercise, in order to demonstrate the best case one might make in favor of a viewpoint that in the end would have to be abandoned.

170. Gyatso 1998, pp. 116, 119.

171. The best example of such a rare case is no doubt Ma-cig Lab-sgron (1055–1143). Several of the works attributed to her authorship are studied in Orofino 1987.

172. *Sa-paṇ gsung-'bum,* vol. 1, p. 681; see also Kapstein in press.

173. This process has yet to be studied in detail. It is clear that during the fifteenth and sixteenth centuries, the contribution of the Sa-skya-pa, Jo-nang-pa, and Bka'-brgyud-pa, to the ongoing development of Tibetan scholasticism remains a vital one, as is seen in the works of masters such as Stag-tshang Lo-tsa-ba Shes-rab-rin-chen (b. 1405), Gser-mdog Paṇ-chen Shākya mchog-ldan (1428–1507), Go-rams-pa Bsod-nams-seng-ge (1429–1489), Karma-pa VII Chos-grags rgya-mtsho (1454–1506), Karma-pa VIII Mi-bskyod rdo-rje (1507–1554), Dwags-po Bkra-shis rnam-rgyal (1512–1587), 'Brug-chen IV Padma dkar-po (1527–1592), and Jo-nang Rje-btsun Tāranātha (1575–1634). After the time of the latter, the creativity of the non-Dge-lugs-pa traditions in Central Tibet seems largely exhausted and picks up again only in the eighteenth and nineteenth centuries, primarily in far eastern Tibet. This is most likely explained by the impact on religious institutions of the struggles of the Dbus-Gtsang civil war, the consolidation of power under the Fifth Dalai Lama, the subsequent state-sponsored promotion of the Dge-lugs-pa sect and restriction of their opponents, and, finally, the devastating effects of the early-eighteenth-century Dzungar invasions (on which see ch. 7, n. 64). On the religious history of this period, refer to Smith 1968, 1970. We should note, too, that even with the revival of non-Dge-lugs-pa scholasticism in eastern Tibet, the general dominance of Dge-lugs-pa thought was often in evidence: see, for instance, Kapstein 1997c on the nineteenth-century Jo-nang-pa master 'Ba'-mda' Dge-legs.

Chapter 7

1. See now esp. Buswell 1989, 1990; Cabezón 1992; Collins 1990.

2. For a useful introduction to the textual traditions called "canon" in recent Buddhist Studies, see Lancaster 1979. As for "apocrypha," Lamotte, 1976, p. 180, referring to the proliferation of sūtras prior to the actual emergence of the Mahāyāna, introduces the term as follows: "D'autre part à coté de sūtra authentiques, dûment classés dans les collections, ont circulé des textes séparés (*muktaka*) et apocryphes (*adhyāropita*). . . . La multiplication des textes apocryphes a conduit les anciens théoriciens du Dharma à formuler des critères d'authenticité. . . ." Consider, too, Warder's remarks (1970, p. 354) on the formation of the Mahāyāna literature itself: "[C]ertain monks felt the need not simply for new interpretations of the original sūtras . . . but for wholesale restatements of the doctrine. For this purpose they rewrote the sūtras, or wrote new sūtras. . . . It is a matter of speculation how far there was deliberate deception in this fabrication of new sūtras."

3. On the background of this popular text (no. 945 in the Taishō Tripiṭaka), refer to Demiéville 1952, pp. 43–52, n. 3; Lamotte 1965, pp. 106–107. Neither writer hesitates to refer to this version of the *Śūraṃgama* as "un apocryphe chinois."

4. Buttrick 1962, vol. 1, pp. 498–499; Hennecke and Schneemelcher 1963, vol. 1, p. 21.

5. Cf. Monier-Williams 1899, p. 1241. For characteristic explanations of the word *sūtra* found in later Buddhist scholastic writings, as known in Tibet, see Rahula 1971, p. 131; Obermiller 1931, p. 31; Dudjom 1991, vol. 1, p. 79.

6. We should note too that, following this definition, large portions of such hallowed collections as the Tibetan Tanjur will have to be regarded as being in some sense extracanonical. This, however, is as it should be, for only a few of the works and authors represented therein are generally thought to be so exalted as to be accorded the authoritative status otherwise reserved for works described as *buddhavacana.* The commentaries, treatises, and literary works making up the Tanjur and similar compilations are canons primarily in the sense in which we speak of "aesthetic canons" or "legal canons"; that is, they provide the models and standards for the specific classes of endeavor that they represent and as such are considered to merit emulation. The degree to which they embody the Buddha's message, however, is subject to discussion and debate and in some cases may be doubted altogether.

7. Cf. the usage of Demiéville and Lamotte in the passages referred to in notes 2 and 3 above; and that of Zürcher 1959, p. 308ff.

8. Hennecke and Schneemelcher 1963, p. 27.

9. There are, however, some exceptions to this, e.g., the "genuine" Chinese sūtras when contrasted with the "spurious" Chinese sūtras, though both classes are agreed not to have originated in Buddhist India. See Mizuno 1982, p. 116ff. (However, the dominant tendency in China was certainly to regard the dichotomy of spurious and genuine as excluding any intervening category; see Kyoku Tokuno, "The Evaluation of Indigenous Scriptures in Chinese Buddhist Bibliographical Catalogues," in Buswell 1990, pp. 31–74.) For a noteworthy exception within the Tibetan tradition, see Tāranātha's comments on the authenticity of the *Maṇi bka'-'bum* in ch. 8 here.

10. The *gter-ma* are considered in more detail later in this chapter. On the term "apocrypha" in Gnostic contexts, see Buttrick 1962, vol. 1, p. 162; Hennecke and Schneemelcher 1963, pp. 25–26. Edward Conze 1967, p. 658, has juxtaposed Gnostic and Mahāyāna ways of authenticating scripture, comparing *gter-ma* to certain Hermetic texts.

11. Cabezón 1992, p. 236, n. 4, takes issue with certain aspects of my discussion here, but I think that his remarks miss the point of this paragraph. My intention is only to emphasize that, when we use the term "apocrypha" to refer to concepts found within Buddhist disputes on scriptural authenticity, we are not using it in just the same way that we do in Jewish and Christian contexts, and that we need to be clear about the semantic shift that has taken place. I am grateful, however, to Cabezón both for his generous comments about this chapter (as it appeared in Kapstein 1989a), and for his contribution to enlarging the scope of reflection on its subject matter through his valuable examination of Vasubandhu's *Vyākhyāyukti.*

12. Cf. *Kathāvatthu* XVIII, 1 ("Of the Buddha and this World") and 2 ("Of how the Norm was taught"), in Aung and Davids 1969, pp. 323–325; and Buddhaghosa's comments in Law 1969, pp. 211–212.

13. *Spyod-'jug rnam-bshad*, pp. 346.4–347.2: *nyan thos pa dag na re/ . . . theg pa chen po'i gzhung de dag ni sangs rgyas kyis gsungs pa'i bka' ma yin te/ Bye brag tu bshad pa chen por/ chos 'khor gnas dang yangs pa can/ sa dkar can dang lha yi gnas . . . zhes bshad pa'i gnas 'di dag tu bzhugs pa na rtag par phyi bzhin 'brang ba'i nyan thos chen po rnams kyis ma thos pa'i phyir . . .*

14. Davidson 1990.

15. *Abhidharmakośam,* vol. 2, pp. 1206–1207: *yo hi granthaḥ sarveṣu nikāyāntareṣv āmnāyate, na ca sūtraṃ dharmatāṃ vā bādhate, so 'smābhir apāṭhān na buddhavacanam iti kevalaṃ sāhasamātram/*

16. As Davidson 1990 rightly points out, one Indian oral tradition, that of the Vedas, was transmitted with verifiable precision. But in the absence of anything like the Vedic system of checks and balances, only an early written tradition could have avoided some of the difficulties faced by the Buddhists in ensuring the authority of their transmissions. For a fine example of the degree of accuracy that was attained in the transmission of some Indian folk traditions, see Grierson and Barnett 1920, pp. 3–4. While the evidence for exactitude here is impressive indeed, we must not forget that the sayings of Lallā form a relatively small collection of verses and so cannot be the basis for a comparison with the extensive prose corpus of ancient Buddhism. Still, the mnemonic achievements of the early Buddhist *bhāṇaka*-s ("reciters") have yet to be considered in detail.

17. Cf. Collingwood 1956, pp. 25–26. There is little doubt that by the time the Buddhists began to commit their scriptures to writing, the lives and teachings of the founder and his original circle of disciples were no longer within the range of scientific history as Collingwood here conceives of it.

18. Cf. Davidson 1990.

19. This is nicely exemplified by Sum-pa mkhan-po: see n. 73 below. A reflection of the same problem may be found in the manner in which some recent Japanese Mahāyānists have treated the distinction between genuine historical claims and genuine spiritual claims, on which see Mizuno 1982, pp. 128–133.

20. Davidson 1990, pp. 305–312.

21. *Ratnagotravibhāga,* IV.

22. *Ratnagotravibhāga,* IV.31–34ab:

> *yathāiva divi devānāṃ pūrvaśuklānubhāvataḥ/*
> *yatna-sthāna-manorūpa-vikalpa-rahitā satī//31//*
> *anitya-duḥkha-nairātmya-śānta-śabdaiḥ pramādinaḥ/*
> *codayaty amarān sarvān asakṛd deva-dundubhiḥ//32//*
> *vyāpya buddhasvareṇāivaṃ vibhur jagad aśeṣataḥ/*
> *dharmaṃ diśati bhavyebhyo yatnādi-rahito 'pi san//33//*
> *devānāṃ divi divya-dundubhir avo yadvat svakarmodbhavo*
> *dharmodāharaṇaṃ muner api tathā loke svakarmodbhavam . . .*

Cf. Dante, *Paradiso,* 29 lines 136–138:

> The Primal Light the whole irradiates,
> And is received therein as many ways
> As there are splendors wherewithal it mates.

Translated in Sayers and Reynolds 1962, p. 313.

23. *Ratnagotravibhāga,* V.18:

> *yad arthavad dharmapadopasaṃhitaṃ tridhātukleśanibarhaṇaṃ vacaḥ/*
> *bhavec ca yac chāntyanuśaṃsadarśakaṃ tad uktam ārṣaṃ viparītam anyathā//*

24. *Rgyud-bla'i rnam-'grel,* fol. 3a.6–3b.5: *gzhung de la zhib mor dpyad na gsum yod de/ dang po ni/ sangs rgyas kyi rang snang gi gsung dbyangs gnyis med kyi ye shes nyid rnam pa thams cad par shar ba'i nang tshan gyi theg chen mdo sde'i ngag gi rnam pa don dam pa de yin la/ 'di ni rang bzhin rnam dag gam bral 'bras chos sku dang ngo bo gcig go// gnyis pa ni/ 'phags pa dang so so skye bo rnams kyi yid la sgra spyi'i rnam par shar ba'i ming tshig yi ge'i tshogs pa dang ldan pa'i theg chen gyi mdo sde'o// gsum pa ni/ de dang mthun par ngag tu brjod pa'i sgra tshig la gzhung theg chen nges don gyi mdo rgyud ces bya'o// phyi ma 'di gnyis ni rang bzhin 'bras bu lam gsum las ngo bo shin tu tha dad mod kyi/ sangs rgyas rnams kyi smon lam las byung ba/ chos kyi sku yi rgyu mthun pa/ sgrib gnyis spong bar byed pa'i nus mthu can yin pa'i phyir/ zag med kyi chos dang/ rnam par byang ba'i dmigs pa dang yongs grub kyi khongs su gtogs pa shes par bya'o//* There appear to be remarkable affinities between the theory of the levels of the text articulated here, and the theory of semantic levels associated with the Indian philosopher Bhartṛhari and later developed in a tantric context by Abhinavagupta. The possible relationships between the linguistic theories of these thinkers and Buddhist speculations on language have yet to be investigated.

25. *Nor-bu ketaka.* The Sanskrit word *ketaka* figuring in the title is used in Tibetan to refer to a mythical gemstone said to be capable of purifying polluted water. According to the colophon (906.6–7), the text was completed during the bright half of the month of phālguna (*dbo-zla'i yar-tshes*) in the water tiger year (*chu-stag-lo*). The exact date is missing. In any case, using the conversion tables found in Schuh 1973, and following the New Phug-pa calendar, this must have been some time during the last half of March 1782.

26. *Ketaka'i byi-dor.* There is also a modern xylographic edition from Rum-btegs, Sikkim, though I have used only the former edition here. According to the colophon (p. 71), the work was completed on the second day of the bright half of the first autumn month (*ston-zla-ra-ba'i yar-tshes bzang-po*) of the same water tiger year (9 September 1782).

27. The traditional history of the Kālacakra cycle is recounted in *BA*, book 10. The authenticity of the *Kālacakratantra* was questioned severely by the great Sa-skya-pa master Red-mda'-ba Gzhon-nu-blo-gros (1349–1412), some of whose remarks on this subject are quoted in *Bdud-'joms chos-'byung*, p. 792.1–4; trans. in Dudjom 1991, vol. 1, p. 930.

28. See in this volume ch. 2, n. 71; ch. 5, n. 7. It should be noted, too, that Khri Srong-lde'u-btsan's rejection of Manichaeism, discussed in Stein 1980, may have turned to some extent on the question of the authenticity of Manichaean scriptures.

29. On some aspects of Śāntarakṣita's role here, see ch. 2 and 3 of this volume.

30. Cf. Mizuno 1982, p. 116ff. But note, too, that in China hermeneutical considerations resulted in certain sūtras and treatises of non-Indic origin being classified as genuine. See Tokuno, cited in n. 9 of this chapter.

31. Karmay 1975a, 1980a, 1980b, 1981, 1985. See, further, Karmay 1988a.

32. This simplifies the view of an extremely complex situation. In particular, the Dge-lugs-pas assessment of the Rnying-ma-pa traditions deserves a more subtle appraisal than it has so far received. The fact is that the Dge-lugs-pa had no fixed party line with respect to the Rnying-ma-pas, for as Sum-pa mkhan-po himself admits: "So it is that although the ancient scholars and saints of Tibet extensively refuted [the Rnying-ma-pas,] the venerable Tsong-kha-pa, his sons, and others among the real Dge-ldan-pas [i.e., Dge-lugs-pas] did not refute or deride them at all. . . ." (*de ltar na bod kyi mkhas grub snga ma dag gis de ltar rgyas par bkag pa las rje tsong kha pa yab sras sogs dge ldan pa dngos dag gis de la dgag smod gang yang byas pa med. . . .*) *Dpag-bsam ljon-bzang*, p. 399.

33. This learned master's view of the Rnying-ma-pa and allied traditions is exceedingly complex. Sa-skya Paṇḍita's foremost polemical work is his *Sa-skya sdom-gsum*, now translated in Rhoton forthcoming. See also R. Jackson 1982; D. Jackson 1990, 1994. What emerges here is that Sa-skya Paṇḍita sought to discredit a tradition that he calls *Rgya-nag rdzogs-chen*, the "Chinese Great Perfection." As Karmay 1975a, p. 152ff., has shown, this was certainly not the Great Perfection of the Rnying-ma-pa and Bon-po, but rather the Chan teaching attributed to Heshang Moheyan. Karmay's conclusion is further reinforced by the consideration that Sa-skya Paṇḍita refers to his own study of the Rdzogs-chen of the "Tibetan elders," without any disparagement, in his *Nga-brgyad-ma'i 'grel-pa*, in *Sa-skya bka'-'bum*, vol. 5, p. 151.2.3. Consider, too, Smith's remarks (1970, pp. 7–8) on Sa-skya Paṇḍita and the Vajrakīla tradition, which was something of a 'Khon family specialty. Finally, we should note that Sa-skya Paṇḍita's nephew Chos-rgyal 'Phags-pa does not hesitate to enumerate the Rnying-ma tantras, without negative comment, in his *Rgyud-sde'i dkar-chag*, in *Sa-skya bka'-'bum*, vol. 7, pp. 136.3–138.2.6.

34. On Rig-pa'i-ral-gri, see also ch. 5. The available evidence suggests that Rig-pa'i-ral-gri, while criticizing the Rnying-ma-pa in some respects, contributed substantially to their defense: see, for instance, *Sog-bzlog-pa* , vol. 1, pp. 500–509, 524–526. The last passage cited, part of a defense of the authenticity of the controversial *Guhyagarbhatantra* (*T* 832), is also given in *Bdud-'joms chos-'byung*, pp. 765.6–768.6; trans. Dudjom 1991, vol. 1, pp. 914–916. It has recently emerged that Thar-pa Lo-tsā-ba's translation of the *Guhyagarbha*, which was commissioned by Rig-pa'-ral-gri, has been preserved as no. 754 of the Phug-brag Bka'-'gyur manuscript kept at the Library of Tibetan Works and Archives, Dharamsala.

35. Aspects of Bu-ston's contributions to the canonicity debates are discussed in *BA*, p. 417, n. 4; Ruegg 1969, pp. 21–35, esp. p. 27, n. 1., pp. 28–30, n. 1. The *Sngags-log sun-'byin*, noted by Ruegg as having been attributed to Bu-ston by Klong-rdol bla-ma and considered to be of questionable authenticity by Sum-pa mkhan-po, has been published in India in a small photo-offset *po-ti* (n.d., n.p.). Doubts about its attribution to Bu-ston are increased by the considerations that Sog-bzlog-pa nowhere mentions it, and by the tract's own character, which is that of a diatribe rather than of a well-reasoned argument. *Thu'u-bkwan grub-*

mtha', p. 74, describes it as follows: "Though it is seemingly authored by Bu-ston, it does not appear in the catalogues of his *Gsung-'bum,* and if one examines its style, there is no experience of its being the work of a scholar. So, it was merely written by some fool and passed off as Bu-ston Rin-po-che's." (*bu ston gyis mdzad pa yin khul zhig 'dug pa/ gsung 'bum gyi dkar chag rnams su mi snang zhing/ tshig sbyor la dpags kyang mkhas pa'i gsung gi nyams mi 'dug pas/ blun po zhig gis bris nas bu ston rin po che la khag yar bar zad do//*)

36. His main polemical work appears to have been *Klong-chen brgal-lan,* though the authorship of this is uncertain. However, related comments are also found inter alia in *Klong-chen rgyud-sde spyi-don,* the attribution of which is reliable.

37. This master, himself a discoverer of spiritual treasures (*gter-ston*), authored a detailed defense of the ancient tantras published as *Rat-gling rtsod-bzlog.*

38. See Dudjom 1991, vol. 1, p. 917.

39. See Karmay 1975a, p. 152.

40. The eighth Karma-pa is famed for having written a furious attack on the Rnying-ma-pa, which, not being satisfactorily refuted by any of the adherents of that sect, he then proceeded to refute himself. The texts are quoted in detail in *Sog-bzlog-pa,* vol. 2, pp. 1–143.

41. *Sog-bzlog-pa,* vol. 1, pp. 261–601; vol. 2, pp. 1–143, 213–241. These works are of particular importance for the documentation they provide of the entire course of the debate from the late tenth century down to the author's own age.

42. An excellent example of this, which devotes much attention to the question of scriptural authenticity, is chapter 7 of *Bdud-'joms chos-'byung;* trans. Dudjom 1991, vol. 1, book 2, pt. 7.

43. There has been a great deal of sectarian dispute among Tibetan refugees in India. Much of this has its roots in the works of Pha-bong-kha-pa Bde-chen snying-po (1878–1937), whose visions of the Dge-lugs-pa protective deity Rdo-rje shugs-ldan seem to have entailed a commitment to oppose actively the other schools of Tibetan Buddhism and the Bon-po. While the status of the protective deity was the ostensive topic of debate initially, all aspects of sectarian rivalry have since been brought into play. The first cannonade was the Dge-lugs-pa partisan Dze-smad sprul-sku's *Bstan-srung byung-brjod.* This was answered, on behalf of the other sects, in T. G. Dhongthog's *Dus-kyi sbrang-char.* The Dge-lugs-pa response came not from Dze-smad, but from a disciple: Yon-tan-rgya-mtsho's *Gdong-lan.* At least two counterattacks then appeared: T. G. Dhongthog's *Dus-kyi me-lce*, and Bya-bral Sangs-rgyas-rdo-rje's *Rdo-rje me-char.* Yon-tan-rgya-mtsho responded in turn with his *Brgal-lan kun-khyab 'brug-sgra.* While these disputes were unfolding, H. H. the Dalai Lama disavowed the opinions of Dze-smad and his followers in a privately distributed mimeographed statement, published later by the government of Bhutan: *Skyabs-mgon bka'-slob.* The Tibetan government in exile in Dharamsala has also published a statement of the Dalai Lama's official position on these matters, *Dol-rgyal-skor gsal-bshad,* and a collection of his pertinent speeches, *Chos-skyong bka'-slob.* For a more general introduction to the controversial opinions of Pha-bong-kha-pa, as presented by his immediate disciples, see *Pha-bong-kha-pa.*

The Dge-lugs-pa sect, both in India and Tibet, has become deeply fissured over the Shugs-ldan issue. During the past several years, the dispute has also become an international cause celèbre, particularly following the gruesome slaying in February 1997 of the principal of the Buddhist dialectical college in Dharamsala, a crime that has been widely blamed on adherents of the Shugs-ldan cult. The controversy has as a result been widely discussed in the press, and on several websites. In November 1997, a special panel was convened to discuss it at the annual meeting of the American Academy of Religion. These developments are conveniently and accurately surveyed in Lopez 1998, pp. 188–196. See now also Dreyfus 1998.

44. On Tominaga Nakamoto and his contributions in this context, see Mizuno 1982, pp. 125–128. In the development of recent Tibetan scholarship, one might compare the impact of the historical writings of Dge-'dun chos-'phel (1903–1951), which met with censure

in many traditional circles during his lifetime but are now more often seen as marking the beginning of modern Tibetan historiography.

45. The colophon (906.6–7) actually says it was his eightieth, but this is an erroneous calculation, as has been indicated by Vostrikov 1970, p. 56, n. 168.

46. *Nor-bu ketaka,* 906.7. The text occupies the last thirteen folios (twenty-six pages) of the fourth volume (*nga-pa*) of his published *Collected Works* (*Gsung-'bum*).

47. Vostrikov 1970, p. 56.

48. Most of these occur in Vostrikov 1970, ch. 4, p. 205ff., concerning the descriptive catalogues (*dkar-chag*) of the canonical collections. Sum-pa mkhan-po's survey of these, *Nor-bu ketaka* (885.2–888.3), is for the purposes of historical research certainly the finest part of the work as a whole.

49. Ariane Macdonald 1968/69, p. 531; Karmay 1975a; Dargyay 1985. The last two authors make use of the *Pag Sam Jon Zang*; it is not altogether clear which work Macdonald is referring to.

50. *Nor-bu ketaka,* 884.4. The text erroneously reads *dag-mi-dgi*, which here is certainly a misprint for *dag-ma-dag* rather than for *dge-mi-dge.*

51. *Nor-bu ketaka,* 884.2–4: *blo gros dang ldan pas rgyal ba'i bka' yin min lung rigs kyis tshig don gnyis ka la phra 'dzin blos rtog dpyod zhib tu bgyis te dag ma dag gi shan legs par phyes nas ma dag pa dang lhad can dang the tshom can rnams dor nas/ gsung rab rnam dag gi glegs bu chung ngu zhig la'ang bkur stir byed pa rjed par byed pa mchod pa ri mor byed pa bsnyen bkur byed pa dang/ de'i tshig nyan pa klog pa kha ton byed pa 'dri* (sic) *ba 'drir* (sic) *'jug pa gzhan la ston pa rang de'i don nyams su len pa la brtson na phral phugs kyi don phun sum tshogs pa mtha' dag bde blag tu 'grub par 'gyur ro//*

52. *Nor-bu ketaka,* 884.4–888.3.

53. *Nor-bu ketaka,* 888.3–906.3.

54. *Nor-bu ketaka,* 888.4–898.7. Sum-pa mkhan-po is not here concerned with the entirely respectable redaction of the *gzungs-'dus* found in, e.g., volumes E and Waṃ of the Sde-dge Kanjur, but with a much lengthier version called the *Rtag-brtan gzungs-'dus,* whose compilation he dates to the age of Tāranātha (1575–1634). This collection appears to be similar to the *Gzungs-mdo'i glegs-bam.*

55. *Nor-bu ketaka,* 899.1–900.7. In the Sde-dge edition, these are contained in three appended volumes.

56. *Nor-bu ketaka,* 904.1–906.3.

57. *Ketaka'i byi-dor,* p. 71.

58. *Ketaka'i byi-dor,* pp. 1–2.

59. *Thu'u-bkwan gsung-'bum.*

60. His famous *Thu'u-bkwan grub-mtha'* evidences the extraordinary range of his interests. More important, however, is the relative impartiality he was able to achieve, despite the fact that he was no doubt limited with respect to his sources for schools other than the Dge-lugs-pa. In this, his work certainly is superior to Sum-pa's *Dpag-bsam ljon-bzang.* The *Thu'u-bkwan grub-mtha',* however, does contain one notable accusation directed against the Rnying-ma-pas: Thu'u-bkwan declares that, for all intents and purposes, the ancient oral tradition (*bka'-ma*) of the Rnying-ma-pas has become a dead lineage. *Bdud-'joms chos-'byung,* pp. 502.3–503.2, trans. Dudjom 1991, vol. 1, pp. 735–736, suggests that this passage was an interpolation in Thu'u-bkwan's text, a possibility here owing to the fact that the work was only published posthumously and so may have suffered at the hands of Thu'u-bkwan's executors. However, Rev. Snyi-shul mkhan-po, a leading Rnying-ma-pa scholar from Khams, has kindly informed me that oral tradition in far eastern Tibet considers Thu'u-bkwan's remarks to reflect accurately the state of affairs existing among the Rnying-ma-pa laity of Amdo during his own day and age. Thorough study of the sources mentioned in the two notes following may eventually contribute to some clarification here.

61. See, for example, Zhabs-dkar's *O-rgyan glegs-bam,* pp. 435.2–439.1, where the entire passage translated later (pp. 132–134) is given and attributed to Chos-kyi-rdo-rje's *Nor-bu ketaka'i byi-dor.* As an Amdo Rnying-ma-pa with a Dge-lugs-pa education writing a tract intended to promote intersectarian understanding, it is most unlikely that Zhabs-dkar would have cited the work of an extremely popular local master if that work were suspected of being forged. Oral reports circulating in some sectarian circles when I lived in India and Nepal during the early 1970s accused the then head of the Nyingmapa sect, H. H. Bdud-'joms Rinpo-che (1904–1987), of having manufactured the text, but given Zhabs-dkar's references to it during the early nineteenth century this was clearly a ludicrous charge.

62. The great 'Jam-dbyangs Mkhyen-brtse'i dbang-po (1820–1892) is quite forthright about this. See *'Jam-dbyangs Mkhyen-brtse,* p. 45.1–2. The late Rev. Mgon-po Tshe-brten, a well-known Rnying-ma-pa master from Amdo, moreover communicated to me that the fourth 'Jam-dbyangs-bzhad-pa'i-rdo-rje, the first two Lcang-skya hierarchs, and the first two Thu'u-bkwan hierarchs are all remembered as protectors of the Rnying-ma-pas in Amdo. Finally, we should recall that Thu'u-bkwan's own preferred tutelary deity (*yi-dam*) was a form of Hayagrīva whose rites belong to the Rnying-ma tradition: see *Thu'u-bkwan gsung-'bum,* vols. 6–7, *Rta-pod.*

63. Petech 1972, pp. 34, 136–137.

64. On these events in general, see Petech 1972, pp. 32–65. Note, in particular, the following remarks, on pp. 53–54: "The general policy that lay at the background of these raids was inspired by the sGo-maṅs Bla-ma Blo-bzaṅ-p'un-tshogs; it was a clear-cut programme of persecution of the rÑiṅ-ma-pa school of Lamaism. Religious persecution was till then little known in Tibet; the struggle between Reds and Yellows had been of a purely political nature. Now these strangers from the north-west, more Lamaist than the lamas, imported into Tibet a full-dress religious intolerence and persecution. All the images, statues, and books of Padmasambhava were burnt. The monasteries of rNam-rgyal-gliṅ and bSam-ldiṅ were stormed, sMin-grol-gliṅ was attacked, all of them rÑiṅ-ma-pa centres. The main centre of that sect, rDo-rje-brag, suffered the same fate; and its incarnate, the Bla-c'en, was killed. . . . Even the Bon-po sanctuary of Ri-rgyal gŚen-dar was pillaged."

65. It must be noted, however, that Sum-pa mkhan-po had a great reputation for upholding the letter of Buddhist monastic discipline, whatever his political opinions may have been. Thus, he is known to have restrained those monks under his authority who sought to take part in military conflict.

66. For Sum-pa mkhan-po's own account of the Dzungar invasions, see Yang 1969, pp. 22–23 (text) and 45–47 (translation). Sum-pa mkhan-po blames Lha-bzang Khan, whom the Dzungars deposed, for having secretly placed his faith in *rnying-chos,* which Yang literally but incorrectly translates as "old religion." Actually, the phrase means here "the doctrine of the Rnying-ma-pas."

67. He did, however, study in Central Tibet, at Sgo-mang Grwa-tshang and elsewhere, while in his early twenties.

68. Petech 1959 would want us to include Sum-pa among them without qualification, but, as my remarks here make clear, I cannot accept this assessment. On p. xv, he writes: "Sum-pa mK'an-po was a typical representative of that group of Mongol churchmen who threw in their lot wholeheartedly with China and linked their fortunes with those of the Manchu dynasty." On Tibetan religious relations with the Qing rulers, see now Rawski 1998.

69. To confirm this, refer to *Zhabs-dkar rnam-thar*; trans. Ricard 1994.

70. *Ketaka'i byi-dor,* p. 2: *deng sang gi skye bo gnad ma go ba'i cal 'drogs mkhan rnams chos la brten pa'i sdig pa'i las gsog par mi 'gyur ba'i ched du. . . .*

71. *Ketaka'i byi-dor,* p. 3: *bstan bcos 'di mdzad pa'i dgos pa ni . . . phyogs 'dir dar che ba'i rnying bon gyi cho ga 'ga' la thar 'dod kyi skyes bu 'jug pa dgag pa'i ched yin. . . .*

72. Cf. P. Williams 1983a, p. 138: "Although it should not be overemphasised, it does seem that too little attention is paid generally to the political/social context of Oriental philosophical ideas."

73. *Nor-bu ketaka,* 884.5–886.1: *bcom ldan 'das bu ram shing pas 'dzam bu'i gling du gsung gi cha shes re res kyang dus gcig tu skal ldan gyi gdul bya grangs med pa la brtsal ba'i chos phung mtha' yas pa bzhugs pa'i nang nas bka' bsdus gsum pa'i dus su mi brjed pa'i gzungs thob pa rnams kyi blo la yod pa rnams yi ger bkod/ de'i phal cher na lan tra'i dgon pa'i chos kyi gandho li gsum na bzhugs pa phyis su bstan par dgra lan gsum byung dus su phal cher nyams kyang lhag ma gang bzhugs pa las/ gangs can gyi mig lta bur gyur ba'i lo tsā ba rnams kyis bod skad du nyung shas shig snga phyir bsgyur ba la bka' 'gyur du grags pa'o//*

74. *Dpag-bsam ljon-bzang,* pp. 37–41, 51–54. Note that Sum-pa mkhan-po is unusual in his insistence, on p. 53 of that work, that "while some explain that after Śākyamuni's passing new tantras emerged, etc., this is difficult to prove." (*la las Shākya thub 'das rjes rgyud rnams gsar du byung bar bshad pa sogs ni 'thad dka'o//*)

75. *Nor-bu ketaka,* 886.1: *phyis kyi blun pos bsres bslad ma byas pa'i rnam dag. . . .*

76. *Nor-bu ketaka,* 887.2–3.

77. Lessing and Wayman 1968. Mkhas-grub-rje's enumerations of valid scriptures are scattered throughout the entire text. It is ironic that Thu'u-bkwan, in rejecting Sum-pa mkhan-po's dependence on the Tibetan catalogues as the criterion of scriptural authenticity, calls attention to Chinese texts of sūtras not available in Tibetan, and the Chinese *Śūraṃgama,* in particular. He further relates that this work was translated into Tibetan by "the Omniscient Lcang-skya." This refers to Lcang-skya Rol-pa'i rdo-rje (1717–1786). The translation in question is preserved in the Snar-thang edition of the Kanjur. (*Ketaka'i byi-dor,* p. 11: *rgya nag tu 'gyur ba'i bka' 'gyur gyi khrod na yang bod du ma 'gyur ba mang du mchis pa las/ dpa' bar 'gro ba'i mdo zhes bya ba zhig Lcang skya thams cad mkhyen pas bod skad du bsgyur bar mdzad la. . . .*)

78. But note, too, Thu'u-bkwan's critiques of these passages (*Ketaka'i byi-dor,* pp. 6–13, 31ff).

79. Vostrikov 1970, pp. 56–57, where his translation of this passage may be found.

80. *Padma bka'-thang*; trans. Toussaint 1933. On Tibetan debates concerning its authenticity, see now Blondeau 1987.

81. *Bka'-thang sde-lnga.*The most thorough discussion of this collection to date will be found in Blondeau 1971.

82. On the questions surrounding the authenticity of this work, see ch. 8 of the present volume.

83. First translated into English in Evans-Wentz 1960 (1927). Lopez 1998, ch. 2, surveys later translations and the Western reception of the so-called *Tibetan Book of the Dead.* Refer to ch. 1, n. 32 here. See now also Blezer 1997.

84. Sum-pa mkhan-po's specific objections to these three short works may be found in *Nor-bu ketaka,* 892.6–893.3.

85. *Nor-bu ketaka,* 901.1–4: *bod kyi bsam yas lha khang thog mar bzhengs skabs su byon pa'i grub chen padma saṃ bha was gangs can du bstan 'chos mang po brtsams pa'i gtam mi snang yang/ padma thang yig dang thang yig sde lnga zhes pa de'i dus su byung na yang deng sang gi de pa lhad zhugs ma zhugs la som nyi mchis/ gzhan Maṇi bka' 'bum dang/ bar do thos grol zhes pa dang/ gong smos gzungs 'dus na yod pa'i nyes pa kun sel/ rnga sgra/ ngan sngags phyir bzlog 'khor lo sogs gangs can du khyab pa'i deng sang gi rnying chos du ma'ang de dag gis brtsams pa min par tshig gi zur yan chad kyis kyang shes sla la/ rnying chos de dag phyis dus su u rgyan padma'i mtshan 'chang ba dang gzhan bka' ma gter bar* [sic] *grags pa snying kham can du mas rgyal gsung gi tshig 'ga' re bsres nas gang 'dod du sbyar bar shes rig dang ldan pa su mthong yang shes sla'o//*

86. Cf. Stein, 1972a, p. 275. But see now esp. Aris 1987.

87. Thu'u-bkwan, rather than referring directly to Sum-pa's main attack on *gter-ma*, cited here earlier, refers instead to a final summary statement: *Nor-bu ketaka*, 905. 3–4.

88. For an example of a non-Rnying-ma-pa tradition based on such teachings, see Kapstein 1980, 1992b, 1997b, on the Shangs-pa Bka'-brgyud.

89. Sum-pa himself affirms its authenticity in *Nor-bu ketaka*, 889.3. The appearance of this text in ancient times is traditionally held to mark the inception of Buddhism's presence in Tibet. See Dudjom 1991, vol. 1, pp. 508–509. Ironically, once more, the text in question is a Chinese apocryphon.

90. There may be some equivocation here: in denouncing "celestial doctrines" (*gnam-chos*), Sum-pa mkhan-po was probably referring not to texts said to have fallen physically from heaven, but rather to the popular *gter-ma* traditions known by this name, which were revealed by Gnam-chos Mi-'gyur-rdo-rje during the mid–seventeenth century and redacted by Karma Chags-med (ca. 1600–1666).

91. These verses paraphrase *Āryamañjuśrīmūlakalpa*, ch. 53, verses 456–459.

92. The original Sanskrit is preserved in *Śikṣāsamuccayaḥ*, p. 105, lines 10–14. Cf. Dōgen: "We receive sutras from mountains, rivers, and the great earth, and we preach them. We receive sutras from the sun, moon, stars, and heavenly bodies, and we preach them." Quoted in Mizuno 1982, p. 121. Interestingly, the concept of the presence of the Dharma in nature, which appears to be involved here, has become a central matter of contestation in the recent Japanese "Critical Buddhism" discussions; see now Hubbard and Swanson 1997, in particular pt. 3. Consider, too, Sigmund K. Sætreng's "ecophilosophical" interpretation of *gter-ma* in Padma Tshewang et al. 1995, pp. 139–158.

93. On Pha-dam-pa (d. 1117), see: Aziz 1979, 1980; Gyatso 1985; Edou 1996; Dudjom 1991, vol. 1, pp. 544–545, 647–648, etc.

94. Cf. *Shes-bya kun-khyab* 1981, vol. 1, p. 421.

95. It appears that this particular precept is a speciality of the Karma Bka'-brgyud-pa tradition. Its history is not discussed in Gtsang-smyon Heruka's biography of Marpa: Nālandā Translation Committee 1982. Gtsang-smyon was an adherent of the 'Brug-pa Bka'-brgyud-pa school.

96. The story of this eleventh-century revelation may be found in *Yi-dam drag-po'i dbang-bshad*, 16b–17a.

97. No further information on this tradition has become available to me.

98. Atiśa's role as a *gter-ston* is discussed in *Gter-ston brgya-rtsa*, pp. 96b.4–97a.6. See also Vostrikov 1970, pp. 28–32. The text he is said to have discovered is the well-known *Ka-chems ka-khol-ma*.

99. No further information. The pillars mentioned are all in the Lhasa Jo-khang.

100. The revelations of this figure (1161–1211), the founder of the 'Brug-pa Bka'-brgyud-pa sect, are described in *BA*, p. 668.

101. *Mtsho maṇḍal nag-po* is elsewhere mentioned as an important site for *gter-ma* discoveries. Compare Kapstein, in Goldstein and Kapstein 1998, p. 100.

102. For the story of these discoveries, which were made in 1316, see *BA*, pp. 717–720; *Gter-ston brgya-rtsa*, pp. 113a.3–b.3.

103. *Gter-ston brgya-rtsa*, pp. 105a.4–b.2. This master seems to have been associated in particular with the spread of the Yogatantras.

104. *Gter-ston brgya-rtsa*, pp. 96a.5–b.4. The lineage of the Guge prince's discoveries was said to have been transmitted through the great translator Rin-chen-bzang-po (958–1055).

105. Dge-ldan-pa, i.e., Dge-lugs-pa.

106. No further information on this is available to me at present.

107. 'Jam-dbyangs-bzhad-pa (1648–1721), the founder of Bla-brang monastery, whose successors were generally remembered among Rnying-ma-pas from Amdo as a protector of

their tradition (Mgon-po Tshe-brtan). For a very brief summary of his career, see Lokesh Chandra 1968, pp. 45–49. The Ma-cig referred to appears to be the celebrated founder of the Gcod tradition, on whom, see Gyatso 1985; Orofino 1987; Edou 1996.

108. Ngag-dbang mchog-ldan (1677–1751) was the fifty-fourth Khri Rin-po-che of Dga'-ldan monastery, his tenure having been during the years 1739–1746. See Petech 1972, pp. 105, 282.

109. *Ketaka'i byi-dor,* pp. 16–21.

110. We should not, of course, expect to find Western debates that are exactly similar to the Tibetan discussions of scripture. A few examples may be useful in order to indicate just what sorts of parallel are to be found. Recalling the argument from consensus found in the passage from Vasubandhu cited in n. 15 above, we may consider the following, from the Jewish polemical work *Niẓẓaḥon Vetus:* "One can also point out that 'a matter is established by two witnesses' (Deut. 19:15), and there are two witnesses for our Torah since both you and the Ishmaelites admit that our Torah is true. However, neither we nor the Ishmaelites admit to the truth of your Torah, and neither we nor you admit to the truth of the Torah of the Ishmaelites. Consequently, there are two witnesses that our Torah is true and that our God is true and eternal" (Berger 1979, p. 203). Regarding the development of normative doctrinal criteria for scriptural authenticity, a good illustration is found in Moses Mendelssohn (1729–1786), here representing a line of thought that can be traced back to the Jewish Averroists of Muslim Spain: "I make the following fundamental distinction between the books of the Old and New Testaments: the former are in harmony with my philosophical views, or at least do not contradict them, while the latter demand a faith I cannot profess" (Lasker, 1977, p. 38). The tendency to exclude, on a priori grounds, the types of revelation characteristic of the scriptures of one's opponents is nicely exemplified by the Byzantine polemicist Barthelemy of Edessa: "Nous, nous ne recevons pas l'Écriture de gens pris de sommeil. Car nul homme doué de sens et maître de sa raison ne néglige ses yeux sensibles et sa connaissance pour admettre les imaginations de ceux qui dorment. Ce n'est pas à des hommes endormis que Dieu demande vertu ou bon jugement. Dieu en effet n'est pas le Dieu de ceux qui dorment mais de ceux qui sont éveillés" (Khoury 1972, p. 214). For further examples from the Latin West and from Islamic authors, see Sweetman 1955, pt. 2, vol. 1, ch. 5.

111. In addition to Sweetman 1955, refer to Rescher 1967, ch. 9, and Southern 1962, pp. 92–94. The crucial comparison is to be made between Sum-pa's point-by-point critique of the texts in the *Gzungs-'dus* and Nicholas's historical approach, which is described by Southern.

112. Accounts and discussions of the *gter-ma* traditions include Aris 1989; Dudjom 1991, vol. 1, book 2, pt. 7; Germano in Goldstein and Kapstein 1998; Germano forthcoming; Gyatso 1986, 1993, 1994, 1998; Padma Tshewang et al. 1995; and Thondup Rinpoche 1986. Lopez 1998, p. 243, n. 32, remarks that "Western scholars of Tibetan Buddhism have been reluctant to directly confront the question of the historical legitimacy of *gter ma,* to consider the rediscovered texts as, in fact, works composed by their discoverers and hidden only to be revealed. . . . The fact that the pious fiction of authenticity has been tacitly maintained for so long by scholars of Tibet is itself a fascinating topic to be considered with the larger issue of mystification."

One important feature of the traditional discourse on *gter-ma* that has unfortunately been too often lost sight of is the tradition's insistence on the bibliographical attribution of the *gter-ma* to their discoverers; I have never seen a Tibetan catalogue (*dkar-chag*) or record of teachings (*gsan-yig*) that simply lumps the *gter-ma* together under their eponymous authors. Thus, for instance, the great nineteenth-century anthology of *gter-ma,* the *Rin-chen gter-mdzod chen-mo,* is arranged within each of its sections according to the historical progression of treasure-discoverers. What must be recalled, therefore, is that the tradition itself tacitly attributes the extant literary form of the *gter-ma* to the discoverer, and not to the "author."

113. Aris 1989, pp. 96–97.

Chapter 8

1. Collins 1998, pp. 121–133, introduces and clarifies this dichotomy in connection with the conception of nirvāṇa in the Pali tradition.

2. The classicist Arthur Adkins (1990), for instance, has suggested that we study, in the context of Greek thought, not the relationship between *mythos* and *philosophia,* but rather the relationship between *mythos* and *logos* within *philosophia.* Lawrence J. Hatab (1990, p. 293), also referring to classical philosophy, concludes: "[T]he idea of rationality *versus* myth is both misleading and at times simply wrong because rationality and myth can overlap. . . . [R]ationality and myth *have* coexisted, *can* coexist and, I would suggest, *should* coexist." (Emphasis in original).

3. Refer to Dundes 1984 for useful surveys of the leading attempts to define "myth," particularly in relation to the categories of "legend" and "folktale," and for general bibliographical background. For more recent work in this area, see especially Lincoln 1989, pt. 1.

4. In this context, readers may wish to reflect on the so-called Gaia-hypothesis of the British chemist James Lovelock, which regards our planet as forming a single organic system. In a popular review of scientific work on Gaia, *The Economist,* vol. 317, no. 7686/7687 (December 22, 1990), 107, commented that "the strongest resistance to Gaia comes from those whose faith is grounded in another metaphor—'natural selection.' Nature is not a goddess who chooses, as Darwin knew full well. But the metaphor of choice was the best way to express his views. . . . Darwin's metaphor provided a great insight into the workings of the world. *If Gaia manages to do the same*—something which looks unlikely at present, but not impossible—then the objections to Dr Lovelock's metaphor will be forgotten, too." (Emphasis added.)

5. Slusser 1982, vol. 1, pp. 364–365.

6. See, in particular, "Pragmatism's Conception of Truth" and "The Will to Believe," both in James 1948.

7. Refer to ch. 4, n. 17, and ch. 7, n. 43. My remarks in the following paragraph are based upon my own observations and conversations with regard to the Rdo-rje Shugs-ldan dispute in recent years.

8. Besides these examples, consider Daniel 1990, where the topic investigated is the virtually ubiquitous presence of myth in early modern philosophy. Daniel's work develops a conception of "myth" essentially similar to that which I am exploring here. In his introduction, p. 3, he writes, "What I mean by myth is a particular mode or group of functions, operative within discourse, that highlight how communication and even thought are themselves possible. Certain functions of discourse are mythic insofar as they reveal how discourse itself is possible."

9. In this chapter I have used the published facsimile edition of the Punakha version of the *Maṇi bka'-'bum.* The blocks for this edition were apparently carved at the request of a certain Mnga'-ris sgrub-chen Ngag-dbang chos-'phel, the disciple of Ngag-dbang bstan-'dzin rab-rgyas (*Maṇi bka'-'bum,* II. 708). Dr. Michael Aris kindly informed me that while the former remains unidentified, "his master . . . was the fourth *'Brug-sDe-srid* (regn. 1680–1695, lived 1638–1696). He was the first in the line of the *Khri-sprul* or *Bla-ma khri-pa* (of which there have been six). The *Lho'i chos-'byung* makes him the first rGyal-tshab, the official stand-ins for (sometimes the incarnations of) the 1st *Zhabs-drung*. He was one of the greatest and most effective Bhutanese rulers. There is an extremely long biography by Ngag-dbang lhun-grub, dated 1720 . . ." (correspondence, July 18, 1980). The Punakha edition is based on an earlier edition from Gung-thang in Mnga'-ris (*Maṇi bka'-'bum,* II. 617), an example of which is preserved in the National Archives of Nepal. I am grateful to Franz-Karl Ehrhard for calling my attention to this rare print.

10. *Thugs-rje-chen-po spyan-ras-gzigs kyi dbang-phyug.*

11. Vostrikov 1970, p. 52.

12. Kőrös 1984, p. 81. Among earlier studies see also Bacot 1934–1935.

13. Vostrikov 1970, p. 55.

14. Ariane Macdonald 1968/69, p. 528.

15. Refer to Aris 1979, pp. 8–24; Blondeau 1984a; Gyatso 1987; Alexander Macdonald 1984a; Per Sørensen 1994. A brief hagiography of Nyang-ral Nyi-ma 'od-zer will be found translated in Dudjom 1991, vol. 1, pp. 755–760.

16. The basic structure of the *Maṇi bka'-'bum* is revealed in its *dkar-chag* (*Maṇi bka'-'bum* I. 9–23). It seems that this *dkar-chag* is of some antiquity and is identical to the *Yer-pa'i dkar-chag* referred to by *Maṇi bka'-'bum*'s editors (I. 19, *mchan*). A similar *dkar-chag* served as the basis for the Fifth Dalai Lama's discussion of the contents of the *Maṇi bka'-'bum*: *Lnga-pa'i gsan-yig*, vol. 3, plates 130–153. *Lnga-pa'i gsan-yig*'s discussion is, for all intents and purposes, a detailed commentary on the *dkar-chag* and reflects the Dalai Lama's great personal interest in the *Maṇi bka'-'bum*. It is noteworthy that at least one group of texts listed in the *dkar-chag* that was not available to the redactors of the *Maṇi bka'-'bum* (II. 616–617) could not be located by the Great Fifth either (*Lnga-pa'i gsan-yig*, 149). The Dalai Lama also mentions one group of texts (*Lnga-pa'i gsan-yig*, 139–140) that are not to be found in the *dkar-chag* but seem to have been in circulation in connection with the *Maṇi bka'-'bum*. For useful summaries of the *Maṇi bka'-'bum*'s contents see also Vostrikov 1970, pp. 53–55; Ariane Macdonald 1968/69, pp. 527–528.

17. In *Maṇi bka'-'bum*, it forms a separate cycle (II. 619–711), where it is entitled *'Phags-pa nam-mkha'i rgyal-po'i mngon-rtogs sogs phran 'ga'*. The title *Gab-pa mngon-phyung gi skor* is given in the *dkar-chag* (I. 22).

18. See esp. Karmay 1988b; Dudjom 1991, vol. 1, pp. 821–824.

19. *las dang skal-bar ldan-pa.*

20. *gtsang-khang byang-ma'i rta-mgrin gyi zhabs 'og-tu sbas.*

21. *gnod-sbyin Nā-ga Ku-be-ra'i dar-sham-'og-gi brla-g.yas-par sbas.*

22. The Tibetan titles of these texts are: *Thugs-rje-chen-po stong-rtsa'i sgrub-thabs, Gab-pa mngon-phyung, Sangs-rgyas stong-rtsa'i bskyed-rdzogs, Thugs-dam mthong-ba'i phan-yon,* and *Srong-btsan 'da'-kha'i bka'-chems.*

23. *Thugs-rje-chen-pos rjes-bzung.*

24. In Dudjom 1991, vol. 2, p. 70, n. 995, it is argued that the correct dating should be 1136–1204. As van der Kuijp 1994 shows, however, Śākyaśrī's arrival in Tibet in 1204 corresponds to the consecration of Nyang-ral's memorial stūpa, and not to his death. The dates 1124–1192 are therefore to be preferred.

25. *Lnga-pa'i gsan-yig*, vol. 3, p. 130. This is a restatement of part of the *dkar-chag* (*Maṇi bka'-'bum*, I. 21–22). It is of interest to note that some of the masters mentioned in connection with the compilations of the *Maṇi bka'-'bum* are also mentioned in connection with the cult of the Lhasa Jo-khang. See *Lha-ldan dkar-chag*, pp. 78–79.

26. Blondeau 1984, p. 81, rightly emphasizes the uncertainty with which the Fifth Dalai Lama proposes this.

27. *Lnga-pa'i gsan-yig*, vol. 3, p. 131.

28. *Bshad-'grel chen-mo*, in *Maṇi bka'-'bum*, I. 498, 584. A.-M. Blondeau has suggested to me that the present version of the *Great Chronicle* is of doubtful attribution. See Blondeau 1984, esp. n. 19.

29. *Maṇi bka'-'bum*, I. 504.

30. Ariane Macdonald has advanced the thesis that Nyi-ma 'od-zer and Mnga'-bdag Myang (= Nyang)-ral were, in fact, two distinct persons, for the latter was used as a familial title among Nyi-ma 'od-zer's descendants. See Ariane Macdonald 1971, p. 203, n. 59. However, the mention of the *siddha* Dngos-grub in connection with the lineage of the *bka'-brgyad* as well as that of the *Maṇi bka'-'bum* leads me to believe that such a view may not, in this in-

stance, be tenable, though we cannot rule out the possibility that one of Nyang-ral's sons has been conflated with his father. See *Gter-ston brgya-rtsa,* pp. 371–372; Dudjom 1991, vol. 1, p. 758. *Nyang-ral,* p. 501, summarizes the *gter-ma* discoveries, possibly including those forming the early portions of the Maṇi bka'-'bum.

31. *Lnga-pa'i gsan-yig,* vol. 3, p. 151, notes that he was a *bhikṣu.* It appears that the Fifth Dalai Lama had access to some specific information about the lesser known figures in the Maṇi bka'-'bum's lineage.

32. *Maṇi bka'-'bum,* II. 651.

33. It should be noted that the *dkar-chag* seems not to have originally listed any of Shakya-'od's discoveries, but that the account of them forms an appended discussion (*Maṇi bka'-'bum* I. 22). Perhaps the "original" *Maṇi bka'-'bum* consisted solely of the discoveries of Dngos-grub and Mnga'-bdag Nyang, as assembled by the latter or one of his school.

34. Compare, for instance, *Shes-bya kun-khyab,* vol. 1, p. 433.

35. *lha'i sgrub-thabs.*

36. *zhal-gdams kyi rtsa-ba-rnams.*

37. *'Phags-pa Spyan-ras-gzigs-kyi bka' dngos.*

38. *pha-chos rnying-ma.*

39. Tāranātha, *Khrid-brgya'i brgyud-pa'i lo-rgyus*, in *Gdams-ngag-mdzod,* vol. 12, pp. 356–357.

40. Among *gter-ma*, the *Maṇi bka'-'bum* is peculiar with respect to its punctuation: it makes use of the ordinary *shad*, instead of the *visarga*-like *gter-shad*. It is of interest to compare, too, Tāranātha's mild suggestion that the treasure-discoverers composed, rather than found, some parts of the *Maṇi bka'-'bum* with Sum-pa Mkhan-po Ye-shes dpal-'byor's vociferous remarks (Vostrikov 1970, pp. 56–57). Cf. ch. 7 here, p. 132.

41. This is confirmed, for instance, by the Central Tibetan *Lnga-pa'i gsan-yig*, the Bhutanese *Maṇi bka'-'bum*, and the many references found throughout *Phyag-rdzogs-zung-'jug*. Karma Chags-med, the author of the latter, who hailed from Nang-chen in Khams, was active during the first half of the seventeenth century.

The exact meaning of the title *Maṇi bka'-'bum* is somewhat problematic; see Vostrikov 1970, pp. 52–53 and Ariane Macdonald 1968/69, p. 527. The biographies of Guru Chos-kyi dbang-phyug (1212–1270) were perhaps the first works to use this title and may provide the key to its precise interpretation. My own rendering is similar to that of A.-M. Macdonald: "The Collected Works (*Bka'-'bum*) of King Srong-btsan sgam-po Concerning the Six-Syllable Mantra (*Oṃ Maṇipadme Hūṃ*)."

42. *Chos-skyong-ba'i rgyal-po Srong-btsan sgam-po'i bka'-'bum.*

43. *Thugs-rje-chen-po yi-ge drug-pa'i chos-skor: Maṇi bka'-'bum,* I. 1, 10. This title seems to confirm the interpretation of the title *Maṇi bka'-'bum* given in n. 41 here.

44. *Rgyal-po-lugs kyi spyan-ras-gzigs.*

45. Dudjom 1991, vol. 1, p. 578.

46. For instance, Bu-ston, in Obermiller 1931–1932, pp. 183–185. Bu-ston's account certainly has some affinity with that of the *Maṇi bka'-'bum*, though there is no reason to assume that he based himself on that source directly. See, too, *BA,* p. 1006, and Per Sørensen 1994.

47. *Thu'u-bkwan grub-mtha',* pp. 57–58. Passages such as this one, found in the work of a leading Dge-lugs-pa hierarch, suggest that the *Maṇi bka'-'bum* did not meet with the condemnation in Dge-lugs-pa circles that the scholar who encounters Sum-pa Mkhan-po's opinion (n. 40, this chapter) may suppose. See, for example, Ariane Macdonald 1968/69, p. 531. Discussions with a number of Tibetan scholars, notably Ven. Dezhung Rinpoche, who himself studied the *Maṇi bka'-'bum* under the Dge-lugs-pa *dge-bshes* Blo-bzang-chos-kyi-dga'-ba, have convinced me that the Great Fifth's love of the *Maṇi bka'-'bum* made a lasting impression on the cult of Srong-btsan sgam-po–Avalokiteśvara within the Dge-lugs-pa sect.

48. *Maṇi bka'-'bum,* I. 22, and *Lnga-pa'i gsan-yig,* vol. 3, p. 131. According to these texts it was Padmasambhava who revealed to Khri srong-lde'u-btsan the works of his ancestor.

49. These issues are taken up at length in Ariane Macdonald 1971 and Imaeda 1979. See also Blondeau 1970; Stein 1986a; and ch. 4 of the present book. There is considerable evidence for the Avalokiteśvara cult in the banner paintings and murals of Dunhuang, but it is difficult to interpret with certainty the ramifications for Tibet. In at least one instance, an exquisite maṇḍala of Avalokiteśvara in the form of Amoghapāśa preserved at the Musée Guimet (MG 26466, reproduced in Giès and Cohen 1995, cat. no. 283), one is tempted to speculate upon a Tibetan connection, although there is unfortunately no evidence linking it positively with Tibet. More telling, perhaps, is Dunhuang cave 14, where Avalokiteśvara in his various forms is the figure emphasized, but where this is clearly due to work that postdates the period of Tibetan occupation. The mural that remains from the Tibetan period is of Vairocana, with whom, as I have argued earlier (ch. 4), Khri Srong-lde'u-btsan and his successors were personally identified. I am inclined to hold that the post-eleventh-century Avalokiteśvara cult drew some of its inspiration from the earlier Vairocana cult and absorbed aspects of it, so that there may be a certain poetic justice in the transformation of Dunhuang cave 14.

50. Lalou 1953. Texts related to the Avalokiteśvara cult that are listed here include numbers 79, 114, 157, 316, 343, 347, 352, 366, 388, 410, 440, 459, 460.

51. My remarks on the *Rnying-ma Bka'-ma* are based on conversations with the late H. H. Bdud-'joms Rin-po-che and with Rev. Mkhan-po Thub-bstan. Avalokiteśvara is one of the eight bodhisattvas in the *maṇḍalas* of the *Sgyu-'phrul zhi-khro,* which is associated with the *Guhyagarbhatantra,* and in the intiatory cycle of the *Mdo dgongs-pa 'dus-pa,* the foremost *Anuyoga-tantra.* In the latter he is also found, with Mañjuśrī and Vajrapāṇi, as one of the Lords of the Three Clans (*rigs-gsum mgon-po*). Avalokiteśvara's wrathful aspect, Hayagrīva, occupies a position of great importance in the *Bka'-ma* tradition, particularly in the *Bka'-brgyad* cycle. When I state that the *Bka'-ma* includes "authentically ancient material," I do so with the understanding that the many threads that are woven together there cannot at present be satisfactorily sorted out. The history of the *Bka'-ma* as seen from a traditional standpoint is recounted in Dudjom 1991, vol. 1, book 2, pt. 5.

52. *Shes-bya kun-khyab,* vol. 1, p. 433. Repeated verbatim in Dudjom 1991, vol. 1, p. 511.

53. These are the *Bka'-gdams lha-bzhi'i spyan-ras-gzigs, Skyer-sgang-lugs kyi spyan-ras-gzigs,* and *Dpal-mo-lugs kyi spyan-ras-gzigs.* Their lineages and precepts have been masterfully summarized by Jo-nang Rje-btsun Kun-dga' grol-mchog: *Gdams-ngag-mdzod,* vol. 12, pp. 252, 256–257, 394–395, 430–432.

54. See *Thugs-rje chen-po dang phyag-rgya chen-po zung-'jug-tu nyams-su-len tshul rjes-gnang dang bcas-pa,* in *Sgrub-thabs-kun-btus,* vol. 3, fol. 1–8; and *BA,* pp. 1006–1046. The *Thugs-rje chen-po rgyal-ba rgya-mtsho* introduced by Ras-chung-pa became particularly popular among the Rnying-ma-pas, and above all among the Karma Bka'-brgyud-pas, whose hierarchs adopted it as their *yi-dam.* There is also a tradition of the *Thugs-rje chen-po rgyal-ba rgya-mtsho* that is traced back to Mitrayogin and is at present a specialty of the Dge-lugs-pa.

55. *Phyag-rdzogs zung-'jug,* p. 265. Compare the tale of La-stod Dmar-po, given in *BA,* pp. 1026–1029, who on requesting teachings in India, probably during the late eleventh century, the very period with which we are here concerned, receives the six-syllable mantra from the master Rdo-rje-gdan-pa and then thinks to himself, "This mantra is repeated throughout Tibet by all old men, women, and even children. This doctrine seems to be a common one." A relatively early Bka'-gdams-pa text, *Bka'-gdams pha-chos,* p. 626, also insists that Avalokiteśvara "certainly is the divine portion of Tibet" (*bod-kyi lha-skal-nyid-du nges*).

56. *Maṇi bka'-'bum,* I. 87.

57. See ch. 4.

58. Ariane Macdonald 1971, p. 388.

59. Ariane Macdonald 1968/69, p. 532.

60. Vostrikov 1970, pp. 28–32, 67–78. Per Sørensen 1994. The *Bka'-chens ka-khol-ma* is traditionally said to have been revealed by Atiśa, a tradition to which *Nyang-ral,* p. 501, already seems to refer.

61. *Maṇi bka'-'bum,* I. 192–193.

62. *Phyag-rdzogs zung-'jug,* pp. 268–269. *Mkhas-pa'i dga'-ston,* vol. 2, p. 894, relates this directly to precedents established by Mnga'-bdag Myang and Guru Chos-dbang. On Karma Pakshi, see, in the present work, ch. 6.

63. The degree to which even ascetics were affected by this unrest is clearly indicated in *Maṇi bka'-'bum,* I. 525, where the yogin is advised to equip his retreat with weaponry. Traditions relating to the Bka'-brgyud Bla-ma Zhang (1122–1193; see D. Jackson 1994) exemplify the martial exploits of certain yogins. The hagiography of Guru Chos-dbang (Dudjom 1991, vol. 1, pp. 764–765; Gyatso 1994) also alludes to the involvement of certain *gter-ston* in military crafts.

64. *Avalokiteśvara-guṇa-karaṇḍavyūha*, p. 265. See, too, the excellent study by Regamey 1971.

65. *Avalokiteśvara-guṇa-karaṇḍavyūha*, pp. 288–292. The *locus classicus* for Atiśa's reported teaching of this vision is found in the *lha-bzhi-la ji-ltar gdams-pa'i le'u* of the *Bka'-gdams pha-chos*, pp. 624–635. The relevant verses may be found quoted in *Phyag-rdzogs zung-'jug,* p. 258. See also n. 53 in the present chapter.

66. *Maṇi bka'-'bum,* I. 34.

67. *Maṇi bka'-'bum,* I. 35–36.

68. *brjod-du-med-pa'i yang brjod-du-med-pa.*

69. *Bkod-pa bar-ma,* consisting of one million worlds of four continents each surrounding a Mount Meru.

70. *dpag-tu-med-pa'i yang dpag-tu-med-pa.*

71. *ba-la-ha,* from Skt. Balāha, the wondrous horse that saved the merchant Sinhala. See Holt 1991, pp. 49–50, for a summary of the story.

72. The green Tārā is identified with the Chinese princess of Wencheng, while the white goddess, Bhṛkuṭī, is the princess of Nepal.

73. *Maṇi bka'-'bum,* I. 29–30.

74. *Maṇi bka'-'bum,* I. 511–2, II. 265–266, 279. (In notes 75 through 82, it is not my intention to provide a comprehensive catalogue of relevant passages, but rather to signal representative examples.)

75. *theg-pa rim-pa dgu. Maṇi bka'-'bum,* I. 496–497, 511–512.

76. *bden-gnyis. Maṇi bka'-'bum,* II. 584–586.

77. *phyag-rgya chen-po. Maṇi bka'-'bum,* II. 288–289, 531, 579–582.

78. *rdzogs-pa chen-po. Maṇi bka'-'bum,* II. 288, 582–584.

79. *lam-rim. Maṇi bka'-'bum,* II. 182–234.

80. *gzhi-lam-'bras-bu gsum. Maṇi bka'-'bum,* I. 514–519.

81. *lta-sgom-spyod gsum. Maṇi bka'-'bum,*. II. 29–30, 279–280, 396–397.

82. *sku-gsum. Maṇi bka'-'bum,* II. 280. More often, however, the *Maṇi bka'-'bum* speaks of the *sku-drug*, six *kāyas*, e.g., II. 26–27, and elsewhere.

83. *man-ngag 'phrul-gyi dum-bu.*

84. *Maṇi bka'-'bum,* I. 18.

85. *gang-zag nyams-su len-pa re-re'i cha-rkyen. Maṇi bka'-'bum,* I. 514.

86. *rang-bzhin-gyi gnas-na bzhugs.*

87. *Maṇi bka'-'bum,* I. 20–21.

88. *Gdams-ngag-mdzod,* vols. 2, 3. The intricate teaching of the Bka'-gdams-pas requires careful study. My statement here is a tentative one, based on the reading of such sources as those brought together by Kong-sprul in the magnificent anthology herein cited.

89. *Maṇi bka'-'bum* I. 470: *rig-pa'i rtsal-kha, ye-shes so-ma rgyun-mi-'chad-pa.*

90. *Maṇi bka'-'bum* II. 27–28.

91. *stong-nyid snying-rje'i snying-po-can,* Skt. *śunyatā karuṇagarbhā.*

92. Having at one time or another attended discourses on Avalokiteśvara given by representatives of all the major Tibetan Buddhist traditions, I cannot but observe that the unifying features of this cult are far more apparent than the distinguishing features of the various lineages involved. It would seem that this unity of the cult is what moved 'Gos Lo-tsā-ba to give it separate treatment in *BA,* pp. 1006–1046, Kong-sprul to anthologize it separately in *Gdams-ngag-mdzod,* vol. 11, and Karma Chags-med to combine freely precepts from its different lineages in his *Phyag-rdzogs zung-'jug.*

93. Kunsang 1990, 1993, translates selections from Nyang-ral's *gter-ma*-s relating to Padmasambhava. Though Gu-ru Chos-dbang is not known to have discovered a biography or historical record along these lines, his liturgical cycle, the *Bla-ma-gsang-'dus,* was undoubtably among the most influential of the early rites for the worship of the precious master.

94. Bischoff 1978 surveys some of the grounds for doubt here.

95. Paul 1982, p. 81, thus rightly remarks that "Guru Rimpoche . . . in many ways, is to be understood as the 'king' of the Sherpas, in that he plays, in a divine, symbolic way, the same ritual role that kings often play in providing the 'center' for a social-cultural system."

96. See ch. 1, nn. 61–62.

97. On this (possibly mythical) tantra, see Mayer 1996, p. 66, n. 1.

98. *Sba-bzhed,* p. 32. According to the remarks of Pa-sangs-dbang-'dus and Hildegard Diemberger, *dBa'-bzhed* (ch. 2, n. 15), pp. 54–59, Padmasambhava's role is apparently even thinner than this.

99. *Sba-bzhed,* p. 81.

100. Above all, the *Zangs-gling-ma,* translated in Kunsang 1993.

101. This is demonstrated by the commentary of the eleveneth-century master Rong-zom-pa, in *Rong-zom gsung-btus.*

102. Refer to Eastman 1983.

103. On the Tibetan cult of Vajrakīla and its literature, see now in particular Boord 1993; Mayer 1996. Traditional accounts of some of the major Vajrakīla lineages are given in Dudjom 1991, vol. 1, pp. 710–716. See also the more detailed *Dpal rdo-rje-phur-pa'i lo-rgyus* in *Sog-bzlog-pa,* vol. 1, pp. 111–201.

104. The history of the early Phur-pa tradition within the 'Khon family is summarized in *Sa-skya'i gdung-rabs,* pp. 14–15.

105. This small and highly interesting text was first noticed by M. Lalou and was later edited and translated by Bischoff and Hartman 1971. I have interpreted the text somewhat differently than they have in a number of places.

106. The manuscript does include a marginal annotation specifying a tiger year, but it is not possible even to guess with which tiger year during the ninth and tenth centuries this may correspond.

107. In this and the following paragraph, for the convenience of nonspecialist readers, I have transcribed the personal and place names as pronounced, where possible using their current forms and not those of *PT* 44 itself. The orthography as given in the manuscript is noted in the index.

108. *PT* 44, 1b–12b.

109. Dudjom 1991, vol. 1, p. 472.

110. Thus, the modern account of Dudjom 1991, vol. 1, p. 481, includes a reference to "four female earth spirits," surely a recollection of the fourfold *Bse* goddess. The porterage of the texts is recounted on p. 472. The narration of the occult powers realized by the adepts (p. 714), though mentioning different persons by name, is striking in its overall similarity to the account found in *PT* 44: "By brandishing the kīla at a brushfire in a sandalwood forest, the great master Padmasambhava restored the forest. By brandishing it at the flooding waters

of the Ganges, Vimalamitra fixed the river's course. By brandishing it at Mount Trakar Kongcen, the Newar Śīlamañju made the rock face crumble to pieces. By thrusting it at the tracks of a wolf, the venerable lady Kharcenza caused the wolf to be swept away in an avalanche. By raising it against the crow which had carried off his rosary, Menu Gyelwei Nyingpo made the bird fall to earth. And by inflicting it upon the yak-hair tents of the Mön army, Lo Pelgi Lodrö overpowered them. In these and other instances, these masters, thrusting the kīla at both enemies and obstacles, were invincible, even in the face of powerful magic." Finally, the mention of Padmasambhava's scattering of gold, an important motif in tales of great tantric masters, is usually associated with his first entry into Tibet, as it is in Dudjom 1991, vol. 1, p. 513. On this theme see also Kapstein 1992b, n. 19.

111. See n. 98 in this chapter.

112. Thus Dudjom 1991, vol. 1, pp. 710–712, enumerates seven lineages specializing in Vajrakīla, of which at least five must have been active at around the beginning of the eleventh century, and this list is certainly not exhaustive.

113. A caveat is required here, for the Padmasambhava cult, while celebrating the monarch Khri Srong-lde'u-btsan also diminishes him by emphatically depicting him as performing obeisance before Padmasambhava. The cult is also frequently at odds with the old ministerial clans, so that its allegiance to the imperial hierarchy is partial at most. The traditions surrounding Srong-btsan-sgam-po seem overall to affirm the imperial order with less reservation, and to treat the ministers as the ruler's disciples and confidants.

114. *Ba-dzra-gu-ru'i phan-yon,* attributed to the discovery of Karma-gling-pa, mid-fourteenth century. Assuming that this dating is approximately correct, the text is of great interest for, among other things, its protest against the current situation in China, Tibet, and Mongolia, and the deleterious effects of this on Tibet.

115. *Oṃ Āḥ Hūṃ Vajraguru Padmasiddhi Hūṃ!*

116. From the *gter-ma* of Ratna-gling-pa, cited in Dudjom 1991, vol. 1, p. 744.

117. Cf. the remarks of Ortner 1989, pp. 33–35, on "egalitarianism and hierarchy: the core contradiction" in Sherpa society. See also Samuel 1993, pp. 123–125, on "horizontal relationships" even within Central Tibet. Of course, I do not mean to suggest that there was an absence of hierarchy on the Tibetan periphery, only that in many instances hierarchy seems to have been more fluid in these regions than in the center.

118. For the example of the authority and prestige accruing to a contemporary *gter-ston,* see Germano in Goldstein and Kapstein 1998. Mkhan-po 'Jigs-phun, the subject of Germano's study, is, however, a rare example of a *gter-ston* who has chosen to remain a monk. But even in this case, some element of the aggrandizement of family power may be seen, for the community of nuns associated with his monastic settlement is directed by a niece who has now herself been recognized as an incarnation.

119. Aris 1989, pp. 105–106.

120. Refer to Karmay 1988b, and Dudjom 1991, vol. 1, pp. 683–684, 821–824, for a glimpse of the Great Fifth's Rnying-ma-pa persona. Throughout the enormous historical and biographical corpus produced by the Fifth and by his spiritual son and regent, Sde-srid Sangs-rgyas-rgya-mtsho, one is struck, too, by the abundant use of prophetic passages culled from the entire range of the *gter-ma* literature in elaborating the ideological justification of the Great Fifth's rule. It is clear that these figures understood very well the enduring authority of those who channeled the voices of the empire.

Chapter 9

1. Aspects of the development of the Buddhist tantric Rudra myth have now been masterfully discussed in Davidson 1991 and Stein 1995. See now also Mayer 1998. For much on

the background of the myth in Indian religions generally, see Hiltebeitel 1989. For interesting speculations on the evolution of the Samantabhadra myth, refer to Germano forthcoming.

2. For an extended example of the traditional polemic concerning authenticity, see Dudjom 1991, vol. 1, book 2, pt. 7.

3. Dudjom 1991, vol. 1, book 2, pt. 2.

4. See, for instance, Karma Pakshi's *Rgya-mtsho mtha'-yas,* vol. 1, p. 402. Nonetheless, Karma Pakshi, like both *Mun-pa'i go-cha,* which work he is probably following, and *Dgongs-'dus 'grel-chen,* is primarily interested in the symbolic dimensions of the Rudra tale.

5. *Bstan-srung rnam-thar*, pp. 4–30. He is concerned here with the variant Buddhist tantric forms of the story of the defeat of Mahādeva (Śiva) by the Buddha or members of the Buddha's retinue, which is clearly the antecedent of the Rudra episode. For a very influential version of the story that is clearly related to that of Rudra, refer to Snellgrove 1987, pp. 134–141.

6. For the general background of Tibetan history during this period, refer to Shakabpa 1967, ch. 4–5; Petech 1990; van der Kuijp 1991.

7. This is particularly evident in the writings of Nyang-ral Nyi-ma 'od-zer (1124–1196) and his associates, on which see esp. Ruegg 1989, pp. 74–92; Kunsang 1990, 1993; Dudjom 1991, pp. 755–759; ch. 8 in this book.

8. On the life and background of Klong-chen-pa, see Guenther 1975–1976, vol. 1, pp. xiii–xxv; Thondup 1989, pp. 145–188; Dudjom 1991, pp. 575–596. All of these accounts may be traced back to the biography authored by Klong-chen-pa's disciple Chos-grags bzang-po. A critical interpretation will be found in Germano forthcoming.

9. This is very clear in the biographical accounts, such as those cited in the preceding note, and in his own poetical works: see, for instance, the colophons found in *Klong-chen gsung-thor-bu,* vol. 1, pp. 95, 137, 149; vol. 2, p. 622. On the influence of Sanskrit *kāvya* in Tibet, see Kapstein in press.

10. There does exist a commentary on the *Uttaratantraśāstra* (*rgyud bla-ma'i bstan-bcos*), by one Blo-gros-mtshungs-med, that has sometimes been attributed to him, though this attribution is doubtful. Reports have recently circulated of the discovery of a manuscript in Tibet that seems surely to be his commentary on Dharmakīrti's *Pramāṇavārttika.*

11. Concerning the major writings, refer to Guenther 1975–1976, vol. 1, pp. xvi–xx; Thondup 1989, pp. 149–58.

12. E.g., Dudjom 1991, vol. 1, pp. 775–779. On O-rgyan-gling-pa's writings, see in particular Blondeau 1971, 1980.

13. *Padma bka'-thang,* Toussaint 1933.

14. Refer to Blondeau 1971.

15. Dudjom 1991, vol. 1, p. 777. The strange tale of the fate of O-rgyan-gling-pa's corpse also has powerful political implications: Dudjom 1991, vol. 1, pp. 777–778.

16. Dudjom 1991, vol. 1, pp. 294–334, provides an extended doxographical account. For historical background, see Karmay 1988a.

17. *Klong-chen gsung-thor-bu,* vol. 1, p. 261. A complete translation of the text from which this passage is taken appears in Berzin, Sherpa Tulku, and Kapstein 1987.

18. *Theg-mchog-mdzod,* fol. 202b–221b.

19. It is important to note, however, that the myth of Samantabhadra is not, and by the Rnying-ma-pa is never taken to be, an actual creation myth: Samantabhadra is neither a creator god nor a demiurge; there is no divine volition posited, through which the ground is thought to give rise to the primordial buddha and to sentient beings. Whereas, in the quotation given later, the ground is itself made to speak in the voice of the original buddha, there is no evidence to suggest that the tradition has ever regarded this to be other than a metaphorical representation. Nevertheless, some contemporary Western scholars have suggested there to be a quasi-theistic standpoint disclosed in certain aspects of Rnying-ma-pa discourse. See, for

instance, Dargyay 1985. I am personally inclined to regard any attribution of literally intended theism to the Rnying-ma-pas as erroneous.

20. *Theg-mchog-mdzod,* fol. 3b–4a.

21. *Theg-mchog-mdzod,* fol. 406b–407a.

22. Lhalungpa 1977, p. 42.

23. Davidson 1991; Stein 1995.

24. Cf. esp. the earliest version, the Buddha's struggle with Namuci, in the *Suttanipāta,* translated in Norman 1985.

25. See Stein 1995. In the Sde-dge edition of the Tibetan Buddhist canon, the *Mdo dgongs-pa 'dus-pa* is given as text no. 829 (Tohoku Catalogue), where the Rudra myth is detailed in ch. 20–31. Commentary may be found in *Mun-pa'i go-cha,* ch. 20–31; *Dgongs-'dus 'grel-chen*, ch. 20–31; and *Rgya-mtsho mtha'-yas*, pp. 401ff. Tibetan traditions concerning the controversial history of the transmission of the *Mdo dgongs-pa 'dus-pa* are detailed in Dudjom 1991, vol. 1, book 2, pt. 5.

26. *Padma bka'-thang,* pp. 29–56; Toussaint 1933, 24–42. The proper names here are transcribed as they are given in the Tibetan text. These names are themselves quite problematic: it is clear that O-rgyan-gling-pa is often engaging in wordplay in his composition of them, and Toussaint has attempted to reflect this in his French translation. Nevertheless, some of Toussaint's interpretations are based on unusual readings that have little textual support (e.g., Ngan-phag, "Evil Pig," for the better-attested Dan-phag, the precise signification of which is uncertain). Because these questions have little bearing on the present discussion, I have preferred not to consider them at length here.

27. The exoteric teachings of the sūtras and the esoteric teachings of the Buddhist tantras.

28. That is, as an adherent of the mantra-vehicle and as a monk. It is of interest to compare here the analysis of the Newari Buddhist priesthood of the Kathmandu Valley in Gellner 1992.

29. Various enumerations of five yogas are found in Rnying-ma-pa works. See, e.g., Dudjom 1991, pp. 280–281, 369.

30. Mkhan-po Nus-ldan-rdo-rje, in his *Dgongs-'dus 'grel-chen,* pp. 630–635, gives two alternative enumerations of the "four matters": in their ordinary sense, they refer to the four prohibited actions of murder, theft, falsehood, and sexual misconduct; esoterically, they are the major categories of tantric vows that are abused when practiced literally and externally.

31. Morality, meditation, and insight.

32. Paul 1982, pp. 53–58. The brief discussion of the myth found in Guenther 1984, 145–146, is surprisingly superficial.

33. Paul 1982, pp. 153–154.

34. This is curiously suggested by a comment found in Bsnubs-chen's *Mun-pa'i go-cha,* pp. 262–263, that "Rudra having been subject to a violation of voluntary obligation, sentient beings became subject to a natural violation." (*rudra ni bcas pa'i ltung bar gyur pas 'gro ba rang bzhin gyis ltung bar gyur to.*) Mkhan-po Nus-ldan-rdo-rje's *Dgongs-'dus 'grel-chen,* p. 660, however, emends this to read: "Rudra was subject to both natural violation and violation of voluntary obligation, and sentient beings became subject to natural violation." (*rudra ni rang bzhin dang bcas pa'i ltung ba gnyis kar gyur la, 'gro ba rnams ni rang bzhin gyi ltung bar gyur to.*) The notion of "natural violation" (Skt. *prakṛtisāvadyam*) in normative Buddhist doctrine has nothing at all to do with Western Christian concepts of "original sin." Natural violations are those that are regarded as being intrinsically wrong, such as murder, quite apart from the specifications of any vows or religious commitments one has voluntarily assumed. Remarkable here is the suggestion found in Bsnubs-chen's wording, and avoided by Mkhan-po Nus-ldan-rdo-rje, that Rudra's violation is perhaps causally related to that of sentient beings.

35. *Ru-tra'i smre-sngags.*

36. These are the obscuration with respect to knowledge (Skt. *jñeyāvaraṇa*) and the obscuration consisting of the psychological and emotional "afflictions" (Skt. *kleśāvaraṇa*).

37. Refer to the commentarial sources cited in n. 25 in this chapter. Throughout his *Dgongs-'dus 'grel-chen*, Mkhan-po Nus-ldan-rdo-rje takes pains to specify which sections of the text he regards to be interpretable (*drang-don*) and which definitive (*nges-don*). His approach to the former is by no means allegorical in any simple fashion, and his interpretations of the texts allow for the contextual transformations of symbolic figures. As a brief example, consider his "demythologized" reading of the birth of Rudra: "Esoterically, [this means that] the Rudra of clinging-to-self has ripened. Losing sight of buddha-nature, the three poisons [aversion, desire and stupidity] adhere to the poisonous tree of the self-aggregates. The child returned to its mother's corpse is the afflicted mind in its relation to the universal ground [the *ālayavijñāna*]. And this universal ground is now seized upon, as self" (*Dgongs-'dus 'grel-chen*, pp. 642–643).

Chapter 10

1. Because the present chapter requires careful attention to particular Tibetan terms, I have in this instance retained the exact transcription of *dran-* and its derivatives, which in any case are pronounced almost as they appear. In the following list of the terms most commonly used here, the approximate pronunciation is given in parenthesis: *dran-* (*dren*), *dran-pa* (*drenpa*), *dran-med* (*drenme*), *dran-pa'i mi* (*drempei mi*), *dran-rig* (*drenrik*).

2. The conception of this chapter owes a great deal to a series of conversations in December 1987 and December 1988 that I was privileged to conduct with Ven. Tulku Urgyen Rinpoche of Nagi Gompa, Nepal, one of the leading contemporary exponents of the Rdzogs-chen. Rinpoche's reflections on *dran-pa* revealed the rich vein of Rdzogs-chen thought centering upon this topic and supplied me with the point of departure for the investigation of the texts here considered. The actual form and content of this chapter, however, represent only my own attempt at understanding the texts explicitly discussed and so do not seek to provide a documentary record of Rinpoche's observations.

3. See ch. 5, n. 50, for relevant scholarship in this area.

4. On Klong-chen-pa and his contributions to Rdzogs-chen thought, see ch. 9, n. 8.

5. Refer to Gyatso 1992 for studies of memory and mindfulness in these and other Buddhist contexts.

6. The most important of the distinctive Rdzogs-chen classifications and concepts, as emphasized in Rnying-ma-pa texts, are surveyed in Dudjom 1991, vol. 1, pp. 294–345.

7. The life of Rig-'dzin Rgod-ldem and his contributions to Rnying-ma-pa Buddhism are summarized in Dudjom 1991, vol. 1, pp. 780–783. Refer now also to Boord 1993. For a more extensive biography in Tibetan, see *Rgod-ldem rnam-thar*. From a traditional standpoint, Rgod-ldem is, of course, the discoverer and not the author of his treasures. But because this entailed his being their redactor, the individual responsible for the precise verbal form in which they have come down to us, I have not insisted on making a distinction that would have no practical role in the context of the present discussion.

8. The edition referred to throughout the present essay is *Dgongs-pa zang-thal*, vol. 5 of which is in fact the *Ka-dag rang-byung rang-shar* collection.

9. *Dgongs-pa zang-thal*, 5. 131–149.

10. Compare, for instance, the conclusions of the following section with the influential analytic philosophical account of memory given in Martin and Deutscher 1966.

11. Refer to ch. 6, n. 10. Rdzogs-chen thought often speaks of this in terms of the "inner radiance that is the body of perfect rapture" (*'od-gsal longs-spyod rdzogs-pa'i sku*).

12. It is not possible in the space of this chapter to examine the difficult doctrines concerning the *dharmakāya* (*chos-kyi sku*, the "body of reality") and its disclosure as the primor-

dial buddha Samantabhadra. For a detailed discussion from a traditional Rnying-ma-pa perspective, see Dudjom 1991, vol. 1, book 1, pt. 2.

13. The Tibetan titles of the chapters are: (1) *'khor 'das gnyis byung tshul* (*Dgongs-pa zang-thal,* V.132.2–135.6); (2) *skal med man ngag 'di dang mi 'phrad pa* (135.6–137.1); (3) *rig pa chos skur ngo sprad pa* (137.1–139.2); (4) *lta ba'i gol sa bcad pa* (139.2–140.5); (5) *lam gyi spyod lam bstan pa* (140.5–143.3); (6) *rkyen gyis chos sku la nye ba* (143.3–145.4); (7) *rtogs pa'i dus bstan pa* (145.4–146.6); (8) *bar dor sangs rgyas thob pa* (146.6–147.5); (9) *gtad rgya* (147.5–148.6); colophons (149.1–6).

14. In this context, we must recall the fundamental role of mnemonic concepts in connection with the entire phenomenon of *gter-ma.* See esp. Gyatso 1986.

15. *ma yengs dran pa'i dpe don blta.* Note that ambiguity in the use of the "genitive" *-'i* and the "instrumental" *-s* is very common in the texts here considered, a characteristic that these works thus share with Tibetan vernacular literature. In this respect, compare the biographies edited and translated in Snellgrove 1967b.

16. *da lta 'khrul pa'i sems 'di la: mngal nas skyes nas da lta'i bar: ci byas dran pa bag chags yin.*

17. *de nyid rang rig chos sku yin: de la rgyun du dran pa yis: legs par brtag cing gtan la dbab.*

18. The puzzlement about reflexivity and its relationship to reference that is involved here has enjoyed a remarkably long history in the writings of the Indian contemplative traditions and their offshoots. Cf. my remarks on some Upaniṣadic references to reference in Kapstein 1989b, esp. p. 244.

19. *mnyam par bzhag pa'i dus nyid na: 'phros te snga ma phyi ma yi: rjes 'brang dran med ma song ba: byings te gnyid rmugs ma song ba'i: rig pa rang gsal ngo bo nyid.*

20. *kun gzhi yangs pa chos sku'i ma: bcos med rig pa chos sku'i bu: bu yi dran pa ma shor na: ma dang 'phrad nas bde ba thob.*

21. *dug lnga thol gyis skyes pa'i tshe: tha mas thog mtha' ngo bor lta: 'bring gis yul snang sgyu mar lta: rab kyi dran pas rang rig lta.*

22. *rig pa cir yang 'char ba 'di: chos sku nyid la thim pa yis: gnyid ni rang byung g.yo med yin: rmi lam snang ba shar ba'i tshe: dran ma thag tu sdug bsngal yal: . . . de ltar rmi lam 'khrul snang mang: sems kyi rang 'od tsam yin te: za zir gyur cing rang la thim: dran pa tsam gyi gzung 'dzin grol: de phyir dran pa myur bar mchog:*

23. Reading here *rtog* for *rtogs.*

24. *mngal dang gnyid dang bar do gsum: ngo bo gcig tu gsal thebs pa: snga phyi'i rtog pa ma shar ba'i: dran pa yang yang gsal btab bo: dran pa rtogs par 'gyur snyams na: phyi rol yul gyi phyir 'brang ba'i: snga phyi'i dran pa rtog pa yin: snga phyir ma shor zhen pa med: yang dag chos sku'i dran pa de: rang byung yin la ye shes yin: chos sku mnyam nyid lta ba yin: rig pa ye shes rang gsal yin:*

25. *snang bar 'khrul pa'i sems shar yang: de ma thag tu dran pas zin: rang byung ngo bo nyid kyi sku: go ba yul shar rtogs par nye:*

26. *rdos pa'i lus 'di bral ma thag: dper na nam langs mun sangs bzhin: bar do dus gsum man ngag dran: ye shes snang bar brtan pa thob: rang rig chos skur gsal bar byung:*

27. Compare, too, the passages just cited from ch. 6 of the *Wide-Open Tantra.* The investigation of the *Dgongs-pa zang-thal* collection has not so far revealed any special signification to the phrase "three temporal phases" (*dus-gsum*) as it is used in this context; the ordinary sense of "past, present, and future" may well be all that is here intended. Moreover, one interesting passage (*Dgongs-pa zang-thal,* IV.367.5–6) concerning the *bar-do* contains the only reference I have found in this material to the canonical doctrine of the *rjes-su dran-pa drug,* the "six recollections" (*anusmṛti*), which are not listed in the ordinary manner, but rather as recollections of the deity (*lha*), path (*lam*), birthplace (*skye-gnas*), meditative concentration (*bsam-gtan*), precepts of the guru (*bla-ma'i man-ngag*), and

dharma (*chos*). I believe that this enumeration in fact strengthens my interpretation in the categories that follow of *dran-pa* B as mindful attentiveness to the conditions for advancement on the path.

28. E.g., *Dgongs-pa zang-thal,* III.120–121: "Mnemic engagement is the ground; amnesis is the path. . . . Mnemic engagement is appearance; amnesis is emptiness. . . . Mnemic engagement is the precept (*gdams-ngag*) of the waking state; amnesis is the precept of sleep. . . ." Some interesting observations on *dran-med* in Indian and Tibetan meditational literature may be found in Ruegg 1989, pp. 94, 99, 115, 155, 160, 183, 202, 207.

29. Knowledge of the importance of repetition as a dimension of soteriological strategy was well established within the Rdzogs-chen tradition. Thus, for example, *Mkha'- lding gshog-rlabs,* fol. 37a, insists that the disciple repeatedly receive guidance in the teaching in order for it to be firmly impressed upon the mind (*yang yang khrid nas yid la 'byor ba dgos*).

30. For a theoretically provocative attempt to characterize abhidharmic discourse and to analyze the role of such discourse, see Griffiths 1990.

31. Neither is it uncommon for the fictitious agents so portrayed to represent dimensions of a single psyche. Cf. Whitman 1981, pp. 63–86, esp. p. 85: "The figures Dante meets are potentialities of his own soul, possibilities which he briefly activates in his personal vision."

32. *rdzogs-pa chen-po man-ngag-gi rgyud thams-cad-kyi thog-ma. Dgongs-pa zang-thal,* III.49–81.

33. *sems kyi gnas tshul dang: dag pa'i lam du 'jug tshul yang dag pa don gyi ngo sprod brda ru bstan pa, Dgongs-pa zang-thal,* III.69.5–79.4.

34. An antecedent for Rig-'dzin Rgod-ldem's version of this allegory is found in an important Rdzogs-chen tantra, the *Rig-pa rang-shar,* discussed in *Theg-mchog-mdzod,* ch. 10, pp. 442–462. See also Guenther 1994.

35. The text, of course, does not make it entirely clear how we are to understand this division. I suspect that "lower vehicle(s)" (*theg-pa 'og-ma*) in this case refers to all eight vehicles that, according to the nine-vehicle system of the Rnying-ma tradition, are ranked below the Great Perfection, or Atiyoga, whose teachings constitute the "higher vehicle(s)" (*theg-pa gong-ma*). See, for instance, the extraordinary passage from the *All-Accomplishing King* (*Kun-byed rgyal-po*) quoted in Dudjom 1991, vol. 1, pp. 295–297, in which the first eight vehicles are criticized in turn for obscuring, through their false projections, the genuine nature of things.

36. Hurvitz, 1976, ch. 3. See, too, the rather neglected monograph, Pye 1978.

37. Note the similarity between the revaluation of deception, as characterized here, and that of *māyā,* so often thought of as an evil deception, in Buddhist yogic literature. The yogic evaluation of *māyā* is considered in some detail in Kapstein 1992b.

38. Barnstone 1984, pp. 308–313.

39. Barnstone 1984, p. 311.

40. Barnstone 1984, p. 311.

41. Guenther 1994, pp. 3–4.

42. Guenther's attempt to historicize traditions of Padmasambhava's origins (1994, pp. 26–27, n. 58), for instance, is fanciful in the extreme.

43. The tantra in question (*Dgongs-pa zang-thal,* IV.81–181) in fact has several titles, of which the one used in the chapter colophons best illustrates the centrality of this work in the *Dgongs-pa zang-thal* corpus overall: *Rdzogs pa chen po kun tu bzang po'i dgongs pa zang thal du bstan pa'i rgyud,* "The Tantra Teaching the Great Perfection, the Penetration of Samantabhadra's Intention."

44. *smon lam stobs po che btab pas: sems can sangs mi rgya ba'i dbang med par bstan pa* (*Dgongs-pa zang-thal,* IV.171.5–177.6). There are many minor variations in the text of this prayer, particularly in its countless vulgate editions. The translation given in the appendix strictly follows the text as found in *Dgongs-pa zang-thal,* however, and the entire text is

translated so as to present some indication of the way in which the topics under consideration are actually distributed in typical passages of *Dgongs-pa zang-thal*. An earlier English translation, with accompanying Tibetan text, may be found in Taklung Tsetul and Kunzang Tenzin 1970, pp. 20–27.

45. van der Leeuw 1986, ch. 62; all uncited quotations in this and the following paragraphs may be found in this chapter.

46. van der Leeuw, 1986, p. 87.

47. See ch. 6, 9, in this book.

48. We should note, too, that the emphasis on reflexivity we find here is entirely consistent with an emphasis on reflexive acts that runs throughout Rdzogs-chen thought. Cf. Kapstein 1988b, pp. 158, 164.

49. *De Trinitate,* XII.xi. Trans. by Arthur West Haddan in Schaff 1905, p. 191.

50. Markus 1964, p. 90.

51. Nor should we ignore, in a more thorough comparative study, the historical and doctrinal roots of the concepts concerned, and the manner in which these contextual considerations may alter our initial understanding of them. Augustine's theory, of course, must be studied in connection with the whole Platonic legacy of speculation on anamnesis.

52. Nietzsche 1969, p. 61.

Chinese Glossary

Omitted from this glossary are the names of dynasties, provinces, and cities commonly used in English writings on China.

An Lushan 安祿山
Anxi Yulin 安西榆林
Chan 禪
Chánshī 禪師
Chaoxian 朝鮮
dānzhū 丹珠
dǎzhāi 打齋
Dunhuang 敦煌
dùnménpài 頓門派
Facheng 法成
fàn 梵
fó 佛
Gaoli 高麗
gōngzhǔ 公主
Guanyin 觀音
hán ("to hold in the mouth") 含
hán ("insertion of gems into the mouths of corpses") 琀
hán zhī kě bù kě 含之可不渴
Heshang Moheyan 和尚 摩訶衍
jiànménpài 漸門派
Jincheng Gongzhu 金城公主
jīng 經
Jiu Tangshu 舊唐書
júe 覺
Kangxi 康熙
Kim Hwa-shang (Ch. Jin Heshang) 金和尚
Lidai fabao ji 歷代法寶記
lùn 論
Nanzhao 南詔
Qianlong 乾隆

Renzong 仁宗
Shiji 史記
Sima Qian 司馬遷
Shujing 書經
Tuzu 土族
Wŏnch'ŭk (Ch. Yuance) 圓測
Wencheng Gongzhu 文城公主
Wutaishan 五臺山
Wuxiang (Kor. Musang) 無相
Wuzhu 無住
Xixia 西夏
Xuanzang 玄奘
Yizhou 益州
yù 玉
zànpŭ 贊普
zhāi 齋
Zhang Daoling 張道陵
Zhendi 眞諦
zhū ("pearl") 珠
zhū ("vermillion") 朱

Bibliography

Tibetan References

Karma-pa'i mdzad-rnam
Chos-rje Karma-pa sku-'phreng rim-byon-gyi rnam-thar mdor-bsdus dpag-bsam khri-shing, in *The Collected Works of Sman-sdong-mtshams-pa Rin-po-che Karma-nges-don-bstan-rgyas,* vol. 2, pp. 1–471. Bir, H. P.: D. Tsondu Senghe, 1976.
Kun-bzang bla-ma
Rdza Dpal-sprul Rin-po-che. *Snying-thig sngon-'gro'i khrid-yig.* Chengdu: Si khron mi rigs dpe skrun khang, 1988.
Ketaka'i byi-dor
Thu'u-bkwan Chos-kyi-nyi-ma. *Gsung-rab rnam-dag chu'i dri-ma sel-byed nor-bu ke-ta-ka'i tshig-don-la dogs-dpyod snyan-sgron-du gsol-ba nor-bu ke-ta-ka'i byi-dor.* Varanasi: Tarthang Tulku, n.d.
Klong-chen rgyud-sde spyi-don
Klong-chen Rab-'byams-pa Dri-med-'od-zer. *Sngags-kyi spyi-don tshangs-dbyangs 'brug-sgra.* Varanasi: Tarthang Tulku, 1967.
Klong-chen brgal-lan
Kloṅ-chen Rab-'byams-pa Dri-med-'od-zer. *Sṅa 'gyur Rñiṅ ma la rgol ṅan log rtog bzlog pa'i bstan bcos.* Nemo, Ladakh: T. S. Tashigang, 1977.
Klong-chen chos-'byung
Klong-chen Rab-'byams-pa Dri-med 'od-zer. *Chos-'byung rin-po-che'i gter-mdzod bstan-pa gsal-bar byed-pa'i nyi-'od. GCRDz* 17 (1991).
Klong-chen gsung-thor-bu
Klong-chen Rab-'byams-pa Dri-med 'od-zer. *Gsuṅ thor bu.* 2 vols. Delhi: Sanje Dorje, 1973.
Klong-rdol gsung-'bum
Klong-rdol Ngag-dbang blo-bzang-gi gsung-'bum. GCRDz 20–21 (1991).
Bka'-chems
Bka'-chems ka-khol-ma. Lanzhou: Kan-su'u mi-rigs dpe-skrun-khang, 1989.
Bka'-thang sde-lnga
Gu-ru U-rgyan-gling-pa. *Bka'-thang sde-lnga.* Beijing: Mi-rigs dpe-skrun-khang, 1986.
Bka'-gdams pha-chos
Jo-bo-rje dpal-ldan A-ti-sha'i rnam-thar bka'-gdams pha-chos. Xining: Mtsho sngon mi rigs dpe skrun khang, 1993.

Bka'-gdams bu-chos
'Brom-ston rgyal-ba'i 'byung-gnas-kyi skyes-rabs bka'-gdams bu-chos. Xining: Mtsho sngon mi rigs dpe skrun khang, 1994.
Bka' yang-dag tshad-ma
Khri Srong-lde'u-bstan. *Bka' yang-dag-pa'i tshad-ma, P* 5839, vol. 144, pp. 97–122.
Sku-gsum rnam-bshad
Karma-pa VIII Mi-bskyod-rdo-rje. *Sku-gsum ngo-sprod-kyi rnam-par-bshad-pa mdo-rgyud bstan-pa mtha'-dag-gi e-waṃ phyag-rgya.* 4 vols. Gangtok: Gonpo Tseten, 1978.
Skyabs-mgon bka'-slob
H. H. the Dalai Lama. *Goṅ-sa skyabs-mgon Ta-lā'i bla-ma-mchog-nas dge-lugs-pa'i chos-skyoṅ rgyal-chen śugs-ldan bkag-'gog gnaṅ-ba'i bka'-slob ma-bcos sor-bźag.* Bhutanese Government Office of Information, 1980.
Mkha'-'gro snying-thig
In *Snying-thig ya-bzhi.* vols. 2–3. New Delhi: Trulku Tsewang, Jamyang, and L. Tashi, 1970.
Mkha'-lding gshog-rlabs
Zhabs-dkar Tshogs-drug rang-grol. *'Od-gsal rdzogs-pa chen-po'i khregs-chod lta-ba'i glu-dbyangs sa-lam ma-lus myur-du bgrod-pa'i rtsal-ldan mkha'-lding gshog-rlabs.* Xylographic edition. Bkra-shis-ljongs, H.P.: India, n.d.
Mkhas-pa Lde'u
Mkhas-pa Lde'u. *Mkhas-pa Lde'us mdzad-pa'i rgya-bod-kyi chos-'byung rgyas-pa. GCRDz* 3 (1987).
Mkhas-pa'i dga'-ston
Dpa'-bo Gtsug-lag phreng-ba. *Chos-'byung mkhas-pa'i dga'-ston.* 2 vols. Beijing: Mi-rigs dpe-skrun-khang, 1986.
Mkhyen-brtse'i gsung-rtsom
'Jam-dbyangs Mkhyen-brtse'i dbang-po'i gsung-rtsom gces-sgrig. Chengdu: Si-khron mi-rigs dpe-skrun-khang, 1989.
Gal-mdo
Gal Mdo: Texts Concerned with the Logical Establishment of the Authenticity of the Rdzogs-chen Teachings of Bon. Dolanji, H. P.: Tibetan Bonpo Monastic Centre, 1972.
Grub-mtha' chen-mo
'Jam-dbyangs-bzhad-pa'i rdo-rje. *Grub-mtha'i rnam-bshad kun-bzang zhing-gi nyi-ma.* Lanzhou: Kan-su'u mi-rigs dpe-skrun-khang, 1994.
Grub-mtha' lhun-po mdzes-rgyan
Lcang-skya Rol-pa'i rdo-rje. *Grub-mtha' thub-bstan lhun-po'i mdzes-rgyan.* Xining: Krung-go bod-kyi shes-rig dpe-skrun-khang, 1989.
Dgongs-gcig yig-cha
Dgoṅs gcig yig cha. 2 vols. Bir: D. Tsondu Senghe, 1975.
Dgongs-'dus 'grel-chen
Mkhan-po Nus-ldan-rdo-rje. *Dpal spyi-mdo dgongs-pa 'dus-pa'i 'grel-pa rnal-'byor nyi-ma gsal-bar byed-pa'i legs-bshad gzi-ldan 'char-kha'i 'od-snang.* Vol. 1. Kalimpong, West Bengal: Dupjung Lama., 1983.
Dgongs-pa zang-thal
A-'dzom chos-sgar xylographic edition, published in facsimile as *Rdzogs pa chen po dgoṅs pa zaṅ thal and Ka dag raṅ byuṅ raṅ śar.* 5 vols. Smanrtsis Shesrig Spendzod Series, vols. 60–64. Leh, Ladakh: S. W. Tashigangpa, 1973.
Rgod-ldem rnam-thar
Sūryabhadra (Ñi-ma-bzaṅ-po). *Sprul-sku rig-'dzin rgod-kyi ldem-'phru-can-gyi rnam-thar gsal-byed ñi-ma'i 'od-zer: The biography of Rig-'dzin Rgod-kyi-ldem-'phru-can.* Paro, Bhutan: Lama Ngodrup and Sherab Drimey, 1985.

Rgya-nag chos-'byung
Mgon-po-skyabs. *Rgya-nag chos-'byung.* Chengdu: Si-khron mi-rigs dpe-skrun-khang, 1983.
Rgya-bod yig-tshang
Dpal-'byor-bzang-po. *Rgya-bod yig-tshang chen-mo.* Chengdu: Si-khron mi-rigs dpe-skrun-khang, 1983.
Rgya-mtsho mtha'-yas
Karma Pakshi (but attributed by the publisher to Karma-pa III Rang-byung-rdo-rje). *Rgya-mtsho mtha'-yas-kyi skor.* 2 vols. Gangtok: Gonpo Tseten, 1978.
Rgyal-rabs gsal-me
Bla-ma-dam-pa Bsod-nams-rgyal-mtshan. *Rgyal-rabs gsal-ba'i me-long.* Beijing: Mi-rigs dpe-skrun-khang, 1982.
Rgyud-bla'i rnam-'grel
'Jam-mgon Kong-sprul Blo-gros-mtha'-yas. *Theg-pa chen-po rgyud-bla-ma'i bstan-bcos snying-po'i don mngon-sum lam-gyi bshad-srol dang sbyar-ba'i rnam-par 'grel-pa phyir mi-ldog-pa seng-ge'i nga-ro.* Xylographic edition. Rum-btegs, Sikkim, n.d.
Sgrub-thabs-kun-'btus
Sgrub-thabs-kun-'dus: A Collection of Sādhanas and Related Texts of the Vajrayāna Traditions of Tibet. Dehradun, UP: G. T. K. Lodoy, N. Gyaltsen, & N. Lungtok, 1970.
Brgal-lan kun-khyab 'brug-sgra
Yon-tan-rgya-mtsho. *Brgal-lan kun-khyab 'brug-sgra.* New Delhi: Yon-tan-rgya-mtsho, 1980.
Lnga-pa'i gsan-yig
Record of Teachings Received: The Gsan-yig of the Fifth Dalai Lama Ṅag-dbaṅ-blo-bzaṅ-rgya-mtsho. 4 vols. Delhi: Nechung and Lakhar, 1971.
Lcang-skya rnam-thar
Thu'u-bkwan Chos-kyi nyi-ma. *Lcang-skya Rol-pa'i rdo-rje'i rnam-thar.* Lanzhou: Kan-su'u mi-rigs dpe-skrun-khang, 1989.
Chags-med ri-chos
Karma Chags-med Rā-ga-a-sya. *Ri chos mtshams kyi zhal gdams.* Rtsib-ri xylographic edition, reproduced in *Rtsib-ri Spar-ma,* compiled by La-dwags Khri-dpon 'Khrul-zhig Padma-rnam-rgyal. Vol. 30. Darjeeling: Kargyud Sungrab Nyamso Khang, 1978.
Chos-skyong bka'-slob
H. H. the Dalai Lama. *Gong-sa skyabs-mgon chen-po mchog nas/ Chos-skyong bsten-phyogs-skor bka'-slob snga-rjes bstsal-pa khag cha-tshang phyogs-bsdebs zhus pa.* Dharamsala: Tibet Cultural Printing Press, 1996.
Jo-nang chos-'byung
Contributions to the Study of Jo-nang-pa History, Iconography, and Doctrine: Selected Writings of 'Dzam-thang Mkhan-po Blo-gros-grags-pa. Vol. 1. Collected and presented by Matthew Kapstein. Dharamsala: Library of Tibetan Works and Archives, 1993.
'Jam-dbyangs Mkhyen-brtse
'Jam-dbyangs Mkhyen-brtse'i dbang-po. *Mkhyen-brtse on the History of the Dharma.* Leh: S. W. Tashigangpa, 1972.
Nyang-ral
Nyang Nyi-ma 'od-zer. *Chos-'byung me-tog snying-po sbrang-rtsi'i bcud. GCRDz* 5 (1988).
Tun-hong bod-yig shog-dril
Bsod-nams-skyid and Dbang-rgyal [Wang Yao]. *Tun-hong-nas thon-pa'i gna'-bo'i bod-yig shog-dril.* Beijing: Mi rigs dpe skrun khang, 1983.
Gter-ston brgya-rtsa
'Jam-mgon Koṅ-sprul Blo-gros-mtha'-yas. *Zab-mo'i gter dang gter-ston grub-thob ji-ltar*

byon-pa'i lo-rgyus mdor-bsdus bkod-pa rin-chen bai-ḍūrya'i phreng-ba, in *Rin-chen gter-mdzod.* Vol. 1. Paro: Ngodrup and Sherap Drimay, 1976.

Bstan-rtsis kun-btus
Tshe-tan zhabs-drung. *Bstan-rtsis kun-las btus-pa.* Xining: Mtsho-sngon mi-rigs dpe-skrun-khang, 1982.

Bstan-srung rnam-thar
Sle-lung Rje-drung Bzhad-pa'i rdo-rje. *Bstan-srung rgya-mtsho'i rnam-thar.* Vol. 1. Smanrtsis Shesrig Spendzod, vol. 104. Leh, Ladakh: T. S. Tashigang, 1979.

Bstan-srung byung-brjod
Dze-smad Blo-bzaṅ-dpal-ldan. *Mthu daṅ stobs-kyi che-ba'i bstan-sruṅ chen-po rdo-rje-śugs-ldan-rtsal-gyi byuṅ-ba brjod-pa pha-rgod bla-ma'i źal-gyi bdud-rtsi'i chu-khur brtsegs-śiṅ 'jigs-ruṅ glog-źags 'gyu-ba'i sprin-nag 'khrugs-pa'i ṅa-ro.* N.p., n.d.

Thu'u-bkwan grub-mtha'
Thu'u-bkwan Blo-bzang chos-kyi nyi-ma. *Thu'u-bkwan grub-mtha' [= Grub-mtha' thams-cad-kyi khungs dang 'dod-tshul ston-pa legs-bshad shel-gyi me-long].* Lanzhou: Kan-su'u mi-rigs dpe-skrun-khang, 1984.

Thu'u-bkwan gsung-'bum
Collected Works of Thu'u-bkwan Blo-bzang-chos-kyi-nyi-ma. 10 vols. New Delhi: Ngawang Gelek Demo, 1969.

Theg-mchog-mdzod
Klong-chen Rab-'byams-pa Dri-med-'od-zer. *Theg-pa'i mchog rin-po-che'i mdzod.* Gangtok: Dodrup Chen Rinpoche, n.d.

Theg-pa spyi-bcings
Dam-pa Bde-gshegs and Ye-shes-rgyal-mtshan. *Theg-pa spyi-bcings rtsa-'grel.* Chengdu: Si-khron mi-rigs dpe-skrun-khang, 1997.

Theg-rim
Theg-pa'i rim-pa mngon-du bshad-pa'i mdo-rgyud, in *Bon po Grub mtha' Material.* Dolanji: Tibetan Bonpo Monastic Centre, 1978.

Dwags-po thar-rgyan
Sgam-po-pa Bsod-nams-rin-chen. *Thar-pa rin-po-che'i rgyan.* Chengdu: Si-khron mi-rigs dpe-skrun-khang, 1989.

Dus-kyi sbrang-char
T. G. Dhongthog. *The Timely Shower: Expression of Unaltered Reality* (*ma bcos dṅos 'brel brjod pa dus kyi sbraṅ char*). Delhi: T. G. Dhongthog, 1974.

Dus-kyi me-lce
T. G. Dhongthog. *The Timely Flame* (*ma bcos dṅos 'brel brjod pa dus kyi me lce*). Delhi: T. G. Dhongthog, 1979.

Deb-ther sngon-po
'Gos-lo Gzhon-nu-dpal. *Deb-ther sngon-po.* 2 vols. Chengdu: Si-khron mi-rigs dpe-skrun-khang, 1984.

Deb-dmar
Tshal-pa Kun-dga'-rdo-rje. *Deb-ther dmar-po-rnams-kyi dang-po hu-lan deb-ther*, ed. Dung-dkar Blo-bzang-'phrin-las. Beijing: Mi-rigs dpe-skrun-khang, 1981.

Deb-dmar gsar-ma
Paṇ-chen Bsod-nams-grags-pa. *Deb-ther dmar-po gsar-ma.* Lhasa: Bod-ljongs mi-dmangs dpe-skrun-khang, 1989.

Dol-po-pa
The 'Dzam-thang Edition of the Collected Works of Kun-mkhyen Dol-po-pa Shes-rab-rgyal-mtshan. Collected and presented by Matthew Kapstein. 10 vols. New Delhi: Shedrup Books and Konchhog Lhadrepa, 1992–1993.

Dol-po-pa'i ri-chos
Dol-po-pa Shes-rab-rgyal-mtshan. *Ri chos ṅes don rgya mtsho: A Treatise on the Philosophical Basis and Practice of Buddhist Contemplation.* Gangtok: Dodrup Sangyey Lama, 1976.
Dol-rgyal-skor gsal-bshad
H. H. the Dalai Lama. *Dol-rgyal-skor gsal-bshad.* Dharamsala: Department of Religion and Culture, 1996.
Gdams-ngag-mdzod
'Jam-mgon Kong-sprul Blo-gros-mtha'-yas. *Gdams ngag mdzod: A Treasury of Instructions and Techniques for Spiritual Realization.* 12 vols. Delhi: N. Lungtok and N. Gyaltsan, 1971.
Gdong-lan
Yon-tan-rgya-mtsho, *Gdoṅ lan luṅ rigs thog mda'.* Delhi: Yonten Gyaltso, 1979.
Bdud-'joms chos-'byung
Bdud-'joms Rin-po-che 'Jigs-bral-ye-shes-rdo-rje. *Gangs-ljongs rgyal-bstan yongs-kyi phyi-mo snga-'gyur rdo-rje theg-pa'i bstan-pa rin-po-che ji-ltar byung-ba'i tshul dag-cing gsal-bar brjod-pa lha-dbang g.yul-las rgyal-ba'i rnga-bo-che'i sgra-dbyangs,* in *Collected Writings and Revelations of Bdud-'joms Rin-po-che,* vol. 1. Kalimpong: Dupjung Lama, 1979.
Rdo-rje me-char
Bya-bral Sangs-rgyas-rdo-rje. *The rain of adamant fire: a holy discourse based upon scriptures and reason, annihilating the poisonous seeds of the wicked speech of Dzeme Trulku Lobsang Palden.* Gangtok: Sherab Gyaltsen, 1979.
Rdor-sems zhu-lan
Gnyan Dpal-dbyangs. *Rdo-rje sems-dpa'i zhu-lan, P* 5082, vol. 87, pp. 163–166.
Lde'u Jo-sras
Lde'u Jo-sras. *Lde'u chos-'byung.* Lhasa: Bod-ljongs mi-dmangs dpe-skrun-khang, 1987.
Ne'u Paṇḍita
Ne'u [or Nel-pa] Paṇḍita Grags-pa smon-lam blo-gros. *Sngon-gyi gtam me-tog phreng-ba,* in *Bod-kyi lo-rgyus deb-ther khag-lnga, GCRDz* 9 (1990): 3–86.
Nor-bu ke-ta-ka
Sum-pa mkhan-po Ye-shes-dpal-'byor. *Gsung-rab rnam-dag chu'i dri-ma sel-byed nor-bu ke-ta-ka,* in Lokesh Chandra, ed., *Collected Works of Sum-pa-mkhan-po,* vol. 4. New Delhi: International Academy of Indian Culture, 1975.
Pakshi'i rang-rnam
The Autobiographical Writings of the Second Karma-pa Karma Pakshi and Spyi-lan ring-mo. Gangtok: Gonpo Tseten, 1978.
Padma bka'-thang
O-rgyan-gling-pa. *Padma bka' thang.* Chengdu: Si khron mi rigs dpe skrun khang, 1987.
Dpag-bsam ljon-bzang
Sarat Chandra Das, ed. *Dpag-bsam ljon-bzang.* Kyoto: Rinsen Book Co., 1984. Reprt. of 1908 Calcutta Presidency Jailhouse Press edition, entitled *Pag Sam Jon Zang.*
Dpe-rgyun dkon-pa tho-yig
A-khu Rin-po-che Shes-rab-rgya-mtsho. *Dpe-rgyun dkon-pa 'ga'-zhig-gi tho-yig,* in Lokesh Chandra, ed., *Materials for a History of Tibetan Literature,* part 3. Śatapiṭaka Series 30. New Delhi: International Academy of Indian Culture, 1963.
Dpe-chos rin-chen spungs-pa.
Dpe-chos dang dpe-chos rin-chen spungs-pa. In the series *Gangs-can rig-brgya'i sgo-'byed lde-mig,* no. 17. Beijing: Mi-rigs dpe-skrun-khang, 1991.
Spa-bstan
Spa-bstan Rgyal-bzang-po. *Bstan-pa'i rnam-bshad dar-rgyas gsal-ba'i sgron-me.* Beijing: Krung-go'i bod-kyi shes-rig dpe-skrun-khang, 1991.

Spyod-'jug rnam-bshad

Sa-bzaṅ Ma-ti Paṇ-chen. *Byaṅ chub sems dpa'i spyod pa la 'jug pa'i rnam bśad gźuṅ don rab gsal snaṅ ba.* Delhi: T. Dorje, 1975.

Pha-bong-kha-pa

The Views of Pha-boṅ-kha-pa Bde-chen-sñiṅ-po. New Delhi: Ngawang Topgay, 1977.

Phyag-rdzogs-zung-'jug

Thugs-rje-chen-po phyag-rdzogs-zung-'jug-gi dmar-khrid, in *The Collected Writings of Karma Chags-med,* vol. 2. Bir, H. P.: Khandro, 1974.

Ba-dzra-gu-ru'i phan-yon

Ba-dzra-gu-ru'i phan-yon, a *gter-ma* discovery attributed to Karma-gling-pa. Xylographic print. Kalimpong, West Bengal: Zangs-mdog-dpal-ri Monastery, n.d.

Bar-do'i gdams-pa

Khyung-po Rnal-'byor. *Bar-do'i gdams-pa,* in *Encyclopedia Tibetica,* vol. 93, pp. 150–67. New Delhi: Tibet House, 1972.

Bu-ston chos-'byung

Bu-ston Rin-chen-grub. *Bu-ston chos-'byung.* Xining: Krung-go'i bod-kyi shes-rig dpe-skrun-khang, 1988.

Be'u-bum sngon-po

Bka'-gdams-kyi man-ngag be'u-bum sngon-po'i rtsa-'grel. In the series *Gangs-can rig-brgya'i sgo-'byed lde-mig,* no. 16. Beijing: Mi-rigs dpe-skrun-khang, 1991.

Bod-kyi deb-ther

Rgyal-ba Lnga-pa-chen-mo (Dalai Lama V) Ngag-dbang-blo-bzang-rgya-mtsho. *Bod-kyi deb-ther dpyid-kyi rgyal-mo'i glu-dbyangs.* Beijing: Mi rigs dpe skrun khang, 1988.

Bod-kyi rdo-ring

Bsod-nams-skyid. *Bod-kyi rdo-ring yi-ge dang dril-bu'i kha-byang.* Beijing: Mi rigs dpe skrun khang, 1984.

Bod-kyi yig-tshags

The Archives of the Tibet Autonomous Region, comp. *Bod-kyi yig-tshags gces-btus.* Beijing: Wenwu Chunbanshe, 1995.

Bon-gyi bstan-'byung

Dpal-tshul. *G.yung-drung bon-gyi bstan-'byung phyogs-bsdus.* Lhasa: Bod-ljongs mi-dmangs dpe-skrun-khang, 1988.

Dbu-'jug 'grel-chen

Red-mda'-ba Gzhon-nu-blo-gros. *Dbu 'jug 'grel chen.* Delhi: Ngawang Topgay, 1974.

Dbu-ma śar-gsum

Phya pa chos kyi seṅ ge, *Dbu ma śar gsum gyi stoṅ thun.* Ed. Helmut Tauscher. Wiener Studien zur Tibetologie und Buddhismuskunde 43. Vienna: Arbeitskreis für Tibetische und Buddhistische Studien Universität Wien, 1999.

Dbon-zhang rdo-ring

Dkon-mchog-tshe-brtan. *Dbon-zhang rdo-ring dang thang-bod-bar-gyi 'brel-ba.* Lanzhou: Kan-su'u mi-rigs dpe-skrun khang, 1986.

'Bri-gung gdan-rabs

'Bri-gung Bstan-'dzin Padma'i rgyal-mtshan. *'Bri-gung gdan-rabs gser-phreng. GCRDz* 8 (1989).

'Brug-pa'i chos-'byung

'Brug-chen Padma-dkar-po. *Chos-'byung bstan-pa'i padma rgyas-pa'i nyin-byed. GCRDz* 19 (1992).

Sba-bzhed

Attr. Sba Gsal-snang. *Sba-bzhed ces-bya-ba-las Sba Gsal-gnang-gi bzhed-pa bzhugs.* Beijing: Mi-rigs dpe-skrun-khang, 1980. See also Stein 1961.

Sbas-pa'i rgum-chung
Namkhai Norbu (Nam-mkha'i nor-bu). *Sbas-pa'i rgum-chung: The Small Collection of Hidden Precepts, a Study of an Ancient Manuscript on Dogchen from Tun-huang.* Arcidosso, Italy: Shang-shung Edizioni, 1984.

Ma-ṇi bka'-'bum
Ma ṇi bka' 'bum: A collection of rediscovered teachings focussing upon the tutelary deity Avalokiteśvara (Mahākāruṇika); Reproduced from a print from the no longer extant Spungs-thang (Punakha) blocks by Trayang and Jamyang Samten. 2 vols. New Delhi, 1975.

Man-ngag lta-phreng
Padmasambhava. *Man-ngag lta-ba'i phreng-ba,* in *Selected Writings of Roṅ-zom Chos-kyi-bzaṅ-po.* Leh: S.W. Tashigangpa, 1973.

Man-ngag rin-chen spungs-pa
Lce-sgom-rdzong-pa Shes-rab-rdo-rje. *Bla-ma rin-po-che Lce-sgom-rdzong-pas mdzad-pa'i Man-ngag rin-chen spungs-pa'i dkar-chag.* Varanasi: Pleasure of Elegant Sayings Printing Press, 1971.

Mun-pa'i go-cha
Bsnubs-chen Sangs-rgyas-ye-shes. *Sangs-rgyas thams-cad-kyi dgongs-pa 'dus-pa mdo'i dka'-'grel mun-pa'i go-cha lde-mig gsal-byed rnal-'byor nyi-ma,* in H. H. Bdud-'joms Rin-po-che, ed., *Rnying ma bka' ma rgyas pa,* vol. 50. Kalimpong, West Bengal: Dupjung Lama, 1987.

Btsan-po Dar-ma
Mkhar-rme'u Bsam-gtan Rgyal-mtshan. *Btsan-po lha-sras Dar-ma dang de'i rjes su byung-ba'i rgyal-rabs mdor-bsdus.* Dharamsala: Library of Tibetan Works and Archives, 1986.

Btsan-po lo-rgyus
Don-grub-rgyal and Khrin Chin-dbyin [Chen Qingying]. *Btsan-po khri sde-srong-btsan-gyi lo-rgyus mdo-tsam brjod-pa.* Beijing: Mi rigs dpe skrun khang, 1984.

Tshad-ma rgyan-gyi me-tog
Bcom-ldan Rig-pa'i Ral-gri, *Tshad-ma sde-bdun rgyan-gyi me-tog.* Xining: Krung-go'i bod-kyi shes-rig dpe-skrun-khang, 1991.

Tshig-mdzod chen-mo
Zhang Yisun, ed. *Bod-rgya tshig-mdzod chen-mo.* 3 vols. Beijing: Mi-rigs dpe-skrun-khang, 1985.

Mdzod-'grel
Mchims 'Jam-pa'i-dbyangs. *Mdzod 'grel mngon pa'i rgyan.* Ed. Rdo-rje-rgyal-po. Xining: Krung go bod kyi shes rig dpe skrun skrun khang, 1989.

'Dzam-gling rgyas-bshad
Btsan-po IV, Bstan-'dzin-phrin-las. *'Dzam gling rgyas bshad,* in Nor-brang O-rgyan, ed., *'Dzam gling rgyas bshad dang spyi bshad gnyis.* Lhasa: Bod rang skyong ljongs spyi tshogs tshan rigs khang bod yig dpe rnying dpe sgrig khang, 1986.

'Dzam-gling spyi-bshad
Sum-pa mkhan-po. *'Dzam-gling spyi-bshad,* in Nor-brang O-rgyan, ed., *'Dzam-gling rgyas bshad dang spyi bshad gnyis.* Lhasa: Bod rang skyong ljongs spyi tshogs tshan rigs khang bod yig dpe rnying dpe sgrig khang, 1986.

Zhe-chen chos-'byung
Zhe-chen rgyal-tshab IV 'Gyur-med Padma Rnam-rgyal. *Zhe-chen rgyal-tshab chos-'byung.* Chengdu: Si-khron mi-rigs dpe-skrun-khang, 1994.

Gzhan-stong khas-len
'Jam-mgon 'Ju Mi-pham-rnam-rgyal. *Gzhan stong mkhas lan seng ge'i nga ro.* Xylographic edition. Ser-lo dgon-pa, Nepal.

Gzhan-stong chen-mo
Contributions to the Study of Jo-nang-pa History, Iconography, and Doctrine: Selected Writings of 'Dzam-thang Mkhan-po Blo-gros-grags-pa. Vol. 2. Collected and presented by Matthew Kapstein. Dharamsala: Library of Tibetan Works and Archives, 1993.

Gzungs-mdo'i glegs-bam
Gzuṅs mdo'i glegs bam dgos 'dod kun 'byuṅ. Delhi: Anu Tshering, c. 1966.

Yar-lung chos-'byung
Shākya Rin-chen-sde. *Yar-lung jo-bo'i chos-'byung.* Lhasa: Bod-ljongs mi-dmangs dpe-skrun-khang, 1988.

Yi-dam drag-po'i dbang-bshad
Karma Chags-med. *Yi-dam drag-po'i mngon-rtogs rdo-rje 'phreng-ba'i dbang-bshad.* Ms. in the author's possession.

Rat-gling rtsod-bzlog
The Nyingmapa Apology of Rin-chen-dpal-bzang-po. Tashijong, H.P.: Sungrab Nyamso Gyunphel Parkhang, 1972.

Rigs-gter dgongs-don
Ngag-dbang-chos-grags. *Tshad-ma rigs-pa'i gter-gyi dgongs-don gsal-bar byed-pa'i legs-bshad ngag-gi dpal-ster.* New Delhi: Ngawang Topgay, 1983.

Rigs-gter gsal-byed
Go-rams-pa Bsod-nams seng-ge. *Sde-bdun mdo dang bcas-pa'i dgongs-pa phyin-ci-ma-log-par 'grel-pa tshad-ma rigs-pa'i gter-gyi don gsal-bar byed-pa.* Mussoorie, U. P.: Sakya College, 1975.

Rigs-gzhung rgya-mtsho
Karma-pa VII Chos-grags-rgya-mtsho. *Tshad-ma'i bstan-chos rigs-gzhung rgya-mtsho.* Lhasa: Bod rang skyong ljongs spyi tshogs tshan rigs khang bod yig dpe rnying dpe sgrig khang, 1987.

Rin-chen gter-mdzod chen-mo
'Jam-mgon Koṅ-sprul Blo-gros-mtha'-yas. *Rin-chen gter-mdzod.* Paro: Ngodrup and Sherap Drimay, 1976.

Ru-tra'i smre-sngags
Khrag-'thung Las-kyi dpa'-bo. *Ru-tra'i smre-sngags bshags-pa.* A recent xylograph from Manali, Himachal Pradesh, in the author's collection.

Rong-zom gsung-btus
Selected Writings of Rong-zom Chos-kyi-bzang-po, Smanrtsis Shesrig Spendzod. Vol. 73. Leh: S.W. Tashigangpa, 1973.

Shangs-pa bla-rabs
Shangs-pa bka'-brgyud bla-rabs-kyi rnam-thar, GCRDz 28 (1996).

Shel-dkar phreng-ba.
Nor-brang O-rgyan. *Bod sil-bu'i byung-ba brjod-pa shel-dkar phreng-ba.* Lhasa: Bod ljongs mi dmangs dpe skrun khang, 1991.

Shes-bya kun-khyab
Kong-sprul Yon-tan-rgya-mtsho [= Blo-gros-mtha'-yas]. *Shes-bya kun-khyab mdzod* Beijing: Minorities Press, 1981.

Sa-skya bka'-'bum
Bsod nams rgya mtsho, ed. *The Complete Works of the Great Masters of the Sa skya Sect of the Tibetan Buddhism* [*sic*]. Tokyo: Toyo Bunko, 1968.

Sa-skya sdom-gsum
Sdom pa gsum gyi rab tu dbye ba, in *Sa-skya bka'-'bum*, vol. 5, pp. 297.1.1–320.4.5.

Sa-skya'i gdung-rabs
['Jam-mgon A-myes-zhabs] Ngag-dbang kun-dga' bsod-nams. *Sa-skya'i gdung-rabs ngo-mtshar bang-mdzod.* Beijing: Mi-rigs dpe-skrun-khang, 1986.

Sa-paṇ gsung-'bum
Sa-skya Paṇḍita Kun-dga'-rgyal-mtshan. *Sa paṇ kun dga' rgyal mtshan gyi gsung 'bum.* 3 vols. *GCRDz* 23–25 (1992).

Sog-bzlog-pa
Collected Writings of Sog-bzlog-pa Blo-gros-rgyal-mtshan. New Delhi: Sanje Dorji, 1975.

Gsang-snying Rgyud-'grel
Commentaries on the Guhyagarbha Tantra and Other Rare Nyingma Texts from the Library of Dudjom Rinpoche. Vol. 1. New Delhi: Sanje Dorje, 1974.

Bsam-gtan mig-sgron
Gnubs-chen Saṅs-rgyas ye-śes. *Sgom gyi gnad gsal bar phye ba bsam gtan mig sgron.* Smanrtsis Shesrig Spendzod series, vol. 74. Leh, 1974.

Lha-ldan dkar-chag
Lha ldan gtsug lag khaṅ gi dkar chag: A Guide to the Great Temple of Lhasa by His Holiness Nag-dbaṅ Blo-bzaṅ rGya-mtsho, the Great Fifth Dalai Lama. Delhi: Ngawang Gelek Demo, n.d.

O-rgyan glegs-bam
O-rgyan sprul-pa'i glegs-bam, in Źabs-dkar Tshogs-drug-raṅ-grol, *Sñigs-dus yoṅs-kyi skyabs-mgon źabs-dkar rdo-rje-'chaṅ chen-po'i rnam-par thar-pa rgyas-par bśad-pa skal-bzaṅ gdul-bya thar-'dod-rnams-kyi re-ba skoṅ-ba'i yid-bźin nor-bu bsam-'phel dbaṅ-gi rgyal-po,* vol. 2. Dolanji, H. P.: Tsering Wangyal, 1975.

Sanskrit References

Abhidharmakośam, ed. Svāmī Dwārikādās Śāstrī. 4 vols. Varanasi: Bauddha Bharati, 1970–1972.

Abhisamayālaṃkārāloka, ed. P. L. Vaidya. *BST* 4 (1960).

Avalokiteśvara-guṇa-karaṇḍavyūha, in *Mahāyānasūtrasaṃgrahaḥ,* ed. P. L. Vaidya. *BST* 17 (1961).

Āryabhadracaripraṇidhānarāja, Skt. and Tib. ed. Suniti Kumar Pathak, Gangtok, Sikkim: Namgyal Institute of Tibetology, 1961.

Āryamañjuśrīmūlakalpa, in *Mahāyānasūtrasaṃgrahaḥ,* ed. P. L. Vaidya. *BST* 18 (1964).

Prasannapadā, ed. P. L. Vaidya. *BST* 10 (1960).

Bodhicaryâvatāra, ed. P. L. Vaidya. *BST* 12 (1960).

Mahāyānasūtrâlaṃkara, ed. S. Bagchi. *BST* 13 (1970).

Ratnagotravibhāga Mahāyānottaratantraśāstra, ed. E. H. Johnston. Patna: Bihar Research Society, 1950.

Laṅkāvatāra, ed. P. L. Vaidya. *BST* 3 (1963).

Vimalaprabhāṭīkā, vol. 1, ed. Jagannatha Upadhyaya. Bibliotheca Indo-Tibetica Series 11. Sarnath: Central Institute of Higher Tibetan Studies, 1986.

Śikṣāsamuccayaḥ, ed. P. L. Vaidya. *BST* 11 (1961).

Sarvadarśanasaṃgraha. Sāyaṇa Mādhava. Ed. Vasudev Abhayankar. Poona: Bhandarkar Oriental Research Institute, 1978.

Chinese References

Dunhuang Wenwu Yanjiusuo, 敦煌文物研究所. comp. *Dunhuang Mogaoku* 4 敦煌莫高窟 四, in the series *Zhongguo shiku* 中國石窟. Beijing: Wenwu Chubanshe, 1987.

Dunhuang Yanjiu-yuan 敦煌研究院. comp. *Anxi Yulinku* 安西榆林窟, in the series *Zhongguo shiku* 中國石窟. Beijing: Wenwu Chubanshe, 1997.

Huo Wei 霍巍, *Xizang gudai muzang zhidu shi* 西藏古代墓葬制度史. Chengdu: Sichuan Renmin Chubanshe, 1995.

Wang Xiaofu 王小甫. *Tang Tufan Dasi zhengzhi guanxi shi* 唐吐蕃大食政治关系史. Beijing: Beijing Daxue Chubanshe, 1992.

Wang Yao 王尧 and Chen Jian 陈践, eds. *Dunhuang Tubowen Shulun Wenji* 敦煌吐蕃文书论文集. Chengdu: Sichuan Minzu Chubanshe, 1988.

Western Language References

Adkins, Arthur W. H. 1990. "Myth, Philosophy, and Religion in Ancient Greece." In Reynolds and Tracy 1990, pp. 95–130.

Adler, Elkan Nathan. 1987. *Jewish Travellers in the Middle Ages: Nineteen Firsthand Accounts.* London: George Routledge, 1930. Rprt., New York: Dover.

Amano, Hirofusa. 1975. *A Study on the Abhisamaya-alaṃkāra-kārikā-śāstra-vṛtti.* Tokyo: Japan Science Press.

Andersen, Dines. 1917. *A Pāli Reader with Notes and Glossary.* Copenhagen. Rprt. Kyoto: Rinsen-Shoten, 1968.

Annas, Julia, and Jonathan Barnes. 1985. *The Modes of Scepticism: Ancient Texts and Modern Interpretations.* Cambridge: Cambridge University Press.

Aris, Michael. 1979. *Bhutan.* Warminster: Aris and Phillips.

Aris, Michael. 1989. *Hidden Treasures and Secret Lives.* London/New York: Kegan Paul International.

Aung, Shwe Zan, and C. A. F. Rhys Davids. 1969. *Points of Controversy.* London: Pali Text Society.

Aziz, Barbara Nimri. 1979. "Indian Philosopher as Tibetan Folk Hero," *Central Asiatic Journal* 23/1–2: 19–37.

Aziz, Barbara Nimri. 1980. "The Work of Pha-dam-pa Sangs-rgyas as Revealed in Ding-ri Folklore," in *TSHHR,* pp. 21–29.

Aziz, Barbara Nimri, and Matthew Kapstein, eds. 1985. *Soundings in Tibetan Civilization.* Delhi: Manohar.

Backus, Charles. 1981. *The Nan-chao Kingdom and T'ang China's Southwestern Frontier.* Cambridge: Cambridge University Press.

Bacot, Jacques. 1934–35. "Le mariage chinois du roi Sroṅ bcan sgam po (extrait du Maṇi bKa' 'bum)," in *Mélanges Chinois et Bouddhiques*, vol. 3, pp. 1–60. Brussels: Institut Belge des Hautes Études Chinoises.

Bacot, Jacques. 1956. "Reconnaissance en Haute Asie septentrionale par cinq envoyés ouigours au VIIIe siècle," *JA* 144: 137–153.

Bacot, J., F. W. Thomas, and Ch. Toussaint. 1940. *Documents de Touen-houang relatifs à l'histoire du Tibet.* Paris: Librairie Orientaliste Paul Geuthner.

Balbir, Jagbans Kishore. 1963. *L'histoire de Rāma en tibétain d'après des manuscrits de Touen-houang.* Paris: Adrien-Maisonneuve.

Barnstone, Willis. 1984. *The Other Bible.* San Francisco: Harper-Collins.

Beckwith, Christopher I. 1979. "The Introduction of Greek Medicine into Tibet in the Seventh and Eighth Centuries," *JAOS* 99/2: 297–313.

Beckwith, Christopher I. 1980. "The Tibetan Empire in the West," in *TSHHR,* pp. 30–38.

Beckwith, Christopher I. 1983. "The Revolt of 755 in Tibet," in *CTLHC,* pp. 1–16.

Beckwith, Christopher I. 1984. "A Hitherto Unnoticed Yüan-Period Collection Attributed to 'Phags-pa," in *TBS,* vol. 1, pp. 9–16.

Beckwith, Christopher I. 1987. *The Tibetan Empire in Central Asia.* Princeton: Princeton University Press.

Beckwith, Christopher I. 1990. "The Medieval Scholastic Method in Tibet and the West," in Lawrence Epstein and Richard F. Sherburne, eds., *Reflections on Tibetan Culture: Essays in Memory of Turrell V. Wylie*, pp. 307–313. Lewiston/Queenston/Lampeter: Edwin Mellen.

Berger, David. 1979. *The Jewish-Christian Debate in the High Middle Ages*. Philadelphia: Jewish Publication Society of America.

Berzin, Alexander, Sherpa Tulku, and Matthew Kapstein, trans. 1987. "The Four-Themed Precious Garland of Longchen Rabjampa," in Stephen Batchelor, ed., *The Jewel in the Lotus: A Guide to the Buddhist Traditions of Tibet*, pp. 137–69. London: Wisdom.

Biraben, J.-N., and J. Le Goff. 1969. "La Peste dans le Haut Moyen Age," *Annales: Economies, Sociétés, Civilisations* 24/6: 1484–1510.

Bischoff, F. A., 1956. *Ārya Mahābala-nāma-mahāyānasūtra*. Buddhica 10. Paris: Librairie Orientaliste Paul Geuthner.

Bischoff, F. A. 1978. "Padmasambhava est-il un personnage historique?" in Louis Ligeti, ed. *Proceedings of the Csoma de Kőrös Symposium*, pp. 27–33. Budapest: Akadémiai Kiadó.

Bischoff, F. A., and Charles Hartman. 1971. "Padmasambhava's Invention of the Phur-bu: Ms. Pelliot tibétain 44," in *ET*, pp. 11–28.

Blezer, Hank. 1997. *Kar gliṅ źi khro: A Tantric Buddhist Concept*. Leiden: Research School CNWS.

Blondeau, Anne-Marie. 1970. "Les religions du Tibet," in Henri-Charles Puech, ed., *Histoire des Religions*, vol. 3. Paris: Bibliothèque de la Pléiade.

Blondeau, Anne-Marie. 1971. "Le Lha-'dre Bka'-thaṅ," in *ET*, pp. 29–126.

Blondeau, Anne-Marie, 1980. "Analysis of the Biographies of Padmasambhava According to Tibetan Tradition: Classification of Sources," in *TSHHR*, pp. 45–58.

Blondeau, Anne-Marie. 1984. "Le 'découvreur' du *Maṇi bka'-'bum* était-il bon-po?" in *TBS*, vol. 1, pp. 77–123.

Blondeau, Anne-Marie. 1987. "Une polémique sur l'authenticité des *Bka' thang* au 17e siècle," in C. I. Beckwith, ed., *Silver on Lapis: Tibetan Literary Culture and History*, pp. 125–161. Bloomington: Tibet Society.

Blondeau, Anne-Marie. 1994. "Bya-rung kha-shor, légende fondatrice du Bouddhisme tibétain," in *TS*, vol. 1, pp. 31–48.

Blondeau, Anne-Marie. 1997. "Que notre enfant revienne! Un rituel méconnu pour les enfants morts en bas-âge," in Karmay and Sagant 1997, pp. 193–220.

Bogoslovskij, V. A. 1972. *Essai sur l'histoire du peuple tibétain, ou la naissance d'une société de classes*. Paris: C. Klincksieck.

Boord, Martin J. 1993. *The Cult of the Deity Vajrakīla*, Buddhica Britannica Series Continua 4. Tring, U.K.: Institute of Buddhist Studies.

Bosson, James. 1969. *Treasury of Aphoristic Jewels*. Indiana University Uralic and Altaic Series, vol. 92. Bloomington: Indiana University Press.

Brandt, J. 1954. *Introduction to Literary Chinese*. New York: Ungar.

Broughton, Jeffrey. 1983. "Early Ch'an Schools in Tibet," in *SCH*, pp. 1–68.

Bussotti, Michela, and Jean-Pierre Drège. 1996. "Essai de bibliographie des travaux sur Dunhuang en langues occidentales," in Jean-Pierre Drège, ed., *De Dunhuang au Japon: Études chinoises et bouddhiques offertes à Michel Soymié*, pp. 411–454. Geneva: Droz.

Buswell, Robert E., Jr. 1989. *The Formation of Ch'an Ideology in China and Korea: The* Vajrasamādhi-Sūtra, *A Buddhist Apocryphon*. Princeton: Princeton University Press.

Buswell, Robert E., Jr., ed. 1990. *Chinese Buddhist Apocrypha*. Honolulu: University of Hawaii Press.

Butterfield, Herbert. 1981. *The Origins of History*. New York: Basic Books.

Buttrick, George Arthur, ed. 1962. *The Interpreter's Dictionary of the Bible.* New York: Abingdon.

Cabezón, José Ignacio. 1992. "Vasubandhu's *Vyākhyāyukti* on the Authenticity of the Mahāyāna *Sūtras,*" in Jeffrey R. Timm, ed., *Texts in Context: Traditional Hermeneutics in South Asia,* pp. 221–243. Albany: State University of New York Press.

Cabezón, José Ignacio. 1994. *Buddhism and Language: A Study of Indo-Tibetan Scholasticism.* Albany: State University of New York Press.

Cabezón, José Ignacio, ed. 1998. *Scholasticism: Cross-Cultural and Comparative Perspectives.* Albany: State University of New York Press.

Cannata, Patrizia. 1990. "La profezia dell'arhat della terra di Li," in Daffinà 1990, pp. 43–79.

Chan, Victor. 1994. *Tibet Handbook: A Pilgrimage Guide.* Chico, Calif.: Moon Publications.

Chayet, Anne. 1988. "Le monastère de bSam-yas: sources architecturales," *ArtsA* 43:19–29.

Chayet, Anne. 1994. *Art et Archéologie du Tibet.* Paris: Picard.

Chimpa, Lama, and Alaka Chattopadhyaya. *Tāranātha's History of Buddhism in India.* Atlantic Highlands, N.J.: Humanities Press.

Chisholm, Roderick, ed. 1960. *Realism and the Background of Phenomenology.* Glencoe, Ill.: Free Press.

Chu Junjie. 1991. "A Study of Bon-po Funeral Ritual in Ancient Tibet: Deciphering the Pelliot Tibetan Mss [*sic!*] 1042," in Hu Tan, ed., *Theses on Tibetology in China*, pp. 91–157, Beijing: China Tibetology Publishing.

Coblin, W. S. 1991. "A Study of the Old Tibetan *Shangshu* Paraphrase," *JAOS* 111: 303–322, 523–539.

Collingwood, R. G. 1956. *The Idea of History.* Oxford: Oxford University Press.

Collins, Steven. 1982. *Selfless Persons.* Cambridge: Cambridge University Press.

Collins, Steven. 1990. "On the Very Idea of the Pali Canon," *Journal of the Pali Text Society* 15: 89–126.

Collins, Steven. 1998. *Nirvana and Other Buddhist Felicities.* Cambridge: Cambridge University Press.

Conze, Edward. 1967. "Buddhism and Gnosis," in *Le Origini dello Gnosticismo*. Studies in the History of Religions, vol. 12. Leiden: E. J. Brill.

Corbin, Henry. 1969. *Creative Imagination in the Sūfism of Ibn 'Arabī.* Princeton: Princeton University Press.

Daffinà, Paolo, ed. 1990. *Indo-Sino-Tibetica: Studi in onore di Luciano Petech.* Rome: Bardi.

Daniel, Stephen H. 1990. *Myth and Modern Philosophy.* Philadelphia: Temple University Press.

Dargyay, Eva K. 1985. "A Rñiṅ-ma Text: The Kun byed rgyal po'i mdo." In Aziz and Kapstein 1985, pp. 283–293.

Davidson, Ronald M. 1981. "The Litany of Names of Mañjuśrī," in *Mélanges Chinois et Bouddhiques*, vol. 20, pp. 1–69. Brussels: Institute Belge des Hautes Études Chinoises.

Davidson, Ronald M. 1990. "An Introduction to the Standards of Scriptural Authenticity in Indian Buddhism," in Buswell 1990, pp. 291–325.

Davidson, Ronald M. 1991. "Reflections on the Maheśvara Subjugation Myth: Indic Materials, Sa-skya-pa Apologetics, and the Birth of Heruka," *JIABS* 14/2:197–235.

Davidson, Ronald M. 1994. "The Eleventh-Century Renaissance in Central Tibet." Unpublished paper presented at the University of Virginia.

Dawa Norbu. 1985. "An Analysis of Sino-Tibetan Relationships, 1245–1911: Imperial Power, Non-coercive Regime, and Military Dependency," in *STC,* pp. 176–195.

Demiéville, Paul. 1952. *Le concile de Lhasa: une controverse sur le quiétisme entre bouddhistes de l'Inde et de la Chine au VIIIe siècle de l'ère chrétienne.* Bibliothèque de l'Institut des Hautes Études Chinoises, vol. VII. Paris: Imprimerie Nationale de France.

Demiéville, Paul. 1957. "Le Bouddhisme et la Guerre." In *Mélanges publiés par l'Institut des Hautes Études Chinoises*. Bibliothèque de l'Institut des Hautes Études Chinoises, vol. XI, pp. 347–385. Paris: Presses Universitaires de France.

Demiéville, Paul. 1973. "La situation religieuse en Chine au temps de Marco Polo," in *Choix d'Études Sinologiques*. Leiden: Brill.

Demiéville, Paul. 1979. "L'introduction au Tibet du Bouddhisme sinisé d'après les manuscrits de Touen-houang: Analyses de récents travaux japonais," in Michel Soymié, ed., *Contributions aux études sur Touen-houang*, pp. 1–16. Genève/Paris: Droz.

Demiéville, Paul. 1987. "The Mirror of Mind," in *SG*, pp. 13–40.

Dietz, Siglinde. 1984. *Die Buddhistische Briefliteratur Indiens*. Asiatische Forschungen 84. Wiesbaden: Otto Harrossowitz.

Douglas, Nik, and Meryl White. 1976. *Karmapa: The Black Hat Lama of Tibet*. London: Luzac.

Dreyfus, Georges. 1994. "Proto-nationalism in Tibet," in *TS*, vol. 1, pp. 205–218.

Dreyfus, Georges. 1997a. *Recognizing Reality*. Albany: State University of New York Press.

Dreyfus, Georges. 1997b. "Tibetan Scholastic Education and the Role of Soteriology," *JIABS* 20/1:31–62.

Dreyfus, Georges. 1998. "The Shuk-den Affair: History and Nature of a Quarrel," *JIABS* 21/2:227–270.

Dudjom Rinpoche, Jikdrel Yeshe Dorje. 1991. *The Nyingma School of Tibetan Buddhism: Its Fundamentals and History*. Trans. Gyurme Dorje and Matthew Kapstein. 2 vols. Boston: Wisdom Publications.

Dundes, Alan, ed. 1984. *Sacred Narrative: Readings in the Theory of Myth*. Berkeley/Los Angeles/London: University of California Press.

Dunnell, Ruth W. 1996. *The Great State of White and High: Buddhism and State Formation in Eleventh-Century Xia*. Honolulu: University of Hawaii Press.

Dutt, Nalinaksha. 1942. *Gilgit Manuscripts*, vol. 3, pt. 2. Rprt. Delhi: Sri Satguru Publications, 1984.

Eastman, K. W. 1983. "Mahāyoga Texts at Tun-huang." *Bulletin of the Institute of Buddhist Cultural Studies* 22, pp. 42–60. Kyoto: Ryukoku University.

Eberhard, Wolfram. 1986. *Dictionary of Chinese Symbols*. London: Routledge and Kegan Paul.

Ecsedy, Hilda. 1964. "Uigurs and Tibetans in Pei-t'ing (790–791 A.D.)," *AOH* 17/1:83–104.

Ecsedy, Ildikó. 1984. "Nanchao: An Archaic State Between China and Tibet," in *TBS*, vol. 1, pp. 165–189.

Edou, Jérôme. 1996. *Machig Labdrön and the Foundations of Chöd*. Ithaca: Snow Lion.

Ehrhard, Franz-Karl. 1990. *"Flügelschläge des Garuḍa: Literar- und ideengeschichtliche Bemerkungen zu einer Liedersammlung des rDzogs-chen*. Tibetan and Indo-Tibetan Studies 3. Stuttgart: Franz Steiner.

Eimer, Helmut. 1983. "Die Auffindung de *bKa' chems ka khol ma*. Quellenkritische Uberlegungen," in *CTLHC*, pp. 45–51.

Eimer, Helmut. 1991. "Eine frühe Quelle zur literarischen Tradition über die 'Debatte von Bsam yas,'" in E. Steinkellner, ed., *Tibetan History and Language: Studies Dedicated to Géza Uray on His Seventieth Birthday*. Vienna: Arbeitskreis fur Tibetische und Buddhistische Studien Universität Wien.

Emmerick, Ronald Eric. 1967. *Tibetan Texts Concerning Khotan*. London: Oxford University Press.

Emmerick, Ronald Eric. 1992. *A Guide to the Literature of Khotan*. 2nd ed. Studia Philologica Buddhica, Occasional Papers 3. Tokyo.

Evans-Wentz, W. Y., ed. 1960. *The Tibetan Book of the Dead*. Trans. Kazi Dawa-Samdup. London: Oxford University Press.

Ferrari, Alfonsa. 1958. *mK'yen brtse's Guide to the Holy Places of Central Tibet.* Ed. Luciano Petech. Serie Orientale Roma 16. Rome: Is.M.E.O.

Finley, M. I. 1973. *The Ancient Economy.* Berkeley/Los Angeles: University of California Press.

Fletcher, Richard. 1997. *The Barbarian Conversion: From Paganism to Christianity.* New York: Holt.

Forte, Antonino. 1976. *Political Propaganda and Ideology in China at the End of the Seventh Century.* Naples: Instituto Universitario Orientale.

Frank, Andre Gunder. 1992. *The Centrality of Central Asia.* Comparative Asian Studies 8. Amsterdam: VU University Press.

Frank, Bernard. 1991. *Le panthéon bouddhique au Japon—Collections d'Emile Guimet.* Paris: Réunion des Musées Nationaux.

Franke, Herbert. 1996. *Chinesischer und Tibetischer Buddhismus im Chine der Yüanzeit.* Munich: Bavarian Academy of Science.

Freemantle, Francesca, and Chogyam Trungpa. 1987. *The Tibetan Book of the Dead.* Boston/London: Shambhala.

French, Rebecca. 1995a. *The Golden Yoke: The Legal Cosmology of Buddhist Tibet.* Ithaca: Cornell University Press.

French, Rebecca. 1995b. "Tibetan Legal Literature: The Law Codes of the dGa' ldan pho brang," in Jackson and Cabézon, 1995, pp. 438–457.

Gellner, David N. 1992. *Monk, Householder, and Tantric Priest: Newar Buddhism and its Hierarchy of Ritual.* Cambridge: Cambridge University Press.

Germano, David. 1994. "Architecture and Absence in the Secret Tantric History of rDzogs Chen," *JIABS* 17/2:203–335.

Germano, David. Forthcoming. *Mysticism and Rhetoric in the Great Perfection: The Transformation of Buddhist Tantra in Ancient Tibet.*

Giès, Jacques, and Monique Cohen. 1995. *Sérinde, Terre de Bouddha.* Paris: Réunion des Musées Nationaux.

Goitein, S. D. 1971. *A Mediterranean Society.* Vol. 2, *The Community.* Berkeley/Los Angeles/London: University of California Press.

Goldstein, Melvyn C. 1989. *A History of Modern Tibet: The Demise of the Lamaist State.* Berkeley: University of California Press.

Goldstein, Melvyn C., and Matthew T. Kapstein, eds. 1998. *Buddhism in Contemporary Tibet: Religious Revival and Cultural Identity.* Berkeley: University of California Press.

Gómez Rodríguez, Luis O. 1981. "Vimalamitra y la doctrina subitista," *EAA* 16/2:254–272.

Gómez, Luis O. 1983a. "Indian Materials on the Doctrine of Sudden Enlightenment," in *ECCT,* pp. 393–434.

Gómez, Luis O. 1983b. "The Direct and Gradual Approaches of Zen Master Mahāyāna: Fragments of the Teachings of Mo-ho-yen," in *SCH,* pp. 69–167.

Gómez, Luis O. 1987. "Purifying Gold: The Metaphor of Effort and Intuition in Buddhist Thought and Practice," in *SG,* pp. 67–165.

Goody, Jack. 1977. *The Domestication of the Savage Mind.* Cambridge: Cambridge University Press.

Goody, Jack. 1986. *The Logic of Writing and the Organization of Society.* Cambridge: Cambridge University Press.

Grierson, George, and Lionel D. Barnett. 1920. *Lallā-vākyāni.* London: Royal Asiatic Society.

Griffiths, Paul. 1990. "Denaturalizing Discourse," in Reynolds and Tracy 1990.

Griffiths, Paul. 1999. *Religious Reading: The Place of Reading in the Practice of Religion.* New York/Oxford: Oxford University Press.

Groot, J. J. M. de. 1892. *The Religious System of China*, vol. 1. Leyden: Brill.

Grossmann, Reinhardt. 1974. *Meinong*. London: Routledge and Kegan Paul.

Gruzinski, Serge. 1993. *The Conquest of Mexico: The Incorporation of Indian Societies into the Western World, Sixteenth–Eighteenth Centuries*. Cambridge: Polity.

Guenther, Herbert V. 1963. *The Life and Teaching of Nāropa*. Oxford: Clarendon.

Guenther, Herbert V., trans. 1971. Sgam.po.pa, *The Jewel Ornament of Liberation*. Berkeley: Shambhala.

Guenther, Herbert V. 1975–1976. *Kindly Bent to Ease Us*. 3 vols. Emeryville, Calif.: Dharma Publications.

Guenther, Herbert V. 1983. "'Meditation' Trends in Early Tibet," in *ECCT*, pp. 351–366.

Guenther, Herbert V. 1984. *Matrix of Mystery: Scientific and Humanistic Aspects of rDzogs-chen Thought*. Boston/London: Shambhala.

Guenther, Herbert V. 1994. *Wholeness Lost and Wholeness Regained: Forgotten Tales of Individuation from Ancient Tibet*. Albany: State University of New York Press.

Gyatso, Janet. 1985. "The Development of the Gcod tradition," in *STC*, pp. 320–342.

Gyatso, Janet. 1986. "Signs, Memory, and History: A Tantric Buddhist Theory of Scriptural Transmission," *JIABS* 9/2: 73–35.

Gyatso, Janet. 1987. "Down with the Demoness: Reflections on the Feminine Ground in Tibet," *Tibet Journal* 12/4: 38–53.

Gyatso, Janet, ed. 1992. *In the Mirror of Memory*. Albany: State University of New York Press.

Gyatso, Janet. 1993. "The Logic of Legitimation in the Tibetan Treasure Tradition," *History of Religions* 33/2: 97–134.

Gyatso, Janet. 1994. "Guru Chos-dbang's *Gter 'byung chen mo:* An Early Survey of the Treasure Tradition and Its Strategies in Discussing Bon Treasure," in *TS*, vol. 1, pp. 275–287.

Gyatso, Janet. 1995. "Drawn from the Tibetan Treasury: The *gTer Ma* Literature," in Jackson and Cabezón, pp. 147–169.

Gyatso, Janet. 1998. *Apparitions of the Self*. Princeton: Princeton University Press.

Haarh, Erik. 1969. *The Yar-luṅ Dynasty*. Copenhagen: G. E. C. Gad.

Hackin, Joseph. 1924. *Formulaire Sanscrit-Tibétain du Xe siècle*. Paris: Librairie Orientaliste Paul Geuthner.

Hahn, Michael. 1997. "A Propos the Term *Gtsug lag*," in Helmut Krasser, et al., eds. *Tibetan Studies*, vol. 1, pp. 347–354. Vienna: Verlag der Österreichischen Akademie der Wissenschaften.

Hakeda, Yoshito S. 1972. *Kūkai: Major Works*. New York/London: Columbia University Press.

Harvey, Peter. 1990. *An Introduction to Buddhism*. Cambridge: Cambridge University Press.

Hatab, Lawrence J. 1990. *Myth and Philosophy: A Contest of Truths*. La Salle, Ill.: Open Court.

Heisig, James W., and John C. Maraldo, eds. 1994. *Rude Awakenings: Zen, the Kyoto School, and the Question of Nationalism*. Honolulu: University of Hawai'i Press.

Heller, Amy. 1994a. "Ninth-Century Buddhist Images Carved at Ldan-ma-brag to Commemorate Tibeto-Chinese Negotiations," in *TS*, vol. 1, pp. 335–349, and appendix to vol. 1, pp. 12–19.

Heller, Amy. 1994b. "Early Ninth-Century Images of Vairochana from Eastern Tibet," *Orientations* 25/6: 74–79.

Heller, Amy. 1997a. "Eighth- and Ninth-Century Temples and Rock Carvings of Eastern Tibet," J. C. Singer and P. Denwood, eds. *Tibetan Art: Towards a Definition of Style*, pp. 86–103. London: Laurence King.

Heller, Amy. 1997b. "Buddhist Images and Rock Inscriptions from Eastern Tibet," in H. Krasser, M. T. Much, E. Steinkellner, and H. Tauscher, eds., *Tibetan Studies: Pro-*

ceedings of the Seventh Seminar of the International Association for Tibetan Studies, vol. 1, pp. 385–403. Vienna: Austrian Academy of Science.

Hennecke, Edgar, and Wilhelm Schneemelcher. 1963. *New Testament Apocrypha.* Philadelphia: Westminster.

Herlihy, David. 1997. *The Black Death and the Transformation of the West.* Cambridge/London: Harvard University Press.

Hiltebeitel, Alf, ed. 1989. *Criminal Gods and Demon Devotees.* Albany: State University of New York Press.

Hobsbawm, E. J. 1992. *Nations and Nationalism since 1780: Programme, Myth, Reality.* 2nd ed. Cambridge: Cambridge University Press.

Hoffman, Helmut. 1950. *Quellen zur Geschichte der tibetischen Bon-Religion,* Abhandlungen der Geistes-und Sozialwissenschaftlichen Klasse 1950/4. Wiesbaden: Akademie der Wissenschaften und der Literatur in Mainz.

Hoffman, Helmut. 1969, 1972. "Kālacakra Studies 1. Manichaeism, Christianity, and Islam in the Kālacakra Tantra," *CAJ* 13: 52–73, and 15: 298–301.

Holt, John Clifford. 1991. *Buddha in the Crown: Avalokiteśvara in the Buddhist Traditions of Sri Lanka.* New York: Oxford University Press.

Hookham, S. K. 1991. *The Buddha Within.* Albany: State University of New York Press.

Hopkins, Jeffrey. 1999. *Emptiness in the Mind-Only School of Buddhism.* Berkeley/Los Angeles/London: University of California Press.

Hopkirk, Peter. 1984. *Foreign Devils on the Silk Road.* London: Oxford University Press.

Horváth, Zoltán. 1984. "Structure and Content of the *Chad-ma rigs-pa'i gter,* an Epistemological Treatise of Saskya Paṇḍita," in *TBS,* vol. 1, pp. 267–302.

Houston, G. W. 1980. *Sources for a History of the bSam yas Debate.* Monumenta Tibetica Historica, ser. 1, vol. 2. Sankt Augustin: VGH Wissenschaftsverlag.

Huang, Wenhuan. 1989. "An Analysis of Ancient Handwritten Copies of Buddhist Scriptures of Sras mkhar dgu thog Monastery," *Tibetan Studies: Journal of the Tibet Academy of Social Sciences.* 1/2: 161–166.

Hubbard, Jamie, and Paul. L. Swanson, eds. 1997. *Pruning the Bodhi Tree: The Storm over Critical Buddhism.* Honolulu: University of Hawai'i Press.

Huber, Toni. 1999. *The Cult of Pure Crystal Mountain.* New York: Oxford.

Huc, M. L'Abbé. 1897. *Christianity in China, Tartary, and Thibet.* 2 vols. New York: P. J. Kenedy.

Hurvitz, Leon, trans. 1976. *Scripture of the Lotus Blossom of the Fine Dharma.* New York: Columbia University Press.

Husserl, Edmund. 1962. *Recherches Logiques.* Trans. Hubert Élie et al. Paris: P.U.F.

Imaeda, Yoshiro. 1975. "Documents tibétains de Touen-houang concernant le concile du Tibet," *JA* 263: 125–146.

Imaeda, Yoshiro. 1979. "Note Preliminare sur la formule *Oṃ Maṇi Padme Hūṃ* dans les Manuscripts Tibetains de Touen-Houang," in Michel Soymié, ed., *Contributions aux études sur Touen-Houang*, pp. 71–76. Geneva/Paris: Droz.

Imaeda, Yoshiro. 1980. "L'identification de l'original chinois du Pelliot tibétain 1291—traduction tibétaine du Zhanguoce," *AOH* 34/1–3: 53–68.

Imaeda, Yoshiro. 1981a. "Un extrait tibétain du *Mañjuśrīmūlakalpa* dans les manuscrits de Touen-houang," in Michel Soymié, ed., *Nouvelles contributions aux études de Touen-houang*, pp. 303–320. Geneva/Paris: Droz.

Imaeda, Yoshiro. 1981b. *Histoire du Cycle de la Naissance et de la Mort.* Geneva/Paris: Droz.

Inaba, Shōju. 1977. "On Chos-grub's Tibetan Translation of the *Chien-chen-mi-chung-shu,*" in Leslie S. Kawamura and Keith Scott, eds., *Buddhist Thought and Asian Civilization: Essays in Honor of Herbert V. Guenther on His Sixtieth Birthday,* pp. 105–113. Emeryville, Calif.: Dharma Publishing.

Ishikawa, Mie. 1990. *A Critical Edition of the* Sgra sbyor bam po gnyis pa, *An Old and Basic Commentary on the* Mahāvyutpatti. Studia Tibetica 18. Tokyo: Toyo Bunko.
Iwasaki, Tsutomu. 1993. "The Tibetan Tribes of Ho-hsi and Buddhism during the Northern Sung Period," *AA* 64:17–37.
Jackson, David. 1983. "Commentaries on the Writings of Sa-skya Paṇḍita: A Bibliographical Sketch," *Tibet Journal* 8/3: 3–23.
Jackson, David. 1987. *The Entrance Gate for the Wise (Section 3): Sa-skya Paṇḍita on Indian and Tibetan Traditions of Pramāṇa and Philosophical Debate.* 2 vols. Wiener Studien zur Tibetologie und Buddhismuskunde 17, 1–2. Vienna: Arbeitskreis für Tibetische und Buddhistische Studien Universität Wien.
Jackson, David. 1990. "Sa-skya Paṇḍita the 'Polemicist': Ancient Debates and Modern Interpretations," *JIABS* 13/2: 17–116.
Jackson, David. 1994. *Enlightenment by a Single Means*. Vienna: Österreichischen Akademie der Wissenschaften.
Jackson, Roger. 1982. "Sa skya Paṇḍita's Account of the bSam yas Debate: History as Polemic," *JIABS* 5: 89–99.
Jackson, Roger, and José Cabezón, eds. 1995. *Tibetan Literature: Studies in Genre.* Ithaca: Snow Lion.
James, William. 1948. *Essays in Pragmatism.* Ed. Alburey Castell. New York: Hafner.
James, William. 1987. *The Varieties of Religious Experience.* Baltimore: Penguin.
Jest, Corneille. 1974a. *Dolpo, communautés de langue tibétaine du Népal.* Paris: CNRS.
Jest, Corneille. 1974b. *Tarap, une vallée dans l'himalaya.* Paris: Seuil.
Jonas, Hans, 1963. *The Gnostic Religion.* Boston: Beacon.
Jong, J. W. de. 1971. "Un fragment de l'histoire de Rāma en Tibétain," in *ET,* pp. 127–141.
Jong, J. W. de. 1989. *The Story of Rāma in Tibet: Text and Translation of the Tun-huang Manuscripts.* Stuttgart: F. Steiner.
Kantorowicz, Ernst H. 1957. *The King's Two Bodies: A Study in Mediaeval Political Theology.* Princeton: Princeton University Press.
Kapstein, Matthew T. 1980. "The Shangs-pa bKa'-brgyud: An Unknown School of Tibetan Buddhism," in *TSHHR,* pp. 138–144.
Kapstein, Matthew T. 1985. "Religious Syncretism in 13th Century Tibet: *The Limitless Ocean Cycle,*" in *STC,* pp. 358–371.
Kapstein, Matthew T. 1986. "Collins, Parfit, and the Problem of Personal Identity in Two Traditions," *Philosophy East and West* 36/3: 289–298.
Kapstein, Matthew T. 1988a. "Mereological Considerations in Vasubandhu's 'Proof of Idealism,'" *Idealistic Studies* 18/1: 32–54.
Kapstein, Matthew T. 1988b. "Mi-pham's Theory of Interpretation," in Donald Lopez, ed., *Buddhist Hermeneutics*, pp. 149–174. Honolulu: University of Hawaii Press.
Kapstein, Matthew T. 1989a. "The Purificatory Gem and Its Cleansing: A Late Tibetan Polemical Discussion of Apocryphal Texts," *History of Religions* 28/3: 217–244.
Kapstein, Matthew T. 1989b. "Indra's Search for the Self and the Beginnings of Philosophical Perplexity in India," *Religious Studies* 24: 239–256.
Kapstein, Matthew T. 1989c. "Śāntarakṣita on the Fallacies of Personalistic Vitalism," *Journal of Indian Philosophy* 17: 43–59.
Kapstein, Matthew T. 1991. "New Sources for Tibetan History," *China Exchange News* 19/3–4: 15–19.
Kapstein, Matthew T. 1992a. "Remarks on the *Maṇi-bka'-'bum* and the Cult of Avalokiteśvara in Tibet," in S. Goodman and R. Davidson, eds., *Tibetan Buddhism: Reason and Revelation*, pp. 79–93, 163–169. Albany: State University of New York Press.
Kapstein, Matthew T. 1992b. "The Illusion of Spiritual Progress," in Robert Buswell, ed., *Paths to Liberation*, pp. 193–224. Honolulu: University of Hawaii Press.

Kapstein, Matthew T. 1992c. "The Amnesic Monarch and the Five Mnemic Men," in Janet Gyatso, ed., *In the Mirror of Memory*, pp. 239–269. Albany: State University of New York Press.

Kapstein, Matthew T. 1992d. "Samantabhadra and Rudra: Innate Enlightenment and Radical Evil in Tibetan Rnying-ma-pa Buddhism," in Frank E. Reynolds and David Tracy, eds., *Discourse and Practice*, pp. 51–82. Albany: State University of New York Press.

Kapstein, Matthew T. 1992e. "The Trouble with Truth: Heidegger on *Aletheia*, Buddhist Thinkers on *Satya*," *Journal of the Indian Council of Philosophical Research* 9/2: 69–85.

Kapstein, Matthew T. 1992f. *The 'Dzam-thang Edition of the Collected Works of Kun-mkhyen Dol-po-pa Shes-rab-rgyal-mtshan Introduction and Catalogue.* New Delhi: Shedrup.

Kapstein, Matthew T. 1995a. "gDams-ngag: Tibetan Technologies of the Self," in Jackson and Cabezón 1995, pp. 275–289.

Kapstein, Matthew T. 1995b. "Weaving the World: The Ritual Art of the *Paṭa* in Pāla Buddhism and Its Legacy in Tibet," *History of Religions* 34/3: 241–262.

Kapstein, Matthew T. 1997a. "Buddhist Perspectives on Ontological Truth," in Eliot Deutsch and Ron Bontekoe, eds., *A Companion to World Philosophies*, pp. 420–433. Oxford: Basil Blackwell.

Kapstein, Matthew T. 1997b. "The Journey to the Golden Mountain," in Donald Lopez, Jr., ed., *Tibetan Religions in Practice,* pp. 178–187. Princeton: Princeton University Press.

Kapstein, Matthew T. 1997c. "From Dol-po-pa to 'Ba'-mda' Dge-legs: Three Jo-nang-pa Masters on the Interpretation of Prajñāpāramitā," in Helmut Krasser, Michael Torsten Much, Ernst Steinkellner, and Helmut Tauscher, eds., *Tibetan Studies: Proceedings of the Seventh Seminar of the International Association for Tibetan Studies*, vol. 1, pp. 457–475. Vienna: Austrian Academy of Science.

Kapstein, Matthew T. In press. "The Indian Literary Identity in Tibet," in Sheldon Pollock, ed., *Literary Cultures in History: Perspectives from South Asia.*

Kapstein, Matthew T. Forthcoming. *Buddhist Thought in Tibet.*

Karma Thinley. 1978. *The History of the Sixteen Karmapas of Tibet.* Boulder: Shambhala.

Karmay, Samten Gyaltsen. 1972. *The Treasury of Good Sayings.* London Oriental Series 26. London: Oxford University Press.

Karmay, Samten Gyaltsen. 1975a. "A Discussion on the Doctrinal Position of rDzogs-chen from the tenth to the thirteenth Centuries," *JA* 263: 147–156.

Karmay, Samten Gyaltsen. 1975b. "A gZer-mig Version of the Interview Between Confucius and Phyva Keṅ-tse," *Bulletin of the School of Oriental and African Studies* 38/3: 562–580.

Karmay, Samten Gyaltsen. 1980a. "The Ordinance of Lha Bla-ma Ye-shes-'od," in *TSHHR,* pp. 150–162.

Karmay, Samten Gyaltsen. 1980b. "An Open Letter by Pho-brang Zhi-ba-'od to the Buddhists in Tibet," *Tibet Journal* 5/3: 3–28.

Karmay, Samten Gyaltsen. 1981. "King Tsa/Dza and Vajrayāna," in Michel Strickmann, ed., *Tantric and Taoist Studies in Honour of R. A. Stein*, Mélanges Chinois et Bouddhiques, vol. 20.

Karmay, Samten Gyaltsen. 1983. "Un témoinage sur le Bon face au Bouddhisme à l'époque des rois tibétains," in *CTBRP,* pp. 89–103.

Karmay, Samten Gyaltsen. 1985. "The Rdzogs-chen in Its Earliest Text: A Manuscript from Tun-huang," in *STC*, pp. 272–282.

Karmay, Samten Gyaltsen. 1988a. *The Great Perfection: A Philosophical and Meditative Teaching of Tibetan Buddhism.* Leiden/New York: Brill.

Karmay, Samten Gyaltsen. 1988b. *Secret Visions of the Fifth Dalai Lama: The Gold Manuscript in the Fournier Collection.* London: Serindia.

Karmay, Samten, and Philippe Sagant. 1997. *Les habitants du Toit du monde: hommage à Alexander W. Macdonald.* Recherches sur la Haute Asie 12. Nanterre: Société d'ethnologie.

Katz, Nathan. 1994. "Contacts Between Jewish and Indo-Tibetan Civilizations Through the Ages," *Judaism* 43/1: 46–60.

Khoury, Adel-Théodore. 1972. *Polémique Byzantine contre l'islam*. Leiden: Brill.

Kimura, Ryūtoku. 1981. "Le dhyāna chinois au Tibet ancien après Mahāyāna," *JA* supplement:183–192.

Klein, Anne C., and Geshe Tenzin Wangyal Rinpoche. 1995. "Preliminary Reflections on *The Authenticity of Innate Awareness (gTan tshigs gal mdo rig pa'i tshad ma)*," *Asiatische Studien/Études Asiatiques* 49/4: 769–792.

Klimberg-Salter, Deborah E. 1998. *Tabo: A Lamp for the Kingdom*. New York: Thames & Hudson.

Klimkeit, Hans Joachim. 1993. *Gnosis on the Silk Road: Gnostic Texts from Central Asia*. Harper: San Francisco.

Könchog Gyaltsen, Khenpo. 1990. *The Great Kagyu Masters: The Golden Lineage Treasury*. Ed. Victoria Huckenpahler. Ithaca: Snow Lion.

Kőrös, Alexander Csoma de. 1984. *Tibetan Studies*. Vol. 4 of *Collected Works of Alexander Csoma de Kőrös*, ed. J. Terjék. Budapest: Akadémiai Kiadó.

Kunsang, Eric Pema, trans. 1990. *Dakini Teachings: Padma Sambhava's Oral Instructions to Lady Tsogyal*. Boston/London: Shambhala.

Kunsang, Eric Pema, trans. 1993. *The Lotus-Born: The Life of Padmasambhava*. Boston/London: Shambhala.

Kuo Li-ying. 1994. *Confession et contrition dans le bouddhisme chinois du Ve au Xe siècle*. Paris: Publications de l'École Française d'Extrême-Orient.

Kværne, Per. 1973. "The A khrid System of Meditation," *Kailash* 1: 18–50 and 247–332.

Kværne, Per. 1980. "A Preliminary Study of Chp. VI of the *Gzer-mig*," in *TSHHR*, pp. 185–191.

Kværne, Per. 1983. "The Great Perfection in the Tradition of the Bonpos," in *ECCT*, pp. 367–392.

Kværne, Per. 1985. *Tibet: Bon Religion*. Iconography of Religions XII, fasc. 13. Leiden: Brill.

Kværne, Per. 1987. "Dualism in Tibetan Cosmogonic Myths and the Question of Iranian Influence," in C. I. Beckwith, ed., *Silver on Lapis: Tibetan Literary Culture and History*, pp. 163–174. Bloomington, Ind.: Tibet Society.

Kværne, Per. 1995. *The Bon Religion of Tibet*. London: Serindia.

Lalou, Marcelle. 1939. "Document tibétain sur l'expansion du dhyāna chinois," *JA* 231: 505–523.

Lalou, Marcelle. 1952. "Rituel Bon-po des funérailles royales," *JA* 240/3: 339–361.

Lalou, Marcelle. 1953. "Les Textes Bouddhiques au Temps du Roi Khri-sroṅ-lde-bcan," *JA* 241/3: 313–353.

Lamasse, H. 1984. *Nouveau manuel de langue chinoise écrite*. 4th ed. Taipei: Li Ming Cultural Enterprise.

Lamotte, Étienne. 1935. *Saṃdhinirmocanasūtra: L'explication des mystères*. Paris: Adrien Maisonneuve.

Lamotte, Étienne. 1965. *La Concentration de la Marche Héroïque*, Vol. 13 of *Mélanges Chinois et Bouddhiques*. Brussels: Institut Belge des Hautes Études Chinoises.

Lamotte, Étienne. 1976. *Histoire du Bouddhisme Indien*. Louvain: Institut Orientaliste.

Lancaster, Lewis. 1979. "Buddhist Literature: Its Canons, Scribes, and Editors," in Wendy Doniger O'Flaherty, ed., *The Critical Study of Sacred Texts*, pp. 215–229. Berkeley Religious Studies Series.

Lasker, Daniel J. 1977. *Jewish Philosophical Polemics Against Christianity in the Middle Ages*. New York: Ktav.

Lauf, Detlef Ingo. 1977. *Secret Doctrines of the Tibetan Books of the Dead*. Boulder/London: Shambhala.

Laufer, Berthold. 1912. *Jade: A Study in Chinese Archaeology and Religion.* Publication 154 of the Field Museum of Natural History, Chicago. Rprt. New York: Dover, 1974.

Law, Bimala Churn. 1969. *The Debates Commentary.* London: Pali Text Society.

Lee, Peter, ed. 1993. *Sourcebook of Korean Civilization.* Volume 1. *From Earliest Times to the Sixteenth Century.* New York: Columbia University Press.

Lessing, Ferdinand D., and Alex Wayman. 1968. *Mkhas grub rje's Fundamentals of the Buddhist Tantras.* The Hague: Mouton.

Lhalungpa, Lobsang P., trans. 1977. *The Life of Milarepa.* New York: Dutton.

Li An-che. 1982. *Labrang: A Study in the Field.* Ed. Chie Nakane. Tokyo: University of Tokyo Institute of Oriental Culture.

Li Fang Kuei, and W. South Coblin. 1987. *A Study of the Old Tibetan Inscriptions.* Institute of History and Philology, Special Publications No. 91. Taipei: Academia Sinica.

Ligeti, Louis. 1968. "Notes sur le lexique Sino-tibétain de Touen-houang en écriture tibétaine," *AOH,* 21: 265–288.

Lincoln, Bruce. 1989. *Discourse and the Construction of Society.* New York/Oxford: Oxford University Press.

Ling, Trevor. 1979. *Buddhism, Imperialism, and War.* London: Allen and Unwin.

Lokesh Chandra. 1968. "The Life and Works of 'Jam-dbyaṅs-bźad-pa," *Central Asiatic Journal* 7: 45–49.

Lopez, Donald S., Jr., ed. 1997. *Tibetan Religions in Practice.* Princeton: Princeton University Press.

Lopez, Donald S., Jr. 1998. *Prisoners of Shangri-la: Tibetan Buddhism and the West.* Chicago/London: University of Chicago Press.

Macdonald, Alexander W. 1984a. "Religion in Tibet at the Time of Srong-btsan sgam-po: Myth as History," in *TBS,* vol. 2, pp. 129–140.

Macdonald, Alexander W. 1984b. "The Autobiography of a Twentieth-Century Rnying-mapa lama." *JIABS* 7: 63–74.

Macdonald, Ariane. 1968/69. *L'annuaire de l'École Pratique des Hautes Études,* 4th section. Paris: EPHE.

Macdonald, Ariane. 1971. "Une lecture des Pelliot tibétain 1286, 1287, 1038, 1047, et 1290: Essai sur la formation et l'emploi des mythes politiques dans la religion royale de Sroṅbcan sgam-po," in *ET,* pp. 190–391.

McItterick, Rosamond. 1989. *The Carolingians and the Written Word.* Cambridge: Cambridge University Press.

McItterick, Rosamond, ed. 1990. *The Uses of Literacy in Early Mediaeval Europe.* Cambridge: Cambridge University Press.

McKeon, Richard, ed. 1941. *The Basic Works of Aristotle.* New York: Random House.

McNeill, William H. 1977. *Plagues and Peoples.* New York: Doubleday.

McRae, John R. 1986. *The Northern School and the Formation of Early Ch'an Buddhism.* Studies in East Asian Buddhism 3. Honolulu: University of Hawaii Press.

Mair, Victor. 1994. "Buddhism and the Rise of the Written Vernacular in East Asia: The Making of National Languages," *Journal of Asian Studies* 53/3: 707–751.

Makransky, John J. 1997. *Buddhahood Embodied: Sources of Controversy in India and Tibet.* Albany: State University of New York Press.

Mala, Guilaine, and Kimura Ryūtoku. 1988. *Un Traité Tibétain de Dhyāna Chinois* (*Chan*). Bulletin de la Maison Franco-Japonaise, nouvelle série 11/1. Louvain: Peeters.

Malandra, Geri H. 1993. *Unfolding a Maṇḍala: The Buddhist Cave Temples at Ellora.* Albany: State University of New York Press.

Margoliouth, D. S. 1907. "The Judeo-Persian Document from Dandān-Uiliq," in M. Aurel Stein, *Ancient Khotan,* vol. 2, pp. 570–574. Oxford: Clarendon.

Markus, R. A. 1964. "Augustine," in D. J. O'Connor, ed., *A Critical History of Western Philosophy*. New York/London: Free Press.
Martin, C. B., and Max Deutscher. 1966. "Remembering," *Philosophical Review* 75: 161–96.
Martin, Dan. 1992. "A Twelfth-Century Tibetan Classic of Mahāmudrā, *The Path of Ultimate Profundity; The Great Seal Instructions of Zhang*," *JIABS* 15/2: 243–319.
Martin, Dan. 1994. *Mandala Cosmogony: Human Body Good Thought and the Revelation of the Secret Mother Tantras of Bon*. Asiatische Forschungen 124. Wiesbaden: Harrassowitz.
Martin, Dan. 1997. *Tibetan Histories: A Bibliography of Tibetan-Language Historical Works*. London: Serindia.
Maspero, Henri. 1971. *Le Taoïsme et les Religions chinoises*. Paris: Gallimard.
Mayer, Robert. 1996. *A Scripture of the Ancient Tantra Collection: The Phur-pa bcu-gnyis*. Oxford: Kiscadale.
Mayer, Robert. 1998. "The Figure of Maheśvara/Rudra in the rÑiṅ-ma-pa Tantric Tradition," *JIABS* 21/2: 271–310.
Mémet, Sébastien. 1988. "Le monastère de bSam-yas: essai de restitution," *ArtsA* 43: 30–32.
Messina, Giuseppe, S. I. 1947. *Cristianismo, Buddhismo, Manicheismo nell'Asia antica*. Rome: Nicola Ruffolo.
Miller, Roy Andrew. 1976. *Studies in the Grammatical Tradition in Tibet*. Amsterdam: John Benjamins.
Miller, Roy Andrew. 1983. "Thon mi Sambhoṭa and His Grammatical Treatises Reconsidered," in *CTLHC*, pp. 183–205.
Miller, Roy Andrew. 1993. *Prolegomena to the First Two Tibetan Grammatical Treatises*. Vienna: Arbeitskreis für Tibetische und Buddhistische Studien, Universität Wien.
Mimaki, Katsumi. 1982. *Blo gsal grub mtha'*. Kyoto: Zinbun Kagaku Kenkyusyo.
Mimaki, Katsumi. 1994. "Doxographie tibétaine et classifications indiennes," in Fukui Fumimasa and Gérard Fussman, eds., *Bouddhisme et cultures locales: Quelques cas de réciproques adaptations*, pp. 115–136. Études thématiques 2. Paris: École française d'Extrême-Orient.
Mirsky, Jeannette. 1977. *Sir Aurel Stein: Archaeological Explorer*. Chicago/London: University of Chicago Press.
Mitra, Debala. 1971. *Buddhist Monuments*. Calcutta: Sahitya Samsad.
Mizuno, Kōgen. 1982. *Buddhist Sutras*. Tokyo: Kōsei.
Moffett, Samuel Hugh. 1992. *A History of Christianity in Asia*. Vol. 1, *Beginnings to 1500*. San Francisco: Harper-Collins.
Momigliano, Arnaldo. 1990. *The Classical Foundations of Modern Historiography*. Berkeley/Los Angeles/Oxford: University of California Press.
Monier-Williams, Monier. 1899. *Sanskrit-English Dictionary*. Oxford: Oxford University Press.
Moriyasu, Takao. 1981. "Qui des Ouigours ou des Tibétains ont gagné en 789–792 à Beš-Balïq?" *JA* supplement: 193–205.
Mumford, Stan. 1989. *Himalayan Dialogue*. Madison: University of Wisconsin Press.
Nālandā Translation Committee. 1982. *The Life of Marpa the Translator*. Boulder: Prajñā Press.
Narkyid, Ngawangthondup. 1983. "The Origin of the Tibetan Script," in *CTLHC*, pp. 207–220.
Nattier, Jan. 1991. *Once Upon a Future Time: Studies in a Buddhist Prophecy of Decline*. Berkeley, Calif.: Asian Humanities Press.
Nebesky-Wojkowitz, Renée de. 1956. *Oracles and Demons of Tibet*. London/The Hague: Mouton.
Nicolas-Vandier, Mme., et al. 1974–1976. *Bannières et Peintures de Touen-houang Conservées au Musée Guimet*. Mission Paul Pelliot 14–15. Paris: Musée Guimet.

Nietzsche, Friedrich. 1969. *On the Geneology of Morals, Ecce Homo*. Ed. (with commentary) Walter Kaufmann. New York: Vintage Books.

Norman, K. R. 1985. *The Rhinocerous Horn and Other Early Buddhist Poems* (*Suttanipāta*). London: Pali Text Society.

Nussbaum, Martha. 1986. *The Fragility of Goodness: Luck and Ethics in Greek Tragedy and Philosophy*. Cambridge: Cambridge University Press.

Nussbaum, Martha. 1990. *Love's Knowledge: Essays on Philosophy and Literature*. Oxford/New York: Oxford University Press.

Obermiller, E. 1931–1932. *History of Buddhism* (*Chos-ḥbyung*) *by Bu-ston. Pt. 1, The Jewelry of Scripture* and *Pt. 2, The History of Buddhism in India and Tibet*. Heidelberg: Harrassowitz. Rprt., Suzuki Research Foundation Reprint Series 5.

Olivelle, Patrick. 1996. *Upaniṣads*. Oxford University Press.

Onoda, Shunzo. 1990. "Abbatial Successions of the Colleges of gSang phu sNe'u thog Monastery," *Bulletin of the National Museum of Ethnology* (Osaka) 15/4: 1049–1071.

Onoda, Shunzo. 1992. *Monastic Debate in Tibet: A Study on the History and Structures of* Bsdus grwa *Logic*. Wiener Studien zur Tibetologie und Buddhismuskunde 27. Vienna: Arbeitskreis für Tibetische und Buddhistische Studien Universität Wien.

Orofino, Giacomella. 1987. *Contributo allo studio dell'insegnamento di Ma gcig lab sgron*. Naples: Instituto Universitario Orientale.

Ortner, Sherry B. 1989. *High Religion: A Cultural and Political History of Sherpa Buddhism*. Princeton: Princeton University Press.

Padma Tshewang, Khenpo Phuntshok Tashi, Chris Butters, and Sigmund K. Sætreng. 1995. *The Treasure Revealer of Bhutan: Pemalingpa, the Terma Tradition, and Its Critics*. Bibliotheca Himalayica III, 8. Kathmandu: EMR.

Parfionovitch, Yuri, Gyurme Dorje, and Fernand Meyer. 1992. *Tibetan Medical Paintings*. London: Serindia.

Paul, Robert A. 1982. *The Tibetan Symbolic World: Psychoanalytic Explorations*. Chicago/London: University of Chicago Press.

Pelliot, Paul. 1961. *Histoire ancienne du Tibet*. Paris: Adrien-Maisonneuve.

Petech, Luciano. 1959. Preface to Lokesh Chandra. Ed. *Dpag-bsam-ljon-bzaṅ*. New Delhi: International Academy of Indian Culture.

Petech, Luciano. 1972. *China and Tibet in the Early XVIIIth Century*. Leiden: Brill.

Petech, Luciano. 1990. *Central Tibetan and the Mongols: The Yüan–Sa-skya Period of Tibetan History*. Serie Orientale Roma 65. Rome: Is.M.E.O.

Petech, Luciano. 1994. "The Disintegration of the Tibetan Kingdom," in *TS*, vol. 2, pp. 649–659.

Piotrovsky, Mikhail, ed. 1993. *Lost Empire of the Silk Road: Buddhist Art from Khara Khoto* (*X–XIIIth Century*). Milan: Thyssen-Bornemisza Foundation/Electa.

Pollock, Sheldon. 1996. "The Sanskrit Cosmopolis, A.D. 300–1300: Transculturation, Vernacularization, and the Question of Ideology," in J. E. M. Houben, ed., *The Ideology and Status of Sanskrit in South and Southeast Asia*. Leiden: Brill.

Pommaret, Françoise. 1989. *Les revenants de l'au-delà dans le monde tibétain*. Paris: CNRS.

Popkin, Richard. 1979. *The History of Scepticism: From Erasmus to Spinoza*. Berkeley/Los Angeles/London: University of California Press.

Powers, John. 1992. "Lost in China, Found in Tibet: How Wonch'uk Became the Author of the *Great Chinese Commentary*," *JIABS* 15/1: 95–103.

Price, Betsey B. 1992. *Medieval Thought: An Introduction*. Cambridge, Mass.: Blackwell.

Pye, Michael. 1978. *Skillful Means: A Concept in Mahayana Buddhism*. London: Duckworth.

Rahula, Walpola. 1971. *Le Compendium de la Super-Doctrine* (*Philosophie*) (*Abhidharmasamuccaya*) *d'Asaṅga*. Paris: École française d'Extrême-Orient.

Randall, John Herman, Jr. 1962. *The Career of Philosophy.* Vol. 1, *From the Middle Ages to the Enlightenment.* New York/London: Columbia University Press.

Rawski, Evelyn. 1998. *The Last Manchu Emperors.* Berkeley/Los Angeles/London: University of California Press.

Reeves, John C. 1992. *Jewish Lore in Manichaean Cosmology: Studies in the* Book of Giants *Traditions.* Cincinnati: Hebrew Union College Press.

Regamey, Constantin. 1971. "Motifs Vichnouïtes et Śivaïtes dans le *Karaṇḍavyūha,*" in *ET*, pp. 411–432.

Renondeau, Gaston. 1957. "Histoire des moines guerriers du Japon," in *Mélanges publiés par l'Institut des Hautes Études Chinoises.* Bibliothèque de l'Institut des Hautes Études Chinoises, vol. 11, pp. 159–345. Paris: Presses Universitaires de France.

Rescher, Nicholas. 1967. *Studies in Arabic Philosophy.* Pittsburgh: University of Pittsburgh Press.

Reynolds, Frank E., and David Tracy, eds. 1990. *Myth and Philosophy.* Albany: State University of New York Press.

Reynolds, Frank E., and David Tracy, eds. 1992. *Discourse and Practice.* Albany: State University of New York Press.

Rhoton, Jared. Forthcoming. *The Three Codes.* Albany: State University of New York Press.

Ricard, Matthieu et al., trans. 1994. *The Life of Shabkar: The Autobiography of a Tibetan Yogin.* Albany: State University of New York Press.

Richardson, Hugh E. 1977. "The Dharma That Came Down From Heaven," in Leslie S. Kawamura and Keith Scott, eds., *Buddhist Thought and Asian Civilization*, pp. 219–229. Emeryville, Calif.: Dharma.

Richardson, Hugh E. 1984. *Tibet and Its History.* Boulder: Shambala.

Richardson, Hugh E. 1985. *A Corpus of Early Tibetan Inscriptions.* London: Royal Asiatic Society.

Richardson, Hugh E. 1993. *Ceremonies of the Lhasa Year.* London: Serindia.

Richardson, Hugh. 1998. *High Peaks, Pure Earth: Collected Writings on Tibetan History and Culture.* Ed. Michael Aris. London: Serindia.

Rockhill, W. Woodville. 1884. *The Life of the Buddha and the Early History of His Order.* Rprt. Varanasi: Orientalia Indica, 1972.

Róna-Tas, A. 1968. "A Brief Note on the Chronology of the Tun-huang Collections," *AOH* 21: 313–316.

Rorty, Richard. 1984. "The Historiography of Philosophy: Four Genres," in Richard Rorty, J. B. Schneewind, and Quentin Skinner, eds. *Philosophy in History*, pp. 49–75. Cambridge: Cambridge University Press.

Rossabi, Morris. 1988. *Khubilai Khan: His Life and Times.* Berkeley: University of California Press.

Rossi, Donnatella. 2000. *The Metaphysical View of the Great Perfection According to the Bon-po Tradition.* Ithaca: Snow Lion.

Ruegg, David Seyfort, trans. 1963. "The Jo naṅ pas: A School of Buddhist Ontologists According to the Grub mtha' šel gyi me loṅ," *JAOS* 83: 73–91.

Ruegg, David Seyfort. 1966. *The Life of Bu ston Rin po che.* Rome: Instituto Italiano per il Medio ed Estremo Oriente.

Ruegg, David Seyfort. 1969. *La théorie du tathāgatagarbha et du gotra.* Publications de l'École française d'Extrême-Orient, vol. 70. Paris.

Ruegg, David Seyfort. 1981. "Autour du *lTa ba'i khyad par* de Ye šes sde (version de Touen-houang, Pelliot tibétain 814)," *JA* supplement: 208–229.

Ruegg, David Seyfort. 1984. "Problems in the Transmission of Vajrayāna Buddhism in the Western Himalaya about the Year 1000," *Acta Indologica* 6: 369–381.

Ruegg, David Seyfort. 1989. *Buddha-nature, Mind, and the Problem of Gradualism in a Comparative Perspective: On the Transmission and Reception of Buddhism in India and Tibet.* London: School of Oriental and African Studies.

Russell, Bertrand. 1919. *An Introduction to Mathematical Philosophy.* New York: Simon & Schuster.

Saeki, P. Y. 1916. *The Nestorian Monument in China.* London: Society for Promoting Christian Knowledge.

Sakaki, R., ed. 1916–25. *Mahāvyutpatti.* Kyoto.

Samuel, Geoffrey. 1990. *Mind, Body, and Culture.* Cambridge: Cambridge University Press.

Samuel, Geoffrey. 1993. *Civilized Shamans: Buddhism in Tibetan Societies.* Washington/London: Smithsonian Institution Press.

Sayers, Dorothy L., and Barbara Reynolds, trans. 1962. *The Divine Comedy of Dante Alighieri, III: Paradise.* Baltimore: Penguin.

Schafer, Edward H. 1963. *The Golden Peaches of Samarkand.* Berkeley/ Los Angeles/London: University of California Press.

Schaff, Philip, ed. 1905. *A Select Library of the Nicene and Post-Nicene Fathers of the Christian Church,* vol. 3. New York: Scribner.

Scharfstein, Ben-Ami. 1989. *The Dilemma of Context.* New York: New York University Press.

Schiefner, F. Anton von. 1905. *Tibetan Tales Derived from Indian Sources.* Trans. W. R. S. Ralston. Rprt. Gurgaon, Haryana: Vintage, 1991.

Schipper, Kristofer. 1993. *The Taoist Body.* Berkeley: University of California Press.

Schopen, Gregory. 1997. *Bones, Stones, and Buddhist Monks: Collected Papers on the Archaeology, Epigraphy, and Texts of Monastic Buddhism in India.* Honolulu: University of Hawai'i Press.

Schuh, Dieter. 1973. *Untersuchungen zur Geschichte der Tibetischer Kalenderrechnung,* Verzeichnis der Orientalischen Handschriften in Deutschland, Supplementband 16. Wiesbaden: Franz Steiner.

Shakabpa, Tsepon W. D. 1967. *Tibet: A Political History.* New Haven/London: Yale University Press.

Shayegan, Daryush. 1990. *Henry Corbin: la topographie spirituelle de l'Islam iranien.* Paris: Éditions de la Différence.

Simonsson, Nils. 1957. *Indo-tibetische Studien.* Uppsala: Almqvist & Wiksells Boktryckeri.

Skorupski, Tadeusz. 1983. *The Sarvadurgatipariśodhanatantra: Elimination of All Evil Destinies.* Delhi: Motilal Banarsidass.

Slusser, Mary Shepard. 1982. *Nepal Mandala: A Cultural Study of the Kathmandu Valley.* Princeton: Princeton University Press.

Smith, E. Gene. 1968. Foreword in Lokesh Chandra, ed., *Tibetan Chronicle of Padma-dkar-po.* New Delhi: International Academy of Indian Culture.

Smith, E. Gene. 1969. "The Biography of Lcang-skya Rol-pa'i-rdo-rje," in *Thu'u-bkwan gsung-'bum,* vol. 1.

Smith, E. Gene. 1970. Introduction in *Kongtrul's Encyclopedia of Indo-Tibetan Culture.* New Delhi: International Academy of Indian Culture.

Snellgrove, David L. 1957. *Buddhist Himalaya.* Oxford: Cassirer.

Snellgrove, David L. 1967a. *The Nine Ways of Bon.* London: Oxford University Press.

Snellgrove, David L. 1967b. *Four Lamas of Dolpo.* 2 vols. Oxford: Cassirer.

Snellgrove, David L. 1987. *Indo-Tibetan Buddhism: Indian Buddhists and Their Tibetan Successors.* 2 vols. Boston: Shambhala.

Snellgrove, David L. 1989. *Himalayan Pilgrimage.* 2nd ed. Boston: Shambhala.

Snellgrove, David L., and Skorupski, Tadeusz. 1977–80. *A Cultural History of Ladakh.* 2 vols. Boulder: Shambhala.

Sohn Pow-key, Kim Chol-choon, and Hong Yi-sup. 1970. *The History of Korea.* Seoul: Korean National Commission for Unesco.

Sørensen, Henrik H. 1993. "Lamaism in Korea During the Late Koryŏ Dynasty," *Korea Journal* 33/3: 67–81.

Sørensen, Per K. 1994. *Tibetan Buddhist Historiography: The Mirror Illuminating the Royal Genealogies.* Wiesbaden: Harrassowitz.

Southern, R. W. 1962. *Western Views of Islam in the Middle Ages.* Cambridge: Harvard University Press.

Sparham, Gareth. 1993. *Ocean of Eloquence.* Albany: State University of New York Press.

Spiro, Melford E. 1982. *Buddhism and Society: A Great Tradition and Its Burmese Vicissitudes.* 2nd ed. Berkeley/Los Angeles/London: University of California Press.

Stearns, Cyrus. 1995. "Dol-po-pa Shes-rab rgyal-mtshan and the Genesis of the *Gzhan-stong* Position in Tibet." *Asiatische Studien/Études Asiatiques* 44/4: 829–852.

Stearns, Cyrus. 1999. *Buddha from Dolpo.* Albany: State University of New York Press.

Stein, M. Aurel. 1933. *On Central Asian Tracks.* London: Macmillan.

Stein, Rolf A. 1956. *L'épopée tibétaine de Gesar dans sa version lamaïque de Ling.* Paris: Presses Universitaires de France.

Stein, Rolf A. 1959. *Recherches su l'épopée et le barde au Tibet.* Paris: Presses Universitaires de France.

Stein, Rolf A. 1961. *Une chronique ancienne de bSam-yas: sBa-bźed.* Paris: Publications de l'Institut des Hautes Études Chinoises.

Stein, Rolf A. 1970. "Un document ancien relatif aux rites funéraires des Bon-po tibétains," *JA* 258: 155–185.

Stein, Rolf A. 1972a. *Tibetan Civilization.* Trans. J. E. Stapleton Driver. Stanford: Stanford University Press.

Stein, Rolf A. 1972b. "Étude du monde chinoise: institutions et concepts," *L'Annuaire du Collège de France* 72: 489–510.

Stein, Rolf A. 1980. "Une mention du Manichéisme dans le choix du Bouddhisme comme religion d'état par le roi tibétain Khri-sroṅ lde-bcan," in *Indianisme et Bouddhisme: Mélanges offerts à Mgr Étienne Lamotte*, pp. 329–337. Louvain: Institut Orientaliste.

Stein, Rolf A. 1981. "'Saint et Divin', un titre tibétain et chinois des rois tibétains," *JA* supplement: 231–275.

Stein, Rolf A. 1983. "Tibetica Antiqua I: Les deux vocabulaires des traductions Indo-tibétaine et Sino-tibétaine dans les Manuscrits de Touen-houang," *BEFEO* 72: 149–236.

Stein, Rolf A. 1984. "Tibetica Antiqua 2: L'usage de métaphores pour les distinctions honorifiques à l'époque des rois tibétains," *BEFEO* 73: 257–272.

Stein, Rolf A. 1985. "Tibetica Antiqua III: A propos du mot *gcug-lag* et de la religion indigène," *BEFEO* 74: 83–133.

Stein, Rolf A. 1986a. "Tibetica Antiqua IV: "La tradition relative au début du Bouddhisme au Tibet," *BEFEO* 75: 169–196.

Stein, Rolf A. 1986b. "Avalokiteśvara/Kouan-yin, un example de transformation d'un dieu en déese," *Cahiers d'Extrême-Asie,* 2: 17–80.

Stein, Rolf A. 1987. "Sudden Illumination or Simultaneous Comprehension: Remarks on Chinese and Tibetan Terminology," in *SG,* pp. 41–65.

Stein, Rolf A. 1988. "Tibetica Antiqua V: "La religion indigène et les *Bon-po* dans les manuscrits de Touen-houang," *BEFEO* 77: 27–56.

Stein, Rolf A. 1995. "La soumission de Rudra et autres contes tantriques," *JA* 283/1: 121–160.

Steinkellner, Ernst. 1988. *Nachweis der Wiedergeburt: Prajñāsenas 'Jig rten pha rol sgrub pa.* 2 vols. Vienna: Österreichischen Akademie der Wissenschaften.

Steinkellner, Ernst. 1989. "Who Was Byaṅ chub rdzu 'phrul? Tibetan and Non-Tibetan Commentaries on the *Saṃdhinirmocanasūtra*—A Survey of the Literature," *Berliner Indologische Studien* 4/5: 229–251.

Strickmann, Michel. 1996. *Mantras et mandarins: Le bouddhisme tantrique en Chine*. Paris: Gallimard.

Strong, John. 1983. *The Legend of King Aśoka.* Princeton: Princeton University Press.

Sweetman, J. Windrow. 1955. *Islam and Christian Theology,* pt. 2, vol. 1. London: Lutterworth.

Szerb, János. 1983. "A Note on the Tibetan-Uigur Treaty of 822/823 A.D.," in *CTLHC*, pp. 375–387.

Takata, Tokio. 1994. "Bouddhisme chinois en écriture tibétain: le Long Rouleau chinois et la communauté sino-tibétaine de Dunhuang," in Fukui Fumimasa and Gérard Fussman, eds., *Bouddhisme et cultures locales: Quelques cas de réciproques adaptations.* Études thématiques 2, pp. 137–144. Paris: École française d'Extrême-Orient.

Takeuchi, Tsuguhito. 1985. "A Passage from the *Shih chi* in the *Old Tibetan Chronicle,*" in *STC,* pp. 135–146.

Taklung Tsetul [Pema Wangyal] Rimpoche and Kunzang Tenzin [Keith Dowman]. 1970. *Ornaments of Illumination, the Sacred Path of Omniscience.* Darjeeling: Keith Dowman.

Takpo Tashi Namgyal. 1986. *Mahāmudrā: The Quintessence of Mind and Meditation.* Trans. Lobsang P. Lhalungpa. Boston/London: Shambhala.

Tambiah, Stanley Jeyaraja. 1992. *Buddhism Betrayed? Religion, Politics, and Violence in Sri Lanka.* Chicago/London: University of Chicago Press.

Tauscher, Helmut. 1995. *Die Lehre von den Zwei Wirklichkeiten in Tsoṅ kha pas Madhyamaka-Werken.* Wiener Studien zur Tibetologie und Buddhismiskunde 36. Vienna: Arbeitskreis für Tibetische und Buddhistische Studien Universität Wien.

Taylor, Charles. 1989. *Sources of the Self: The Making of the Modern Identity.* Cambridge: Harvard University Press.

Teiser, Stephen F. 1988. *The Ghost Festival in Medieval China.* Princeton: Princeton University Press.

Tenzin Gyatso, the Fourteenth Dalai Lama. 1975. *The Buddhism of Tibet.* London: Allen and Unwin.

Tenzin Gyatso, the Dalai Lama, and Jeffrey Hopkins. 1988. *Kalachakra Tantra: Rite of Initiation.* London/Boston: Wisdom.

Thomas, F. W. 1935. *Tibetan Literary Texts and Documents Concerning Chinese Turkestan.* Pt. 1, *Literary Texts.* London: Royal Asiatic Society.

Thomas, F. W. 1948. *Nam: An Ancient Language of the Sino-Tibetan Borderland.* Publication 15. London: Philological Society.

Thomas, F. W. 1951. *Tibetan Literary Texts and Documents Concerning Chinese Turkestan.* Pt. 2, *Documents.* London: Luzac.

Thondup Rinpoche, Tulku. 1986. *Hidden Teachings of Tibet: An Explanation of the Terma Tradition of the Nyingma School of Buddhism.* Ed. by Harold Talbott. London: Wisdom.

Thondup Rinpoche, Tulku. 1989. *Buddha Mind.* Ithaca: Snow Lion.

Thurman, Robert A. F. 1984. *Tsong Khapa's Speech of Gold in the Essence of True Eloquence.* Princeton: Princeton University Press.

Tillemans, Tom J. F., and Toru Tomabechi. 1995. "Le *dBu ma'i byuṅ tshul* de Śākya mchog ldan," *Asiatische Studien/Études Asiatiques* 44/4: 891–918.

Toussaint, Gustave-Charles, trans. 1933. *Le Dict de Padma, Padma thang yig, Ms. de Lithang.* Bibliothèque de l'Institut de Hautes Études Chinoises, vol. 3. Paris: Leroux. [Trans. from the French by Kenneth Douglas and Gwendolyn Bays as *The Life and Liberation of Padmasambhava.* 2 vols. Emeryville, Calif.: Dharma Publications, 1978.]

Tucci, Giuseppe. 1949. *Tibetan Painted Scrolls.* 3 vols. Rome: Libreria dello Stato.

Tucci, Giuseppe. 1950. *The Tombs of the Tibetan Kings.* Serie Orientale Roma 1. Rome: Is.M.E.O.

Tucci, Giuseppe. 1956–1958. *Minor Buddhist Texts,* pts. 1 and 2. Serie Orientale Roma 9 (1956 and 1958). Rprt. Kyoto: Rinsen, 1978.

Tucci, Giuseppe. 1971a. *Deb t'er dmar po gsar ma: Tibetan Chronicles by bSod nams grags pa.* Serie Orientale Roma 24. Rome: Is.M.E.O.

Tucci, Giuseppe. 1971b. *Opera Minora.* 2 vols. Rome: Giovanni Bardi.

Tucci, Giuseppe. 1971c. *Minor Buddhist Texts,* Pt. 3. Serie Orientale Roma 43. Rome: Is.M.E.O.

Tucci, Giuseppe. 1973. *The Ancient Civilization of Transhimalaya.* Trans. James Hogarth. London: Barrie & Jenkins.

Tucci, Giuseppe. 1980. *The Religions of Tibet.* Trans. Geoffrey Samuel. Berkeley/Los Angeles: University of California Press.

Uebach, Helga. 1980. "Notes on the Tibetan Kinship Term *Dbon,*" in *TSHHR,* pp. 301–309.

Uebach, Helga. 1987. *Nel-pa Paṇḍitas Chronik Me-tog Phreṅ-ba.* Studia Tibetica 1. Munich: Bavarian Academy of Science.

Uebach, Helga. 1990. "On Dharma-Colleges and Their Teachers in the Ninth-Century Tibetan Empire," in Daffinà 1990, pp. 393–417.

Uebach, Helga. 1997. "Eminent Ladies of the Tibetan Empire According to Old Tibetan Texts," in Karmay and Sagant 1997, pp. 53–74.

Ueyama, Daishun. 1981. "Études des manuscrits tibétains de Dunhuang relatifs au Bouddhisme de Dhyāna: bilan et perspectives," *JA* supplement: 287–295.

Ueyama, Daishun. 1983. "The Study of Tibetan Ch'an Manuscripts Recovered from Tunhuang: A Review of the Field and Its Prospects," in *ECCT,* pp. 327–349.

Uray, Géza. 1972a. "Queen Sad-mar-kar's Songs in the Old Tibetan Chronicle," *AOH* 25: 5–38.

Uray, Géza. 1972b. "The Narrative of Legislation and Organization of the Mkhas-pa'i Dga'-ston: The Origins of the Traditions Concerning Sroṅ-brcan Sgam-po as First Legislator and Organizer of Tibet," *AOH* 26: 11–68.

Uray, Géza. 1975. "L'annalistique et la pratique bureaucratique au Tibet ancien," *JA* 263: 157–170.

Uray, Géza. 1979. "The Old Tibet Sources of the History of Central Asia up to 751 A.D.: A Survey," in J. Harmatta, ed., *Prolegomena to the Sources on the History of Pre-Islamic Central Asia,* pp. 275–305. Budapest: Akadémiai Kiadó.

Uray, Géza. 1983. "Tibet's connections with Nestorianism and Manicheism in the 8th–10th Centuries," in *CTLHC,* pp. 399–429.

Uray, Géza. 1992. "The Structure and Genesis of the *Old Tibetan Chronicle* of Dunhuang," in Alfredo Cadonna, ed., *Turfan and Tun-huang: The Texts.* Florence: Leo S. Olschki Editore.

van der Kuijp, Leonard W. J. 1983. *Contributions to the Development of Tibetan Buddhist Epistemology.* Wiesbaden: Franz Steiner.

van der Kuijp, Leonard W. J. 1984. "Miscellanea to a Recent Contribution on the Bsam-yas Debate," *Kailash* 11/3–4: 149–184.

van der Kuijp, Leonard W. J. 1986. "On the Sources for Sa-skya Paṇḍita's Notes on the bSam-yas Debate," *JIABS* 9: 147–153.

van der Kuijp, Leonard W. J. 1987. "An Early Tibetan View of the Soteriology of Buddhist Epistemology: The Case of 'Bri-gung 'Jig-rten mgon-po," *Journal of Indian Philosophy* 15: 57–70.

van der Kuijp, Leonard W. J. 1989. Introduction to Gtsang-nag-pa, *Tshad ma rnam par nges pa'i ṭī ka legs bshad bsdus pa.* Otani University Tibetan Works Series. Kyoto: Otani University.

van der Kuijp, Leonard W. J. 1991. "On the Life and Political Career of Ta'i-si-tu Byang-chub rgyal-mtshan," in E. Steinkellner, ed., *Tibetan History and Language: Studies Dedicated to Géza Uray on His Seventieth Birthday.* Vienna: Arbeitskreis fur Tibetische und Buddhistische Studien Universität Wien.

van der Kuijp, Leonard W. J. 1992. "Dating the Two Lde'u Chronicles of Buddhism in India and Tibet," *Asiatische Studien/Études Asiatiques* 46/1: 468–491.

van der Kuijp, Leonard W. J. 1994. "On the *Lives* of Śākyaśrībhadra (?–?1225)," *JAOS* 114/4: 599–616.

van der Kuijp, Leonard W. J. 1996. "The Tibetan Script and Derivatives," in Peter T. Daniels and William Bright, eds., *The World's Writing Systems.* New York/Oxford: Oxford University Press.

van der Leeuw, G. 1986. *Religion in Essence and Manifestation.* Trans. J. E. Turner. Princeton: Princeton University Press.

Verhagen, Pieter C. 1992a. "'Royal' Patronage of Sanskrit Grammatical Studies in Tibet," in A. W. van der Hoek, D. H. A. Kolff, and M. S. Oort, eds., *Ritual, State, and History in South Asia: Essays in Honour of J. C. Heesterman*, pp. 375–392. Leiden/New York: Brill.

Verhagen, Pieter C. 1992b. "A Ninth-Century Tibetan Summary of the Indo-Tibetan Model of Case-semantics," in Ihara Shōren and Yamaguchi Zuihō, eds., *Tibetan Studies: Proceedings of the fifth Seminar of the International Association for Tibetan Studies, Narita 1989*, vol. 2, pp. 833–844. Narita: Naritasan Shinshoji.

Verhagen, Pieter C. 1994. *A History of Sanskrit Grammatical Literature in Tibet.* Vol. 1, *Transmission of the Canonical Literature.* Leiden/New York: Brill.

Vitali, Roberto. 1990. *Early Temples of Central Tibet.* London: Serindia.

Vitali, Roberto. 1996. *The Kingdoms of Gu.ge Pu.hrang.* Dharamsala: Tho ling dpe med lhun gyis grub pa'i gtsug lag khang lo 1000 'khor ba'i rjes dran mdzad sgo'i go sgrig tshogs chung.

Vostrikov, A. I. 1970. *Tibetan Historical Literature.* Trans. Harish Chandra Gupta. Calcutta: Indian Studies Past & Present.

Warder, A. K. 1970. *Indian Buddhism.* Delhi: Motilal Banarsidass.

Watt, James C. Y., and Anne E. Wardwell. 1997. *When Silk Was Gold: Central Asian and Chinese Textiles.* New York: Metropolitan Museum of Art.

Weber, Max. 1964. *The Sociology of Religion.* Trans. by Ephraim Fischoff. Boston: Beacon.

Whitman, Jon. 1981. "From the Cosmographia to the Divine Comedy: An Allegorical Dilemma," in Morton W. Bloomfield, ed., *Allegory, Myth, and Symbol.* Harvard English Studies 9. Cambridge/London: Harvard University Press.

Williams, C. A. S. 1941. *Outlines of Chinese Symbolism and Art Motives.* 3rd rev. ed. Rprt. New York: Dover, 1976.

Williams, Michael Allen. 1996. *Rethinking "Gnosticism": An Argument for Dismantling a Dubious Category.* Princeton: Princeton University Press.

Williams, Paul. 1983a. "A Note on Some Aspects of Mi Bskyod Rdo Rje's Critique of Dge Lugs Pa Madhyamaka," *Journal of Indian Philosophy* 11: 125–145.

Williams, Paul. 1983b. "On rang rig," in *CTBRP,* pp. 321–332.

Wu Chi-yu. 1996. "Le manuscrit Hébreu de Touen-houang," in Jean-Pierre Drège, ed., *Du Dunhuang au Japon: Études chinoises et bouddhiques offertes à Michel Soymié*, pp. 259–292. Geneva: Droz.

Wylie, Turrell V. 1958. "Dating the Tibetan Geography *'Dzam gling rgyas bshad* Through Its Description of the Western Hemisphere," *Central Asiatic Journal* 4: 300–311.

Wylie, Turrell V. 1959. "A Standard System of Tibetan Transcription," *Harvard Journal of Asiatic Studies* 22: 261–267.

Wylie, Turrell V. 1962. *The Geography of Tibet According to the 'Dzam-gling rgyas-bshad.* Series Orientale Roma. 25. Rome: Is.M.E.O.

Wylie, Turrell V. 1977. "Etymology of Tibetan: *Bla-ma*," *Central Asiatic Journal,* 21/2: 145–148.

Yamaguchi, Zuihō. 1977–88. *A Catalogue of the Tibetan Manuscripts Collected by Sir Aurel Stein.* 12 pts. Tokyo: Tokyo University.

Yamaguchi, Zuihō. 1996. "The Fiction of King Dar-ma's Persecution of Buddhism," in Jean-Pierre Drège, ed., *Du Dunhuang au Japon: Études chinoises et bouddhiques offertes à Michel Soymié*, pp. 231–258. Geneva: Droz.

Yampolsky, Philip. 1983. "New Japanese Studies in Early Ch'an History," in *ECCT*, pp. 1–11.

Yanagida Seizan. 1983a. "The *Li-Tai Fa-Pao Chi* and the Ch'an Doctrine of Sudden Awakening," in *ECCT*, pp. 13–49.

Yanagida Seizan. 1983b. "The 'Recorded Sayings' Texts of Chinese Ch'an Buddhism," in *ECCT*, pp. 185–205.

Yang Han-Sung, Jan Yün-Hua, Iida Shotaro, and Laurence W. Preston. n.d. *The Hye Ch'o Diary: Memoir of the Pilgrimage to the Five Regions of India.* Berkeley: Asian Humanities Press.

Yang, Ho-chin. 1969. *The Annals of Kokonor*. Uralic and Altaic Series, vol. 106. Bloomington: Indiana University Press.

Zürcher, Erik. 1959. *The Buddhist Conquest of China.* Leiden: Brill.

Zürcher, Erik. 1962. *Buddhism: Its Origin and Spread in Words, Maps, and Pictures.* New York: St. Martin's.

Index

References to illustrations are given in **boldface.**

Printed in the United States
39494LVS00004B/45

9 780195 152272